THE INDISPENSABLE PILL BOOK

The Pill Book gives you the answers to the questions millions of Americans are asking about the pills their physicians are prescribing for them and their families.

This newly revised, updated 3rd edition of the two-million-copy bestseller gives you the essentials about all the revolutionary new drugs and drug types.

Now, thanks to *The Pill Book*, the general public can easily understand and accurately identify the medicines their doctors prescribe. *The Pill Book* describes practically everything you should know about over 1600 prescription drugs, including generic and brand names, usual dosages, side effects, adverse effects, cautions and warnings, overdose potential, interactions with other drugs, and much more. It includes new, vital information on drugs considered ineffective by the U.S. government.

It is based on the same information your physician and pharmacist rely on—information seldom available to patients. *The Pill Book* synthesizes the most important facts about each drug in a concise, readable entry. Warnings about drug use are given special prominence.

THE PILL BOOK
3rd Edition

NO HOME SHOULD BE WITHOUT IT!

THE PILL BOOK

3rd EDITION

BERT STERN

Producer

LAWRENCE D. CHILNICK

Editor-in-Chief

Text By

GILBERT I. SIMON,

Sc.D.

HAROLD M. SILVERMAN,

Pharm. D.

Additional Text
LAWRENCE D. CHILNICK

Photography
**THIERRY GRIHAULT DES FONTAINES
FRANCK THIERY**

Production
**RONA HUNTER
JULIE SELEMAN-SURREY
DANIEL MONTOPOLI
CARYL MACKLER**

BANTAM BOOKS
TORONTO • NEW YORK • LONDON • SYDNEY • AUCKLAND

THE PILL BOOK
A Bantam Book / June 1979

15 printings through September 1981
Bantam Revised edition / October 1982
7 printings through October 1985
Bantam 3rd Revised edition / March 1986

This revised edition was published simultaneously in trade paperback and mass market paperback by Bantam, March 1986

ISBN 0-553-24955-X

Published simultaneously in the United States and Canada

Bantam Books are published by Bantam Books, Inc. Its trademark, consisting of the words "Bantam Books" and the portrayal of a rooster, is Registered in U.S. Patent and Trademark Office and in other countries. Marca Registrada. Bantam Books, Inc., 666 Fifth Avenue, New York, New York 10103.

PRINTED IN THE UNITED STATES OF AMERICA

0   0 9 8 7 6 5 4 3 2

Contents

ACKNOWLEDGMENTS

The staff of The Pill Book wish to acknowledge the following people whose professional assistance and dedication has contributed to the value of the 3rd edition of this book: Dr. George Piltz, Henry Resnick, Jeff Packer and Dave Phillips—Carlyle Chemists, N.Y.C., Sidney Abromowitz and the staff of First Avenue Pharmacy, N.Y.C., Toni Burbank, Judy Knipe, Janet S. Chilnick, James Miglino, Barry Secunda, Noel Silverman, Kenneth Youngstein, Ned Leavitt, Jay Acton, Donna Ruvituso, Yook Louie, Nick Miglino, Joy Dermanjian.

The purpose of this book is to provide educational information to the public concerning the majority of various types of prescription drugs which are presently utilized by physicians. It is not intended to be complete or exhaustive or in any respect a substitute for personal medical care. *Only a physician may prescribe these drugs and the exact dosage which should be taken.*

While every effort has been made to reproduce products on the cover and insert of this book in an exact fashion, certain variations of size or color may be expected as a result of the photographic process. Furthermore, pictures identified as brand name drugs should not be confused with their generic counterparts, and vice versa. *In any event, the reader should not rely upon the photographic image to identify any pills depicted herein, but should rely solely upon the physician's prescription as dispensed by the pharmacist.*

THE
PILL BOOK

How to Use This Book

The Pill Book, like pills themselves, should be used with caution. Used properly, this book can save you money and perhaps your life.

Our book contains a section of life-sized pictures of the drugs most often prescribed in the United States. New drugs that have had an important impact on medical care, such as cancer chemotherapy and heart drugs, are included in this edition.

The Pill Book's product identification system is designed to help you check that the drug you're about to take is the right drug. Included are the most prescribed brand-name drugs and some of the more frequently prescribed generic versions of those drugs. Although many dosage forms are included, not all dosage forms of a certain drug have been shown.

Organized by color, each drug has been as faithfully reproduced as possible. While every effort has been made to depict the products accurately, certain variations of size or color may be expected as a result of the photographic process. In any event, readers should not rely solely upon the photographic image to identify any pills, but should check with their pharmacist if they have any questions about identification.

Most, although not all drugs, in the color section can be matched with the pill you have by checking to see if:

* the imprinted company logos (e.g. "Lilly," "Roche,") are the same;
* the product strengths (e.g. "250 mg.," "10 mg.,") which are frequently printed on the pills are the same;
* and if any product code numbers, which may be imprinted, are the same.

Note: Because many generic drugs look the same as their

brand-name counterparts, some manufacturers have begun to print the product name on a drug.

To find out more about the drugs depicted, check the descriptive material in the text (page numbers are given). The pill profiles provide a complete description of over 1,300 generic and brand-name drugs. These are the drugs most often prescribed to Americans. The descriptions should give you a detailed explanation of what your doctor and pharmacist have told you about your prescription. Most drugs are listed alphabetically under their generic classification; however, when a drug is a combination of two or more active ingredients, the listing is under the major brand name. Every brand and generic name is cross-referenced in the Index beginning on page 772.

Each drug profile contains the following information:

Generic or **Brand Name:** The generic name, the common name or chemical description of the drug approved by the Food and Drug Administration, is listed along with the current brand names available for each generic drug.

Most prescription drugs are sold in more than one strength. Some, such as the oral contraceptive drugs, come in packages containing different numbers of pills. A few manufacturers reflect this fact by adding letters and/or numbers to the basic drug name; others do not. An example: Norlestrin 21 1/50, Norlestrin 21 2.5/50, Norlestrin 28 1/50, Norlestrin 28 2.5/50. (The numbers here refer to the number of tablets in each monthly supply—28 or 21—and the strength of medication found in the tablets.) Other drugs come in different strengths: this is often indicated by a notation such as "DS" (double strength) or "Forte" (stronger).

The Pill Book lists only the generic or brand names (e.g., Norlestrin) where there are no differences in the basic ingredients, only in amounts of ingredients.

Type of Drug: Describes the general pharmacologic use of each drug: "antidepressant," "tranquilizer," "decongestant," "expectorant," and so on. A separate index begins on page 795 and gives page references for all the pills of a particular type.

Prescribed for: The reasons for which a drug is most often prescribed. Most drugs are given for certain symptoms, but often a drug may be prescribed in combination with another for a quite different reason. Check with your doctor if you are not sure why you have been given a certain pill.

Cautions and Warnings: Any drug can be harmful if the patient is sensitive to any of its actions. The information given alerts you to possible allergic reactions and to certain personal physical conditions such as pregnancy and heart disease which should be taken into consideration if the drug is prescribed for you.

Possible Side Effects: These are the more common side effects to be expected from a drug.

Possible Adverse Drug Effects: More uncommon effects of a pill that can be cause for concern. If you are not sure whether you are experiencing an adverse reaction, ALWAYS call your doctor.

Drug Interactions: This section tells you what other drugs should not be taken at the same time as the drug under discussion. This important information is also summarized in a general interaction chart. Drug interactions with other pills, alcohol, food, or other substances can cause death. Interactions are more common than overdoses. Obviously, it is important to be careful when taking alcohol with any medication or when taking several medications at the same time. Be sure to inform your doctor of any medication that you have been taking. Your pharmacist should also keep a record of all your prescription and non-prescription medicines. This listing, generally called a Patient Drug Profile, is used to review your record for any potential problems. You may want to keep your own drug profile and bring it to your pharmacist for review whenever a new medicine is added to it.

Food Interactions: This section includes information on foods to avoid while taking a medication.

Usual Dose: The maximum and minimum amounts of a drug usually prescribed; however, you may be given different dosage instructions by your doctor. It is important to check with your doctor if you are confused about how often to take a pill and when, or why a different dosage than indicated in the book has been prescribed. You should not change the prescribed dosages for a drug you are taking without first calling your doctor. Dosages differ for different age groups, and this information is also given.

Overdosage: Symptoms of an overdose of drugs and the immediate steps to take in that event.

Special Information: Facts to help you take your medicine more safely, symptoms to watch for, and special instructions.

The Pill Book also describes how some of the most common drug types work. It suggests some questions you may want to ask your doctor or pharmacist about your medicine.

This book is a unique visual reference tool. Its use, however, is only intended to amplify the information given by your doctor and pharmacist.

If you read something in *The Pill Book* which does not jibe with your instructions, call your doctor. Any drug can have serious side effects if abused or used improperly.

In an Emergency!

Each year some 1.5 million people are poisoned in the United States; about 70,000 of the poisonings are drug-related. In fact, drug overdose is a leading cause of fatal poisoning in this country, with about 7,000 deaths recorded each year. Sedatives, barbiturates, benzodiazepine tranquilizers, and topically applied medicines are responsible for the bulk of the drug-related poisonings or overdoses.

Although each of the product information descriptions in the new revised edition of *The Pill Book* has specific information on overdose management, there are also some general rules to remember if you are confronted with someone who has been poisoned.

Do the following:

1. Make sure the victim is breathing—call for medical help immediately.
2. When calling for help, the place to call is your local poison control center. The telephone number can be obtained from information; just ask for "poison control." When you call, be prepared to tell the person who answers:

   - What was taken and how much.
   - What the victim is doing (conscious or sleeping, vomiting, having convulsions, etc.).
   - The approximate age and weight of the victim.
   - Any chronic medical problems of the victim (such as diabetes, epilepsy, or high blood pressure), if you know them.
   - What medicines, if any, the victim takes regularly.

3. Remove anything that could interfere with breathing. A person who has poor oxygen supply will turn blue (the fingernails or tongue change color first). If this happens, lay the victim on his back, open the collar, place one hand

5

under the neck, and lift, pull, or push the victim's jaw so that it juts outward. This will open the airway between the mouth and lungs as wide as possible. If the victim is not breathing, begin mouth-to-mouth resuscitation.

4. If the victim is unconscious or having convulsions, call for medical help immediately. While waiting for the ambulance, lay the victim on the stomach and turn the head to one side. This will prevent inhalation of vomit should the victim throw up. Do not give an unconscious victim anything by mouth. Keep the victim warm.

5. If the victim is conscious, call for medical help and give the victim an 8-ounce glass of water to drink. This will dilute the poison.

Only a small percent of poisoning victims require hospitalization. Most can be treated with simple actions or need no treatment at all.

Depending on what was taken, you may be instructed to make the patient vomit. The best way to do this is to use syrup of ipecac, which can be purchased without a prescription at any pharmacy. Specific instructions on how much to give infants, children, or adults are printed on the label and will also be given by your poison control center. Remember, *do not* make the victim vomit unless you have been instructed to do so. Never make the victim vomit if the victim is unconscious, is having a convulsion, has a painful, burning feeling in the mouth or throat, or has swallowed a corrosive poison. (Corrosive poisons include bleach—liquid or powder—washing soda, drain cleaner, lye, oven cleaner, toilet bowl cleaner, and dishwasher detergent.) If a corrosive poison has been taken and the victim can still swallow, give milk or water to dilute the poison. The Poison Control Center will give you further instructions.

If the victim has swallowed a petroleum derivative such as gasoline, kerosene, machine oil, lighter fluid, furniture polish, or cleaning fluids, do not do anything. Call the Poison Control Center for instructions.

If the poison or chemical has spilled onto the skin, remove any clothing or jewelry that has been contaminated and wash the area with plenty of warm water for at least 15 minutes. Then wash the area thoroughly with soap and water. The Poison Control Center will give you more instructions.

Be Prepared

The best way to deal with a poisoning is to be ready for it. Do the following *now*:

1. Get the telephone number of your local Poison Control Center and write it down with your other emergency phone numbers.
2. Decide which hospital you will go to, if necessary, and how you will get there.
3. Buy 1 ounce of syrup of ipecac from your pharmacy. The pharmacist will explain how to use it, if needed. Remember, this is a potent drug to be used only if directed.
4. Learn to give mouth-to-mouth resuscitation. You may have to use this on a victim of poisoning.

In order to reduce the possibility of poisoning, do the following:

- Keep all medicine, household cleaners, disinfectants, insecticides, gardening products, and similar products out of the reach of young children, in a locked place.
- Do not store poisonous materials in containers that have contained food.
- Do not remove the labels from bottles so that the contents cannot be read.
- Discard all medicines after you no longer need them.
- Do not operate a car engine or other gasoline engine in an unventilated space. Do not use a propane heater indoors.
- If you smell gas, call the gas company immediately.

Poison prevention is best achieved by common sense. If you follow the simple advice given in this chapter, you will have taken a giant step toward assuring household safety for you and your family members.

The Most Commonly Prescribed Drugs in the United States, Generic and Brand Names, with Complete Descriptions of Drugs and Their Effects

Generic Name

Acebutelol

Brand Name

Sectral

Type of Drug

Beta-adrenergic blocking agent.

Prescribed for

High blood pressure, abnormal heart rhythms. It may also be used to treat angina pectoris.

General Information

Acebutelol is a relatively weak beta blocker and is, therefore, given in larger doses than the other 7 beta-blocking drugs available in the United States. Otherwise, Acebutelol is remarkably similar to other beta blockers in its ability to lower blood pressure and treat abnormal heart rhythms (arrhythmias).

Cautions and Warnings

If you have asthma, severe heart failure, reduced heart rate, and heart block, you should be cautious about taking Acebutelol because it can aggravate these conditions. However, compared with the other beta blockers, Acebutelol has less of an effect on the pulse and the bronchial muscles, less of a rebound effect when the drug is discontinued, and tends to produce less tiredness, depression and exercise intolerance. This may make it useful for people who have been unable to tolerate other beta-blocking drugs.

People with angina who take acebutelol for high blood pressure should have their dose reduced gradually over 1–2 weeks rather than suddenly discontinued to avoid possible aggravation of the angina.

Animal studies on rats and rabbits with doses greater than those normally given to humans have revealed no adverse effects of Acebutelol on the developing fetus. However, Acebutelol should be avoided by pregnant women or women who may become pregnant while using it. In those situa-

11

tions where it is deemed essential, the potential risk of the drug must be carefully weighed against any benefit it might produce. Nursing mothers must observe their infants for any possible drug effect while taking Acebutelol, since small amounts of the medication will pass into breast milk.

Acebutelol should be used with caution if you have liver disease because your ability to eliminate the drug from your body may be impaired.

Possible Side Effects

Most Acebutelol side effects develop early in the course of treatment, are relatively mild, and rarely force drug discontinuation. Side effects increase with increasing dose and include: dizziness, tingling of the scalp, nausea, vomiting, upset stomach, taste distortion, fatigue, sweating, male impotence, urinary difficulty, diarrhea, bile duct blockage, bronchial spasm, breathing difficulty, muscle weakness, cramps, dry eyes, blurred vision, skin rash, swelling of the face, and loss of hair.

Possible Adverse Drug Effects

Less frequent adverse effects include: aggravation of lupus erythematosus (a disease of body connective tissue) and stuffy nose. Like other beta blockers, Acebutelol has some potential to cause mental depression, confusion and disorientation, loss of short-term memory, emotional instability, colitis, drug allergy (fever, sore throat, breathing difficulty), and reduction in the levels of white blood cells and blood platelets.

Drug Interactions

Acebutelol may prevent normal signs of low blood sugar from appearing and can also interfere with the action of oral antidiabetes drugs.

The combination of Acebutelol with a tricyclic antidepressant drug can cause tremor.

Acebutelol may interfere with the effectiveness of some anti-asthma drugs, especially Ephedrine, Isoproterenol and other beta stimulants.

Cimetidine increases the amount of Acebutelol absorbed into the blood stream from oral tablets.

Acebutelol may increase the blood pressure lowering effect of Nitroglycerin.

Food Interactions

This medicine may be taken with food if it upsets your stomach.

Usual Dose

Starting dose: 400 milligrams per day, taken all at once or in 2 divided doses, which may be gradually increased.

Maintenance dose: 400 to 800 milligrams per day, but sometimes up to 1200 milligrams per day.

Elderly: Older patients may respond to lower doses of the drug and should be treated more cautiously, beginning with 200 milligrams per day.

Overdosage

Symptoms are slowed heart rate and dizziness or faintness caused by an excessive drop in blood pressure. The possible consequences of these effects can only be treated in a hospital emergency room. ALWAYS bring the medicine bottle with you.

Special Information

Senior citizens tend to absorb more Acebutelol than younger adults and may require only half as much medication to achieve the same effect.

Acebutelol is meant to be taken on a continuing basis. Do not stop taking it unless instructed to do so by your doctor. Weakness, breathing difficulty or other side effects should be reported to your doctor as soon as possible. Most side effects are not serious, but a small number of people have to switch to another drug.

Minor side effects like scalp tingling, fatigue, dizziness and nausea usually subside with no other treatment and do not require dosage reduction or a change of medications.

Generic Name

Acetaminophen

Brand Names

A'Cenol	Mejoral
Acephen	without Aspirin
Aceta	Neopap Supprettes
Actamin	Oraphen-PD
Amphenol	Panadol, Children's Panadol
Anacin-3,	Panex
Children's Anacin-3	Pedric Wafers
Anuphen	Peedee
APAP	Phenaphen
Banesin	SK-APAP
Bayapap	St. Joseph Aspirin-Free
Bromo Seltzer	Sudoprin
Conacetol	Suppap
Dapa	Tapanol
Datril	Tapar
Dolanex	Tempra
Febrinol	Tenol
Genebs	Tylenol, Children's Tylenol
Halenol	Tylenol Extra Strength
Liquiprin	Ty-tabs
Medatab	Valadol
Mejoralito	Valorin

(Also available in generic form)

Type of Drug

Antipyretic analgesic.

Prescribed for

Symptomatic relief of pain and fever for people who cannot take Aspirin.

General Information

Acetaminophen is generally used to provide symptomatic relief from pain and fever associated with the common cold, flu, viral infections, or other disorders where pain or fever may be a problem. It is also used to relieve pain in people with an Aspirin allergy or those who cannot take Aspirin because of potential interactions with other drugs such as oral anticoagulants. It can be used to relieve pain from a variety of sources including arthritis, headache, and tooth and periodontic pain.

Cautions and Warnings

Do not take Acetaminophen if you are allergic or sensitive to it. Do not take Acetaminophen for more than 10 consecutive days unless directed by your doctor. Do not take more than is prescribed for you or recommended on the package.

Use with caution in patients with impaired liver function.

This drug may cause birth defects or interfere with your baby's development. Check with your doctor before taking it if you are, or might be, pregnant.

Possible Side Effects

This drug is relatively free from side effects. For this reason it has become extremely popular, especially among those who cannot take Aspirin.

Possible Adverse Drug Effects

Taking large doses of Acetaminophen for a long time may cause rash, itching, fever, lowered blood sugar, stimulation, and/or yellowing of the skin or whites of the eyes. Other effects of overuse may include a change in the composition of your blood.

Usual Dose

Adult: 300 to 650 milligrams 3 to 4 times per day. Avoid taking doses greater than 2.6 grams (8 of the 325-milligram tablets) per day for long periods of time.

Child (age 7 to 12): 162 to 325 milligrams 3 to 4 times per day. Do not take more than 1.6 grams per day.

Child (age 3 to 6): 120 milligrams 3 to 4 times per day. Do not take more than 800 milligrams per day.

Child (age 1 to 3): 80 to 120 milligrams 3 to 4 times per day.

Child (under age 1): 60 milligrams 3 to 4 times per day.

Overdosage

Symptoms are development of bluish color of the lips, fingertips, etc., rash, fever, stimulation, excitement, delirium, depression, nausea and vomiting, abdominal pain, diarrhea, yellowing of the skin and/or eyes, convulsions, and coma. Victims of Acetaminophen overdose should be made to vomit with Syrup of Ipecac and taken to a hospital emergency room. ALWAYS bring the medicine bottle.

Special Information

Unless abused, Acetaminophen is a beneficial, effective, and relatively nontoxic drug.

Generic Name

Acetaminophen with Codeine

Brand Name

Tylenol with Codeine

Ingredients

Acetaminophen
Codeine Phosphate

Other Brand Names

Aceta with Codeine	Panadol with Codeine
Anacin-3 with Codeine	Phenaphen with Codeine
Bayapap with Codeine	Proval #3
Capital with Codeine	Rid-a-Pain with Codeine
Codap	SK-APAP with Codeine
Empracet with Codeine	Ty-Tab #3

(Also available in generic form)

Type of Drug

Narcotic analgesic combination.

Prescribed for

Relief of mild to moderate pain.

General Information

Acetaminophen with Codeine is generally prescribed for the patient who requires a greater analgesic effect than Acetaminophen alone can deliver, and/or is allergic to Aspirin.

Acetaminophen with Codeine is probably not effective for arthritis or other pain caused by inflammation because the ingredient Acetaminophen does not reduce inflammation. Aspirin with Codeine will produce an anti-inflammatory effect, and this is the major difference between these two products.

Cautions and Warnings

Do not take Acetaminophen with Codeine if you know you are allergic or sensitive to it. Use this drug with extreme caution if you suffer from asthma or other breathing problems. Long-term use of Acetaminophen with Codeine may cause drug dependence or addiction. Codeine is a respiratory depressant and affects the central nervous system, producing sleepiness, tiredness, and/or inability to concentrate. Be careful if you are driving, operating machinery, or performing other functions requiring concentration. If you are pregnant or suspect that you are pregnant do not take this drug.

Acetaminophen has not caused problems when used during pregnancy or breast-feeding. However, the regular use of Codeine may cause the unborn child to become addicted. If used during labor, it may cause breathing problems in the infant.

Possible Side Effects

Most frequent: light-headedness, dizziness, sleepiness, nausea, vomiting, loss of appetite, sweating. If these effects occur, consider calling your doctor and asking him about lowering the dose of Codeine you are taking. Usually the side effects disappear if you simply lie down.

More serious side effects of Acetaminophen with Codeine are shallow breathing or difficulty in breathing.

Possible Adverse Drug Effects

Euphoria (feeling high), weakness, sleepiness, headache, agitation, uncoordinated muscle movement, minor hallucinations, disorientation and visual disturbances, dry mouth, loss of appetite, constipation, flushing of the face, rapid heart-beat, palpitations, faintness, urinary difficulties or hesitancy, reduced sex drive and/or potency, itching, rashes, anemia, lowered blood sugar, yellowing of the skin and/or whites of the eyes. Narcotic analgesics may aggravate convulsions in those who have had convulsions in the past.

Drug Interactions

Because of its depressant effect and potential effect on breathing, Acetaminophen with Codeine should be taken with extreme care in combination with alcohol, sleeping medicine, tranquilizers, antihistamines, or other drugs producing sedation.

Food Interactions

Acetaminophen with Codeine is best taken with food or at least ½ glass of water to prevent stomach upset.

Usual Dose

Adult: 1 to 2 tablets every 4 hours.

Child (2 to 6 years): 2.5 milligrams to 5 milligrams every 4 to 6 hours. Not to exceed 30 milligrams in 24 hours.

Child (6 to 12 years): 5 to 10 milligrams every 4 to 6 hours. Not to exceed 60 milligrams in 24 hours.

Overdosage

Symptoms are depression of respiration (breathing), extreme tiredness progressing to stupor and then coma, pinpointed pupils of the eyes, no response to stimulation such as a pin stick, cold and clammy skin, slowing down of the heart rate, lowering of blood pressure, yellowing of the skin and/or whites of the eyes, bluish color in skin of hands and feet, fever, excitement, delirium, convulsions, cardiac arrest, and liver toxicity (shown by nausea, vomiting, pain in the abdomen, and diarrhea). The patient should be made to vomit with Syrup of Ipecac and taken to a hospital emergency room immediately. ALWAYS bring the medicine bottle.

Generic Name

Acetazolamide

Brand Names

Cetazol	Dazamide
AK-Zol	Diamox

(Also available in generic form)

Type of Drug

Carbonic anhydrase inhibitor.

Prescribed for

General elimination of excess body water. Treatment of glaucoma where it is desirable to lower the pressure inside the eye.

Prophylactic treatment of mountain sickness at high altitudes. This drug has also been used in treating some convulsive disorders such as petit mal epilepsy and other unlocalized seizures. How Acetazolamide works for these disorders is not fully known.

Different brands of this drug may not be absorbed into the body in exactly the same amounts. According to some studies these (bioequivalence) problems can be serious enough to alter the drug's effect on your body. Do not indiscriminately switch brands.

General Information

Acetazolamide inhibits an enzyme in the body called carbonic anhydrase. This effect allows the drug to be used as a weak diuretic, and as part of the treatment of glaucoma by helping to reduce pressure inside the eye. The same effect on carbonic anhydrase is thought to make Acetazolamide a useful drug in treating certain epileptic seizure disorders. The exact way in which the effect is produced is not understood.

Cautions and Warnings

Do not take Acetazolamide if you have serious kidney, liver, or Addison's disease. This drug should not be used by people with low blood sodium or potassium.

This drug may cause birth defects or interfere with your baby's development. Check with your doctor before taking it if you are, or might be, pregnant.

Possible Side Effects

Side effects of short-term Acetazolamide therapy are usually minimal. Those which have been noted include tingling feeling in the arms or legs or at lips, mouth, or anus, loss of appetite, increased frequency in urination (to be expected, since this drug has a weak diuretic effect), occasional drowsiness and/or convulsion. Transient myopia has been reported.

Since this drug is chemically considered to be a sulfa drug it can cause all of the side effects of the sulfa drugs: fever, rash, the formation of drug crystals in the urine, and adverse effects of the drug.

Possible Adverse Drug Effects

Infrequent: itching, rash, blood in stool or urine, increased blood sugar, convulsions, diarrhea, loss of weight, nausea, vomiting, constipation, weakness, nervousness, depression, dizziness, dry mouth, disorientation, muscle spasms, ringing in the ears, loss of taste or smell, not feeling well.

Drug Interactions

Avoid over-the-counter drug products which contain stimulants or anticholinergics, which tend to aggravate glaucoma or cardiac disease. Ask your pharmacist about ingredients contained in the over-the-counter drugs.

Acetazolamide may increase the effect of Quinidine and predispose patients to Digitalis toxicity by increasing potassium losses.

Food Interactions

May be taken with food to minimize stomach upset. Acetazolamide may increase potassium loss. Take this drug with foods that are rich in potassium, like apricots, bananas, orange juice, or raisins.

Usual Dose

250 milligrams to 1 gram per day, according to disease and patient's condition.

Special Information

Acetazolamide may cause minor drowsiness and confusion, particularly during the first 2 weeks of therapy. Take care while performing tasks which require concentration, such as driving or operating appliances or machinery.

Call your doctor if you develop sore throat, fever, unusual bleeding or bruises, tingling in the hands or feet, rash, or unusual pains. These can be signs of important drug side effects.

Brand Name

Actifed-C Expectorant

Ingredients

Codeine Phosphate   Pseudoephedrine Hydrochloride
Guiafenesin   Triprolidine Hydrochloride

(Also available in generic form)

Type of Drug

Decongestant; expectorant; cough suppressant.

Prescribed for

Relief of cough, nasal congestion, runny nose, and other symptoms associated with the common cold, viruses, or other upper respiratory diseases. The drug may also be used to treat allergies, ear infections, or sinus infections.

General Information

Actifed-C is one of almost 100 products marketed to relieve the symptoms of the common cold and other upper respiratory infections and is available without prescription. These products contain ingredients to relieve congestion, act as an antihistamine, relieve or suppress cough, and help cough up mucus. They may contain medicine for each purpose, or may contain a combination of medicines. Some combinations leave out the antihistamine, the decongestant, or the expectorant. You must realize while taking Actifed-C or similar products that these drugs are good only for the relief of symptoms and do not treat the underlying problem, such as a cold virus or other infections.

Cautions and Warnings

Can cause excessive tiredness or drowsiness.

The regular use of Codeine during pregnancy may lead to addiction by the fetus. If used during labor, the infant may have breathing difficulty.

The antihistamines, Pseudoephedrine and Triprolidine Hydrochloride pass into mother's milk and may cause excitement or irritability in breast-fed infants. Actifed is not recommended for nursing mothers.

This drug may cause birth defects or interfere with your baby's development. Check with your doctor before taking it if you are, or might be, pregnant.

Possible Side Effects

Dry mouth, blurred vision, difficulty passing urine, (possibly) constipation, nervousness, restlessness or inability to sleep.

Drug Interactions

Taking Actifed-C with an MAO inhibitor can produce severe interaction. Consult your doctor first.

Do not take this drug with sedatives, tranquilizers, antihistamines, sleeping pills, thyroid medicine, or antihypertensive drugs such as Reserpine or Guanethidine.

Since Actifed-C contains ingredients which may cause sleepiness or difficulty in concentration, do not drink alcoholic beverages while taking this drug. The combination can cause excessive drowsiness or sleepiness, and result in inability to concentrate and carry out activities requiring extra concentration and coordination.

Usual Dose

1 to 2 teaspoons 4 times per day.

Special Information

Take with a full glass of water to remove excessive mucus from the throat and reduce stomach upset.

Brand Name

Actifed Tablets

Ingredients

Pseudoephedrine Hydrochloride
Triprolidine

Other Brand Names

Actacin	Suhist Tablets
Actagen	Tagafed
Actamine Tablets	Triafed
Actifed	Trifed
Actihist	Triphed
Allerfrin	Tripodrine
Norafed	Triposed
Pseudophedrine Plus	

(Also available in generic form)

Type of Drug

Antihistamine decongestant combination.

Prescribed for

Relief of sneezing, runny nose, and nasal congestion associated with the common cold, allergy, or other upper respiratory condition.

General Information

Actifed is one of many products marketed to relieve the symptoms of the common cold and is available without a prescription. Most of these products contain ingredients to relieve nasal congestion or to dry up runny noses or relieve a scratchy throat; and several of them may contain ingredients to suppress cough, or to help eliminate unwanted mucus. All these products are good only for the relief of symptoms and do not treat the underlying problem, such as a cold virus or other infections.

Cautions and Warnings

Can cause excessive tiredness or drowsiness, restlessness, nervousness with an inability to sleep.

This drug may cause birth defects or interfere with your baby's development. Check with your doctor before taking it if you are, or might be, pregnant.

Possible Side Effects

Tremor, headache, palpitations, elevation of blood pressure, sweating, sleeplessness, loss of appetite, nausea, vomiting, dizziness, constipation.

Drug Interactions

Interaction with alcoholic beverages may cause excessive drowsiness and/or sleepiness, or inability to concentrate. Do not take this drug with alcohol, sedatives, tranquilizers, antihistamines, sleeping pills, thyroid medicine, or antihypertensive drugs such as Reserpine or Guanethidine.

Do not self-medicate with over-the-counter drugs for the relief of cold symptoms: taking Actifed with such drugs may aggravate high blood pressure, heart disease, diabetes, or thyroid disease.

Do not take Actifed if you are taking or suspect you may be taking a monoamine oxidase (MAO) inhibitor; severe elevation in blood pressure may result.

Food Interactions

If this drug upsets your stomach it should be taken with food.

Usual Dose

Adult: 1 tablet 2 to 3 times per day. Syrup preparation, 1 to 2 teaspoons 3 times per day.

Child (over age 6): 1 tablet 3 times per day. Syrup preparation, 2 teaspoons 3 times per day.

Child (age 4 months to 6 years): 1 teaspoon 3 times per day.

Child (under age 4 months): ½ teaspoon 3 times per day.

Special Information

Since drowsiness may occur during use of Actifed Tablets, be cautious while performing mechanical tasks requiring concentration and alertness.

Generic Name

Acetohydroxamic Acid

Brand Name

Lithostat

Type of Drug

Urinary anti-infective.

Prescribed for

Chronic urinary tract infection.

General Information

This product applies a unique mechanism of action to the treatment of chronic urinary infections. It is always taken together with an antibiotic or another urinary anti-infective. It works by inhibiting the bacterial enzyme urease and interfering with the process responsible for making ammonia. Ammonia interferes with most urinary anti-infectives, so this medicine can only enhance the effect of other drugs; it cannot treat a urinary infection by itself.

Cautions and Warnings

As many as 15 percent of all people taking this drug may develop laboratory signs of hemolytic anemia, a severe condition. A much smaller percentage (3 percent) of people go on to develop the disease itself. Signs of hemolytic anemia include nausea, vomiting, loss of appetite, and a general feeling of ill health. Your doctor should perform complete blood count and platelet count tests every 3 months while you are taking this medicine.

This drug should not be used if your condition can be treated surgically or if it may respond to other anti-infective therapy. It must be used with caution if you have impaired kidney function because Acetohydroxamic Acid is eliminated from the body via the kidneys.

This product should not be used by women who are pregnant or who might become pregnant because it is known to cause harm to a developing baby when taken during pregnancy. Since it is not known if this drug passes into breast milk, a nursing mother should either change feeding methods or not take the drug.

Possible Side Effects

Most side effects are mild and not serious enough to interfere with drug treatment. The most common: mild headaches during the first 2 days of treatment, depression, anxiety, nervousness, tremulousness, nausea, vomiting, a sickly feeling, and increase in red-blood-cell counts.

Possible Adverse Drug Effects

Vein irritations, small blood clots in the lungs (in people who have had past instances of clots in their blood vessels), rash.

Drug Interactions

Acetohydroxamic Acid interferes with the absorption of iron from both food and iron pills. If you develop iron-deficiency anemia during treatment and extra iron is needed, it may have to be given by injection.

Alcoholic beverages will enhance the rash associated with Acetohydroxamic Acid.

Usual Dose

Adult: 250 milligrams 3 or 4 times per day, increasing to no more than 1500 milligrams per day.

Child: 4.5 milligrams per pound of body weight per day in divided doses.

The daily dosage must be reduced for people with reduced kidney function.

Overdosage

The symptoms of overdosage are a sickly feeling, loss of appetite, lethargy, tremulousness, nausea, and vomiting. The drug is very rapidly absorbed into the blood, and home measures, including the induction of vomiting with Syrup of Ipecac, are generally ineffective as early as 15 minutes after the overdose has been taken. Victims who have overdose symptoms must be taken to a hospital emergency room for treatment. ALWAYS bring the prescription bottle with you.

Special Information

Do not drink alcoholic beverages while taking this drug. Be

sure to report any unusual side effects to your doctor. The overall incidence of side effects is fairly high, and as many as 6 of every 100 people taking the drug may have to stop because of severe side effects.

Generic Name

Acyclovir

Brand Name

Zovirax

Type of Drug

Antiviral; antiherpes.

Prescribed for

Both types of herpes simplex infections of the genitalia and of mucous membrane tissues.

General Information

Acyclovir is the only drug that can reduce the rate of growth of the herpes virus and its relatives, Epstein-Barr virus, cytomegalovirus, and varicella-zoster.

The ointment works only on the viral blisters of an initial infection by interfering with viral DNA. It has little effect on recurrent infection and will not prevent the infection from coming back once it has healed. The drug must be given by mouth or by intravenous injection in a hospital to treat both local and systemic symptoms. The capsules can be taken every day to reduce the number and severity of herpes attacks in people who usually suffer 10 or more a year and may be used to treat intermittent attacks as they occur, but the drug must be started as soon as possible to have the greatest effect.

Cautions and Warnings

Acyclovir ointment should not be applied to your skin if you have had an allergic reaction to it or to the major component of the ointment base, Polyethylene Glycol. Acyclovir ointment should not be used to treat a herpes infection of the eye because it is not specifically formulated for that purpose.

Very small amounts of the drug are absorbed into the blood after application in the ointment form. While there is no information to indicate that Acyclovir ointment affects a developing baby, you should not use this medication during pregnancy unless it is specifically prescribed by your doctor. Acyclovir capsules and injections have been given to lab animals and found to cause no birth defects. However, Acyclovir has not been studied in pregnant women and should not be used unless the possible benefits clearly outweigh any possible adverse effects. It is not known if Acyclovir passes into breast milk. Mothers who must take this medicine should not breast-feed.

High doses of Acyclovir taken over long periods of time have caused reduced sperm count in lab animals, but this effect has not yet been reported in men.

Possible Side Effects

The ointment has few side effects, the most common of which are mild burning, irritation, rash, and itching. Women are 4 times more likely to experience burning than men, and it is more likely to occur when applied during an initial herpes attack than during a recurrent attack.

The most common side effects of Acyclovir capsules are nausea, vomiting, and headache. Additional side effects that may be experienced by people taking the drug continuously are diarrhea and aching joints.

Possible Adverse Drug Effects

The ointment should not be applied inside the vagina because the Polyethylene Glycol base can irritate and cause swelling of those sensitive tissues.

Acyclovir capsules may occasionally cause dizziness, loss of appetite, fatigue, swelling and fluid retention, rash, leg pains, swollen lymph glands in the groin and elsewhere, sore throat, a bad taste in your mouth, sleeplessness, heart palpitations, menstrual abormalities, superficial blood clots, hair loss, depression, fever, muscle cramps, and acne.

Drug Interactions

Do not apply Acyclovir with any other ointment or topical medicine.

Oral Probenecid may decrease the elimination of Acyclovir from your body and increase drug blood levels, when the Acyclovir is taken by mouth or by injection.

Usual Dose

Capsules: For treatment of an initial herpes attack or an occasional herpes attack: 1 capsule every 4 hours, 5 times per day for 10 days. For maximum benefit, start treatment as soon as possible.

As supressive therapy, for people who suffer from chronic herpes infection: 1 capsule 3 to 5 times per day, every day.

Ointment: Apply the ointment every 3 hours, 6 times per day for 7 days, in sufficient quantity to cover all visible lesions. About ½ inch of Acyclovir ointment should cover 4 square inches of skin lesions. Your doctor may prescribe a longer course of treatment to prevent the delayed formation of new lesions during the duration of an attack.

Overdosage

The chance of toxic side effects from swallowing Acyclovir ointment is quite small because of the limited amount of drug contained in the ointment (only 50 milligrams per gram). There is no information on Acyclovir overdose, but doses of up to 4.8 grams per day for 5 days have been taken without serious adverse effects. Observe the overdose victim for side effects and call your local Poison Control Center for more detailed information and advice.

Special Information

Use a finger cot when applying the ointment to protect against inadvertently spreading the virus, and be sure to apply the medicine exactly as directed and to completely cover all lesions. If you skip several doses or a day or more of treatment, the therapy will not exert its maximum effect.

Call your doctor if the drug does not relieve your condition, if side effects become severe or intolerable, or if you become pregnant or want to begin breast-feeding.

To avoid transmitting the condition, do not have intercourse while visible herpes lesions are present.

Generic Name

Albuterol

Brand Names

Proventil
Ventolin

Type of Drug

Bronchodilator.

Prescribed for

Asthma and bronchial muscle spasms.

General Information

Albuterol is one of the newer bronchodilator drugs. It is similar to Metaproterenol and Isoetharine but it has a weaker effect on nerve receptors in the heart and blood vessels, and for this reason it is somewhat safer for people with heart conditions.

Albuterol tablets begin to work within 30 minutes and continue working for about 4 hours. Albuterol inhalation begins working within 15 minutes, and continues for 3 to 4 hours.

Cautions and Warnings

Albuterol should be used with caution by people with a history of angina, heart disease, high blood pressure, stroke or seizure, diabetes, thyroid disease, prostate disease, or glaucoma. Older patients are especially sensitive to the side effects of Albuterol and generally require less medicine to achieve desired effects. Excessive use of Albuterol inhalants can lead to worsening of your asthmatic or other respiratory condition.

This drug should be avoided by pregnant women or those who become pregnant while using it. It is not known if Albuterol causes birth defects in humans, but it has caused defects in pregnant-animal studies. When it is deemed essential, the potential risk of taking Albuterol must be carefully weighed against any benefit it might produce. It is not known if Albuterol passes into breast milk. Nursing mothers must observe for any possible drug effect on their infants while taking Albuterol. You may want to consider using an alternate feeding method.

Possible Side Effects

Albuterol's side effects are similar to those of other bronchodilators, except that its effects on the heart and blood vessels are not as pronounced. Most common: restlessness, weakness, anxiety, fear, tension, sleeplessness, tremors, convulsions, dizziness, headache, flushing, loss of appetite, pallor, sweating, nausea, vomiting, and muscle cramps.

Possible Adverse Drug Effects

Angina, abnormal heart rhythms, heart palpitations, high blood pressure, and urinary difficulty.

Drug Interactions

Albuterol's effects may be increased by MAO inhibitor drugs, antidepressants, thyroid drugs, other bronchodilator drugs, and some antihistamines. It is antagonized by the beta-blocking drugs (Propranolol and others).

Albuterol may antagonize the effects of blood-pressure-lowering drugs, especially Reserpine, Methyldopa, and Guanethidine.

Food Interactions

Albuterol tablets are more effective taken on an empty stomach, 1 hour before or 2 hours after meals, but can be taken with food or meals if they upset your stomach. Do not inhale Albuterol if you have food or anything else in your mouth.

Usual Dose

Adult and child (age 12 and over): Inhalation: 2 puffs every 4 to 6 hours (each puff delivers 90 milligrams of Albuterol). Asthma brought on by exercise may be prevented by taking 2 puffs 15 minutes before the exercise is to begin.

Tablets: 6 to 16 milligrams per day in divided doses to start; the dosage may be slowly increased until it controls patient's asthma, to a maximum of 32 milligrams per day.

Elderly: 6 to 8 milligrams per day to start, but increase to the maximum daily adult dosage, if tolerated.

Child (under age 12): not recommended.

Overdosage

Overdose of Albuterol inhalation usually results in exaggerated side effects, including heart pains and high blood pressure, although the pressure may drop to a low level after a short period of elevation. People who inhale too much Albuterol should see a doctor, who may prescribe a beta-blocking drug, such as Atenolol or Metoprolol.

Overdose of Albuterol tablets is more likely to lead to side effects of changes in heart rate, palpitations, unusual heart rhythms, heart pains, high blood pressure, fever, chills, cold sweats, nausea, vomiting, and dilation of the pupils. Convulsions, sleeplessness, anxiety, and tremors may also develop and the victim may collapse.

If the overdose was taken within the past half hour, give the victim Syrup of Ipecac to induce vomiting and remove any remaining medicine from the stomach. DO NOT GIVE SYRUP OF IPECAC IF THE VICTIM IS UNCONSCIOUS OR CONVULSING. If symptoms have already begun to develop, the victim may have to be taken to a hospital emergency room for treatment. ALWAYS bring the prescription bottle with you.

Special Information

If you are inhaling Albuterol, be sure to follow patient instructions that come with the product. The drug should be inhaled during the second half of your breath, since this will allow it to reach deeper down into your lungs. Wait about 5 minutes between puffs, if you use more than 1 puff per dose.

Do not take more Albuterol than prescribed by your doctor. Taking more than you need could actually result in worsening of your symptoms.

Call your doctor immediately if you develop chest pains, palpitations, rapid heart beat, muscle tremors, dizziness, headache, facial flushing, or urinary difficulty, or if you continue to experience difficulty in breathing after using the medicine.

Brand Name

Aldactazide

Ingredients

Hydrochlorothiazide
Spironolactone

Other Brand Names

Alazide
Spiractazide
Spironazide
Spironolactone with Hydrochlorothiazide
Spirozide

(Also available in generic form)

Type of Drug

Diuretic.

Prescribed for

High blood pressure or any condition where it is desirable to eliminate excess fluid from the body.

General Information

Aldactazide is a combination of two diuretics and is a convenient, effective approach for the treatment of diseases where the elimination of excess fluids is required. One of the ingredients in Aldactazide has the ability to hold potassium in the body while producing a diuretic effect. This balances off the other ingredient, Hydrochlorothiazide, which normally causes a loss of potassium from outside sources.

Combination drugs such as Aldactazide should only be used when you need the exact amount of ingredients contained in the product and when your doctor feels you would benefit from taking one dose per day.

Cautions and Warnings

Do not use Aldactazide if you have nonfunctioning kidneys, if you may be allergic to this drug or any sulfa drug, or if you have a history of allergy or bronchial asthma.

Aldactazide may be used to treat specific conditions in pregnant women, but the decision to use this medication by pregnant women should be weighed carefully because the drug may cross the placental barrier into the blood of the unborn child. This drug may cause birth defects or interfere with your baby's development. Check with your doctor before taking it if you are, or might be, pregnant.

Do not take any potassium supplements together with Aldactazide unless specifically directed to do so by your doctor.

Possible Side Effects

Drowsiness, lethargy, headache, gastrointestinal upset, cramping and diarrhea, rash, mental confusion, fever, feeling of ill health, enlargement of the breasts, inability to achieve or maintain erection in males, irregular menstrual cycles or deepening of the voice in females.

Possible Adverse Drug Effects

Loss of appetite, headache, tingling in the toes and fingers, restlessness, anemias or other effects on components of the blood, unusual sensitivity to sunlight, dizziness when rising quickly from a sitting position. Aldactazide can also produce muscle spasms, gout, weakness, and blurred vision.

Drug Interactions

Aldactazide will increase (potentiate) the action of other blood-pressure-lowering drugs. This is beneficial, and is frequently used to help lower blood pressure in patients with hypertension.

The possibility of developing imbalances in body fluids (electrolytes) is increased if you take other medications such as Digitalis and adrenal corticosteroids while you are taking Aldactazide.

If you are taking an oral antidiabetic drug and begin taking Aldactazide, the antidiabetic dose may have to be altered.

Lithium Carbonate taken with Aldactazide should be monitored carefully as there may be an increased risk of Lithium toxicity.

Avoid over-the-counter cough, cold, or allergy remedies containing stimulant drugs which can aggravate your condition.

Aldactazide may interfere with the oral blood-thinning drugs (like Warfarin) by making the blood more concentrated (thicker).

Usual Dose

2 to 4 tablets per day, adjusted by your doctor until the desired therapeutic effect is achieved.

Special Information

This drug may cause drowsiness or sleepiness. Do not drive or operate machinery. Call your doctor if you develop muscle or stomach cramps, dizziness, nausea, diarrhea, unusual thirst, headache, rash, voice changes, breast enlargement, or unusual menstrual period. This drug may be taken with food to reduce stomach upset.

Brand Name

Aldoril

Ingredients

Hydrochlorothiazide
Methyldopa

Type of Drug

Antihypertensive combination.

Prescribed for

High blood pressure.

General Information

Be sure to take this medicine exactly as prescribed: if you don't, it cannot exert its maximum effect.

An ingredient in this drug can cause loss of potassium. Potassium loss leads to a condition known as hypokalemia. Warning signs of hypokalemia or other electrolyte imbalances that can be due to Aldoril are dryness of the mouth, excessive thirst, weakness, drowsiness, restlessness, muscle pains or cramps, muscular fatigue, lack of urination, abnormal heart rhythms, and upset stomach. If this happens, call your doctor. You may have to take extra potassium to supplement loss due to Aldoril. This may be taken as a potassium supplement (tablet, powder, liquid) or by increasing certain foods in your diet such as bananas, citrus fruits, melons, and tomatoes.

Cautions and Warnings

Do not take Aldoril if you are allergic to either of its ingredients, if you have any liver diseases such as hepatitis or active cirrhosis (liver disease), or if previous therapy with Methyldopa has been associated with signs of liver reaction (jaundice or unexplained fever).

This drug will pass into the unborn child and can be found in mother's milk. Pregnant women should use this drug only if it is absolutely necessary. Women taking Aldoril should not breast-feed their infants.

This drug may cause birth defects or interfere with your baby's development. Check with your doctor before taking it if you are, or might be, pregnant.

Possible Side Effects

Loss of appetite, stomach upset, nausea, vomiting, cramps, diarrhea, constipation, dizziness, headache, tingling in the extremities, restlessness, chest pains, abnormal heart rhythms, drowsiness during the first few days of therapy.

Possible Adverse Drug Effects

Aldoril can cause abnormal liver function in the first 2 to 3 months of therapy. Watch for jaundice (yellowing of the skin or whites of the eyes), with or without fever. If you are taking Aldoril for the first time, be sure the doctor checks your liver function, particularly during the first 6 to 12 weeks of therapy. If fever or jaundice appears, notify your doctor immediately and discontinue therapy. Other adverse effects: stuffy nose, breast enlargement lactation (in females), impotence or decreased sex drive, mild arthritis, skin reactions such as mild eczema, stomach gas, dry mouth, a sore tongue, fever.

Drug Interactions

Interaction with Digitalis or Quinidine can result in the development of abnormal heart rhythms.

Interaction with Lithium products can lead to Lithium toxicity unless appropriate dose adjustments are made.

Do not self-medicate with over-the-counter cough, cold, or allergy remedies containing stimulant drugs which may raise your blood pressure. If you are not sure which over-the-counter drugs are safe for you, ask your pharmacist.

Usual Dose

Individualized to suit the patient. The usual starting dose, 1 tablet 2 to 3 times per day for the first 2 days, is adjusted up or down as needed.

Special Information

Aldoril may cause temporary mild sedation. Contact your doctor if your normal urine output is dropping or you are less hungry or nauseated.

Be aware that Aldoril can cause orthostatic hypotension (dizziness when rising from a sitting or lying position). Alcohol will worsen this effect, so avoid alcohol at the beginning of Aldoril therapy.

You may take this drug with food to reduce upset stomach. Call your doctor if you develop muscle weakness, cramps, nausea, dizziness, fever, or tiredness.

Generic Name

Allopurinol

Brand Names

Lopurin
Zyloprim

(Also available in generic form)

Type of Drug

Anti-gout, anti-uric medication.

Prescribed for

To prevent formation of uric acid by the body.

General Information

Unlike other anti-gout drugs which affect the elimination of uric acid from the body, Allopurinol acts on the system that manufactures uric acid in your body. A high level of uric acid can mean that you have gout or that you have one of many other diseases, including various cancers and malignancies, or psoriasis. High uric acid levels can be caused by taking some drugs, including diuretic medicines. The fact that you have a high blood level of uric acid does not point to a specific disease.

Cautions and Warnings

Do not take this medication if you have ever developed a severe reaction to it. If you develop a rash or any other adverse effects while taking Allopurinol, stop taking the medication immediately and contact your doctor.

Allopurinol should be used by children only if they have high uric acid levels due to neoplastic disease. A nursing mother should not take this medication, since it will pass through the mother's milk into the child.

This drug may cause birth defects or interfere with your baby's development. Check with your doctor before taking it if you are, or might be, pregnant.

Possible Side Effects

You may develop rash. Such rashes have been associated with severe, allergic, or sensitivity reactions to Allopurinol. If you develop an unusual rash or other sign of drug toxicity, stop taking this medication and contact your doctor. Other side effects: nausea, vomiting, diarrhea, intermittent stomach pains, effects on blood components, drowsiness or lack of ability to concentrate, and, rarely, effects on the eyes.

Possible Adverse Drug Effects

Loss of hair, fever, chills, arthritis-like symptoms, itching.

Drug Interactions

Avoid taking Allopurinol with iron tablets or vitamins with iron: Allopurinol can cause iron to concentrate in your liver. Megadoses of Vitamin C may increase the possibility of kidney stone formation.

Interaction with drugs used to treat cancer is important and should be taken into account by your physician.

Allopurinol may interact with anticoagulant (blood-thinning) medication such as Dicoumarol. The importance of this interaction is not yet known.

Food Interactions

Take each dose with a full glass of water and drink 10 to 12 glasses of water, juices, soda, or other liquids each day to avoid the formation of crystals in your urine and/or kidneys.

This drug may be taken with food to reduce upset stomach.

Usual Dose

Adult: 200 to 600 milligrams per day, depending on disease and patient's response.

Child (age 6 to 10): 300 milligrams per day.

Child (under age 6): 150 milligrams per day.

The dose should be reviewed periodically by your doctor to be sure that it is producing the desired therapeutic effect.

Special Information

Allopurinol can make you sleepy or make it difficult for you to concentrate: take care while driving a car or using other equipment or machinery.

Generic Name

Alprazolam

Brand Name

Xanax

Type of drug

Tranquilizer.

Prescribed for

Relief of symptoms of anxiety, tension, fatigue and agitation.

General Information

Alprazolam is a member of the chemical group of drugs known as benzodiazepines. These drugs are used either as antianxiety agents, anticonvulsants, or sedatives (sleeping pills). They exert their effects by relaxing the large skeletal muscles and by a direct effect on the brain. In doing so, they can relax you and make you either more tranquil or sleepier, depending upon which drug you use and how much you take. Many doctors prefer the benzodiazepines to other drugs that can be used for the same effects because benzodiazepines tend to be safer, have fewer side effects, and are usually as, if not more, effective. The benzodiazepines are generally prescribed in any situation where they can be a useful adjunct.

The benzodiazepines, including Alprazolam, can be abused if taken for long periods of time, and it is possible to experience withdrawal symptoms if you stop taking the drug abruptly. Withdrawal symptoms include tremor, muscle cramp, stomach cramps, vomiting, insomnia, and convulsions.

Cautions and Warnings

Do not take Alprazolam if you know you are sensitive or allergic to this drug or other benzodiazepines such as Diazepam, Oxazepam, Chlorazepate, Temazepam, Halazepam, Lorazepam, Prazepam, Flurazepam, and Clonazepam. Alprazolam and other members of this group can aggravate narrow angle glaucoma, but if you have open angle glaucoma you may take the drug. In any case, check with your doctor. Alprazolam can cause tiredness, drowsiness, inability to concentrate, or similar symptoms. Be careful if you are driving, operating machinery, or performing other activities which require concentration.

This drug may cause birth defects or interfere with your baby's development. Check with your doctor before taking it if you are, or might be, pregnant.

Possible Side Effects

Most common: mild drowsiness during the first few days of therapy, especially in the elderly or debilitated. If drowsiness persists, contact your doctor.

Possible Adverse Drug Effects

Major adverse effects: confusion, depression, lethargy, disorientation, headache, inactivity, slurred speech, stupor, dizziness, tremor, constipation, dry mouth, nausea, inability to control urination, sexual difficulties, irregular menstrual cycle, changes in heart rhythm, lowered blood pressure, fluid retention, blurred or double vision, itching, rash, hiccups, nervousness, inability to fall asleep, and occasional liver dysfunction. If you experience any of these symptoms, stop taking the medicine and contact your doctor immediately.

Drug Interactions

Alprazolam is a central nervous system depressant. Avoid alcohol, other tranquilizers, narcotics, barbiturates, MAO inhibitors, antihistamines, and medicine used to relieve depression. Taking Alprazolam with these drugs may result in excessive depression, tiredness, sleepiness, difficulty breathing, or similar symptoms. Smoking may reduce the effectiveness of Alprazolam by increasing the rate at which it is broken down by the body. The effects of Alprazolam may be prolonged when taken together with Cimetidine.

Usual Dose

0.75 to 4 milligrams per day. The dose must be tailored to the individual needs of the patient. Elderly or debilitated patients will require less of the drug to control anxiety or tension. This drug should not be used in children.

Overdosage

Symptoms are confusion, sleepiness, lack of response to pain such as a pin stick, shallow breathing, lowered blood pressure, and coma. The patient should be taken to a hospital emergency room for treatment. ALWAYS bring the medicine bottle with you.

Special Information

Do not drink alcoholic beverages while taking Alprazolam. Sleeping pills, narcotics, barbiturates, other tranquilizers, or any other drug which produces central nervous depression should be used with caution while taking Alprazolam. Tell your doctor if you become pregnant or are nursing an infant.

Generic Name

Amitriptyline

Brand Names

Amitrip
Elavil
Emitrip
Endep
SK-Amitriptyline

(Also available in generic form)

Type of Drug

Antidepressant.

Prescribed for

Depression with or without symptoms of anxiety.

General Information

Amitriptyline and other members of this group are effective in treating symptoms of depression. They can elevate mood, increase physical activity and mental alertness, improve appetite and sleep patterns in a depressed patient. These drugs are mild sedatives and therefore useful in treating mild forms of depression associated with anxiety. You should not expect instant results with this medicine: results are usually seen after 2 to 4 weeks. If symptoms are not affected after 6 to 8 weeks, contact your doctor. Occasionally this drug and other members of the group of drugs have been used in treating nighttime bed-wetting in the young child, but they do not produce long-lasting relief and therapy with one of them for nighttime bed-wetting is of questionable value.

Cautions and Warnings

Do not take Amitriptyline if you are allergic or sensitive to this or other members of this class of drug: Doxepin, Nortriptyline, Imipramine, Desipramine, and Protriptyline. The drugs should not be used if you are recovering from a heart attack. Amitriptyline may be taken with caution if you have a history of epilepsy or other convulsive disorders, difficulty in urination, glaucoma, heart disease, or thyroid disease. Amitriptyline can interfere with your ability to perform tasks which require concentration, such as driving or operating machinery. Do not stop taking this medicine without first discussing it with your doctor, since stopping may cause you to become nauseated, weak, and headachy.

This drug may cause birth defects or interfere with your baby's development. Check with your doctor before taking it if you are, or might be, pregnant.

Possible Side Effects

Changes in blood pressure (both high and low), abnormal heart rates, heart attack, confusion, especially in elderly patients, hallucinations, disorientation, delusions, anxiety, restlessness, excitement, numbness and tingling in the extremities, lack of coordination, muscle spasms or tremors, seizures and/or convulsions, dry mouth, blurred vision, constipation, inability to urinate, rash, itching, sensitivity to bright light or sunlight, retention of fluids, fever, allergy, changes in composition of blood, nausea, vomiting, loss of appetite, stomach upset, diarrhea, enlargement of the breasts in males and females, increased or decreased sex drive, increased or decreased blood sugar.

Possible Adverse Drug Effects

Infrequent: agitation, inability to sleep, nightmares, feeling of panic, a peculiar taste in the mouth, stomach cramps, black coloration of the tongue, yellowing eyes and/or skin, changes in liver function, increased or decreased weight, excessive perspiration, flushing, frequent urination, drowsiness, dizziness, weakness, headache, loss of hair, nausea, not feeling well.

Drug Interactions

Interaction with monoamine oxidase (MAO) inhibitors can cause high fevers, convulsions, and occasionally death. Don't take MAO inhibitors until at least 2 weeks after Amitriptyline has been discontinued.

In patients who require concomitant use of Amitriptyline and an MAO inhibitor, close medical observation is warranted.

Amitriptyline interacts with Guanethidine and Clonidine, drugs used to treat high blood pressure: if your doctor prescribes Amitriptyline and you are taking medicine for high blood pressure, be sure to discuss this with him.

Amitriptyline increases the effects of barbiturates, tranquilizers, other sedative drugs, and alcohol. Don't drink alcoholic beverages if you take this medicine.

Taking Amitriptyline and thyroid medicine will enhance the effects of the thyroid medicine. The combination can cause abnormal heart rhythms. The combination of Amitriptyline and Reserpine may cause overstimulation.

Large doses of Vitamin C (Ascorbic Acid), oral contraceptives, or smoking can reduce the effect of Amitriptyline. Drugs such as Bicarbonate of Soda, Acetazolamide, Quinidine, or Procainamide will increase the effect of Amitriptyline. Ritalin and phenothiazine drugs such as Thorazine and Compazine block the metabolism of Amitriptyline, causing it to stay in the body longer. This can cause possible overdose.

The combination of Amitriptyline with large doses of the sleeping pill Ethchlorvynol has caused patients to experience passing delirium.

Usual Dose

Adult: 25 milligrams 3 times per day, which may be increased to 150 milligrams per day if necessary. The medication must be tailored to the needs of the patient.

Adolescent or elderly: lower doses are recommended—generally, 30 to 50 milligrams per day.

Overdosage

Symptoms are confusion, inability to concentrate, hallucinations, drowsiness, lowered body temperature, abnormal heart rate, heart failure, enlarged pupils of the eyes, convulsions, severely lowered blood pressure, stupor, and coma (as well as agitation, stiffening of body muscles, vomiting, and high fever). The patient should be taken to a hospital emergency room immediately. ALWAYS bring the medicine bottle.

Generic Name

Amobarbital

Brand Name

Amytal

(Also available in generic form)

Type of Drug

Hypnotic; sedative; anticonvulsive.

Prescribed for

Daytime sedation, sedation before surgery, sleeping medication, control of convulsive disorders.

General Information

Amobarbital, like the other barbiturates, appears to act by interfering with nerve impulses to the brain. When used as an anticonvulsive, Amobarbital is not very effective by itself; but when used with anticonvulsive agents such as Phenytoin, the combined action of Amobarbital and Phenytoin is dramatic. This combination has been used very successfully to control epileptic seizures.

Cautions and Warnings

Amobarbital may slow down your physical and mental reflexes; be extremely careful when operating machinery, driving an automobile, or performing other potentially dangerous tasks. Amobarbital is classified as a barbiturate; long-term or unsupervised use may cause addiction. Elderly people on Amobarbital may exhibit nervousness and confusion at times. Barbiturates are neutralized in the liver and eliminated from the body through the kidneys; consequently, people who have liver or kidney disorders—namely, difficulty in forming or excreting urine—should be carefully monitored by their doctor when taking Amobarbital.

If you have known sensitivities or allergies to barbiturates, or if you have previously been addicted to sedatives or hypnotics, or if you have a disease affecting the respiratory system, you should not take Amobarbital.

This drug has not been found to be safe for use during pregnancy and can affect a developing infant at any time. Remember, you should check with your doctor before taking any drug if you are pregnant.

Possible Side Effects

Difficulty in breathing, rash, and general allergic reaction such as running nose, watering eyes, and scratchy throat.

Possible Adverse Drug Effects

Drowsiness, lethargy, dizziness, hangover, nausea, vomiting, diarrhea. More severe adverse reactions may include anemia and yellowing of the skin and eyes.

Drug Interactions

Interaction with alcohol, tranquilizers, or other sedatives increases the effect of Amobarbital.

Interaction with anticoagulants (blood-thinning agents) can reduce their effect. This is also true of muscle relaxants, painkillers, and other anticonvulsants.

Usual Dose

Daytime sedative: up to 150 milligrams per day.
Sleeping medication: up to 200 milligrams at bedtime.
Anticonvulsant: 65 milligrams 2 to 4 times a day.
Sedation before surgery: 200 milligrams 1 to 2 hours before surgery.

Overdosage

Symptoms are difficulty in breathing, decrease in size of the pupils of the eyes, lowered body temperature progressing to fever as time passes, fluid in the lungs, and eventually coma.

Anyone suspected of having taken an overdose must be taken to the hospital for immediate care. ALWAYS bring the medicine bottle to the emergency room physician so he can quickly and correctly identify the medicine and start treatment. Severe overdosage of this medication can kill; the drug has been used many times in suicide attempts.

Generic Name

Amoxapine

Brand Name

Asendin

Type of Drug

Antidepressant.

Prescribed for

Depression with or without symptoms of anxiety.

General Information

Amoxapine and other members of this group are effective in treating symptoms of depression. They can elevate mood, increase physical activity and mental alertness, improve appetite and sleep patterns in a depressed patient. These drugs are mild sedatives and therefore useful in treating mild forms of depression associated with anxiety. You should not expect instant results with this medicine: results are usually seen after 1 to 4 weeks. If symptoms are not affected after 6 to 8 weeks, contact your doctor. Occasionally this drug and other members of the group of drugs have been used in treating nighttime bed-wetting in the young child, but they do not produce long-lasting relief, and therapy with one of them for nighttime bed-wetting is of questionable value.

Cautions and Warnings

Do not take Amoxapine if you are allergic or sensitive to this or other members of this class of drug: Doxepin, Nortriptyline, Imipramine, Desipramine, and Amitriptyline. The drugs should not be used if you are recovering from a heart attack. Amoxapine may be taken with caution if you have a history of epilepsy or other convulsive disorders, difficulty in urination, glaucoma, heart disease, or thyroid disease. Amoxapine can interfere with your ability to perform tasks which require concentration, such as driving or operating machinery.

This drug may cause birth defects or interfere with your

baby's development. Check with your doctor before taking it
if you are, or might be, pregnant.

Amoxapine may pass into breast milk. Nursing mothers
should use an alternative feeding method.

Possible Side Effects

Changes in blood pressure (both high and low), abnormal
heart rates, heart attack, confusion, especially in elderly
patients, hallucinations, disorientation, delusions, anxiety, restlessness, excitement, numbness and tingling in the extremities, lack of coordination, muscle spasms or tremors, seizures
and/or convulsions, dry mouth, blurred vision, constipation,
inability to urinate, rash, itching, sensitivity to bright light or
sunlight, retention of fluids, fever, allergy, changes in composition of blood, nausea, vomiting, loss of appetite, stomach upset, diarrhea, enlargement of the breasts in males and
females, increased or decreased sex drive, increased or decreased blood sugar.

Possible Adverse Drug Effects

Infrequent: agitation, inability to sleep, nightmares, feeling
of panic, a peculiar taste in the mouth, stomach cramps,
black coloration of the tongue, yellowing eyes and/or skin,
changes in liver function, increased or decreased weight,
perspiration, flushing, frequent urination, drowsiness, dizziness, weakness, headache, loss of hair, nausea, not feeling
well.

Drug Interactions

Interaction with monoamine oxidase (MAO) inhibitors can
cause high fevers, convulsions, and occasionally death. Don't
take MAO inhibitors until at least 2 weeks after Amoxapine
has been discontinued.

Certain patients may require concomitant use of Amoxapine
and an MAO inhibitor, and in these situations close medical
observation is warranted.

Amoxapine interacts with Guanethidine, a drug used to
treat high blood pressure: if your doctor prescribes Amoxapine
and you are taking medicine for high blood pressure, be
sure to discuss this with him.

Amoxapine increases the effects of barbiturates, tranquilizers, other depressive drugs, and alcohol. Don't drink alcoholic beverages if you take this medicine.

Taking Amoxapine and thyroid medicine will enhance the effects of the thyroid medicine. The combination can cause abnormal heart rhythms.

Large doses of Vitamin C (Ascorbic Acid) can reduce the effect of Amoxapine. Drugs such as Bicarbonate of Soda or Acetazolamide will increase the effect of Amoxapine.

Usual Dose

Adult: 150 to 400 milligrams per day. Hospitalized patients may need up to 600 milligrams per day. The dose of this drug must be tailored to patient's need.

Elderly: lower doses are recommended; for people over 60 years of age, usually 75 to 300 milligrams per day.

This drug should not be given to patients under age 16.

Overdosage

Symptoms are confusion, inability to concentrate, hallucinations, drowsiness, lowered body temperature, abnormal heart rate, heart failure, large pupils of the eyes, convulsions, severely lowered blood pressure, stupor, and coma (as well as agitation, stiffening of body muscles, vomiting, and high fever). The patient should be taken to a hospital emergency room immediately. ALWAYS bring the medicine bottle.

Generic Name

Amoxicillin

Brand Names

Amoxil	Trimox
Larotid	Utimox
Polymox	Wymox
Sumox	

(Also available in generic form)

Type of Drug

Penicillin-type antibiotic.

Prescribed for

Gram-positive bacterial infections. Gram-positive bacteria (pneumococci, streptococci, and staphylococci) are organisms which usually cause diseases such as pneumonia, infections of the tonsils and throat, venereal disease, meningitis (infection of the spinal column), and septicemia (general infection of the bloodstream).

Infections of the urinary tract and some infections of the gastrointestinal tract can also be treated with Amoxicillin.

General Information

Amoxicillin is manufactured in the laboratory by fermentation and by general chemical reaction and is classified as a semisynthetic antibiotic. Because the effectiveness of the antibiotic is determined by the drug's ability to destroy the cell wall of the invading bacteria, it is very important that the patient completely follow the doctor's prescribing directions. These directions include spacing of doses as well as the number of days the patient should continue taking the medicine. If they are not followed, the effect of the antibiotic is severely reduced. To ensure the maximum effect of this drug, you should take the medication on an empty stomach, either 1 hour before or 2 hours after meals.

Cautions and Warnings

If you have a known history of allergy to Penicillin you should avoid taking Amoxicillin, since the drugs are chemically very similar. The most common allergic reaction to Amoxicillin, as well as to the other penicillins, is a hivelike rash over the body with itching and redness. It is important to tell your doctor if you have ever taken this drug or penicillins before and if you have experienced any adverse reaction to the drug such as rash, itching, or difficulty in breathing.

This drug may cause birth defects or interfere with your baby's development. Check with your doctor before taking it if you are, or might be, pregnant.

Amoxicillin passes into breast milk and may cause problems in breast-fed infants, such as allergy reactions, fungal infections, skin rashes, or diarrhea. Therefore, it is not recommended for nursing mothers.

Possible Side Effects

Common: stomach upset, nausea, vomiting, diarrhea, and possible rash. Less common: hairy tongue, itching or irritation around the anus and/or vagina. If these symptoms occur, you should contact your doctor immediately.

Drug Interactions

The effect of Amoxicillin can be significantly reduced when it is taken with other antibiotics. Consult your doctor if you are taking both. Otherwise, Amoxicillin is generally free of interaction with other medications.

Usual Dose

Adult: 250 milligrams every 8 hours.

Child: 9 to 18 milligrams per pound of body weight per day in 3 divided doses (every 8 hours). Amoxicillin pediatric drops (under 3 pounds), 1 milliliter every 8 hours; (3 to 4 pounds), 2 milliliters every 8 hours. Dose may be halved for less serious infections or doubled for severe infections.

Storage

Amoxicillin can be stored at room temperature.

Special Information

Do not take Amoxicillin after the expiration date on the label.

Food Interactions

Amoxicillin may be taken with food or meals if it upsets your stomach.

Generic Name

Ampicillin

Brand Names

Amcap	Polycillin
Amcill	Principen
D-Amp	SK-Ampicillin
Omnipen	Supen
Pfizerpen A	Totacillin

(Also available in generic form)

Type of Drug

Penicillin-type antibiotic.

Prescribed for

Gram-positive bacterial infections. Gram-positive bacteria (pneumococci, streptococci, and staphylococci) are organisms which usually cause diseases such as pneumonia, infections of the tonsils and throat, venereal disease, meningitis (infection of the spinal column), and septicemia (general infection of the bloodstream).

Infections of the urinary tract and some infections of the gastrointestinal tract can also be treated with Ampicillin.

General Information

Ampicillin is manufactured in the laboratory by the process known as fermentation and by general chemical reaction and is classified as a semisynthetic antibiotic. Because the effectiveness of the antibiotic is determined by the drug's ability to destroy the cell wall of the invading bacteria, it is very important that the patient completely follow the doctor's prescribing directions. These directions include spacing of doses as well as the number of days the patient should continue taking the medicine. If they are not followed, the effect of the antibiotic is severely reduced.

Cautions and Warnings

If you have a known history of allergy to Penicillin you should avoid taking Ampicillin, since the drugs are chemically very similar. The most common allergic reaction to Ampicillin, as well as to the other penicillins, is a hivelike rash over the body with itching and redness. It is important to tell your doctor if you have ever taken this drug or penicillins before and if you have experienced any adverse reaction to the drug such as skin rash, itching, or difficulty in breathing.

This drug may cause birth defects or interfere with your baby's development. Check with your doctor before taking it if you are, or might be, pregnant.

Ampicillin passes into breast milk and may cause problems in breast-fed infants, such as allergy reactions, fungal infections, skin rashes, or diarrhea. Therefore the drug is not recommended for nursing mothers.

Possible Side Effects

Common: stomach upset, nausea, vomiting, diarrhea, and possible rash. Less common: itching or irritation around the anus and/or vagina. If these symptoms occur, you should contact your doctor immediately.

Drug Interactions

The effect of Ampicillin can be significantly reduced when taken with other antibiotics. Consult your doctor if you are taking both. Otherwise, Ampicillin is generally free of interaction with other medications.

Food Interactions

To ensure the maximum effect of this drug, you should take the medication on an empty stomach, either 1 hour before or 2 hours after meals. However, it may be taken with small amounts of food if it upsets your stomach.

Usual Dose

Adult: 250 to 500 milligrams every 6 hours.

Child (44 pounds and over): same as adult.

Child (under 44 pounds): 25 to 50 milligrams per pound per day.

Storage

Ampicillin can be stored at room temperature.

Special Information

Do not take Ampicillin after the expiration date on the label.
The safety of the drug in pregnancy has not been established.

Type of Drug

Antacids

Brand Names

Aluminum Antacids

Alagel
AlternaGel
Aluminum Hydroxide Gel
Alu-Cap
Alu-Tab
Amphojel

Basaljel
Dialume
Nephrox
Phosphaljel
Rolaids

Calcium Antacids

Alka-2
Amitone
Calcilac
Calcium Carbonate
Calglycine
Chooz
Dicarbosil
Equilet

Gustalac
Mallamint
Pama
Titracid
Titralac
Tums
Tums E-X

Magnesium Antacids

Magnesium Carbonate
Magnesium Oxide
Magnesium Trisilicate
Mag-Ox 400

Maox
Milk of Magnesia
Par-Mag
Uro-Mag

Sodium Bicarbonate Antacids

Bell/ans
Soda Mint
Sodium Bicarbonate

Aluminum + Magnesium Antacids

Algemol	Magmalin
Algenic Alka	Magnagel
Alma-Mag	Magnatril
Aludrox	Mintox
Alumid	Neutracomp
Creamalin	Noralac
Delcid	Riopan
Escot	Rolox
Estomul-M	Rulox
Gaviscon	Tralmag
Gelamal	Triconsil
Kolantyl	WinGel
Kudrox	
Maalox	

Calcium + Magnesium Antacids

Alkets	Marblen
Bisodol	Ratio
Lo-Sol	Spastosed

Aluminum + Calcium + Magnesium Antacids

Camalox
Duracid

Aluminum + Magnesium + Simethicone (an antigas ingredient) Antacids

Almacone	Mi-Acid
Alumid Plus	Mygel
Antagel	Mylanta
Di-Gel	Riopan Plus
Gelusil	Silain Gel
Low Sium Plus	Simaal
Maalox Plus	Simeco

Aluminum + Magnesium + Calcium + Simethicone

Tempo

Effervescent Powders or Tablets Antacids

Alka-Seltzer without aspirin	Citrocarbonate
Bisodol Powder	ENO
Bromo Seltzer	

(Also available in generic form)

Type of Drug

Gastrointestinal acid antagonist.

Prescribed for

Relief of heartburn, acid indigestion, sour stomach, or other conditions related to an upset stomach. These drugs are also prescribed for excess acid in the stomach or intestine associated with ulcer, gastritis, esophagitis, and hiatal hernia. Antacid therapy will help these conditions to heal more quickly. Aluminum antacids are prescribed for kidney failure patients to prevent phosphate from being absorbed into the body. Only Aluminum Hydroxide Gel (any brand) and Basalgel have been shown to be useful as phosphate binders.

General Information

In spite of the large number of antacid products available on the market, there are basically only a few different kinds. All antacids work against stomach acid in the same way—by neutralizing the acid through a chemical reaction. The choice of an antacid is based upon its "neutralizing capacity," that is, how much acid is neutralized by a given amount of antacid. Sodium and calcium have the greatest capacity but should not be used for long-term or ulcer therapy because of the effects large amounts of sodium and calcium can have on your body. Of the other products, Magnesium Hydroxide has the greatest capacity. Next come mixtures of magnesium and aluminum compounds, Magnesium Trisilicate, Aluminum Hydroxide, and Aluminum Phosphates, in that order. The neutralizing capacity of an antacid product also depends upon how it is formulated, how much antacid is put in the mixture, and what the form of the mixture is. Antacid suspensions have greater neutralizing capacity than powders or tablets. Antacid tablets should be thoroughly chewed before they are swallowed.

In most cases, the choice of an antacid product is based purely upon advertising, packaging, convenience, taste, or price. The similarity among so many products accounts for the vast amounts of advertising and promotion put behind antacid products.

Cautions and Warnings

People with high blood pressure or heart failure, and those on low sodium diets, must avoid antacids with a high sodium content. Many antacids are considered to be low in sodium, with Riopan having the lowest sodium content of all antacids. Your pharmacist can advise you which of these drugs are considered low-sodium antacids.

Sodium Bicarbonate is easily absorbed and may result in a condition called systemic alkalosis if it is taken for a long period of time. Magnesium antacids must be used with caution by patients with kidney disease.

This drug may cause birth defects or interfere with your baby's development. Check with your doctor before taking it if you are, or might be, pregnant.

Possible Side Effects

Diarrhea (magnesium products); constipation (aluminum and calcium products). Aluminum/magnesium combinations are usually used to avoid affecting the bowel.

Kidney failure patients who take magnesium antacids may develop magnesium toxicity.

Calcium and sodium antacids may cause a rebound effect, with more acid produced after the antacid is stopped than before it was started.

Magnesium Trisilicate antacids used over long periods may result in the development of silicate renal stones.

Drug Interactions

Antacids can interfere with the absorption of most drugs into the body. Intake of antacids should be separated from that of other oral drugs by 1 to 2 hours. Those drugs with which antacids are known to interfere are anticholinergic drugs, phenothiazines, Digoxin, Phenytoin, Isoniazid, Quinidine, Warfarin, iron-containing products, and tetracycline-type antibiotics.

Usual Dose

The dose of antacids must be individualized to the patient's requirement. For ulcers, antacids are given every hour for the first 2 weeks (during waking hours) and 1 to 3 hours after meals and at bedtime thereafter.

Special Information

If you are using antacid tablets, be sure they are completely chewed. Swallow with milk or water.

Aluminum antacids may cause speckling or add a whitish coloration to the stool.

Brand Name

Anusol-HC

Ingredients

Balsam Peru
Benzyl Benzoate
Bismuth Resorcin Compound

Bismuth Subgallate
Hydrocortisone Acetate
Zinc Oxide

(Also available in generic form)

Type of Drug

Hemorrhoid relief compound.

Prescribed for

Relief of rectal pain and itching due to hemorrhoids or local itching.

General Information

Although its ingredients are unique, Anusol-HC is one of many products available for the relief of rectal pain and itching. The bismuth compounds and Zinc Oxide act to help shrink hemorrhoids, and the Hydrocortisone acts to reduce inflammation throughout the general area. This and similar products provide effective relief but do not treat the underlying cause of the problem.

Cautions and Warnings

Do not use if the area is infected or if you have herpes cold sores, tuberculosis of the skin or other generalized skin infections, or glaucoma. Use with caution if you experience urinary difficulties, are elderly, or suffer from prostate disease.

This drug may cause birth defects or interfere with your

baby's development. Check with your doctor before taking it if you are, or might be, pregnant.

Possible Side Effects

Local irritation, aggravation of glaucoma, or infection.

Possible Adverse Drug Effects

A lot of the Hydrocortisone in this drug will be absorbed into the bloodstream and it is possible to experience the adverse effects seen when a corticosteroid drug is taken by mouth. This will not become a serious problem except in cases where the medicine is used for too long or when it is used by someone also taking corticosteroids by mouth.

Usual Dose

Children: should be used with caution by children under age 6.

Cream: apply locally twice a day for up to 7 days.

Suppository: 1 suppository twice a day for up to 7 days.

Storage

Keep away from excessive heat.

Special Information

Do not use for more than 7 days unless specifically directed to do so. Stop taking or call your doctor if you experience dry mouth, blurred vision, eye pain, or dizziness.

Generic Name

A.P.C. with Codeine

Ingredients

Aspirin	Codeine Sulfate
Caffeine	Phenacetin

Brand Names

Tabloid APC with Codeine   *Combinations containing
                                 only Aspirin and Codeine:*
                                 Emcodiene
                                 Emprin w/Codeine

(Also available in generic form)

Type of Drug

Narcotic analgesic and cough suppressant.

Prescribed for

Relief of mild to moderate pain.

General Information

A.P.C. with Codeine is one of many combination products
containing narcotics and analgesics. These products often
contain barbiturates or tranquilizers, and Acetaminophen may be substituted for Aspirin and/or Caffeine may be
omitted.

Cautions and Warnings

Do not take Codeine if you know you are allergic or sensitive
to it. Use this drug with extreme caution if you suffer from
asthma or other breathing problems. Long-term use of this
drug may cause drug dependence or addiction. Codeine is a
respiratory depressant and affects the central nervous system, producing sleepiness, tiredness, and/or inability to concentrate.

This drug is known to cause birth defects or interfere with
your baby's development. It is not considered safe for use
during pregnancy.

Possible Side Effects

Most frequent: light-headedness, dizziness, sleepiness, nausea, vomiting, loss of appetite, sweating. If these occur,
consider calling your doctor and asking him about lowering
the dose of Codeine you are taking. Usually the side effects
disappear if you simply lie down.

More serious side effects of A.P.C. with Codeine are shallow breathing or difficulty in breathing.

Possible Adverse Drug Effects

Euphoria (feeling "high"), weakness, sleepiness, headache, agitation, uncoordinated muscle movement, minor hallucinations, disorientation and visual disturbances, dry mouth, loss of appetite, constipation, flushing of the face, rapid heartbeat, palpitations, faintness, urinary difficulties or hesitancy, reduced sex drive and/or potency, itching, rashes, anemia, lowered blood sugar, yellowing of the skin and/or whites of the eyes. Narcotic analgesics may aggravate convulsions in those who have had convulsions in the past.

Drug Interactions

Interaction with alcohol, tranquilizers, barbiturates, or sleeping pills produces tiredness, sleepiness, or inability to concentrate, and seriously increases the depressive effect of A.P.C. with Codeine.

The Aspirin component of A.P.C. with Codeine can affect anticoagulant (blood-thinning) therapy. Be sure to discuss this with your doctor so that the proper dosage adjustment can be made.

Interaction with adrenal cortical steroids, Phenylbutazone, or alcohol can cause severe stomach irritation with possible bleeding.

Food Interactions

Take with food or ½ glass of water to prevent stomach upset.

Usual Dose

1 to 2 tablets 3 to 4 times per day.

Overdosage

Symptoms are depression of respiration (breathing), extreme tiredness progressing to stupor and then coma, pinpointed pupils of the eyes, no response to stimulation such as a pin stick, cold and clammy skin, slowing down of the heartbeat, lowering of blood pressure, convulsions, and cardiac arrest. The patient should be taken to a hospital emergency room immediately. ALWAYS bring the medicine bottle.

Special Information

Drowsiness may occur: be careful when driving or operatin
hazardous machinery.

The Phenacetin ingredient of A.P.C. with Codeine may b
toxic to your kidneys: do not take this medication for longe
than 10 days unless so directed by your doctor.

Brand Name

Apresazide

Ingredients

Hydralazine
Hydrochlorothiazide

(Also available in generic form)

Other Brand Names

Apresodex   Hydral
Apresoline-Esidrix
Aprozide

Type of Drug

Antihypertensive combination.

Prescribed for

High blood pressure.

General Information

This is a combination of two drugs used for the treatment o
high blood pressure. Together, they are more effective tha
either drug taken alone. Since many people take the indivic
ual ingredients for high blood pressure, the combinatio
may be a more convenient way to take their medicine.

This is a good example of a drug which takes advantage o
a drug interaction. Both of the drugs work by different mech
anisms to lower blood pressure. Hydrochlorothiazide is
diuretic which works through its effects on muscles in th
walls of the blood vessels and its effect on lowering flui
levels in the body. Hydralazine works by affecting the mus
cles in the walls of the arteries and lowers blood pressure b
dilating, or widening, these blood vessels.

Cautions and Warnings

Do not take Apresazide if you are allergic to either of the ingredients or to sulfa drugs. It should not be used if you have certain kinds of heart disease, including rheumatic heart, or severe kidney disease. It must be used with care in patients who have severe liver disease.

This drug, in a few patients, may produce symptoms of a serious disease called lupus erythematosus. The symptoms of this are aching muscles and joints, skin rash and other complications, fever, anemia, and spleen enlargement. If these occur, the drug must be stopped immediately.

Apresazide must be used with caution by women who are pregnant or breast-feeding, and only when absolutely necessary.

This drug may cause birth defects or interfere with your baby's development. Check with your doctor before taking it if you are, or might be, pregnant. Avoid sudden changes in posture.

Possible Side Effects

One of the ingredients in this drug can cause the lowering of potassium levels in the body. Signs of this are dryness of the mouth, thirst, weakness, lethargy, drowsiness, restlessness, muscle pains or cramps, muscle tiredness, low blood pressure, decreased frequency of urination, abnormal heart rate, and stomach upset, including nausea and vomiting. To prevent this, potassium supplements are given in the form of tablets, liquid, or powders, or by increasing consumption of high-potassium foods such as bananas, citrus fruits, melons, and tomatoes. This drug can also cause loss of appetite, diarrhea, rapid heartbeat, and chest pain.

Possible Adverse Drug Effects

Stuffy nose, flushing, tearing, itching, and redness of the eyes, numbness and tingling in the hands or feet, dizziness, tremors, muscle cramps, depression, disorientation, anxiety. The drug can also cause nausea, vomiting, cramps and diarrhea, constipation, dizziness, headache, tingling in the arms, hands, legs, or toes, changes in blood composition, sensitivity to the sun, rash, itching, fever, drug allergy, difficulty in breathing, blurred vision, weakness, and dizziness when rising from a sitting or lying position.

Drug Interactions

This combination should be used with caution by people taking an MAO inhibitor drug.

The possibility of developing imbalances in body fluids is increased if you take medicines like the digitalis drugs or adrenal corticosteroids with Apresazide. This problem can be avoided by periodic laboratory monitoring of the blood.

One of the ingredients in Apresazide will affect oral antidiabetic drugs. If you are already taking an oral drug for diabetes and start taking Apresazide, your dose of diabetes medicine may have to be changed.

Lithium drugs should be monitored closely if given together with Apresazide because of the increased possibility of Lithium toxicity.

Food Interactions

Apresazide may antagonize Vitamin B_6, pyridoxine, which can result in peripheral neuropathy including tremors, tingling and numbness of the fingers, toes, or other extremities. If these occur, your doctor may advise you to take a vitamin containing Vitamin B_6.

This drug may be taken with meals if it causes upset stomach.

Usual Dose

1 to 2 tablets per day. The exact dose must be tailored to your needs. This drug comes in several different dosage strengths.

Overdosage

Symptoms: very low blood pressure, rapid heartbeat, headache, flushing of the skin, chest pain, abnormal heart rhythms, fatigue, and coma may develop. In case of an overdose take the patient to a hospital emergency room immediately. ALWAYS bring the medicine bottle.

Special Information

Always take your medicine exactly as directed.

Avoid over-the-counter drugs containing stimulants; most

of these are for colds and allergies. If you are in doubt, ask your pharmacist.

You may develop headache or heart palpitations, especially during the first few days of therapy with Apresazide.

If you develop weakness, muscle cramps, nausea, dizziness, or other signs of potassium loss, or if you develop fever or muscle aches or chest pains, call your doctor.

Do not stop taking this medication unless told to do so by your physician.

Generic Name
Aspirin, Buffered Aspirin

Brand Names

A.S.A.	Arthritis Bayer
A.S.A. Enseals	Arthritis Pain Formula
A.S.A. Pulvules	Alka-Seltzer
Aspergum	Arthritis Strength Bufferin
Bayer	Ascriptin
Bayer Children's Aspirin	Ascriptin A/D
Bayer Timed-Release Aspirin	Asperbuf
Norwich Extra-Strength	Buff-A
Cosprin	Buffaprin
Easprin	Bufferin
Ecotrin	Buffex
Empirin Analgesic	Buffinol
Hipirin	Buf-Tabs
Measurin	Cama Arthritis Pain Reliever
Zorprin	Wesprin Buffered

(Also available in generic form)

Type of Drug

Analgesic, anti-inflammatory.

Prescribed for

Mild to moderate pain; fever; inflammation of bones, joints, or other body tissues; reducing the probability that people who have had a stroke or TIA (oxygen shortage to the brain) because of a problem with blood coagulation will have another such attack. Aspirin may also be prescribed as an anticoagulant (blood-thinning) drug, or in people with unstable angina, to protect against heart attack, although it has not been approved by the government for this purpose.

General Information

Aspirin is probably the closest thing we have to a wonder drug. It has been used for more than a century as a pain and fever remedy but is now used for its effect on the blood as well.

Aspirin is the standard against which all other drugs are compared for pain relief. Chemically, Aspirin is a member of the group called Salicylates. Other Salicylates include Sodium Salicylate, Sodium Thiosalicylate, Choline Salicylate, and Magnesium Salicylate (Trilisate). These drugs are no more effective than regular Aspirin, although two of them (Choline Salicylate and Magnesium Salicylate) may be a little less irritating to the stomach. They are all more expensive than Aspirin.

Scientists think that they have finally discovered how Aspirin works. It reduces fever by causing the blood vessels in the skin to open, thereby allowing heat from our body to leave more rapidly. Its effects on pain and inflammation are thought to be related to its ability to prevent the manufacture of complex body hormones called prostaglandins. Of all the Salicylates, Aspirin has the greatest effect on prostaglandin production.

Many people find that they can take Buffered Aspirin but not regular Aspirin. The addition of antacids to Aspirin can be important to patients who must take large doses of Aspirin for chronic arthritis or other conditions. In many cases, Aspirin is the only effective drug and it can be tolerated only with the antacids present.

Cautions and Warnings

People with liver damage should avoid Aspirin. People who are allergic to Aspirin may also be allergic to drugs such as Indomethacin, Sulindac, Ibuprofen, Fenoprofen, Naproxen, Tolmetin, and Meclofenamate Sodium, or to products containing tartrazine (a commonly used orange dye and food coloring). People with asthma and/or nasal polyps are more likely to be allergic to Aspirin.

Reye's syndrome is a life-threatening condition characterized by vomiting and stupor or dullness and may develop in children with influenza (flu) or chicken pox if treated with Aspirin or other Salicylates.

The Surgeon General, Centers for Disease Control, and pediatric physicians associations advise against the use of Aspirin or other Salicylates in children with flu or chicken pox. Acetaminophen-containing products are suggested instead.

Aspirin can interfere with normal blood coagulation and should be avoided for 1 week before surgery for this reason. It would be wise to ask your surgeon or dentist their recommendation before taking Aspirin for post-surgical pain.

This drug may cause birth defects or interfere with your baby's development. Check with your doctor before taking it if you are, or might be, pregnant.

Possible Side Effects

Nausea, upset stomach, heartburn, loss of appetite, and loss of small amounts of blood in the stool. Aspirin may contribute to the formation of a stomach ulcer and bleeding.

Drug Interactions

People taking anticoagulants (blood-thinning drugs) should avoid Aspirin. The effect of the anticoagulant will be increased.

Aspirin may increase the possibility of stomach ulcer when taken together with adrenal corticosteroids, Phenylbutazone, or alcoholic beverages. Aspirin will counteract the uric acid eliminating effect of Probenecid and Sulfinpyrazone.

Food Interactions

Since Aspirin can cause upset stomach or bleeding, take each dose with food, milk, or a glass of water.

Usual Dose

Adult: aches, pains, and fever, 325 to 650 milligrams every 4 hours; arthritis and rheumatic conditions, up to 5200 milligrams (16 325-milligram tablets) per day; rheumatic fever, up to 7800 milligrams (24 325-milligram tablets) per day; to prevent recurrence of stroke or TIA in men, 325 milligrams 2 to 4 times per day.

Child: 30 milligrams per pound per day, in 4 to 6 divided doses.

Overdosage

Symptoms of mild overdosage are rapid and deep breathing, nausea, vomiting, dizziness, ringing or buzzing in the ears, flushing, sweating, thirst, headache, drowsiness, diarrhea, and rapid heartbeat.

Severe overdosage may cause fever, excitement, confusion, convulsions, coma, or bleeding.

The initial treatment of Aspirin overdose involves making the patient vomit to remove any Aspirin remaining in the stomach. Further therapy depends on how the situation develops and what must be done to maintain the patient. DO NOT INDUCE VOMITING UNTIL YOU HAVE SPOKEN WITH YOUR DOCTOR OR POISON CONTROL CENTER. If in doubt, go to a hospital emergency room.

Special Information

Contact your doctor if you develop a continuous stomach pain or a ringing or buzzing in the ears.

Generic Name

Atenolol

Brand Name

Tenormin

Type of Drug

Beta-adrenergic blocking agent.

Prescribed for

High blood pressure.

General Information

This drug is very much like Metoprolol, another beta-adrenergic blocker with specific effects on the heart and less specific effects on receptors in the blood vessels and respiratory tract than Propranolol, the first beta-adrenergic blocker marketed in the United States. The exact way that these drugs lower blood pressure is not known, but it is thought to be the result of their effect on the heart and body hormone systems. Atenolol and Metoprolol cause fewer side effects than Propranolol because of their specificity on receptors in the heart.

Cautions and Warnings

Atenolol should be used with care if you have a history of asthma or upper respiratory disease, seasonal allergies, or other respiratory conditions which may be worsened by this drug. Do not take this drug if you are allergic to any of the beta-adrenergic blocking drugs.

Atenolol may aggravate or worsen an existing condition of congestive heart failure. It may induce spasms in the bronchial muscles, which will make any existing asthmatic or respiratory condition worse.

This drug may cause birth defects or interfere with your baby's development. Check with your doctor before taking it if you are, or might be, pregnant.

Possible Side Effects

Coldness in the hands or feet, dizziness, tiredness, depression, decreased heart rate, dizziness on rising quickly from a sitting or lying position, leg pains, light-headedness, lethargy, drowsiness, unusual dream patterns, diarrhea, nausea, difficulty breathing, wheezing, tingling in the extremities, visual disturbances, hallucinations, short-term memory loss, or abdominal cramps.

Possible Adverse Drug Effects

Atenolol can cause adverse effects on the blood system, drug allergy (fever, aching, sore throat, and difficulty breathing), emotional instability or personality changes, hair loss (reversible when the drug is stopped), rash.

Drug Interactions

Atenolol is not generally recommended to be given with MAO inhibitors.

Atenolol, unlike other beta-blocking drugs, does not increase the blood sugar lowering effect of Insulin. Atenolol may reduce the effectiveness of digitalis drugs on your heart. Any dose of digitalis medication will have to be altered. If you are taking Digitalis for a purpose other than congestive heart failure, the effectiveness of the Digitalis may be increased by Atenolol, and the Digitalis dose reduced. Atenolol will interact with other blood pressure lowering drugs to yield an enhanced effect. This is an interaction with positive results and is used in treating patients for high blood pressure.

Do not self-medicate with over-the-counter cold, cough, or allergy remedies which may contain stimulant drugs that will aggravate certain types of heart disease and high blood pressure, or other ingredients that may antagonize the effects of Atenolol. Check with your pharmacist before taking an over-the-counter medication.

Atenolol may interact with calcium channel blockers. Close medical supervision is advised.

Usual Dose

50 to 100 milligrams given once a day. Patients with kidney disease may need only 50 milligrams every other day. The dosage must be tailored to individual patient need.

Overdosage

Symptoms are slowed heart rate, heart failure, lowered blood pressure, and spasms of the bronchial muscles which make it difficult to breathe. The patient should be taken to a hospital emergency room for treatment. ALWAYS bring the medicine bottle with you.

Special Information

This drug may make you tired, so take care while driving or doing anything that requires coordination. Call your doctor if you become dizzy or develop diarrhea. Do not stop taking this medicine abruptly. The dose should be reduced gradually over a period of time. Serious heart pain may develop if you do not taper the dosage.

Brand Name
Augmentin

Ingredients

Amoxicillin
Clavulanic Acid

Type of Drug

Antibiotic.

Prescribed for

Treatment of infections of the lungs, middle ear, skin and soft tissue, and urinary tract. It can also be used for sinusitis caused by organisms usually sensitive to Amoxicillin or Ampicillin.

General Information

This medicine represents a novel approach to the treatment of resistant infections by adding an "augmentor" to the antibiotic. Clavulanic Acid is a weak antibiotic that is chemically similar to Ampicillin and other Penicillin-type antibiotics. However, at low concentrations it has the unique ability to inactivate enzymes produced by bacteria that can neutralize Amoxicillin or Ampicillin before it can kill the bacteria. Clavulanic Acid combined with Amoxicillin or another Penicillin-type antibiotic will increase the antibiotic's effectiveness against organisms that may have developed some degree of resistance to it over the years.

Cautions and Warnings

This product cannot be taken by anyone who is sensitive or allergic to Amoxicillin, Ampicillin, Hetacillin, Bacampicillin, or to any member of the penicillin group.

This drug should not be taken by women who are or may become pregnant while using it. In situations where it is deemed essential, the drug's potential risk must be carefully weighed against any benefit it might produce. Nursing mothers should watch for any possible drug effect on their infants while taking this medicine.

Possible Side Effects

The side effects of this combination are essentially the same as those associated with Amoxicillin. Most common are upset stomach and diarrhea, more frequent than with plain Amoxicillin. Skin rash may also develop, but is not necessarily a sign of drug allergy. More definite signs of drug allergy include wheezing, sneezing, itching, and severe difficulty breathing.

Possible Adverse Drug Effects

Less frequent effects of this product include those associated with the other penicillins. The vast majority of people taking this product will tolerate it without any problems. Detailed information can be found in the Amoxicillin monograph on page 50.

Drug Interactions

The effect of this combination will be reduced if it is taken together with Tetracycline or another bacteriostatic antibiotic, one which works by slowing the growth of an organism rather than killing it, as Amoxicillin and other penicillin-type antibiotics do.

Probenecid (Benemid) will reduce the rate at which Amoxicillin is eliminated from your body, extending its effect.

Augmentin can cause false positive test results for urine sugar if Clinitest or similar products are used. It will not interfere with the enzyme method used by Tes-Tape or Clinistix.

Food Interactions

Augmentin may be taken with food if it upsets your stomach because it is unaffected by food in the stomach.

Usual Dose

250 to 500 milligrams every 8 hours. Each tablet, regardless of the amount of Amoxicillin it contains, also has 125 milligrams of Clavulanic Acid in it. Children may be given 9 to 18 milligrams per pound each day, in divided doses. The dose is based on Amoxicillin content.

Overdosage

The most frequent effects of overdose are nausea, vomiting, and stomach pain. For most people, the symptoms can be treated simply by taking milk or an antacid. Severe and

llergic reactions must be treated in a hospital emergency
oom. ALWAYS bring the medicine bottle with you.

Special Information

Take the full course of treatment prescribed by your doctor, even if you feel better within a day or two of beginning
therapy.

Call your doctor if you begin to itch or if hives, skin rash,
or breathing difficulty develop.

All antibiotics, including Augmentin, are best taken at even
intervals around the clock.

Brand Name

Auralgan

Ingredients

Antipyrine
Benzocaine
Glycerin

Other products with the same ingredients in different
concentrations:

Auromid
OTO (also contains Chlorobutanol)

(Also available in generic form)

Type of Drug

Analgesic.

Prescribed for

Earache.

General Information

This drug is a combination product containing a local anesthetic to deaden nerves inside the ear which transmit painful
impulses, an analgesic to provide additional pain relief, and
Glycerin to remove any water present in the ear. This drug is

often used to treat painful conditions where water is presen
in the ear canal, such as "swimmer's ear." This drug doe
not contain any antibiotics and should not be used to trea
any infection.

Cautions and Warnings

Do not use Auralgan if you are allergic to any of its ingredients
   This drug may cause birth defects or interfere with you
baby's development. Check with your doctor before taking
if you are, or might be, pregnant.

Possible Side Effects

Local irritation.

Usual Dose

Place drops of Auralgan in the ear canal until it is fillec
Saturate a piece of cotton with Auralgan and put it in the ea
canal to keep the drug from leaking out. Leave the drug i
the ear for several minutes. Repeat 3 to 4 times per day.

Special Information

Before using, warm the bottle of eardrops to body tempera
ture by holding it in your hand for several minutes. Do no
warm the bottle to a temperature above normal bod
temperature. Protect the bottle from light.
   Call your doctor if you develop a burning or itching feelin
or if the pain does not go away.

Brand Name

AVC Cream

Ingredients

Allantoin
Aminacrine
Sulfanilamide

Other Brand Names

AAS-Suppositories	Sufamal
Amide-VC	Vag
Benegyn	Vagacreme
Cervex	Vagidine
Deltavac	Vagi-Nil
Femguard	Vagitrol
Par	

Type of Drug

Vaginal anti-infective.

Prescribed for

Relief of vaginal infection.

General Information

AVC Cream should only be used to treat vaginal irritation due to an infection. In such cases there may be relief within a few days, but the drug should be used through an entire menstrual cycle. If no relief occurs within a few days, or if the symptoms return, do not continue this drug. Consult your doctor, as a new medication may be required.

Cautions and Warnings

Do not use if you are allergic to sulfa drugs. If a rash develops, stop using the drug and consult your doctor.

This drug may cause birth defects or interfere with your baby's development. Check with your doctor before taking it if you are, or might be, pregnant.

Possible Side Effects

Most frequent: vaginal burning or discomfort. Less frequent: rash or other side effects associated with sulfa drug toxicity.

Usual Dose

1 applicator full of cream inserted into the vagina once or twice per day.

Generic Name

Azatadine Maleate

Brand Name
Optimine

Type of Drug
Antihistamine.

Prescribed for
Seasonal allergy, stuffed and runny nose, itching of the eyes, scratching of the throat caused by allergy, and other allergic symptoms such as itching, rash, or hives.

General Information
Antihistamines generally, including Azatadine, act by blocking the release of histamine from the cell at the H_1 histamine receptor site. Antihistamines work by drying up the secretions of the nose, throat, and eyes.

Cautions and Warnings
Azatadine Maleate should not be used if you are allergic to this drug. It should be avoided or used with extreme care if you have narrow angle glaucoma (pressure in the eye), stomach ulcer or other stomach problems, enlarged prostate, or problems passing urine. It should not be used by people who have deep-breathing problems such as asthma.

Azatadine Maleate can cause dizziness, drowsiness, and lowering of blood pressure, particularly in the elderly patient. Young children can show signs of nervousness, increased tension, and anxiety.

This drug may cause birth defects or interfere with your baby's development. Check with your doctor before taking it if you are, or might be, pregnant.

Possible Side Effects
Occasionally seen: itching, rash, sensitivity to light, excessive perspiration, chills, dryness of the mouth, nose, and

throat, lowering of blood pressure, headache, rapid heart-beat, sleeplessness, dizziness, disturbed coordination, confusion, restlessness, nervousness, irritability, euphoria (feeling high), tingling of the hands and feet, blurred vision, double vision, ringing in the ears, stomach upset, loss of appetite, nausea, vomiting, constipation, diarrhea, difficulty in urination, tightness of the chest, wheezing, nasal stuffiness.

Possible Adverse Drug Effects

Use with care if you have a history of asthma, glaucoma, thyroid disease, heart disease, high blood pressure, or diabetes.

Drug Interactions

Azatadine Maleate should not be taken with the MAO inhibitors.

Interactions with tranquilizers, sedatives, and sleeping medication will increase the effect of these drugs; it is extremely important that you discuss this with your doctor so that doses of these drugs can be properly adjusted.

Be extremely cautious when drinking alcohol while taking Azatadine Maleate, which will enhance the intoxicating effect of alcohol. Alcohol also has a sedative effect.

Usual Dose

1 to 2 milligrams twice per day.

Overdosage

Symptoms are depression or stimulation (especially in children), dry mouth, fixed or dilated pupils, flushing of the skin, and stomach upset. Take the patient to a hospital emergency room immediately, if you cannot make him vomit. ALWAYS bring the medicine bottle.

Special Information

Antihistamines produce a depressing effect: be extremely cautious when driving or operating heavy equipment.

The safety of Azatadine Maleate in pregnancy has not been established. A breast-feeding mother should avoid taking this medication, since it is known to pass from the mother to the baby through the milk.

Brand Name

Azo Gantrisin

Ingredients

Phenazopyridine
Sulfisoxazole

Other Brand Names

Azo-Sulfisoxazole
Suldiazo

Type of Drug

Urinary anti-infective.

Prescribed for

Urinary tract infections.

General Information

Azo Gantrisin is one of many combination products used to treat urinary tract infections. The primary active ingredient is Sulfisoxazole. The other ingredient, Phenazopyridine, is added as a pain reliever.

Cautions and Warnings

Do not take Azo Gantrisin if you know you are allergic to sulfa drugs, salicylates, or similar agents or if you have the disease porphyria. Azo Gantrisin should not be considered if you have advanced kidney disease.

   This drug may cause birth defects or interfere with your baby's development. Check with your doctor before taking it if you are, or might be, pregnant.

Possible Side Effects

Headache, itching, rash, sensitivity to strong sunlight, nausea, vomiting, abdominal pains, feeling of tiredness or lassitude, hallucinations, dizziness, ringing in the ears, chills, feeling of ill health.

Possible Adverse Drug Effects

Blood diseases or alterations of normal blood components, itching of the eyes, arthritis-type pain, diarrhea, loss of appetite, stomach cramps or pains, hearing loss, drowsiness, fever, chills, hair loss, yellowing of the skin and/or eyes, reduction in sperm count.

Drug Interactions

When Azo Gantrisin is taken with an anticoagulant (blood-thinning) drug, any drug used to treat diabetes, Methotrexate, Phenylbutazone, salicylates (Aspirin-like drugs), Phenytoin, or Probenecid, it will cause unusually large amounts of these drugs to be released into the bloodstream, possibly producing symptoms of overdosage. If you are going to take Azo Gantrisin for an extended period, your physician should reduce the dosage of these interactive drugs. Also, avoid large doses of Vitamin C.

Usual Dose

Adult: first dose, 4 to 6 tablets, then 2 tablets every 4 hours. Take each dose with a full glass of water.

Overdosage

Induce vomiting and give a rectal enema; then take the patient to a hospital emergency room. ALWAYS bring the medicine bottle.

Special Information

Azo Gantrisin can cause photosensitivity—a severe reaction to strong sunlight. Avoid prolonged exposure to strong sunlight while taking it.

Sore throat, fever, unusual bleeding or bruising, rash, and feeling tired are early signs of serious blood disorders and should be reported to your doctor immediately.

The Phenazopyridine ingredient in Azo Gantrisin is an orange-red dye and will color the urine. Do not be worried, since this is a normal effect of the drug; but note that if you are diabetic, the dye may interfere with testing your urine for sugar. This dye may also appear in your sweat and tears. Note that this dye may discolor certain types of contact lenses.

Generic Name

Beclomethasone

Brand Names

Beclovent
Beconase
Vancenase
Vanceril

Type of Drug

Adrenal cortical steroid.

Prescribed for

Treatment of chronic asthma.

General Information

Beclomethasone is used as an inhaler by mouth and as an intranasal product to relieve symptoms associated with seasonal allergy. It works by reducing inflammation of the mucosal lining within the bronchi, thereby making it easier to breathe. This drug should not be used more than 3 weeks if it has not worked within that time. Beclomethasone will not work immediately, as a decongestant would; it may take several days to exert its effect.

Cautions and Warnings

Do not use this drug if you are allergic to Beclomethasone. This drug cannot be used as the primary treatment of severe asthma. It is only for people who usually take Prednisone, or another adrenal cortical steroid, by mouth and those who are taking other asthma drugs but are still having asthmatic attacks.

Even though this drug is taken by inhaling directly into the lungs, it should be considered a potent adrenal corticosteriod drug. During periods of severe stress, you may have to go back to taking steroid drugs by mouth if Beclomethasone does not control your asthma.

Large amounts of Beclomethasone used during pregnancy or breast-feeding may slow the growth of newborn babies. This drug may cause birth defects or interfere with your baby's development. Check with your doctor before taking it if you are, or might be, pregnant.

Possible Side Effects

Dry mouth, hoarseness.

Possible Adverse Drug Effects

Deaths have occurred in patients taking adrenal corticosteroid tablets or syrup and being switched to Beclomethasone by inhalation due to failure of the adrenal gland. This is a rare complication and usually results from stopping the liquid or tablets too quickly. They must be stopped gradually over a long period of time.

This drug can also cause rash or spasm of the bronchial muscles.

Usual Dose

Intra-nasal inhalation:
  Adult and child (over age 12): 1 inhalation in each nostril 2 to 4 times per day. Not recommended for children under 12 years of age.
Oral inhalation:
  Adult and child (over age 12): 6 to 20 inhalations per day.
  Child (age 6 to 12): 3 to 10 inhalations per day.

Special Information

People using both Beclomethasone and a bronchodilator by inhalation should use the bronchodilator first, wait a few minutes, then use the Beclomethasone. This will allow more Beclomethasone to be absorbed.

This drug is for preventive therapy only and will not affect an asthma attack. Beclomethasone must be inhaled regularly, as directed. Wait at least 1 minute between inhalations.

Dry mouth or hoarseness may be reduced by rinsing the mouth after each use of the inhaler.

Shake well before each use.

Brand Name

Bentyl with Phenobarbital

Ingredients

Dicyclomine Hydrochloride
Phenobarbital

Other Brand Names

Byclomine with Phenobarbital

(Also available in generic form)

Type of Drug

Gastrointestinal anticholinergic agent.

Prescribed for

Symptomatic relief of stomach upset and spasms.

General Information

Bentyl with Phenobarbital works by reducing spasms in muscles of the stomach and other parts of the gastrointestinal tract. In doing so, it helps relieve some of the uncomfortable symptoms associated with peptic ulcer, irritable bowel and/or colon, spastic colon, and other gastrointestinal disorders. It only relieves symptoms. It does not cure the underlying disease.

Cautions and Warnings

Bentyl with Phenobarbital should not be used if you know you are sensitive or allergic to Dicyclomine Hydrochloride. Do not use this medicine if you have glaucoma, asthma, obstructive disease of the gastrointestinal tract, or other serious gastrointestinal disease. Because this drug reduces your ability to sweat, its use in hot climates may cause heat exhaustion.

This drug may cause birth defects or interfere with your baby's development. Check with your doctor before taking it if you are, or might be, pregnant.

Possible Side Effects

Occasional: difficulty in urination, blurred vision, rapid heartbeat, palpitations, sensitivity to light, headache, flushing, nervousness, dizziness, weakness, drowsiness, inability to sleep, nausea, vomiting, fever, nasal congestion, heartburn, constipation, feeling of being bloated. There is also occasionally drug allergy or a drug idiosyncratic reaction, which may include itching or other skin manifestations.

Possible Adverse Drug Effects

Use of this drug in elderly patients may be associated with some degree of mental confusion and/or excitement.

Drug Interactions

Interaction with antihistamines, benzodiazepines, phenothiazines, tranquilizers, antidepressants, and some narcotic painkillers may cause blurred vision, dry mouth, or drowsiness.

Do not use with Tranylcypromine Sulfate (Parnate), Isocarboxazid (Marplan), Phenelzine Sulfate (Nardil), or other MAO inhibitor drugs, which will tend to prevent excretion of Bentyl with Phenobarbital from the body and thus potentiate it (increase its effects).

Avoid use with antacids as they may interfere with absorption of Bentyl with Phenobarbital.

Usual Dose

1 capsule or 1 tablet every 3 to 4 hours as needed for relief of symptoms. If necessary, capsules may be given up to 8 times per day, tablets up to 4 times per day.

Syrup: 1 teaspoon 3 to 4 times per day, but as many as 8 teaspoons per day may be required.

Special Information

Dry mouth produced by Bentyl with Phenobarbital can be relieved by chewing gum or sucking hard candy; constipation can be treated with a stool softener (rather than a harsh cathartic).

Brand Name

Benylin Cough Syrup

Ingredients

Ammonium Chloride
Diphenhydramine Hydrochloride
Sodium Citrate

Other Brand Names

Diphen Cough	Noradryl Cough Syrup
Diphenhydramine Hydro- chloride Cough Syrup	Tusstat Valdrene

(Also available in generic form)

Type of Drug

Cough syrup.

Prescribed for

Coughs associated with the common cold and other upper
respiratory infections.

General Information

Benylin Cough Syrup is one of many products marketed for
the relief of coughs. Its major active ingredient is an antihistamine; therefore, the drug is most effective in relieving the
symptoms of excess histamine product. Basically, Benylin
Cough Syrup is only able to help you feel well. It cannot help
you recover more quickly, only more comfortably.

Cautions and Warnings

Do not use Benylin Cough Syrup if you have narrow angle
glaucoma.
   This drug may cause birth defects or interfere with your
baby's development. Check with your doctor before taking it
if you are, or might be, pregnant.

Possible Side Effects

Tiredness, inability to concentrate, blurred vision, dry mouth, difficulty in urination, constipation.

Drug Interactions

Benylin Cough Syrup contains an antihistamine and may produce some depression, drowsiness, or inability to concentrate. Don't drink large quantities of alcoholic beverages, which can increase this depressant effect.

Usual Dose

1 to 2 teaspoons 4 times per day.

Special Information

Take with a full glass of water to reduce stomach upset and help loosen mucus that may be present in the breathing passages.

Generic Name

Benzphetamine Hydrochloride

Brand Name

Didrex

Type of Drug

Central nervous system stimulant.

Prescribed for

Short-term (2 to 3 weeks) aid to diet control, minimal brain dysfunction in children, narcolepsy (uncontrollable and unpredictable desire to sleep).

General Information

When taking this medicine as part of a weight control program it is usual to experience *less* appetite reduction as time goes on. This is because your body is breaking down the drug faster. Do not increase the amount of drug you are taking: simply stop taking the medicine.

The use of Benzphetamine Hydrochloride (as well as other drugs) in the treatment of minimal brain dysfunction in children is extremely controversial and must be undertaken only on the advice of a physician qualified to treat the disorder. Children whose problems are judged to have been produced by their surroundings or by primary psychiatric disorders may not be helped by Benzphetamine Hydrochloride.

Cautions and Warnings

Benzphetamine Hydrochloride is highly abusable and addictive. It must be used with extreme caution. People with hardening of the arteries (arteriosclerosis), heart disease, high blood pressure, thyroid disease, or glaucoma, or who are sensitive or allergic to any amphetamine, should not take this medication.

This drug is known to cause birth defects or interfere with your baby's development. It is not considered safe for use during pregnancy.

Possible Side Effects

Palpitations, restlessness, overstimulation, dizziness, sleeplessness, increased blood pressure, rapid heartbeat.

Possible Adverse Drug Effects

Euphoria, hallucinations, muscle spasms and tremors, headache, dryness of the mouth, unpleasant taste, diarrhea, constipation, stomach upset, itching, loss of sex drive, (rarely) psychotic drug reactions.

Drug Interactions

Benzphetamine Hydrochloride should not be given at the same time or within 14 days following the use of MAO inhibitors. To do so may cause severe lowering of blood pressure.

Benzphetamine Hydrochloride may also decrease the effectiveness of Guanethidine Sulfate, and other antihypertensive agents.

Usual Dose

25 to 150 milligrams per day.

Overdosage

Symptoms are tremors, muscle spasms, restlessness, exaggerated reflexes, rapid breathing, hallucinations, confusion, panic, and overaggressive behavior, followed by depression and exhaustion after the central nervous system stimulation wears off, as well as abnormal heart rhythms, changes in blood pressure, nausea, vomiting, diarrhea, convulsions, and coma. The patient should be taken to a hospital emergency room immediately. ALWAYS bring the medicine container.

Special Information

Do not take this medicine after 6 to 8 hours before you plan to go to sleep, or it will interfere with a sound and restful night's sleep.

Generic Name

Benztropine Mesylate

Brand Name

Cogentin

Type of Drug

Anticholinergic.

Prescribed for

Treatment of Parkinson's disease or prevention or control of muscle spasms caused by other drugs, particularly phenothiazine drugs.

General Information

Benztropine Mesylate has an action on the body similar to that of Atropine Sulfate (see p. 227), but side effects are less frequent and less severe. It is an anticholinergic and has the ability to reduce muscle spasms. This property makes the drug useful in treating Parkinson's disease and other diseases associated with spasms of skeletal muscles.

Cautions and Warnings

Benztropine Mesylate should be used with caution if you

have narrow angle glaucoma, stomach ulcers, obstructions in the gastrointestinal tract, prostatitis, or myasthenia gravis.

Benztropine may decrease the amount of milk produced in nursing mothers.

This drug may cause birth defects or interfere with your baby's development. Check with your doctor before taking it if you are, or might be, pregnant.

Possible Side Effects

The same as with any other anticholinergic drug: difficulty in urination, constipation, blurred vision, and increased sensitivity to strong light. The effects may increase if Benztropine Mesylate is taken with antihistamines, phenothiazines, antidepressants, or other anticholinergic drugs.

Drug Interactions

Interaction with other anticholinergic drugs, including tricyclic antidepressants or phenothiazine drugs, may cause severe stomach upset or unusual abdominal pain. If this happens, contact your doctor. Avoid over-the-counter remedies which contain Atropine or similar drugs. Your pharmacist can tell you the ingredients of over-the-counter drugs.

This drug should be used with caution by people taking barbiturates. Use alcoholic beverages with care while taking this drug.

This drug may reduce the absorption and therefore the effect of some drugs, including Levodopa, Haloperidol, and phenothiazines.

Usual Dose

0.5 to 6 milligrams per day, depending upon the disease being treated and patient's response.

Special Information

Side effects of dry mouth, constipation, and increased sensitivity to strong light may be relieved by, respectively, chewing gum or sucking on hard candy, taking a stool softener, and wearing sunglasses. Such side effects are easily tolerated in the absence of undesirable drug interaction.

Generic Name

Betamethasone Topical Ointment/ Cream/Lotion/Gel/Aerosol

Brand Names

Alphatrex
Benisone Cream/Gel/
    Ointment/Lotion
Beta-Val Cream
Betatrex Cream/Ointment/
    Lotion
Celestone Cream
Diprolene

Diprosone Dipropionate
    Ointment/Cream/Lotion/
    Aerosol
Uticort Cream/Gel/Lotion/
    Ointment
Valisone Ointment/Cream/
    Lotion/Aerosol
Valnac

Type of Drug

Corticosteroid.

Prescribed for

Relief of skin inflammation, itching, or other skin problems in a localized area.

General Information

Betamethasone is one of many adrenal cortical steroids used today. The major differences between Betamethasone and other adrenal cortical steroids are potency of medication and variation in some secondary effects. In most cases the choice of adrenal cortical steroids to be used in a specific disease is a matter of doctor preference and past experience. Other adrenal cortical steroids include Cortisone, Hydrocortisone, Prednisone, Prednisolone, Triamcinolone, Methylprednisolone, Meprednisone, Paramethasone, Fluprednisolone, Dexamethasone, and Fludrocortisone.

Cautions and Warnings

Betamethasone should not be used if you have viral diseases of the skin (herpes), fungal infections of the skin (athlete's foot), or tuberculosis of the skin, nor should it be used in the ear if the eardrum is perforated. People with a history of allergies to any of the components of the ointment, cream, or gel should not use this drug.

This drug may cause birth defects or interfere with your baby's development. Check with your doctor before taking it if you are, or might be, pregnant.

Possible Side Effects

Burning sensations, itching, irritation, dryness and redness of the skin, secondary infection.

Special Information

Clean the skin before applying Betamethasone, to prevent secondary infection. Apply in a very thin film (effectiveness is based on contact area and not on the thickness of the layer applied).

Generic Name

Brompheniramine Maleate

Brand Names

Brombay	Diamine T. D.
Bromphen	Dimetane
	Veltane

(Also available in generic form)

Type of Drug

Antihistamine.

Prescribed for

Seasonal allergy, stuffed and runny nose, itching of the eyes, scratchy throat caused by allergy, and other allergic symptoms such as itching, rash, or hives.

General Information

Antihistamines, including Brompheniramine, generally act by antagonizing histamine at the site where histamine works. This site is often called the H_1 histamine receptor. Antihistamines work by drying up the secretions of the nose, throat, and eyes.

Cautions and Warnings

Brompheniramine Maleate should not be used if you are allergic to this drug. It should be avoided or used with extreme care if you have narrow-angle glaucoma (pressure in the eye), stomach ulcer or other stomach problems, enlarged prostate, or problems passing urine. It should not be used by people who have deep-breathing problems such as asthma.

Brompheniramine Maleate can cause dizziness, drowsiness, and lowering of blood pressure, particularly in the elderly patient. Young children can show signs of nervousness, increased tension, and anxiety.

This drug may cause birth defects or interfere with your baby's development. Check with your doctor before taking it if you are, or might be, pregnant.

Brompheniramine Maleate is not recommended in nursing mothers because it passes into breast milk and may cause excitement or irritability in the breast-fed infant.

Possible Side Effects

Occasionally seen: itching, rash, sensitivity to light, perspiration, chills, dryness of the mouth, nose, and throat, lowering of blood pressure, headache, rapid heartbeat, sleeplessness, dizziness, disturbed coordination, confusion, restlessness, nervousness, irritability, euphoria (feeling "high"), tingling of the hands and feet, blurred vision, double vision, ringing in the ears, stomach upset, loss of appetite, nausea, vomiting, constipation, diarrhea, difficulty in urination, tightness of the chest, wheezing, nasal stuffiness.

Possible Adverse Drug Effects

Use with care if you have a history of asthma, glaucoma, thyroid disease, heart disease, high blood pressure, or diabetes.

Drug Interactions

Brompheniramine Maleate should not be taken with MAO inhibitors.

Interaction with tranquilizers, sedatives, and sleeping medication will increase the effects of these drugs; it is extremely important that you discuss this with your doctor so that doses of these drugs can be properly adjusted.

Be extremely cautious when drinking while taking Brompheniramine Maleate, which will enhance the intoxicating effect of the alcohol. Alcohol also has a sedative effect.

Usual Dose

Adult: 4 milligrams 3 to 4 times per day.

Child (age 6 to 12): 2 to 4 milligrams 3 to 4 times per day.

Child (under age 6): ¼ milligram per pound per day in divided doses.

Time-release doses are as follows:

Adult: 8 to 12 milligrams at bedtime or every 8 to 12 hours during the day.

Child (age 6 to 12): 8 milligrams during the day or at bedtime.

Overdosage

Symptoms are depression or stimulation (especially in children), dry mouth, fixed or dilated pupils, flushing of the skin, and stomach upset. Take the patient to a hospital emergency room immediately, if you cannot make him vomit. ALWAYS bring the medicine bottle.

Special Information

Antihistamines produce a depressing effect: be extremely cautious when driving or operating heavy equipment.

The safety of Brompheniramine Maleate in pregnancy has not been established. A breast-feeding mother should avoid taking this medication, since it is known to pass from the mother to the baby through the milk.

Generic Name

Bumetanide

Brand Name

Bumex

Type of Drug

Diuretic.

Prescribed for

Congestive heart failure, cirrhosis of the liver, kidney dysfunction, high blood pressure, and other conditions where it may be desirable to rid the body of excess fluid.

General Information

Bumetanide is a potent diuretic that works in the same way as Furosemide and Ethacrynic Acid. Not only do these drugs affect the same part of the kidney as the more commonly used thiazide diuretics, they also affect the portion of the kidney known as the Loop of Henle. This double action makes Bumetanide and the other "loop" diuretics extremely powerful drugs. All three loop diuretics can be used for the same purposes, but their doses are quite different. One milligram of Bumetanide is equivalent to about 40 milligrams of Furosemide and about 50 milligrams of Ethacrynic Acid.

Cautions and Warnings

Excessive amounts of Bumetanide can lead to dehydration and severe imbalances in your body levels of potassium, sodium, and chloride. Warning signs of dehydration are dry mouth, excessive thirst, loss of appetite, weakness, lethargy, drowsiness, restlessness, tingling in the hands or feet, muscle weakness, pain or cramps, low blood pressure, reduced urinary volume, rapid heartbeat, abnormal heart rhythms, nausea, and vomiting.

Animals given doses between 3.4 and 3400 times the maximum human dose showed some effect on developing embryos. Bumetanide has not caused adverse effects on developing infants and may even be prescribed to treat severe pregnancy-induced high blood pressure when other treatments fail. In general, though, this drug should be avoided by pregnant women or women who may become pregnant while using it. In those situations where it is deemed essential, the potential risk of taking Bumetanide must be carefully weighed against any benefit it might produce. It is not known if Bumetanide passes into breast milk. It is recommended that women taking Bumetanide use alternative feeding methods.

Do not use Bumetanide if you have had an allergic reaction to it in the past. People who are allergic to or cannot tolerate Furosemide may receive a prescription for Bumetanide as an alternative diuretic.

People with severe kidney or liver disease who take this medicine should maintain close contact with their doctor because the drug can accentuate some conditions affecting these organs.

Elderly patients may be more sensitive to Bumetanide side effects than younger adults and should be treated with doses at the low end of the recommended range.

Possible Side Effects

Loss of appetite, nausea, vomiting, diarrhea, inflammation of the pancreas, yellowing of the skin or whites of the eyes, dizziness, headache, blurred vision, ringing or buzzing in the ears, and reduction of blood-platelet and white-blood-cell levels.

Possible Adverse Drug Effects

Bumetanide may worsen liver or kidney disease, cause abdominal pains, dry mouth, impotence, muscle weakness or cramps, arthritislike pains in the joints, low blood pressure, changes in heart rhythm, and chest pains. The loop diuretics (Bumetanide, Ethacrynic Acid and Furosemide) have been associated with mild ear congestion, diminished hearing, and hearing loss. But these are rare and usually only follow rapid intravenous injection of these drugs.

Drug Interactions

Because Bumetanide may enhance the effects of drugs that lower blood pressure, this interaction is beneficial and is often used to treat high blood pressure. Bumetanide increases the side effects of Lithium by interfering with the elimination of that drug from the body.

Alcohol, barbiturate-type sleeping pills, and narcotic pain relievers can cause excessive low blood pressure when taken with potent diuretics like Bumetanide.

The possibility of losing body potassium with Bumetanide is increased by combining it with Digoxin (for the heart) and adrenal corticosteroids (for inflammation). Potassium loss also increases the chances of Digoxin side effects.

Probenecid reduces the effectiveness of Bumetanide by interfering with its action on the kidneys. Indomethacin and other nonsteroidal anti-inflammatory drugs such as Naproxen, Sulindac, and Ibuprofen may also reduce Bumetanide effectiveness.

People taking Bumetanide for high blood pressure or heart failure should take care to avoid nonprescription medicines that might aggravate those conditions, such as decongestants, cold and allergy treatments, and diet pills, all of which can contain stimulants. If you are unsure about which medicine to choose, ask your pharmacist.

Food Interactions

Bumetanide may cause loss of body potassium (hypokalemia), a complication that can be avoided by adding foods high in potassium to your diet. Some potassium-rich foods are tomatoes, citrus fruits, melons, and bananas. Hypokalemia can also be prevented by taking a potassium supplement in pill, powder, or liquid form.

Bumetanide may be taken with food if it upsets your stomach.

Usual Dose

0.5 to 2 milligrams per day. It may also be taken every other day or for 3 to 4 consecutive days followed by 1 to 2 medicine-free days.

Overdosage

The major symptoms of overdose are related to the potent diuretic effect of Bumetanide: lethargy, weakness, dizziness, confusion, cramps, loss of appetite, and vomiting. Victims of Bumetanide overdose should be taken to a hospital emergency room for treatment. ALWAYS bring the medicine bottle with you.

Special Information

Take your daily dose no later than 10:00 A.M. If taken later in the day, this potent diuretic could interfere with your sleep by keeping you up to go to the bathroom.

Call your doctor if any warning signs of dehydration develop while you are taking Bumetanide. The warning signs are dry mouth, excessive thirst, loss of appetite, weakness, lethargy, drowsiness, restlessness, tingling in the hands or feet, muscle weakness, pain or cramps, low blood pressure, reduced urinary volume, rapid heartbeat, abnormal heart rhythms, nausea, and vomiting.

Generic Name

Butabarbital

Brand Names

Butalan   Butisol Sodium
Butatran   Sarisol
Buticaps

(Also available in generic form)

Type of Drug

Hypnotic; sedative; anticonvulsive.

Prescribed for

Epileptic seizures, convulsions: as an anticonvulsive or a daytime sedative; as a mild hypnotic (sleeping medication); and for eclampsia (toxemia in pregnancy).

General Information

Butabarbital, like the other barbiturates, appears to act by interfering with nerve impulses to the brain. When used as an anticonvulsive, Butabarbital is not very effective by itself, but when used with anticonvulsive agents such as Phenytoin, the combined action of Butabarbital and Phenytoin is dramatic. This combination has been used very successfully to control epileptic seizures.

Cautions and Warnings

Butabarbital may slow down your physical and mental reflexes, so you must be extremely careful when operating machinery, driving an automobile, or performing other potentially dangerous tasks. Elderly patients on Butabarbital exhibit nervousness and confusion at times. Barbiturates are neutralized in the liver and eliminated from the body through the kidneys; consequently, people who have liver or kidney disorders—namely, difficulty in forming or excreting urine— should be monitored by their doctor when taking Butabarbital. Butabarbital is classified as a barbiturate; long-term or unsupervised use may cause addiction.

If you have known sensitivities or allergies to barbiturates, or if you have previously been addicted to sedatives or hypnotics, or if you have a disease affecting the respiratory system, you should not take Butabarbital.

Nursing mothers should not use Butabarbital because it passes into breast milk and may cause increased tiredness, shortness of breath, or a slow heartbeat in the breast-fed baby.

Butabarbital may be required to be used if a serious situation arises which threatens the mother's life.

This drug may cause birth defects or interfere with your baby's development. Check with your doctor before taking it if you are, or might be, pregnant.

Possible Side Effects

Difficulty in breathing, rash, and general allergic reaction such as running nose, watering eyes, and scratchy throat.

Possible Adverse Drug Effects

Drowsiness, lethargy, dizziness, hangover, nausea, vomiting, diarrhea. More severe adverse reactions may include anemia and yellowing of the skin and eyes.

Drug Interactions

Interaction with alcohol, tranquilizers, or other sedatives increases the sedative effect of Butabarbital.

Interaction with anticoagulants (blood-thinning agents) can reduce their effect. This is also true of muscle relaxants and painkillers.

Effects of Butabarbital may be increased if given with Valproic Acid.

Usual Dose

Adult: daytime sedative, 15 to 30 milligrams 3 to 4 times per day: hypnotic sleep, 50 to 100 milligrams at bedtime.

Child: 7.5 to 30 milligrams as determined by age, weight, and degree of sedation desired.

Overdosage

Symptoms are difficulty in breathing, decrease in size of the pupils of the eyes, lowered body temperature progressing to fever as time passes, fluid in the lungs, and eventually coma.

Anyone suspected of having taken an overdose must be taken to the hospital for immediate care. ALWAYS bring the medicine bottle to the emergency room physician so he can quickly and correctly identify the medication and start treatment. Severe overdosage of this medication can kill; the drug has been used many times in suicide attempts.

Generic Name

Captopril

Brand Name

Capoten

Type of Drug

Antihypertensive.

Prescribed for

Patients who have high blood pressure which cannot be controlled with other drugs or who suffer from unacceptable side effects of other drugs. Low doses may be used to treat mild to moderate high blood pressure. Captopril should be used together with a diuretic drug.

Captopril has also been used in the treatment of congestive heart failure.

General Information

This drug is the first member of a new class of drugs which work by preventing the conversion of a potent hormone called Angiotensin I. This directly affects the production of other hormones and enzymes which participate in the regulation of blood pressure. The effect is to lower blood pressure relatively quickly, within 1 to 1½ hours after taking the medicine.

Cautions and Warnings

This drug can cause kidney disease, especially loss of protein in the urine. Patients should have the amount of protein in their urine measured during the first month and monthly for a few months afterward. The drug can also cause reduction in the white-blood-cell count, and this can result in increased susceptibility to infection. Captopril should be used with caution by people who have kidney disease or diseases of the immune/collagen system (particularly lupus erythematosus), or who have taken other drugs which affect the white-blood-cell count.

The use of this drug by women who are pregnant or breast-feeding or by children is recommended only when absolutely necessary. Nursing mothers who must take the drug should find an alternate way to feed their children.

Possible Side Effects

Rash (usually mild), itching, fever, loss of taste perception (which usually returns in 2 to 3 months), and gastric irritation.

Possible Adverse Drug Effects

Adverse effects on the kidney including protein in the urine, kidney failure, excessive or frequent urination, reduction in the amount of urine produced; adverse effect on the blood system, especially white blood cells; swelling of the face, mucous membranes of the mouth, or arms and legs, flushing or pale color of skin. Captopril may also cause low blood pressure, adverse effects on the heart (chest pain, abnormal heartbeats, spasms of blood vessels, heart failure).

Drug Interactions

The blood pressure effect of Captopril is additive with diuretic drugs. Some other hypertensive drugs can cause severe blood pressure drops when used with large amounts of Captopril. They should be used with extreme caution. Beta-adrenergic blocking drugs may add some blood-pressure-lowering effect to Captopril.

Captopril may increase serum potassium, especially if given with potassium-sparing diuretics and/or potassium supplements. Avoid over-the-counter cough, cold, and allergy remedies containing drugs which may aggravate your condition.

Food Interactions

Do not take this medicine with food or meals. It must be taken at least 1 hour before or 2 hours after meals.

Usual Dose

75 milligrams per day to start. Dose may be increased up to 450 milligrams per day, if needed. The dose of this medicine must be tailored to your needs.

Overdosage

The primary effect of Captopril overdosage is very low blood pressure. A person who has taken a Captopril overdose must be taken to a hospital emergency room for treatment. ALWAYS bring the medicine bottle with you.

Special Information

Call your doctor if you develop fever, sore throat, mouth sores, abnormal heart beat, or chest pain, or if you have persistent rash or loss of taste perception.

This drug may cause dizziness when you rise quickly from sitting or lying down.

Avoid strenuous exercise and/or very hot weather as heavy sweating and/or dehydration can cause a rapid drop in blood pressure.

Do not abruptly stop taking this medication.

Generic Name

Carisoprodol

Brand Names

Rela
Soma
Soprodol
(Also available in generic form)

Type of Drug

Skeletal muscle relaxant.

Prescribed for

Partial treatment for the relief of pain and other discomforts associated with acute conditions such as sprains, strains, or bad backs.

General Information

Carisoprodol is one of several drugs available for the relief of pain caused by spasms of large skeletal muscles. These drugs give symptomatic relief only. They should not be the only form of therapy used. If you are taking Carisoprodol, follow any other instructions given by your doctor about rest, physical therapy, or other measures to help relieve your problem.

Cautions and Warnings

The effect of Carisoprodol on the pregnant female has not been studied. It may have an effect on the unborn child: if you are pregnant, you should not use this medicine unless it is absolutely necessary and this problem has been considered by your physician. Do not use this drug if you are allergic to it or to Meprobamate and Mebutamate.

This drug should not be used if you have the disease porphyria.

This drug may cause a rare, unusual reaction within minutes or hours after taking the first dose. The reaction consists of extreme weakness, momentary loss of control over arms and legs, dizziness, double vision or temporary loss of vision, agitation, confusion, a ''high'' feeling, and loss of orientation. Although the reaction usually goes away within a few hours, hospitalization may be necessary.

This drug may cause birth defects or interfere with your baby's development. Check with your doctor before taking it if you are, or might be, pregnant.

Possible Side Effects

Most common: light-headedness, dizziness, drowsiness, loss of muscle control, tremors, agitation, headache, depression, sleeplessness, rash, itching, fever, weakness, difficulty in breathing, low blood pressure. If one of these occurs, call your doctor immediately.

Possible Adverse Drug Effects

Rapid heartbeat, flushing of the face, dizziness when rising quickly from a sitting or lying position, nausea, vomiting, upset stomach, hiccups. This drug may cause adverse effects on the blood system.

Drug Interactions

Other drugs which, like Carisoprodol, may cause drowsiness, sleepiness, or lack of ability to concentrate must be taken with extreme caution: sleeping pills, tranquilizers, benzodiazepines, barbiturates, narcotics, and alcoholic beverages.

Food Interactions

May be taken with food to reduce stomach upset.

Usual Dose

350 milligrams 4 times per day.

Overdosage

Symptoms are central nervous system depression, desire to sleep, weakness, lassitude, and difficulty in breathing. The patient should be taken to a hospital immediately. ALWAYS bring the medicine bottle.

Special Information

Carisoprodol may cause drowsiness, sleepiness, and inability to concentrate: this can affect you if you drive or operate any sort of appliance, equipment, or machinery.

Generic Name

Cefaclor

Brand Name

Ceclor

Type of Drug

Cephalosporin antibiotic.

Prescribed for

Bacterial infections susceptible to this medication. Cefaclor is generally prescribed for respiratory tract infections, infections of the middle ear, infections of the skin and other soft tissues, bone infections, and infections of the urinary tract.

General Information

Cefaclor is manufactured in the laboratory by the process known as fermentation and by general chemical reaction, and is classified as a semisynthetic antibiotic. Because the effectiveness of the antibiotic is determined by the drug's ability to destroy the cell wall of the invading bacteria, it is very important that the patient completely follow the doctor's prescribing directions. These directions include spacing of doses as well as the number of days the patient should continue taking the medicine. If directions are not followed, the effect of the antibiotic is severely reduced.

Cefaclor is a member of the group of antibiotics known as cephalosporins. All the members of this group have the same basic effects and are excellent drugs. Most experts consider the forms of these drugs that are taken by mouth to be equivalent in effectiveness for most infections. The cephalosporins are chemical cousins of Penicillin.

Cautions and Warnings

If you know that you are allergic or feel that you might be allergic to Penicillin, you might be allergic to Cefaclor too. The most common allergic effect experienced with any of the antibiotics similar to Penicillin is a hivelike rash over large areas of the body, with itching and redness. It is extremely important that you tell your doctor if you have ever taken this drug or any of the penicillins before, and if you have experienced any adverse effects to the drug such as rash, itching, or difficulty in breathing.

The safe use of Cefaclor in pregnant females has not been definitely established and it should be used only if there is a specific need for it, since it is possible that this drug may cross the blood barrier into the unborn child. These drugs will also pass into the milk of a nursing mother.

Possible Side Effects

If you are taking Cefaclor you may experience one or more of the following allergic reactions ranging from mild to life-threatening. Most often, however, reactions are quite mild: itching, rashes, occasional fever, chills, and reactions of one or more of the components of the blood. Serious reactions are called anaphylactic reactions; although they are quite rare, some deaths have been reported from anaphylactic reactions to this or another member of the cephalosporin class.

Possible Adverse Drug Effects

Cefaclor and other cephalosporin antibiotics have been known to induce adverse effects on the blood system; it is the other antibiotics in this group that have been more definitely associated with decrease in kidney function. Taking Cefaclor induces nausea, vomiting, or diarrhea in about one-third of patients. Less frequent adverse effects: cramps in the abdomen, upset stomach, headache, not feeling well, dizziness, difficulty in breathing, tingling in the extremities, and (occasional) enlargement of the liver.

Drug Interactions

Cefaclor, which works by killing microorganisms which cause infections, may be inhibited by antibiotics, such as Erythromycin and Tetracycline, which do not kill but simply stop the growth of microorganisms. The two types should be avoided if possible.

Food Interactions

The drug has maximum effect if taken 1 hour before or 2 hours after meals, but if upset stomach occurs the drug can be taken with meals.

Usual Dose

Adult: 250 to 1000 milligrams every 8 hours.

Child: up to 9 milligrams per pound per day in 3 divided doses; maximum dose is 1000 milligrams per day.

Doses may be doubled for severe infections.

Special Information

Cefaclor, to be effective, must be taken continuously for 7 to 10 days; so take it exactly as prescribed.

Generic Name

Cefadroxil

Brand Name

Duricef
Ultracef

Type of Drug

Cephalosporin antibiotic.

Prescribed for

Bacterial infections susceptible to this medication. Cefadroxil is usually prescribed for infections of the respiratory tract, skin, middle ear and other soft tissue, bone, and urinary tract. Like all other antibiotics, it should NEVER be prescribed to treat an infection caused by a virus.

General Information

Cefadroxil is a member of the most widely used group of antibiotics, the cephalosporins, many members of which are given in hospitals by injection to cure life-threatening infections. Cephalosporins are chemical cousins to the Penicillin family. However, this and other cephalosporin antibiotics that can be taken by mouth are virtually identical to the kinds of infections they can be used to treat and their ability to produce a cure.

Cefadroxil works by interfering with the process by which a growing bacteria manufactures its cell wall. Since the drug must always be present in sufficient amounts to yield this effect, it is essential that you take the medicine exactly as prescribed, including the number of days and time between doses. If the directions are not followed, the effect of the antibiotic is severely reduced.

Cautions and Warnings

Avoid Cefadroxil if you know you are allergic to other cephalosporins or to Penicillin, although the chances of a cross-reaction between Penicillin and this medicine are relatively small. The most common allergic reaction is a hivelike rash over large areas of the body, with itching and redness. It is very important that you tell your doctor if you have ever taken this or another cephalosporin or Penicillin before, especially if you have any adverse effects, including rash, itching, or difficulty breathing.

This drug should not be taken by pregnant women or women who may become pregnant while using it. In those situations where its need has been established, discuss with your doctor the potential risk of using the drug weighed against any benefit it might produce. Cefadroxil may pass into breast milk, nursing mothers should watch for any possible drug effect on their infants.

Possible Side Effects

Upset stomach, nausea, vomiting, diarrhea, loss of appetite, itching, and rash. Most sensitivity reactions are mild, including itching, rashes, chills, and occasional fever.

Possible Adverse Drug Effects

Cephalosporin antibiotics taken by mouth have rarely affected blood components, but it is possible for the levels of some white blood cells, red blood cells, and blood platelets to be temporarily reduced.

Drug Interactions

This drug's effect may be inhibited by Tetracycline or Erythromycin, if taken together.

Taking Probenecid together with this drug will slow the rate at which cephalosporin is eliminated from the body.

Occasionally, people drinking alcohol while taking a cephalosporin antibiotic have experienced flushing, throbbing in the head and neck, breathing difficulty, sweating, extreme thirst, chest pains, heart palpitations, increased heart rate, dizziness, weakness, and low blood pressure.

Food Interactions

You may take this medication with food, milk, or an antacid if it upsets your stomach.

Usual Dose

250 to 500 milligrams every 6 hours.

Overdosage

The most frequent overdose effects are nausea, vomiting, and upset stomach. These symptoms can be treated by stopping the antibiotic and drinking milk or taking an antacid. Call your doctor before completely discontinuing the medication.

Special Information

Make sure you take the complete course of treatment prescribed by your doctor to obtain maximum benefit from the drug.

Tell your doctor if you have ever had a reaction to a penicillin or cephalosporin antibiotic and make sure to call if any severe or unusual side effects develop, especially diarrhea containing pus or blood.

Generic Name

Cephalexin

Brand Name

Keflex

Type of Drug

Cephalosporin antibiotic.

Prescribed for

Bacterial infections susceptible to this medication. Cephalexin is generally prescribed for respiratory tract infections, infec-

tions of the middle ear, infections of the skin and other soft
tissues, bone infections, and infections of the urinary tract.

General Information

Cephalexin is manufactured in the laboratory by the process
known as fermentation and by general chemical reaction,
and is classified as a semisynthetic antibiotic. Because the
effectiveness of the antibiotic is determined by the drug's
ability to destroy the cell wall of the invading bacteria, it is
very important that the patient completely follow the doctor's prescribing directions. These directions include spacing
of doses as well as the number of days the patient should
continue taking the medicine. If they are not followed, the
effect of the antibiotic is severely reduced.

Cautions and Warnings

If you know that you are allergic or feel that you might be
allergic to Penicillin, you might be allergic to Cephalexin
too. The most common allergic effect experienced with any
of the antibiotics similar to Penicillin is a hivelike rash over
large areas of the body with itching and redness. It is extremely important that you tell your doctor if you have ever
taken this drug or any of the penicillins before, and if you
have experienced any adverse effects to the drug such as
rash, itching, or difficulty in breathing.

Although problems have not been seen in pregnant women
or nursing mothers using Cephalexin, the safe use of this
drug in pregnant females has not been definitely established
and it should be used only if there is a specific need for it,
since it is possible that this drug may cross the blood barrier
into the unborn child. This drug will also pass into the milk
of a nursing mother and should be used with caution by a
breast-feeding woman.

Possible Side Effects

If you are taking Cephalexin you may experience one or
more of the following allergic reactions ranging from mild to
life-threatening. Most often, however, reactions are quite
mild: itching, rashes, occasional fever, chills, and reactions
of one or more of the components of the blood. Serious
reactions are called anaphylactic reactions; although they

are quite rare, some deaths have been reported from anaphylactic reactions to this or another member of the cephalosporin class.

Possible Adverse Drug Effects

Cephalexin and other cephalosporin antibiotics have been
known to induce adverse effects on the blood system; it is
the others that have been more definitely associated with
decrease in kidney function. Taking Cephalexin induces nausea, vomiting, or diarrhea in about one-third of patients.
Less frequent adverse effects: cramps in the abdomen, upset stomach, headache, not feeling well, dizziness, difficulty
in breathing, tingling in the extremities, and (occasional)
enlargement of the liver.

Drug Interactions

Cephalexin, which works by killing microorganisms which
cause infections, may be inhibited by antibiotics, such as
Erythromycin and Tetracycline, which do not kill but simply
stop the growth of microorganisms. The two types should
be avoided if possible.

Probenecid will slow down the excretion rate of cephalosporins.

Food Interactions

The drug has maximum effect if taken 1 hour before or
2 hours after meals, but if upset stomach occurs the drug
can be taken with meals.

Usual Dose

Adult: 1 to 4 grams per day in divided doses.

Child: 12½ to 25 milligrams per pound of body weight per
day in 4 divided doses.

Doses may be doubled for severe infections.

Special Information

Cephalexin, to be effective, must be taken continuously for 7
to 10 days; so take it exactly as prescribed.

Generic Name

Cephradine

Brand Names

Anspor
Velosef

Type of Drug

Cephalosporin antibiotic.

Prescribed for

Bacterial infections susceptible to this medication. Cephradine is generally prescribed for respiratory tract infections, infections of the middle ear, infections of the skin and other soft tissues, bone infections, and infections of the urinary tract.

General Information

Cephradine is manufactured in the laboratory by the process known as fermentation and by general chemical reaction, and is classified as a semisynthetic antibiotic. Because the effectiveness of the antibiotic is determined by the drug's ability to destroy the cell wall of the invading bacteria, it is very important that the patient completely follow the doctor's prescribing directions. These directions include spacing of doses as well as the number of days the patient should continue taking the medicine. If they are not followed, the effect of the antibiotic is severely reduced.

Cephradine is a member of the group of antibiotics known as cephalosporins. All the members of this group have the same basic effects and are excellent drugs. Most experts consider the forms of these drugs that are taken by mouth to be equivalent in effectiveness for most infections. The cephalosporins are chemical cousins of Penicillin.

Cautions and Warnings

If you know that you are allergic or feel that you might be allergic to Penicillin, you might be allergic to Cephradine too. The most common allergic effect experienced with any of the antibiotics similar to Penicillin is a hivelike rash over large areas of the body, with itching and redness. It is extremely important that you tell your doctor if you have ever taken this drug or any of the penicillins before, and if you have experienced any adverse effects to the drug such as rash, itching, or difficulty in breathing.

Although problems have not been seen in pregnant women or nursing mothers using Cephradine the safe use of this drug in pregnant females has not been definitely established and it should be used only if there is a specific need for it, since it is possible that this drug may cross the blood barrier into the unborn child. This drug will also pass into the milk of a nursing mother and should be used with caution by a breast-feeding woman.

Possible Side Effects

If you are taking Cephradine you may experience one or more of the following allergic reactions ranging from mild to life-threatening. Most often, however, reactions are quite mild: itching, rashes, occasional fever, chills, and reactions of one or more of the components of the blood. Serious reactions are called anaphylactic reactions; although they are quite rare, some deaths have been reported from anaphylactic reactions to this or another member of the cephalosporin class.

Possible Adverse Drug Effects

Cephradine and other cephalosporin antibiotics have been known to induce adverse effects on the blood system; it is the others that have been more definitely associated with decrease in kidney function. Taking Cephradine induces nausea, vomiting, or diarrhea in about one-third of patients. Less frequent adverse effects: cramps in the abdomen, upset stomach, headache, not feeling well, dizziness, difficulty in breathing, tingling in the extremities, and (occasional) enlargement of the liver.

Drug Interactions

Cephradine, which works by killing microorganisms which cause infections, may be inhibited by antibiotics, such as Erythromycin and Tetracycline, which do not kill but simply stop the growth of microorganisms. The two types should be avoided if possible.

Probenicid will slow down the excretion rate of cephalosporins.

Food Interactions

The drug has maximum effect if taken 1 hour before or 2 hours after meals, but if upset stomach occurs the drug can be taken with meals

Usual Dose

Adult: 250 milligrams every 6 hours.

Child: 9 to 25 milligrams per pound per day in 4 divided doses; maximum dose is 4000 milligrams per day.

Doses may be doubled for severe infections.

Special Information

Cephradine, to be effective, must be taken continuously for 7 to 10 days; so take it exactly as prescribed.

Generic Name

Chenodiol

Brand Name

Chenix

Type of Drug

Gallstone dissolver.

Prescribed for

People with choesterol gallstones that are readily identifiable by x-ray examination and in whom surgery might be risky.

General Information

Chenodiol is a natural bile acid found in our bodies. It suppresses the production of cholesterol and cholic acid in the liver, leading to the gradual withdrawal of cholesterol from gallstones, which causes them to dissolve. The success of this therapy varies according to the characteristics of individual gallstones, but is most successful in people whose stones are small and float. Over-all, about one-third of all people who take this medicine will achieve complete dissolution of their gallstones. But the drug is most successful in small, thin women whose cholesterol level is above 227, and who have a small number of floatable gallstones and can tolerate 24 months of drug therapy.

Cautions and Warnings

Before taking this drug, it is important that your doctor perform a complete gallbladder examination, including X-ray tests, to be sure that your bile duct is functioning normally and that your condition is not amenable to surgery.

Chenodiol can be toxic to people with liver conditions such as hepatitis or cirrhosis. Also, it can cause liver damage on its own. Some people may be more susceptible to Chenodiol-induced liver damager than others. Your doctor should perform liver-function tests while you are taking this medication to determine your susceptibility and discontinue the drug at the first negative signs.

Chenodiol may contribute to the development of colon and liver cancer in some people.

Chenodiol should not be used by women who are pregnant or who might become pregnant while using it because it may harm the developing baby. Animal studies in monkeys and baboons have revealed serious effects on fetal liver, kidneys, and adrenal glands. Although such damage has not occurred in humans, the potential risks of taking Chenodiol while pregnant must be weighed heavily against the possible benefits it will produce. It is not known if Chenodiol passes into breast milk. Therefore, nursing mothers must observe for any possible drug effect on their infants while taking this medication.

Possible Side Effects

Liver inflammation, as indicated by an increase in the levels of some liver enzymes, develops in almost one-third of all people who take this medication. Most inflammation is minor and resolves on its own after about 6 months, but 2 to 3 percent of people who take this drug experience more severe inflammation. In virtually all people, the test results return to normal after the medicine is stopped. Other side effects are diarrhea that worsens as the dosage increases and subsides as the dosage is reduced, increase in blood cholesterol levels, and reduction in blood triglyceride levels.

Possible Adverse Drug Effects

Cramps, heartburn, constipation, nausea, vomiting, loss of appetite, abdominal discomfort and pain, upset stomach, stomach and intestinal gas, and reductions in the white-blood-cell count.

Drug Interactions

Cholestyramine or Cholestipol, two products used to remove bile acids from the stomach, will interfere with the action of Chenodiol by preventing it from being absorbed into the system. Antacids containing aluminum may also have this effect.

Estrogens, oral contraceptive pills, and Clofibrate increase the amount of cholesterol that passes through the bile ducts into the intestines and all three are associated with an increased risk of cholesterol gallstones. These medicines should not be taken while you are on Chenodiol therapy because they can counteract its effectiveness.

Food Interactions

Follow your doctor's instructions for dietary limitations while under treatment for gallstones. A low-cholesterol diet is often prescribed. Chenodiol is best taken on an empty stomach.

Usual Dose

250 milligrams morning and night to start. This dose is gradually increased in weekly steps of 250 milligrams until the maximum recommended dose of 6 to 7.25 milligrams per pound of body weight per day is reached, or until side effects develop.

Total daily doses of less than 4.5 milligrams per pound of body weight per day are ineffective and are actually associated with an increased need for gallstone surgery.

Overdosage

The are no reports of accidental or intentional overdose with Chenodiol. Call your local Poison Control Center for specific advice on what to do in the event of a Chenodiol overdose.

Special Information

You must take this drug exactly as prescribed to get the maximum benefit from it.

Report any side effects to your doctor. Especially important are abdominal pains, severe and sudden pain in the right upper abdominal area that travels to your shoulder, nausea, and vomiting. Minor side effects such as diarrhea may be controlled by reducing your total daily dose, but you must not adjust the dose on your own.

It is essential that you return to your doctor for periodic tests of liver function and tests (ultrasonogram or oral cholecystogram) that allow your doctor to verify that your stones are being dissolved.

It is important for you to realize that this treatment is not a permanent cure. About half of all people whose original stones are completely dissolved by Chenodiol therapy will have another gallstone attack within 5 years.

Generic Name

Chloral Hydrate

Brand Names

Noctec
Oradrate
SK-Chloral Hydrate

(Also available in generic form)

Type of Drug

Sedative-hypnotic.

Prescribed for

Insomnia, or as a daytime sedative.

General Information

Chloral Hydrate is very effective in producing sleep. Most people will fall asleep within an hour after taking this medicine. This drug usually does not cause the morning "hangover" seen with other sleeping pills.

Cautions and Warnings

Do not take Chloral Hydrate if you have liver or kidney disease, severe heart disease, or stomach problems, or if you are sensitive or allergic to this or similar drugs.

Chloral Hydrate may be habit-forming or addictive. It should only be taken when absolutely necessary and only in the amounts prescribed.

This drug is known to cause birth defects or interfere with your baby's development. It is not considered safe for use during pregnancy.

Possible Side Effects

Most common: reduction in alertness. If you plan to drive a car or operate other machinery, do so with extreme caution.

Possible Adverse Drug Effects

Headache, hangover, hallucinations, drowsiness, stomach upset, nausea, vomiting, difficulty in walking, bad taste in the mouth, feeling of excitement, itching, light-headedness, dizziness, nightmares, feeling unwell, changes in the composition of the blood.

Drug Interactions

Taking Chloral Hydrate with blood-thinning drugs may require a change of dosage of the latter: consult your doctor. Chloral Hydrate is a potent depressant, so avoid drinking alcohol or taking other drugs with depressant properties such as tranquilizers, barbiturates, or sleeping pills.

Food Interactions

Stomach upset can be minimized if you take Chloral Hydrate with a full glass of water, juice, or other liquid and never chew or break the capsule.

Usual Dose

Adult: sleeping medicine, 500 milligrams to 1 gram ½ hour before sleep. Daytime sedative, 250 milligrams 3 times per day after meals. Daily dose should not exceed 2 grams.

Child: sleeping medicine, 20 milligrams per pound of body weight (maximum of 1 gram). Daytime sedative, half the dose for sleeping, divided into 3 equal doses.

Overdosage

Symptoms are listed in "Possible Adverse Drug Effects" above. The patient should be taken to a hospital emergency room immediately. ALWAYS bring the medicine bottle.

Storage

Store at room temperature in a night table drawer, not in an area that is hot and/or humid, such as a bathroom.

Special Information

The combination of Chloral Hydrate and alcohol is notorious as the Mickey Finn. Avoid it.

Generic Name

Chlordiazepoxide

Brand Names

A-poxide   Lipoxide
Libritabs   Reposans-10
Librium   SK-Lygen

(Also available in generic form)

Type of Drug

Minor tranquilizer.

Prescribed for

Relief of symptoms of anxiety, tension, fatigue, or agitation.

General Information

Chlordiazepoxide is a member of the chemical group of

drugs known as benzodiazepines. These drugs are used as either antianxiety agents, anticonvulsants, or sedatives (sleeping pills). They exert their effects by relaxing the large skeletal muscles and by a direct effect on the brain. In doing so, they can relax you and make you either more tranquil or sleepier, depending on the drug and how much you use. Many doctors prefer Chlordiazepoxide and the other members of this class to other drugs that can be used for the same effect. Their reason is that the benzodiazepines tend to be safer, have fewer side effects, and are usually as, if not more, effective.

These drugs are generally used in any situation where they can be a useful adjunct.

Benzodiazepine tranquilizing drugs can be abused if taken for long periods of time and it is possible to develop withdrawal symptoms if you discontinue the therapy abruptly. Withdrawal symptoms include tremor, muscle cramps, stomach cramps, vomiting, insomnia, agitation, sweating, and even convulsions.

Cautions and Warnings

Do not take Chlordiazepoxide if you know you are sensitive or allergic to this drug or to other benzodiazepines such as Diazepam, Oxazepam, Clorazepate, Lorazepam, Prazepam, Flurazepam, Clonazepam, and Temazepam.

Chlordiazepoxide and other members of this drug group may aggravate narrow angle glaucoma, but if you have open angle glaucoma you may take the drugs. In any case, check this information with your doctor. Chlordiazepoxide can cause tiredness, drowsiness, inability to concentrate, or similar symptoms. Be careful if you are driving, operating machinery, or performing other activities which require concentration.

This drug may cause birth defects or interfere with your baby's development. Check with your doctor before taking it if you are, or might be, pregnant.

Possible Side Effects

Most common: mild drowsiness during the first few days of therapy, especially in the elderly or debilitated. If drowsiness persists, contact your doctor.

Possible Adverse Drug Effects

Major adverse reactions: confusion, depression, lethargy, disorientation, headache, inactivity, slurred speech, stupor, dizziness, tremor, constipation, dry mouth, nausea, inability to control urination, changes in sex drive, irregular menstrual cycle, changes in heart rhythm, lowered blood pressure, retention of fluids, blurred or double vision, itching, rash, hiccups, nervousness, inability to fall asleep, (occasional) liver dysfunction. If you experience any of these reactions stop taking the medicine and contact your doctor immediately.

Drug Interactions

Chlordiazepoxide is a central nervous system depressant. Avoid alcohol, tranquilizers, narcotics, barbiturates, MAO inhibitors, antihistamines, and other medicines used to relieve depression. Smoking may reduce the effectiveness of Chlordiazepoxide. The effects of Chlordiazepoxide may be prolonged when taken together with Cimetidine.

Usual Dose

Adult: 5 to 100 milligrams per day. This tremendous range in dosage exists because of varying response of individuals, related to age, weight, severity of disease, and other characteristics.

Child (over age 6): may be given this drug if it is deemed appropriate by the physician. Initial dose, lowest available (5 milligrams 2 to 4 times per day). Later, may increase in some children to 30 to 40 milligrams per day. The dose must be individualized to obtain maximum benefit.

Overdosage

Symptoms are confusion, sleep or sleepiness, lack of response to pain such as a pin stick, shallow breathing, lowered blood pressure, and coma. The patient should be taken to a hospital emergency room immediately. ALWAYS bring the medicine bottle.

Generic Name

Chlorothiazide

Brand Names

Diachlor
Diuril
SK-Chlorothiazide

(Also available in generic form)

Type of Drug

Diuretic.

Prescribed for

Congestive heart failure, cirrhosis of the liver, kidney malfunction, high blood pressure, and other conditions where it is necessary to rid the body of excess fluid.

General Information

This drug is a member of the class known as thiazide diuretics. Thiazides act on the kidneys to stimulate the production of large amounts of urine. They also cause you to lose bicarbonate, sodium chloride, and potassium ions from the body. They are used as part of the treatment of any disease where it is desirable to eliminate large quantities of body water. These diseases include heart failure, some kidney diseases, and liver disease.

Cautions and Warnings

Do not take Chlorothiazide if you are allergic or sensitive to this drug, similar drugs of this group, or sulfa drugs. If you have a history of allergy or bronchial asthma, you may also have a sensitivity or allergy to Chlorothiazide.

Although the drug has been used to treat specific conditions in pregnancy, unsupervised use by pregnant women should be avoided. This drug may cause birth defects or interfere with your baby's development. Check with your doctor before taking it if you are, or might be, pregnant.

Possible Side Effects

Chlorothiazide will cause a lowering of potassium in the

ody. Signs of low potassium levels are dryness of the
mouth, thirst, weakness, lethargy, drowsiness, restlessness,
muscle pains or cramps, gout, muscular tiredness, low blood
pressure, decreased frequency of urination and decreased
amount of urine produced, abnormal heart rate, and stom-
ch upset including nausea and vomiting.

To treat this, potassium supplements are given in the form
f tablets, liquids, or powders, or by increased consumption
f foods such as bananas, citrus fruits, melons, and tomatoes.

ossible Adverse Drug Effects

oss of appetite, stomach upset, nausea, vomiting, cramp-
ng, diarrhea, constipation, dizziness, headache, tingling of
ne toes and fingers, restlessness, changes in blood compo-
ition, sensitivity to sunlight, rash, itching, fever, difficulty in
reathing, allergic reactions, dizziness when rising quickly
om a sitting or lying position, muscle spasms, weakness,
lurred vision.

rug Interactions

hlorothiazide will increase (potentiate) the action of other
lood-pressure-lowering drugs. This is beneficial, and is fre-
uently used to help lower blood pressure in patients with
ypertension.

The possibility of developing imbalances in body fluids
electrolytes) is increased if you take medication such as
igitalis and adrenal corticosteroids while you take Chloro-
niazide.

If you are taking an oral antidiabetic drug and begin taking
hlorothiazide, the antidiabetic dose may have to be altered.

Lithium Carbonate should not be taken with Chlorothia-
de because the combination may increase the risk of Lith-
im toxicity.

If you are taking Chlorothiazide for the treatment of high
lood pressure or congestive heart failure, avoid over-the-
ounter medicines for the treatment of coughs, colds, and
llergies: such medicines may contain stimulants. If you are
nsure about them, ask your pharmacist.

sual Dose

Adult: 0.5 to 1 gram 1 to 2 times per day. Often people

respond to intermittent therapy; that is, getting the drug on alternate days or 3 to 5 days per week. This reduces side effects.

Child: 10 milligrams per pound of body weight each day in 2 equal doses.

Infant (under age 6 months): up to 15 milligrams per pound per day in 2 equal doses.

Overdosage

Symptoms are large amount of urination, fatigue, and coma. The patient should be taken to a hospital emergency room immediately. ALWAYS bring the medicine bottle.

Generic Name

Chlorphenesin Carbamate

Brand Name

Maolate

Type of Drug

Skeletal muscle relaxant.

Prescribed for

A part of the treatment for pain and discomfort of skeletal muscle disorders and spasms.

General Information

This drug should always be used together with rest, physical therapy, and other measures designed to treat lower back and other musculoskeletal disorders. The exact way this drug works is not known, but its results may be associated with the sedative effects it exerts.

Cautions and Warnings

This drug may interfere with normal concentration and usual day-to-day tasks. Do not take this drug if you are allergic to it. The safe use of Chlorphenesin Carbamate beyond 8 weeks has not been definitely established. Patients with liver disease should use this drug with caution.

This drug may cause birth defects or interfere with your baby's development. Check with your doctor before taking it if you are, or might be, pregnant.

Possible Side Effects

Drowsiness, dizziness, nausea, confusion, upset stomach, sleeplessness, stimulation, rash, itching, fever, low blood pressure.

Possible Adverse Drug Effects

May cause adverse effects on the blood system.

Drug Interactions

Other drugs which, like Chlorphenesin Carbamate, may cause drowsinesss, sleepiness, or lack of ability to concentrate must be taken with extreme caution: sleeping pills, tranquilizers, barbiturates, narcotics, and alcoholic beverages.

Usual Dose

800 milligrams 3 times per day to start. Dose may be reduced to 400 milligrams 4 times per day after desired effect is obtained.

Overdosage

Symptoms are central nervous system depression, desire to sleep, weakness, lassitude, and difficulty in breathing. The patient should be taken to a hospital immediately. ALWAYS bring the medicine bottle.

Special Information

Take care while driving or performing other activities requiring concentration: avoid alcohol and other depressant drugs.

Generic Name

Chlorpheniramine Maleate

Brand Names

Alermine	Chlor-Trimeton
Aller-Chlor	Hal Chlor
Allerid	Histrey
Chlo-Amine	Isoclor
Chloramate	Phenetron
Chlorate	Phenetron Lanacaps
Chlor-Niramine	T.D. Alermine
Chlorspan	Teldrin Spansules
Chlortab	Trymegen

(Also available in generic form)

Type of Drug

Antihistamine.

Prescribed for

Seasonal allergy, stuffed and runny nose, itching of the eyes, scratching of the throat caused by allergy, and other allergic symptoms such as itching, rash, or hives.

General Information

Antihistamines, including Chlorpheniramine, generally act by antagonizing histamine at the site where histamine works. This site is often called the H_1 histamine receptor. Antihistamines work by drying up the secretions of the nose, throat, and eyes.

Cautions and Warnings

Chlorpheniramine Maleate should not be used if you are allergic to this drug. It should be avoided or used with extreme care if you have narrow angle glaucoma (pressure in the eye), stomach ulcer or other stomach problems, enlarged prostate, or problems passing urine. It should not be used by people who have deep-breathing problems such as asthma.

Chlorpheniramine Maleate can cause dizziness, drowsiess, and lowering of blood pressure, particularly in the elderly patient. Young children can show signs of nervousness, increased tension, and anxiety.

This drug may cause birth defects or interfere with your baby's development. Check with your doctor before taking it if you are, or might be, pregnant.

Chlorpheniramine Maleate crosses over to breast-fed infants and may cause excitement or irritability. For this reason, Chlorpheniramine Maleate is not recommended in nursing mothers.

Possible Side Effects

Occasionally seen: itching, rash, sensitivity to light, perspiration, chills, dryness of the mouth, nose, and throat, lowering of blood pressure, headache, rapid heartbeat, sleeplessness, dizziness, disturbed coordination, confusion, restlessness, nervousness, irritability, euphoria (feeling high), tingling of the hands and feet, blurred vision, double vision, ringing in the ears, stomach upset, loss of appetite, nausea, vomiting, constipation, diarrhea, difficulty in urination, tightness of the chest, wheezing, nasal stuffiness.

Possible Adverse Drug Effects

Use with care if you have a history of asthma, glaucoma, thyroid disease, heart disease, high blood pressure, or diabetes.

Drug Interactions

Chlorpheniramine Maleate should not be taken with MAO inhibitors.

Interaction with tranquilizers, benzodiazepines, sedatives, and sleeping medication will increase the effect of these drugs; it is extremely important that you discuss this with your doctor so that doses of these drugs can be properly adjusted.

Be extremely cautious when drinking alcohol while taking Chlorpheniramine Maleate, which will enhance the intoxicating effect of alcohol. Alcohol also has a sedative effect.

Usual Dose

Adult: 4-milligram tablet 3 to 4 times per day.
Child (age 6 to 12): 2-milligram tablet 3 to 4 times per day.

Time-release doses (capsules or tablets) are as follows:

Adult: 8 to 12 milligrams at bedtime or every 8 to 10 hour during the day.

Child (age 6 to 12): 8 milligrams during the day or a bedtime.

Overdosage

Symptoms are depression or stimulation (especially in chi dren), dry mouth, fixed or dilated pupils, flushing of the skin and stomach upset. Take the patient to a hospital emergenc room immediately, if you cannot make him vomit. ALWAY bring the medicine bottle.

Special Information

Antihistamines produce a depressing effect: be extremel cautious when driving or operating heavy equipment.

The safety of Chlorpheniramine Maleate in pregnancy ha not been established. A breast-feeding mother should avoi taking this medication, since it is known to pass from th mother to the baby through the milk.

Generic Name

Chlorpromazine

Brand Names

BayChlor	Thorazine
Promapar	Thor-Prom
Promaz	

(Also available in generic form)

Type of Drug

Phenothiazine Antipsychotic.

Prescribed for

Psychotic disorders, moderate to severe depression with anx iety, control of agitation or aggressiveness of disturbed chi dren, alcohol withdrawal symptoms, intractable pain, an senility. Chlorpromazine may also be used to relieve nausea vomiting, hiccups, and restlessness, and/or apprehension before surgery or other special therapy.

General Information

Chlorpromazine and other members of the phenothiazine group act on a portion of the brain called the hypothalamus. They affect parts of the hypothalamus that control metabolism, body temperature, alertness, muscle tone, hormone balance, and vomiting, and may be used to treat problems related to any of these functions.

Cautions and Warnings

Chlorpromazine should not be taken if you are allergic to one of the drugs in the broad classification known as phenothiazine drugs. Do not take Chlorpromazine if you have any blood, liver, kidney, or heart disease, very low blood pressure, or Parkinson's disease. This medication is a tranquilizer and can have a sedative effect, especially during the first few days of therapy. Care should be taken when performing activities requiring a high degree of concentration, such as driving.

This drug should be used with caution and under strict supervision of your doctor if you have glaucoma, epilepsy, ulcers, or difficulty passing urine.

Avoid insecticides and extreme exposure to heat.

This drug may cause birth defects or interfere with your baby's development. Check with your doctor before taking it if you are, or might be, pregnant.

Possible Side Effects

Most common: drowsiness, especially during the first or second week of therapy. If the drowsiness becomes troublesome, contact your doctor.

Possible Adverse Drug Effects

Chlorpromazine can cause jaundice (yellowing of the whites of the eyes or skin), usually in 2 to 4 weeks. The jaundice usually goes away when the drug is discontinued, but there have been cases when it did not. If you notice this effect or if you develop symptoms such as fever and generally not feeling well, contact your doctor immediately. Less frequent: changes in components of the blood including anemias, raised or lowered blood pressure, abnormal heart rates, heart attack, feeling faint or dizzy.

Phenothiazines can produce "extrapyramidal effects," such as spasm of the neck muscles, rolling back of the eyes, convulsions, difficulty in swallowing, and symptoms associated with Parkinson's disease. These effects look very serious but disappear after the drug has been withdrawn; however, symptoms of the face, tongue, and jaw may persist for as long as several years, especially in the elderly with a history of brain damage. If you experience extrapyramidal effects contact your doctor immediately.

Chlorpromazine may cause an unusual increase in psychotic symptoms or may cause paranoid reactions, tiredness, lethargy, restlessness, hyperactivity, confusion at night, bizarre dreams, inability to sleep, depression, and euphoria. Other reactions are itching, swelling, unusual sensitivity to bright lights, red skin, and rash. There have been cases of breast enlargement, false positive pregnancy tests, changes in menstrual flow in females, and impotence and changes in sex drive in males, as well as stuffy nose, headache, nausea, vomiting, loss of appetite, change in body temperature, loss of facial color, excessive salivation, excessive perspiration, constipation, diarrhea, changes in urine and stool habits, worsening of glaucoma, blurred vision, weakening of eyelid muscles, spasms in bronchial and other muscles, increased appetite, excessive thirst, and changes in the coloration of skin, particularly in exposed areas.

Drug Interactions

Chlorpromazine should be taken with caution in combination with barbiturates, sleeping pills, narcotics, other tranquilizers, or any other medication which may produce a sedative effect. Avoid alcohol.

Usual Dose

Adult: 30 to 1000 milligrams or more per day, individualized according to disease and patient's response.

Child: 0.25 milligram per pound of body weight every 4 to 6 hours up to 200 milligrams or more per day (by various routes including rectal suppositories), depending on disease, age, and response to therapy.

This drug may turn the color of your urine pink or reddish brown.

Overdosage

Symptoms are depression, extreme weakness, tiredness, desire to go to sleep, coma, lowered blood pressure, uncontrolled muscle spasms, agitation, restlessness, convulsions, fever, dry mouth, and abnormal heart rhythms. The patient should be taken to a hospital emergency room immediately. ALWAYS bring the medicine bottle.

Generic Name

Chlorpropamide

Brand Name

Diabinese

(Also available in generic form)

Type of Drug

Oral antidiabetic.

Prescribed for

Diabetes mellitus (sugar in the urine).

General Information

Chlorpropamide is one of several oral antidiabetic drugs that work by stimulating the production and release of insulin from the pancreas. The action of these agents is also related to improved Insulin sensitivity of peripheral tissues. The primary difference between these drugs lies in the duration of action. Because they do not lower blood sugar directly, they require some function of pancreas cells.

Cautions and Warnings

Mild stress such as infection, minor surgery, or emotional upset reduces the effectiveness of Chlorpropamide. Remember that while you are taking this drug you should be under your doctor's continuous care.

Chlorpropamide is an aid to, not a substitute for, a diet.

Diet remains of primary importance in the treatment of your diabetes. Follow the diet plan your doctor has prescribed for you.

Chlorpropamide and similar drugs are not oral Insulin, nor are they a substitute for Insulin. They do not lower blood sugar by themselves.

This drug should not be used if you have serious liver, kidney or endocrine disease.

This drug may cause birth defects or interfere with your baby's development. Check with your doctor before taking it if you are, or might be, pregnant. For control of diabetes in pregnant women, the use of insulin and diet is recommended. Nursing women who must take this drug should find an alternative method of feeding their children.

Possible Side Effects

Common: loss of appetite, nausea, vomiting, stomach upset. At times, you may experience weakness or tingling in the hands and feet. These effects can be eliminated by reducing the daily dose of Chlorpropamide or, if necessary, by switching to a different oral antidiabetic drug. This decision must be made by your doctor.

Possible Adverse Drug Effects

Chlorpropamide may produce abnormally low levels of blood sugar when too much is taken for your immediate requirements. (Other factors which may cause lowering of blood sugar are liver or kidney disease, malnutrition, age, drinking alcohol, and diseases of the glands.)

Chlorpropamide may cause a yellowing of the whites of the eyes or skin, itching, rash, or changes in the results of laboratory tests made by your doctor. Usually these reactions will disappear in time. If they persist you should contact your doctor.

Drug Interactions

Thiazide diuretics may lessen the effect of Chlorpropamide, while Insulin, sulfa drugs, Oxyphenbutazone, Phenylbutazone, and MAO inhibitor drugs prolong and enhance the action of Chlorpropamide.

Interaction with alcoholic beverages may cause flushing of the face and body, throbbing pain in the head and neck, difficult breathing, nausea, vomiting, sweating, thirst, chest pains, palpitations, lowered blood pressure, weakness, dizziness, blurred vision, and confusion. If you experience these reactions, contact your doctor immediately.

Because of the stimulant ingredients in many over-the-counter drug products for the relief of coughs, colds, and allergies, avoid them unless your doctor advises otherwise.

Response to Chlorpropamide may be reduced if beta-blocking agents such as Propranolol (Inderal) are given to the same patient.

Usual Dose

Adult: 250 milligrams daily.
Elderly: 100 to 250 milligrams daily.
For severe cases: 500 milligrams daily.

Overdosage

A mild overdose of Chlorpropamide lowers the blood sugar, which can be treated by consuming sugar in such forms as candy and orange juice. A patient with a more serious overdose should be taken to a hospital emergency room immediately. ALWAYS bring the medicine bottle.

Special Information

The treatment of diabetes is your responsibility. You should follow all instructions about diet, body weight, exercise, personal hygiene, and all measures to avoid infection. If you are not feeling well, or if you have symptoms such as itching, rash, yellowing of the skin or eyes, abnormally light-colored stools, a low-grade fever, sore throat, or diarrhea—contact your doctor immediately.

Do not discontinue taking this medication unless advised by your physician.

Generic Name

Chlorthalidone

Brand Names

Hygroton
Hylidone
Thalitone

(Also available in generic form)

Type of Drug

Diuretic.

Prescribed for

Congestive heart failure, cirrhosis of the liver, kidney malfunction, high blood pressure, and other conditions where it is necessary to rid the body of excess fluid.

General Information

This drug is a member of the class known as thiazide diuretics. Thiazides act on the kidneys to stimulate the production of large amounts of urine. They also cause you to lose bicarbonate, sodium chloride, and potassium ions from the body. They are used as a part of the treatment of any disease where it is desirable to eliminate large quantities of body water. These diseases include heart failure, some kidney diseases, and liver diseases.

Cautions and Warnings

Do not take Chlorthalidone if you are allergic or sensitive to this drug, similar drugs of this group, or sulfa drugs. If you have a history of allergy or bronchial asthma, you may also have a sensitivity or allergy to Chlorthalidone.

This drug may cause birth defects or interfere with your baby's development. Check with your doctor before taking it if you are, or might be, pregnant. Chlorthalidone will cross the placenta and pass into the unborn child, possibly causing side effects such as blood problems (jaundice) and low potassium. Chlorthalidone passes into breast milk. Nursing mothers should use an alternative feeding method.

Possible Side Effects

Chlorthalidone will cause a lowering of potassium in the body. Signs of low potassium are dryness of the mouth, thirst, weakness, lethargy, drowsiness, restlessness, muscle pains or cramps, muscular tiredness, low blood pressure, gout, decreased frequency of urination and decreased amount of urine produced, abnormal heart rate, and stomach upset including nausea and vomiting.

To treat this, potassium supplements are given in the form of tablets, liquids, or powders, or by increased consumption of foods such as bananas, citrus fruits, melons, and tomatoes.

Possible Adverse Drug Effects

Loss of appetite, stomach upset, nausea, vomiting, cramping, diarrhea, constipation, dizziness, headache, tingling of the toes and fingers, restlessness, changes in blood composition, sensitivity to sunlight, rash, itching, fever, difficulty in breathing, allergic reactions, dizziness when rising quickly from a sitting or lying position, muscle spasms, weakness, blurred vision.

Drug Interactions

Chlorthalidone will add to (potentiate) the action of other blood-pressure-lowering drugs. This is beneficial, and is frequently used to help lower blood pressure in patients with hypertension.

The possibility of developing imbalances in body fluids (electrolytes) is increased if you take medications such as Digitalis and adrenal corticosteroids while you take Chlorthalidone.

If you are taking an oral antidiabetic drug and begin taking Chlorthalidone, the antidiabetic dose may have to be altered.

Lithium Carbonate should not be taken with Chlorthalidone because the combination may increase the risk of Lithium toxicity.

If you are taking this drug for the treatment of high blood pressure or congestive heart failure, avoid over-the-counter medicines for the treatment of coughs, colds, and allergies: such medicines may contain stimulants. If you are unsure about them, ask your pharmacist.

Usual Dose

50 to 100 milligrams per day; or 100 milligrams on alternate days or 3 days per week.

Some patients may require 150 or 200 milligrams per day; doses of more than 200 milligrams per day generally do not produce greater response. A single dose is taken with food in the morning. Dose often declines from the initial dose, according to patient's need.

Overdosage

Symptoms are excessive urination, fatigue, and coma. The patient should be taken to a hospital emergency room immediately. ALWAYS bring the medicine bottle.

Generic Name

Ciclopirox Olamine

Brand Name

Loprox

Type of Drug

Antifungal.

Prescribed for

Fungus and yeast infections of the skin, including those responsible for athlete's foot, candida, and other fungus infections.

General Information

This drug slows the growth of a wide variety of fungus organisms and yeasts and kills many others. Ciclopirox Olamine penetrates the skin very well and is present in levels sufficient to kill or inhibit most fungus organisms. In addition, it penetrates the hair, hair follicles, and skin sweat glands.

Cautions and Warnings

Do not use if you are allergic to this product.

When the drug was given by mouth to animals in doses 10 times the amount normally applied to the skin, it was found to be nontoxic to the developing fetus. As with all drugs, caution should be exercised when using Ciclopirox Olamine during pregnancy. It is not known if Ciclopirox Olamine passes into human breast milk.

Possible Side Effects

Burning, itching, and stinging in the areas to which the cream has been applied.

Usual Dose

Apply enough of the cream to cover affected areas twice a day and massage it into the skin.

Overdosage

This cream should not be swallowed. If it is swallowed, the victim may be nauseated and have an upset stomach. Little is known about Ciclopirox Olamine overdose, and you should call your local Poison Control Center for more information.

Special Information

Clean the affected areas before applying Ciclopirox Olamine cream, unless otherwise directed by your doctor.

Call your doctor if the affected area burns, stings, or becomes red after using this product. Also, notify your doctor if your symptoms don't clear up after 4 weeks of treatment, since it is unlikely that, after that length of treatment, the cream will be effective at all.

This product is quite effective and can be expected to relieve symptoms within the first week of use. Follow your doctor's directions for the complete 2-to-4-week course of treatment to gain maximum benefit from this product. Stopping it too soon may not completely eliminate the fungus and can lead to a relapse.

Generic Name

Cimetidine

Brand Name

Tagamet

Type of Drug

Histamine H_2 Antagonist.

Prescribed for

Part of the treatment of ulcers. Also used in the treatment of other conditions characterized by secretions of large amounts of gastrointestinal fluids.

Cautions and Warnings

Do not take Cimetidine if you know you are allergic to it.

Although problems in pregnant women or nursing mothers have not been seen when using Cimetidine, this drug should be used with extreme caution if you are pregnant or if you might become pregnant while taking it. Cimetidine should not be used by nursing mothers.

Possible Side Effects

Most frequent: mild diarrhea, muscle pains and cramps, dizziness, rash, nausea, vomiting, headache, mental confusion, drowsiness.

Possible Adverse Drug Effects

Changes in heart rhythm, adverse effects on the blood system, hepatitis, kidney disorders, impotence, hair loss, hallucinations, double vision. A few patients have reported breast enlargement.

Drug Interactions

Cimetidine may increase the effects of blood-thinning drugs like Warfarin, tranquilizers of the benzodiazepine group, phenytoin beta blockers, quinidine, caffeine and Theophylline. Separate Cimetidine from antacid doses by about 3 hours. Metoclopramide slows Cimetidine absorption into the blood stream.

Usual Dose

300 milligrams 4 times per day, with meals and at bedtime.

Overdosage

Symptoms are rapid heart beat and difficulty breathing. The patient should be taken to a hospital emergency room immediately. ALWAYS bring the medicine bottle.

Special Information

Many doctors believe that Cimetidine, properly used, will decrease the amount of ulcer surgery because the drug reduces the amount of irritating secretions produced by stomach glands. Report any unusual side effects of this drug to your doctor immediately.

Food Interactons

Take Cimetidine with or immediately after a meal to get maximum effect from the drug.

Generic Name

Clindamycin

Brand Name

Cleocin
Cleocin T Topical Solution

Type of Drug

Antibiotic.

Prescribed for

Serious infections caused by bacteria which are generally found to be susceptible to this drug.

General Information

This is one of the few drugs, given by mouth, which is effective against anaerobic organisms: bacteria which grow only in the absence of oxygen and are frequently found in infected wounds, lung abscesses, abdominal infections, and infections of the female genital tract. It is also effective against the organisms usually treated by Penicillin or Erythromycin.

Clindamycin may be useful for treating certain skin or soft tissue infections where susceptible organisms are present.

Cautions and Warnings

Do not take Clindamycin if you are allergic to it or to Lincomycin, another antibiotic drug. It may cause a severe intestinal irritation called colitis, which may be fatal. Because of this, Clindamycin should be reserved for serious infections due to organisms known to be affected by it. It should not be taken for the casual treatment of colds or other moderate infections, or for infections which can be successfully treated with other drugs. If you develop severe diarrhea or stomach pains, call your doctor at once.

This drug may cause birth defects or interfere with your baby's development. Check with your doctor before taking it if you are, or might be, pregnant.

Possible Side Effects

Stomach pain, nausea, vomiting, diarrhea, pain when swallowing.

Possible Adverse Drug Effects

Itching and rash or more serious signs of drug sensitivity, such as difficulty in breathing; also yellowing of the skin or whites of the eyes, occasional effects on components of the blood, and joint pain.

Drug Interactions

Clindamycin may antagonize Erythromycin; these drugs should not be taken together.

Usual Dose

Adult: 150 to 450 milligrams every 6 hours.

Child: 2 to 11 milligrams per pound of body weight per day in divided doses. No child should be given less than 37.5 milligrams 3 times per day, regardless of weight.

Special Information

Safety in pregnant women has not been established. Since this drug is transferred to the breast milk of nursing mothers, its use by them should be carefully considered. Unsupervised use of this drug or other antibiotics can cause secondary infections from susceptible organisms such as fungi.

Like any antibiotic treatment, take for the full course of therapy as indicated by your physician.

Generic Name

Clofibrate

Brand Name

Atromid-S

Type of Drug

Antihyperlipidemic.

Prescribed for

Reduction of high blood levels of cholesterol and/or triglycerides, in patients not responding to diet, weight control, and exercise measures to control their diabetes.

General Information

Although we don't know exactly how Clofibrate works, we know that it works on blood cholesterol and triglycerides. The lowering of blood levels of these fatty materials may be beneficial, and may have an effect on the development of heart disease. No one knows for sure. However, it is generally considered better to have low levels of cholesterol and triglycerides in the blood. Clofibrate is only part of the therapy for high blood levels of cholesterol and/or triglycerides. Diet and weight control are also very important. You must remember that taking this medicine is not a substitute for other activities or dietary restrictions which have been prescribed for you by your doctor.

Cautions and Warnings

Clofibrate should not be used if you have severe liver or kidney disease, are pregnant, or are a nursing mother. There is the possibility that this medication may pass from you into your baby and build up in the unborn child to cause an adverse effect.

Clofibrate causes liver cancer in rats and may do the same to human patients. Its use has not been definitely associated with reductions in death from heart disease; therefore, this drug should be used only by patients whose diets and other activities have not solved their triglyceride or cholesterol problems. Some studies have reported a large increase in death rates and drug side effects when people have taken Clofibrate over a long term.

Possible Side Effects

The most frequent side effect of Clofibrate is nausea. Other gastrointestinal reactions may be experienced: loose stools, stomach upset, stomach gas, abdominal pain. Less frequent: headache, dizziness, tiredness, cramped muscles, aching and weakness, rash, itching, brittle hair and loss of hair.

Possible Adverse Drug Effects

Abnormal heart rhythms, blood clots in the lungs or veins, enlargement of the liver, gallstones (especially in patients who have taken Clofibrate for a long time), decreased sex drive, sexual impotence. If you suffer from angina pectoris, a specific type of chest pain, Clofibrate may either increase or decrease this pain. It may cause you to produce smaller amounts of urine than usual, and has been associated with blood in the urine, tiredness, weakness, drowsiness, dizziness, headache, and increased appetite. Clofibrate has been accused of causing stomach ulcers, stomach bleeding, arthritislike symptoms, uncontrollable muscle spasms, increased perspiration, blurred vision, breast enlargement, and some effects on the blood.

Drug Interactions

If you are taking an anticoagulant and get a new prescription for Clofibrate, your anticoagulant dose will have to be reduced by as much as a third to a half. It is absolutely essential that your doctor knows you are taking these drugs in combination so that the proper dose adjustments can be made.

Food Interactions

This drug may be taken with food or milk if it causes upset stomach.

Usual Dose

4 capsules per day in divided doses.

Storage

Clofibrate capsules are covered with soft gelatin that must

be protected from heat and moisture. They should not be
stored in the refrigerator, or in a bathroom medicine chest
where there may be a lot of heat or moisture in the air, but
in a dresser or night table where room temperature is normal.

Special Information

Call your doctor if you develop chest pains, difficulty in
breathing, abnormal heart rates, severe stomach pains with
nausea and vomiting, fever and chills, sore throat, blood in
the urine, swelling of the legs, weight gain, or change in
urine habits.

Follow your diet and limit your intake of alcoholic beverages.

Generic Name

Clonazepam

Brand Name

Clonopin

Type of Drug

Anticonvulsant.

Prescribed for

Control of petit mal seizures.

General Information

Clonazepam is a member of the family of drugs known as
benzodiazepines. Other members of the family include Diazepam, Chlordiazepoxide, Flurazepam, and Triazolam. Clonazepam is used only to control petit mal seizures in people
who have not responded to other drug treatments, such as
Ethosuximide. Clonazepam is generally considered a safe
and effective treatment for such seizures and shares many of
the same side effects, precautions, and interactions as its
benzodiazepine cousins.

Cautions and Warnings

When stopping Clonazepam treatments, it is essential that

the drug be discontinued gradually over a period of time to allow for safe withdrawal. Abrupt discontinuation of any benzodiazepine, including Clonazepam, may lead to drug withdrawal symptoms. In the case of Clonazepam, the withdrawal symptoms can include severe seizures. Other symptoms include tremors, abdominal cramps, muscle cramps, vomiting, and sweating.

This drug should be avoided by women who may become pregnant while using it and by pregnant and nursing mothers. It will cross into the developing infant, and the possible adverse effects are not known. In those situations where it is deemed essential, the potential risk of the drug must be carefully weighed against any benefit it might produce.

Recent reports suggest a strong association between the use of anticonvulsant drugs and birth defects. Although most of the information pertains to Phenytoin and Phenobarbital, not Clonazepam, other reports indicate a general association between all anticonvulsant drug treatments and birth defects. It is possible that the epileptic condition itself or genetic factors common to people with seizure disorders may also figure in the higher incidence of birth defects. Mothers taking Clonazepam should not breast-feed because of the possibility that the drug will pass into their breast milk and affect the baby. Use an alternative feeding method.

Clonazepam should be used with caution if you have a chronic respiratory illness because the drug tends to increase salivation and other respiratory secretions and can make breathing more labored.

Possible Side Effects

Drowsiness, poor muscle control, and behavior changes.

Possible Adverse Drug Effects

Abnormal eye movements, loss of voice and/or the ability to express a thought, double vision, coma, a glassy-eyed appearance, headache, temporary paralysis, labored breathing, shortness of breath, slurred speech, tremors, dizziness, fainting, confusion, depression, forgetfulness, hallucination, increased sex drive, hysteria, sleeplessness, psychosis, suicidal acts, chest congestion, stuffy nose, heart palpitations, hair loss, hairiness, rash, swelling of the face or ankles, changes in appetite and body weight (increased or decreased), coated tongue, constipation, diarrhea, involuntary passing feces, dry mouth, stomach irritation, nausea, sore gums, difficulty urinating, pain on urination, bedwetting, getting up at night to urinate, muscle weakness or pain, reduced red- and white-blood-cell and platelet levels, enlarged liver, liver inflammation, dehydration, a deterioration in general health, fever, and swollen lymph glands.

Drug Interactions

The depressant effects of Clonazepam are increased by tranquilizers, sleeping pills, narcotic pain relievers, antihistamines, alcohol, MAO inhibitors, antidepressants, and other anticonvulsants.

The combination of Valproic Acid and Clonazepam may produce severe petit mal seizures.

Phenobarbital or Phenytoin may reduce Clonazepam effectiveness by increasing the rate at which it is eliminated from the body.

Clonazepam treatment may increase the requirement for other anticonvulsant drugs, because of its effects on people who suffer from multiple types of seizures.

Avoid alcoholic beverages, which increase the depressant effects of this medicine.

Food Interactions

Clonazepam is best taken on an empty stomach but may be taken with food if it upsets your stomach.

Usual Dose

Adult and Child (over age 10): 0.5 milligram 3 times per day to start. The dose is increased in steps of 0.5 to 1 milligram every 3 days until seizures are controlled or side effects develop. The maximum daily dose is 20 milligrams.

Infant and *child* (up to age 10, or 66 pounds): 0.004 to 0.013 milligram per pound of body weight per day to start. The dosage can be gradually increased to a maximum of 0.045 to 0.09 milligram per pound of body weight.

The dosage of Clonazepam must be reduced in people with impaired kidney function since this drug is primarily released from the body via the kidneys.

143

overdose will cause confusion, coma, poor reflexes, drowsiness, low blood pressure, labored breathing, and other depressive effects. If the overdose is discovered immediately, it may be helpful to make the victim vomit with Syrup of Ipecac to remove any remaining medicine from the stomach. All victims of Clonazepam overdose *must* be taken to a hospital emergency room for treatment. ALWAYS bring the prescription bottle with you.

Special Information

Clonazepam may interfere with your ability to drive a car or perform other complex tasks because it can cause drowsiness and difficulty concentrating.

Your doctor should perform periodic blood counts and liver-function tests while you are taking this drug to check for possible adverse drug effects.

Do not suddenly stop taking the medicine, since to do so could result in severe seizures. The dosage must be discontinued gradually by your doctor.

Carry identification or wear a bracelet indicating that you suffer from a seizure disorder for which you take Clonazepam.

Generic Name

Clonidine

Brand Name

Catapres

Type of Drug

Antihypertensive.

Prescribed for

High blood pressure.

General Information

Clonidine acts in the brain by causing the dilation of certain blood vessels, thereby decreasing blood pressure. The drug produces its effect very quickly, causing a decline in blood pressure within 1 hour. If you abruptly stop taking Clonidine you may experience an unusual increase in blood pressure with symptoms of agitation, headache, and nervousness. These effects can be reversed by simply resuming therapy or by taking another drug to lower the blood pressure. Under no circumstances should you stop taking Clonidine without your doctor's knowledge. People who abruptly stop taking this medication may suffer severe reactions and even die. Be sure you always have an adequate supply on hand.

Clonidine has also been used in the treatment of tourette syndrome, migraine headaches and Methadone/opiate detoxification.

Cautions and Warnings

Some people develop a tolerance to their usual dose of Clonidine. If this happens to you your blood pressure may increase, and you will require a change in the Clonidine dose. Clonidine is not recommended for use by women who are pregnant or who plan to become pregnant.

Possible Side Effects

Most common: dry mouth, drowsiness, sedation, constipation, dizziness, headache, fatigue. These effects tend to diminish as you continue taking the drug.

Possible Adverse Drug Effects

Infrequent: loss of appetite, not feeling well, nausea, vomiting, weight gain, breast enlargement, various effects on the heart, changes in dream patterns, nightmares, difficulty sleeping, nervousness, restlessness, anxiety, mental depression, rash, hives, itching, thinning or loss of scalp hair, difficulty urinating, impotence, dryness and burning of the eyes.

Drug Interactions

Clonidine has a depressive effect and will increase the depressive effects of alcohol, barbiturates, sedatives, and tranquilizers. Avoid them.

Antidepressant drugs may counteract the effects of Clonidine.

Usual Dose

Starting dose of 0.1 milligram twice per day may be raised

by 0.1 to 0.2 milligram per day until maximum control is achieved. The dose must be tailored to your individual needs. It is recommended that no one should take more than 2.4 milligrams per day.

Overdosage

Symptoms are severe lowering of blood pressure, weakness, and vomiting. The patient should be taken to a hospital emergency room immediately. ALWAYS bring the medicine bottle.

Special Information

Clonidine causes drowsiness in about 35 percent of those who take it: be extremely careful while driving or operating any sort of appliance or machinery. The effect is prominent during the first few weeks of therapy, then tends to decrease.

Avoid taking nonprescription cough and cold medicine unless so directed by your doctor.

Generic Name

Clorazepate

Brand Names

Azene
Tranxene
Tranxene-SD

Type of Drug

Tranquilizer.

Prescribed for

Relief of symptoms of anxiety, tension, fatigue, or agitation.

General Information

Clorazepate is a member of the chemical group of drugs known as benzodiazepines. These drugs are used as either antianxiety agents, anticonvulsants, or sedatives (sleeping pills). They exert their effects by relaxing the large skeletal muscles and by a direct effect on the brain. In doing so, they can relax you and make you either more tranquil or sleepier, depending on the drug and how much you use. Many doctors prefer Clorazepate and the other members of this class to other drugs that can be used for the same effect. Their reason is that the benzodiazepines tend to be safer, have fewer side effects, and are usually as, if not more, effective.

These drugs are generally used in any situation where they can be a useful adjunct.

Benzodiazepine tranquilizing drugs can be abused if taken for long periods of time, and it is possible to develop withdrawal symptoms if you discontinue the therapy abruptly. Withdrawal symptoms include tremor, muscle cramps, stomach cramps, vomiting, insomnia, agitation, sweating, and even convulsions.

Cautions and Warnings

Do not take Clorazepate if you know you are sensitive or allergic to this drug or other benzodiazepines such as Diazepam, Chlordiazepoxide, Oxazepam, Lorazepam, Prazepam, Flurazepam, Clonazepam, and Temazepam. Clorazepate and other members of this drug group may aggravate narrow angle glaucoma, but if you have open angle glaucoma you may take the drugs. In any case, check this information with your doctor. Clorazepate can cause tiredness, drowsiness, inability to concentrate, or similar symptoms. Be careful if you are driving, operating machinery, or performing other activities which require concentration. Avoid taking this drug during the first 3 months of pregnancy except under strict supervision of your doctor. Although an increased chance of birth defects has not been seen, there is a risk factor to be considered. Other drugs similar to Clorazepate have been shown to cause birth defects.

The baby may become dependent on Clorazepate if it is used continually during pregnancy. If used during the last weeks of pregnancy or during breast-feeding, the baby may be overly tired, short of breath, or have a low heartbeat.

Use during labor may cause weakness in the newborn.

Possible Side Effects

Most common: mild drowsiness during the first few days of

therapy, especially in the elderly or debilitated. If drowsiness persists, contact your doctor.

Possible Adverse Drug Effects

Major adverse reactions: confusion, depression, lethargy, disorientation, headache, inactivity, slurred speech, stupor, dizziness, tremor, constipation, dry mouth, nausea, inability to control urination, changes in sex drive, irregular menstrual cycle, changes in heart rhythm, lowered blood pressure, retention of fluids, blurred or double vision, itching, rash, hiccups, nervousness, inability to fall asleep, (occasional) liver dysfunction. If you experience any of these reactions stop taking the medicine and contact your doctor immediately.

Drug Interactions

Clorazepate is a central nervous system depressant. Avoid alcohol, tranquilizers, narcotics, barbiturates, MAO inhibitors, antihistamines, and other medicines used to relieve depression. Smoking may reduce the effectiveness of Clorazepate. The effects of Clorazepate may be prolonged when taken together with Cimetidine.

Usual Dose

15 to 60 milligrams daily; average dose, 30 milligrams in divided quantities. Must be adjusted to individual response for patient to receive maximum effect.

Tranxene-SD, a long-acting form of Clorazepate, may be given as a single dose, either 11.25 or 22.5 milligrams once every 24 hours. The daily dose of Azene, another brand name, is slightly different, from 12 to 52 milligrams per day according to patient's response. The drug may be given as a single daily dose at bedtime; usual starting dose for helping patients go to sleep is 13 milligrams.

Overdosage

Symptoms are confusion, sleep or sleepiness, lack of response to pain such as a pin stick, shallow breathing, lowered blood pressure, and coma. The patient should be taken to a hospital emergency room immediately. ALWAYS bring the medicine bottle.

Generic Name

Clotrimazole

Brand Names

Gyne-Lotrimin
Lotrimin
Mycelex

(Also available in generic form)

Type of Drug

Antifungal.

Prescribed for

Fungus infections of the skin and vaginal tract.

General Information

Clotrimazole is one of the newer antifungal drugs in the U.S., although it has been available in other parts of the world for some time. This drug is especially useful against a wide variety of fungus organisms which other drugs do not affect.

Cautions and Warnings

If Clotrimazole causes local itching and/or irritation, stop using it. Do not use in the eyes. Women who are in the first three months of pregnancy should use this drug only if directed to do so by their doctors.

Possible Side Effects

Side effects do not occur very often and are usually mild. Cream or solution: redness, stinging, blistering, peeling, itching and swelling of local areas. Vaginal tablets: mild burning, skin rash, mild cramps, frequent urination, and burning or itching in a sexual partner.

Usual Dose

Cream or solution: apply to affected areas, morning and night.

   Vaginal cream: one applicatorful at bedtime for 7 to 14 days.
   Vaginal tablets: 1 tablet inserted into the vagina at bedtime for 7 days, or 2 tablets a day for 3 days.

Special Information

If treating a vaginal infection, you should refrain from sexual activity or be sure that your partner wears a condom until the treatment is finished. Call your doctor if burning or itching develop or if the condition does not show improvement in 7 days.

Generic Name

Codeine

(Available only in generic form)

Type of Drug

Narcotic analgesic cough suppressant combination.

Prescribed for

Relief of moderate to moderately severe pain, and as a cough suppressant.

General Information

Codeine is a narcotic drug with some pain-relieving and cough-suppressing activity. As an analgesic it is useful for mild to moderate pain. 30 to 60 milligrams of Codeine is approximately equal in pain-relieving effect to 2 Aspirin tablets (650 milligrams). Codeine may be less active than Aspirin for types of pain associated with inflammation, since Aspirin reduces inflammation and Codeine does not. Codeine suppresses the cough reflex but does not cure the underlying cause of the cough. In fact, sometimes it may not be desirable to overly suppress a cough, because cough suppression reduces your ability to naturally eliminate excess mucus produced during a cold or allergy attack. Other narcotic cough suppressants are stronger than Codeine, but Codeine remains the best cough medicine available today.

Cautions and Warnings

Do not take Codeine if you know you are allergic or sensitive to it. Use this drug with extreme caution if you suffer from asthma or other breathing problems. Long-term use of this drug may cause drug dependence or addiction. Codeine is a respiratory depressant and affects the central nervous system, producing sleepiness, tiredness, and/or inability to concentrate. Be careful if you are driving, operating machinery, or performing other functions requiring concentration.

This drug may cause birth defects or interfere with your baby's development. Check with your doctor before taking it if you are, or might be, pregnant.

Possible Side Effects

Most frequent: light-headedness, dizziness, sleepiness, nausea, vomiting, loss of appetite, sweating. If these occur, consider calling your doctor and asking him about lowering the dose of Codeine you are taking. Usually the side effects disappear if you simply lie down.

More serious side effects of Codeine are shallow breathing or difficulty in breathing.

Possible Adverse Drug Effects

Euphoria (feeling high), sleepiness, headache, agitation, uncoordinated muscle movement, minor hallucinations, disorientation and visual disturbances, dry mouth, loss of appetite, constipation, flushing of the face, rapid heartbeat, palpitations, faintness, urinary difficulties or hesitancy, reduced sex drive and/or potency, itching, rashes, anemia, lowered blood sugar, yellowing of the skin and/or whites of the eyes. Narcotic analgesics may aggravate convulsions in those who have had convulsions in the past.

Drug Interactions

Because of its depressant effect and potential effect on breathing, Codeine should be taken with extreme care in combination with alcohol, sleeping medicine, tranquilizers, or other depressant drugs.

Food Interactions

Codeine may be taken with food to reduce stomach upset.

Usual Dose

Adult: 15 to 60 milligrams 4 times per day for relief of pain; 10 to 20 milligrams every few hours as needed to suppress cough.

Child: 1 to 2 milligrams per pound of body weight in divided doses for relief of pain; 0.5 to 0.75 milligram per pound of body weight in divided doses to suppress cough.

Overdosage

Symptoms are depression of respiration (breathing), extreme tiredness progressing to stupor and then coma, pinpointed pupils of the eyes, no response to stimulation such as a pin stick, cold and clammy skin, slowing down of the heartbeat, lowering of blood pressure, convulsions, and cardiac arrest. The patient should be taken to a hospital emergency room immediately. ALWAYS bring the medicine bottle.

Special Information

Avoid alcohol while taking Codeine. Call your doctor if you develop constipation or dry mouth.

Generic Name

Colchicine

Brand Name

Colsalide

(Also available in generic form)

Type of Drug

Reduces the inflammatory response to gout.

Prescribed for

Gouty arthritis.

General Information

While no one knows exactly how Colchicine works, it appears to affect gout by reducing the body's inflammatory response to gout. Unlike drugs that affect uric-acid levels, Colchicine will not block the progression of gout to chronic gouty arthritis, but it will relieve the pain of acute attacks and lessen the frequency and severity of attacks.

Cautions and Warnings

Notify your doctor if you experience skin rash, sore throat, fever, unusual bleeding or bruising, tiredness, numbness or tingling.

Stop taking Colchicine as soon as gout pain is relieved or at the first sign of nausea, vomiting, stomach pain, or diarrhea. If you experience these side effects, contact your doctor.

Do not use Colchicine if you suffer from serious kidney, liver, stomach, or cardiac disorder.

Colchicine should be used with great caution by the elderly.

Colchicine can harm the fetus; use by pregnant women should be considered only when the benefits clearly outweigh the potential hazards to the fetus.

Safety and effectiveness for use by children has not been established.

Periodic blood counts should be done when you are taking Colchicine for long periods of time.

Possible Side Effects

Vomiting, diarrhea, stomach pain, nausea, hair loss, skin rash.

Possible Adverse Drug Effects

Disorders of the blood may occur in patients undergoing long-term Colchicine therapy.

Drug Interactions

Colchicine has been shown to cause poor absorption of Vitamin B_{12}, a condition that is reversible.

Colchicine may increase sensitivity to central-nervous-system depressants such as tranquilizers and alcohol.

Usual Dose

To relieve an acute attack of gout: 1 to 1.2 milligrams. This dose may be followed by 0.5 to 1.2 milligrams every 1 to 2 hours until pain is relieved. The total amount usually needed to control pain and inflammation during an attack varies from 4 to 8 milligrams.

To prevent gout attacks: 0.3 to 1.2 milligrams daily.

Overdosage

Symptoms may include nausea; vomiting; stomach pain; burning sensations in the throat, stomach and skin; diarrhea (which may be severe and bloody). If you think you are experiencing an overdose, contact your doctor immediately, or go to a hospital emergency room. ALWAYS bring the medicine bottle with you.

Brand Name

Combid

Ingredients

Isopropamide
Prochlorperazine

Type of Drug

Gastrointestinal anticholinergic agent.

Prescribed for

Excess acid in the stomach, spasms of the stomach and small intestine, and relief of anxiety and tension or nausea and vomiting associated with gastrointestinal disease.

General Information

The antinauseant in Combid works to relieve and prevent nausea and vomiting and the anticholinergic works to prevent and treat stomach and intestinal spasms. By relieving these spasms, Combid can prevent or treat stomach or intestinal pains. Combid spansules release their ingredients over an 8-to-12-hour period; only 2 capsules per day are usually required.

Cautions and Warnings

Do not take Combid if you have narrow angle glaucoma.

Other disorders where an anticholinergic drug such as Combid may be damaging are prostatic hypertrophy, pyloric obstruction, bladder-neck obstruction, and obstructive lesions of the intestine. Nausea and vomiting may be a drug side effect or a sign of disease: if you have this medication at home, do not self-medicate for nausea and vomiting until you have checked with your doctor. The safety of this drug for pregnant or nursing women has not been established.

When used by pregnant women, Combid has caused side effects in newborns such as jaundice (yellowing of skin and eyes) and twitching. These medications should be stopped 1 to 2 weeks before expected delivery to avoid this. Combid has not been shown to cause problems during breast-feeding.

Possible Side Effects

Primary: sleepiness or drowsiness, dry mouth, blurred vision, increased sensitivity to strong light, difficulty in urination, loss of sense of taste.

Possible Adverse Drug Effects

Rare: sore throat, fever, unusual bleeding or bruising, rash, yellowing of the skin or whites of the eyes. If you experience any of these, contact your doctor immediately.

Drug Interactions

Combid can cause sleepiness, tiredness, or difficulty in concentration. Do not aggravate the problem by taking alcoholic beverages, tranquilizers, sedatives, and other drugs that cause tiredness.

Usual Dose

1 capsule every 12 to 24 hours.

Overdosage

Symptoms (from either ingredient in Combid) are central nervous system depression possibly to the point of coma, lowered blood pressure, agitation, restlessness, convulsions, fever, dry mouth, severe stomach cramps, abnormal heart rhythms, difficulty in swallowing, extreme thirst, blurred vision, sensitivity to bright light, flushed, hot dry skin, rash, high blood pressure, confusion, and delirium. The patient should be taken to a hospital emergency room immediately. ALWAYS bring the medicine bottle.

Brand Name

Combipres

Ingredients

Chlorthalidone
Clonidine

Type of Drug

Antihypertensive.

Prescribed for

High blood pressure.

General Information

This drug is a combination of two effective antihypertensive drugs. One of them works by causing the dilation of certain blood vessels. The other is a diuretic which lowers blood pressure through its effect on body ions (sodium and potassium). Although it is convenient to take the two drugs in one tablet, it may not be in your best interest. If you need more or less of one of the ingredients than are available in the Combipres tablets, you must take the drugs as separate pills. Often, doctors are able to lower your blood pressure most effectively by manipulating the doses of one drug or the other.

Cautions and Warnings

Do not take Combipres if you are allergic to either of the ingredients or to sulfa-type drugs.

Some people develop a tolerance to the effect of one of the ingredients in this product. If this happens, your blood pressure may increase and you may require a change of dose or medicine.

This drug should not be taken by women planning to become pregnant, pregnant women, or nursing mothers. Chlorthalidone, if used during pregnancy, may cause side effects in the newborn infant; they are jaundice, blood problems, and low potassium. Chlorthalidone passes into breast milk. Nursing mothers should use an alternate feeding method.

Possible Side Effects

One of the ingredients in this drug can cause loss of potassium from the body (hypokalemia). The signs of this problem are dryness of the mouth, weakness, lethargy, drowsiness, restlessness, muscle pains or cramps, muscular tiredness, stomach upset, nausea and vomiting, and abnormal heart rhythms. To prevent or treat hypokalemia, potassium supplements, in the form of tablets, powders, or liquids, are given every day. You may increase your potassium intake naturally by eating more bananas, citrus fruits, melons, or tomatoes.

Combipres may also cause constipation or headache.

Possible Adverse Drug Effects

Loss of appetite, feeling of ill health, nausea, vomiting, weight gain, breast enlargement, adverse effects on the heart, changes in dream patterns, nightmares, difficulty sleeping, anxiety, depression, rash, hives, itching, thinning or loss of hair, dryness or burning of the eyes, sexual impotence. Other possible adverse effects from this combination are tingling of the toes or fingers, changes in blood composition, sensitivity to sunlight, difficulty in breathing, drug allergy, dizziness when rising quickly from a sitting or lying position, muscle spasms, weariness, blurred vision.

Drug Interactions

May interact with Digitalis to cause abnormal heart rhythms. The effect of an oral antidiabetic medicine may be altered by Combipres. People taking Lithium drugs should be careful about also taking Combipres since the combination may lead to Lithium toxicity. Avoid alcohol, barbiturates, sedatives, and tranquilizers while taking Combipres. Their action may be increased by one of the ingredients in Combipres.

Usual Dose

2 tablets per day (of either strength). The dose of this drug

must be tailored to your individual needs for maximum effectiveness.

Overdosage

Symptoms are excessive urination, fatigue, and extreme lowering of blood pressure. The patient should be taken immediately to a hospital emergency room. ALWAYS bring the medicine bottle.

Special Information

Avoid over-the-counter drugs containing stimulant drugs. If you are unsure which ones to avoid, ask your pharmacist.

One of the ingredients in Combipres causes drowsiness in about 35 percent of those who take it. Be extremely careful while driving or operating any equipment. This effect is most prominent during the first few weeks of therapy.

Do not suddenly stop taking this medication.

Generic Name

Conjugated Estrogens

Brand Names

Conjugated Estrogenic
  Substances
Estrocon
Evestrone
Premarin
Progeus

(Also available in generic form)

Type of Drug

Estrogen.

Prescribed for

Moderate to severe symptoms associated with menopause and prevention of post-menopausal osteoporosis. There is no evidence that this drug is effective for nervous symptoms or depression occurring during menopause: it should not be used to treat this condition. Conjugated Estrogens may also be used to treat various types of cancer in selected patients;

and other conditions where supplementation of normal estrogenic substances is required.

General Information

Because of the potential development of secondary disease after a long period of taking Conjugated Estrogens, the decision to take this medication chronically should be made cautiously by you and your doctor.

Cautions and Warnings

Estrogens have been reported to increase the risk of certain types of cancer in postmenopausal women taking this type of drug for prolonged periods of time: the risk tends to depend upon the duration of treatment and the dose of the estrogen being taken. When long-term estrogen therapy is indicated for the treatment of menopausal symptoms, the lowest effective dose should be used. If you have to take Conjugated Estrogens for extended periods of time, you should see your doctor at least twice a year so that he can assess your current condition and your need to continue the drug therapy.

If you are taking an estrogenic product and experience vaginal bleeding of a recurrent, abnormal, or persistent nature, contact your doctor immediately. If you are pregnant do not use this or any other estrogenic substance, since these drugs, if used during the earlier stages of pregnancy, may seriously damage the offspring. Estrogens may reduce the flow of breast milk and the effects on nursing infants are not predictable.

If you have active thrombophlebitis or any other disorder associated with the formation of blood clots, you probably should not take this drug. If you feel that you have a disorder associated with blood clots and you have been taking Conjugated Estrogens or a similar product, you should contact your doctor immediately so that he can evaluate your situation and decide about stopping the drug therapy.

Prolonged continuous administration of estrogenic substances to certain animal species has increased the frequency of cancer in these animals, and there is evidence that these drugs may increase the risk of various cancers in humans. This drug should be taken with caution by women with a strong family history of breast cancer or those who have breast nodules, fibrocystic disease of the breast, or abnormal mammogram. Furthermore, long-term taking of Conjugated Estrogens may expose a woman to a two- to threefold increase in chance of developing gallbladder disease. It is possible that women taking Conjugated Estrogens for extended periods of time may experience some of the same development of long-term adverse effects as women who have taken oral contraceptives for extended periods of time. These long-term problems may include thromboembolic disease or the development of various disorders associated with the development of blood clots, liver cancer or other liver tumors, high blood pressure, glucose intolerance or a development of a symptom similar to diabetes or the aggravation of diabetes in patients who had this disease before they started the estrogen, and high blood levels of calcium in certain classes of patients.

Possible Side Effects

Breakthrough bleeding, spotting, changes in menstrual flow, dysmenorrhea, premenstrual-type syndrome, amenorrhea, vaginal infection with candida, cystitislike syndrome, enlargement or tenderness of the breasts, nausea, vomiting, abdominal cramps, feeling of bloatedness, jaundice or yellowing of the skin or whites of the eyes, rash, loss of scalp hair, development of new hairy areas. Lesions of the eye have been associated with estrogen therapy. If you wear contact lenses and are taking estrogens, it is possible that you will become intolerant to the lenses. You may also experience headache—possibly migraine headache—dizziness, depression, weight changes, retention of water, and changes in sex drive.

Drug Interactions

Vitamin C (in doses of 1 gram a day or more) may increase the effect of estrogen.

Phenytoin, Ethotoin, and Mephenytoin may interfere with estrogen effects.

Estrogens may force a dosage change in oral anticoagulant (blood-thinning) drugs, which your doctor can do with a simple blood test.

Estrogens may increase the side effects of antidepressants and phenothayine-type tranquilizers. Low estrogen doses may increase estrogen effectiveness.

Food Interactions

This drug may be taken with food to reduce upset stomach.

Usual Dose

0.3 to 3.75 milligrams per day, depending on the disease and patient's response.

Overdosage

Overdosage may cause nausea and withdrawal bleeding in adult females. Accidental overdosage in children has not resulted in serious adverse effects.

Special Information

Call your doctor if you develop chest pain, difficulty breathing, pain in the groin or calves, unusual vaginal bleeding, missed menstrual period, lumps in the breast, sudden severe headaches, dizziness or fainting, disturbances in speech or vision, weakness or numbness in the arms or legs, abdominal pains, depression, yellowing of the skin or whites of the eyes. Call your doctor if you think you are pregnant.

Brand Name

Cortisporin Otic

Other Brand Names

Otobione
Ortega Otic M

Ingredients

Hydrocortisone
Neomycin Sulfate
Polymyxin-B

(Also available in generic form)

Type of Drug

Steroid antibiotic combination product.

Prescribed for

Superficial infections, inflammation, itching, and other problems involving the outer ear.

General Information

Cortisporin Otic contains a steroid drug to reduce inflammation and two antibiotics to treat local infections. This combination can be quite useful for local infections and inflammations of the ear because of its dual method of action and its relatively broad, nonspecific applicability.

Cautions and Warnings

This drug has been found to be safe for use during pregnancy. Remember, you should check with your doctor before taking any drug if you are pregnant.

Possible Side Effects

Local irritation such as itching or burning can occur if you are sensitive or allergic to one of the ingredients in this drug.

Usual Dose

2 to 4 drops in the affected ear 3 to 4 times per day.

Special Information

Use only when specifically prescribed by a physician. Overuse of this or similar products can result in the growth of other organisms such as fungi. If new infections or new problems appear during the time you are using this medication, stop using the drug and contact your doctor.

Generic Name

Cyclandelate

Brand Names

Cyclospasmol
Cyclan

(Also available in generic form)

Type of Drug

Vasodilator.

Prescribed for

Nighttime leg cramps. Also prescribed to dilate large blood vessels in the brain so that more blood can be delivered to it.

General Information

Cyclandelate relaxes various smooth muscles: it slows their normal degree of responsiveness but does not paralyze muscle cells. Cyclandelate may directly widen blood vessels in the brain and other areas, increasing the flow of blood and oxygen to these areas.

These actions should be considered as possibly effective.

Cautions and Warnings

Do not take Cyclandelate if you are allergic or sensitive to it. Do not take Cyclandelate if you have a history of glaucoma, or of heart or other disease in which major blood vessels have been partly or completely blocked.

This drug may cause birth defects or interfere with your baby's development. Check with your doctor before taking it if you are, or might be, pregnant.

Possible Side Effects

The most common side effect of Cyclandelate is mild stomach upset, but this can be avoided by taking the medicine with food or antacid. Cyclandelate can produce mild flushing, particularly in the face and extremities. It can also cause headache, feeling of weakness, and rapid heartbeat, especially during the first few weeks of therapy.

Possible Adverse Drug Effects

Cyclandelate can make you feel weak, dizzy, or faint when you rise quickly from a lying or sitting position: this is called orthostatic hypotension and is caused by a sudden drop in the amount of blood being supplied to your brain. You can usually avoid orthostatic hypotension by getting up slowly. If the symptom becomes a problem, contact your doctor so that he can adjust your dose or prescribe a different medicine for you.

Drug Interactions

Avoid taking over-the-counter drugs for cough, cold, or allergy as some of these drugs can aggravate heart disease or other diseases related to blocked blood vessels. Contact your doctor or pharmacist for more specific information about over-the-counter products which could be a problem.

Food Interactions

This drug may be taken with food or antacids to reduce stomach upset.

Usual Dose

Starting dose: 1200 to 1600 milligrams per day in divided doses before meals and at bedtime. As you begin to respond to the medication, the dose may be reduced to a lowest effective level of, usually, 400 to 800 milligrams per day given in 2 to 4 divided doses. Improvement takes several weeks to appear; do not look for immediate benefits. Use of this medication for less than several weeks is usually of little or no value and certainly of no permanent value.

Generic Name

Cyclobenzaprine

Brand Name

Flexeril

Type of Drug

Skeletal muscle relaxant.

Prescribed for

Painful muscle spasm associated with certain conditions.

General Information

This drug can relieve painful muscle spasm and does not interfere with muscle function. It should be used for only 2 to 3 weeks because the kind of conditions for which the drug is used generally do not last longer and it has not been studied in depth for any longer period of use. It should be used until muscle spasm and pain have been relieved, the patient has regained full movement, and complete daily activities have been restored. This drug is a chemical cousin to tricyclic antidepressant drugs.

Cautions and Warnings

Do not use if you are allergic to this drug, are taking MAO inhibitor drugs (or have been taking them within the last 2 weeks), are just recovering from a heart attack, or have abnormal heart rhythms, heart failure, or an overactive thyroid.

This drug may cause birth defects or interfere with your baby's development. Check with your doctor before taking it if you are, or might be, pregnant.

Possible Side Effects

Drowsiness occurs in 40 percent of people taking this drug. It can also cause dry mouth, dizziness, increased heart rate, and weakness.

Possible Adverse Drug Effects

Sweating, muscle aches, difficulty in breathing, abdominal

pain, constipation, coated tongue, tremors, poor muscle control, nervousness, feeling of euphoria, disorientation, confusion, headache, difficulty in urination, depression, hallucination, rash, itching, swelling of the face or tongue.

Drug Interactions

Cyclobenzaprine may interact with MAO inhibitors to produce high fever and convulsions. It may increase the depressive effect of alcohol, sleeping pills, tranquilizers, or other depressant drugs. It may block the effect of Guanethidine and other blood-pressure-lowering drugs. It may interact with Atropine or atropinelike (anticholinergic) drugs to produce symptoms of anticholinergic overdose (dry mouth, difficult urination, thirst).

Usual Dose

20 to 60 milligrams per day.

Overdosage

Symptoms of overdose include temporary confusion, stiff muscles, vomiting, very high fever, drowsiness, heart abnormalities, difficulty in concentrating, hallucinations, and agitation, as well as low body temperature, dilated pupils, convulsions, low blood pressure, and coma.

The drug must be eliminated from the body as quickly as possible. Call your doctor or poison control center for more information. The patient may have to be taken to a hospital emergency room. ALWAYS bring the medicine bottle with you.

Special Information

This drug can cause drowsiness, dizziness, or blurred vision. Be careful while driving or operating any kind of equipment.

Do not use alcohol or any other depressant while taking Cyclobenzaprine.

Generic Name

Cyclosporine

Brand Name

Sandimmune

Type of Drug

Immunosuppressant.

Prescribed for

Prevention of the body's rejection of a transplanted kidney, heart, or liver. Used with or without corticosteroids for those who have previously been given other drug treatments. Cyclosporine has had limited success in bone marrow, heart-lung, and pancreas transplants, all of which are considered non-approved uses for the drug.

Many researchers think that Cyclosporine may help in the treatment of other immunologic diseases such as diabetes, psoriasis, myasthenia gravis, multiple sclerosis, rheumatoid arthritis, lupus, and others. The drug is not approved by the FDA for treating these conditions.

General Information

Cyclosporine is the first new drug approved in the U.S. in over 20 years to prevent rejection of transplanted organs. A product of fungus metabolism, Cyclosporine was proved a potent immunosuppressant in 1972. First given to human kidney- and bone-marrow-transplant patients in 1978, it selectively inhibits cells known as T-lymphocytes and prevents the production of a compound known as interlukein-II, which activates T-lymphocyte cells. T-lymphocytes are an integral part of the body's defense mechanism that actually destroy invading cells.

Cautions and Warnings

This drug should be prescribed only by doctors experienced in immunosuppressive therapy and the care of organ-transplant patients. It is always used with adrenal corticosteroid drugs. Cyclosporine should not be given with other immunosuppressants since oversuppression of the immune system can result in lymphoma or extreme susceptibility to infection.

The oral form of the drug is poorly and erraticaly absorbed into the bloodstream. Because of this, it must be taken in doses 3 times larger than the injectable dose. People taking this drug orally over a period of time should have their blood checked for Cyclosporine levels so that the dose can be adjusted, if necessary.

This drug should be avoided by pregnant women or women who may become pregnant while using it. In those situations where it is deemed essential, the potential risk of the drug must be carefully weighed against any benefit it might produce. Cyclosporine passes into breast milk. Nursing mothers who take this medicine should use an alternative feeding method.

Possible Side Effects

Kidney toxicity: Cyclosporine is known to be extremely toxic to the kidneys. this effect is seen in 25 percent of all kidney transplants, 38 percent of heart transplants, and 37 percent of liver transplants where the drug is used. Mild toxicity is generally seen 2 to 3 months after the transplant and is often reversed by reducing the Cyclosporine dose.

Severe toxicity usually develops soon after transplantation and may be difficult to differentiate from organ rejection. Drug toxicity responds to a reduction in Cyclosporine dosage, while rejection does not. If the toxic effect does not respond to dosage reduction, your doctor will probably switch to a different drug. All people treated with Cyclosporine should be tested periodically for kidney function.

Liver toxicity: This is much less common than kidney toxicity, but still occurs in many people receiving Cyclosporine. Liver toxicity is usually present in 4 percent of kidney transplants, 7 percent of heart transplants, and 4 percent of liver transplants, usually during the first month of therapy, when doses tend to be the highest.

Lymphoma may develop in people whose immune systems are excessively suppressed. Almost 85 percent of all people treated with this medicine will develop an infection, compared with 94 percent on other forms of immunosuppressive therapy.

Other frequent Cyclosporine side effects are: high blood pressure, increased hair growth, growth of the gums, and tremors.

Possible Adverse Drug Effects

Common: cramps, acne, brittle hair or fingernails, convulsions, headache, confusion, diarrhea, nausea and vomiting, tingling in the hands or feet, facial flushing, reduction in blood counts of white cells and platelets, sinus inflammation, swollen and painful male breasts, drug allergy, conjuctivitis (red-eye), fluid retention and swelling, ringing or buzzing in the ears, hearing loss, high blood sugar, muscle pains.

Rare: blood in the urine, heart attack, itching, anxiety, depression, lethargy, weakness, mouth sores, difficulty swallowing, intestinal bleeding, constipation, pancreas inflammation, night sweats, chest pain, joint pains, visual disturbances, weight loss.

Drug Interactions

Cyclosporine is so new that relatively few drug interactions have been reported in the medical literature. The chances are that many more will be discovered in the next few years.

Cyclosporine should be used carefully with other drugs known to be toxic to the kidneys. Cimetidine, for ulcers, and Ketoconazole and Amphotericin B, both antifungal agents, will increase blood levels of Cyclosporine. Phenytoin, for seizure disorders, reduces Cyclosporine blood levels.

Excessive immunosuppression may result from the use of Cyclosporine with any immune-suppressing drug other than a corticosteroid.

Food Interactions

The oral form of this drug comes in an oily base derived from caster oil. You should mix it in a glass (not paper or plastic) with whole milk, chocolate milk, or orange juice at room temperature to make it taste better. Drink immediately after mixing, add more of the dilutent, and drink that to be sure that the entire dose has been taken.

Cyclosporine is best taken on an empty stomach but may be taken with food if it upsets your stomach.

Usual Dose

The usual oral dose of Cyclosporine is 6.8 milligrams per pound of body weight per day, given 4 to 12 hours before the transplant operation. This dosage is continued after the operation for a week or two and then gradually reduced (5 percent per week) to 2.25 to 4.5 milligrams per pound of body weight. Use the method described in Food Interactions. Injectable Cyclosporine is given to people who can't take or tolerate the oral form, in one-third the dose of the oral liquid.

Overdosage

Victims of Cyclosporine overdose can be expected to develop drug side effects and symptoms of extreme immunosuppression. Patients taking an overdose of this drug must be made to vomit with Syrup of Ipecac (available at any pharmacy) to remove any remaining drug from the stomach. Call your doctor or a Poison Control Center before doing this. If you must go to a hospital emergency room, ALWAYS bring the medicine bottle.

Special Information

Call your doctor at the first sign of fever, sore throat, tiredness, unusual bleeding, or bruising.

This medicine should be continued as long as prescribed by your doctor. Do not stop taking it because of side effects or other problems. If you cannot tolerate the oral form, it can be given by injection.

Generic Name

Cyproheptadine Hydrochloride

Brand Name

Periactin

(Also available in generic form)

Type of Drug

Phenothiazine-type antihistamine.

Prescribed for

Relief of symptoms associated with allergies, drug allergies, colds or upper respiratory infections, infection or itching of the extremities, insect bites, and general itching.

It has also been used to stimulate appetite and for the treatment of headaches.

General Information

Cyproheptadine Hydrochloride is an antihistamine. Any effect it exerts is due to its ability to counteract the effects of histamine, a chemical released by the body as part of allergic or sensitivity reactions. Histamine is also released as a part of the body's reaction to the common cold or similar respiratory infections. Cyproheptadine Hydrochloride is especially useful in treating symptoms of allergy, itching, and the common cold. It has been reported to cause weight gain and has even been tried as an appetite stimulant.

Cautions and Warnings

Do not take Cyproheptadine Hydrochloride if you are allergic to it or to other phenothiazine-type drugs such as Chlorpromazine and Prochlorperazine. Signs of allergies to phenothiazines include sore throat, fever, unusual bleeding or bruising, rash, blurred vision, and yellowing of the skin.

Although this drug is usually not a problem for people with heart, liver, and stomach problems, they would do well to avoid taking it.

This drug may cause birth defects or interfere with your baby's development. Check with your doctor before taking it if you are, or might be, pregnant.

Possible Side Effects

Most frequent: sedation, sleeplessness, dizziness, disturbed coordination. Less common: itching, rash, drug allergy, sensitivity to sunlight, excessive perspiration, chills, dryness of the mouth, nose, and throat. Other possible side effects: lowered blood pressure, headache, palpitations, rapid heartbeat.

Possible Adverse Drug Effects

Effects on the blood system, confusion, restlessness, excitation, nervousness, irritability, sleeplessness, euphoria, tingling in the hands and feet, blurred vision, double vision, ringing in the ears, convulsions, stomach upset, loss of appetite, vomiting, nausea, diarrhea, constipation, thickening of mucus and other bronchial secretions resulting in tightness in the chest, wheezing, stuffy nose. Cyproheptadine Hydrochloride may also produce adverse effects common to the phenothiazine class of drugs, such as tremors, a spastic, uncontrollable motion, and (rarely) a form of jaundice (yellowing of the skin and eyes).

Drug Interactions

Alcohol will increase the drowsiness or sleepiness that can be produced by Cyproheptadine Hydrochloride, so avoid drinking excessive amounts of alcoholic beverages. Taking Cyproheptadine Hydrochloride with another sedative, tranquilizer, barbiturate, or hypnotic drug can increase drowsiness and other symptoms of depression.

Cyproheptadine Hydrochloride can influence the effectiveness of any high blood pressure medicine you are taking.

If you have Parkinson's disease, you probably should not be taking this type of antihistamine; it is known to produce specific adverse drug effects in people with Parkinson's disease. An MAO inhibitor may interact with Cyproheptadine Hydrochloride to prolong the drying effect of the antihistamine, causing dry mouth and blurred vision.

Usual Dose

Adult: 4 to 20 milligrams daily.

Child (age 7 to 14): 4 milligrams 2 to 3 times per day.

Child (age 2 to 6): 2 to 3 milligrams per day.

The maximum daily dose for adults is 32 milligrams; for children age 7 to 14, 16 milligrams; for children age 2 to 6, 12 milligrams.

The liquid form of this medicine is very bitter. To improve the taste you can mix it with fruit juice, milk, or a carbonated beverage.

Overdosage

Symptoms are depression or stimulation (especially in children), dry mouth, fixed or dilated pupils, flushing of the skin, and stomach upset. Take the patient to a hospital emergency room immediately. ALWAYS bring the medicine container to the hospital. Do not induce vomiting. After having taken this drug the patient might breathe in the vomit, causing serious lung damage.

Special Information

Cyproheptadine Hydrochloride can produce sleepiness. Be careful if you are driving or operating hazardous machinery.

Brand Name

Darvocet-N

Ingredients

Acetaminophen
Propoxyphene Napsylate

Other Brand Names

Note: The following products have the same combination of ingredients in different concentrations.
Dolene-AP 65
Genagesic
Lorcet
SK-65 APAP
Wygesic

(Also available in generic form)

Type of Drug

Analgesic.

Prescribed for

Relief of mild to moderate pain.

General Information

Propoxyphene Napsylate, the major ingredient in this product, is a chemical derivative of Methadone, a narcotic used for pain relief. It is estimated that Propoxyphene Napsylate is about half to two-thirds as strong a pain reliever as Codeine and about as effective as Aspirin.

Cautions and Warnings

Do not take this drug if you are allergic to either ingredient.

It may produce physical or psychological drug dependence (addiction) after long periods of time. The major sign of dependence is anxiety when the drug is suddenly stopped. Darvocet-N abuse can lead to toxic effects on the kidneys and liver from the Acetaminophen ingredient of this drug (see "Possible Adverse Drug Effects" below).

Darvocet-N is not recommended for pregnant women as it may lead to addiction in the unborn child. This drug may cause birth defects or interfere with your baby's development. Check with your doctor before taking it if you are, or might be, pregnant.

Possible Side Effects

Dizziness, sedation, nausea, vomiting. These effects usually disappear if you lie down and relax for a few moments.

Possible Adverse Drug Effects

Darvocet-N can produce constipation, abdominal pain, skin rash, light-headedness, weakness, headache, euphoria, and minor visual disturbances. Long-term use may lead to adverse effects caused by the Acetaminophen portion of Darvocet-N: anemias and changes in the composition of blood. Allergic reactions are rash, itching, and fever.

Drug Interactions

Interaction with alcohol, tranquilizers, sedatives, hypnotics, or antihistamines may produce tiredness, dizziness, light-headedness, and other signs of depression.

Food Interactions

Take with a full glass of water or with food to reduce the possibility of stomach upset.

Usual Dose

1 to 2 tablets every 4 hours to relieve pain.

Overdosage

Symptoms are restlessness and difficulty in breathing, leading to stupor or coma, blue color of the skin, anemia, yellowing of the skin and/or whites of the eyes, rash, fever, stimulation, excitement, and delirium followed by depression, coma, and convulsions. The patient should be taken to a hospital emergency room immediately. ALWAYS bring the medicine bottle.

Special Information

Do not drink excessive amounts of alcohol when taking this medicine. Be extra careful when driving or operating machinery.

Brand Name

Darvon Compound-65

Ingredients

Aspirin
Caffeine
Propoxyphene Hydrochloride

Other Brand Names

Bexophene
Darvon Compound-65
Dolene Compound 65
Doxaphene Compound

Propoxyphene Hydrochloride
  Compound
SK-65 Compound

(Also available in generic form)

Type of Drug

Analgesic combination.

Prescribed for

Relief of mild to moderate pain.

General Information

Propoxyphene Hydrochloride, the major ingredient in this product, is a chemical derivative of Methadone, a narcotic used for pain relief. It is estimated that Propoxyphene Hydrochloride is about half to two-thirds as strong a pain reliever as Codeine and about as effective as Aspirin.

Cautions and Warnings

Do not take Darvon Compound-65 if you know you are allergic or sensitive to it. Long-term use of this medicine may cause drug dependence or addiction. Use this drug with extreme caution if you suffer from asthma or other breathing problems. Darvon Compound-65 affects the central nervous system, producing sleepiness, tiredness, and/or inability to concentrate.

Darvon has been shown to cause birth defects in animals. But we don't know if this occurs in humans. When a woman takes large amounts of narcotic drugs during pregnancy or breast-feeding, the baby may become dependent on the narcotic. Narcotics may also cause breathing problems in the infant during delivery. Do not take this medicine if you are pregnant or think you may be pregnant.

Possible Side Effects

Most frequent: light-headedness, dizziness, sleepiness, nausea, vomiting, loss of appetite, sweating. If these effects occur, consider calling your doctor and asking him about lowering the dose you are taking. Usually the side effects disappear if you simply lie down.

More serious side effects of Darvon Compound-65 are shallow breathing or difficulty in breathing.

Possible Adverse Drug Effects

Euphoria (feeling high), weakness, sleepiness, headache, agitation, uncoordinated muscle movement, minor hallucinations, disorientation and visual disturbances, dry mouth, loss of appetite, constipation, flushing of the face, rapid heartbeat, palpitations, faintness, urinary difficulties or hesitancy, reduced sex drive and/or potency, itching, skin rashes.

Drug Interactions

Interaction with alcohol, tranquilizers, barbiturates, or sleeping pills produces tiredness, sleepiness, or inability to concentrate, and seriously increases the depressive effect of Darvon Compound-65.

The Aspirin component of Darvon Compound-65 can affect anticoagulant (blood-thinning) therapy. Be sure to discuss this with your doctor so that the proper dosage adjustment can be made.

Food Interactions

Take with food or ½ glass of water to prevent stomach upset.

Usual Dose

1 capsule every 4 hours as needed for pain.

Overdosage

Symptoms are depression of respiration (breathing), extreme tiredness progressing to stupor and then coma, cold and clammy skin, slowing down of the heartbeat, convulsions, and cardiac arrest. The patient should be taken to a hospital emergency room immediately. ALWAYS bring the medicine bottle.

Special Information

Drowsiness may occur: be careful when driving or operating machinery.

Do not drink excessive amounts of alcohol when taking this medicine.

Brand Name

Deconamine SR

Ingredients

Pseudoephedrine Hydrochloride
Chlorpheniramine Maleate

Other Brand Names

- **Allerid DC Capsules
- *Anafed
- *Anamine TD
- *Brexin LA
- *Chlorafed Adult Timecells
- **Chlorafed Half-Strength Timecelles
- **Chlor-Trimeton Decongestant Repetabs
- *Codimal-LA Capsules
- *Duralex Capsules
- **Fedahist Gyrocaps
- **Hournaze Capsules
- **Isocaps
- *Isoclor Timesules
- **Kronofed-A Jr. Kronocaps
- *Kronofed-A Kronocaps
- *ND Clear Capsules
- *Novafed A Capsules
- **Rhinosyn
- *Rinade BID Caps

*Contains both active ingredients in the exact strengths present in Deconamine SR.
**Contains both active ingredients, but in slightly different strengths than Deconamine SR

Type of Drug

Antihistamine decongestant combination.

Prescribed for

Relief of symptoms of the common cold, allergy, or other upper respiratory condition, including sneezing, watery eyes, runny nose, itchy or scratchy throat, and nasal congestion.

General Information

Deconamine SR and its generic equivalent products are only a few of the several hundred different cold and allergy remedies available on both a prescription-only and a nonprescription basis. The basic formula that appears in each of these is always the same: an antihistamine to relieve allergy symptoms and a decongestant to treat the symptoms of either a cold or an allergy.

The only thing that distinguishes this product from others using the same combination is the strength of its two active ingredients, twice that found in the most potent nonprescription products, which allows it to be taken less often each day. Since nothing can cure a cold or an allergy, the best you can hope to achieve from this or any other cold or allergy remedy is simply symptom relief.

Cautions and Warnings

This product can cause excessive drowsiness, or it can cause you to become overly anxious and nervous and may interfere with sleep. Elderly patients are more likely to suffer from dizziness, sedation, low blood pressure, and confusion than younger adults using it.

This drug should be avoided by pregnant women or women who may become pregnant while using it. In those situations where it is deemed essential, the potential risk of the drug must be carefully weighed against any benefit it might produce. Nursing mothers must observe for any possible drug effect on their infants while taking Deconamine SR, since both ingredients may pass into breast milk.

Possible Side Effects

Restlessness, sleeplessness, excitation, nervousness, drowsiness, sedation, dizziness, poor coordination, upset stomach, and worsening of bronchial congestion (if present before the pill is taken).

Possible Adverse Drug Effects

Low blood pressure, heart palpitations, chest pain, rapid heartbeat and abnormal heart rhythm, anemia, fatigue, confusion, tremors, headache, irritability, a "high" feeling, tingling or heaviness in the hands, tingling in the feet or legs, blurred or double vision, convulsions, hysterical reactions, ringing or buzzing in the ears, fainting, changes in appetite (increase or decrease), nausea, vomiting, diarrhea or constipation, frequent urination, difficulty urinating, early menstrual periods, loss of sex drive, difficulty breathing, wheezing with chest tightness, stuffy nose, dry mouth, nose, and throat, itching, rashes, unusual sensitivity to the sun, chills, and excessive sweating.

Drug Interactions

Interaction with alcoholic beverages, tranquilizers, antianxiety drugs, and narcotic-type pain relievers may lead to excessive drowsiness or inability to concentrate.

This product should be avoided if you are taking an MAO inhibitor for depression or high blood pressure because the MAO inhibitor may cause a very rapid rise in blood pressure or increase some side effects (dry mouth and nose, blurred vision, abnormal heart rhythms).

The decongestant portion of this product may interfere with the normal effects of blood-pressure-lowering medicines and can aggravate diabetes, heart disease, hyperthyroid disease, high blood pressure, a prostate condition, stomach ulcers, and urinary blockage.

Usual Dose

1 capsule (120 milligrams of Pseudoephedrine Hydrochloride and 8 milligrams of Chlorpheniramine Maleate) every 8 to 12 hours.

Overdosage

The main symptoms of Deconamine SR overdose are drowsiness, chills, dry mouth, fever, nausea, nervousness, irritability, rapid or irregular heartbeat, heart pains, and urinary difficulty. Most cases of overdose are not severe. Patients taking an overdose of this drug must be made to vomit with Syrup of Ipecac (available at any pharmacy) to remove any remaining drug from the stomach. Call your doctor or a Poison Control Center before doing this. If you must go to a hospital emergency room, ALWAYS bring the medicine bottle.

Special Information

Since the antihistamine component of this medicine can slow down your central nervous sytem, you must use extra caution while doing anything that requires concentration, such as driving a car. Take your pill with food if it causes an upset stomach.

Call your doctor if your side effects are severe or gradually become intolerable. There are so many different cold and allergy products available to choose from that one is sure to be the right combination for you.

Brand Name

Demazin

Ingredients

Chlorpheniramine Maleate
Phenylephrine

Other Brand Names

Histaspan-Plus
Dristan 12 Hour
Novohistine LP
These products contain same ingredients but in slightly different strengths.

(Also available in generic form)

Type of Drug

Decongestant; antihistamine.

Prescribed for

Relief of sneezing, runny nose, and nasal congestion associated with the common cold, allergy, or other upper respiratory conditions.

General Information

Demazin is one of many products marketed to relieve the
symptoms of the common cold. Most of these products
contain ingredients to relieve a scratchy throat; and several
of them may contain ingredients to suppress cough, or to
help eliminate unwanted mucus. All these products are good
only for the relief of symptoms and do not treat the underlying problem such as the cold virus or other infections.

Demazin may be bought over the counter, without a
prescription.

Cautions and Warnings

Can cause excessive tiredness or drowsiness, restlessness,
and nervousness with inability to sleep.

This drug may cause birth defects or interfere with your
baby's development. Check with your doctor before taking it
if you are, or might be, pregnant.

Possible Side Effects

Tremor, headache, palpitations, elevation of blood pressure,
sweating, sleeplessness, loss of appetite, nausea, vomiting,
dizziness, constipation.

Drug Interactions

Interaction with alcoholic beverages may produce excessive
drowsiness and/or sleepiness, or inability to concentrate.

Do not self-medicate with additional over-the-counter drugs
for the relief of cold symptoms: taking Demazin with such
drugs may result in aggravation of high blood pressure,
heart disease, diabetes, or thyroid disease.

Do not take Demazin if you are taking or suspect you may
be taking a monoamine oxidase (MAO) inhibitor: severe
elevation in blood pressure may result.

Usual Dose

Adult and child (over age 6): 2 teaspoonfuls every 4 hours.
Child (under age 6): 1 teaspoonful every 4 to 6 hours.

Overdosage

The main symptoms of Demazin overdose are drowsiness, chills, dry mouth, fever, nausea, nervousness, irritability, rapid or irregular heartbeat, heart pains, and urinary difficulty. Most cases of overdose are not severe. Patients taking an overdose of this drug must be made to vomit with Syrup of Ipecac (available at any pharmacy) to remove any remaining drug from the stomach. Call your doctor or a Poison Control Center before doing this. If you must go to a hospital emergency room, ALWAYS bring the medicine bottle.

Special Information

Since the antihistamine component of this medicine can slow down your central nervous system, you must use extra caution while doing anything that requires concentration, such as driving a car.

Call your doctor if your side effects are severe or gradually become intolerable. There are so many different cold and allergy products available to choose from that one is sure to be the right combination for you.

Food Interactions

Take your pill with food if it causes an upset stomach.

Generic Name

Demeclocycline

Brand Name

Declomycin

Type of Drug

Broad-spectrum antibiotic effective against gram-positive and gram-negative organisms. It belongs to the general class of antibiotics known as Tetracycline.

Prescribed for

Bacterial infections such as gonorrhea, infections of the mouth, gums, and teeth, Rocky Mountain spotted fever and other fevers caused by ticks and lice from a variety of carriers, urinary tract infections, and respiratory system infections such as pneumonia and bronchitis.

These diseases are produced by gram-positive and gram-negative organisms such as diplococci, staphylococci, streptococci, gonococci, *E. coli,* and *Shigella.*

Demeclocycline has also been used successfully to treat some skin infections, but it is not considered the first-choice antibiotic for the treatment of general skin infections or wounds.

Demeclocycline has been used experimentally to treat the disease syndrome of inappropriate antidiuretic hormone (SIADH), where excess amounts of antidiuretic hormone are produced by the body.

General Information

Demeclocycline works by interfering with the normal growth cycle of the invading bacteria, preventing them from reproducing and thus allowing the body's normal defenses to fight off the infection. This process is referred to as bacteriostatic action. Demeclocycline has also been used along with other medicines to treat amoebic infections of the intestinal tract, known as amoebic dysentery. It is also prescribed for diseases caused by ticks, fleas, and lice.

Demeclocycline has been successfully used for the treatment of adolescent acne, in small doses over a long period of time. Adverse effects or toxicity in this type of therapy are almost unheard of.

Since the action of this antibiotic depends on its concentration within the invading bacteria, it is imperative that you completely follow your doctor's directions.

Cautions and Warnings

You should not use Demeclocycline if you are pregnant, especially during the last 4½ months. Do not use while breast-feeding because Demeclocycline may have an adverse effect on the formation of an infant's bones and teeth. Demeclocycline when used in children has been shown to interfere with the development of the long bones and may retard growth.

Exceptions would be when Demeclocycline is the only effective antibiotic available and all risk factors have been made known to the patient.

Demeclocycline should not be given to people with known liver disease or kidney or urine excretion problems. You should avoid taking high doses of Demeclocycline or undergoing extended Demeclocycline therapy if you will be exposed to sunlight for a long period, because this antibiotic can interfere with your body's normal sun-screening mechanism, possibly causing a severe sunburn. If you have a known history of allergy to Demeclocycline, you should avoid taking this drug or other drugs within this category such as Aureomycin, Terramycin, Rondomycin, Vibramycin, Tetracycline, and Minocycline.

This drug is very likely to cause skin sensitivity, which has the appearance of a severe sunburn.

Possible Side Effects

As with other antibiotics, the common side effects of Demeclocycline are stomach upset, nausea, vomiting, diarrhea, and rash. Less common side effects include hairy tongue and itching and irritation of the anal and/or vaginal region. If these symptoms appear, consult your physician immediately. Periodic physical examinations and laboratory tests should be given to patients who are on long-term Demeclocycline.

Possible Adverse Drug Effects

Loss of appetite, peeling of the skin, sensitivity to the sun, fever, chills, anemia, possible brown spotting of the skin, decrease in kidney function, weakness, thirst, excessive urination, damage to the liver.

Drug Interactions

Demeclocycline (a bacteriostatic drug) may interfere with the action of bactericidal agents such as Penicillin. It is not advisable to take both during the same course of therapy.

Don't take multivitamin products containing minerals at the same time as Demeclocycline, or you may reduce the antibiotic's effectiveness. You may take these two medicines at least 2 hours apart.

People receiving anticoagulation therapy (blood-thinning agents) should consult their doctor, since Demeclocycline will interfere with this form of therapy. An adjustment in the anticoagulant dosage may be required.

Food Interactions

The antibacterial effect of Demeclocycline is neutralized when taken with food, some dairy products, including milk and cheese, and antacids.

Usual Dose

Adult: 600 milligrams per day.

Child (age 9 and over): 3 to 6 milligrams per pound per day.

Child (under age 8): should avoid Demeclocycline, as it has been shown to produce serious discoloration of the permanent teeth.

Take on an empty stomach 1 hour before or 2 hours after meals.

Storage

Demeclocycline can be stored at room temperature.

Special Information

Do *not* take after the expiration date on the label. The decomposition of Demeclocycline produces a highly toxic substance which can cause serious kidney damage.

Generic Name

Desipramine

Brand Names

Norpramin
Pertofrane

Type of Drug

Antidepressant.

Prescribed for

Depression with or without symptoms of anxiety.

General Information

Desipramine and other members of this group are effective in treating symptoms of depression. They can elevate mood, increase physical activity and mental alertness, improve appetite and sleep patterns in a depressed patient. These drugs are mild sedatives and therefore useful in treating mild forms of depression associated with anxiety. You should not expect instant results with this medicine: benefits are usually seen after 1 to 4 weeks. If symptoms are not affected after 6 to 8 weeks, contact your doctor. Occasionally this drug and other members of the group of drugs have been used in treating nighttime bed-wetting in the young child, but they do not produce long-lasting relief, and therapy with one of them for nighttime bed-wetting is of questionable value.

Cautions and Warnings

Do not take Desipramine if you are allergic or sensitive to this or other members of this class of drug: Doxepin, Nortriptyline, Imipramine, Protriptyline, and Amitriptyline. The drugs should not be used if you are recovering from a heart attack. Desipramine may be taken with caution if you have a history of epilepsy or other convulsive disorders, difficulty in urination, glaucoma, heart disease, or thyroid disease. Desipramine can interfere with your ability to perform tasks which require concentration, such as driving or operating machinery.

This drug may cause birth defects or interfere with your baby's development. Check with your doctor before taking it if you are, or might be, pregnant. Desipramine may pass into breast milk. Nursing women should consider alternate feeding methods.

Possible Side Effects

Changes in blood pressure (both high and low), abnormal heart rates, heart attack, confusion, especially in elderly patients, hallucinations, disorientation, delusions, anxiety, restlessness, excitement, numbness and tingling in the extremities, lack of coordination, muscle spasms or tremors, seizures and/or convulsions, dry mouth, blurred vision, constipation, inability to urinate, rash, itching, sensitivity to bright light or sunlight, retention of fluids, fever, allergy, changes in composition of blood, nausea, vomiting, loss of appetite, stomach upset, diarrhea, enlargement of the breasts in males and females, increased or decreased sex drive, increase or decrease of blood sugar.

Possible Adverse Drug Effects

Infrequent: agitation, inability to sleep, nightmares, feeling of panic, peculiar taste in the mouth, stomach cramps, black coloration of the tongue, yellowing eyes and/or skin, changes in liver function, increased or decreased weight, perspiration, flushing, frequent urination, drowsiness, dizziness, weakness, headache, loss of hair, nausea, not feeling well.

Drug Interactions

Interaction with monoamine oxidase (MAO) inhibitors can cause high fevers, convulsions, and occasionally death. Don't take MAO inhibitors until at least 2 weeks after Desipramine has been discontinued. Certain patients may require concomitant use of Desipramine and an MAO inhibitor, and in these cases close medical observation is warranted.

Desipramine interacts with Guanethidine, a drug used to treat high blood pressure: if your doctor prescribes Desipramine and you are taking medicine for high blood pressure, be sure to discuss this with him.

Desipramine increases the effects of barbiturates, tranquilizers, other depressive drugs, and alcohol. Don't drink alcohol if you take this medicine.

Taking Desipramine and thyroid medicine will enhance the effects of the thyroid medicine. The combination can cause abnormal heart rhythms.

Large doses of Vitamin C (Ascorbic Acid) can reduce the effect of Desipramine. Drugs such as Bicarbonate of Soda or Acetazolamide will increase the effect of Desipramine.

Usual Dose

Adult: 75 to 300 milligrams per day. The dose of this drug must be tailored to patient's need. Patients taking high doses of this drug should have regular heart examinations to check for side effects.

Adolescent or elderly: lower doses are recommended, usually 25 to 150 milligrams per day.

This drug should not be taken by children.

Overdosage

Symptoms are confusion, inability to concentrate, hallucinations, drowsiness, lowered body temperature, abnormal heart
rate, heart failure, large pupils of the eyes, convulsions,
severely lowered blood pressure, stupor, and coma (as well
as agitation, stiffening of body muscles, vomiting, and high
fever). The patient should be taken to a hospital emergency
room immediately. ALWAYS bring the medicine bottle.

Generic Name

Dexamethasone

Brand Names

Baycadron   Hexadrol
Decadron   SK-Dexamethasone
Dexone

(Also available in generic form)

Type of Drug

Adrenal cortical steroid.

Prescribed for

Reduction of inflammation. There is a wide range of disorders for which Dexamethasone is prescribed, from skin rash
to cancer. The drug may be used as a treatment for adrenal
gland disease, since one of the hormones produced by the
adrenal gland is very similar to Dexamethasone. If patients
are not producing sufficient adrenal hormones, Dexamethasone may be used as replacement therapy. It may also be
prescribed for the treatment of bursitis, arthritis, severe skin
reactions such as psoriasis or other rashes, severe allergic
conditions, asthma, drug or serum sickness, severe, acute
or chronic allergic inflammation of the eye and surrounding
areas such as conjunctivitis, respiratory diseases including
pneumonitis, blood disorders, gastrointestinal diseases including ulcerative colitis, and inflammation of the nerves, heart
or other organs.

General Information

Dexamethasone is one of many adrenal cortical steroids used in medical practice today. The major differences between Dexamethasone and other adrenal cortical steroids are potency of medication and variation in some secondary effects. Choice of an adrenal cortical steroid to be used for a specific disease is usually a matter of doctor preference and past experience. Other adrenal cortical steroids include Cortisone, Hydrocortisone, Prednisolone, Triamcinolone, Methylprednisolone, Meprednisone, Paramethasone, Fluprednisolone, Prednisone, Betamethasone, and Fludrocortisone.

Dexamethasone may be used as eyedrops, eye ointment, topical cream, intranasal spray, or for oral inhalation as well as in an oral tablet.

Cautions and Warnings

Because of the effect of Dexamethasone on your adrenal gland, it is essential that the dose be tapered from a large dose down to a small dose over a period of time. Do not stop taking this medication suddenly and/or without the advice of your doctor. If you do, you may cause a failure of the adrenal gland with extremely serious consequences.

Dexamethasone has a strong anti-inflammatory effect, and may mask some signs of infection. If new infections appear during the use of Dexamethasone therapy, they may be difficult to diagnose and may grow more rapidly due to your decreased resistance. If you think you are getting an infection during the time that you are taking Dexamethasone, you should contact your doctor, who will prescribe appropriate therapy.

If you are taking Dexamethasone, you should not be vaccinated against any infectious diseases, because of inability of the body to produce the normal reaction to vaccination. Discuss this with your doctor before he administers any vaccination.

If you suspect that you are pregnant and are taking Dexamethasone, report it immediately to your doctor. If you are taking Dexamethasone and have just given birth, do not nurse; used prepared formulas instead. Large amounts of Dexamethasone taken during pregnancy or breast-feeding may slow the growth of newborn babies.

Possible Side Effects

Stomach upset is one of the more common side effects of Dexamethasone, which may in some cases cause gastric or duodenal ulcers. If you notice a slight stomach upset when you take your dose of Dexamethasone, take this medication with food or a small amount of antacid. If stomach upset continues or bothers you, notify your doctor. Other side effects: water retention, heart failure, potassium loss, muscle weakness, loss of muscle mass, loss of calcium which may result in bone fractures and a condition known as aseptic necrosis of the femoral and humoral heads (this means the ends of the large bones in the hip may degenerate from loss of calcium), slowing down of wound healing, black-and-blue marks on the skin, increased sweating, allergic skin rash, itching, convulsions, dizziness, headache.

Possible Adverse Drug Effects

May cause irregular menstrual cycles, slowing down of growth in children, particularly after the medication has been taken for long periods of time, depression of the adrenal and/or pituitary glands, development of diabetes, increased pressure of the fluid inside the eye, hypersensitivity or allergic reactions, blood clots, insomnia, weight gain, increased appetite, nausea, and feeling of ill health. Psychic derangements may appear which range from euphoria to mood swings, personality changes, and severe depression. Dexamethasone may also aggravate existing emotional instability.

Drug Interactions

Dexamethasone and other adrenal corticosteroids may interact with Insulin and oral antidiabetic drugs, causing an increased requirement of the antidiabetic drugs.

Interaction with Phenobarbital, Ephedrine, and Phenytoin may reduce the effect of Dexamethasone by increasing its removal from the body.

If a doctor prescribes Dexamethasone you should discuss any oral anticoagulant (blood-thinning) drugs you are taking: the dose of them may have to be changed.

Interaction with diuretics such as Hydrochlorothiazide may cause you to lose blood potassium. Be aware of signs of lowered potassium level such as weakness, muscle cramps and tiredness, and report them to your physician. Eat high potassium foods such as bananas, citrus fruits, melons, and tomatoes.

Usual Dose

Initial dose: 0.75 to 9 milligrams per day. The dose of this medicine must be individualized to the patient's need, although it is always desirable to take the lowest effective dose of Dexamethasone. Stressful situations may cause a need for a temporary increase in your Dexamethasone dose. This drug must be tapered off slowly and not stopped abruptly. This drug may be taken every other day instead of every day. It is best to take Dexamethasone in the morning, if prescribed once a day.

Overdosage

There is no specific treatment for overdosage of adrenal cortical steroids. Symptoms are anxiety, depression and/or stimulation, stomach bleeding, increased blood sugar, high blood pressure, and retention of fluid. The patient should be taken to a hospital emergency room immediately, where stomach pumping, oxygen, intravenous fluids, and other supportive treatments are available. ALWAYS bring the medicine bottle.

Generic Name

Dexchlorpheniramine Maleate

Brand Name

Dexclor
Doladex T. D.
Polaramine

(Also available in generic form)

Type of Drug

Antihistamine.

Prescribed for

Seasonal allergy, stuffed and runny nose, itching of the eyes, scratchy throat caused by allergy, and other allergic symptoms such as itching, rash, or hives.

General Information

Antihistamines generally, and Dexchlorpheniramine Maleate specifically, act by antagonizing at the site where histamine works. This site is often called the H_1 histamine receptor. Antihistamines work by drying up the secretions of the nose, throat, and eyes.

Cautions and Warnings

Dexchlorpheniramine Maleate should not be used if you are allergic to this drug. It should be avoided or used with extreme care if you have narrow angle glaucoma (pressure in the eye), stomach ulcer or other stomach problems, enlarged prostate, or problems passing urine. It should not be used by people who have deep-breathing problems such as asthma.

Dexchlorpheniramine Maleate can cause dizziness, drowsiness, and lowering of blood pressure, particularly in the elderly patient. Young children can show signs of nervousness, increased tension, and anxiety.

Although Dexchlorpheniramine Maleate has not been shown to cause problems for unborn children, it should be used only if essential during the first 6 months of pregnancy and not at all during the last 3 months. The ingredients in Dexchlorpheniramine Maleate cross over to breast-fed infants and may cause excitement or irritability. Dexchlorpheniramine Maleate is not recommended in nursing mothers.

Possible Side Effects

Occasional: itching, rash, sensitivity to light, excessive perspiration, chills, dryness of mouth, nose, and throat, lowering of blood pressure, headache, rapid heartbeat, sleeplessness, dizziness, disturbed coordination, confusion, restlessness, nervousness, irritability, euphoria (feeling high), tingling of the hands and feet, blurred vision, double vision, ringing in the ears, stomach upset, loss of appetite, nausea, vomiting, constipation, diarrhea, difficulty in urination, tightness of the chest, wheezing, nasal stuffiness.

Possible Adverse Drug Effects

Use with care if you have a history of asthma, glaucoma, thyroid disease, heart disease, high blood pressure, or diabetes.

Drug Interactions

Dexchlorpheniramine Maleate should not be taken with MAO inhibitors.

Interaction with tranquilizers, sedatives, and sleeping medication will increase the effects of these drugs: it is extremely important that you discuss this with your doctor so that doses of these drugs can be properly adjusted.

Be extremely cautious when drinking while taking Dexchlorpheniramine Maleate, which will enhance the intoxicating effect of alcohol. Alcohol also has a sedative effect.

Usual Dose

Adult: 2 milligrams 3 to 4 times per day.
Child (under age 12): 1 milligram 3 to 4 times per day.
Infant: 0.5 milligram 3 to 4 times per day.

Overdosage

Symptoms are depression or stimulation (especially in children), dry mouth, fixed or dilated pupils, flushing of the skin, and stomach upset. Take the patient to a hospital emergency room immediately, if you cannot make him vomit. ALWAYS bring the medicine bottle.

Special Information

Antihistamines produce a depressing effect: be extremely cautious when driving or operating heavy equipment.

Generic Name

Dextroamphetamine (D-Amphetamine)

Brand Names

Dexampex
Dexedrine
Ferndex
Oxydess
Spancap

(Also available in generic form)

Type of Drug

Central nervous system stimulant.

Prescribed for

Short-term (a couple of weeks) aid to diet control, abnormal behavioral syndrome in children, narcolepsy (uncontrollable and unpredictable desire to sleep).

General Information

When taking this medicine as part of a weight control program it is usual to experience a decrease in drug effectiveness because your body is breaking down the drug faster. Do not increase the amount of drug you are taking: simply stop taking the medicine.

The use of D-Amphetamine (as well as other drugs) in the treatment of minimal brain dysfunction in children is extremely controversial and must be judged by a physician qualified to treat the disorder. Children whose problems are judged to have been produced by their surroundings or by primary psychiatric disorders may not be helped by D-Amphetamine.

Cautions and Warnings

D-Amphetamine is highly abusable and addictive. It must be used with extreme caution. People with hardening of the arteries (arteriosclerosis), heart disease, high blood pressure, thyroid disease, or glaucoma, or who are sensitive or allergic to any amphetamine, should not take this medication.

This drug is known to cause birth defects or interfere with

your baby's development. It is not considered safe for use during pregnancy.

Possible Side Effects

Palpitations, restlessness, overstimulation, dizziness, sleeplessness, increased blood pressure, rapid heartbeat.

Possible Adverse Drug Effects

Euphoria, hallucinations, muscle spasms and tremors, headache, dryness of the mouth, unpleasant taste, diarrhea, constipation, stomach upset, itching, loss of sex drive, (rarely) psychotic drug reactions.

Drug Interactions

D-Amphetamine should not be given at the same time or within 14 days following the use of MAO inhibitors. This may cause severe lowering of the blood pressure.

D-Amphetamine may also decrease the effectiveness of Guanethidine.

If D-Amphetamine is taken with Insulin, Insulin requirements may be altered.

Usual Dose

Narcolepsy: 5 to 60 milligrams per day, depending on individual need.

Abnormal behavior syndrome: 2.5 to 40 milligrams per day, depending on child's age and response to the drug.

Weight control: 5 to 30 milligrams per day in divided doses ½ to 1 hour before meals; or, as a long-acting dose, once in the morning.

Overdosage

Symptoms are tremors, muscle spasms, restlessness, exaggerated reflexes, rapid breathing, hallucinations, confusion, panic, and overaggressive behavior, followed by depression and exhaustion after the central nervous system stimulation wears off, as well as abnormal heart rhythms, changes in blood pressure, nausea, vomiting, diarrhea, convulsions, and coma. The patient should be taken to a hospital emergency room immediately. ALWAYS bring the medicine container.

Special Information

Do not take this medicine after 6 to 8 hours before you plan to go to sleep, or it will interfere with a sound and restful night's sleep.

Do not crush or chew the sustained-release formulations.

Generic Name

Dextrothyroxine Sodium

Brand Name

Choloxin

Type of Drug

Antihyperlipidemic.

Prescribed for

Lowering blood cholesterol levels. Triglyceride levels may also be affected by Dextrothyroxine Sodium. May also be used to treat thyroid disease in patients who cannot take other thyroid drugs.

General Information

This drug is interesting in that it is a close cousin to Levothyroxine Sodium, a thyroid drug. It is thought to lower blood cholesterol by stimulating the liver to remove more cholesterol from the blood than usual. The lowering of blood cholesterol levels may have an effect on the development of heart disease, although no one knows for sure. This drug is only part of the therapy for high blood cholesterol levels. Diet and weight control are also very important. Remember, this medicine is not a substitute for dietary restrictions or other activities prescribed by your doctor.

Cautions and Warnings

Dextrothyroxine Sodium should not be taken by people with heart disease of any kind, severe high blood pressure, advanced liver or kidney disease, or a history of iodism.

Although no serious effects have been reported, this drug

should not be used by women who are pregnant or breast-feeding.

This drug is not meant to help people lose weight. In large doses, it will not reduce appetite but can cause serious side effects.

This drug should be discontinued for 2 weeks before surgery. It could interact with the general anesthetic drugs to cause heart problems.

Possible Side Effects

The fewest side effects from Dextrothyroxine Sodium are experienced by people with normal thyroid function and no heart disease. The risk of side effects is increased if you have an underactive thyroid gland and is greatest if you have both thyroid and heart disease.

The most common side effects are heart palpitations and other effects related to heart function. Other side effects include sleeplessness, nervousness, weight loss, sweating, flushing, increased body temperature, hair loss, menstrual irregularity, and an unusual need to urinate. Dextrothyroxine Sodium can also cause upset stomach, nausea and vomiting, constipation, diarrhea, and loss of appetite.

Possible Adverse Drug Effects

Headache, change in sex drive (increase or decrease), hoarseness, dizziness, ringing or buzzing in the ears, swelling of the arms and legs, not feeling well, tiredness, visual disturbances, psychic changes, tingling in the hands or feet, muscle pain, rashes. Some rather bizarre subjective complaints have been linked to this drug.

Drug Interactions

May interact with digitalis drugs to yield adverse effects on the heart. Dextrothyroxine Sodium may increase the effects of the oral anticoagulant drugs. Some patients may need their anticoagulant dose reduced by 30 percent. Dextrothyroxine Sodium will increase the effect of other drugs being given for underactive thyroid.

The drug may increase blood sugar levels in diabetic patients. Diabetics may need an adjustment in their Insulin or oral antidiabetic drug therapy while taking Dextrothyroxine Sodium.

Usual Dose

Adult: up to 8 milligrams per day.

Child: up to 4 milligrams per day; approximately 0.05 milligrams per pound.

Overdosage

Symptoms are headache, irritability, nervousness, sweating, and rapid heartbeat, with unusual stomach rumbling with or without cramps, chest pains, heart failure, and shock. The patient should be taken to a hospital emergency room immediately. ALWAYS bring the medicine bottle.

Special Information

Contact your doctor if you develop chest pain, heart palpitations, sweating, diarrhea, or a rash.

Generic Name

Diazepam

Brand Names

Valium
Valrelease

(Also available in generic form)

Type of Drug

Minor tranquilizer.

Prescribed for

Relief of symptoms of anxiety, tension, fatigue, or agitation.

General Information

Diazepam is a member of the chemical group of drugs known as benzodiazepines. These drugs are used as either antianxiety agents, anticonvulsants, or sedatives (sleeping pills). They exert their effects by relaxing the large skeletal muscles and by a direct effect on the brain. In doing so, they can relax you and make you either more tranquil or sleepier, depending on the drug and how much you use. Many doctors prefer Diazepam and the other members of this class to other drugs that can be used for the same effect. Their reason is that the benzodiazepines tend to be safer, have fewer side effects, and are usually as, if not more, effective.

These drugs are generally used in any situation where they can be a useful adjunct.

Benzodiazepine tranquilizing drugs can be abused if taken for long periods of time and it is possible to develop withdrawal symptoms if you discontinue the therapy abruptly. Withdrawal symptoms include tremor, muscle cramps, stomach cramps, vomiting, insomnia, agitation, sweating, and even convulsions.

Cautions and Warnings

Do not take Diazepam if you know you are sensitive or allergic to this drug or to other benzodiazepines such as Chlordiazepoxide, Oxazepam, Clorazepate, Lorazepam, Prazepam, Flurazepam, Clonazepam, and Temazepam.

Diazepam and other members of this drug group may aggravate narrow angle glaucoma, but if you have open angle glaucoma you may take the drugs. In any case, check this information with your doctor. Diazepam can cause tiredness, drowsiness, inability to concentrate, or similar symptoms. Be careful if you are driving, operating machinery, or performing other activities which require concentration.

Avoid taking this drug during the first 3 months of pregnancy except under strict supervision of your doctor. Taken during the first 3 months of pregnancy, Diazepam has been shown to increase the chance of birth defects. The baby may become dependent on Diazepam if it is used continually during pregnancy. If used during the last weeks of pregnancy or during breast-feeding, the baby may be overly tired, be short of breath, or have a low heartbeat. Use during labor may cause weakness in the newborn.

Possible Side Effects

Most common: mild drowsiness during the first few days of therapy, especially in the elderly or debilitated. If drowsiness persists, contact your doctor.

Possible Adverse Drug Effects

Major adverse reactions: confusion, depression, lethargy, disorientation, headache, inactivity, slurred speech, stupor, dizziness, tremor, constipation, dry mouth, nausea, inability to control urination, changes in sex drive, irregular menstrual cycle, changes in heart rhythm, lowered blood pressure, retention of fluids, blurred or double vision, itching, rash, hiccups, nervousness, inability to fall asleep, (occasional) liver dysfunction. If you experience any of these reactions stop taking the medicine and contact your doctor immediately.

Drug Interactions

Diazepam is a central nervous system depressant. Avoid alcohol, tranquilizers, narcotics, barbiturates, MAO inhibitors, antihistamines, and other medicines used to relieve depression. Smoking may reduce the effectiveness of Diazepam. The effects of Diazepam may be prolonged when taken together with Cimetidine.

Usual Dose

Adult: 2 to 40 milligrams per day as individualized for maximum benefit, depending on symptoms and response to treatment.

Elderly: if debilitated, will usually require less of the drug to control tension and anxiety.

Child: 1 to 2.5 milligrams 3 to 4 times per day; possibly more if needed to control anxiety and tension. Diazepam should not be given to children under age 6 months.

Overdosage

Symptoms are confusion, sleep or sleepiness, lack of response to pain such as a pin stick, shallow breathing, lowered blood pressure, and coma. The patient should be taken to a hospital emergency room immediately. ALWAYS bring the medicine bottle.

Special Information

Do not drink alcohol or take other depressive drugs, such as tranquilizers, sleeping pills, narcotics, or barbiturates, when taking Diazepam.

Generic Name

Dicloxacillin Sodium

Brand Names

Dycill
Dynapen
Pathocil
Veracillin

(Also available in generic form)

Type of Drug

Penicillin-type antibiotic.

Prescribed for

Gram-positive bacterial infections. Gram-positive bacteria (pneumococci, streptococci, and staphylococci) are organisms which usually cause diseases such as pneumonia, infections of the tonsils and throat, venereal disease, meningitis (infection of the spinal column), and septicemia (general infection of the bloodstream). This drug is best used to treat certain infections resistant to Penicillin, although it may be used as initial treatment for some patients.

General Information

Dicloxacillin Sodium is manufactured in the laboratory by fermentation and by general chemical reaction, and is classified as a semisynthetic antibiotic. Because the effectiveness of the antibiotic is determined by the drug's ability to affect the cell wall of the invading bacteria, it is very important that the patient completely follow the doctor's prescribing directions. These directions include spacing of doses as well as the number of days the patient should continue taking the medicine. If they are not followed, the effect of the antibiotic is severely reduced. Another antibiotic closely related is Cloxacillin Sodium (Tegopen). This drug is taken in the same doses and exerts the same effect as Dicloxacillin Sodium.

Food Interactions

To ensure the maximum effect, you should take the medication on an empty stomach, either 1 hour before or 2 hours after meals.

Cautions and Warnings

If you have a known history of allergy to Penicillin you should avoid taking Dicloxacillin Sodium, since the drugs are chemically similar. The most common allergic reaction to Dicloxacillin Sodium, as well as to the other penicillins, is a hivelike rash over the body with itching and redness. It is important to tell your doctor if you have ever taken this drug or any other penicillin before and if you have experienced any adverse reaction to the drug such as rash, itching, or difficulty in breathing.

Although Dicloxacillin Sodium has not been shown to harm the developing fetus, the drug should be used during pregnancy only if considered essential. This medicine is excreted in breast milk and should be used with caution by nursing mothers.

Possible Side Effects

Common: stomach upset, nausea, vomiting, diarrhea, possible rash. Less common: hairy tongue, itching or irritation around the anus and/or vagina, stomach pain with or without bleeding.

Drug Interactions

The effect of Dicloxacillin Sodium can be significantly reduced when taken with other antibiotics. Consult your doctor if you are taking both during the same course of therapy. Otherwise, Dicloxacillin Sodium is generally free of interactions with other medications.

Usual Dose

Adult (and child weighing 88 pounds or more): 125 to 250 milligrams every 6 hours. In severe infections, 500 milligrams may be needed.

Child (less than 88 pounds): 5.5 to 11 milligrams per pound of body weight per day in divided doses.

Storage

Dicloxacillin Sodium can be stored at room temperature.

Special Information

Do not take Dicloxacillin Sodium after the expiration date on the label.

Generic Name

Dicyclomine Hydrochloride

Brand Names

A-Spas	Di-cyclonex
Antispas	Di-Spaz
Bentyl	
Byclomine	
Dibent	
Dicen	

(Also available in generic form)

Type of Drug

Gastrointestinal anticholinergic agent.

Prescribed for

Relief of stomach upset and spasms. This medication is sometimes prescribed to treat morning sickness during the early months of pregnancy.

General Information

Dicyclomine Hydrochloride works by reducing spasms in muscles of the stomach and other parts of the gastrointestinal tract. In doing so, it helps relieve some of the uncomfortable symptoms associated with peptic ulcer, irritable bowel and/or colon, spastic colon, and other gastrointestinal disorders. It only relieves symptoms. It does not cure the underlying disease.

Cautions and Warnings

Dicyclomine Hydrochloride should not be used if you know you are sensitive or allergic to it. Do not use this medicine if you have narrow-angle glaucoma, asthma, obstructive disease of the gastrointestinal tract, or other serious gastrointestinal disease. Because this drug reduces your ability to sweat, its use in hot climates may cause heat exhaustion.

The safety of this drug for pregnant or nursing women has not been established. To date, problems in pregnant women or nursing mothers using Dicyclomine Hydrochloride have not been seen.

Possible Side Effects

Difficulty in urination, blurred vision, rapid heartbeat, rash, sensitivity to light, headache, flushing of the skin, nervousness, dizziness, weakness, drowsiness, nausea, vomiting, fever, nasal congestion, heartburn, constipation, loss of sense of taste.

Possible Adverse Drug Effects

Elderly patients taking this drug may develop mental confusion or excitement.

Drug Interactions

Interaction with antihistamines, phenothiazines, long-term use of corticosteroids, tranquilizers, antidepressants, and some narcotic painkillers may cause blurred vision, dry mouth, or drowsiness. Antacids should not be taken together with Dicyclomine Hydrochloride, or they will reduce the absorption of the Dicyclomine Hydrochloride.

Do not use with MAO inhibitor drugs, which will tend to prevent excretion of Dicyclomine Hydrochloride from the body and thus increase its effect.

Usual Dose

10 to 30 milligrams 3 to 4 times per day.

Special Information

Dry mouth from Dicyclomine Hydrochloride can be relieved by chewing gum or sucking hard candy; constipation can be treated by using a stool-softening laxative.

Generic Name

Diethylpropion Hydrochloride

Brand Names

Depletite	Tepanil
Tenuate	Tepanil Ten-Tab
Tenuate Dospan	

(Also available in generic form)

Type of Drug

Nonamphetamine appetite depressant.

Prescribed for

Suppression of appetite and treatment of obesity.

General Information

Although Diethylpropion Hydrochloride is not an amphetamine, it can produce the same adverse effects as the amphetamine appetite suppressants.

Cautions and Warnings

Do not use Diethylpropion Hydrochloride if you have heart disease, high blood pressure, thyroid disease, or glaucoma, or if you are sensitive or allergic to this or similar drugs. Furthermore, do not use this medication if you are emotionally agitated or have a history of drug abuse.

This drug may cause birth defects or interfere with your baby's development. Check with your doctor before taking it if you are, or might be, pregnant.

Possible Side Effects

Palpitations, high blood pressure, overstimulation, nervousness, restlessness, drowsiness, sedation, weakness, dizziness, inability to sleep, tremor, headache, dry mouth, nausea, vomiting, diarrhea and other intestinal disturbances, rash, itching, changes in sex drive, hair loss, muscle pain, difficulty in passing urine, sweating, chills, blurred vision, fever.

Usual Dose

25 milligrams 3 times per day 1 hour before meals; an additional tablet may be given in midevening, if needed to suppress the desire for midnight snacks. Sustained-release tablets or capsules of 75 milligrams (Tenuate Dospan, Tepanil Ten-Tab, WehLess Timecelles); 1 per day usually in mid-morning.

Overdosage

Symptoms are restlessness, tremor, shallow breathing, confusion, hallucinations, and fever, followed by fatigue and depression, with additional symptoms such as high or possibly low blood pressure, cold and clammy skin, nausea, vomiting, diarrhea, and stomach cramps. The patient should be taken to a hospital emergency room immediately. ALWAYS bring the medicine bottle.

Special Information

Use for only a few weeks as an adjunct to diet, under strict supervision of your doctor.

Medicine alone will not take off weight. You must limit and modify your food intake, preferably under medical supervision.

Do not crush or chew sustained-release products.

Generic Name

Diethylstilbestrol

Brand Names

DES

(Also available in generic form)

Type of Drug

Estrogen.

Prescribed for

Hormone replacement.

General Information

Because of the potential development of secondary disease after a long period of taking Diethylstilbestrol, the decision to take this medication chronically should be made cautiously by you and your doctor.

Cautions and Warnings

Estrogens have been reported to increase the risk of certain types of cancer in postmenopausal women taking this type of drug for prolonged periods of time: this risk tends to depend upon the duration of treatment and on the dose of the estrogen being taken. When long-term estrogen therapy is indicated for the treatment of menopausal symptoms, the lowest effective dose should be used. If you have to take Diethylstilbestrol for extended periods of time, you should see your doctor at least twice a year so that he can assess your current condition and your need to continue the drug therapy. If you are taking an estrogenic product and experience vaginal bleeding of a recurrent, abnormal, or persistent nature, contact your doctor immediately.

If you are pregnant and do not want to cause spontaneous abortion, you should not use this or any other estrogenic substance, since these drugs, if used during the earlier stages of pregnancy, may seriously damage the offspring. Estrogens may reduce the flow of breast milk. If estrogen is considered essential for a nursing mother, she should use an alternative method of feeding her infant.

If you have active thrombophlebitis or any other disorder associated with the formation of blood clots, you probably should not take this drug. If you feel that you have a disorder associated with blood clots and you have been taking Diethylstilbestrol or a similar product, you should contact your doctor immediately so that he can evaluate your situation and decide about stopping the drug therapy.

Prolonged continuous administration of estrogenic substances to certain animal species has increased the frequency of cancer in these animals, and there is evidence that these drugs may increase the risk of various cancers in humans. This drug should be taken with caution by women with a strong family history of breast cancer or those who have breast nodules, fibrocystic disease of the breast, or abnormal mammogram. Furthermore, long-term use of Diethylstilbestrol may expose a woman to a two- to threefold increase in chance of developing gallbladder disease. It is possible that women taking Diethylstilbestrol for extended periods of time may experience some of the same development of long-term adverse effects as women who have taken oral contraceptives for extended periods of time. These long-term problems may include thromboembolic disease or the development of various disorders associated with the development of blood clots, liver cancer or other liver tumors, high blood pressure, glucose intolerance or a development of a symptom similar to diabetes or the aggravation of diabetes in patients who had this disease before they started the estrogen, and high blood levels of calcium in certain classes of patients.

Possible Side Effects

Breakthrough bleeding, spotting, changes in menstrual flow, dysmenorrhea, premenstrual-type syndrome, resumption of menorrhea, vaginal infection with candida, cystitislike syndrome, enlargement or tenderness of the breasts, nausea, vomiting, abdominal cramps, feeling of bloatedness, jaundice or yellowing of the skin or whites of the eyes, skin rash, loss of scalp hair, development of new hairy areas. Lesions of the eye have been associated with estrogen therapy. If you wear contact lenses and are taking estrogens, it is possible that you will become intolerant to the lenses. You may also experience headache—possibly migraine—dizziness, depression, weight changes, retention of water, and changes in sex drive.

Drug Interactions

Vitamin C (in doses of 1 gram a day or more) may increase the effect of estrogen.

Phenytoin, Ethotoin, and Mephenytoin may interfere with estrogen effects.

Estrogens may force a dosage change in oral anticoagulant (blood-thinning) drugs, which your doctor can do with a simple blood test.

Estrogens may increase the side effects of antidepressants and phenothayine-type tranquilizers. Low estrogen doses may increase estrogen effectiveness.

Usual Dose

0.2 to 3 milligrams per day, depending upon the disease being treated and patient's response. Some diseases or patients may require up to 15 milligrams per day.

Overdosage

Overdose may cause nausea and withdrawal bleeding in adult females. Serious adverse effects have not been reported after accidental overdosage in children.

Generic Name

Digitoxin

Brand Names

Crystodigin
Purodigin

(Also available in generic form)

Type of Drug

Cardiac glycoside.

Prescribed for

Congestive heart failure and other heart abnormalities.

General Information

This medication is generally used for long periods of time.

Cautions and Warnings

Do not use this drug if you know you are allergic or sensitive to Digitalis. Long-term use of Digitoxin can cause the body to lose potassium, especially since Digitoxin is generally used in combination with a diuretic drug. For this reason, be sure to eat a well-balanced diet and emphasize foods which are high in potassium such as bananas, citrus fruits, melons, and tomatoes.

This drug may cause birth defects or interfere with your baby's development. Check with your doctor before taking it if you are, or might be, pregnant.

Possible Side Effects

Most common: loss of appetite, nausea, vomiting, diarrhea, blurred or disturbed vision. If you experience any of these problems, discuss them with your doctor immediately.

Possible Adverse Drug Effects

Enlargement of the breasts has been reported after long-term use of Digitoxin, but this is uncommon. Allergy or sensitivity to Digitoxin is also uncommon.

Drug Interactions

Diuretics (drugs which increase the production of urine) including Bumetanide, Furosemide, Chlorothiazide, and Hydrochlorothiazide can reduce the potassium in your blood and interact with Digitoxin.

If you are a long-term Digitoxin user, avoid over-the-counter drugs used to relieve coughs, colds, or allergies if they contain stimulants which may aggravate your heart condition. If you feel you must have medication to relieve the symptoms of colds, ask your doctor or pharmacist which medicines do not contain stimulants.

Usual Dose

Adult: The first dose—known as the digitalizing dose—is 2 milligrams over about 3 days, or 0.4 milligram per day for 4 days. Maintenance dose ranges from 0.05 to 0.03 milligram daily.

Elderly: Lower doses, as the elderly are more sensitive to adverse effects.

Infant or child: The first dose depends on age but can be from 0.01 milligram per pound to 0.02 milligram per pound. Maintenance dose is one-tenth the first dose.

Overdosage

Symptoms are loss of appetite, nausea, vomiting, diarrhea,

headache, weakness, feeling of not caring, blurred vision, yellow or green spots before the eyes, yellowing of the skin and eyes, or changes in heartbeat. Contact your doctor immediately if any of these symptoms appear. An early sign of overdose in children is change in heart rhythm. Vomiting, diarrhea, and eye trouble are frequently seen in older people.

Special Information

Do not stop taking this medicine unless your doctor tells you to. Avoid nonprescription medicine containing stimulants. Your pharmacist can tell you which nonprescription medicine is safe for you. Call your doctor if you develop loss of appetite, stomach pains, nausea or vomiting, diarrhea, unusual tiredness or weakness, visual disturbances, or mental depression. There are considerable variations among Digitoxin tablets made by different manufacturers. Do not change brands of Digitoxin without telling your doctor.

Generic Name

Digoxin

Brand Names

Lanoxicaps
Lanoxin
SK-Digoxin

(Also available in generic form)

Type of Drug

Cardiac glycoside.

Prescribed for

Congestive heart failure, and other heart abnormalities.

General Information

This medication is generally used for long periods of time.

Cautions and Warnings

Do not use this drug if you know you are allergic or sensitive to Digitalis. Long-term use of Digoxin can cause the body to lose potassium, especially since Digoxin is generally used in combination with a diuretic drug. For this reason, be sure to eat a well-balanced diet and emphasize foods which are high in potassium, such as bananas, citrus fruits, melons, and tomatoes.

This drug may cause birth defects or interfere with your baby's development. Check with your doctor before taking it if you are, or might be, pregnant.

Possible Side Effects

Most common: loss of appetite, nausea, vomiting, diarrhea, blurred or disturbed vision. If you experience any of these problems, discuss them with your doctor immediately.

Possible Adverse Drug Effects

Enlargement of the breasts has been reported after long-term use of Digoxin, but this is uncommon. Allergy or sensitivity to Digoxin is also uncommon.

Drug Interactions

Diuretics (drugs which increase the production of urine), including Bumetanide, Furosemide, Chlorothiazide, and Hydrochlorothiazide, can reduce the potassium in your blood and interact with Digoxin.

If you are a long-term Digoxin user avoid over-the-counter drugs used to relieve cough, colds, or allergies if they contain stimulants which may aggravate your heart condition. If you feel you must have medication to relieve the symptoms of colds, contact your doctor or pharmacist for information about medicine which does not contain stimulating ingredients.

Food Interactions

Taking Digoxin with foods high in fiber content may decrease the absorption of Digoxin.

Usual Dose

Adult: the first dose—known as the digitalizing dose—is 1 to 1.5 milligrams. Maintenance dose ranges from 0.125 to 0.5 milligram.

Elderly: lower dose, as the elderly are more sensitive to adverse effects.

Infant or child: substantially lower dose.

Overdosage

If symptoms of loss of appetite, nausea, vomiting, diarrhea, headache, weakness, feeling of not caring, blurred vision, yellow or green spots before the eyes, yellowing of the skin and eyes, or changes in heartbeat appear, contact your doctor immediately. An early sign of overdose in children is change in heart rhythm. Vomiting, diarrhea, and eye trouble are frequently seen in older people.

Special Information

Do not stop taking this medicine unless your doctor tells you to. Avoid nonprescription medicine containing stimulants. Your pharmacist can tell you which nonprescription medicine is safe for you. Call your doctor if you develop loss of appetite, stomach pains, nausea or vomiting, diarrhea, unusual tiredness or weakness, visual disturbances, or mental depression. There are considerable variations among Digoxin tablets made by different manufacturers. Do not change brands of Digoxin without telling your doctor.

Generic Name

Diltiazem Hydrochloride

Brand Name

Cardizem

Type of Drug

Calcium channel blocker.

Prescribed for

Angina pectoris; high blood pressure.

General Information

Diltiazem Hydrochloride is one of three calcium channel blockers sold in the United States, the others being Nifedipine and Verapamil. These drugs work by slowing the passage of calcium into muscle cells. This causes muscles in the blood vessels that supply your heart to open wider, allowing more blood to reach heart tissues. The drugs also decrease muscle spasm in those blood vessels. Diltiazem Hydrochloride also reduces the speed at which electrical impulses are carried through heart tissue, adding to its ability to slow the heart and prevent the pain of angina. This drug can help to reduce high blood pressure by causing blood vessels throughout the body to widen, allowing blood to flow more easily through them, especially when combined with a diuretic, beta blocker, or other blood-pressure-lowering drug.

Cautions and Warnings

Diltiazem Hydrochloride can slow your heart and interfere with normal electrical conduction. For people with a condition called sick sinus syndrome, this can result in temporary heart stoppage; most people will not develop this effect.

Animal studies with Diltiazem Hydrochloride have revealed a definite potential to harm a developing fetus, usually at doses greater than the usual human dose. As the dose was increased, adverse effects became more frequent and more severe. Diltiazem Hydrochloride should not be taken by pregnant women or women who may become pregnant while using it. In those situations where it is deemed essential, the potential risk of the drug must be carefully weighed against any benefit it might produce. Nursing mothers should watch for any possible drug effect on their infants while taking this medication, since it is not known if Diltiazem Hydrochloride passes into breast milk.

Diltiazem Hydrochloride can cause severe liver damage and should be taken with caution if you have had hepatitis or any other liver condition. Caution should also be exercised if you have a history of kidney problems, although no clear tendency toward causing kidney damage exists.

Possible Side Effects

Abnormal heart rhythms, fluid accumulation in the hands, legs, or feet, headache, fatigue, nausea, and rash.

Possible Adverse Drug Effects

Low blood pressure, dizziness, fainting, changes in heart rate (increase or decrease), heart failure, light-headedness, nervousness, tingling in the hands or feet, hallucinations, temporary memory loss, difficulty sleeping, weakness, diarrhea, vomiting, constipation,-upset stomach, itching, unusual sensitivity to sunlight, painful or stiff joints, liver inflammation, and increased urination, especially at night.

Drug Interactions

Taking Diltiazem Hydrochloride together with a beta-blocking drug for high blood pressure is usually well tolerated, but may lead to heart failure in people with already weakened hearts.

Calcium channel blockers, including Diltiazem Hydrochloride, may add to the effects of Digoxin, although this effect is not observed with any consistency and only affects people with a lot of Digoxin already in their systems.

Food Interactions

Diltiazem Hydrochloride is best taken on an empty stomach, at least 1 hour before or 2 hours after meals.

Usual Dose

30 to 60 milligrams 4 times per day.

Overdosage

The two major symptoms of Diltiazem Hydrochloride overdose are very low blood pressure and reduced heart rate. Patients poisoned with this drug must be made to vomit within 30 minutes of the actual dose with Syrup of Ipecac (available at any pharmacy) to remove the drug from the stomach. If overdose symptoms have developed or more than 30 minutes has passed, vomiting is of little value. You must go to a hospital emergency room for treatment. ALWAYS bring the medicine bottle.

Special Information

Call your doctor if you develop any of the following symptoms: swelling of the hands, legs, or feet, severe dizziness, constipation or nausea, or very low blood pressure.

Brand Name

Dimetapp Extentabs

Ingredients

Brompheniramine
Phenylpropanolamine

Type of Drug

Long-acting combination antihistamine-decongestant.

Prescribed for

Relief of cough, nasal congestion, runny nose, and other symptoms associated with the common cold, viruses, or other upper respiratory diseases.

General Information

Dimetapp Extentabs is one of many non-prescription products marketed to relieve the symptoms of the common cold. These products contain medicine to relieve nasal congestion or to dry up runny noses or relieve a scratchy throat; and several of them may contain ingredients to suppress cough, or to help eliminate unwanted mucus. All these products are good only for the relief of symptoms and will not treat the underlying problem, such as a cold virus or other infections.

Cautions and Warnings

Can cause excessive tiredness or drowsiness.

This product should not be used for newborn infants or taken by pregnant or nursing mothers. People with glaucoma or difficulty in urinating should avoid this drug and other drugs containing antihistamines.

Possible Side Effects

Mild drowsiness has been seen in patients taking Dimetapp.

Possible Adverse Drug Effects

Infrequent: restlessness, tension, nervousness, tremor, weakness, inability to sleep, headache, palpitations, elevation of blood pressure, sweating, sleeplessness, loss of appetite, nausea, vomiting, dizziness, constipation.

Drug Interactions

Interaction with alcoholic beverages may produce excessive drowsiness and/or sleepiness, or inability to concentrate. Also avoid sedatives, tranquilizers, antihistamines, and sleeping pills.

Do not self-medicate with additional over-the-counter drugs for the relief of cold symptoms; taking Dimetapp Extentabs with such drugs may result in aggravation of high blood pressure, heart disease, diabetes, or thyroid disease.

Do not take Dimetapp Extentabs if you are taking or suspect you may be taking a monoamine oxidase (MAO) inhibitor: severe elevation in blood pressure may result.

Usual Dose

1 tablet morning and night.

Special Information

Since drowsiness may occur during use of Dimetapp Extentabs, be cautious while performing mechanical tasks requiring alertness.

Generic Name

Diphenhydramine Hydrochloride

Brand Names

Belix	Fynex Cough
Benadryl	Hydril Cough
Benaphen	Nordryl Cough
Bendylate	Phen-Amin
Benylin Cough	SK-Diphenhydramine
Diahist	Tusstat
Diphen Cough	Valdrene
Fenylhist	

(Also available in generic form)

Type of Drug

Antihistamine.

Prescribed for

Seasonal allergy, stuffed and runny nose, itching of the eyes, scratchy throat caused by allergy, and other allergic symptoms such as itching, rash, or hives. In addition, Diphenhydramine Hydrochloride has been used for motion sickness and, with other drugs, for Parkinson's disease.

General Information

Antihistamines generally, and Diphenhydramine Hydrochloride specifically, act by antagonizing histamine at the site of the H_1 histamine receptor.

Antihistamines work by drying up the secretions of the nose, throat, and eyes.

Cautions and Warnings

Diphenhydramine Hydrochloride should not be used if you are allergic to this drug. It should be avoided or used with extreme care if you have narrow angle glaucoma (pressure in the eye), stomach ulcer or other stomach problems, enlarged prostate, or problems passing urine. It should not be used by people who have deep-breathing problems such as asthma.

Diphenhydramine Hydrochloride can cause dizziness, drowsiness, and lowering of blood pressure, particularly in the elderly patient. Young children can show signs of nervousness, increased tension, and anxiety.

This drug may cause birth defects or interfere with your baby's development. Check with your doctor before taking it if you are, or might be, pregnant.

Possible Side Effects

Occasional: itching, rash, sensitivity to light, perspiration, chills, dryness of the mouth, nose, and throat, lowering of blood pressure, headache, rapid heartbeat, sleeplessness, dizziness, disturbed coordination, confusion, restlessness, nervousness, irritability, euphoria (feeling high), tingling of the hands and feet, blurred vision, double vision, ringing in the ears, stomach upset, loss of appetite, nausea, vomiting, constipation, diarrhea, difficulty in urination, tightness of the chest, wheezing, nasal stuffiness.

Possible Adverse Drug Effects

Use with care if you have a history of asthma, glaucoma, thyroid disease, heart disease, high blood pressure, or diabetes.

Drug Interactions

Diphenhydramine Hydrochloride should not be taken with MAO inhibitors.

Interaction with tranquilizers, sedatives, and sleeping medication will increase the effects of these drugs; it is extremely important that you discuss this with your doctor so that doses of these drugs can be properly adjusted.

Be extremely cautious when drinking while taking Diphenhydramine Hydrochloride, which will enhance the intoxicating effect of the alcohol. Alcohol also has a sedative effect.

Usual Dose

Adult: 25 to 50 milligrams 3 to 4 times per day.

Child (over 20 pounds): 12.5 to 25 milligrams 3 to 4 times per day.

Overdosage

Symptoms are depression or stimulation (especially in children), dry mouth, fixed or dilated pupils, flushing of the skin, and stomach upset. Take the patient to a hospital emergency room immediately, if you cannot make him vomit. ALWAYS bring the medicine bottle.

Special Information

Antihistamines produce a depressant effect: be extremely cautious when driving or operating heavy equipment.

Generic Name

Dipyridamole

Brand Names

Persantine
Pyridamole

(Also available in generic form)

Type of Drug

Antianginal agent; antiplatelet.

Prescribed for

Prevention of attacks of angina pectoris; generally used for chronic treatment of angina, not for the immediate pain of an attack.

   Also used for the prevention of myocardial reinfarction.

General Information

Dipyridamole is one of many drugs used in the treatment of angina and is also being studied as a possible addition to the treatment of stroke. In such studies, the drug is examined for its possible ability to affect platelets, a component of blood involved in clotting. When used for angina, Dipyridamole increases the flow of blood to the heart muscle in order to provide the heart with sufficient oxygen.

   This drug may cause birth defects or interfere with your baby's development. Check with your doctor before taking it if you are, or might be, pregnant.

Possible Side Effects

Headache, dizziness, nausea, flushing, weakness, mild stomach upset, possible skin rash.

Possible Adverse Drug Effects

Dipyridamole has, on rare occasions, been reported to aggravate angina pectoris.

Drug Interactions

May interact with anticoagulant (blood-thinning drugs); patients taking anticoagulants and Dipyridamole should be checked periodically by their physician. Aspirin has an effect similar to Dipyridamole on the platelets and may increase the chances of bleeding due to loss of platelet effectiveness when taken with Dipyridamole.

Usual Dose

50 milligrams 3 times per day 1 hour before meals with a full glass of water.

Special Information

Dipyridamole may take 2 or 3 months to exert a therapeutic effect.

Generic Name

Disopyramide

Brand Names

Norpace
Norpace CR

Type of Drug

Antiarrhythmic.

Prescribed for

Abnormal heart rhythms.

General Information

Disopyramide slows the rate at which nerve impulses are carried through heart muscle, reducing the response of heart muscle to those impulses. It acts on the heart similarly to the more widely used antiarrhythmic medicines, Procainamide Hydrochloride and Quinidine Sulfate. Disopyramide is often used as an alternative to one of these medications for people who do not respond to other antiarrhythmic drugs. It may be prescribed for people who have had a heart attack (infarction) because it helps infarcted areas to respond more like adjacent, healthy heart tissue to nerve impulses.

Cautions and Warnings

This drug can exacerbate heart failure or produce severe reductions in blood pressure. It should only be used in combination with another antiarrhythmic agent or beta blocker, such as Propranolol Hydrochloride, when single-drug treatment has not been effective or the arrhythmia may be life-threatening.

In rare instances, Disopyramide has caused a reduction in blood-sugar levels. Because of this, the drug should be used with caution by diabetics, older adults (who are more susceptible to this effect), and people with poor kidney or liver function. Blood-sugar levels should be measured periodically in people with heart failure, liver or kidney disease, those who are malnourished, and those taking a beta-blocking drug.

Disopyramide should be used with caution by people who have severe difficulty urinating (especially men with a severe prostate condition), glaucoma, or myasthenia gravis.

Do not take this drug if you are pregnant or planning to become pregnant while using it, because it will pass from mother to child. If Disopyramide is considered essential, discuss the potential risks of taking it with your doctor. Nursing women should not take Disopyramide, as it passes into breast milk.

Possible Side Effects

Heart failure, low blood pressure, and urinary difficulty are the most serious side effects of this drug. Other frequent side effects are dry mouth, constipation, blurred vision, dry nose, eyes, and throat, frequent urination and feeling a need to urinate frequently, dizziness, fatigue, headache, nervousness, difficulty breathing, chest pain, nausea, stomach bloating, gas, and pain, loss of appetite, diarrhea, vomiting, itching, rashes, muscle weakness, generalized aches and pains, a feeling of ill health, low blood levels of potassium, increases in blood cholesterol and trigylceride levels.

Possible Adverse Drug Effects

Male impotence, painful urination, stomach pain, reduction in heart activity, anemia (reduced levels of blood hemoglobin and hematocrit), reduced white-blood-cell counts (rare), sleeplessness, depression, psychotic reactions (rare), liver inflammation and jaundice, numbness and tingling in the hands or feet, elevated BUN and creatinine (blood tests for kidney function), low blood sugar, fever, swollen, painful male breasts, drug allergy, glaucoma.

Drug Interactions

Phenytoin and Rifampin may increase the rate at which your body removes Disopyramide from the blood. Your doctor may need to alter your Disopyramide dose if this combination is used. Other drugs known to increase drug breakdown by the liver, such as barbiturates and Primidone, may also have this effect.

Food Interactions

Disopyramide may cause symptoms of low blood sugar: anxiety, chills, cold sweats, cool, pale skin, drowsiness, excessive hunger, nausea, nervousness, rapid pulse, shakiness, unusual weakness, or tiredness. If this happens to you, eat some chocolate candy or other high-sugar food and call your doctor at once.

Usual Dose

Adult: 200 to 300 milligrams every 6 hours. In severe cases, 400 milligrams every 4 hours may be required. People with reduced kidney function should receive a reduced dosage, depending on the degree of kidney failure present. People with liver failure should receive 400 milligrams per day.

Child: 2.5 to 14 milligrams per pound of body weight per day, depending on age and condition.

Overdosage

Symptoms are breathing difficulty, abnormal heart rhythms, unconsciousness, and, in severe cases, death. Patients taking an overdose of this drug must be made to vomit with Syrup of Ipecac (available at any pharmacy) to remove any remaining drug from the stomach. Call your doctor or a Poison Control Center before doing this. If you must go to a hospital emergency room, ALWAYS bring the medicine bottle. Prompt and vigorous treatment can make the difference between life and death in severe overdose cases.

Special Information

Disopyramide can cause dry mouth, urinary difficulty, constipation, and blurred vision. Call your doctor if these symptoms become severe or intolerable, but don't stop taking this medicine without your doctor's knowledge and approval.

Brand Name

Diupres

Ingredients

Chlorothiazide
Reserpine

Other Brand Names

Chlorserpine

(Also available in generic form)

Type of Drug

Antihypertensive.

Prescribed for

High blood pressure.

General Information

Diupres is a good example of a drug taking advantage of a drug interaction. Each of the drug ingredients works by different mechanisms to lower your blood pressure. The Chlorothiazide relaxes the muscles in your veins and arteries and also helps reduce the volume of blood flowing through those blood vessels. Reserpine works on the nervous system to reduce the efficiency of nerve transmissions which are contributing to the increased pressure. These drugs complement each other so that their combined effect is better than the effect of either one alone.

It is essential that you take your medicine exactly as prescribed for maximum benefit.

An ingredient in this drug may cause excessive loss of

potassium, which may lead to a condition called hypokalemia. Warning signs are dryness of mouth, excessive thirst, weakness, drowsiness, restlessness, muscle pains or cramps, muscular fatigue, lack of urination, abnormal heart rhythms, and upset stomach. If warning signs occur, call your doctor. You may need potassium from some outside source. This may be done by either taking a potassium supplement or by eating foods such as bananas, citrus fruits, melons, and tomatoes, which have high concentrations of potassium.

This drug should be stopped at the first sign of despondency, early morning insomnia, loss of appetite, or sexual impotence. Drug-induced depression may persist for several months after the drug has been discontinued; it has been known to be severe enough to result in suicide attempts. This drug should be used with care by women of childbearing age.

Cautions and Warnings

Do not take this drug if you have a history of mental depression, active peptic ulcer, or ulcerative colitis, or if you are sensitive or allergic to either of its ingredients, to similar drugs of the Chlorothiazide group, or to sulfa drugs. If you have a history of allergy or bronchial asthma, you may also have a sensitivity or allergy to the Chlorothiazide ingredient.

Although Chlorothiazide has been used to treat specific conditions in pregnancy, unsupervised use by pregnant women should be avoided; the drug will cross the placenta and pass into the unborn child, possibly causing problems. Chlorothiazide will also pass into the breast milk of nursing mothers.

Possible Side Effects

Loss of appetite, stomach irritation, nausea, vomiting, cramps, diarrhea, constipation, dizziness, headache, tingling in the arms and legs, restlessness, chest pains, abnormal heart rhythms, drowsiness, depression, nervousness, anxiety, nightmares, glaucoma, blood disorders, itching, fever, difficulty in breathing, muscle spasms, gout, weakness, high blood sugar, sugar in urine, blurred vision, stuffy nose, dryness of the mouth, rash. Occasional: impotence or decreased sex drive.

Drug Interactions

Interaction with Digitalis or Quinidine may cause abnormal heart rhythms.

Interaction with drugs containing Lithium may lead to toxic effects of Lithium.

Avoid over-the-counter cough, cold, or allergy remedies containing stimulant drugs which may raise your blood pressure.

Usual Dose

Must be individualized to patient's response.

Brand Name

Donnagel-PG

Ingredients

Alcohol	Pectin
Atropine Sulfate	Powdered Opium
Hyoscyamine Sulfate	Scopolamine Hydrobromide
Kaolin	

Other Brand Names

Amogel-PG
Kaodonna-PG
Kapectolin-PG
Quiagel PG

(Also available in generic form)

Type of Drug

Antidiarrheal.

Prescribed for

Relief of diarrhea.

General Information

Donnagel-PG works by reducing the mobility of the intestine, reducing secretions from the stomach and other parts of the gastrointestinal tract, and absorbing excessive fluids and other unusual materials which may be present in the stomach. This is one of many products available for the symptomatic treatment of diarrhea. Although it is effective in reducing diarrhea, it does not treat the underlying causes of the problem.

Cautions and Warnings

Do not take Donnagel-PG if you are allergic to any of its ingredients or if you have glaucoma or serious kidney or liver disease.

Safety for use of this medicine in pregnant and nursing women has not been established. Consult a physician.

Possible Side Effects

Blurred vision, dry mouth, and difficulty in urination will occur only in a small number of people, usually when the recommended dosage is exceeded.

Drug Interactions

Donnagel-PG should not be taken at the same time as any other drug. The Kaolin and Pectin in this product will prevent other medications from being absorbed into the bloodstream. This is especially true of antibiotics.

Donnagel-PG occasionally interacts with large quantities of alcoholic beverages to cause excessive sleepiness, drowsiness, and inability to concentrate.

The Atropine Sulfate and Hyoscyamine Sulfate in Donnagel-PG can interact with antihistamines and drugs with side effects similar to those of antihistamines, exaggerating such effects as dry mouth, difficulty urinating, constipation, and blurred vision. If this becomes a problem, consult your doctor.

Usual Dose

Adult: 2 tablespoons taken immediately after each episode of diarrhea; then 2 tablespoons every 3 hours as needed.

Child (30 pounds and over): 1 to 2 teaspoons every 3 hours as needed.

Child (10 to 30 pounds): 1 teaspoon every 3 hours as needed.

Child (up to 10 pounds): ½ teaspoon every 3 hours as needed.

Brand Name

Donnatal

Ingredients

Atropine Sulfate
Hyoscyamine Hydrobromide
Phenobarbital
Scopolamine Hydrobromide

Other Brand Names

Bellalphen	Seds
Bellastal	Spaslin
Hyosophen	Spasmolin
Malatal	Spasmophen
Relaxadon	Susano

(Also available in generic form)

Products with slightly different concentrations of the same ingredients are:

Barbidonna	Kinesed
Donnatal No 2	Palbar
Donphen Tablets	
Hybephen	

(Also available in generic form)

Type of Drug

Anticholinergic combination.

Prescribed for

Symptomatic relief of stomach spasm and other forms of cramps. Donnatal may also be prescribed for the treatment of motion sickness.

General Information

Donnatal is a mild antispasmodic sedative drug. It is only used to relieve symptoms, not to treat the cause of the symptoms. In addition to the brand names listed above, there are 40 to 50 other drug products which are anticholinergic combinations with the same properties. All are used to relieve cramps, and all are about equally effective. Some have additional ingredients to reduce or absorb excess gas in the stomach, to coat the stomach, or to control diarrhea.

Cautions and Warnings

Donnatal should not be used by people with glaucoma, rapid heartbeat, severe intestinal disease such as ulcerating colitis, serious kidney or liver disease, or a history of allergy to any of the ingredients of this drug. Donnatal and other drugs of this class can reduce the patient's ability to sweat. Therefore if you take this type of medication, avoid extended heavy exercise and the excessive high temperature of summer.

This drug may cause birth defects or interfere with your baby's development. Check with your doctor before taking it if you are, or might be, pregnant. Regularly using Donnatal during the last 3 months of pregnancy may cause drug dependency of the newborn. Labor may be prolonged and delivery may be delayed as well as breathing problems in the newborn if Donnatal is used. Breast-feeding while using Donnatal may cause increased tiredness, shortness of breath, or a slow heartbeat in the baby. Nursing mothers should use alternate feeding methods.

Possible Side Effects

Most common: blurred vision, dry mouth, difficulty in urination, flushing, dry skin.

Possible Adverse Drug Effects

Infrequent: rapid or unusual heartbeat, increased sensitivity to strong light, loss of taste sensation, headache, difficulty in passing urine, nervousness, tiredness, weakness, dizziness, inability to sleep, nausea, vomiting, fever, stuffy nose, heartburn, loss of sex drive, decreased sweating, constipation, bloated feeling, allergic reactions such as fever and rash.

Drug Interactions

Although Donnatal contains only a small amount of Phenobarbital, it is wise to avoid excessive amounts of alcohol or other drugs which are sedative in action. Be careful when driving or operating equipment. Other Phenobarbital interactions are probably not significant, but are possible with anticoagulants, adrenal corticosteroids, tranquilizers, narcotics, sleeping pills, Digitalis or other cardiac glycosides, and antihistamines.

Some phenothiazine drugs, tranquilizers, antidepressants, and narcotics may increase the side effects of the Atropine Sulfate contained in Donnatal, causing dry mouth, difficulty in urination, and constipation.

Usual Dose

Adult: 1 to 2 tablets, capsules, or teaspoons 3 to 4 times per day.

Child: Half the adult dose, if necessary.

Overdosage

Symptoms are dry mouth, difficulty in swallowing, thirst, blurred vision, sensitivity to strong light, flushed, hot dry skin, rash, fever, abnormal heart rate, high blood pressure, difficulty in urination, restlessness, confusion, delirium, and difficulty in breathing. The patient should be taken to a hospital emergency room immediately. ALWAYS bring the medicine bottle.

Special Information

Dry mouth from Donnatal can be relieved by chewing gum or sucking hard candy; constipation can be treated with a stool-softening laxative.

Generic Name

Doxepin Hydrochloride

Brand Names

Adapin
Sinequan

Type of Drug

Antidepressant.

Prescribed for

Primary depression or depression secondary to disorders

such as alcoholism, major organic diseases such as cancer, or other illnesses which may have a strong psychological impact on a patient.

General Information

Doxepin Hydrochloride and other members of this group are effective in treating symptoms of depression. They can elevate your mood, increase physical activity and mental alertness, and improve appetite and sleep patterns in a depressed patient. The drugs are mild sedatives and therefore useful in treating mild forms of depression associated with anxiety. You should not expect instant results with this medicine: benefits are usually seen after 1 to 4 weeks of therapy. If symptoms are not changed after 6 to 8 weeks, contact your doctor.

Cautions and Warnings

Unlike other tricyclic antidepressants, Doxepin Hydrochloride should not be given to children under age 12 and cannot be used to treat nighttime bed-wetting. Do not take Doxepin Hydrochloride if you are allergic or sensitive to this or other members of this class of drug: Imipramine, Nortriptyline, Amitriptyline, Desipramine, and Protriptyline. The drugs should not be used if you are recovering from a heart attack. Doxepin Hydrochloride may be taken with caution if you have a history of epilepsy or other convulsive disorders, difficulty in urination, glaucoma, heart disease, or thyroid disease. Doxepin Hydrochloride can interfere with your ability to perform tasks which require concentration, such as driving or operating machinery. Do not stop taking this medicine without first discussing it with your doctor, since stopping may cause you to become nauseated, weak, and headachy.

This drug may cause birth defects or interfere with your baby's development. Check with your doctor before taking it if you are, or might be, pregnant.

Possible Side Effects

Changes in blood pressure (both high and low), abnormal heart rate, heart attack, confusion, especially in elderly patients, hallucinations, disorientation, delusions, anxiety, restlessness, excitement, numbness and tingling in the extremities, lack of coordination, muscle spasm or tremors, seizures and/or convulsions, dry mouth, blurred vision, constipation, inability to urinate, rash, itching, sensitivity to bright light or sunlight, changes in composition of blood, nausea, vomiting, loss of appetite, stomach upset, diarrhea, enlargement of the breasts in males and females, increased or decreased sex drive, and increased or decreased blood sugar.

Possible Adverse Drug Effects

Infrequent: agitation, inability to sleep, nightmares, feeling of panic, peculiar taste in the mouth, stomach cramps, black coloration of the tongue, yellowing eyes and/or skin, changes in liver function, increased or decreased weight, excessive perspiration, flushing, frequent urination, drowsiness, dizziness, weakness, headache, loss of hair, nausea, not feeling well.

Drug Interactions

Interaction with MAO inhibitors can cause high fevers, convulsions, and (occasionally) death. Don't take MAO inhibitors until at least 2 weeks after Doxepin Hydrochloride has been discontinued.

Certain patients may require concomitant use of Doxepin Hydrochloride and an MAO inhibitor, and in these cases close medical observation is warranted.

Doxepin Hydrochloride interacts with Guanethidine and Clonidine, drugs used to treat high blood pressure: if your doctor prescribes Doxepin Hydrochloride and you are taking medicine for high blood pressure, be sure to discuss this with him.

Doxepin Hydrochloride increases the effects of barbiturates, tranquilizers, other depressive drugs, and alcohol. Don't drink alcoholic beverages if you take Doxepin Hydrochloride.

Taking Doxepin Hydrochloride and thyroid medicine will enhance the effects of the thyroid medicine. The combination can cause abnormal heart rhythms. The combination of Doxepin Hydrochloride and Reserpine may cause overstimulation.

Large doses of Vitamin C (Ascorbic Acid), oral contraceptives, or smoking can reduce the effect of Doxepin Hydrochloride. Drugs such as Bicarbonate of Soda, Acetazolamide,

Quinidine, or Procainamide will increase the effect of Doxepin Hydrochloride. Ritalin and phenothiazine drugs such as Thorazine and Compazine block the metabolism of Doxepin Hydrochloride, causing it to stay in the body longer. This can cause possible overdose.

The combination of Doxepin Hydrochloride with large doses of the sleeping pill Ethchlorvynol has caused patients to experience passing delirium.

Usual Dose

Initial dose is a moderate 10 to 25 milligrams 3 times per day; the low dose reduces drowsiness during the first few days. The doctor may then increase or decrease the dose according to individual response, giving 50 to 300 milligrams per day. This drug should not be given to children under age 12.

Overdosage

Symptoms are confusion, inability to concentrate, hallucinations, drowsiness, lowered body temperature, abnormal heart rate, heart failure, large pupils of the eyes, convulsions, severely lowered blood pressure, stupor, and coma (as well as agitation, stiffening of body muscles, vomiting, and high fever). The patient should be taken to a hospital emergency room immediately. ALWAYS bring the medicine bottle.

Special Information

Liquid Doxepin Hydrochloride should not be diluted until just before use. Dilute in about 4 ounces of water or juice just before you take it.

Generic Name

Doxycycline

Brand Names

Doxy-Caps   Vibramycin
Doxychel   Vibra-Tabs
Doxy-Tabs

(Also available in generic form)

Type of Drug

Broad-spectrum antibiotic effective against gram-positive and
gram-negative organisms; Tetracycline-type antibiotic.

Prescribed for

Bacterial infections such as gonorrhea, infections of the mouth,
gums, and teeth, Rocky Mountain spotted fever and other
fevers caused by ticks and lice from a variety of carriers,
urinary tract infections, and respiratory system infections
such as pneumonia and bronchitis.

These diseases may be produced by gram-positive or gram-
negative organisms such as diplococci, staphylococci, streptococci, gonococci, E. coli, and Shigella.

Doxycycline has also been used successfully to treat some
skin infections, but is not considered the first-choice antibiotic for the treatment of general skin infections or wounds. It
may be used to prevent "traveler's diarrhea."

General Information

Doxycycline works by interfering with the normal growth
cycle of the invading bacteria, preventing them from reproducing and thus allowing the body's normal defenses to
fight off the infection. This process is referred to as bacteriostatic action. Doxycycline has also been used along with
other medicines to treat amoebic infections of the intestinal
tract, known as amoebic dysentery. It is also prescribed for
diseases caused by ticks, fleas, and lice.

Doxycycline has been successfully used for the treatment
of adolescent acne, in small doses over a long period of
time. Adverse effects or toxicity in this type of therapy are
almost unheard of.

Since the action of this antibiotic depends on its concentration within the invading bacteria, it is imperative that you
completely follow the doctor's directions.

Cautions and Warnings

You should not use Doxycycline if you are pregnant. Doxycycline is not recommended for use during the last half of
pregnancy or during breast-feeding, when the infant's bones
and teeth are being formed.

In general, children up to age 8 should also avoid Doxycycline as it has been shown to produce serious discoloration of the permanent teeth. Doxycycline when used in children has been shown to interfere with the development of long bones and may retard growth.

Exceptions would be when Doxycycline is the only effective antibiotic available and all risk factors have been made known to the patient.

Doxycycline should not be given to people with known liver disease. You should avoid taking high doses of Doxycycline therapy if you will be exposed to sunlight for a long period because this antibiotic may interfere with your body's normal sun-screening mechanism, possibly causing severe sunburn. If you have a known history of allergy to Doxycycline you should avoid taking this drug or other drugs within this category such as Aureomycin, Terramycin, Rondomycin, Vibramycin, Demeclocycline, Tetracycline, and Minocycline.

Possible Side Effects

As with other antibiotics, the common side effects of Doxycycline are stomach upset, nausea, vomiting, diarrhea, and rash. Less common side effects include hairy tongue and itching and irritation of the anal and/or vaginal region. If these symptoms appear, consult your physician immediately. Periodic physical examinations and laboratory tests should be given to patients who are on long-term Doxycycline.

Possible Adverse Drug Effects

Loss of appetite, peeling of the skin, sensitivity to the sun, fever, chills, anemia, possible brown spotting of the skin, decrease in kidney function, damage to the liver.

Drug Interactions

Doxycycline (a bacteriostatic drug) may interfere with the action of bactericidal agents such as Penicillin. It is not advisable to take both.

Don't take multivitamin products containing minerals at the same time as Doxycycline, or you will reduce the antibiotic's effectiveness. Space the taking of these two medicines at least 2 hours apart.

People receiving anticoagulation therapy (blood-thinning agents) should consult their doctor, since Doxycycline will interfere with this form of therapy. An adjustment in the anticoagulant dosage may be required.

Anticonvulsant drugs such as Carbamazepine, Phenytoin, and barbiturates may increase the elimination of Doxycycline from the body, requiring higher or more frequent doses of the antibiotic.

Food Interactions

You may take Doxycycline with food or milk to reduce stomach upset.

Usual Dose

Adult: first day, 200 milligrams given as 100 milligrams every 12 hours. Maintenance, 100 milligrams per day in 1 to 2 doses. The maintenance dose may be doubled in severe infections.

Child (101 pounds and over): the usual adult dose may be given.

Child (under 101 pounds): first day, 2 milligrams per pound of body weight divided in 2 doses. Maintenance, 1 milligram per pound as a single daily dose. (Double the maintenance dose for severe infections.)

An increased incidence of side effects is observed if the dose is over 200 milligrams per day.

Storage

Doxycycline can be stored at room temperature.

Special Information

Do *not* take after the expiration date on the label. The decomposition of Doxycycline produces a highly toxic substance which can cause serious kidney damage.

Brand Name

Drixoral

Ingredients

Dexbrompheniramine Maleate
Pseudoephedrine Sulfate

(Also available in generic form)

Other Brand Names

Desihist SA	Disophrol
Desobrom	Drisen T.D.
Dexaphen SA	Efedra P.A.

Type of Drug

Long-acting combination antihistamine-decongestant.

Prescribed for

Relief of sneezing, runny nose, and nasal congestion associated with the common cold, allergy, or other upper respiratory condition.

General Information

Drixoral is one of many products marketed to relieve the symptoms of the common cold. Most of these products contain ingredients to relieve nasal congestion or to dry up runny noses or relieve a scratchy throat; and several of them may contain ingredients to suppress cough, or to help eliminate unwanted mucus. All these products are good only for the relief of symptoms and do not treat the underlying problem, such as a cold virus or other infections.

Cautions and Warnings

This drug may cause birth defects or interfere with your baby's development. Check with your doctor before taking it if you are, or might be, pregnant.

Possible Side Effects

Mild drowsiness has been seen in patients taking Drixoral.

Possible Adverse Drug Effects

Infrequent: restlessness, tension, nervousness, tremor, weakness, inability to sleep, headache, palpitations, elevation of blood pressure, sweating, sleeplessness, loss of appetite, nausea, vomiting, dizziness, constipation.

Drug Interactions

Interaction with alcoholic beverages may cause excessive drowsiness and/or sleepiness, or inability to concentrate. Also avoid sedatives, tranquilizers, antihistamines, sleeping pills, thyroid medicine, or antihypertensive drugs such as Reserpine or Guanethidine.

Do not self-medicate with over-the-counter drugs for the relief of cold symptoms: taking Drixoral with such drugs may aggravate high blood pressure, heart disease, diabetes, or thyroid disease.

Do not take Drixoral if you are taking or suspect you may be taking a monoamine oxidase (MAO) inhibitor; severe elevation in blood pressure may result.

Food Interactions

If this drug upsets your stomach it should be taken with food.

Usual Dose

Adult and child (age 12 and over): 1 tablet morning and night.

Child (under age 12): not recommended.

Special Information

Since drowsiness may occur during use of Drixoral, be cautious while performing mechanical tasks requiring alertness.

Generic Name

Dronabinol

Brand Name

Marinol

Type of Drug

Antinauseant.

Prescribed for

Relief of nausea and vomiting associated with cancer chemotherapy. Has been studied as a treatment for glaucoma.

General Information

Dronabinol is the first legal form of marijuana available to
the American public. The psychoactive chemical ingredient
in marijuana, it is also known as delta-9-THC. It has been
studied for several years as an antinauseant in people receiving cancer chemotherapy who have not responded to
other antinausea drugs. Dronabinol has all of the psychological effects of marijuana and is, therefore, considered to be a
highly abusable drug. Its ability to cause personality changes,
feelings of detachment, hallucinations and euphoria have
made Dronabinol relatively unacceptable among older adults
and others who feel they must be in control of their environment at all times. Younger adults have reported greater
success rate with Dronabinol, probably because they are able
to tolerate these effects.

Most people start on Dronabinol while in the hospital
because the doctor needs to monitor closely their response
to the medication and possible adverse effects.

Cautions and Warnings

Dronabinol should not be used to treat nausea and vomiting
caused by anything other than cancer chemotherapy. It should
not be used by people who are allergic to it, to marijuana or
to sesame oil. Dronabinol has a profound effect on its users'
mental status and will impair your ability to operate complex
equipment, or engage in any activity that requires intense
concentration, sound judgment and coordination.

Like other abusable drugs, Dronabinol produces a definite
set of withdrawal symptoms. Tolerance to the drug's effects
develops after a month of use. Withdrawal symptoms can
develop within 12 hours of the drug's discontinuation and
include restlessness, sleeplessness and irritability. Within a
day after the drug has been stopped, stuffy nose, hot flashes,
sweating, loose stools, hiccups and appetite loss may be
evident. The symptoms will subside within 4 days.

Studies of Dronabinol in pregnant animals taking doses 10 to 400 times the human dose have shown no adverse effects on the developing fetus. However, Dronabinol should not be taken by a pregnant woman unless it is absolutely necessary. Dronabinol passes into breast milk and can affect a nursing infant. Nursing mothers either should not use the drug or should change the method of feeding their child.

Dronabinol causes reduced fertility in animal studies and may have a similar effect on women. It may also affect the potency of male sperm, actually reducing the number of sperm produced.

Dronabinol should be used with caution by people with a manic-depressive or schizophrenic history because of the possibility that Dronabinol will aggravate the underlying disease.

Possible Side Effects

Most frequent: drowsiness, a "high" feeling (easy laughing, elation, and heightened awareness), dizziness, anxiety, muddled thinking, perceptual difficulties, poor coordination, irritability, a weird feeling, depression, weakness, sluggishness, headache, hallucinations, memory lapse, loss of muscle coordination, unsteadiness, paranoia, depersonalization, disorientation and confusion, rapid heart beat, dizziness when rising from a sitting or lying position.

Possible Adverse Drug Effects

Difficulty talking, flushing of the face, perspiring, nightmares, ringing or buzzing in the ears, speech slurring, fainting, diarrhea, loss of ability to control bowel movement, muscle pains.

Drug Interactions

Dronabinol will increase the psychological effects of alcoholic beverages, tranquilizers, sleeping pills, sedatives and other depressants. It will also enhance the effects of other psychoactive drugs.

Usual Dose

5 to 10 milligrams 1 to 3 hours before starting chemotherapy treatment, repeated every 2 to 4 hours after chemotherapy has been given, for a total of 4 to 6 doses per day. The daily

dose may be increased up to 30 miligrams a day if needed, but psychiatric side effects increase dramatically at higher doses.

Overdosage

Overdosage symptoms can occur at usual doses or at higher doses taken if the drug is being abused. The primary symptoms of overdosage are the psychiatric symptoms listed under Possible Side Effects. No deaths have been caused by either marijuana or Dronabinol. Dronabinol treatment may be restarted at lower doses if other antinauseants are ineffective.

Special Information

Avoid alcoholic beverages, tranquilizers, sleeping pills and other depressants while taking Dronabinol.

Dronabinol may impair your ability to drive a car, to perform complex tasks, or to operate complex equipment.

Dronabinol can cause acute psychiatric or psychological effects and you should be aware of this possibility while taking the drug. Be sure to remain in close contact with your doctor and call him or her if any such side effects develop.

Dronabinol capsules must be stored in the refrigerator.

Brand Name

Dyazide

Ingredients

Hydrochlorothiazide
Triamterene

Other Brand Name

Maxzide
Contains slightly different concentrations of the same ingredients.

Type of Drug

Diuretic.

Prescribed for

High blood pressure or any condition where it is desirable to eliminate excess fluid from the body, and at the same time minimize potassium loss.

General Information

Dyazide is a combination of two diuretics and is a convenient, effective approach for the treatment of diseases where the elimination of excess fluids is required. One of the ingredients in Dyazide has the ability to hold potassium in the body while producing a diuretic effect. This balances off the other ingredient, Hydrochlorothiazide, which normally causes a loss of potassium from outside sources.

Cautions and Warnings

Do not use Dyazide if you have nonfunctioning kidneys, if you may be allergic to this drug or any sulfa drug, or if you have a history of allergy or bronchial asthma. Dyazide may be used to treat specific conditions in pregnant women, but the decision to use this medication by pregnant women should be weighed carefully because the drug may cross the placental barrier into the blood of the unborn child. Dyazide may appear in the breast milk of nursing mothers. Do not take any potassium supplements together with Dyazide unless specifically directed to do so by your doctor.

Possible Side Effects

Drowsiness, lethargy, headache, gastrointestinal upset, cramping and diarrhea, rash, mental confusion, fever, feeling of ill health, enlargement of the breasts, inability to achieve or maintain erection in males, irregular menstrual cycles, or deepening of the voice in females.

Possible Adverse Drug Effects

Loss of appetite, headache, tingling in the toes and fingers, restlessness, anemias or other effects on components of the blood, unusual sensitivity to sunlight, dizziness when rising quickly from a sitting position. Dyazide can also produce muscle spasms, gout, weakness, and blurred vision.

Drug Interactions

Dyazide will increase (potentiate) the action of other blood-pressure-lowering drugs. This is beneficial, and the drug is frequently used to help lower blood pressure in patients with hypertension.

The possibility of developing imbalances in body fluids

(electrolytes) is increased if you take other medications such as Digitalis and adrenal corticosteroids while you are taking Dyazide.

If you are taking an oral antidiabetic drug and begin taking Dyazide, the antidiabetic dose may have to be altered.

Lithium Carbonate should not be taken with Dyazide because the combination may increase the risk of Lithium toxicity.

Avoid over-the-counter cough, cold, or allergy remedies containing stimulant drugs which can aggravate your condition.

Usual Dose

1 capsule twice per day.

Special Information

Take Dyazide exactly as prescribed.

Generic Name

Econazole Nitrate

Brand Name

Spectazole

Type of Drug

Antifungal.

Prescribed for

Fungus infections of the skin, including those responsible for athlete's foot and many other common infections.

General information

This drug is similar to another antifungal agent, Miconazole Nitrate. However, unlike Miconazole Nitrate, Econazole Nitrate is available only as a cream for application to the skin. Very small amounts of Econazole Nitrate are absorbed into the bloodstream, but quite a bit of the drug penetrates to the middle and inner layers of the skin, where it can kill fungus organisms that may have penetrated to deeper layers.

Cautions and Warnings

This product is generally safe, but belongs to a family known to cause liver damage. Therefore, the long-term application of this product to large areas of skin might produce an adverse effect on the liver.

When the drug was given by mouth to pregnant animals in doses 10 to 40 times the amount normally applied to the skin, Econazole Nitrate was found to be toxic to the developing fetus. Because of this, Econazole Nitrate should be avoided by women during the first 3 months of pregnancy. It should be used during the last 6 months of pregnancy only if absolutely necessary. It is not known if Econazole Nitrate passes into human breast milk. However, animals given this drug by mouth did show passage of the drug and its breakdown products into milk. As a precaution, nursing mothers either should not use the drug or should change the method of feeding their children.

Possible Side Effects

Burning, itching, stinging, and redness in the areas to which the cream has been applied.

Usual Dose

Apply enough of the cream to cover affected areas once or twice a day.

Overdosage

This cream should not be swallowed. If it is swallowed, the victim may be nauseated and have an upset stomach. Other possible effects are drowsiness, liver inflammation and damage. Little is known about Econazole Nitrate overdose, and you should call your local Poison Control Center for more information.

Special Information

Clean the affected areas before applying Econazole Nitrate cream, unless otherwise directed by your doctor.

Call your doctor if the affected area burns, stings, or becomes red after using this product.

This product is quite effective and can be expected to relieve symptoms within a day or two after you begin using it. Follow your doctor's directions for the complete 2-to-4-week course of treatment to gain maximum benefit from the product. Stopping it too soon may not completely eliminate the fungus and can lead to a relapse.

Brand Name

Entex LA

Ingredients

Guiafenesin
Phenylpropanolamine

Other Brand Names

*Dura-Vent
**Head and Chest
*Contains both active ingredients in the exact strengths found in Entex LA
**Contains both active ingredients, but in smaller amounts than found in Entex LA, and can be bought without a prescription.

Type of Drug

Decongestant expectorant combination.

Prescribed for

Relief of some symptoms of the common cold, allergy, or other upper respiratory condition, including nasal congestion and stuffiness and runny nose. The ingredient Guiafenesin is supposed to help loosen thick mucus that may contribute to your feeling of chest congestion. But the effectiveness of this and other expectorant drugs has not been established.

General Information

Entex LA and its generic equivalent products are only a few of the several hundred cold and allergy remedies available on both a prescription-only and a nonprescription basis.

There are a variety of different formulas employed in these products, such as the combination used in Entex LA. The decongestant ingredient, Phenylpropanolamine, will produce the most dramatic effect in reducing congestion and stuffiness. The expectorant, Guiafenesin, may help relieve chest congestion. There are other products using this same general formula, an expectorant plus a decongestant, on the market, but they use different decongestants or a combination of decongestants in combination with the expectorant Guiafenesin.

These products should not be used over extended periods to treat a persistent or chronic cough, especially one that may be caused by cigarette smoking, asthma, or emphysema. Information on other decongestant-expectorant combinations can be obtained from your pharmacist.

Since nothing can cure a cold or an allergy, the best you can hope to achieve from taking this or any other cold or allergy remedy is symptom relief.

Cautions and Warnings

Entex LA can cause you to become overly anxious and nervous and may interfere with your sleep. This is especially true when it is taken by elderly patients, who are more susceptible to side effects and toxic effects (hallucinations, convulsions, tiredness, sleepiness, weakness) than younger adults.

Do not use these products if you have diabetes, heart disease, high blood pressure, thyroid disease, glaucoma, or a prostate condition.

Entex LA should be avoided by pregnant women or women who may become pregnant while using it. Discuss the potential risks with your doctor.

Nursing mothers must observe for any possible drug effect on their infants while taking Entex LA, since the decongestant Phenylpropanolamine may pass into breast milk.

Possible Side Effects

Fear, anxiety, restlessness, sleeplessness, tenseness, excitation, nervousness, dizziness, drowsiness, headaches, tremors, hallucinations, psychological disturbances, and convulsions.

Possible Adverse Drug Effects

Nausea, vomiting, upset stomach, low blood pressure, heart palpitations, chest pain, rapid heartbeat, abnormal heart rhythms, irritability, feeling "high", eye irritation and tearing, hysterical reactions, reduced appetite, difficulty urinating in men with a prostate condition, weakness, loss of facial color, and breathing difficulty.

Drug Interactions

This product should be avoided if you are taking an MAO inhibitor for depression or high blood pressure because the MAO inhibitor may cause a very rapid rise in blood pressure or increase some side effects (dry mouth and nose, blurred vision, abnormal heart rhythms).

The decongestant portion of this product may interfere with the normal effects of blood-pressure-lowering medicines. It can also aggravate diabetes, heart disease, hyperthyroid disease, high blood pressure, a prostate condition, stomach ulcers, and urinary blockage.

Food Interactions

Take this medicine with food if it causes an upset stomach.

Usual Dose

1 tablet (Entex LA; Voxin-PG) or capsule (Dura-Vent) 2 times per day.

Overdosage

The main symptoms of overdose are sedation, sleepiness, sweating, and increased blood pressure. Hallucinations, convulsions, and nervous-system depression are particularly prominent in older adults, and breathing may become more difficult. Most cases of overdose are not severe. Patients taking an overdose of this drug must be made to vomit with Syrup of Ipecac (available at any pharmacy) to remove any remaining drug from the stomach. Call your doctor or a Poison Control Center before doing this. If you must go to a hospital emergency room, ALWAYS bring the medicine bottle.

Special Information

Call your doctor if your side effects are severe or gradually become intolerable.

Brand Name

Equagesic

Ingredients

Aspirin
Meprobamate

Other Brand Names

Equazine-M   Micrainin
Mepro Compound   Tranquigesic
Meprogesic-Q

(Also available in generic form)

Type of Drug

Analgesic combination.

Prescribed for

Pain relief in patients who suffer muscle spasms, sprains, strains, or bad backs.

General Information

Equagesic is a combination product containing a tranquilizer and Aspirin; it is used for the relief of pain associated with muscle spasms. The tranquilizer (Meprobamate) in this combination opens it to many drug interactions, especially with other tranquilizers or depressant drugs, which can result in habituation and possible drug dependence. Equagesic may be effective in providing temporary relief from pain and muscle spasm. If you are taking Equagesic, you must follow any other instructions your doctor gives you to help treat the basic problem.

Cautions and Warnings

Do not take Equagesic if you are allergic to any of the ingredients contained in it. If you are pregnant or are nursing, talk to your physician before you take Equagesic, because this combination may cause adverse effects in the unborn infant or child.

Possible Side Effects

Most frequent: nausea, vomiting, stomach upset, dizziness, drowsiness. Less frequent: allergy, itching, rash, fever, fluid in the arms and/or legs, occasional fainting spells, spasms of bronchial muscles leading to difficulty in breathing.

Possible Adverse Drug Effects

People taking Equagesic have occasionally experienced effects on components of the blood system. Equagesic has also caused blurred vision.

Drug Interactions

Meprobamate may cause sleepiness, drowsiness, or, in high doses, difficulty in breathing. Avoid interaction with other drugs that produce the same effect, for example, barbiturates, narcotics, tranquilizers, sleeping pills, and some antihistamines. Do not drink alcoholic beverages with Equagesic, because the depressive effect of the alcohol will be increased.

If you are taking an anticoagulant (blood-thinning medication) and have been given a new prescription for Equagesic, be sure that your doctor is aware that there is Aspirin in Equagesic. Aspirin affects the ability of your blood to clot and can necessitate a change in the dose of your anticoagulant.

Food Interactions

If you experience stomach upset with Equagesic, take each dose with food or water

Usual Dose

1 or 2 tablets 3 to 4 times per day as needed for the relief of pain associated with skeletal muscle spasms.

Overdosage

Equagesic overdoses are serious. Symptoms are drowsiness, feeling of light-headedness, desire to go to sleep, nausea, and vomiting. The patient should be taken to a hospital emergency room immediately. ALWAYS bring the medicine bottle.

Generic Name

Ergot Alkaloids Dihydrogenated

Brand Names

Circanol

Deapril-ST

Hydergine

Hydroloid

Niloric

(Also available in generic form)

Type of Drug

Psychotherapeutic.

Prescribed for

Alzheimer's disease; depression, confusion, forgetfulness, antisocial behavior, and dizziness in the elderly.

General Information

Ergot Alkaloids Dihydrogenated has improved the supply of blood to the brain in test animals and reduces heart rate and muscle tone in blood vessels. Some studies have shown the drug to be very effective in relieving mild symptoms of mental impairment, while others have found it to be only moderately effective. It has been most beneficial in patients whose symptoms are due to the effects of high blood pressure in the brain.

Cautions and Warnings

Do not use this drug if you are allergic or sensitive to Ergot or any of its derivatives.

This drug may cause birth defects or interfere with your baby's development. Check with your doctor before taking it if you are, or might be, pregnant.

Possible Side Effects

Ergot Alkaloids Dihydrogenated does not produce serious side effects. Since some forms of this drug are taken under the tongue, you may experience some irritation, nausea, or stomach upset.

Usual Dose

1 milligram taken 3 times a day.

Special Information

The results of this drug are gradual. Frequently they are not seen for 3 to 4 weeks.

Dissolve sublingual tablets under the tongue: they are not effective if swallowed whole.

Generic Name

Erythromycin

Brand Names

Bristamycin	Ethril
E.E.S.	Ilosone
E-Mycin	Ilotycin
Eramycin	Pediamycin
ERYC	Pfizer-E
Erypar	Robimycin
EryPed	RP-Mycin
Ery-Tab	SK-Erythromycin
Erythrocin	Wyamycin
Erythromycin Ethyl-succinate	

(Also available in generic form)

Type of Drug

Bacteriostatic antibiotic, effective against gram-positive organisms such as streptococcus, staphylococcus, and gonococcus.

Prescribed for

Infections of the upper and lower respiratory tract; infections of the mouth, gums, and teeth; infections of the nose, ears, and sinuses. May be used for mild to moderate skin infections, but is not considered the antibiotic of choice. Can also be effective against amoebas of the intestinal tract, which cause amoebic dysentery and legionnaire's disease.

Erythromycin is a relatively safe antibiotic. It is used instead of Penicillin for mild to moderate infections in people who are allergic to the penicillin class of antibiotics.

Note: Erythromycin is not the antibiotic of choice for severe infections.

General Information

Erythromycin works by interfering with the normal growth cycle of the invading bacteria, preventing them from reproducing and thus allowing the body's normal defenses to fight off the infection. This process is referred to as bacteriostatic action.

Erythromycin is absorbed from the gastrointestinal tract, but it is deactivated by the acid content of the stomach. Because of this, the tablet form of this drug is formulated in such a way as to bypass the stomach and dissolve in the intestine.

Erythromycin is used primarily for infections of the mouth, nose, ears, sinuses, throat, and lungs. It can also be used to treat venereal disease and pelvic inflammatory disease in people who have allergies and/or sensitivity to the penicillin class of antibiotics.

Because the action of this antibiotic depends on its concentration within the invading bacteria, it is imperative that you follow the doctor's directions regarding the spacing of the doses as well as the number of days you should continue taking the medication. The effect of the antibiotic is severely reduced if these instructions are not followed.

Cautions and Warnings

Erythromycin is excreted primarily through the liver. People with liver disease or damage should exercise caution. Those on long-term therapy with Erythromycin are advised to have periodic blood tests.

Erythromycin is available in a variety of formulations. One formula, Erythromycin Estolate, has occasionally produced fatigue, nausea, vomiting, abdominal cramps, and fever. If you are susceptible to stomach problems, Erythromycin may cause mild to moderate stomach upset. Discontinuing the drug will reverse this condition.

This drug may cause birth defects or interfere with your baby's development. Check with your doctor before taking it if you are, or might be, pregnant. Nursing mothers should consider using an alternate feeding method.

Possible Side Effects

Most common: nausea, vomiting, stomach cramps, diarrhea. Less common: hairy tongue, itching, irritation of the anal and/or vaginal region. If any of these symptoms appear, consult your physician immediately.

Possible Adverse Drug Effects

Erythromycin should not be given to people with known sensitivity to this antibiotic. It may cause a yellowing of the skin and eyes. If this occurs, discontinue the drug and notify your doctor immediately.

Drug Interactions

Erythromycin is relatively free of interactions with other medicines. However, there seems to be a neutralizing effect between it and Lincomycin and Clindamycin. Erythromycin interferes with the elimination of Theophylline from the body. This may cause toxic effects of Theophylline overdose.

Food Interactions

Food in the stomach will decrease the absorption rate of some Erythromycin products. In general, Erythromycin is best taken on an empty stomach.

Usual Dose

Adult: 250 to 500 milligrams every 6 hours.

Children: 50 to 200 milligrams per pound of body weight per day in divided doses, depending upon age, weight, and severity of infection.

Take 1 hour before or 2 hours after meals.

Doses of E.E.S., Pediamycin, and Wyamycin are 60 percent higher, due to different chemical composition of the Erythromycin formulation.

Generic Name

Ethchlorvynol

Brand Name

Placidyl

Type of Drug

Sedative-hypnotic.

Prescribed for

Short-term hypnotic therapy for insomnia.

General Information

Sleep is produced within 30 minutes and lasts 4 to 8 hours.

Cautions and Warnings

Patients who are allergic to this drug and patients with rash
or porphyria should not take Ethchlorvynol. Continued use
may cause physical and psychological dependence.

Pregnant women should not use the drug; Ethchlorvynol
has caused problems to the unborn child if taken during
pregnancy. Some of these problems are slow heartbeat,
breathing difficulty, and side effects due to dependency on
Ethchlorvynol. It is possible that Ethchlorvynol is excreted in
breast milk, and the decision to nurse while taking it should
be weighed against the possible risks to the infant.

Possible Side Effects

Skin rash, dizziness.

Possible Adverse Drug Effects

There have been reports of nausea, morning hangover, excitation, and blurring of the vision.

Drug Interactions

The combination of Ethchlorvynol and Amitriptyline can make
you delirious. Avoid combining them.

Do not take this drug with alcohol, antihistamines, or other
depressants.

Usual Dose

Adult: 500 milligrams by mouth at bedtime; for severe insomnia, 750 or even 1000 milligrams. Patients may be instructed, if they awaken during the night, to take an additional 100 to 200 milligrams to help them get back to sleep. Only the smallest effective dose of Ethchlorvynol should be used, since the drug can be abused and can be addictive.

Overdosage

Large amounts of Ethchlorvynol can be fatal, and the drug is frequently used in suicide attempts. Symptoms are coma, lowered body temperature followed by fever, absence of normal reflexes and pain responses after pinches and needle or pin sticks, and shallow breathing. The patient should be taken to a hospital emergency room immediately. ALWAYS bring the medicine bottle.

People who have taken Ethchlorvynol for a long time may show signs of chronic overdosage: loss of memory, inability to concentrate, shakes, tremors, loss of reflexes, slurring of speech, and general sense of depression. Abrupt discontinuation of Ethchlorvynol often causes withdrawal reactions of nervousness, anxiety, seizures, cramping, chills, numbness of the extremities, and general behavior changes. Chronic overdosage is best treated by withdrawing of the drug over a period of days or weeks.

Storage

Ethchlorvynol capsules must be protected from heat and moisture. They should not be refrigerated. The best place to keep them is at room temperature; for example, in a night or bed table.

Special Information

If you feel giddy or get an upset stomach from this drug, take it after eating.

Generic Name

Ethosuximide

Brand Name

Zarontin

Type of Drug

Anticonvulsant.

Prescribed for

Control of petit mal seizures

General Information

Ethosuximide and the other succinimide-type anticonvulsants control petit mal seizures by slowing the transmission of impulses through certain areas of the brain. The succinimides are first choice of treatment for this type of seizure, which may then be treated by Clonazepam if the succinimides are not sufficient.

Cautions and Warnings

Ethosuximide may be associated with severe reductions in white-blood-cell and platelet counts. Your doctor should perform periodic blood counts while you are taking this medicine.

In patients with grand mal and petit mal, succinimide-type anticonvulsants, when used alone, may increase the number of grand mal seizures, necessitating more medicine to control those seizures.

Abrupt withdrawal of any anticonvulsant may lead to severe seizures. It is important that your dosage be gradually reduced by your doctor.

This drug should be avoided by women who may become pregnant while using it and by pregnant and nursing mothers, since it will cross into the developing infant, and possible adverse effects on the infant are not known. In those situations where it is deemed essential, the potential risk of the drug must be carefully weighed against any benefit it might produce.

Recent reports suggest a strong association between the use of anticonvulsant drugs and birth defects. Although most of the information pertains to Phenytoin and Phenobarbital, not Ethosuximide, other reports indicate a general association between all anticonvulsant-drug treatments and birth defects. It is possible that the epileptic condition itself or genetic factors common to people with seizure disorders may also figure in the higher incidence of birth defects. Mothers taking Ethosuximide should not breast-feed because of the possibility that the drug will pass into their breast milk and affect the baby. Use an alternative feeding method.

Possible Side Effects

Nausea, vomiting, upset stomach, stomach cramps and pain, loss of appetite, diarrhea, constipation, weight loss, drowsiness, dizziness, and poor muscle control.

Possible Adverse Drug Effects

Reductions in white-blood-cell and platelet counts, nervousness, hyperactivity, sleeplessness, irritability, headache, blurred vision, unusual sensitivity to bright lights, hiccups, a euphoric feeling, a dreamlike state, lack of energy, fatigue, confusion, mental instability, mental slowness, depression, sleep disturbances, nightmares, loss of the ability to concentrate, aggressiveness, constant concern with well-being and health, paranoid psychosis, suicidal tendencies, increased sex drive, rash, itching, frequent urination, kidney damage, blood in the urine, swelling around the eyes, hair loss, hairiness, muscle weakness, nearsightedness, vaginal bleeding, and swelling of the tongue and/or gums.

Drug Interactions

The depressant effects of Ethosuximide are increased by tranquilizers, sleeping pills, narcotic pain relievers, antihistamines, alcohol, MAO inhibitors, antidepressants, and other anticonvulsants.

Ethosuximide may increase the action of Phenytoin by increasing the blood levels of that drug. Your doctor should be sure that your dosages of the two drugs are appropriate to your condition.

Carbamazepine, another medicine prescribed to treat seizure disorders, may interfere with Ethosuximide action by increasing the rate at which it is removed from the body.

The action of Ethosuximide may be increased by Isoniazid, prescribed to prevent tuberculosis, and by Valproic Acid, another anticonvulsant drug, possibly leading to an increase in drug side effects when both drugs are taken together.

Avoid alcoholic beverages, which increase the depressant effects of this medicine.

Food Interactions

Ethosuximide is best taken on an empty stomach but may be taken with food if it upsets your stomach.

Usual Dose

Adult and *child* (over age 6): 500 milligrams per day to start.

Child (age 3 to 6): 250 milligrams per day to start.

The dose is increased in steps of 250 milligrams every 4 to 7 days until seizures are controlled or side effects develop. The maximum daily dose is 1500 milligrams.

Dosage adjustments may be required for people with reduced kidney or liver function.

Overdosage

Ethosuximide overdose will cause exaggerated side effects. If the overdose is discovered immediately, it may be helpful to make the victim vomit with Syrup of Ipecac to remove any remaining medicine from the stomach. But all victims of Ethosuximide overdose must be taken to a hospital emergency room for treatment. ALWAYS bring the prescription bottle with you.

Special Information

Call your doctor if side effects become intolerable. Especially important are sore throat, joint pains, unexplained fever, rashes, unusual bleeding or bruising, drowsiness, dizziness, and blurred vision. Be sure to tell your doctor if you become pregnant while taking this medicine.

Ethosuximide may interfere with your ability to drive a car or perform other complex tasks because it can cause drowsiness and difficulty concentrating.

Your doctor should perform periodic blood counts while you are taking this drug to check for possible adverse drug effects.

Do not suddenly stop taking the medicine, since this can result in severe seizures. The dosage must be discontinued gradually by your doctor.

Carry identification or wear a bracelet indicating that you suffer from a seizure disorder for which you take Ethosuximide.

Generic Name

Fenoprofen Calcium

Brand Name

Nalfon

Type of Drug

Nonsteroid anti-inflammatory.

Prescribed for

Relief of pain and inflammation of joints and muscles; arthritis, both rheumatoid and osteoarthritis, mild to moderate pain of menstrual cramps, dental surgery, and extractions, and athletic injuries such as sprains and strains.

General Information

Fenoprofen Calcium is one of several nonsteroid antiinflammatory drugs used to reduce inflammation, relieve pain, or reduce fever. Nonsteroid anti-inflammatory drugs share the same side effects and may be used by patients who cannot tolerate Aspirin. Choice of one of these drugs over another depends on disease response, side effects seen in a particular patient, convenience of times to be taken, and cost. Different drugs or different doses of the same drug may be tried to produce the greatest effectiveness with the fewest side effects.

Cautions and Warnings

Do not take Fenoprofen Calcium if you are allergic or sensitive to this drug, Aspirin, or other nonsteriod anti-inflammatory drugs. Fenoprofen Calcium may cause stomach ulcers. This drug should not be used by patients with severe kidney disease.

Fenoprofen Calcium taken by pregnant women has caused heart and blood problems in the unborn child. Fenoprofen Calcium may also make pregnancy and labor longer. Since most of these drugs are excreted in mother's milk, nursing mothers who must use Fenoprofen Calcium should change feeding method for their infants.

Possible Side Effects

Stomach upset, blurred vision, darkening of stool, changes in color vision, rash, weight gain, retention of fluids.

Possible Adverse Drug Effects

Most frequent: stomach upset, dizziness, headache, drowsiness, ringing in the ears. Others: heartburn, nausea, vomiting, bloating, gas in the stomach, stomach pain, diarrhea, constipation, dark stool, nervousness, insomnia, depression, confusion, tremor, loss of appetite, fatigue, itching, rash, double vision, abnormal heart rhythm, anemia or other changes in the composition of the blood, changes in liver function, loss of hair, tingling in the hands and feet, fever, breast enlargement, lowered blood sugar, effects on the kidneys. If symptoms appear, stop taking the medicine and see your doctor immediately.

Drug Interactions

Fenoprofen Calcium increases the action of Phenytoin, sulfa drugs, drugs used to control diabetes, and drugs used to thin the blood. If you are taking any of these medicines, be sure to discuss it with your doctor, who will probably change the dose of the other drug.

An adjustment in the dose of Fenoprofen Calcium may be needed if you take Phenobarbital.

Usual Dose

Adult: 300 to 600 milligrams 4 times per day, to start. Arthritis: 300 to 600 milligrams 3 to 4 times per day; up to 3200 milligrams per day. Mild to moderate pain: 200 milligrams every 4 to 6 hours.

Child: not recommended.

Generic Name

Ferrous Sulfate

Brand Names

Feosol	Ferusal
Fer-In-Sol	Heatinic
Fer Iron	Iromal
Ferospace	Mol-Iron
Ferralyn	Slow F E
Fero-Gradumet	

(Also available in generic form)

Type of Drug

Iron-containing product.

Prescribed for

Iron deficiency of the blood.

General Information

Ferrous Sulfate is used to treat anemias due to iron deficiency. Other anemias will not be affected by this drug. Ferrous Sulfate works by being incorporated into red blood cells where it can help carry oxygen throughout the body. Iron is absorbed only in a small section of the gastrointestinal tract called the duodenum. Sustained-release preparations of iron should only be used to help minimize the stomach discomfort that Ferrous Sulfate can cause, since any drug which passes the duodenum (in the upper part of the small intestine) cannot be absorbed.

Other drugs may also provide a source of iron to treat iron deficiency anemia. The iron in these products may be combined with other vitamins or with special extracts as in the product Triniscon, where iron is combined with Vitamin B_{12}, Folic Acid and Intrinsic Factor.

Cautions and Warnings

Do not take Ferrous Sulfate if you have a history of stomach upset, peptic ulcer, or ulcerative colitis.

This drug has been found to be safe for use during pregnancy. Remember, you should check with your doctor before taking any drug if you are pregnant.

Possible Side Effects

Stomach upset and irritation, nausea, diarrhea, constipation.

Drug Interactions

Ferrous Sulfate will interfere with absorption of oral Tetracycline. Separate the doses by at least 2 hours.

Antacids will interfere with the absorption of iron; again, separate doses by 2 hours.

In either case, avoid taking iron supplements (unless absolutely necessary) until your other medical condition clears up.

Food Interactions

Iron salts and iron-containing products are best absorbed on an empty stomach; but if they upset your stomach, take with meals or immediately after meals.

Usual Dose

1 to 3 tablets per day.

Overdosage

Symptoms appear after 30 minutes to several hours: lethargy (tiredness), vomiting, diarrhea, stomach upset, change in pulse to weak and rapid, and lowered blood pressure—or, after massive doses, shock, black and tarry stools due to massive bleeding in the stomach or intestine, and pneumonia. Quickly induce vomiting and feed the patient eggs and milk until he can be taken to a hospital for stomach pumping. Be sure to call a doctor right away. The patient must be taken to the hospital as soon as possible, since stomach pumping should not be performed after the first hour of iron ingestion because there is a danger of perforation of the stomach wall. In the hospital emergency room measures to treat shock, loss of water, loss of blood, and respiratory failure may be necessary. ALWAYS bring the medicine bottle.

Special Information

Iron salts impart a black color to stools and are slightly

constipating. If stools become black and tarry in consistency, however, there may be some bleeding in the stomach or intestine. Discuss it with your doctor.

Brand Name

Fiorinal

Ingredients

Aspirin
Butalbital
Caffeine

Other Brand Names

Buff-A Comp	Marnal
Butal Compound	Protension
Isollyl	Tenstan
Lanorinal	

(Also available in generic form)

Type of Drug

Nonnarcotic analgesic combination.

Prescribed for

Relief of headache pain or other types of pain.

General Information

Fiorinal is one of many combination products containing barbiturates and analgesics. These products often also contain tranquilizers or narcotics, and Acetaminophen may be substituted for Aspirin.

Cautions and Warnings

Fiorinal can cause drug dependence or addiction. Use this drug with caution if you have asthma or problems in breathing. It can affect your ability to drive a car or operate machinery. Do not drink alcoholic beverages while taking Fiorinal. The Aspirin component in this drug can interfere with the normal coagulation of blood. This is especially important if you are taking blood-thinning medication.

There is an increased chance of birth defects while using Fiorinal during pregnancy. Fiorinal may be required to be used if a serious situation arises which threatens the mother's life.

Regularly using Fiorinal during the last 3 months of pregnancy may cause drug dependency of the newborn. Pregnant women using Fiorinal may experience prolonged labor and delayed delivery and breathing problems may afflict the newborn. If taken during the last 2 weeks of pregnancy, Fiorinal may cause bleeding problems in the newborn child. Problems may also be seen in the mother herself, including bleeding.

Breast-feeding while using Fiorinal may cause increased tiredness, shortness of breath, or a slow heartbeat in the baby.

Caffeine can cause birth defects in animals but has not been shown to cause problems in humans.

Possible Side Effects

Major: light-headedness, dizziness, sedation, nausea, vomiting, sweating, stomach upset, loss of appetite, (possible) mild stimulation.

Possible Adverse Drug Effects

Weakness, headache, sleeplessness, agitation, tremor, uncoordinated muscle movements, mild hallucinations, disorientation, visual disturbances, feeling high, dry mouth, loss of appetite, constipation, flushing of the face, changes in heart rate, palpitations, faintness, difficulty in urination, skin rashes, itching, confusion, rapid breathing, diarrhea.

Drug Interactions

Interaction with alcohol, tranquilizers, barbiturates, sleeping pills, or other drugs that produce depression can cause tiredness, drowsiness, and inability to concentrate.

Interaction with Prednisone, steroids, Phenylbutazone, or alcohol can irritate your stomach.

The dose of anticoagulant (blood-thinning) drugs will have to be changed by your physician if you begin taking Fiorinal, which contains Aspirin.

Usual Dose

1 to 2 tablets or capsules every 4 hours or as needed. Maximum of 6 doses per day.

Take with a full glass of water or with food to reduce the possibility of stomach upset.

Overdosage

Symptoms are difficulty in breathing, nervousness progressing to stupor or coma, pinpointed pupils of the eyes, cold clammy skin and lowered heart rate and/or blood pressure, nausea, vomiting, dizziness, ringing in the ears, flushing, sweating, and thirst. The patient should be taken to a hospital emergency room immediately. ALWAYS bring the medicine bottle.

Special Information

Drowsiness may occur.

Brand Name

Fiorinal with Codeine

Ingredients

Aspirin	Caffeine
Butalbital	Codeine Phosphate

Other Brand Names

Buff-A-Comp
Isollyl with Codeine

(Also available in generic form)

Type of Drug

Narcotic analgesic combination.

Prescribed for

Relief of headache pain or other types of pain.

General Information

Fiorinal with Codeine is one of many combination products containing barbiturates and analgesics. These products often also contain tranquilizers or narcotics, and Acetaminophen may be substituted for Aspirin.

Cautions and Warnings

Fiorinal with Codeine can cause drug dependence or addiction. Use this drug with caution if you have asthma or problems in breathing. It can affect your ability to drive a car or operate machinery.

There is an increased chance of birth defects while using Fiorinal with Codeine during pregnancy. Fiorinal with Codeine may be required to be used if a serious situation arises which threatens the mother's life.

Regularly using Fiorinal with Codeine during the last 3 months of pregnancy may cause drug dependency of the newborn. Pregnant women using Fiorinal with Codeine may experience prolonged labor and delayed delivery and breathing problems may afflict the newborn. If taken during the last 2 weeks of pregnancy, Fiorinal with Codeine may cause bleeding problems in the newborn child. Problems may also be seen in the mother herself, including bleeding.

Breast-feeding while using Fiorinal with Codeine may cause increased tiredness, shortness of breath, or a slow heartbeat in the baby.

Caffeine can cause birth defects in animals but has not been shown to cause problems in humans.

Codeine can cause addiction in the unborn child if used regularly during pregnancy.

Possible Side Effects

Major: light-headedness, dizziness, sedation, nausea, vomiting, sweating, stomach upset, loss of appetite, (possible) mild stimulation.

Possible Adverse Drug Effects

Weakness, headache, sleeplessness, agitation, tremor, uncoordinated muscle movements, mild hallucinations, disorientation, visual disturbances, feeling high, dry mouth, loss of appetite, constipation, flushing of the face, changes in heart rate, palpitations, faintness, difficulty in urination, rashes, itching, confusion, rapid breathing, diarrhea.

Drug Interactions

Interaction with alcohol, tranquilizers, barbiturates, sleeping pills, or other drugs that produce depression can cause tiredness, drowsiness, and inability to concentrate.

Interaction with Prednisone, steroids, Phenylbutazone, or alcohol can irritate your stomach.

The dose of anticoagulant (blood-thinning) drugs will have to be changed by your physician if you begin taking Fiorinal with Codeine, which contains Aspirin.

Usual Dose

1 to 2 tablets or capsules every 4 hours or as needed. Maximum of 6 doses per day.

Take with a full glass of water or with food to reduce the possibility of stomach upset.

Overdosage

Symptoms are difficulty in breathing, nervousness progressing to stupor or coma, pinpointed pupils of the eyes, cold clammy skin and lowered heart rate and/or blood pressure, nausea, vomiting, dizziness, ringing in the ears, flushing, sweating, and thirst. The patient should be taken to a hospital emergency room immediately. ALWAYS bring the medicine bottle.

Special Information

Drowsiness may occur.

Generic Name

Fluocinolone Acetonide

Brand Names

Fluocet	Synalar
Fluonid	Synalar-HP
Flurosyn	Synemol

(Also available in generic form)

Type of Drug

Topical corticosteroid.

Prescribed for

Relief of local skin inflammation, itching, or other skin problems.

General Information

Fluocinolone Acetonide is one of many adrenal cortical steroids used in medical practice today. The major differences between Fluocinolone Acetonide and other adrenal cortical steroids are potency of medication and variation in some secondary effects. In most cases the choice of adrenal cortical steroids to be used in a specific disease is a matter of doctor preference and past experience. Other adrenal cortical steroids include Cortisone, Hydrocortisone, Prednisone, Prednisolone, Triamcinolone, Methylprednisolone, Meprednisone, Paramethasone, Fluprednisolone, Dexamethasone, Betamethasone, and Fludrocortisone.

Cautions and Warnings

Fluocinolone Acetonide should not be used if you have viral diseases of the skin (herpes), fungal infections of the skin (athlete's foot), or tuberculosis of the skin, nor should it be used in the ear if the eardrum is perforated. People with a history of allergies to any of the components of the ointment, cream, or gel should not use this drug.

This drug has been found to be safe for use during pregnancy. Remember, you should check with your doctor before taking any drug if you are pregnant.

Possible Side Effects

Itching, irritation, dryness, and redness of the skin.

Special Information

Clean the skin before applying Fluocinolone Acetonide to prevent secondary infection. Apply in a very thin film (effectiveness is based on contact area and not on the thickness of the layer applied).

Generic Name

Fluocinonide Ointment/Cream/Gel

Brand Names

Lidex
Lidex-E

Type of Drug

Topical corticosteroid.

Prescribed for

Relief of local skin inflammation, itching, or other skin problems.

General Information

Fluocinonide is used to relieve the symptom of any itching, rash, or inflammation of the skin. It does not treat the underlying cause of the skin problem, only the symptom. It exerts this effect by interfering with natural body mechanisms that produce the rash, itching, etc., in the first place. If you use this drug without finding the cause of the problem, the condition may return after you stop using the drug. Fluocinonide should not be used without your doctor's consent because it could cover an important reaction, one that may be valuable to him in treating you.

Cautions and Warnings

Fluocinonide should not be used if you have viral diseases of the skin (herpes), fungal infections of the skin (athlete's foot), or tuberculosis of the skin, nor should it be used in the ear if the eardrum is perforated. People with a history of allergies to any of the components of the ointment, cream, or gel should not use this drug.

   This drug has been found to be safe for use during pregnancy. Remember, you should check with your doctor before taking any drug if you are pregnant.

Possible Side Effects

Itching, irritation, dryness and redness of the skin.

Special Information

Clean the skin before applying Fluocinonide to prevent secondary infection. Apply a very thin film (effectiveness is based on contact area and not on the thickness of the layer applied).

Generic Name

Fluoxymesterone

Brand Names

Android-F
Halotestin
Ora-Testryl

(Also available in generic form)

Type of Drug

Androgenic (male) hormone.

Prescribed for

Diseases in which male hormone replacement or augmentation is needed; male menopause.

General Information

This is a member of the androgenic or male hormone group, which includes Testosterone, Methyl Testosterone, Calusterone, and Dromostanolone Propionate. (The last two are used primarily to treat breast cancer in women.) Females taking any androgenic drug should be careful to watch for deepening of the voice, oily skin, acne, hairiness, increased libido, and menstrual irregularities, effects related to the so-called virilizing effects of these hormones. Virilization is a sign that the drug is starting to produce changes in secondary sex characteristics. The drugs should be avoided if possible by young boys who have not gone through puberty.

Cautions and Warnings

Men with unusually high blood levels of calcium, known or suspected cancer of the prostate, or prostate destruction or disease, cancer of the breast, or with liver, heart, or kidney disease should not use this medication.

Fluoxymesterone is not recommended for use during pregnancy or breast-feeding. Fluoxymesterone may cause unwanted problems in babies such as the development of male features in female babies.

Possible Side Effects

In males: Inhibition of testicle function, impotence, chronic erection of the penis, enlargement of the breast.

In females: unusual hairiness, baldness in a pattern similar to that seen in men, deepening of the voice, enlargement of the clitoris. These changes are usually irreversible once they have occurred. Females also experience increases in blood calcium and menstrual irregularities.

In both sexes: changes in libido, flushing of the skin, acne, habituation, excitation, chills, sleeplessness, water retention, nausea, vomiting, diarrhea. Symptoms resembling stomach ulcer may develop. Fluoxymesterone may affect levels of blood cholesterol.

Drug Interactions

Fluoxymesterone may increase the effect of oral anticoagulants; dosage of the anticoagulant may have to be decreased. It may have an effect on the glucose tolerance test, a blood test used to screen for diabetes mellitus.

Food Interactions

Take with meals if the drug upsets your stomach taken alone.

Usual Dose

2 to 30 milligrams per day, depending upon the disease being treated and patient's response.

Special Information

Fluoxymesterone and other androgens are potent drugs. They must be taken only under the close supervision of your doctor and never used casually. The dosage and clinical effects of the drug vary widely and require constant monitoring.

Generic Name

Fluphenazine Hydrochloride

Brand Names

Permitil
Prolixin

Type of Drug

Phenothiazine antipsychotic.

Prescribed for

Psychotic disorders, moderate to severe depression with anxiety, control of agitation or aggressiveness of disturbed children, alcohol withdrawal symptoms, intractable pain, and senility.

General Information

Fluphenazine Hydrochloride and other members of the phenothiazine group act on a portion of the brain called the hypothalamus. The drugs affect parts of the hypothalamus that control metabolism, body temperature, alertness, muscle tone, hormone balance, and vomiting, and may be used to treat problems related to any of these functions.

Cautions and Warnings

Fluphenazine Hydrochloride should not be taken if you are allergic to one of the drugs in the broad classification of phenothiazine drugs. Do not take it if you have blood, liver, kidney, or heart disease, very low blood pressure, or Parkinson's disease. This medication is a tranquilizer and can have a depressive effect, especially during the first few days of therapy. Care should be taken when performing activities requiring a high degree of concentration, such as driving. If you are taking this medication and become pregnant, contact your doctor immediately.

Fluphenazine Hydrochloride used by pregnant women has caused side effects in newborns such as jaundice (yellowing of skin and eyes), and twitching. This medication should be stopped 1 to 2 weeks before expected delivery to avoid this. Fluphenazine has not been shown to cause problems during breast-feeding.

Possible Side Effects

Most common: drowsiness, especially during the first or second week of therapy. If the drowsiness becomes troublesome, contact your doctor.

Possible Adverse Drug Effects

Can cause jaundice (yellowing of the whites of the eyes or skin), usually in 2 to 4 weeks. The jaundice usually goes away when the drug is discontinued, but there have been cases when it did not. If you notice this effect or if you develop symptoms such as fever and generally not feeling well, contact your doctor immediately. Less frequent: changes in components of the blood including anemias, raised or lowered blood pressure, abnormal heart rate, heart attack, feeling faint or dizzy.

Phenothiazines can produce "extrapyramidal effects," such as spasms of the neck muscles, severe stiffness of the back muscles, rolling back of the eyes, convulsions, difficulty in swallowing, and symptoms associated with Parkinson's disease. These effects look very serious, but disappear after the drug has been withdrawn; however, symptoms of the face, tongue, and jaw may persist for as long as several years, especially in the elderly with a history of brain damage. If you experience extrapyramidal effects, contact your doctor immediately.

Fluphenazine Hydrochloride may cause an unusual increase in psychotic symptoms or may cause paranoid reactions, tiredness, lethargy, restlessness, hyperactivity, confusion at night, bizarre dreams, inability to sleep, depression, and euphoria. Other reactions are itching, swelling, unusual sensitivity to bright lights, red skin, and rash. There have been cases of breast enlargement, false positive pregnancy tests, changes in menstrual flow in females, and impotence and changes in sex drive in males. Fluphenazine Hydrochloride may also cause dry mouth, stuffy nose, headache, nausea, vomiting, loss of appetite, change in body temperature, loss of facial color, excessive salivation, excessive perspiration, constipation, diarrhea, changes in urine and stool habits, worsening of glaucoma, blurred vision, weakening of eyelid muscles, and spasms in bronchial and other muscles, as well as increased appetite, fatigue, excessive thirst, and changes in the coloration of skin, particularly in exposed areas.

Drug Interactions

Fluphenazine Hydrochloride should be taken with caution in combination with barbiturates, sleeping pills, narcotics, or any other medication which may produce a depressive effect. Avoid alcohol.

Usual Dose

Adult: 0.5 to 10 milligrams per day in divided doses. (The lowest effective dose should be used.) Few people will require more than 3 milligrams per day, although some have required 20 milligrams or more per day.

Elderly: Geriatric patients usually require lower doses of this drug than younger adults because they metabolize it more slowly.

Overdosage

Symptoms are depression, extreme weakness, tiredness, desire to go to sleep, coma, lowered blood pressure, uncontrolled muscle spasms, agitation, restlessness, convulsions, fever, dry mouth, and abnormal heart rhythms. The patient should be taken to a hospital emergency room immediately. ALWAYS bring the medicine bottle.

Generic Name

Flurandrenolide

Brand Names

Cordran Ointment/Lotion/Tape
Cordran SP Cream

Type of Drug

Corticosteroid.

Prescribed for

Relief of local inflammation of the skin, itching, or other skin problems.

General Information

Flurandrenolide is used to relieve the symptom of any itching, rash, or inflammation of the skin. It does not treat the underlying cause of the skin problem, only the symptom. It exerts this effect by interfering with natural body mechanisms that produced the rash, itching, etc., in the first place. If you use this drug without finding the cause of the problem, the condition may return after you stop using the drug. Flurandrenolide should not be used without your doctor's consent because it could cover an important reaction, one that may be valuable to him in treating you.

Cautions and Warnings

Flurandrenolide should not be used if you have viral diseases of the skin (herpes), fungal infections of the skin (athlete's foot), or tuberculosis of the skin, nor should it be used in the ear if the eardrum has been perforated. Don't use this medicine if you are allergic to any of the components of the ointment, cream, lotion, or tape.

This drug has been found to be safe for use during pregnancy. Remember, you should check with your doctor before taking any drug if you are pregnant.

Possible Side Effects

Burning sensations, itching, irritation, dryness of the skin, secondary infection.

Special Information

Clean the skin before applying Flurandrenolide in a very thin film (effectiveness is based on contact area and not on the thickness of the layer applied).

Generic Name

Flurazepam

Brand Name

Dalmane

Type of Drug

Sedative-sleeping medicine.

Prescribed for

Insomnia or sleeplessness, frequent nighttime awakening, or waking up too early in the morning.

General Information

Flurazepam is a member of the chemical group of drugs known as benzodiazepines. These drugs are used as either antianxiety agents, anticonvulsants, or sedatives (sleeping pills). They exert their effects by relaxing the large skeletal muscles and by a direct effect on the brain. In doing so, they can relax you and make you either more tranquil or sleepier, depending on the drug and how much you use. Many doctors prefer Flurazepam and the other members of this class to other drugs that can be used for the same effect. Their reason is that the benzodiazepines tend to be safer, have fewer side effects, and are usually as, if not more, effective.

These drugs are generally used in any situation where they can be a useful adjunct.

Benzodiazepine tranquilizing drugs can be abused if taken for long periods of time, and it is possible to develop withdrawal symptoms if you discontinue the therapy abruptly. Withdrawal symptoms include convulsions, tremor, muscle cramps, stomach cramps, insomnia, agitation, diarrhea, vomiting, sweating, and even convulsions.

Cautions and Warnings

Do not take Flurazepam if you know you are sensitive or allergic to this drug or to other benzodiazepines such as Chlordiazepoxide, Oxazepam, Clorazepate, Diazepam, Lorazepam, Prazepam, Clonazepam, and Temazepam.

Flurazepam and other members of this drug group may

aggravate narrow angle glaucoma, but if you have open angle glaucoma you may take the drugs. In any case, check this information with your doctor. Flurazepam can cause tiredness, drowsiness, inability to concentrate, or similar symptoms. Be careful if you are driving, operating machinery, or performing other activities which require concentration.

Avoid taking this drug during the first 3 months of pregnancy except under strict supervision of your doctor.

The baby may become dependent on Flurazepam, if it is used continually during pregnancy. If used during the last weeks of pregnancy or during breast feeding the baby may be overly tired, be short of breath, or have a low heartbeat.

Use during labor may cause weakness in the newborn.

Possible Side Effects

Most common: mild drowsiness during the first few days of therapy, especially in the elderly or debilitated. If drowsiness persists, contact your doctor.

Possible Adverse Drug Effects

Major adverse reactions: confusion, depression, lethargy, disorientation, headache, lack of activity, slurred speech, stupor, dizziness, tremor, constipation, dry mouth, nausea, inability to control urination, changes in sex drive, irregular menstrual cycle, changes in heart rhythm, lowered blood pressure, retention of fluids, blurred or double vision, itching, rash, hiccups, nervousness, inability to fall asleep, (occasional) liver dysfunction. If you experience any of these reactions stop taking the medicine and contact your doctor immediately.

Drug Interactions

Flurazepam is a central nervous system depressant. Avoid alcohol, tranquilizers, narcotics, sleeping pills, barbiturates, MAO inhibitors, antihistamines, and other medicines used to relieve depression.

Cimetidine may increase the effect of Flurazepam.

Usual Dose

15 to 30 milligrams at bedtime. Must be individualized for maximum benefit.

Elderly: Initiate therapy with 15 milligrams at bedtime.

Overdosage

Symptoms are confusion, sleep or sleepiness, lack of response to pain such as a pin stick, shallow breathing, lowered blood pressure, and coma. The patient should be taken to a hospital emergency room immediately. ALWAYS bring the medicine bottle.

Generic Name

Furosemide

Brand Name

Lasix

(Also available in generic form)

Type of Drug

Diuretic.

Prescribed for

Congestive heart failure, cirrhosis of the liver, kidney dysfunction, high blood pressure, and other conditions where it may be desirable to rid the body of excess fluid.

General Information

Furosemide causes the production of urine by affecting the kidneys. It may also cause lowered blood pressure. Furosemide is particularly useful as a very strong drug with great diuretic potential, when a drug with less diuretic potential would fail to produce the desired therapeutic effect.

Cautions and Warnings

Furosemide if given in excessive quantities will cause depletion of water and electrolytes. It should not be taken without constant medical supervision and unless the dose has been adjusted to your particular needs. You should not take this drug if your production of urine has been decreased abnormally by some type of kidney disease, or if you feel you may be allergic to it or if you have experienced an allergic reaction to it in the past.

Morgan

Daily

Thyroid 3gr   1

Hydroxyzine HCL 2.5mg 3

Zantac   150 mg   2

Lozol   2.5 mg   1

Carafate   1 gram   4

Lasix (Feursosemide)20mg 1

Tranzene (Clarazpate) 3.75 2

K - Tab 10 mg (750 mg) 1

Tylenol - Extra Strength   3a more

Prednisone   10 mg

Although Furosemide has been used to treat specific conditions in pregnancy, it should generally not be used to treat a pregnant woman because of its potential effects on the unborn child. Although this effect has not been seen in humans, Furosemide can cause kidney problems in unborn animals if given to animals during pregnancy. If your doctor feels that your case warrants the use of Furosemide, the decision to use this drug must be made by you and your doctor based on the potential benefits derived from this drug as opposed to the potential problems that may be associated with its use. If you must take this drug during the period that you are nursing a newborn baby, you should stop nursing and feed the baby prepared formulas.

Excessive use of Furosemide will result in dehydration or reduction in blood volume, and may cause circulatory collapse and other related problems, particularly in the elderly. In addition, because of the potent effect that this drug has on the electrolytes in the blood—potassium, sodium, carbon dioxide, and others—frequent laboratory evaluations of these electrolytes should be performed during the few months of therapy, and periodically afterward.

Possible Side Effects

If you are taking Furosemide you should be aware that changes may develop in potassium and other electrolyte concentrations in your body. In the case of lower potassium produced by Furosemide (hypokalemia), you may observe these warning signs: dryness of the mouth, thirst, weakness, lethargy, drowsiness, restlessness, muscle pains or cramps, muscular tiredness, low blood pressure, decreased frequency of urination and decreased amount of urine produced, abnormal heart rate, and stomach upset including nausea and vomiting. To treat this, potassium supplements are given in the form of tablets, liquids, or powders or by increased consumption of potassium-rich foods such as bananas, citrus fruits, melons, and tomatoes.

Furosemide may alter the metabolism of sugar in your body. If you have diabetes mellitus, you may develop high blood sugar or sugar in the urine while you are taking the drug. To treat this problem, the dose of drugs that you are taking to treat your diabetes will have to be altered.

In addition, people taking Furosemide have experienced one or more of the following side effects: abdominal discomfort, nausea, vomiting, diarrhea, rash, dizziness, lightheadedness, weakness, headache, blurred vision, fatigue, jaundice or yellowing of the skin or whites of the eyes, acute attacks of gout, ringing in the ears, reversible periodic impairment in hearing. There have also been some reported cases of irreversible hearing loss.

Possible Adverse Drug Effects

Dermatitis, unusual skin reactions, tingling in the extremities, postural hypotension (or dizziness on rising quickly from a sitting or lying position), anemia of various types. Rare: a sweet taste in the mouth, burning feeling in the stomach and/or mouth, thirst, increased perspiration, frequent urination.

Drug Interactions

Furosemide will increase (potentiate) the action of other blood-pressure-lowering drugs. This is beneficial, and is frequently used to help lower blood pressure in patients with hypertension.

The possibility of developing electrolyte imbalances in body fluids is increased if you take other medications such as Digitalis and adrenal corticosteroids while you are taking Furosemide.

If you are taking Furosemide because of congestive heart failure and are also taking Digitalis, loss of potassium may significantly affect the toxicity of Digitalis.

If you are taking an oral antidiabetic drug and begin taking Furosemide, the antidiabetic dose may have to be altered.

If you are taking Lithium Carbonate, you should probably not take a diuretic, which by reducing the elimination of Lithium from the blood adds a high risk of lithium toxicity.

Interaction with aminoglycoside antibiotics may cause periodic hearing losses; make sure your doctor knows you are taking Furosemide before he gives you an injection of an aminoglycoside.

If you are taking high doses of Aspirin to treat arthritis or similar diseases, and you begin to take Furosemide, you may have to lower the dose of Aspirin because of the effect Furosemide has on passage of Aspirin through the kidneys.

If you are taking Furosemide for the treatment of high blood pressure or congestive heart failure, avoid over-the-counter drug products for the treatment of coughs, colds, and allergies which may contain stimulant drugs. Check with your pharmacist, who can give you accurate information about any over-the-counter drug and its potential interactions with Furosemide.

Food Interactions

Foods which are high in potassium, including bananas, citrus fruits, melons, and tomatoes, should be given high priority in your daily diet.

Usual Dose

Adult: 20 to 80 milligrams per day, depending on disease and patient's response. Doses of 600 milligrams per day or even more have been prescribed.

Infant or child: 4 to 5 milligrams per pound of body weight daily in a single dose. If therapy is not successful, the dose may be increased by steps of 2 to 5 milligrams, but not to more than 14 to 15 milligrams per day.

Maintenance doses are adjusted to the minimum effective level.

Special Information

If the amount of urine you produce each day is dropping or if you suffer from significant loss of appetite, muscle weakness, tiredness, or nausea while taking this drug, contact your doctor immediately.

Generic Name

Gamma Benzene Hexachloride (Lindane)

Brand Names

Kwell
Scabene

(Also available in generic form)

Type of Drug

Parasiticide.

Prescribed for

Topical treatment of head lice, crab lice, and scabies.

General Information

Gamma Benzene Hexachloride is considered to be the most effective agent against lice and scabies by many authorities. It should only be used when prescribed by a physician because it cannot prevent infestation, it can only treat it. Also, this medication is extremely irritating, particularly when applied to the eyelids and genital areas. If allowed to remain in contact with the skin for too long, Gamma Benzene Hexachloride will be absorbed directly into the bloodstream, causing signs of drug overdose.

Lindane is absorbed through the skin and may: cause unwanted effects in both pregnant mother and unborn baby; it is not recommended for use during pregnancy.

Possible Side Effects

Skin rash.

Usual Dose

For head lice: pour 1 ounce of shampoo on the affected area; rub vigorously; be sure to wet all hairy areas. Wet hair with warm water and work into a full lather for at least 4 minutes. Rinse hair thoroughly and rub with a dry towel. Comb with a fine-tooth comb to remove any remaining nit shells. A second application is usually not needed, but may be made after 24 hours if necessary. The drug should not be used more than twice in 1 week. The shampoo may also be used for crab lice.

For crab lice: after a bath or shower, apply a thin layer of lotion to hairy areas and over the skin of adjacent areas. Leave on for 12 to 24 hours, then wash thoroughly and put on freshly laundered or dry-cleaned clothing. Repeat after 4 days if necessary.

For scabies: after a bath or shower, apply a thin layer of the lotion over the entire skin surface. Leave on for 24 hours, then wash thoroughly. If necessary, a second and third weekly application may be made.

Overdosage

Anyone who ingests this drug accidentally should be taken to a hospital emergency room immediately. When taken internally, Gamma Benzene Hexachloride is a stimulant; the patient may require Phenobarbital or a similar depressant to neutralize the effect.

If contact with your eyes occurs during shampoo or other use, flush the eyes and surrounding area with water. If irritation or sensitization occurs, discontinue use and call a doctor.

Special Instructions

Do not apply to face. Flush thoroughly with water if medication comes in contact with eyes. Do not exceed prescribed dose.

Brand Name

Gaviscon

Ingredients

Alginic Acid	Magnesium Trisilicate
Aluminum Hydroxide Dried Gel	Sodium Bicarbonate

Type of Drug

Antacid.

Prescribed for

Heartburn, acid indigestion, or sour stomach.

General Information

Gaviscon is one of many commercial antacid products on the market. Antacids are used by many people for the relief of temporary symptoms associated with indigestion caused by drugs, food, or disease. For more information on Antacids see page 54.

Cautions and Warnings

Do not use this antacid if you are on a sodium-restricted diet.

This drug may cause birth defects or interfere with your baby's development. Check with your doctor before taking it if you are, or might be, pregnant.

Possible Side Effects

Occasional constipation or diarrhea if taken in large quantities.

Drug Interactions

Do not take this drug at the same time as a Tetracycline derivative, antibiotic, Digoxin, Phenytoin, Quinidine, Warfarin, or oral iron supplement. The antacid may interfere with the effective absorption of these drugs.

Take other drugs 1 hour before or 2 hours after taking an antacid.

Usual Dose

Chew 2 to 4 tablets 4 times per day, as needed. Do not take more than 16 tablets per day.

Overdosage

Take the patient to an emergency facility. Bring the medication.

Storage

Store the medication at room temperature in a dry place.

Special Information

Do not swallow these tablets whole—they must be chewed.

Generic Name

Gemfibrozil

Brand Name

Lopid

Type of Drug

Antihyperlipidemic (blood-fat reducer).

Prescribed for

People with excessively high levels of blood triglycerides.

General Information

Gemfibrozil consistently reduces blood triglyceride levels, but is usually prescribed only for people with very high blood-fat levels who have not responded to dietary changes or other therapies. Normal levels range between 50 and 200 milligrams. People with very high levels of blood trigly-cerides are likely to have severe abdominal pains and pancreas inflammation. Gemfibrozil usually has little effect on blood cholesterol levels, although it may reduce blood cholesterol in some people.

Gemfibrozil works by affecting the breakdown of body fats and by reducing the amount of triglyceride manufactured by the liver. However, it is not known if these two mechanisms are solely responsible for the drug's effect on triglyceride levels.

Cautions and Warnings

Gemfibrozil should not be taken by people with severe liver or kidney disease or by those who have had allergic reac-tions to the drug. Gemfibrozil users may have an increased chance of developing gallbladder disease and should realize that this drug, like other blood-fat reducers, including Clofi-brate and Probucol, has not been proven to reduce the chances of fatal heart attacks.

Long-term studies of male rats in which the animals were given between 1 and 10 times the maximum human dose showed a definite increase in liver tumors, both cancerous and noncancerous. Other studies on male rats, in which 3 to 10 times the human dose was given for 10 weeks, showed that the drug reduced sperm activity, although this effect has not been reported in humans.

There are no Gemfibrozil studies involving pregnant women. However, it should be avoided by pregnant women or women who may become pregnant while using it. In those situations where its use is considered essential, the potential risk of the drug must be carefully weighed against any benefit it might produce. Because of the tumor-stimu-lating effect of Gemfibrozil, it is recommended that nursing mothers consider bottle-feeding while taking this drug.

Possible Side Effects

Most common: abdominal and stomach pains and gas, diar
rhea, nausea, and vomiting.

Possible Adverse Drug Effects

Rash and itching, dizziness, blurred vision, anemia, reduce
levels of certain white blood cells, increased blood sugar
and muscle pains, especially in the arms and legs. Othe
adverse reactions are dry mouth, constipation, loss of appe
tite, upset stomach, sleeplessness, tingling in the hands o
feet, ringing or buzzing in the ears, back pains, painful mus
cles and/or joints, swollen joints, fatigue, a feeling of il
health, reduction in blood potassium, and abnormal live
function. People taking this drug may be more susceptible t
the common cold or other viral or bacterial infections.

Drug Interactions

Gemfibrozil increases the effects of oral anticoagulant (blood
thinning) drugs, and your doctor will have to reduce you
anticoagulant dosage when Gemfibrozil treatment is started

Food Interactions

Follow your doctor's instructions for dietary restrictions.

  Gemfibrozil is best taken on an empty stomach 30 minute
before meals, but may be taken with food if it upsets you
stomach.

Usual Dose

900 to 1500 milligrams per day, in 2 divided doses taken 2
minutes before breakfast and the evening meal.

Overdosage

There are no reports of Gemfibrozil overdosage, but victim
might be expected to develop exaggerated versions of th
drug's side effects. Patients taking an overdose of this drug
must be made to vomit with Syrup of Ipecac (available a
any pharmacy) to remove any remaining drug from the stom
ach. Call your doctor or a Poison Control Center befor
doing this. If you must go to a hospital emergency room
ALWAYS bring the medicine bottle.

Special Information

Your doctor should perform periodic blood counts during the first year of Gemfibrozil treatment to check for anemia or other blood effects. Liver-function tests are also necessary. Blood-sugar levels should be checked periodically while you are taking Gemfibrozil, especially if you are diabetic or have a family history of diabetes.

Gemfibrozil may cause dizziness or blurred vision. Use caution while driving or doing anything else that requires concentration and alertness.

Call your doctor if any drug side effects become severe or intolerable, especially diarrhea, nausea, vomiting, or stomach pains and/or gas. These may disappear by reducing the drug dose.

Generic Name

Glipizide

Brand Name

Glucotrol

Type of Drug

Oral antidiabetic.

Prescribed for

Diabetes mellitus (high sugar levels in the blood and urine) that develops during adulthood.

General Information

Glipizide is a "second-generation" antidiabetes drug that was sold in Europe and Canada for several years before the F.D.A. approved its use in the United States. It belongs to the same chemical class as earlier oral antidiabetic drugs, but is more potent, so that less medication is required to accomplish the same effect as the other products. Other minor differences between the first- and second-generation drugs are not considered clinically important at this time. Glipizide and the other second-generation drug, Glyburide, offer no advantage over first-generation agents (Acetohexamide, Chlor-propamide, Tolazamide, and Tolbutamide) available in the United States.

The major differences among all antidiabetes drugs are in the time it takes for the drugs' action to begin and the duration of their effect. All currently available antidiabetes drugs work by stimulating the cells in the pancreas that release Insulin into the blood to increase their production. These antidiabetics require a functioning pancrease to produce their effect. However, they may be used together with Insulin injections in certain cases.

Cautions and Warnings

Mild stress, such as infection, minor surgery, or emotional upset, reduces the effectiveness of Glipizide. Remember that while you are taking this medication, you should be under your doctor's continuous care.

The long-term (several years) use of oral antidiabetes drugs has been associated with more heart disease than has treatment with diet or diet plus Insulin. For this reason, many physicians consider diet or diet plus Insulin to be superior to an oral antidiabetes drug.

Glipizide is an aid to, not a substitute for, dietary control. Dietary restriction is still of primary importance in treating diabetes. Follow the diet plan your doctor has prescribed.

Glipizide and the other oral antidiabetes drugs are not oral Insulin, nor are they a substitute for Insulin. they do not lower blood sugar by themselves.

Treating diabetes is your responsibility. Following all of your doctor's instructions with regard to diet, body weight, exercise, personal hygiene, and measures to avoid infection is of paramount importance.

Glipizide should not be used if you have severe kidney, liver, or endocrine (hormone) system disease. This drug should be avoided by women who may become pregnant while using it, and pregnant and nursing mothers. In those situations where it is deemed essential, the potential risk of the drug must be carefully weighed against any benefit it might produce. Bear in mind that diabetic mothers are known to be 3 to 4 times more likely to have children with birth defects than are nondiabetic women.

If you are pregnant or nursing, attempts should be made to control your diabetes with diet and/or Insulin during this time. If you take Glipizide during pregnancy, it should be stopped at least 1 month before the expected birth date to avoid very low blood sugar in your newborn baby.

Possible Side Effects

Most common: appetite loss, nausea, vomiting, heartburn, and upset stomach. You may experience tingling in your hands or feet and itching and rash. These effects can be treated by reducing the daily Glipizide dose or switching to another antidiabetes drug.

Possible Adverse Drug Effects

Glipizide can produce abnormally low blood-sugar levels if too much is taken. Other factors that can contribute to low blood sugar are age, kidney or liver disease, malnutrition, consumption of alcoholic beverages, and glandular disorders.

Glipizide may produce liver inflammation shown by a yellow discoloration of your skin or the whites of your eyes, but this is rare. Other side effects are relatively infrequent, but can include weakness, fatigue, dizziness, headache, loss of some kidney function, mild reduction in levels of white blood cells and platelets (involved in clotting), and drug allergy (itching and rash).

Drug Interactions

The action of Glipizide may be enhanced by Insulin, sulfa drugs, Oxyphenbutazone, Phenylbutazone, Clofibrate, Aspirin and other Salicylates, Probenecid, Dicumarol, Bishydroxycoumarin, Warfarin, Phenyramidol, and MAO inhibitor drugs, requiring a reduction in Glipizide dosage.

Thiazide-type diuretics, Corticosteroids, Phenothiazine tranquilizers, drugs for underactive thyroids, estrogens, oral contraceptives, Phenytoin, Nicotinic Acid, calcium channel blockers, Isoniazid, and the stimulant ingredients added for their decongestant effects to many nonprescription cough, cold, and allergy medicines can increase blood-sugar levels, calling for a possible increase in Glipizide dosage. Check with your doctor or pharmacist before taking any such over-the-counter products.

Beta blockers, prescribed for high blood pressure and some forms of heart disease, may counteract the effects of oral antidiabetes drugs. The outward signs of low blood sugar may also be reversed by these drugs.

Alcoholic beverages can either increase or decrease blood-sugar levels and should be avoided. Also, alcoholic beverages can interact with this medication to cause flushing of the face and body, throbbing pain in the head and neck, breathing difficulty, nausea, vomiting, sweating, chest pains, thirst, low blood pressure, heart palpitations, weakness, dizziness, blurred vision, and confusion. Contact your doctor at once if you experience any of these symptoms.

Food Interactions

Dietary restriction is an essential part of the treatment of diabetes. Be sure to follow the diet your doctor prescribes. Glipizide is best taken on an empty stomach but may be taken with food if it upsets your stomach.

Usual Dose

5 milligrams once per day.

Overdosage

Mild Glipizide overdosage lowers blood sugar and can be treated by consuming sugar in such forms as candy and orange juice. More serious overdosage must be treated in a hospital emergency room. ALWAYS bring the prescription bottle with you.

Special Information

This medicine should not be discontinued without your doctor's knowledge and advice. It should be taken as a part of a program for the treatment of your condition, including diet, exercise, personal hygiene, measures to avoid infection, and periodic testing of your urine for sugar and ketones. Your doctor may also want you to measure blood sugar periodically, which can be conveniently accomplished at home using an appropriate device.

Contact your doctor if you are not feeling well or if you develop symptoms such as yellowing of the skin or whites of the eyes, an abnormally light-colored stool, low-grade fever, unusual bleeding or bruising, sore throat, or diarrhea.

Abnormally low blood sugar may be evidenced by fatigue, hunger, profuse sweating, and numbness in your hands or feet.

Abnormally high blood sugar may be evidenced by excessive thirst and/or frequent urination, and very high levels of sugar or ketones in your urine.

Generic Name

Glutethimide

Brand Name

Doriden

(Also available in generic form)

Type of Drug

Sedative-hypnotic.

Prescribed for

Inability to sleep.

General Information

Sleep is produced within 30 minutes and lasts 4 to 8 hours.

Cautions and Warnings

Glutethimide should not be used if you are sensitive or allergic to it. It can be addictive.

This drug is known to cause birth defects or interfere with your baby's development. It is not considered safe for use during pregnancy. If used during breast feeding the baby may become overly tired, be short of breath, or have a low heartbeat.

Possible Side Effects

Skin rash.

Possible Adverse Drug Effects

There have been reports of nausea, morning hangover, rash, excitation, and blurred vision.

Drug Interactions

Do not take this drug with alcohol and/or other depressants such as sedatives, hypnotics, and antihistamines which may produce drowsiness or sleepiness.

Doses of anticoagulant (blood-thinning) drugs such as Warfarin may require adjustment because of increased effects. Dosage adjustment will also be required when you stop taking Glutethimide.

Usual Dose

1 tablet at bedtime; if necessary, repeat after 4 hours.

Overdosage

Large amounts of Glutethimide can be fatal, and the drug is frequently used in suicide attempts. Symptoms are coma, lowered body temperature followed by fever, absence of normal reflexes and pain responses after pinches and needle or pin sticks, and shallow breathing. The patient should be taken to a hospital emergency room immediately.

People who have taken Glutethimide for a long time may show signs of chronic overdosage: loss of memory, inability to concentrate, shakes, tremors, loss of reflexes, slurring of speech, and general sense of depression. Abrupt discontinuation of Glutethimide often causes withdrawal reactions of nervousness, anxiety, seizures, cramping, chills, numbness of the extremities, and general behavior changes. Chronic overdosage is best treated by withdrawing the drug over a period of days or weeks.

Generic Name

Glyburide

Brand Names

DiaBeta
Micronase

Type of Drug

Oral antidiabetic.

Prescribed for

Diabetes mellitus (high sugar levels in the blood and urine) that develops during adulthood.

General Information

Glyburide is a "second-generation" antidiabetes drug that was sold in Europe and Canada for several years before the F.D.A. approved its use in the United States. It belongs to the same chemical class as earlier oral antidiabetic drugs, but is more potent, so that less medication is required to accomplish the same effect as the other products. Other minor differences between the first- and second-generation drugs are not considered clinically important at this time. Glyburide and the other second-generation drug, Glipizide, offer no advantage over first-generation agents (Acetohexamide, Chlorpropamide, Tolazamide, and Tolbutamide) available in the United States.

The major differences among all antidiabetes drugs are in the time it takes for the drugs' action to begin and the duration of their effect. All currently available antidiabetes drugs work by stimulating the cells in the pancreas that release Insulin into the blood to increase their production. These antidiabetics require a functioning pancreas to produce their effect. However, they may be used together with Insulin injections in certain cases.

Cautions and Warnings

Mild stress, such as infection, minor surgery, or emotional upset, reduces the effectiveness of Glyburide. Remember that while you are taking this medication, you should be under your doctor's continuous care.

The long-term (several years) use of oral antidiabetes drugs has been associated with more heart disease than has treatment with diet or diet plus Insulin. For this reason, many physicians consider diet or diet plus Insulin to be superior to an oral antidiabetes drug.

Glyburide is an aid to, not a substitute for, dietary control. Dietary restriction is still of primary importance in treating diabetes. Follow the diet plan your doctor has prescribed.

Glyburide and the other oral antidiabetes drugs are not

oral Insulin, nor are they a substitute for Insulin. They do not lower blood sugar on their own.

Treating diabetes is your responsibility. Following all of your doctor's instructions with regard to diet, body weight, exercise, personal hygiene, and measures to avoid infection is of paramount importance.

Glyburide should not be used if you have severe kidney, liver, or endocrine (hormone) system disease.

Unlike the older oral antidiabetes drugs, Glyburide has been tested in animals and found to produce no damage to the developing fetus. Other oral antidiabetes drugs produce birth defects but the exact relationship is unclear because children of diabetic mothers are 3 to 4 times more prone to birth defects than are children of nondiabetic women. Nevertheless, there is no corresponding proof of safety in humans, and Glyburide should be taken with extreme caution if you are pregnant, might become pregnant during its use, or are nursing. Attempts should be made to control your diabetes with diet and/or Insulin during this time. If you take Glyburide during pregnancy, it should be stopped at least 2 weeks before the expected birth to avoid very low blood sugar in the newborn baby.

Possible Side Effects

Most common: appetite loss, nausea, vomiting, heartburn, and upset stomach. You may experience tingling in your hands or feet and itching and rash. These effects can be treated by reducing the daily Glyburide dose or switching to another antidiabetes drug.

Possible Adverse Drug Effects

Glyburide can produce abnormally low blood-sugar levels if too much is taken. Other factors that can contribute to low blood sugar are age, kidney or liver disease, malnutrition, consumption of alcoholic beverages, and glandular disorders.

Glyburide may produce liver inflammation shown by a yellow discoloration of your skin or the whites of your eyes, but this is rare. Other side effects are relatively infrequent, but can include weakness, fatigue, dizziness, headache, loss of some kidney function, mild reduction in levels of white blood cells and platelets (involved in clotting), and drug allergy (itching and rash).

Drug Interactions

The action of Glyburide may be enhanced by Insulin, sulfa drugs, Oxyphenbutazone, Phenylbutazone, Clofibrate, Aspirin and other Salicylates, Probenecid, Dicumarol, Bishydroxycoumarin, Warfarin, Phenyramidol, and MAO inhibitor drugs, requiring a reduction in Glyburide dosage.

Thiazide-type diuretics, Corticosteroids, Phenothiazine tranquilizers, drugs for underactive thyroids, estrogens, oral contraceptives, Phenytoin, Nicotinic acid, calcium channel blockers, Isoniazid, and the stimulant ingredients added for their decongestant effects to many nonprescription cough, cold, and allergy medicines can increase blood-sugar levels, calling for a possible increase in Glyburide dosage. Check with your doctor or pharmacist before taking any such over-the-counter products.

Beta blockers, prescribed for high blood pressure and some forms of heart disease, may counteract the effects of oral antidiabetes drugs. The outward signs of low blood sugar may also be reversed by these drugs.

Alcoholic beverages can either increase or decrease blood-sugar levels and should be avoided. Also, alcoholic beverages can interact with this medication to cause flushing of the face and body, throbbing pain in the head and neck, breathing difficulty, nausea, vomiting, sweating, chest pains, thirst, low blood pressure, heart palpitations, weakness, dizziness, blurred vision, and confusion. Contact your doctor at once if you experience any of these symptoms.

Food Interactions

Dietary restriction is an essential part of the treatment of diabetes. Be sure to follow the diet your doctor prescribes. Glyburide is best taken on an empty stomach but may be taken with food if it upsets your stomach.

Usual Dose

2.5 to 5 milligrams once per day.

Overdosage

Mild Glyburide overdosage lowers blood sugar and can be treated by consuming sugar in such forms as candy and orange juice. More serious overdosage must be treated in a hospital emergency room. ALWAYS bring the prescription bottle with you.

Special Information

This medicine should not be discontinued without your doctor's knowledge and advice. It should be taken as a part of a program for the treatment of your condition, including diet, exercise, personal hygiene, measures to avoid infection, and periodic testing of your urine for sugar and ketones. Your doctor may also want you to measure blood sugar periodically, which can be conveniently accomplished at home using an appropriate device.

Contact your doctor if you are not feeling well or if you develop symptoms such as yellowing of the skin or whites of the eyes, an abnormally light-colored stool, low-grade fever, unusual bleeding or bruising, sore throat, or diarrhea.

Abnormally low blood sugar may be evidenced by fatigue, hunger, profuse sweating, and numbness in your hands or feet.

Abnormally high blood sugar may be evidenced by excessive thirst and/or frequent urination, and very high levels of sugar or ketones in your urine.

Generic Name

Guanabenz Acetate

Brand Name

Wytensin

Type of Drug

Antihypertensive.

Prescribed for

High blood pressure.

General Information

This drug works by stimulating certain nerve receptors in the central nervous system, resulting in a lessening of general nervous-system stimulation by the brain. The immediate blood-pressure reduction occurs without a major effect on blood vessels. However, chronic use of Guanabenz Acetate can result in widening of blood vessels and a slight reduction in pulse rate. It can be taken alone or in combination with a thiazide diuretic.

Cautions and Warnings

Do not take Guanabenz Acetate if you are sensitive to it.

Reports of the effects of this drug in pregnant women have yielded conflicting results. Because it may adversely affect a developing baby, this drug should be avoided by pregnant women or women who may become pregnant while using it. In those situations where it is deemed essential, the potential risk of the drug must be carefully weighed against any benefit it might produce. Nursing mothers should not use this drug, since it is not known if it passes into breast milk. Consider an alternative feeding method if you must take Guanabenz Acetate.

Possible Side Effects

The incidence and severity of side effects increase with increases in the daily dosage. The side effects are drowsiness, sedation, dry mouth, dizziness, weakness, and headache.

Possible Adverse Drug Effects

Chest pains, swelling in the hands, legs, or feet, heart palpitations and abnormal heart rhythms, stomach and abdominal pains and discomfort, nausea, diarrhea, vomiting, constipation, anxiety, poor muscle control, depression, difficulty sleeping, stuffy nose, blurred vision, muscle aches and pains, difficulty breathing, frequent urination, male impotence, unusual taste in the mouth, and swollen and painful male breasts.

Drug Interactions

The effect of this drug is increased by taking it together with other blood-pressure lowering agents. Its sedative effects will be increased by taking it together with tranquilizers, sleeping pills, or other nervous system depressants.

People taking Guanabenz Acetate for high blood pressure

should avoid nonprescription medicines that might aggravate hypertension, such as decongestants, cold and allergy treatments, and diet pills, all of which may contain stimulants. If you are unsure about which medicine to choose, ask your pharmacist.

Food Interactions

This drug is best taken on an empty stomach but may be taken with food if it upsets your stomach.

Usual Dose

4 milligrams 2 times per day to start, with a gradual increase to a maximum of 32 milligrams twice per day, although doses this large are rarely needed.

Overdosage

Guanabenz Acetate will cause sleepiness, lethargy, low blood pressure, irritability, pinpoint pupils, and reduced heart rate.

Patients taking an overdose of this drug must be made to vomit with Syrup of Ipecac (available at any pharmacy) to remove any remaining drug from the stomach. Call your doctor or a Poison Control Center before doing this. If you must go to a hospital emergency room, ALWAYS bring the medicine bottle.

Special Information

Take this drug exactly as prescribed for maximum benefit. If any side effects become severe or intolerable, contact your doctor, who may reduce your daily dosage to eliminate the side effect.

Generic Name

Guanadrel Sulfate

Brand Name

Hylorel

Type of Drug

Antihypertensive.

Prescribed for

High blood pressure.

General Information

This drug is similar to Guanethidine Sulfate and works by preventing the release of the neurohormone norepinephrine from nervous-system storage sites. This relaxes blood-vessel muscles and lowers blood pressure by preventing blood-vessel constriction. Guanadrel Sulfate is usually taken with other medicines, such as diuretics.

Cautions and Warnings

Guanadrel Sulfate must not be taken by people who are sensitive or allergic to its effects, who have heart failure (the drug can cause you to retain salt and water), or those with a tumor of the adrenal glands known as pheochromocytoma. Asthmatics and people with stomach ulcers may find their conditions are worsened by this drug.

This drug should be avoided by pregnant women or women who may become pregnant while using it. In those situations where it is deemed essential, the potential risk of the drug must be carefully weighed against any benefit it might produce. Nursing mothers should watch for any possible drug effect on their infants while taking this medication. It is not known if Guanadrel Sulfate passes into breast milk.

Possible Side Effects

Difficulty breathing with or without physical exertion, heart palpitations, chest pains, coughing, fatigue, headache, feeling faint, drowsiness, visual disturbances, tingling in the hands or feet, confusion, increased bowel movements, gas pains, indigestion, constipation, loss of appetite, inflammation of the tongue, nausea, vomiting, frequent urination, a feeling that you need to urinate, nighttime urination, fluid retention and swelling in the arms, legs, or feet, male impotence, aching arms or legs, leg cramps, and excessive changes in body weight (up or down).

Possible Adverse Drug Effects

Psychological changes, depression, difficulty sleeping, fainting, dry mouth, dry throat, blood in the urine, joint pains or inflammation, backache, and neckache.

Drug Interactions

Guanadrel Sulfate should be discontinued 2 to 3 days before surgery to avoid potentially severe interaction with anesthetic agents.

It should not be taken together with MAO inhibitor drugs or within a week of MAO inhibitor therapy because of the possible enhancement of MAO side effects.

The effects of Guanadrel Sulfate may be reversed by tricyclic antidepressant drugs, Ephedrine, Phenylpropanolamine, and the phenothiazine tranquilizers. Avoid nonprescription medicines that might aggravate your condition, such as decongestants, cold and allergy treatments, asthma remedies, and diet pills, all of which may contain stimulants. If you are unsure about which medicine to choose, ask your pharmacist.

Guanadrel Sulfate's effects may be increased by beta-blocking drugs and Reserpine.

Drug Interactions

Alcoholic beverages are likely to increase the chances of dizziness and fainting associated with Guanadrel Sulfate.

Food Interactions

This drug is best taken on an empty stomach but may be taken with food if it upsets your stomach.

Usual Dose

5 milligrams twice per day to start. The daily dosage will be increased in small steps until blood-pressure control is achieved or side effects become intolerable. Most people require between 20 and 75 milligrams per day. Larger daily amounts may be required but should be divided into 3 or 4 doses per day.

Overdosage

Extreme dizziness and blurred vision are the hallmarks of Guanadrel Sulfate overdose. Lie down until the symptoms subside. If the symptoms are more severe and include a rapid drop in blood pressure, take the victim to the hospital at once for treatment. ALWAYS bring the prescription bottle with you.

Special Information

Guanadrel Sulfate frequently causes weakness and dizziness in someone who has been sitting or lying down and then rises quickly. This is more likely to happen early in the morning, during hot weather, if you have been sitting or reclining for a long period of time, or if you have been drinking alcoholic beverages. You can minimize this reaction by getting up as slowly as possible. When you get up from lying down, sit on the edge of your bed for several minutes with your feet dangling, then stand slowly. Call your doctor if the problem continues; your daily drug dosage may have to be reduced.

People taking this drug for long periods of time may become tolerant to its effects. If this happens, your doctor will increase your daily dose slightly to achieve the same degree of blood-pressure control.

Generic Name

Guanethidine Sulfate

Brand Name

Ismelin

Type of Drug

Antihypertensive.

Prescribed for

High blood pressure.

General Information

Guanethidine Sulfate affects the section of the nervous system which controls pressure in the major blood vessels. Its blood-pressure-lowering effect is enhanced when taken along with other medicines, such as diuretics.

Cautions and Warnings

Patients who may be allergic to this drug, who are taking an MAO inhibitor, or who also have a tumor called a pheochromocytoma should not take Guanethidine Sulfate.

This drug may cause birth defects or interfere with your baby's development. Check with your doctor before taking it if you are, or might be, pregnant.

Possible Side Effects

Dizziness, weakness, especially on rising quickly from a sitting or prone position, slowed heartbeat, increased bowel movements, possibly severe diarrhea, male impotence (difficult ejaculation), retention of fluid in the body.

Possible Adverse Drug Effects

Difficulty in breathing, fatigue, nausea, vomiting, increased frequency of nighttime urination, difficulty in controlling urinary function, itching, rash, loss of scalp hair, dry mouth, involuntary lowering of eyelids, blurred vision, muscle aches and spasms, mental depression, chest pains (angina pectoris), tingling in the chest, stuffy nose, weight gain, asthma in some patients. This drug may affect kidney function.

Drug Interactions

Guanethidine Sulfate may interact with digitalis drugs to slow heart rates excessively. When taken with other blood-pressure-lowering drugs it can lower pressure excessively. Otherwise, this is a useful interaction that is sometimes used in treating hypertension (high blood pressure).

Drugs with stimulant properties (antidepressants, decongestants), oral contraceptives, and some antipsychotic drugs (phenothiazines, etc.) may reduce the effectiveness of Guanethidine Sulfate. The drug should not be taken together with MAO inhibitors, which should be stopped at least 1 week before taking Guanethidine Sulfate.

Avoid over-the-counter cough, cold, or allergy medicines which may contain stimulants. Check with your doctor or pharmacist before combining these medicines.

Usual Dose

10 milligrams per day to start. Dose is adjusted according to

patient's need. Average daily requirement is 25 to 50 milligrams.

Overdosage

Symptoms are basically exaggerated or prolonged side effects, including dizziness, weakness, slowed heartbeat, and possible diarrhea. Call your doctor immediately if the symptoms appear or if you think you have these symptoms.

Special Information

Do not stop taking this medication unless specifically directed to. Call your doctor if you develop frequent diarrhea or are often dizzy or faint. Alcoholic beverages, heat, and strenuous exercise may increase the chances of dizziness or faintness developing.

Generic Name

Halazepam

Brand Name

Paxipam

Type of Drug

Minor tranquilizer.

Prescribed for

Relief of symptoms of anxiety, tension, fatigue, and agitation.

General Information

Halazepam is a member of the chemical group of drugs known as benzodiazepines. These drugs are used either as antianxiety agents, anticonvulsants, or sedatives (sleeping pills). They exert their effects by relaxing the large skeletal muscles and by a direct effect on the brain. In doing so, they can relax you and make you either more tranquil or sleepier, depending upon which drug you use and how much you take. Many doctors prefer the benzodiazepines to other drugs that can be used for the same effects. Their reason is that these drugs tend to be safer, have fewer side effects, and are usually as, if not more, effective. The benzodiazepines are generally prescribed in any situation where they can be a useful adjunct.

The benzodiazepines, including Halazepam, can be abused if taken for long periods of time and it is possible to experience withdrawal symptoms if you stop taking the drug abruptly. Withdrawal symptoms include tremor, muscle cramps, stomach cramps, vomiting, insomnia, and convulsions.

Cautions and Warnings

Do not take Halazepam if you know you are sensitive or allergic to this drug or other benzodiazepines such as Diazepam, Oxazepam, Chlorazepate, Lorazepam, Prazepam, Flurazepam, Temazepam, and Clonazepam. Halazepam and other members of this group can aggravate narrow angle glaucoma, but if you have open angle glaucoma you may take the drug. In any case, check with your doctor. Halazepam can cause tiredness, drowsiness, inability to concentrate, or similar symptoms. Be careful if you are driving, operating machinery, or performing other activities which require concentration.

This drug may cause birth defects or interfere with your baby's development. Check with your doctor before taking it if you are, or might be, pregnant.

If used during breast feeding the baby may be overly tired, be short of breath, or have a low heartbeat.

Possible Side Effects

Most common: mild drowsiness during the first few days of therapy, especially in the elderly or debilitated. If drowsiness persists, contact your doctor.

Possible Adverse Drug Effects

Major adverse reactions: confusion, depression, lethargy, disorientation, headache, inactivity, slurred speech, stupor, dizziness, tremor, constipation, dry mouth, nausea, inability to control urination, changes in sex drive, irregular menstrual cycle, changes in heart rhythm, lowered blood pressure, fluid retention, blurred or double vision, itching, rash, hiccups, nervousness, inability to fall asleep, and occasional liver dysfunction. If you experience any of these symptoms, stop taking the medicine and contact your doctor immediately.

Drug Interactions

Halazepam is a central nervous system depressant. Avoid alcohol, other tranquilizers, narcotics, barbiturates, MAO inhibitors, antihistamines, and medicine used to relieve depression. Taking Halazepam with these drugs may result in excessive depression, tiredness, sleepiness, difficulty breathing, or similar symptoms. Smoking may reduce the effectiveness of Halazepam by increasing the rate at which it is broken down in the body. The effects of Halazepam may be prolonged when taken together with Cimetidine.

Usual Dose

60 to 160 milligrams per day. The dose must be tailored to the individual needs of the patient. Elderly or debilitated patients will require less of the drug to control anxiety and tension. This drug should not be used in children.

Overdosage

Symptoms are confusion, sleepiness, lack of response to pain such as a pin stick, shallow breathing, lowered blood pressure, and coma. The patient should be taken to a hospital emergency room. ALWAYS bring the medicine bottle.

Special Information

Do not drink alcoholic beverages or take other depressive drugs, such as tranquilizers, sleeping pills, narcotics, or barbiturates when taking Halazepam. Tell your doctor if you become pregnant or are nursing an infant. Take care while driving or operating machinery.

Generic Name

Haloperidol

Brand Name

Haldol

Type of Drug

Butyrophenone antipsychotic.

Prescribed for

Psychotic disorders and to help control an unusual disorder: Gilles de la Tourette's syndrome; short-term treatment of hyperactive children.

General Information

Haloperidol is one of many nonphenothiazine agents used in the treatment of psychosis. The drugs in this group are usually about equally effective when given in therapeutically equivalent doses. The major differences are in type and severity of side effects. Some patients may respond well to one and not at all to another: this variability is not easily explained and is thought to result from inborn biochemical differences.

Cautions and Warnings

Haloperidol should not be used by patients who are allergic to it. Patients with blood, liver, kidney, or heart disease, very low blood pressure, or Parkinson's disease should avoid this drug.

Avoid this drug if you are pregnant. Haloperidol has not been studied in pregnant women; however, serious problems have been seen in pregnant animals given large amounts of Haloperidol. Nursing baby animals have also shown problems such as tiredness and body movement problems. Haloperidol is not recommended during nursing.

Possible Side Effects

Most common: drowsiness, especially during the first or second week of therapy. If the drowsiness becomes troublesome, contact your doctor.

Possible Adverse Drug Effects

Halperidol can cause jaundice (yellowing of the whites of the eyes or skin), usually in 2 to 4 weeks. The jaundice usually goes away when the drug is discontinued, but there have been cases when it did not. If you notice this effect or if you develop fever and generally do not feel well, contact your doctor immediately. Less frequent: changes in components of the blood including anemias, raised or lowered blood pressure, abnormal heartbeat, heart attack, feeling faint or dizzy.

Butyrophenone drugs can produce extrapyramidal effects such as spasms of the neck muscles, severe stiffness of the back muscles, rolling back of the eyes, convulsions, difficulty in swallowing, and symptoms associated with Parkinson's disease. These effects look very serious but disappear after the drug has been withdrawn; however, symptoms of the face, tongue, and jaw may persist for several years, especially in the elderly with a long history of brain disease. If you experience these extrapyramidal effects contact your doctor immediately.

Haloperidol may cause an unusual increase in psychotic symptoms or may cause paranoid reactions, tiredness, lethargy, restlessness, hyperactivity, confusion at night, bizarre dreams, inability to sleep, depression, or euphoria. Other reactions are itching, swelling, unusual sensitivity to bright lights, red skin, and rash. There have been cases of breast enlargement, false positive pregnancy tests, changes in menstrual flow in females, impotence and changes in sex drive in males.

Haloperidol may also cause dry mouth, stuffy nose, headache, nausea, vomiting, loss of appetite, change in body temperature, loss of facial color, excessive salivation, excessive perspiration, constipation, diarrhea, changes in urine and stool habits, worsening of glaucoma, blurred vision, weakening of eyelid muscles, and spasms in bronchial and other muscles, as well as increased appetite, fatigue, excessive thirst, and changes in the coloration of skin, particularly in exposed areas.

Drug Interactions

Haloperidol should be taken with caution in combination

with barbiturates, sleeping pills, narcotics, or any other medication which produces a depressive effect. Avoid alcohol.

Haloperidol may increase the need for anticonvulsant medicine in patients who must take both drugs. It may interfere with oral anticoagulant drugs. Any dosage adjustment necessary can easily be made by your doctor.

Usual Dose

Adult: .5 to 2 milligrams 2 to 3 times per day. Dose may be increased according to patient's need up to 100 milligrams per day.

Child: not recommended.

Overdosage

Symptoms are depression, extreme weakness, tiredness, desire to go to sleep, coma, lowered blood pressure, uncontrolled muscle spasms, agitation, restlessness, convulsions, fever, dry mouth, and abnormal heart rhythms. The patient should be taken to a hospital emergency room immediately. ALWAYS bring the medicine bottle.

Generic Name

Hydralazine Hydrochloride

Brand Name

Alazine
Apresoline

(Also available in generic form)

Type of Drug

Antihypertensive.

Prescribed for

Aortic insufficiency, congestive heart failure, essential hypertension (high blood pressure), heart valve replacement.

General Information

Although the mechanism of action is not completely understood, it is felt that Hydralazine Hydrochloride lowers blood pressure by enlarging the blood vessels throughout the body.

Cautions and Warnings

Long-term administration of large doses of Hydralazine Hydrochloride may produce an arthritislike syndrome in some people, although symptoms of this problem usually disappear when the drug is discontinued. Fever, chest pain, not feeling well, or other unexplained symptoms should be reported to your doctor.

This drug may cause birth defects or interfere with your baby's development. Check with your doctor before taking it if you are, or might be, pregnant.

Possible Side Effects

Common: headache, loss of appetite, nausea, vomiting, diarrhea, rapid heartbeat, chest pain.

Possible Adverse Drug Effects

Most frequent: stuffy nose, flushing, tearing in the eyes, itching and redness of the eyes, numbness and tingling of the hands and feet, dizziness, tremors, muscle cramps, depression, disorientation, anxiety. Less frequent: itching, rash, fever, chills, (occasional) hepatitis, constipation, difficulty in urination, adverse effects on the normal composition of the blood.

Drug Interactions

Hydralazine Hydrochloride should be used with caution by patients who are taking MAO inhibitors.

Food Interactions

Hydralazine Hydrochloride may antagonize Vitamin B_6, pyridoxine, which can result in peripheral neuropathy including tremors, tingling and numbness of the fingers, toes, or other extremities. If these occur, your doctor may consider pyridoxine supplementation.

Usual Dose

Tailored to your needs, like other antihypertensive drugs. Most people begin with 40 milligrams per day for the first few days, then increase to 100 milligrams per day for the rest of the first week. Dose increases until the maximum effect is seen.

Overdosage

If symptoms of extreme lowering of blood pressure, rapid heartbeat, headache, generalized skin flushing, chest pains, and poor heart rhythms appear, contact your doctor immediately.

Special Information

Take this medicine exactly as prescribed.

Do not self-medicate with over-the-counter cough, cold, or allergy remedies whose stimulant ingredients will increase blood pressure.

This drug should not be used if you are pregnant unless it is very strictly monitored by your doctor.

Generic Name

Hydrochlorothiazide

Brand Names

Aquazide	Hydromal
Chlorzide	Hydro-Z
Diaqua	Mictrin
Diu-Scrip	Oretic
Esidrix	SK Hydrochlorothiazide
Hydro-Chlor	Thianal
HydroDiuril	Thiuretic
Hydro-t	Zide

(Also available in generic form)

Type of Drug

Diuretic.

Prescribed for

Congestive heart failure, cirrhosis of the liver, kidney malfunction, high blood pressure, and other conditions where it is necessary to rid the body of excess fluid.

General Information

This drug is a member of the class known as thiazide diuretics. Thiazides act on the kidneys to stimulate the production of large amounts of urine. They also cause you to lose bicarbonate, chloride, and potassium ions from the body. They are used as part of the treatment of any disease where it is desirable to eliminate large quantities of body water. These diseases include heart failure, some kidney diseases, and liver disease.

Cautions and Warnings

Do not take Hydrochlorothiazide if you are allergic or sensitive to this drug, similar drugs of this group, or sulfa drugs. If you have a history of allergy or bronchial asthma, you may also have a sensitivity or allergy to Hydrochlorothiazide.

Although this drug has been used to treat specific conditions in pregnancy, unsupervised use by pregnant patients should be avoided. Hydrochlorothiazide will cross the placenta and can cause side effects in the newborn infant, such as jaundice, blood problems and low potassium. Birth defects have not been seen in animal studies. Hydrochlorothiazide passes into breast milk. Nursing mothers should use an alternate feeding method.

Possible Side Effects

Hydrochlorothiazide will cause a lowering of potassium in the body. Signs of low potassium are dryness of the mouth, thirst, weakness, lethargy, drowsiness, restlessness, muscle pains or cramps, muscular tiredness, low blood pressure, decreased frequency of urination and decreased amount of urine produced, abnormal heart rate, stomach upset including nausea and vomiting.

To treat this, potassium supplements are given in the form of tablets, liquids, or powders, or by increased consumption of foods such as bananas, citrus fruits, melons, and tomatoes.

Possible Adverse Drug Effects

Loss of appetite, stomach upset, nausea, vomiting, cramping, diarrhea, constipation, dizziness, headache, tingling of the toes and fingers, restlessness, changes in blood composition, sensitivity to sunlight, rash, itching, fever, difficulty in breathing, allergic reactions, dizziness when rising quickly from a sitting or lying position, muscle spasms, weakness, blurred vision.

Drug Interactions

Hydrochlorothiazide will increase (potentiate) the action of other blood-pressure-lowering drugs. This is beneficial, and is frequently used to help lower blood pressure in patients with hypertension.

The possibility of developing imbalances in body fluids (electrolytes) is increased if you take medications such as Digitalis and adrenal corticosteroids while you take Hydrochlorothiazide.

If you are taking an oral antidiabetic drug and begin taking Hydrochlorothiazide, the antidiabetic dose may have to be altered.

Lithium Carbonate taken with Hydrochlorothiazide should be monitored carefully by a doctor as there may be an increased risk of Lithium toxicity.

If you are taking Hydrochlorothiazide for the treatment of high blood pressure or congestive heart failure, avoid over-the-counter medicines for the treatment of coughs, colds, and allergies: such medicines may contain stimulants. If you are unsure about them, ask your pharmacist.

Usual Dose

Adult: 25 to 200 milligrams per day, depending on condition treated. Maintenance dose, 25 to 100 milligrams per day; some patients may require up to 200 milligrams per day. It is recommended that you take this drug early in the morning, thus avoiding the possibility of your sleep being disturbed by the need to urinate.

Child: 1 milligram per pound of body weight per day in 2 doses.

Infant (under age 6 months): 1.5 milligrams per pound per day in 2 doses.

The dose, individualized to your response, must be altered until maximum therapeutic response at minimum effective dose is reached.

Overdosage

Symptoms are large amount of urination, fatigue, and coma. The patient should be taken to a hospital emergency room immediately. ALWAYS bring the medicine bottle.

Brand Name

Hydropres

Other Brand Names

Hydro-Plus
Hydro-Serp
Hydroserpine

Hydrosine
Hydrotensin
Mallopress

(Also available in generic form)

Ingredients

Hydrochlorothiazide
Reserpine

Type of Drug

Antihypertensive.

Prescribed for

High blood pressure.

General Information

Hydropres is a good example of a drug taking advantage of a drug interaction. Each of the drug ingredients works by different mechanisms to lower your blood pressure. The Hydrochlorothiazide relaxes the muscles in your veins and arteries and also helps reduce the volume of blood flowing through those blood vessels. Reserpine works on the nervous system to reduce the efficiency of nerve transmissions which are contributing to the increased pressure. These drugs complement each other so that their combined effect is better than the effect of either one alone.

It is essential that you take your medicine exactly as prescribed for maximum benefit.

An ingredient in this drug may cause excessive loss of potassium, which may lead to a condition called hypokalemia. Warning signs are dryness of mouth, excessive thirst, weakness, drowsiness, restlessness, muscle pains or cramps, muscular fatigue, lack of urination, abnormal heart rhythms, and upset stomach. If warning signs occur, call your doctor.

This drug should be stopped at the first sign of despondency, early morning insomnia, loss of appetite, or sexual impotence. Drug-induced depression may persist for several months after the drug has been discontinued; it has been known to be severe enough to result in suicide attempts. This drug should be used with care by women of childbearing age.

Cautions and Warnings

Do not take this drug if you have a history of mental depression, active peptic ulcer, or ulcerative colitis, or if you are sensitive or allergic to either of its ingredients, to similar drugs of the Hydrochlorothiazide group, or to sulfa drugs. If you have a history of allergy or bronchial asthma, you may also have a sensitivity or allergy to the Hydrochlorothiazide ingredient.

Although the Hydrochlorothiazide ingredient has been used to treat specific conditions in pregnancy, unsupervised use by pregnant women should be avoided; the drug will cross the placenta and pass into the unborn child, possibly causing problems such as jaundice and low potassium. The Hydrochlorothiazide ingredient will pass into breast milk of nursing mothers, who should consider alternate feeding methods.

Possible Side Effects

Loss of appetite, stomach irritation, nausea, vomiting, cramps, diarrhea, constipation, dizziness, headache, tingling in the arms and legs, restlessness, chest pains, abnormal heart rhythms, drowsiness, depression, nervousness, anxiety, nightmares, glaucoma, blood disorders, rash, itching, fever, difficulty in breathing, muscle spasms, gout, weakness, high blood sugar, sugar in urine, blurred vision, stuffy nose, dryness of the mouth. Occasional: impotence or decreased sex drive.

Drug Interactions

Interaction with Digitalis or Quinidine may cause abnormal heart rhythms.

Interaction with drugs containing Lithium may lead to toxic effects of Lithium.

Avoid over-the-counter cough, cold, or allergy remedies containing stimulant drugs which may raise your blood pressure.

Food Interactions

You may need potassium from some outside source. This may be done by either taking a potassium supplement or by eating foods such as bananas, citrus fruits, melons, and tomatoes, which have high concentrations of potassium.

Usual Dose

Must be individualized to patient's response.

Generic Name

Hydroxyzine Hydrochloride

Brand Names

Anxanil	Hydroxyzine Pamoate
Atarax	Hy-Pam
Atozine	Vamate
Durrax	Vistaril

(Also available in generic form)

Type of Drug

Antihistamine with antinausea and antianxiety properties.

Prescribed for

Nausea and vomiting; the management of emotional stress such as anxiety, tension, agitation or itching caused by allergies.

General Information

Hydroxyzine Hydrochloride may be of value in relieving temporary anxiety such as stress of dental or other minor surgical procedures, acute emotional problems, and the management of anxiety associated with stomach and digestive disorders, skin problems, and behavior difficulties in children. This drug has also been used in the treatment of alcoholism.

Cautions and Warnings

Hydroxyzine Hydrochloride should not be used if you know you are sensitive or allergic to this drug.

Hydroxyzine Hydrochloride is not recommended during the early months of pregnancy.

This drug may cause birth defects or interfere with your baby's development. Check with your doctor before taking it if you are, or might be, pregnant.

Possible Side Effects

The primary side effect of Hydroxyzine Hydrochloride is drowsiness, but this disappears in a few days or when the dose is reduced. At higher doses, you may experience dry mouth and occasional tremors or convulsions.

Drug Interactions

Hydroxyzine Hydrochloride has a depressive effect on the nervous system, producing drowsiness and sleepiness. It should not be used with alcohol, sedatives, tranquilizers, antihistamines, or other depressants.

Usual Dose

Adult: 25 to 100 milligrams 3 to 4 times per day.

Child (age 6 and over): 5 to 25 milligrams 3 to 4 times per day.

Child (under age 6): 5 to 10 milligrams 3 to 4 times per day.

Special Information

Be aware of the depressive effect of Hydroxyzine Hydrochloride: be careful when driving or operating heavy or dangerous machinery.

Generic Name

Ibuprofen

Brand Names

Advil	Nuprin
Motrin	Rufen

(Also available in generic form)

Type of Drug

Nonsteroid anti-inflammatory.

Prescribed for

Relief of pain and inflammation of joints and muscles; arthritis, mild to moderate pain of menstrual cramps, dental surgery and extractions, and athletic injuries such as sprains and strains.

General Information

Ibuprofen is one of several nonsteroid anti-inflammatory drugs used to reduce inflammation, relieve pain, or reduce fever. All nonsteroid anti-inflammatory drugs share the same side effects and may be used by patients who cannot tolerate Aspirin. Choice of one of these drugs over another depends on disease response, side effects seen in a particular patient, convenience of times to be taken, and cost. Different drugs or different doses of the same drug may be tried until the greatest effectiveness is seen with the fewest side effects.

In 1984 a reduced strength, 200 milligrams of Ibuprofen, became available without a prescription (Advil or Nuprin). These products are intended for the relief of mild to moderate pain and fever reduction, much the same way Aspirin would be used.

Cautions and Warnings

Do not take Ibuprofen if you are allergic or sensitive to this drug, Aspirin, or other nonsteroid anti-inflammatory drugs. Ibuprofen may cause stomach ulcers. This drug should not be used by patients with severe kidney disease.

This drug may cause birth defects or interfere with your

baby's development. Check with your doctor before taking it if you are, or might be, pregnant.

Ibuprofen may also make labor longer. This drug should not be taken by nursing mothers.

Possible Side Effects

Stomach upset, blurred vision, darkening of stool, changes in color vision, rash, weight gain, retention of fluids.

Possible Adverse Drug Effects

Most frequent: stomach upset, dizziness, headache, drowsiness, ringing in the ears. Others: heartburn, nausea, vomiting, bloating, gas in the stomach, stomach pain, diarrhea, constipation, dark stool, nervousness, insomnia, depression, confusion, tremor, loss of appetite, fatigue, itching, rash, double vision, abnormal heart rhythm, anemia or other changes in the composition of the blood, changes in liver function, loss of hair, tingling in the hands and feet, fever, breast enlargement, lowered blood sugar, effects on the kidneys. If symptoms appear, stop taking the medicine and see your doctor immediately.

Drug Interactions

Ibuprofen increases the action of Phenytoin, sulfa drugs, drugs used to control diabetes, and drugs used to thin the blood. If you are taking any of these medicines, be sure to discuss it with your doctor, who will probably change the dose of the other drug.

An adjustment in the dose of Ibuprofen may be needed if you take Phenobarbital.

Food Interactions

Take with meals to reduce stomach upset.

Usual Dose

900 to 1600 or even 2400 milligrams per day.

Generic Name

Imipramine

Brand Names

Janimine
SK-Pramine
Tipramine

Tofranil
Tofranil-PM (long-acting
dosage form)

(Also available in generic form)

Type of Drug

Antidepressant.

Prescribed for

Depression with or without symptoms of anxiety.

General Information

Imipramine and other members of this group are effective in treating symptoms of depression. They can elevate your mood, increase physical activity and mental alertness, improve appetite and sleep patterns. These drugs are mild sedatives and therefore useful in treating mild forms of depression associated with anxiety. You should not expect instant results with this medicine: benefits are usually seen after 1 to 4 weeks. If symptoms are not affected after 6 to 8 weeks, contact your doctor. Occasionally this drug and other members of the group of drugs have been used in treating nighttime bed-wetting in the young child, but they do not produce long-lasting relief, and therapy with one of them for nighttime bed-wetting is of questionable value.

Cautions and Warnings

Do not take Imipramine if you are allergic or sensitive to this or other members of this class of drug: Doxepin, Nortriptyline, Amitriptyline, Desipramine, and Protriptyline. The drugs should not be used if you are recovering from a heart attack. Imipramine may be taken with caution if you have a history of epilepsy or other convulsive disorders, difficulty in urination, glaucoma, heart disease, or thyroid disease. Imipramine can interfere with your ability to perform tasks which require concentration, such as driving or operating machinery. Do not stop taking this medicine without first discussing it with your doctor, since stopping may cause you to become nauseated, weak, and headachy.

This drug may cause birth defects or interfere with your baby's development. Check with your doctor before taking it if you are, or might be, pregnant.

Imipramine passes into breast milk. Nursing mothers should consider alternative feeding methods.

Possible Side Effects

Changes in blood pressure (both high and low), abnormal heart rates, heart attack, confusion, especially in elderly patients, hallucinations, disorientation, delusions, anxiety, restlessness, excitement, numbness and tingling in the extremities, lack of coordination, muscle spasms or tremors, seizures and/or convulsions, dry mouth, blurred vision, constipation, inability to urinate, rash, itching, sensitivity to bright light or sunlight, retention of fluids, fever, allergy, changes in composition of blood, nausea, vomiting, loss of appetite, stomach upset, diarrhea, enlargement of the breasts in males and females, increased or decreased sex drive, increased or decreased blood sugar.

Possible Adverse Drug Effects

Infrequent: agitation, inability to sleep, nightmares, feeling of panic, peculiar taste in the mouth, stomach cramps, black coloration of the tongue, yellowing eyes and/or skin, changes in liver function, increased or decreased weight, perspiration, flushing, frequent urination, drowsiness, dizziness, weakness, headache, loss of hair, nausea, not feeling well.

Drug Interactions

Interaction with Monoamine oxidase (MAO) inhibitors can cause high fevers, convulsions, and occasionally death. Don't take MAO inhibitors until at least 2 weeks after Imipramine has been discontinued.

Imipramine interacts with Guanethidine and Clonidine, drugs used to treat high blood pressure: if your doctor prescribes Imipramine and you are taking medicine for high blood pressure, be sure to discuss this with him.

Imipramine increases the effects of barbiturates, tranquilizers, other depressive drugs, and alcohol. Don't drink alcoholic beverages if you take this medicine.

Taking Imipramine and thyroid medicine will enhance the effects of the thyroid medicine. The combination can cause abnormal heart rhythms. The combination of Imipramine and Reserpine may cause overstimulation.

Large doses of Vitamin C (Acsorbic Acid), oral contraceptives, or smoking can reduce the effect of Imipramine. Drugs such as Bicarbonate of Soda, Acetazolamide, Quinidine, or Procainamide will increase the effect of Imipramine. Ritalin and phenothiazine drugs such as Thorazine and Compazine block the metabolism of Imipramine, causing it to stay in the body longer. This can cause possible overdose.

The combination of Imipramine with large doses of the sleeping pill Ethchlorvynol has caused patients to experience passing delirium.

Usual Dose

Adult: initial dose, about 75 milligrams per day in divided doses; then increased or decreased as judged necessary by your doctor. The individualized dose may be less than 75 or up to 200 milligrams. Long-term patients being treated for depression may be given extended-acting medicine daily at bedtime or several times per day.

Adolescent or elderly: initial dose, 30 or 40 milligrams per day. These patients require less of the drug because of increased sensitivity. Maintenance dose is usually less than 100 milligrams per day.

Child: dose for nighttime bed-wetting is 25 milligrams per day (age 6 and over), an hour before bedtime. If relief of bed-wetting does not occur within 1 week, the dose is increased to a daily 50 to 75 milligrams, depending on age; often in midafternoon and at bedtime. (A dose greater than 75 milligrams will increase side effects without increasing effectiveness.) The medication should be gradually tapered off; this may reduce the probability that the bed-wetting will return.

Overdosage

Symptoms are confusion, inability to concentrate, hallucinations, drowsiness, lowered body temperature, abnormal heart rate, heart failure, large pupils of the eyes, convulsions, severely lowered blood pressure, stupor, and coma (as well as agitation, stiffening of body muscles, vomiting, and high fever). The patient should be taken to a hospital emergency room immediately. ALWAYS bring the medicine bottle.

Generic Name

Indapamide

Brand Name

Lozol

Type of Drug

Diuretic.

Prescribed for

Congestive heart failure, cirrhosis of the liver, high blood pressure, and other conditions where it is necessary to rid the body of excess fluids.

General Information

This diuretic is most similar to the thiazide diuretics in its action and effects on the body. Thiazides work on the kidneys to promote the release of sodium from the body, carrying water with it. They also cause you to lose potassium ions, chloride, and bicarbonate. There are no major differences between Indapamide and other thiazide diuretics.

Cautions and Warnings

Do not take Indapamide if you are allergic or sensitive to it or to any other thiazide drug or any sulfa drug. If you have a history of allergy or bronchial asthma, you may also have a sensitivity or allergy to Indapamide. Do not take this drug if you have kidney or liver disease.

This drug should not be taken by pregnant women or women who may become pregnant whie using it since it will pass into the blood system of the fetus. In those situations where it is deemed essential, the potential risk of the drug must be carefully weighed against any benefit it might produce. Thiazide diuretics are known to pass into breast milk. Nursing mothers should either not take the drug or change the feeding method.

Possible Side Effects

Loss of body potassium, leading to dry mouth, thirst, weakness, drowsiness, restlessness, muscle pains, cramps, or tiredness, low blood pressure, decreased frequency of urination, abnormal heart rhythm, and upset stomach. Other side effects are loss of appetite, nausea, vomiting, stomach bloating or cramps, diarrhea, constipation, yellowing of the skin or whites of the eyes, pancreas inflammation, liver inflammation (hepatitis), frequent urination (especially at night), headache, dizziness, fatigue, loss of energy, tiredness, a feeling of ill health, numbness in the hands or feet, nervousness, tension, anxiety, irritability, and agitation.

Possible Adverse Drug Effects

Kidney inflammation, impotence, reduced sex drive, light-headedness, drowsiness, fainting, difficulty sleeping, depression, tingling in the hands or feet, blurred vision, reduced levels of white blood cells and platelets, dizziness when rising quickly from a sitting or lying position, heart palpitations, chest pain, gout attacks, chills, stuffy nose, facial flushing, and weight loss.

Drug Interactions

Indapamide increases the effects of other blood-pressure-lowering drugs. This interaction is beneficial and often used to help treat people with high blood pressure.

The chances of losing body potassium are increased if you take Indapamide with Digoxin or with a corticosteroid anti-inflammatory drug. If you are taking medicine to treat diabetes and begin taking Indapamide, the dose of your diabetes medicine may have to be adjusted.

Indapamide will increase the effects of Lithium and the chances of developing Lithium toxicity by preventing it from passing out of your body.

People taking Indapamide for high blood pressure or heart failure should take care to avoid nonprescription medicines that might aggravate those conditions, such as decongestants, cold and allergy treatments, and diet pills, all of which may contain stimulants. If you are unsure about which medicine to choose, ask your pharmacist.

Dizziness when rising from a sitting or lying position may be worsened by taking Indapamide with alcoholic beverages, barbiturate-type sleeping pills, or narcotic pain relievers.

The effects of Indapamide may be counteracted by Indomethacin because of its effect on the kidneys. Colestipol Hydrochloride or Cholestyramine, taken at the same time as Indapamide, will reduce the drug's effect by preventing it from being absorbed into the bloodstream.

Taking more than one diuretic drug at a time can result in an excessive and prolonged diuretic effect. This is especially true when a thiazide diuretic is combined with a "loop" diuretic such as Bumetanide, Ethacrynic Acid, or Furosemide.

Taking Indapamide and other thiazide-type diuretics with calcium or Vitamin D could result in excessive levels of calcium in the blood.

Sulfa drugs may increase the effects of Indapamide by increasing the amount of diuretic drug in the bloodstream.

Indapamide may increase the effect of Quinidine, taken for abnormal heart rhythms, by interfering with its release from the body via the kidneys.

Food Interactions

Indapamide may cause loss of body potassium (hypokalemia), a complication that can be avoided by adding foods high in potassium to your diet. Some potassium-rich foods are tomatoes, citrus fruits, melons, and bananas. Hypokalemia can also be prevented by taking a potassium supplement in pill, powder, or liquid form. Indapamide may be taken with food or meals if it upsets your stomach.

Usual Dose

2.5 to 5 milligrams per day.

Overdosage

The primary symptom of overdose is potassium deficiency and dehydration: confusion, dizziness, muscle weakness, upset stomach, excessive thirst, loss of appetite, lethargy (rare), drowsiness, restlessness (rare), tingling in the hands or feet, rapid heartbeat, nausea, and vomiting. Patients taking an overdose of this drug must be made to vomit with Syrup of Ipecac (available at any pharmacy) to remove any remaining drug from the stomach. Call your doctor or a Poison Control Center before doing this. If you must go to a hospital emergency room, ALWAYS bring the medicine bottle. If overdose symptoms have developed or more than 1 hour has passed since the overdose was taken, do not make the victim vomit, just go to an emergency room.

Special Information

Always take your daily dose of Indapamide by 10:00 A.M. Taking it later in the day will increase the chances that you will be kept awake at night by the need to urinate frequently.

Call your doctor if muscle weakness, cramps, nausea, dizziness, or other severe side effects develop.

Brand Name

Inderide

Ingredients

Hydrochlorothiazide
Propranolol

Type of Drug

Antihypertensive.

Prescribed for

High blood pressure.

General Information

Inderide is a combination of two proven antihypertensive drugs. One of these works by directly affecting the dilation of the blood vessels; the other works by affecting the nerves which control the dilating of the blood vessels. The more dilated (open) these vessels are, the lower the blood pressure. This combination is good so long as both ingredients are present in the right amounts. If you need more or less of one ingredient than the other, you must take the ingredients as separate pills. Often, doctors are able to lower your blood pressure most effectively by manipulating the doses of one drug or the other.

Cautions and Warnings

Do not take this drug if you are allergic to either of the active ingredients or to sulfa drugs. If you have a history of heart failure, asthma, or upper respiratory disease, Inderide may aggravate the situation.

This drug may cause birth defects or interfere with your baby's development. Check with your doctor before taking it if you are, or might be, pregnant.

If this drug is considered essential for a nursing mother, she should change the method of feeding her infant.

Possible Side Effects

May decrease the heart rate, aggravate heart failure or some other heart diseases, cause a tingling in the hands or feet, light-headedness, depression, sleeplessness, weakness, tiredness, feeling of not caring, hallucinations, visual disturbances, disorientation, loss of short-term memory, nausea, vomiting, upset stomach, cramps, diarrhea, constipation, allergic reactions including: sore throat, rash, and fever. Inderide can also cause adverse effects on the blood.

Inderide can cause a lowering of body potassium (hypokalemia). The signs of this include dryness of the mouth, weakness, thirst, lethargy, drowsiness, restlessness, muscle pains or cramps, muscle tiredness, low blood pressure, decreased frequency of urination. To treat this, potassium supplements are given as tablets, liquids, or powders.

Possible Adverse Drug Effects

Loss of appetite, dizziness, headache, increased sensitivity to the sun, dizziness when rising quickly from a sitting or lying position, muscle spasms and loss of hearing (it comes back after the drug has been stopped).

Drug Interactions

Inderide may interact with Reserpine and similar drugs to

cause very low blood pressure, slowed heart rate, and dizziness.

Inderide may cause a need for the alteration of your daily dose of oral antidiabetic drug.

Inderide should not be taken with Lithium drugs since there is an increased possibility of Lithium toxicity. This drug may interact with digitalis drugs to cause abnormal heart rhythms. This effect results from potassium loss and may be prevented by taking extra potassium.

Food Interactions

You may increase your natural consumption of potassium by eating more bananas, citrus fruits, melons, or tomatoes.

Usual Dose

4 tablets of either strength per day. The dose of this drug must be tailored to your needs for maximum benefit.

Overdosage

In case of overdosage contact your doctor or Poison Control Center immediately. The patient may have to be taken to a hospital emergency room for treatment. ALWAYS bring the medicine bottle with you.

Special Information

Do not stop taking this medicine unless your doctor tells you to.

If you develop rash, severe muscle pains, or difficulty in breathing, call your doctor.

Avoid any over-the-counter drugs containing stimulants. If you are unsure which ones to avoid, ask your pharmacist.

Generic Name

Indomethacin

Brand Name

Indocin

(Also available in generic form)

Type of Drug

Nonsteroid anti-inflammatory.

Prescribed for

Arthritis and other forms of inflammation of joints and muscles.

General Information

Indomethacin has pain-relieving, fever-lowering, and inflammation-reducing effects, but we do not know exactly how these effects are produced. Part of these actions may be due to Indomethacin's prostaglandin-inhibitory effects. It also can produce serious side effects at high doses. For this reason, the drug should be taken with caution.

Cautions and Warnings

Use Indomethacin with extra caution if you have a history of ulcers, bleeding diseases, or allergic reaction to Aspirin. Indomethicin may cause heart and blood problems in the unborn child. It may also make pregnancy and labor longer. Indomethacin should be avoided by pregnant women, nursing mothers, children under age 14, and patients with nasal polyps. This drug is not a simple pain reliever; it should be used only under the strict supervision of your doctor.

Possible Side Effects

Indomethacin may produce severe stomach upset or other reactions. It has caused ulcers in all portions of the gastrointestinal tract, including the esophagus, stomach, small intestine, and large intestine. For this reason any unusual stomach upset, nausea, vomiting, loss of appetite, gas, gaseous feeling, or feeling of being bloated must be reported immediately to your doctor. Indomethacin may cause blurred vision; this is an important side effect and must be reported to your doctor immediately. If you develop a persistent headache while taking Indomethacin, report this to your doctor immediately and stop taking the drug.

Indomethacin may aggravate preexisting psychiatric disturbances, epilepsy, or Parkinson's disease. It may cause reduction in mental alertness and coordination which can affect you particularly while driving, operating a machine or appliance, or engaging in any activity requiring alertness and concentration.

Possible Adverse Drug Effects

On rare occasions Indomethacin can cause effects on the liver, and anemia or other effects on components of the blood. People who are allergic to the drug can develop reactions including a rapid fall in blood pressure, difficulty in breathing, itching, and rashes. It has also caused ringing in the ears, retention of fluids in the body, elevation of blood pressure, passing of blood in the urine, loss of hair, (occasional) vaginal bleeding, and increased blood sugar.

Drug Interactions

Avoid alcohol, which will aggravate any problem with drowsiness or lack of alertness.

Probenecid (Benemid) increases the amount of Indomethacin in your blood by reducing its elimination from the body. This interaction will reduce the amount of Indomethacin required.

If you are taking an anticoagulant (blood-thinning) drug and start taking Indomethacin, you probably will experience no serious interaction, but your doctor should know that you are taking both drugs so he can monitor the anticoagulant during the first week or two of Indomethacin therapy, in case dosage adjustment may be required.

Since Indomethacin causes stomach upset in many patients and can be a source of ulcers, it should be taken with food or antacids. Adrenal corticosteroids, Aspirin, or other drugs may aggravate this problem. Space Indomethacin and such drugs at least 2 to 3 hours apart to minimize irritating effects on the stomach.

Usual Dosage

50 to 150 milligrams per day, individualized to patient's needs.

Special Information

If you are allergic to Aspirin, you may be allergic to Indomethacin.

Generic Name

Insulin

Brand Names

Insulin for Injection

Beef Regular Iletin II	Regular Iletin
Humulin R	Regular Insulin
Novolin R	Regular Purified Pork Insulin
Pork Regular Iletin II	Velosulin

Insulin Zinc Suspension

Lente Iletin	Lente Purified Pork Insulin
Lente Iletin II	Novolin L
Lente Insulin	Purified Beef Insulin Zinc

Insulin Zinc Suspension, Extended

Ultralente Iletin
Ultralente Insulin
Ultralente Purified Beef

Insulin Zinc Suspension, Prompt

Semilente Iletin
Semilente Insulin
Semilente Purified Beef

Isophane Insulin Suspension and Insulin Injection

Mixtard

Isophane Insulin Suspension (NPH)

Beef NPH Iletin II	NPH Insulin
Humulin N	NPH Purified Pork
Insulatard NPH	Pork NPH Iletin II
Novolin N	Protaphane
NPH Iletin	

Protamine Zinc Insulin Suspension

Protamine Zinc and Iletin II (Beef)	Protamine Zinc and Iletin (Beef and Pork)
Protamine Zinc and Iletin II (Pork)	

Type of Drug

Antidiabetic.

Prescribed for

Diabetes mellitus that cannot be controlled by dietary restriction. Insulin may also be used in a hospital to treat hyperkalemia (high blood potassium levels).

General Information

Insulin is a complex hormone normally produced by the pancreas. Diabetes develops when we do not make enough Insulin or when the Insulin we do make is not effective in our bodies. At the present, most of the Insulin we use as a drug we get from animals. Insulin derived from pork is closer in chemical structure to our own Insulin than that derived from beef. It causes fewer reactions.

Insulin used for injection is the unmodified material derived from the animal source. It starts to work quickly, and lasts only 6 to 8 hours. People using only Insulin injection must take several injections per day. Pharmaceutical scientists have been able to add on to the Insulin molecule so as to help extend the time over which the drug can exert its effect. Insulin Zinc Suspension, like Insulin for injection, is considered rapid-acting. It starts to work in 30 to 60 minutes and lasts 12 to 16 hours.

Intermediate-acting Insulin starts working 1 to 1½ hours after injection and continues to work for 24 hours. Isophane Insulin Suspension and Insulin Zinc Suspension are intermediate-acting forms of Insulin. Long-acting Insulin begins working 4 to 8 hours after injection and its effect lasts for 36 hours or more. Protamine Zinc Insulin Suspension and Insulin Zinc Suspension, Extended, are long-acting types of Insulin.

Other factors have a definite influence on patients' response to Insulin: diet, amount of regular exercise, and other medicines being used.

Because Insulin is derived from a natural source, there are a number of normal contaminants in the products. In recent years, processes have been developed to remove many of these contaminants. The first process resulted in single-peak Insulin, with only one high point of drug effect, making the action of the drug more predictable and therefore safer.

Today, all Insulin sold in the United States is single-peak. The second refinement resulted in purified Insulin. Several purified Insulin products are available. The advantage of purified Insulin over single-peak is that it produces fewer reactions at the injection site.

Recent developments in recombinant DNA research have led to the production of human Insulin. This product has the potential of fewer allergic reactions as compared to older Insulins manufactured from pork and/or beef sources.

Cautions and Warnings

Patients taking Insulin *must* also follow the diet that has been prescribed. Be sure to take exactly the dose prescribed. Too much Insulin will cause lowering of the blood sugar and too little will not control the diabetes. Avoid alcoholic beverages.

This drug has been found to be safe for use during pregnancy. Remember, you should check with your doctor before taking any drug if you are pregnant. Pregnant diabetic women must exactly follow their doctor's directions for Insulin use.

Possible Side Effects

Allergic reactions.

Drug Interactions

Insulin may affect blood potassium levels and can therefore affect digitalis drugs. Patients on Insulin who begin taking oral contraceptive pills, adrenal corticosteroids (by mouth), Epinephrine, or thyroid hormones may have an increased need for Insulin. Thiazide diuretic drugs can raise blood-sugar levels and cause a need for more Insulin. The blood-sugar-lowering effects of Insulin can be increased by MAO inhibitor drugs, Phenylbutazone, Sulfinpyrazone, Tetracycline, alcoholic beverages, and anabolic steroid drugs (Oxymetholone, Oxandrolone, Methandrostenolone, Ethylestrenol, Stanozolol, Nandrolone). Patients taking these drugs may require a decrease in their Insulin dosage.

Usual Dose

The dose and kind of Insulin must be individualized to the

patient's need. Insulin is generally injected ½ hour before meals; the longer-acting forms are taken ½ hour before breakfast. Since Insulin can only be given by injection, patients must learn to give themselves their Insulin subcutaneously (under the skin) or have a family member or friend give them their injection. Hospitalized patients may receive Insulin injection directly into a vein.

Special Information

You may develop low blood sugar if you take too much Insulin, work or exercise more strenuously than usual, skip a meal, take Insulin too long before a meal, or vomit before a meal. Signs of low blood sugar may be fatigue, headache, drowsiness, nausea, tremulous feeling, sweating, or nervousness. If you develop any of these signs while taking Insulin, your blood sugar may be too low. The usual treatment for low blood sugar is eating a candy bar or lump of sugar, which diabetics should carry with them at all times. If the signs of low blood sugar do not clear up within 30 minutes, call your doctor. You may need further treatment.

If your Insulin is in suspension form, you must evenly distribute the suspended particles throughout the liquid before taking the dose out. Do this by rotating the vial and turning it over several times. Do not shake the vial too strenuously.

Insulin products are generally stable at room temperatures for about 2 years. They must be kept away from direct sunlight. Most manufacturers, however, still recommend that Insulin be stored in a refrigerator or a cool place whenever possible. Insulin should not be put in a freezer or exposed to very high temperatures; this can affect its stability. Partly used vials of Insulin should be thrown away after several weeks if not used.

Some Insulin products can be mixed. Do it only if so directed by your doctor. Insulin for injection may be mixed with Isophane Insulin Suspension and Protamine Zinc Insulin in any proportion. Insulin Zinc Suspension, Insulin Zinc Suspension (Prompt), and Insulin Zinc Suspension (Extended) may also be mixed in any proportions. Insulin for injection and Insulin Zinc Suspension must be mixed immediately before using.

Generic Name

Isosorbide Dinitrate

Brand Names

Dilatrate-SR
Iso-Bid
Isonate
Isordil
Isordil Sublingual
Isordil Tembids
Isordil Titradose

Isotrate Timecelles
Onset
Sorate
Sorbide T.D.
Sorbitrate
Sorbitrate SA

(Also available in generic form)

Type of Drug

Antianginal agent.

Prescribed for

Relief of heart or chest pain associated with angina pectoris; also, control or prevention of recurrence of chest or heart pain, and in reducing heart work in congestive heart failure and other similar conditions.

General Information

Isosorbide Dinitrate belongs to the class of drugs known as nitrates, which are used to treat pain associated with heart problems. The exact nature of their action is not fully understood. However, they are believed to relax muscles of veins and arteries.

Cautions and Warnings

If you know that you are allergic or sensitive to this drug or other drugs for heart pain such as Nitroglycerin, do not use Isosorbide Dinitrate. Anyone who has a head injury or has recently had a head injury should use this drug with caution.

This drug may cause birth defects or interfere with your baby's development. Check with your doctor before taking it if you are, or might be, pregnant.

Possible Side Effects

Flushing of the skin and headache are common, but should disappear after your body has had an opportunity to get used to the drug. You may experience dizziness and weakness in the process.

There is a possibility of blurred vision and dry mouth; if this happens stop taking the drug and call your physician.

Possible Adverse Drug Effects

Nausea, vomiting, weakness, sweating, rash with itching, redness, possible peeling. If these signs appear, discontinue the medication and consult your physician.

Drug Interactions

If you take Isosorbide Dinitrate, do not self-medicate with over-the-counter cough and cold remedies, since many of them contain ingredients which may aggravate heart disease.

Interaction with large amounts of whiskey, wine, or beer can cause rapid lowering of blood pressure resulting in weakness, dizziness, and fainting.

Usual Dose

Average daily dose, 10 to 20 milligrams 4 times per day. The drug may be given in doses from 5 milligrams to 40 milligrams 4 times per day.

Special Information

Take Isosorbide Dinitrate on an empty stomach unless you get a headache which cannot be controlled by the usual means, when the medication can be taken with meals. If you take this drug sublingually (under the tongue) be sure the tablet is fully dissolved before swallowing the drug.

Generic Name

Isotretinoin

Brand Name

Accutane

Type of Drug

Antiacne.

Prescribed for

Severe cystic acne that has not responded to other treatments, including medicines applied to the skin and antibiotics.

Isotretinoin has been used experimentally to treat a variety of other skin disorders involving the process of keratinization, or hardening of skin cells, and a condition known as mycosis fungoides that begins in the skin and can progress to a form of leukemia. Isotretinoin treatment is usually successful for these conditions, but relatively high doses are usually needed.

General Information

Isotretinoin is one of the first specialized products of vitamin research to be released for prescription by doctors. Researchers have long known that several vitamins, including A and D, have special properties that make them attractive treatments for specific conditions. However, the vitamins themselves are not appropriate treatments for these conditions because of the side effects that would develop if you took the quantities needed to produce the desired effects.

It is not known exactly how Isotretinoin works in cases of severe cystic acne. But its effect is to reduce the amount of sebum (the oily substance that serves as the skin's natural lubricant) in the skin, shrink the skin glands that produce sebum, and inhibit the process of keratinization, in which skin cells become hardened and block the flow of sebum onto the skin. Keratinization is key to the problem of severe acne because it leads to the buildup of sebum within skin follicles and causes the formation of closed comedos (whiteheads). Sebum production may be permanently reduced after Isotretinoin treatment, but no one knows why it has this effect.

Cautions and Warnings

This product should never be used by women who are pregnant or who might become pregnant while using it because it is known to cause harm to the developing baby when taken during pregnancy. Specifically, Isotretinoin can cause abnormalities of the head, brain, eye, ear, and hearing mechanisms. Several cases of spontaneous abortion have been linked to Isotretinoin.

Before taking this drug, women of childbearing age or potential should take a simple urinary pregnancy test to confirm that they are not pregnant. Also, you must be absolutely certain that effective birth control is used for 1 month before and during, and 1 month after Isotretinoin treatment. Accidental pregnancy during Isotretinoin therapy should be considered possible grounds for a therapeutic abortion. *Discuss this with your doctor immediately*. Nursing mothers should not take Isotretinoin because of the possibility that it will affect the nursing infant. It is not known if Isotretinoin passes into breast milk.

People allergic or sensitive to Vitamin A, any Vitamin A product, or to Paraben preservatives used in Accutane should not use Isotretinoin.

Isotretinoin has been associated with several cases of increased fluid pressure inside the head. The symptoms of this condition, known as pseudotumor cerebri, are severe headaches, nausea, vomiting, and visual disturbances. Isotretinoin may cause temporary opaque spots on the cornea of your eye, causing visual disturbances. These generally go away by themselves within 2 months after the drug has been stopped. Several cases of severe bowel inflammation, indicated by abdominal discomfort and pain, severe diarrhea, or bleeding from the rectum, have developed in people taking Isotretinoin.

Possible Side Effects

The frequency of side effects increases with your daily dose, the most severe effects occurring at daily doses above 0.45 milligrams per pound of body weight per day. The most common side effects are dry, chapped, and inflamed lips, dry mouth, dry nose, nosebleeds, eye irritation and conjunctivitis (red-eye), dry and flaky skin, rash, itching, peeling of skin from the face, palms of the hands, and soles of the feet, unusual sensitivity to sunlight, temporary skin discoloration, dry mucous membranes of the mouth and nose, brittle nails, inflammation of the nailbed or bone under the nail of either the hands or feet, temporary thinning of the hair, nausea, vomiting, and abdominal pains, tiredness, lethargy, sleeplessness, headache, tingling in the hands or feet, dizziness, protein, blood, and white blood cells in the urine, blurred vision, urinary difficulty, bone and joint aches and pains, muscle pains, and stiffness.

Isotretinoin causes extreme elevations of blood triglycerides and milder elevations of other blood fats, including cholesterol. It also can cause an increased blood-sugar and uric-acid level and an increase in liver-function-test values.

Possible Adverse Drug Effects

Crusting over wounds caused by an exaggerated healing response stimulated by the drug, hair problems other than thinning, loss of appetite, upset stomach or intestinal discomfort, severe bowel inflammation, stomach or intestinal bleeding, weight loss, visual disturbances, pseudotumor cerebri (see Cautions and Warnings for symptoms), mild bleeding or easy bruising, fluid retention, infections of the lungs or respiratory system; several people taking Isotretinoin have developed widespread herpes simplex infections.

Drug Interactions

Supplemental Vitamin A increases Isotretinoin side effects and must be avoided while you are taking this medicine.

Alcohol should be avoided while you are taking Isotretinoin since the combination can cause severe elevations of blood triglyceride levels.

People taking Isotretinoin who have developed pseudotumor cerebri have usually been taking a Tetracycline antibiotic. Although the link has not been definitely established, you should avoid Tetracycline antibiotics while taking this medicine.

Food Interactions

Isotretinoin should be taken with food or meals.

Avoid eating beef liver, calf's liver, or chicken liver while taking Isotretinoin. Liver contains extremely large amounts of Vitamin A. Foods with moderate amounts of Vitamin A that you need not avoid but should limit your intake of are apricots, broccoli, cantaloupe, carrots, endive, persimmon, pumpkin, spinach, and winter squash.

Usual Dose

0.45 to 0.9 milligrams per pound of body weight per day, in 2 divided doses for 15 to 20 weeks. Lower doses may be effective, but relapses are more common. Since Isotretinoin, like Vitamin A, dissolves in body fat, people weighing more than 155 pounds may need doses at the high end of the usual range.

If the total cyst count drops by 70 percent before 15 to 20 weeks, the drug may be stopped. Treatment should stop for 2 months after the 15-to-20 week treatment. A second course of treatment may be given if the acne doesn't clear up.

Overdosage

Isotretinoin overdose is likely to cause nausea, vomiting, lethargy, and other frequent side effects. Patients taking an overdose of this drug must be made to vomit with Syrup of Ipecac (available at any pharmacy) to remove any remaining drug from the stomach. Call your doctor or a Poison Control Center before doing this. If you must go to a hospital emergency room, ALWAYS bring the medicine bottle.

Special Information

You may become unusually sensitive to sunlight while taking this drug. Use a sunscreen and wear protective clothing until your doctor can determine if you are likely to develop this effect.

Be sure your doctor knows if you are pregnant or plan to become pregnant while taking Isotretinoin, if you are breast-feeding a baby, if you are a diabetic, if you are taking a Vitamin A supplement (as a multivitamin or Vitamin A alone), or if you or any family member has a history of high blood triglyceride levels.

Call your doctor if any severe side effects develop. Abdominal pain, bleeding from the rectum, severe diarrhea, headache, nausea and vomiting, visual difficulty of any kind, severe muscle or bone and joint aches or pains, and unusual sensitivity to sunlight or to ultraviolet light are especially important.

Sometimes, acne actually gets a little worse when Isotretinoin treatment begins, but subsequently it starts to improve. Don't be alarmed if this happens, but be sure to tell your doctor, who will want to know.

Generic Name

Isoxsuprine Hydrochloride

Brand Name

Vasodilan
Voxsuprine

(Also available in generic form)

Type of Drug

Vasodilator.

Prescribed for

Relief of symptoms arising from chronic organic brain syndrome; specifically, loss of memory and other intellectual functions. Also used to prevent the progress of this disease and at times to help reverse the disease process.

General Information

Isoxsuprine Hydrochloride works by helping to increase the amount of blood supplied to the brain, by acting on the nerves that control muscles in the major blood vessels, which relaxes the muscles and allows more blood to flow to the brain. Many studies have questioned the effectiveness of this drug. However, it continues to be widely used and prescribed.

Cautions and Warnings

This drug may cause birth defects or interfere with your baby's development. Check with your doctor before taking it if you are, or might be, pregnant.

Possible Side Effects

Isoxsuprine Hydrochloride can cause low blood pressure. In this condition blood tends to stay in the arms and legs and less is available to the brain, resulting in light-headedness or dizziness. To avoid this, if you are taking Isoxsuprine Hydrochloride or any other vasodilator do not stand for long periods and be careful not to get out of bed or stand up too quickly.

Possible Adverse Drug Effects

Rapid heartbeat, nausea, vomiting, dizziness, stomach distress, severe rash. If you develop a rash, stop taking the drug and consult your doctor immediately.

Drug Interactions

Alcoholic beverages increase the effect of Isoxsuprine Hydrochloride and can cause dizziness or faintness.

Usual Dose

10 to 20 milligrams 3 to 4 times per day.

Generic Name

Ketoconazole

Brand Name

Nizoral

Type of Drug

Antifungal.

Prescribed for

Thrush and other systemic fungus infections, including candidiasis, histoplasmosis, and blastomycosis. Ketoconazole may also be prescribed for fungus infections of the skin, fingernails, and vagina.

General Information

This medicine is effective against a wide variety of fungus

organisms. It works by disrupting the fungus cell's membrane, ultimately destroying the cell. Ketoconazole is most efficiently absorbed into the bloodstream when mixed with an acid medium. For this reason, the drug should be taken with meals or food, which stimulates the release of stomach acid.

Cautions and Warnings

Ketoconazole has been associated with liver inflammation and damage. At least 1 of every 10,000 people who take the drug will develop this condition. In most cases, the inflammation subsides when the drug is discontinued. Do not take Ketoconazole if you have had an allergic reaction to it. It should not be used to treat fungus infections of the nervous system because only small amounts of the drug will enter that part of the body.

Animals given doses of Ketoconazole larger than the maximum human dose have shown some damage in their developing offspring. This drug should be avoided by pregnant women or women who may become pregnant while using it. In those situations where it is deemed essential, the potential risk of the drug must be carefully weighed against any benefit it might produce. Nursing mothers who must take Ketoconazole should find an alternative method of feeding their infants since the drug probably passes into breast milk.

Possible Side Effects

Nausea, vomiting, upset stomach, abdominal pain or discomfort, itching, swelling of male breasts. Most of these side effects are mild, and only a small number of people (1.5 percent) have to stop taking the drug because of severe side effects.

Possible Adverse Drug Effects

Headache, dizziness, drowsiness or tiredness, fever, chills, unusual sensitivity to bright lights, diarrhea, reduced sperm count, male impotence, and reduced levels of blood platelets.

Drug Interactions

Antacids, histamine H_2 antagonists, and other drugs that

reduce the amount of acid in the stomach will counteract the effects of Ketoconazole by preventing it from being absorbed. This drug requires an acid environment to pass into the blood.

When Ketoconazole is taken together with Rifampin, both drugs lose their effectiveness.

The combination of Isoniazid and Ketoconazole causes a neutralization of the Ketoconazole's effect. These interactions occur even when drug doses are separated by 12 hours.

Food Interactions

Ketoconazole should be taken with food or meals to increase the amount absorbed into the blood. This happens because food stimulates acid release, and Ketoconazole is absorbed much more efficiently when there is acid in the stomach.

Usual Dose

Adult: 200 to 400 milligrams taken once per day. Dosage may continue for several months, depending on the type of infection being treated.

Child (age 2 and up): 1.5 to 3 milligrams per pound of body weight once per day. Children under the age of 2 should not take Ketoconazole.

Overdosage

The most likely effects of Ketoconazole overdose are liver damage and exaggerated versions of the drug's side effects. Victims of Ketoconazole overdose should be immediately given Bicarbonate of Soda or any other antacid to reduce the amount of drug absorbed into the blood. Call your local Poison Control Center for more information. If you take the victim to a hospital emergency room for treatment, ALWAYS bring the prescription bottle.

Special Information

If you must take antacids or other ulcer treatments, separate doses of those medicines from Ketoconazole doses by at least 2 hours. Anything that reduces your stomach-acid levels will reduce the amount of Ketoconazole absorbed into the blood.

Use caution while doing anything that requires intense

concentration, like driving a car, or operating machinery. This drug can cause headaches, dizziness, and drowsiness.

Call your doctor if you develop pains in the stomach or abdomen, severe diarrhea, a high fever, unusual tiredness, loss of appetite, nausea, vomiting, yellow discoloration of the skin or whites of the eyes, pale stools, or dark urine.

Generic Name

Labetalol Hydrochloride

Brand Names

Normodyne
Trandate

Type of Drug

Alpha-beta adrenergic blocking agent.

Prescribed for

High blood pressure.

General Information

This drug, first studied for its effect as a beta blocker, is a unique approach to high-blood-pressure treatment because it selectively blocks both alpha and beta adrenergic impulses. This combination of actions contributes to its ability to reduce your blood pressure. It may be better than other beta-blocking drugs because it rarely affects heart rate. Other drugs can increase or decrease heart rate.

Cautions and Warnings

People with asthma, severe heart failure, reduced heart rate, and heart block should not take Labetalol Hydrochloride.

People with angina who take Labetalol Hydrochloride for high blood pressure should have their dose reduced gradually over a 1-to-2-week period, instead of having it discontinued suddenly, to avoid possible aggravation of the angina.

This drug should be avoided by women who may become pregnant while using it and pregnant and nursing mothers.

In those situations where it is deemed essential, the potential risk of the drug must be carefully weighed against any benefit it might produce. Nursing mothers must observe for any possible drug effect on their infants while taking Labetalol Hydrochloride, since small amounts of the medication will pass into breast milk.

Labetalol Hydrochloride should be used with caution if you have liver disease because your ability to eliminate the drug from your body may be impaired.

Possible Side Effects

Most Labetalol Hydrochloride side effects develop early in the course of treatment and increase with larger doses. Side effects include dizziness, tingling of the scalp, nausea, vomiting, upset stomach, taste distortion, fatigue, sweating, male impotence, urinary difficulty, diarrhea, bile-duct blockage, bronchial spasm, breathing difficulty, muscle weakness, cramps, dry eyes, blurred vision, rash, swelling of the face, and loss of hair.

Possible Adverse Drug Effects

Less frequent adverse effects of Labetalol Hydrochloride include aggravation of lupus erythematosus, a disease of body connective tissue, and stuffy nose. Because this drug is a beta blocker, it has the potential to cause mental depression, confusion and disorientation, loss of short-term memory, emotional instability, colitis, drug allergy (fever, sore throat, breathing difficulty), and reduction in the levels of white blood cells and blood platelets.

Drug Interactions

Labetalol Hydrochloride may prevent normal signs of low blood sugar from appearing and can also interfere with the action of oral antidiabetes drugs.

The combination of Labetalol Hydrochloride and a tricyclic antidepressant drug can cause tremor.

This drug may interfere with the effectiveness of some antiasthma drugs, especially Ephedrine, Isoproterenol, and other beta stimulants.

Cimetidine increases the amount of Labetalol Hydrochloride absorbed into the bloodstream from oral tablets.

Labetalol Hydrochloride may increase the blood-pressure-lowering effect of Nitroglycerin.

Food Interactions

This medicine may be taken with food if it upsets your stomach because it is unaffected by food in the stomach. In fact, food increases the amount of Labetalol Hydrochloride absorbed into your blood.

Usual Dose

The usual starting dose is 100 milligrams taken twice per day. The dosage may be increased gradually to as much as 1200 milligrams twice per day, but the usual maintenance dose is in the range of 200 to 400 milligrams twice daily.

Overdosage

Labetalol Hydrochloride overdose slows your heart rate and causes an excessive drop in blood pressure. The possible consequences of these effects can be treated only in a hospital emergency room. ALWAYS bring the medicine bottle with you.

Special Information

Elderly patients tend to absorb more of this medicine than do younger adults and may require slightly lower doses to achieve the same effect.

This medication is meant to be taken on a continuing basis. Do not stop it unless instructed to do so by your doctor. Weakness, breathing difficulty, or other side effects should be reported to your doctor as soon as possible. Most side effects are not serious, but a small number of people (about 7 in 100) have to switch to another medicine because of drug side effects.

Minor side effects, such as tingling scalp, fatigue, dizziness, and nausea, usually subside without treatment and do not require dosage reduction or switching medicines.

Generic Name

Levodopa (L-Dopa)

Brand Names

Dopar
Larodopa

(Also available in generic form)

Type of Drug

Anti-Parkinsonian.

Prescribed for

Parkinson's disease; relief of pain associated with Shingles (Herpes Zoster).

General Information

Parkinson's disease can develop as a result of changes in the utilization of dopamine in the brain or damage to the central nervous system caused by carbon monoxide poisoning or manganese poisoning. It usually develops in the elderly because of hardening of the arteries. In many cases, the cause of Parkinson's disease is not known. Levodopa works by entering into the brain where it is converted to dopamine, a chemical found in the central nervous system. The new dopamine replaces what is deficient in people with Parkinson's disease. Another drug used to treat Parkinson's disease is Amantadine (Symmetrel). It has been shown to increase the amount of dopamine released in the brain.

Cautions and Warnings

Patients with severe heart or lung disease, asthma, or kidney, liver, or hormone diseases should be cautious about using this drug. Do not take it if you have a history of stomach ulcer. People with a history of psychosis must be treated with extreme care; this drug can cause depression with suicidal tendencies. Levodopa has not been studied in humans; however, studies show problems with the babies' growth in pregnant and nursing animals. Pregnant women should take this drug only if it is absolutely necessary. Women taking this drug must not breast-feed their infants.

High doses of Amantidine (Symmetrel), another drug used to treat Parkinson's disease, have been shown to cause birth defects and harm the unborn child.

Nursing while using Amantidine is not recommended since it can cause skin rashes, vomiting, or urination problems in the baby.

Possible Side Effects

Muscle spasms, inability to control arms, legs, or facial muscles, loss of appetite, nausea, vomiting (with or without stomach pain), dry mouth, difficulty eating, dribbling saliva from the corners of the mouth (due to poor muscle control), tiredness, hand tremors, headache, dizziness, numbness, weakness and a faint feeling, confusion, sleeplessness, grinding of the teeth, nightmares, euphoria, hallucinations, delusions, agitation and anxiousness, feeling of general ill health.

Possible Adverse Drug Effects

Heart irregularities or palpitations, dizziness when standing or arising in the morning, mental changes (depression, with or without suicidal tendencies; paranoia; loss of some intellectual function), difficulty urinating, muscle twitching, burning of the tongue, bitter taste, diarrhea, constipation, unusual breathing patterns, double or blurred vision, hot flashes, weight gain or loss, darkening of the urine or sweat.

Rare adverse effects include stomach bleeding, development of an ulcer, high blood pressure, convulsions, adverse effects on the blood, difficulty controlling the eye muscles, feeling of being stimulated, hiccups, loss of hair, hoarseness, decreasing size of male genitalia, and retention of fluids.

Drug Interactions

The effect of Levodopa is increased when it is used together with an anticholinergic drug (such as Trihexyphenidyl). If one of these drugs is stopped, the change must be gradual to allow for adjustments in the other one. Levodopa can interact with drugs for high blood pressure to cause further lowering of pressure. Dosage adjustments in the high blood pressure medication may be needed. Methyldopa (a drug for high blood pressure) may increase the effects of Levodopa.

The effects of Levodopa may be antagonized by Reserpine, benzodiazepine drugs, phenothiazine-type tranquilizing drugs, Phenytoin, Papaverine, and Vitamin BF.

Patients taking MAO inhibitor drugs should stop taking them 2 weeks before starting to take Levodopa.

Levodopa may increase the effects of stimulants such as amphetamines, Ephedrine, Epinephrine, Isoproterenol, and the triclyclic antidepressant drugs.

Levodopa will affect the blood sugar of diabetic patients. Adjustments in dosages of antidiabetic medicine may be needed.

Food Interactions

Do not take vitamin preparations which contain Vitamin B_6, pyridoxine. Vitamin B_6 will decrease the effectiveness of Levodopa.

This drug can cause upset stomach; each dose should be taken with food.

Usual Dose

0.5 to 8 grams per day. Dosage must be individualized to patient's need.

Overdosage

People taking an overdose of Levodopa must be treated in a hospital emergency room. ALWAYS bring the prescription bottle with you.

Special Information

Be careful while driving or operating any machinery.

Call your doctor *immediately* if any of the following occur: abnormal urine test for sugar (diabetics), uncontrollable movement of the face, eyelids, mouth, tongue, neck, arms, hands, or legs, mood changes, palpitations or irregular heartbeats, difficulty urinating, severe nausea or vomiting.

Generic Name

Levothyroxine Sodium

Brand Names

Levothroid
Synthroid

Synthrox
Syroxine
Thyrolar

(Also available in generic form)

Type of Drug

Thyroid replacement.

Prescribed for

Replacement of thyroid hormone or low output of hormone from the thyroid gland.

General Information

Levothyroxine Sodium is one of several thyroid replacement products available. The major difference between these products is in effectiveness in treating certain phases of thyroid disease.

Cautions and Warnings

If you have hyperthyroid disease or high output of thyroid hormone you should not use Levothyroxine Sodium. Symptoms of hyperthyroid disease include headache, nervousness, sweating, rapid heartbeat, chest pains, and other signs of central nervous system stimulation. If you have heart disease or high blood pressure, thyroid therapy should not be used unless it is clearly indicated and supervised by your physician. If you develop chest pains or other signs of heart disease while you are taking thyroid medication, contact your doctor immediately.

This drug may cause birth defects or interfere with your baby's development. Check with your doctor before taking it if you are, or might be, pregnant.

Possible Side Effects

Most common: palpitations of the heart, rapid heartbeat, abnormal heart rhythms, weight loss, chest pains, shaking of the hands, headache, diarrhea, nervousness, menstrual irregularity, inability to sleep, sweating, inability to stand heat. These symptoms may be controlled by adjusting the dose of the medication. If you are suffering from one or more side effects, you must contact your doctor immediately so that the proper dose adjustment can be made.

Drug Interactions

Interaction of Levothyroxine Sodium with Cholestyramine (Questran) can be avoided by spacing the two doses at least 4 hours apart.

Avoid over-the-counter products containing stimulant drugs, such as many drugs used to treat coughs, colds, or allergies, which will affect your heart and may cause symptoms of overdosage.

Thyroid replacement therapy may increase the effect of anticoagulant (blood-thinning) drugs such as Warfarin or Bishydroxycoumarin. Be sure you report this to your physician as it will be necessary to reduce the dose of your anticoagulant drug by approximately one-third at the beginning of thyroid therapy (to avoid hemorrhage). Further adjustments may be made later after your doctor reviews your blood tests.

Diabetics may have to increase their dose of Insulin or oral antidiabetic drugs. Changes in dose must be made by a doctor.

Usual Dose

Initial dose, as little as 25 micrograms per day; then increased in steps of 25 micrograms once every 3 to 4 weeks, depending upon response, with final dose of 100 to 200 micrograms per day, or even 300 to 400 micrograms if needed to achieve normal function.

Overdosage

Symptoms are headache, irritability, nervousness, sweating, rapid heartbeat with unusual stomach rumbling and with or without cramps, chest pains, heart failure, and shock. The patient should be taken to a hospital emergency room immediately. ALWAYS bring the medicine bottle.

Brand Name

Librax

Ingredients

Chlordiazepoxide
Clidinium Bromide

(Also available in generic form)

Type of Drug

Anticholinergic combination.

Prescribed for

Anxiety and spasms associated with gastrointestinal disease. Librax may be specifically prescribed as an adjunct in the treatment of organic or functional gastrointestinal disorders and in the management of peptic ulcers, gastritis, irritable bowel syndrome, spastic colon, and mild ulcerative colitis.

General Information

Librax is one of many combinations of this class containing an anticholinergic or antispasmodic drug and a minor tranquilizer such as Chlordiazepoxide. All the drugs in this class will provide symptomatic relief only, and will not treat an underlying disease: it is important that you realize while taking this medication that you should actively pursue the treatment of the underlying cause of this problem if one is present and can be found.

Cautions and Warnings

Librax should not be used if you know you are sensitive or allergic to either of its ingredients, Chlordiazepoxide (Librium) and Clidinium Bromide (Quarzan), or to any benzodiazepine drug, which is related to Chlordiazepoxide. Do not use this medicine if you have glaucoma, or if you have a history of prostatic hypertrophy and bladder-neck obstruction.

   Some people may develop dependence on Librax because of its tranquilizer components.

   This drug may cause birth defects or interfere with your baby's development. Check with your doctor before taking it if you are, or might be, pregnant.

Possible Side Effects

Most common: mild drowsiness (usually experienced during the first few days of therapy), dry mouth, difficulty in urination, constipation. These side effects may be accentuated in the elderly or debilitated person. If they persist, discuss these problems with your doctor, since it is possible that you may be taking too much of the drug for your system—or the side effects may be so bothersome as to suggest the possibility of using a different medication.

Possible Adverse Drug Effects

Infrequent: confusion, depression, lethargy, disorientation, headache, lack of activity, slurring of speech, stupor, dizziness, tremor, constipation, nausea, difficulty in urination, changes in sex drive, menstrual irregularity, changes in heart rhythm, stuffy nose, fever, heartburn, suppression of lactation in females, bloated feeling, drug allergy or allergic reaction to the drug including itching, rash, and less common manifestations. Most people taking Librax experience few truly bothersome effects and although the effects listed may be a problem, in most patients they do not constitute a severe difficulty.

Drug Interactions

The central nervous system depressant (tranquilizer) or the atropinelike drug (anticholinergic) in Librax may interact with alcoholic beverages or depressant drugs such as other tranquilizers, narcotics, barbiturates, or even antihistamines, causing excessive tiredness or sleepiness.

Both Librax ingredients may be potentiated (increased in effect) by MAO inhibitors: you may wish to discuss with your doctor the possibility of avoiding the combination.

The anticholinergic ingredient in Librax may be inhibited by certain drugs used to treat high blood pressure, including Guanethidine (Ismelin) and Reserpine. Discuss this with your doctor.

Cimetidine may exaggerate the effects expected from Chlordiazepoxide.

Usual Dose

1 to 2 capsules 3 to 4 times per day, usually before meals

and at bedtime. Amount and scheduling of medication may vary according to disease and patient's response.

Overdosage

Symptoms are dry mouth, difficulty in swallowing, thirst, blurred vision, inability to tolerate bright lights, flushed, hot dry skin, rash, high temperatures, palpitations and other unusual heart rhythms, feeling that you must urinate but difficulty in doing so, restlessness or depression, confusion, delirium, possible coma and/or lack of reflexes, and lowered respiration (breathing) and blood pressure. The patient should be taken to a hospital emergency room immediately. ALWAYS bring the medicine bottle.

Brand Name

Limbitrol

Ingredients

Amitriptyline
Chlordiazepoxide

Type of Drug

Antianxiety-antidepressant combination.

Presribed for

Moderate to severe anxiety and depression.

General Information

This combination contains two drugs often used by them selves. Some reports have stated that this combination takes effect sooner than other treatments. Symptoms that may respond to this treatment are sleeplessness, feelings of guilt or worthlessness, agitation, anxiety, suicidal thoughts, and appetite loss.

Cautions and Warnings

Do not take this drug if you are allergic to either of the ingredients or related drugs. It should be used with caution if you have a history of heart disease, epilepsy or other convulsive disorder, difficulty urinating, glaucoma, or thyroid disease.

This combination can cause drowsiness or dizziness. While taking this drug, drive and operate equipment with extreme caution. Avoid alcoholic beverages.

This drug may cause birth defects or interfere with your baby's development. Check with your doctor before taking it if you are, or might be, pregnant.

If used during breast feeding the baby may be overly tired, be short of breath, or have a low heartbeat.

Possible Side Effects

Mild drowsiness, changes in blood pressure, abnormal heart rates, heart attacks, confusion (especially in elderly patients), hallucinations, disorientation, delusions, anxiety, restlessness, excitement, numbness and tingling in the extremities, blurred vision, constipation, difficult urination, lack of coordination, muscle spasms, seizures or convulsions, dry mouth, blurred vision, rash, itching, sensitivity to the sun or bright light, retention of fluids, fever, drug allergy, changes in blood composition, nausea, vomiting, loss of appetite, stomach upset, diarrhea, enlargement of the breasts, changes in sex drive, changes in blood sugar.

Possible Adverse Drug Effects

Confusion, depression, lethargy, disorientation, headache, inactivity, slurred speech, stupor, dizziness, changes in menstrual cycle, blurred or double vision, inability to fall asleep, nightmares, feeling of panic, peculiar taste in the mouth, stomach cramps, black coloration of the tongue, yellowing of the eyes or skin, changes in liver function, changes in weight, sweating, flushing, loss of hair, feeling of ill health.

Drug Interactions

Avoid MAO inhibitors while taking this combination. The addition of MAO inhibitors can cause fever and convulsions. Do not take this drug together with Guanethidine. If you are taking high blood pressure medicine with this combination, consult with your doctor. Do not take this combination with alcohol, sleeping pills, or other depressive drugs.

Large doses of Vitamin C can reduce the effect of Amitriptyline, one ingredient of Limbitrol.

Usual Dose

1 tablet 3 to 4 times per day.

Overdosage

May cause confusion, drowsiness, difficulty concentrating, abnormal heart rate, convulsions, and coma. Bring the patient to a hospital emergency room and ALWAYS bring the medicine bottle.

Generic Name

Lithium

Brand Names

Cibalith-S Syrup	Lithium Citrate Syrup
Eskalith	Lithobid
Lithane	Lithonate
Lithium Carbonate	Lithotabs

(Also available in generic form)

Type of Drug

Antipsychotic, antimanic.

Prescribed for

Treatment of the manic phase of manic-depressive illness.

Lithium has also been used for treating certain types of cancer and migraine headaches.

General Information

Lithium is the only medicine which is effective as an antimanic drug. It reduces the level of manic episodes and may produce normal activity within the first 3 weeks of treatment. Typical manic symptoms include rapid speech, elation, hyperactive movements, need for little sleep, grandiose ideas, poor judgment, aggressiveness, and hostility.

Cautions and Warnings

This drug should not be given to patients with heart or kidney disease, dehydration, low blood sodium, or to patients who take diuretic drugs. If such patients require Lithium they must be very closely monitored by their doctors.

Lithium may affect routine mental or physical activity. Take care while driving or operating machinery.

This drug may cause birth defects or interfere with your baby's development. Check with your doctor before taking it if you are, or might be, pregnant.

Possible Side Effects

Side effects of Lithium are directly associated with the amount of this drug in the blood. At usual doses, the patient may develop a fine hand tremor, thirst, and excessive urination. Mild nausea and discomfort may be present during the first few days of treatment. At higher levels, diarrhea, vomiting, drowsiness, muscle weakness and poor coordination, giddiness, ringing in the ears, and blurred vision, may occur.

Possible Adverse Drug Effects

The following body systems can be affected by Lithium, producing symptoms which tend to become worse with more of this drug in the body: muscles, nerves, central nervous system (blackouts, seizures, dizziness, incontinence, slurred speech, coma), heart and blood vessels, stomach and intestines, kidney and urinary tract, skin, thyroid gland. Lithium can also cause changes in tests used to monitor heart-brain function and can cause dry mouth and blurred vision.

Drug Interactions

When combined with Haloperidol, Lithium may cause an unusual set of symptoms including weakness, tiredness, fever and confusion. In a few patients these symptoms have been followed by permanent brain damage.

Lithium may reduce the effect of Chlorpromazine.

The drug is counteracted by Sodium Bicarbonate, Acetazolamide, Urea, Mannitol, and Aminophylline, which increase the rate at which Lithium is released from the body.

Long-term use of thiazide diuretic drugs may decrease the clearance of Lithium from the body. Salt (sodium chloride) is directly related to this drug in the body. You will retain more of the drug than normal if the salt level in your body is low, and will hold less if you have a high salt level.

Food Interactions

It is essential to maintain a normal diet, including salt and fluid intake, while taking Lithium, since it can cause a natural reduction in body salt levels.

Usual Dose

Must be individualized to each patient's need. Most patients will respond to 600 milligrams 3 times per day at first, then will require 300 milligrams 3 to 4 times per day.

Overdosage

Toxic levels of Lithium are only slightly above the levels required for treatment. If diarrhea, vomiting, tremors, drowsiness, or poor coordination occur, stop taking the medicine and call your doctor immediately.

Special Information

Lithium may cause drowsiness. If you are taking this drug be cautious while driving or operating any machinery.

Brand Name

Lomotil

Ingredients

Atropine Sulfate
Diphenoxylate

Other Brand Names

Diphenatol	Lonox
Enoxa	Lo-Trol
Latropine	Low-Quel
Lofene	Nor-Mil
Lomanate	SK-Diphenoxylate

(Also available in generic form)

Type of Drug

Antidiarrheal.

Prescribed for

Symptomatic treatment of diarrhea.

General Information

Lomotil and other antidiarrheal agents should only be used for short periods: they will relieve the diarrhea, but not its underlying causes. Sometimes these drugs should not be used even though there is diarrhea present: people with some kinds of bowel, stomach, or other disease may be harmed by taking antidiarrheal drugs. Obviously, the decision to use Lomotil must be made by your doctor. Do not use Lomotil without his advice.

Cautions and Warnings

Do not take Lomotil if you are allergic to this medication or any other medication containing Atropine Sulfate, or if you are jaundiced (yellowing of the whites of the eyes and/or skin) or are suffering from diarrhea caused by antibiotics such as Clindamycin or Lincomycin.

This drug has been found to be safe for use during pregnancy. Remember, you should check with your doctor before taking any drug if you are pregnant.

Possible Side Effects

Most common: dryness of the skin inside the nose or mouth, flushing or redness of the face, fever, unusual heart rates, inability to urinate.

Possible Adverse Drug Effects

People taking Lomotil for extended periods may experience abdominal discomforts, swelling of the gums, interference with normal breathing, feeling of numbness in the extremities, drowsiness, restlessness, rashes, nausea, sedation, vomiting, headache, dizziness, depression, feeling unwell, lethargy, loss of appetite, euphoria, itching, and coma.

Drug Interactions

Lomotil, a depressant on the central nervous system, may

cause tiredness or inability to concentrate, and may thus increase the effect of sleeping pills, tranquilizers, and alcohol. Avoid drinking large amounts of alcoholic beverages while taking Lomotil.

Usual Dose

Adult: 4 tablets per day until diarrhea has stopped; then reduce to the lowest level that will control diarrhea (usually 2 tablets per day or less).

For children age 2 to 12 the liquid form, supplied with a dropper calibrated to deliver medication as desired in milliliters, is used.

Child (age 8 to 12, or about 60 to 80 pounds): 4 milliliters 5 times per day.

Child (age 5 to 8, or about 45 to 60 pounds): 4 milliliters 4 times per day.

Child (age 2 to 5, or about 26 to 45 pounds): 4 milliliters 3 times per day.

Child (under age 2): not recommended.

Overdosage

Lomotil overdose is generally accidental: patients, feeling that the prescribed amount has not cured their diarrhea, will take more medication on their own. Symptoms of overdosage (particularly effects on breathing) may not be evident until 12 to 30 hours after the medication has been taken. Symptoms are dryness of skin, mouth, and/or nose, flushing, fever and abnormal heart rates with possible lethargy, coma, or depression of breathing. The patient should be taken to a hospital emergency room immediately. ALWAYS bring the medicine bottle.

Special Information

Lomotil may cause drowsiness and difficulty concentrating: be careful while driving or operating any appliance or equipment.

Generic Name

Loperamide

Brand Name

Imodium

Type of Drug

Antidiarrheal.

Prescribed for

Symptomatic treatment of diarrhea.

General Information

Loperamide and other antidiarrheal agents should only be used for short periods: they will relieve the diarrhea, but not its underlying causes. Sometimes these drugs should not be used even though there is diarrhea present: people with some kinds of bowel, stomach, or other disease may be harmed by taking antidiarrheal drugs. Obviously, the decision to use the drug must be made by your doctor; do not use it without his advice.

Cautions and Warnings

Do not use Loperamide if you are allergic or sensitive to it or if you suffer from diarrhea associated with colitis. Also, do not use when intestinal toxins from bacteria such as *E. coli*, *Salmonella*, or *Shigella* are present or with certain drugs such as Clindamycin. Pregnant women and nursing mothers should avoid taking this drug. Loperamide is not known to be addictive.

Possible Side Effects

The incidence of side effects from Loperamide is low. Stomach and abdominal pain, bloating or other discomfort, constipation, dryness of the mouth, dizziness, tiredness, nausea and vomiting, and rash are possible.

Drug Interactions

Loperamide, a depressant on the central nervous system,

may cause tiredness and inability to concentrate, and may thus increase the effect of sleeping pills, tranquilizers, and alcohol. Avoid drinking large amounts of alcoholic beverages while taking Loperamide.

Usual Dose

Adult or child (age 12 and over): 2 capsules to start, followed by 1 capsule after each loose stool, up to 8 capsules per day maximum. Improvement should be seen in 2 days. People with long-term (chronic) diarrhea usually need 2 to 4 capsules per day. This drug usually is effective within 10 days or not at all.

Child (under age 12): not recommended.

Overdosage

Symptoms are constipation, irritation of the stomach and tiredness. Large doses cause vomiting. The patient should be taken to the emergency room immediately. ALWAYS bring the medicine bottle.

Special Information

Loperamide may cause drowsiness and difficulty concentrating: be careful while driving or operating any appliance or equipment.

Generic Name

Lorazepam

Brand Name

Ativan

Type of Drug

Minor tranquilizer.

Prescribed for

Relief of symptoms of anxiety, tension, fatigue, or agitation.

General Information

Lorazepam is a member of the chemical group of drugs known as benzodiazepines. These drugs are used as either antianxiety agents, anticonvulsants, or sedatives (sleeping pills). They exert their effects by relaxing the large skeletal muscles and by a direct effect on the brain. In doing so, they can relax you and make you either more tranquil or sleepier, depending on the drug and how much you use. Many doctors prefer Lorazepam and the other members of this class to other drugs that can be used for the same effect. Their reason is that the benzodiazepines tend to be safer, have fewer side effects, and are usually as, if not more, effective.

These drugs are generally used in any situation where they can be a useful adjunct.

Benzodiazepine tranquilizing drugs can be abused if taken for long periods of time and it is possible to develop withdrawal symptoms if you discontinue the therapy abruptly. Withdrawal symptoms include convulsions, tremor, muscle cramps, stomach cramps, vomiting, and sweating.

Cautions and Warnings

Do not take Lorazepam if you know you are sensitive or allergic to this drug or to other benzodiazepines such as Chlordiazepoxide, Oxazepam, Clorazepate, Diazepam, Prazepam, Flurazepam, Clonazepam, and Temazepam.

Lorazepam and other members of this drug group may aggravate narrow angle glaucoma, but if you have open angle glaucoma you may take the drugs. In any case, check this information with your doctor. Lorazepam can cause tiredness, drowsiness, inability to concentrate, or similar symptoms. Be careful if you are driving, operating machinery, or performing other activities which require concentration.

Avoid taking this drug during the first 3 months of pregnancy except under strict supervision of your doctor. The baby may become dependent on Lorazepam if it is used continually during pregnancy. If used during the last weeks of pregnancy or during breast-feeding the baby may be overly tired, be short of breath, or have a low heartbeat. Use during labor may cause weakness in the newborn.

Possible Side Effects

Most common: mild drowsiness during the first few days of

therapy, especially in the elderly or debilitated. If drowsiness persists, contact your doctor.

Possible Adverse Drug Effects

Major: confusion, depression, lethargy, disorientation, headache, lack of activity, slurred speech, stupor, dizziness, tremor, constipation, dry mouth, nausea, inability to control urination, changes in sex drive, irregular menstrual cycle, changes in heart rhythm, lowered blood pressure, retention of fluids, blurred or double vision, itching, rash, hiccups, nervousness, inability to fall asleep, (occasional) liver dysfunction. If you experience any of these reactions stop taking the medicine and contact your doctor immediately.

Drug Interactions

Lorazepam is a central nervous system depressant. Avoid alcohol, tranquilizers, narcotics, sleeping pills, barbiturates, MAO inhibitors, antihistamines, and other medicines used to relieve depression.

Usual Dose

Adult: 2 to 10 milligrams per day as individualized for maximum benefit, depending on symptoms and response to treatment, which may call for a dose outside the range given. Most people require 2 to 6 milligrams per day. 2 to 4 milligrams may be taken at bedtime for sleep.

Elderly: usually require less of the drug to control anxiety and tension.

Child: not recommended.

Overdosage

Symptoms are confusion, sleep or sleepiness, lack of response to pain such as a pin stick, shallow breathing, lowered blood pressure, and coma. The patient should be taken to a hospital emergency room immediately. ALWAYS bring the medicine bottle.

Generic Name

Maprotiline

Brand Name

Ludiomil

Type of Drug

Antidepressant.

Prescribed for

Depression with or without symptoms of anxiety.

General Information

Maprotiline and other members of this group are effective in treating symptoms of depression. They can elevate your mood, increase physical activity and mental alertness, improve appetite and sleep patterns. These drugs are mild sedatives and therefore useful in treating mild forms of depression associated with anxiety. You should not expect instant results with this medicine: benefits are usually seen after 1 to 4 weeks. If symptoms are not affected after 6 to 8 weeks, contact your doctor. Occasionally other members of this group of drugs have been used in treating nighttime bed-wetting in the young child, but they do not produce long-lasting relief, and therapy with one of them for nighttime bed-wetting is of questionable value.

Cautions and Warnings

Do not take Maprotiline if you are allergic or sensitive to this or other members of this class of drug: Doxepin, Nortriptyline, Imipramine, Desipramine, Protriptyline, and Amitriptyline. The drugs should not be used if you are recovering from a heart attack. Maprotiline may be taken with caution if you have a history of epilepsy or other convulsive disorders, difficulty in urination, glaucoma, heart disease, or thyroid disease. Maprotiline can interfere with your ability to perform tasks which require concentration, such as driving or operating machinery.

This drug may cause birth defects or interfere with your

baby's development. Check with your doctor before taking it if you are, or might be, pregnant.

Possible Side Effects

Changes in blood pressure (both high and low), abnormal heart rates, heart attack, confusion, especially in elderly patients, hallucinations, disorientation, delusions, anxiety, restlessness, excitement, numbness and tingling in the extremities, lack of coordination, muscle spasms or tremors, seizures and/or convulsions, dry mouth, blurred vision, constipation, inability to urinate, rash, itching, sensitivity to bright light or sunlight, retention of fluids, fever, allergy, changes in composition of blood, nausea, vomiting, loss of appetite, stomach upset, diarrhea, enlargement of the breasts in males and females, increased or decreased sex drive, increased or decreased blood sugar.

Possible Adverse Drug Effects

Infrequent: agitation, inability to sleep, nightmares, feeling of panic, development of a peculiar taste in the mouth, stomach cramps, black coloration of the tongue, yellowing eyes and/or skin, changes in liver function, increased or decreased weight, increased perspiration, flushing, frequent urination, drowsiness, dizziness, weakness, headache, loss of hair, nausea, not feeling well.

Drug Interactions

Interaction with monoamine oxidase (MAO) inhibitors can cause high fevers, convulsions, and occasionally death. Don't take MAO inhibitors until at least 2 weeks after Maprotiline has been discontinued.

Maprotiline interacts with Guanethidine, a drug used to treat high blood pressure: if your doctor prescribes Maprotiline and you are taking medicine for high blood pressure, be sure to discuss this with him.

Maprotiline increases the effects of barbiturates, tranquilizers, other depressive drugs, and alcohol. Don't drink alcoholic beverages if you take this medicine.

Taking Maprotiline and thyroid medicine will enhance the effects of the thyroid medicine. The combination can cause abnormal heart rhythms.

Large doses of Vitamin C (Ascorbic Acid) can reduce the effect of Maprotiline. Drugs such as Bicarbonate of Soda or Acetazolamide will increase the effect of Maprotiline.

Usual Dose

Adult: 75 to 225 milligrams per day. Hospitalized patients may need up to 300 milligrams per day. The dose of this drug must be tailored to patient's need.

Elderly: lower doses are recommended for people over 60 years of age, usually 50 to 75 milligrams per day.

Overdosage

Symptoms are confusion, inability to concentrate, hallucinations, drowsiness, lowered body temperature, abnormal heart rate, heart failure, large pupils of the eyes, convulsions, severely lowered blood pressure, stupor, and coma (as well as agitation, stiffening of body muscles, vomiting, and high fever). The patient should be taken to a hospital emergency room immediately. ALWAYS bring the medicine bottle.

Brand Name

Marax

Ingredients

Ephedrine Sulfate
Hydroxyzine Hydrochloride
Theophylline

Other Brand Names

Hydrophed	T.E.H. Compound
Moxy compound	Theozine

(Also available in generic form)

Type of Drug

Antiasthmatic combination product.

Prescribed for

Relief of asthma symptoms or other upper respiratory disorders.

General Information

Marax is one of several antiasthmatic combination products prescribed for the relief of asthmatic symptoms and other breathing problems. These products contain drugs which help relax the bronchial muscles, drugs which increase the diameter of the breathing passages, and a mild tranquilizer to help relax the patient. Other products in this class may contain similar ingredients along with other medicine to help eliminate mucus from the breathing passages.

Cautions and Warnings

This drug should not be taken if you have severe kidney or liver disease.

This drug may cause birth defects or interfere with your baby's development. Check with your doctor before taking it if you are, or might be, pregnant.

Possible Side Effects

Large doses of Marax can produce excitation, shakiness, sleeplessness, nervousness, rapid heartbeat, chest pains, irregular heartbeat, dizziness, dryness of the nose and throat, headache, and sweating. Occasionally people have been known to develop hesitation or difficulty in urination. Marax may also cause stomach upset, diarrhea, and possible bleeding, so you are advised to take this drug with food.

Possible Adverse Drug Effects

Excessive urination, heart stimulation, drowsiness, muscle weakness, muscle twitching, unsteady walk. These effects can usually be controlled by having your doctor adjust the dose.

Drug Interactions

Marax may cause sleeplessness or drowsiness. Do not take this drug with alcoholic beverages.

Taking Marax or similar medicines with an MAO inhibitor can produce severe interaction. Consult your doctor first.

Marax or similar products taken together with Lithium Carbonate will increase the excretion of Lithium; they have neutralized the effect of Propranolol. Erythromycin and similar antibiotics cause the body to hold Theophylline, leading to possible side effects.

Food Interactions

Take the drug with food to help prevent stomach upset.

Actions and side effects of Marax may be enhanced by ingestion of caffeine from sources which include various teas, coffee, chocolate, and soft drinks.

Usual Dose

Adult: 1 tablet 2 to 4 times per day.

Child (over age 5): ½ tablet 2 to 4 times per day. Syrup, 1 teaspoon 3 to 4 times per day.

Child (age 2 to 5): Syrup, ½ teaspoon 3 to 4 times per day.

Take doses at least 4 hours apart. The dose is adjusted to severity of disease and patient's ability to tolerate side effects.

Generic Name

Meclizine

Brand Names

Antivert
Bonine
Dizmiss
Motion Cure
Wehvert

(Also available in generic form)

Type of Drug

Antiemetic, antivertigo agent.

Prescribed for

Relief of nausea, vomiting, and dizziness associated with motion sickness or disease affecting the middle ear.

General Information

Meclizine is an antihistamine used to treat or prevent nausea, vomiting, and motion sickness. It takes a little longer to start working than most other drugs of this type but its effects last much longer (1 to 2 days). The specific method by which Meclizine acts on the brain to prevent dizziness and the nausea associated with it is not fully understood. In general, Meclizine does a better job of preventing motion sickness than of treating the symptoms once they are present.

Use with caution in children as a treatment for vomiting or nausea. This drug may obscure symptoms important in reaching the diagnosis of underlying disease. Meclizine is one of several drugs prescribed for the relief of nausea, vomiting, or dizziness that do not cure any underlying problems.

Cautions and Warnings

Do not take this medication if you think you are allergic to it.

Women who are pregnant or who feel they may become pregnant while they are taking this medication should not take Meclizine. Meclizine has been associated with birth defects in children. Nursing mothers may use this medicine.

Possible Side Effects

Most common: drowsiness, dry mouth, blurred vision.

Possible Adverse Drug Effects

Infrequent: difficulty in urination, constipation. Adverse effects are usually not cause for great concern. If they become serious, discuss them with your doctor.

Drug Interactions

Meclizine may cause sleepiness, tiredness, or inability to concentrate. Avoid tranquilizers, sleeping pills, alcoholic beverages, barbiturates, narcotics, and antihistamines, which can add to these effects.

Usual Dose

25 to 50 milligrams 1 hour before travel; repeat every 24 hours for duration of journey. For control of dizziness (diseases affecting middle ear, etc.), 25 to 100 milligrams per

day in divided doses. This drug should not be given to
children.

Special Information

Meclizine may cause tiredness, sleepiness, and inability to
concentrate. Be extremely careful while driving or operating
any machinery, appliances, or delicate equipment.

Generic Name

Meclofenamate Sodium

Brand Name

Meclomen

Type of Drug

Nonsteroid anti-inflammatory.

Prescribed for

Arthritis, mild to moderate pain of menstrual cramps, dental
surgery and extractions, and athletic injuries such as sprains
and strains.

General Information

Meclofenamate Sodium is one of 10 nonsteroid anti-inflam-
atory drugs available in the United States for the treatment
of pain and inflammation of arthritis and osteoarthritis. Many
people find they must try several of these nonsteriod anti-
inflammatory agents before they find the one that is right for
their condition. Meclofenamate Sodium must be taken for
several days before it exerts any effect and will take 2 to 3
weeks for the maximum effect to develop.

As a group, these drugs reduce inflammation and ease
pain via the same mechanism and share many side effects,
the most common of which are stomach upset and irritation.
In fact, the potential effect of Meclofenamate Sodium on
your stomach and intestines is so severe that it is recommended for use only after other medications have proven
ineffective for controlling your symptoms. Many doctors also

prescribe the nonsteroid anti-inflammatory agents to treat mild to moderate pain, menstrual cramps and pain, dental pain, and strains and sprains. However, you should check with your doctor before using Meclofenamate Sodium for any of these purposes.

Cautions and Warnings

Do not use Meclofenamate Sodium if you have had an allergic reaction to it or to any other nonsteroid anti-inflammatory drugs. Also, people allergic to Aspirin should not take Meclofenamate Sodium.

Older patients should be treated with a reduced daily dosage because they are more likely to be sensitive to the side effects. Report any side effects to your doctor at once. People with reduced kidney function should also receive lower than the usual dose because their ability to remove the drug from the body is impaired. Also, their kidney function should be monitored by periodic measurements of blood creatinine levels.

This drug should be avoided by pregnant women, women who may become pregnant while using it, and nursing mothers, since this drug passes into breast milk. In those situations where it is deemed essential, the potential risk of the drug must be carefully weighed against any benefit it might produce.

Possible Side Effects

Most common: nausea, vomiting, and diarrhea, which may be severe. Other possible side effects are heartburn, stomach pain and discomfort, stomach ulcer, bleeding in the stomach or intestines, liver inflammation and jaundice, dizziness, headache, and rashes.

Possible Adverse Drug Effects

Light-headedness, nervousness, tension, fainting, tingling in the hands or feet, muscle weakness and aches, tiredness, a feeling of ill health, difficulty sleeping, drowsiness, strange dreams, confusion, loss of the ability to concentrate, depression, personality changes, stuffy nose, changes in taste perception, heart failure, low blood pressure, fluid retention, cystitis, urinary infection, changes in kidney function, nosebleeds, hemorrhage, easy bruising, reduction in the count of some white blood cells, itching, hair loss, appetite and body-weight changes, increased sugar in the blood or urine, increased need for Insulin in diabetic patients, flushing or sweating, menstrual difficulty, vaginal bleeding.

Drug Interactions

Meclofenamate Sodium may enhance the activity of oral anticoagulants (blood-thinning agents), Phenytoin and other antiseizure drugs, oral antidiabetes drugs, and sulfa drugs by increasing the amounts of these agents in the blood-stream. People taking Meclofenamate Sodium in combination with any of these medications may require a reduction in the dosage of their anticoagulant, antiseizure, sulfa, or antidiabetes drug.

Aspirin reduces the effectiveness of Meclofenamate Sodium. These two drugs should never be taken together.

Probenecid may increase the action of Meclofenamate Sodium in your blood and cause side effects. People taking this combination should report any side effects or adverse effects to their doctor at once.

Food Interactions

Meclofenamate Sodium may be taken with food or meals if it upsets your stomach. If your stomach is still irritated, your dosage may have to be reduced, or you may have to change to another nonsteroid anti-inflammatory drug.

Usual Dose

200 to 400 milligrams per day.

Overdosage

The primary symptom of overdosage is acute stomach and intestinal distress. Symptoms generally develop within an hour of the overdose and resolve on their own within another 24 hours. Patients taking an overdose of this drug must be made to vomit with Syrup of Ipecac (available at any pharmacy) to remove any remaining drug from the stomach if the overdose was taken within the past hour. Call your doctor or a Poison Control Center before doing this. If more than an hour has passed, go to a hospital emergency room. ALWAYS bring the medicine bottle.

Special Information

Meclofenamate Sodium may cause blurred vision or drowsiness. Because of this, you should be especially careful while driving or doing anything else that requires concentration.

Call your doctor if you develop severe stomach or intestinal irritation, sudden weight gain, rash, itching, swelling, black or tarry bowel movements, or intense headaches.

Generic Name

Medroxyprogesterone Acetate

Brand Names

Amen
Curretab
Provera

(Also available in generic form)

Type of Drug

Progestogen.

Prescribed for

Irregular menstrual bleeding.

General Information

Because of the potential development of secondary disease after a long period of taking Medroxyprogesterone Acetate, the decision to take this medication chronically should be made cautiously by you and your doctor. Your continued need for chronic therapy with Medroxyprogesterone Acetate should be evaluated at least every 6 months to be sure that this therapy is absolutely necessary.

Cautions and Warnings

Do not take this drug if you have a history of blood clots or similar disorders, a history of convulsions, liver disease, known or suspected breast cancer, undiagnosed vaginal bleeding or miscarriage.

This drug is known to cause birth defects or interfere with your baby's development. It is not considered safe for use during pregnancy.

Possible Side Effects

Breakthrough bleeding, spotting, changes in or loss of menstrual flow, retention of water, increase or decrease in weight, jaundice, rash (with or without itching), mental depression.

Possible Adverse Drug Effects

A significant association has been demonstrated between the use of progestogen drugs and the following serious adverse effect: development of blood clots in the veins, lungs, or brain. Other possible adverse effects: changes in libido or sex drive, changes in appetite and mood, headache, nervousness, dizziness, tiredness, backache, loss of scalp hair, growth of hair in unusual quantities or places, itching, symptoms similar to urinary infections, unusual rashes.

Usual Dose

5 to 10 milligrams per day for 5 to 10 days beginning on what is assumed to be the 16th to 21st day of the menstrual cycle.

Special Information

At the first sign of sudden, partial, or complete loss of vision, leg cramps, water retention, unusual vaginal bleeding, migraine headache, or depression, or if you think you have become pregnant, stop the drug immediately and call your doctor.

Generic Name

Megestrol Acetate

Brand Name

Megace

Type of Drug

Progestational hormone.

Prescribed for

Cancer of the breast or endometrium.

General Information

Magestrol Acetate has been used quite successfully in the treatment of the cancers cited above. It exerts its effect by acting as a hormonal counterbalance in areas rich in estrogen (breast and endometrium). Other progestational hormones such as Norethindrone (Norlutin, Norlutate) may be used to treat cancer of the endometrium or uterus or to correct hormone imbalance.

Cautions and Warnings

This drug should only be used for its two specifically approved indications. The use of this drug should be accompanied by close, continued contact with your doctor.

Do not use this drug if you are planning to become pregnant or during the first 4 months of pregnancy.

Possible Side Effects

Back or stomach pain, headache, nausea, vomiting. If any of these symptoms appear, contact your doctor immediately.

Possible Adverse Drug Effects

Should be used with caution if you have a history of blood clots in the veins.

Usual Dose

40 to 320 milligrams per day.

Generic Name

Meperidine

Brand Names

Demerol
Meperidine Hydrochloride
Pethadol

(Also available in generic form)

Type of Drug

Narcotic analgesic.

Prescribed for

Moderate to severe pain.

General Information

Meperidine is a narcotic drug with potent pain-relieving effect. It is also used before surgery to reduce patient anxiety and help bring the patient into the early stages of anesthesia. Meperidine is probably the most commonly used narcotic analgesic in American hospitals. Its effects compare favorably with those of Morphine Sulfate, the standard against which other narcotics are judged.

Meperidine is a narcotic drug with some pain-relieving and cough-suppressing activity. As an analgesic it is useful for mild to moderate pain. 25 to 50 milligrams of Meperidine are approximately equal in pain-relieving effect to 2 Aspirin tablets (650 milligrams). Meperidine may be less active than Aspirin for types of pain associated with inflammation, since Aspirin reduces inflammation and Meperidine does not. Meperidine suppresses the cough reflex but does not cure the underlying cause of the cough. In fact, sometimes it may not be desirable to overly suppress cough, because cough suppression reduces your ability to naturally eliminate excess mucus produced during a cold or allergy attack.

Cautions and Warnings

The side effects of narcotic drugs are exaggerated when the patient has a head injury, brain tumor, or other head problem. Narcotics can also hide the symptoms of head injury. They should be used with extreme caution in patients with head injuries.

This drug may cause birth defects or interfere with your baby's development. Check with your doctor before taking it if you are, or might be, pregnant.

Possible Side Effects

Most frequent: light-headedness, dizziness, sleepiness, nausea, vomiting, loss of appetite, sweating. If these occur, consider calling your doctor and asking him about lowering your present dose of Meperidine. Usually the side effects disappear if you simply lie down.

More serious side effects of Meperidine are shallow breathing or difficulty in breathing.

Possible Adverse Drug Effects

Euphoria (feeling high), weakness, sleepiness, headache, agitation, uncoordinated muscle movement, minor hallucinations, disorientation and visual disturbances, dry mouth, loss of appetite, constipation, flushing of the face, rapid heartbeat, palpitations, faintness, urinary difficulties or hesitancy, reduced sex drive and/or potency, itching, skin rashes, anemia, lowered blood sugar, and a yellowing of the skin and/or whites of the eyes. Narcotic analgesics may aggravate convulsions in those who have had convulsions in the past.

Drug Interactions

Because of its depressant effect and potential effect on breathing, Meperidine should be taken with extreme care in combination with alcohol, sleeping medicine, tranquilizers, or other depressant drugs.

Food Interactions

This drug may be taken with food to reduce stomach upset.

Usual Dose

Adult: 50 to 150 milligrams every 3 to 4 hours as needed.

Child: 0.5 to 0.8 milligram per pound every 3 to 4 hours as needed, up to the adult dose.

Overdosage

Symptoms are depression of respiration (breathing), extreme tiredness progressing to stupor and then coma, pinpointed pupils of the eyes, no response to stimulation such as a pin stick, cold and clammy skin, slowing down of the heartbeat, lowering of blood pressure, convulsions, and cardiac arrest. The patient should be taken to a hospital emergency room immediately. ALWAYS bring the medicine bottle.

Special Information

If you are taking Meperidine, be extremely careful while

driving or operating machinery. Avoid alcoholic beverages. Call your doctor if this drug makes you very nauseated or constipated or if you have trouble breathing.

Generic Name

Meprobamate

Brand Names

Equanil
Mepriam
Meprospan
Miltown
Neuramate

Neurate
Sedabamate
SK-Bamate
Tranmep

(Also available in generic form)

Type of Drug

Minor tranquilizer.

Prescribed for

Relief of anxiety and tension, and to promote sleep in anxious or tense patients.

General Information

Meprobamate and the other drugs in its chemical group are used as either antianxiety agents, anticonvulsants, or sedatives (sleeping pills). This drug exerts effects by relaxing the large skeletal muscles and by a direct effect on the brain. In doing so, it can relax you and make you either more tranquil or sleepier, depending on the drug and how much you use.

Meprobamate is generally used in any situation where it can be a useful adjunct.

Meprobamate can be abused if taken for long periods of time and it is possible to develop withdrawal symptoms if you discontinue the therapy abruptly. Withdrawal symptoms include convulsions, tremor, muscle or stomach cramps, vomiting, and sweating.

Cautions and Warnings

You should not take Meprobamate if you are allergic to it or if you feel that you may be allergic to a related drug such as Carisoprodol, Mebutamate, or Carbromal. Severe physical and psychological dependence has been experienced by people taking Meprobamate for long periods of time. The drug can produce chronic intoxication after prolonged use or if used in greater than recommended doses, leading to adverse effects such as slurred speech, dizziness, and general sleepiness or depression. Sudden withdrawal of Meprobamate after prolonged and excessive use may result in drug withdrawal symptoms including severe anxiety, loss of appetite, sleeplessness, vomiting, tremors, muscle twitching, severe sleepiness, confusion, hallucinations, and possibly convulsions. Such withdrawal symptoms usually begin 12 to 48 hours after Meprobamate has been stopped and may last 1 to 4 days. When someone has taken this medication in excessive quantities for weeks, months, or longer, the medication must be gradually reduced over a period of 1 or 2 weeks in order to avoid these withdrawal symptoms.

If you are taking Meprobamate you should be aware that this drug may cause inability to perform usual tasks which require coordination, such as driving or operating machinery, and you must be extremely careful when performing such tasks.

Use with extreme caution if you are in the first 3 months of pregnancy or if you suspect that you may be pregnant; Meprobamate has been shown to increase the chance of birth defects and may cause tiredness in nursing infants. If you are pregnant and are taking this medication, you should discuss it with your doctor.

Possible Side Effects

Most common: drowsiness, sleepiness, dizziness, slurred speech, headache, weakness, tingling in the arms and legs, euphoria, and possibly excitement or paradoxical reactions such as overstimulation.

Possible Adverse Drug Effects

Infrequent: nausea, vomiting, diarrhea, abnormal heart rhythms, low blood pressure, itching, rash, effects on various components of the blood. Quite rarely there has been severe hypersensitivity or allergic reactions producing high fever, chills, closing of the throat (bronchospasm), loss of urinary function, and other severe symptoms.

Drug Interactions

Interactions with other drugs that produce depression of the central nervous system can cause sleepiness, tiredness, and tranquilization. Interaction with other tranquilizers, alcoholic beverages in excessive quantities, narcotics, barbiturates and other sleeping pills, or antihistamines can cause excessive depression, sleepiness, and fatigue.

Usual Dose

Adult (when used as a tranquilizer): 1200 to 1600 milligrams per day in divided doses; maximum permissible, 2400 milligrams per day.

Child (age 6 to 12): 100 to 200 milligrams 2 to 3 times per day.

Should not be given to children under age 6.

Overdosage

In attempted suicide or accidental overdose, symptoms are extreme drowsiness, lethargy, stupor, and coma, with possible shock and respiratory collapse (breathing stops).

The overdosed patient must be taken to a hospital emergency room immediately. ALWAYS bring the medicine bottle. Some people have died after taking 30 tablets, others have survived after taking 100.

The overdose is much worse if there is interaction with alcohol or another depressant: a much smaller dose of Meprobamate can produce fatal results.

After a large overdose, the patient will go to sleep very quickly and blood pressure, pulse, and breathing levels will be greatly reduced. After the patient is taken to the hospital his stomach should be pumped and respiratory assistance and other supportive therapy given.

Special Information

Elderly or debilitated (physically below par) people are espe-

cially sensitive to Meprobamate and should take it with care.
The same dose taken in the past may produce excessive
depression and be uncomfortable or dangerous.

Generic Name

Mesoridazine

Brand Name

Serentil

Type of Drug

Phenothiazine antipsychotic.

Prescribed for

Psychotic disorders, moderate to severe depression with anx
iety, control of agitation or aggressiveness of disturbed chil
dren, alcohol withdrawal symptoms, intractable pain, and
senility.

General Information

Mesoridazine and other members of the phenothiazine group
act on a portion of the brain called the hypothalamus. They
affect parts of the hypothalamus that control metabolism,
body temperature, alertness, muscle tone, hormone balance,
and vomiting, and may be used to treat problems related to
any of these functions.

Cautions and Warnings

Mesoridazine should not be taken if you are allergic to one
of the drugs in the broad classification known as phenothi
azine drugs. Do not take Mesoridazine if you have any blood,
liver, kidney, or heart disease, very low blood pressure, or
Parkinson's disease. This medication is a tranquilizer and
can have a depressive effect, especially during the first few
days of therapy. Care should be taken when performing
activities requiring a high degree of concentration, such as
driving.

If you are taking this medication and become pregnant

ontact your doctor immediately. Mesoridazine when used by pregnant women has caused side effects in newborns such as jaundice (yellowing of skin and eyes) and twitching. Mesoridazine has not been shown to cause problems during breast-feeding. These medications should be stopped 1 to 2 weeks before expected delivery to avoid this.

This drug should be used with caution and under strict supervision of your doctor if you have glaucoma, epilepsy, ulcers, or difficulty passing urine.

Avoid exposure to extreme heat because this drug can impair your ability to accomodate to high temperatures.

Possible Side Effects

Most common: drowsiness, especially during the first or second week of therapy. If the drowsiness becomes troublesome, contact your doctor.

Possible Adverse Drug Effects

Mesoridazine can cause jaundice (yellowing of the whites of the eyes or skin), usually in 2 to 4 weeks. The jaundice usually goes away when the drug is discontinued, but there have been cases when it did not. If you notice this effect or if you develop symptoms such as fever and generally not feeling well, contact your doctor immediately. Less frequent: changes in components of the blood including anemias, raised or lowered blood pressure, abnormal heart rates, heart attack, feeling faint or dizzy.

Phenothiazines can produce "extrapyramidal effects," such as spasm of the neck muscles, rolling back of the eyes, convulsions, difficulty in swallowing, and symptoms associated with Parkinson's disease. These effects look very serious but go away after the drug has been withdrawn; however, symptoms of the face, tongue, and jaw may persist for as long as several years, especially in the elderly with a history of brain damage. If you experience extrapyramidal effects, contact your doctor immediately.

Mesoridazine may cause an unusual increase in psychotic symptoms or may cause paranoid reactions, tiredness, lethargy, restlessness, hyperactivity, confusion at night, bizarre dreams, inability to sleep, depression, and euphoria. Other reactions are itching, swelling, unusual sensitivity to bright lights, red skin (particularly in exposed areas) and rash. There have been cases of breast enlargement, false positive pregnancy tests, changes in menstrual flow in females, and impotence and changes in sex drive in males, stuffy nose, headache, nausea, vomiting, loss of appetite, change in body temperature, loss of facial color, excessive salivation and perspiration, constipation, diarrhea, changes in urine and stool habits, worsening of glaucoma, blurred vision, weakening of eyelid muscles and spasms in bronchial and other muscles, increased appetite, and excessive thirst.

Drug Interactions

Mesoridazine should be taken with caution in combination with barbiturates, sleeping pills, narcotics, other tranquilizers, or any other medication which may produce a depressive effect. Avoid alcohol.

Usual Dose

30 to 400 milligrams per day, depending on the condition being treated.

Overdosage

Symptoms are depression, extreme weakness, tiredness, desire to go to sleep, coma, lowered blood pressure, uncontrolled muscle spasms, agitation, restlessness, convulsions, fever, dry mouth, and abnormal heart rhythms. The patient should be taken to a hospital emergency room immediately. ALWAYS bring the medicine bottle.

Special Information

This drug may turn the color of your urine to pink or reddish brown.

Generic Name

Metaproterenol

Brand Names

Alupent
Metaprel

(Also available in generic form)

Type of Drug

Bronchodilator.

Prescribed for

Asthma and spasm of the bronchial muscles.

General Information

Metaproterenol can be taken both as a tablet and by inhalation. This drug may be used together with other drugs to produce the desired relief from asthmatic symptoms. It begins working 15 to 30 minutes after a dose and its effects may last for up to 4 hours.

Cautions and Warnings

This drug should be used with caution by patients who have angina, heart disease, high blood pressure, a history of stroke or seizures, diabetes, thyroid disease, prostate disease, or glaucoma.

This drug should be used by women who are pregnant or breast-feeding only when absolutely necessary. The potential hazard to the unborn child or nursing infant is not known at this time because it has not been studied in humans. However, it has caused birth defects when given in large amounts to pregnant animals.

Older patients, over age 60, are more likely to experience the adverse effects of this drug.

Possible Side Effects

Restlessness, anxiety, fear, tension, sleeplessness, tremors, convulsions, weakness, dizziness, headache, flushing, pallor, sweating, nausea; also vomiting, loss of appetite, muscle cramps, urinary difficulties.

Possible Adverse Drug Effects

Metaproterenol can cause some side effects on the heart and cardiovascular system, such as high blood pressure, abnormal heart rhythms, and angina. It is less likely to cause these effects than some of the older drugs.

Drug Interactions

The effect of this drug may be increased by antidepressant drugs, some antihistamines, and Levothyroxine. This drug may antagonize the effects of Reserpine or Guanethidine.

Food Interactions

If the tablets cause an upset stomach, take each dose with food.

Usual Dose

Oral doses are as follows:
Adult and Child (over 60 pounds, or over age 9): 60 to 80 milligrams per day.
Child (under 60 pounds, or age 6 to 9): 30 to 40 milligrams per day.
Inhalation doses are as follows:
Adult and Child (over age 12): 2 or 5 puffs every 3 to 4 hours.
Do not use more than 12 puffs per day. The inhalation form of the drug is not recommended for children under age 12.

Overdosage

Symptoms of Metaproterenol overdose are palpitation, abnormal heart rhythms, rapid or slow heartbeat, chest pain, high blood pressure, fever, chills, cold sweat, blanching of the skin, nausea, vomiting, sleeplessness, delirium, tremor, pinpoint pupils, convulsions, coma, and collapse. If you or someone you know has taken an overdose of this drug call your doctor or bring the patient to a hospital emergency room. ALWAYS remember to bring the prescription bottle or inhaler with you.

Special Information

Do not take more than the amount prescribed for you.

Generic Name

Methenamine Hippurate

Brand Names

Hiprex
Mandelamine
Urex

(Also available in generic form)

Type of Drug

Urinary anti-infective.

Prescribed for

Chronic urinary tract infections.

General Information

This drug and other methenamine salts work by turning into formaldehyde and ammonia when the urine is acidic. It is the formaldehyde that kills the bacteria in the urinary tract. These drugs do not break down in the blood. Acidification of the urine may be necessary with 4 to 12 grams per day of Ascorbic Acid (Vitamin C) or Ammonium Chloride tablets.

Cautions and Warnings

Patients with kidney disease, dehydration, or severe liver disease should not use this drug. Pregnant women should only take this drug if absolutely necessary. Studies suggest it may be safe during the last 3 months of pregnancy, but are not conclusive.

Possible Side Effects

Large doses for long periods of time may cause bladder

irritation, painful and frequent urination, and protein or blood in the urine. This drug may cause elevation in liver enzymes.

Possible Adverse Drug Effects

Upset stomach, rash.

Drug Interactions

Do not take with sulfa drugs, since the sulfas can form a precipitate in the urine when mixed with Methenamine Hippurate, which may lead to a kidney stone.

Sodium Bicarbonate and Acetazolamide will decrease the effect of Methenamine Hippurate by making the drug less acidic.

Food Interactions

The action of Methenamine Hippurate will be decreased by foods which reduce urine acidity, including milk and dairy products. Avoid these agents in large quantities when taking Methenamine Hippurate.

Take Methenamine Hippurate with food to minimize upset stomach.

Usual Dose

Adult: 1 gram twice per day.
Child (age 6 to 12): .5 to 1 gram twice per day.

Special Information

Take each dose every 12 hours with plenty of water. Call your doctor if you develop pain when urinating or severe upset stomach.

Generic Name

Methocarbamol

Brand Names

Delaxin
Marbaxin
Robaxin
SK-Methocarbamol

(Also available in generic form)

Type of Drug

Skeletal muscle relaxant.

Prescribed for

Partial treatment for the relief of pain and other discomforts associated with acute conditions such as sprains, strains, or bad backs.

General Information

Methocarbamol is one of several drugs available for the relief of pain caused by spasms of large skeletal muscles. These drugs give symptomatic relief only. They should not be the only form of therapy used. If you are taking Methocarbamol, follow any other instructions given by your doctor about rest, physical therapy, or other measures to help relieve your problem.

Cautions and Warnings

The effect of Methocarbamol on the pregnant female has not been studied. It may have an effect on the unborn child: if you are pregnant, you should not use this medicine unless it is absolutely necessary and this problem has been considered by your physician.

Methocarbamol has not been shown to cause problems in breast-fed infants.

Possible Side Effects

Most common: light-headedness, dizziness, drowsiness, nausea, drug allergy (itching and rash), conjunctivitis with nasal congestion, blurred vision, headache, fever.

Drug Interactions

Other drugs which, like Methocarbamol, may cause drowsiness, sleepiness, or lack of ability to concentrate must be taken with extreme caution: sleeping pills, tranquilizers, barbiturates, narcotics, and alcoholic beverages.

Usual Dose

Adult: initial dose, 1500 milligrams 4 times per day for 48 to 72 hours; then 1500 milligrams 3 times per day, 1000 milligrams 4 times per day, or 750 milligrams every 4 hours.

Overdosage

Symptoms are central nervous system depression, desire to sleep, weakness, lassitude, and difficulty in breathing. The patient should be taken to a hospital immediately. ALWAYS bring the medicine bottle.

Special Information

Methocarbamol may cause drowsiness, sleepiness, and inability to concentrate: this can affect you if you drive or operate any sort of appliance, equipment, or machinery.

Generic Name

Methsuximide

Brand Name

Celontin

Type of Drug

Anticonvulsant.

Prescribed for

Control of petit mal seizures.

General Information

Methsuximide and the other succinimide-type anticonvulsants control petit mal seizures by slowing the transmission of impulses through certain areas of the brain. The succinimides are first choice of treatment for this type of seizure, although Methsuximide is used only after Ethosuximide. If Methsuximide doesn't work, the condition may be treated with Clonazepam.

Cautions and Warnings

Methsuximide may be associated with severe reductions in white-blood-cell and platelet counts. Your doctor should perform periodic blood counts while you are taking this medicine.

In patients with grand mal and petit mal, succinimide-type

anticonvulsants, when used alone, may increase the number of grand mal seizures and necessitate more medicine to control those seizures.

Abrupt withdrawal of any anticonvulsant may lead to severe seizures. It is important that your dosage be gradually reduced by your doctor.

This drug should be avoided by women who may become pregnant while using it and by pregnant and nursing mothers, since it will cross into the developing infant's circulation, and possible adverse effects on the infant are not known. In those situations where it is deemed essential, the potential risk of the drug must be carefully weighed against any benefit it might produce.

Recent reports suggest a strong association between the use of anticonvulsant drugs and birth defects. Although most of the information pertains to Phenytoin and Phenobarbital, not Methsuximide, other reports indicate a general association between all anticonvulsant drug treatments and birth defects. It is possible that the epileptic condition itself or genetic factors common to people with seizure disorders may also be a factor in the higher incidence of birth defects. Mothers taking Methsuximide should not breast-feed because of the possibility that the drug will pass into their breast milk and affect the baby. Use an alternative feeding method.

Possible Side Effects

Nausea, vomiting, upset stomach, stomach cramps and pain, loss of appetite, diarrhea, constipation, weight loss, drowsiness, dizziness, and poor muscle control.

Possible Adverse Drug Effects

Reductions in white-blood-cell and platelet counts, nervousness, hyperactivity, sleeplessness, irritability, headache, blurred vision, unusual sensitivity to bright lights, hiccups, a euphoric feeling, a dreamlike state, lack of energy, fatigue, confusion, mental instability, mental slowness, depression, sleep disturbances, nightmares, loss of the ability to concentrate, aggressiveness, constant concern with well-being and health, paranoid psychosis, suicidal tendencies, increased sex drive, rash, itching, frequent urination, kidney damage, blood in the urine, swelling around the eyes, hair loss, hairiness, muscle weakness, nearsightedness, vaginal bleeding, and swelling of the tongue and/or gums.

Drug Interactions

The depressant effects of Methsuximide are increased by tranquilizers, sleeping pills, narcotic pain relievers, antihistamines, alcohol, MAO inhibitors, antidepressants, and other anticonvulsants.

Methsuximide may increase the action of Phenytoin by increasing the blood levels of that drug. Your doctor should be sure that your dosages of the two drugs are appropriate to your condition.

Carbamazepine, another medicine prescribed to treat seizure disorders, may interfere with Methsuximide action by increasing the rate at which it is removed from the body.

The action of Methsuximide may be increased by Isoniazid, prescribed to prevent tuberculosis, and by Valproic Acid, another anticonvulsant drug, possibly leading to an increase in drug side effects when both drugs are taken together.

Avoid alcoholic beverages, which increase the depressant effects of this medicine.

Food Interactions

Methsuximide is best taken on an empty stomach but may be taken with food if it upsets your stomach.

Usual Dose

300 milligrams per day to start. If needed, the dose may be increased in steps of 300 milligrams every 7 days until seizures are controlled or side effects develop. The maximum daily dose is 1200 milligrams.

Dosage adjustments may be required for people with reduced kidney or liver function.

Overdosage

Methsuximide overdose will cause exaggerated side effects. If the overdose is discovered immediately, if may be helpful to induce vomiting with Syrup of Ipecac to remove any remaining medicine from the stomach. But all victims of Methsuximide overdose must be taken to a hospital emergency room for treatment. ALWAYS bring the prescription bottle with you.

Special Information

Call your doctor if side effects become intolerable. Especially important are sore throat, joint pains, unexplained fever, rashes, unusual bleeding or bruising, drowsiness, dizziness, and blurred vision. Be sure to tell your doctor if you become pregnant while taking this medicine.

Methsuximide may interfere with your ability to drive a car or perform other complex tasks because it can cause drowsiness and difficulty concentrating.

Your doctor should perform periodic blood counts while you are taking this drug to check for possible adverse drug effects.

Do not suddenly stop taking the medicine, since to do so can result in severe seizures. The dosage must be discontinued gradually by your doctor.

Carry identification or wear a bracelet indicating that you suffer from a seizure disorder for which you take Methsuximide.

Generic Name

Methyclothiazide

Brand Names

Aquatensen
Enduron
Ethon

(Also available in generic form)

Type of Drug

Diuretic.

Prescribed for

Congestive heart failure, cirrhosis of the liver, kidney malfunction, high blood pressure, and other conditions where it is necessary to rid the body of excess fluid.

General Information

This drug is a member of the class known as thiazide diuretics. Thiazides act on the kidneys to stimulate the production of large amounts of urine. They also cause you to lose bicarbonate, chloride, and potassium ions from the body. They are used as part of the treatment of any disease where it is desirable to eliminate large quantities of body water. These diseases include heart failure, some kidney diseases, and liver disease.

Cautions and Warnings

Do not take Methyclothiazide if you are allergic or sensitive to this drug, similar drugs of this group, or sulfa drugs. If you have a history of allergy or bronchial asthma, you may also have a sensitivity or allergy to Methyclothiazide.

This drug may cause birth defects or interfere with your baby's development. Check with your doctor before taking it if you are, or might be, pregnant.

Possible Side Effects

Methyclothiazide will cause a lowering of potassium in the body. Signs of low potassium levels are dryness of the mouth, thirst, weakness, lethargy, drowsiness, restlessness, muscle pains or cramps, muscular tiredness, low blood pressure, decreased frequency of urination and decreased amount of urine produced, abnormal heart rate, and stomach upset including nausea and vomiting.

To treat this, potassium supplements are given in the form of tablets, liquids, or powders, or by increased consumption of foods such as bananas, citrus fruits, melons, and tomatoes.

Possible Adverse Drug Effects

Loss of appetite, stomach upset, nausea, vomiting, cramping, diarrhea, constipation, dizziness, headache, tingling of the toes and fingers, restlessness, changes in blood composition, sensitivity to sunlight, rash, itching, fever, difficulty in breathing, allergic reactions, dizziness when rising quickly from a sitting or lying position, muscle spasms, weakness, blurred vision.

Drug Interactions

Methyclothiazide will increase (potentiate) the action of other blood-pressure-lowering drugs. This is beneficial, and is frequently used to help lower blood pressure in patients with hypertension.

The possibility of developing imbalances in body fluids (electrolytes) is increased if you take medications such as Digitalis and adrenal corticosteroids while you take Methyclothiazide.

If you are taking an oral antidiabetic drug and begin taking Methyclothiazide, the antidiabetic drug dose may have to be altered.

Lithium Carbonate should not be taken with Methyclothiazide because the combination may increase the risk of Lithium toxicity.

If you are taking this drug for the treatment of high blood pressure or congestive heart failure, avoid over-the-counter medicines for the treatment of coughs, colds, and allergies: such medicines may contain stimulants. If you are unsure about them, ask your pharmacist.

Usual Dose

Adult: 2.5 to 10 milligrams per day. Thiazide diuretic doses must be adjusted toward maximum effect with minimum medication. Eventual dose is often 5 milligrams or less.

Overdosage

Symptoms are unusually frequent and excessive urination, fatigue, and coma. The patient should be taken to a hospital emergency room. ALWAYS bring the medicine bottle.

Generic Name

Methyldopa

Brand Name

Aldomet

(Also available in generic form)

Type of Drug

Antihypertensive.

Prescribed for

High blood pressure.

General Information

Methyldopa is usually prescribed with one or more of the other high blood pressure medications or a diuretic.

Cautions and Warnings

You should not take Methyldopa if you have hepatitis or active cirrhosis or if you have ever developed a sign or symptom of reaction to Methyldopa. No unusual effects have been noted in patients using the drug while they are pregnant, but since Methyldopa crosses the placental barrier and appears in breast milk the possibility of damage to the unborn and nursing child should be kept in mind.

Possible Side Effects

Most people have little trouble with Methyldopa, but it can cause transient sedation during the first few weeks of therapy or when the dose is increased. Transient headache or weakness are other possible early symptoms.

Possible Adverse Drug Effects

Dizziness, light-headedness, tingling in the extremities, unusual muscle spasms, decreased mental acuity, and psychic disturbances including nightmares, mild psychosis, or depression; also changes in heart rate, increase of pain associated with angina pectoris, retention of water, resulting weight gain, and orthostatic hypotension (dizziness when rising suddenly from a sitting or lying position), as well as nausea, vomiting, constipation, diarrhea, mild dryness of the mouth, and sore and/or black tongue. The drug may cause liver disorders: you may develop jaundice (yellowing of the skin and/or whites of the eyes), with or without fever, in the first 2 to 3 months of therapy. If you are taking Methyldopa for the first time, be sure your doctor checks your liver function, especially during the first 6 to 12 weeks of therapy. If you develop fever or jaundice, stop taking the drug and contact your physician immediately: if the reactions are due to Methyldopa, your temperature and/or liver abnormalities will reverse toward normal as soon as the drug is discontinued.

Still other adverse effects are stuffy nose, breast enlargement, lactation (in females), impotence or decreased sex drive, mild symptoms of arthritis, and skin reactions.

Drug Interactions

Methyldopa will increase the effect of other blood pressure-lowering drugs. This is a desirable interaction which benefits patients with high blood pressure.

Avoid over-the-counter cough, cold, and allergy preparations containing stimulant drugs that can aggravate your high blood pressure. Information on over-the-counter drugs that are safe for you can be obtained from your pharmacist.

Methyldopa may increase the blood sugar, lowering effect of Tolbutamine or other oral antidiabetic drugs. If given together, with phenoxybenzamine, inability to control one's bladder (urinary incontinence) may result. The combination of Methyldopa and Lithium may cause symptoms of Lithium overdose, even though blood levels of Lithium do not change. Methyldopa when given together with Haloperidol may produce irritability, aggressiveness, assaultive behavior or other psychiatric symptoms.

Usual Dose

Adult: Starting dose, 250-milligram tablet 2 to 3 times per day for first 2 days. Dosage may be increased or decreased until blood pressure control is achieved. Maintenance dose, 500 milligrams to 3000 milligrams per day in 2 to 4 divided doses, per patient's needs.

Child: 5 milligrams per pound of body weight per day in 2 to 4 divided doses per patient's needs. Maximum dose, 30 milligrams per pound of body weight per day, up to 3 grams per day.

Special Information

Take this drug exactly as prescribed by your doctor so you can maintain maximum control over your high blood pressure.

A mild sedative effect is to be expected from Methyldopa and will resolve within several days.

Do not stop taking this medicine unless you are told to by your doctor. Avoid nonprescription cough and cold medicines or diet pills which contain stimulants. Your pharmacist can give you more information on those nonprescription drugs to be avoided. Call your doctor if you develop fever, prolonged general tiredness, or unusual dizziness.

Generic Name

Methylphenidate

Brand Name

Ritalin

(Also available in generic form)

Type of Drug

Central nervous system stimulant.

Prescribed for

Minimal brain dysfunction in children; psychological, educational, or social disorders; narcolepsy and mild depression.

General Information

Chronic or abusive use of Methylphenidate can cause the development of drug dependence or addiction; also the drug can cause severe psychotic episodes. The primary use for Methylphenidate is the treatment of minimal brain dysfunction or attention deficit disorders in children. Common signs of this disease are short attention span, easy distractibility, emotional instability, impulsiveness, and moderate to severe hyperactivity. Children who suffer from this disorder will find it difficult to learn. There are many who feel that Methylphenidate is only a temporary solution because it does not permanently change patterns of behavior. When Methylphenidate is used, it must be used with other special measures.

Cautions and Warnings

Do not take Methylphenidate if you are extremely tense or agitated, have glaucoma, are allergic to this drug, have high blood pressure, or have a history of epilepsy or other seizures.

Women of child-bearing age should consult with a doctor before taking this drug.

This drug is known to cause birth defects or interfere with

your baby's development. It is not considered safe for use during pregnancy.

Possible Side Effects

Most common in adults: nervousness and inability to sleep, which are generally controlled by reducing or eliminating the afternoon or evening dose. Most common in children: loss of appetite, stomach pains, weight loss (especially during prolonged periods of therapy), difficulty sleeping, and abnormal heart rhythms.

Possible Adverse Drug Effects

Infrequent in adults: skin rash, itching, fever, symptoms similar to arthritis, loss of appetite, nausea, dizziness, abnormal heart rhythms, headache, drowsiness, changes in blood pressure or pulse, chest pains, stomach pains, psychotic reactions, effects on components of the blood, loss of some scalp hair.

Drug Interactions

Methylphenidate will decrease the effectiveness of Guanethidine, a drug used to treat high blood pressure.

Interaction with MAO inhibitors may vastly increase the effect of Methylphenidate and cause problems.

If you take Methylphenidate regularly, avoid alcoholic beverages; they will add to the drowsiness problem.

Interaction with anticoagulants (blood-thinning drugs), some drugs used to treat epilepsy or other kinds of convulsions, Phenylbutazone and Oxyphenbutazone, and antidepressant drugs will slow the rate at which these drugs are broken down by the body, making more of them available in the bloodstream. Thus it may be necessary to lower the dose of them.

Usual Dose

Adult: 10 or 20 to 30 or even 60 milligrams per day in divided doses 2 to 3 times per day, preferably 30 to 45 minutes before meals.

Child (over age 6): Initial dose, 5 milligrams before breakfast and lunch; then increase in steps of 5 to 10 milligrams each week as required, but not to exceed 60 milligrams per day.

Doses should be tailored to individual needs; the doses listed here are only guidelines.

Overdosage

Symptoms are stimulation of the nervous system such as vomiting, agitation, tremors (uncontrollable twitching of the muscles), convulsions followed by coma, euphoria, confusion, hallucinations, delirium, sweating, flushing (face, hands, and extremities will be red), headache, high fever, abnormal heart rate, high blood pressure, and dryness of the mouth and nose. The patient should be taken to a hospital emergency room. ALWAYS bring the medicine bottle.

Special Information

Methylphenidate can cause temporary drowsiness: be careful while driving or operating an automobile, machine, or appliance.

Generic Name

Methylprednisolone

Brand Name

Medrol

(Also available in generic form)

Type of Drug

Adrenal cortical steroid.

Prescribed for

Reduction of inflammation. The variety of disorders for which Methylprednisolone is prescribed is almost endless, from skin rash to cancer. The drug may be used as a treatment for adrenal gland disease, since one of the hormones produced by the adrenal gland is very similar to Methylprednisolone. If patients are not producing sufficient adrenal hormones, Methylprednisolone may be used as replacement therapy. It may also be prescribed for the treatment of bursitis, arthritis, severe skin reactions such as psoriasis or other rashes, severe allergic conditions, asthma, drug or serum sickness, severe acute or chronic allergic inflammation of the eye and surrounding areas such as conjunctivitis, respiratory diseases including pneumonitis, blood disorders, gastrointestinal diseases including ulcerative colitis, and inflammation of the nerves, heart, or other organs.

General Information

Methylprednisolone is one of many adrenal cortical steroids used in medical practice today. The major differences between Methylprednisolone and other adrenal cortical steroids are potency of medication and variation in some secondary effects. In most cases the choice of adrenal cortical steroids to be used in a specific disease is a matter of doctor preference and past experience. Other adrenal cortical steroids include Cortisone, Hydrocortisone, Prednisone, Prednisolone, Triamcinolone, Meprednisone, Paramethasone, Fluprednisolone, Dexamethasone, Betamethasone, and Fludrocortisone.

Cautions and Warnings

Because of the effect of Methylprednisolone on your adrenal gland, it is essential that the dose be tapered from a large dose down to a small dose over a period of time. Do not stop taking this medication suddenly and/or without the advice of your doctor. If you do, you may cause a failure of the adrenal gland with extremely serious consequences. Methylprednisolone has a strong anti-inflammatory effect, and may mask some signs of infections. If new infections appear during the use of Methylprednisolone therapy, they may be difficult to discover and may grow more rapidly due to your decreased resistance. If you think you are getting any kind of infection during the time that you are taking Methylprednisolone, you should contact your doctor, who will prescribe appropriate therapy.

If you are taking Methylprednisolone you should not be vaccinated against infectious disease, because of a potential inability of the body to produce the normal reaction to the vaccination. Discuss this with your doctor before he administers any vaccination.

If you suspect that you have become pregnant and are taking Methylprednisolone, report it immediately to your doctor. Large amounts of Methylprednisolone during pregnancy or breast-feeding may slow the growth of newborn babies. If you are taking Methylprednisolone and have just given birth, do not nurse; use prepared formulas instead.

Possible Side Effects

Stomach upset is one of the more common side effects of Methylprednisolone, which may in some cases cause gastric or duodenal ulcers. Other side effects: retention of water, heart failure, potassium loss, muscle weakness, loss of muscle mass, loss of calcium from bones which may result in bone fractures and a condition known as aseptic necrosis of the femoral and humoral heads (this means the ends of the large bones in the hip may degenerate from loss of calcium), slowing down of wound healing, black-and-blue marks on the skin, increased sweating, allergic skin rash, itching, convulsions, dizziness, headache.

Possible Adverse Drug Effects

May cause irregular menstrual cycles, slowing down of growth in children, particularly after the medication has been taken for long periods of time, depression of the adrenal and/or pituitary glands, development of diabetes, increased pressure of the fluid inside the eye, hypersensitivity or allergic reactions, blood clots, insomnia, weight gain, increased appetite, nausea, and feeling of ill health. Psychic derangements may appear which range from euphoria to mood swings, personality changes, and severe depression. Methylprednisolone may also aggravate existing emotional instability.

Drug Interactions

Methylprednisolone and other adrenal corticosteroids may interact with Insulin or oral antidiabetic drugs, causing an increased requirement of the antidiabetic drugs.

Interaction with Phenobarbital, Ephedrine, and Phenytoin may reduce the effect of Methylprednisolone by increasing its removal from the body.

If a doctor prescribes Methylprednisolone you should discuss any oral anticoagulant (blood-thinning) drugs you are taking; their dose may have to be changed.

Interaction with diuretics such as Hydrochlorothiazide may cause you to lose blood potassium. Be aware of signs of lowered potassium level such as weakness, muscle cramps, and tiredness, and report them to your physician.

Food Interactions

If you notice a slight stomach upset when you take your dose of Methylprednisolone, take this medication with food or with a small amount of antacid. If stomach upset continues, notify your doctor.

It is recommended that you eat high-potassium foods such as bananas, citrus fruits, melons, and tomatoes.

Usual Dose

Initial dose, 4 to 48 milligrams; maintenance dose, as determined by your doctor based on your response.

Overdosage

There is no specific treatment for overdosage of adrenal cortical steroids. Symptoms are anxiety, depression and/or stimulation, stomach bleeding, increased blood sugar, high blood pressure, and retention of fluid. The patient should be taken to a hospital emergency room immediately, where stomach pumping, oxygen, intravenous fluids, and other supportive treatment are available.

Generic Name

Methyltestosterone

Brand Names

Android	Oreton
Metandren	Testred
Methyl	Virilon

(Also available in generic form)

Type of Drug

Androgenic (male) hormone.

Prescribed for

Diseases in which male hormone replacement or augmentation is needed; male menopause.

General Information

This is a member of the androgenic or male hormone group, which includes Testosterone, Calusterone, and Dromostanolone Propionate. (The last two are used primarily to treat breast cancer in women.) Females taking any androgenic drug should watch for deepening of the voice, oily skin, acne, hairiness, increased libido, and menstrual irregularities, which may be related to the so-called virilizing effects of these hormones. Virilization is a sign that the drug is starting to produce changes in secondary sex characteristics. The drugs should be avoided if possible by boys who have not gone through puberty.

Cautions and Warnings

Men who have an unusually high blood level of calcium, known or suspected cancer of the prostate, or prostate destruction or disease, cancer of the breast, liver, heart, or kidney disease should not use this medication. Women who are pregnant or breast-feeding should not use Methyltestosterone, since it may cause unwanted problems in babies, such as the development of male features in female babies.

Possible Side Effects

In males: inhibition of testicle function, impotence, chronic erection of the penis, enlargement of the breast.

In females: unusual hairiness, baldness in a pattern similar to that seen in men, deepening of the voice, enlargement of the clitoris. These changes are usually irreversible once they have occurred. Females also experience menstrual irregularities and increases in blood calcium.

Possible Adverse Drug Effects

In both sexes: changes in libido, flushing of the skin, acne, mild dependence on the drug, excitation, chills, sleeplessness, water retention, nausea, vomiting, diarrhea. Symptoms resembling stomach ulcer may develop. Methyltestosterone may affect level of blood cholesterol.

Drug Interactions

Methyltestosterone may increase the effect of oral anticoagulants; dosage of the anticoagulant may have to be decreased. The drug may have an effect on the glucose tolerance test, a blood test used to screen people for diabetes mellitus.

Usual Dose

10 to 300 milligrams per day, depending upon the disease being treated and patient's response.

Special Information

Methyltestosterone and other androgens are potent drugs. They must be taken only under the close supervision of your doctor and never used casually. The dosage and clinical effects of the drug vary widely and require constant monitoring.

Generic Name

Methyprylon

Brand Name

Noludar

Type of Drug

Sedative-hypnotic.

Prescribed for

Inability to sleep.

General Information

This drug works in about 45 minutes. Its effect lasts for 5 to 8 hours. It should not be used continuously for long periods of time.

Cautions and Warnings

Methyprylon should not be used if you are sensitive or allergic to it. It can be addictive.

This drug may cause birth defects or interfere with your

baby's development. Check with your doctor before taking it if you are, or might be, pregnant.

Possible Side Effects

Skin rash.

Possible Adverse Drug Effects

People who have taken Methyprylon for a long time may show signs of chronic overdosage: loss of memory, inability to concentrate, shakes, tremors, loss of reflexes, slurred speech, and general sense of depression. Abrupt discontinuation of Methyprylon often causes withdrawal reactions of nervousness, anxiety, seizures, cramping, chills, numbness of the extremities, and general behavior changes. Chronic overdosage is best treated by withdrawing the drug over a period of days or weeks.

There have been reports of nausea, morning hangover, rash, excitation, and blurred vision.

Drug Interactions

Do not take this drug with alcohol and/or other depressants such as sedatives, hypnotics, and antihistamines which may produce drowsiness or sleepiness.

Doses of anticoagulant (blood-thinning) drugs such as Warfarin may require adjustment because of increased effects. Dosage adjustment will also be required when you stop taking Methyprylon.

Usual Dose

200 to 400 milligrams at bedtime.

Overdosage

Large amounts of Methyprylon can be fatal, and the drug is frequently used in suicide attempts. Symptoms are coma, lowered body temperature followed by fever, absence of normal reflexes and pain responses after pinches and needle or pin sticks, and shallow breathing. The patient should be taken to a hospital emergency room immediately. ALWAYS bring the medicine bottle.

Generic Name

Metoclopramide

Brand Name

Reglan

(Also available in generic form)

Type of Drug

Gastrointestinal stimulant.

Prescribed for

Symptoms of diabetic gastroparesis (stomach paralysis), including nausea, vomiting, fullness after meals, and loss of appetite. Also used to facilitate certain X-ray diagnostic procedures. Used for the relief of nausea and vomiting. This drug is also used by nursing mothers to improve lactation and is used to treat certain cases of stomach ulcers and anorexia nervosa.

General Information

This drug stimulates movement of the upper gastrointestinal tract but does not stimulate excess stomach acids or other secretions. It has been investigated in the United States as an antinauseant for patients receiving anticancer drugs. It has been used extensively for this purpose in Europe and South America. Although it is not known exactly how the drug works, its results may be caused by the direct effect of Metoclopramide on special receptors in the brain. Its value as an antiemetic is about the same as that of other currently available drugs.

Cautions and Warnings

This drug should not be used where stimulation of the gastrointestinal tract could be dangerous (bleeding ulcers, etc.) and should not be used if you are allergic to the drug. This drug can cause "extrapyramidal" side effects similar to those caused by phenothiazine drugs. Do not take the two classes of drugs together. Extrapyramidal effects occur in only about 0.2 percent of the people taking the drug and usually include restlessness and involuntary movements of arms and legs, face, tongue, lips, or other parts of the body. This drug should be used by pregnant women or nursing mothers only when absolutely necessary.

Possible Side Effects

Restlessness, drowsiness, tiredness.

Possible Adverse Drug Effects

Sleeplessness, headache, dizziness, nausea, upset stomach.

Drug Interactions

The effects of Metoclopramide on the stomach are antagonized by narcotics and anticholinergic drugs. Metoclopramide may interact with alcohol, sedatives, or other depressant drugs to produce excessive sleepiness or tiredness. Because of its effects on the gastrointestinal tract, this drug may affect the passage of drugs through the stomach or intestines into the bloodstream.

Usual Dose

Adult: 1 to 2 tablets before meals and at bedtime. Single doses of 1 to 2 tablets are used before X-ray diagnostic procedures.

Child (age 6 to 14): One-quarter to half the adult dose.

Child (under age 6): 0.05 milligram per pound of body weight per dose.

Overdosage

Symptoms are drowsiness, disorientation, restlessness, or uncontrollable muscle movements. Symptoms usually disappear within 24 hours after the drug has been stopped. Anticholinergic drugs will antagonize these symptoms.

Special Information

Take exactly as directed. When taking this drug for nausea, be sure to take the medicine 30 minutes before meals and at bedtime.

Generic Name

Metolazone

Brand Names

Diulo
Zaroxolyn

Type of Drug

Diuretic.

Prescribed for

Congestive heart failure, cirrhosis of the liver, high blood pressure, and other conditions where it is necessary to rid the body of excess fluids.

General Information

This diuretic is most similar to the thiazide diuretics in its action and effects on the body. It works on the kidneys to promote the release of sodium from the body, and to stimulate the production of large amounts of urine. Thiazides also cause you to lose potassium, chloride, and bicarbonate from the body. There are no major differences between Metolazone and other thiazide diuretics.

Cautions and Warnings

Do not take Metolazone if you are allergic or sensitive to it or to any other thiazide drug or any sulfa drug. If you have a history of allergy or bronchial asthma, you may also have a sensitivity or allergy to Metolazone. Avoid this drug if you have kidney or liver disease.

This drug should not be taken by pregnant women or women who may become pregnant while using it since it will pass into the blood system of the fetus. In those situations where it is deemed essential, the potential risk of the drug must be carefully weighed against any benefit it might produce. Nursing mothers who must take thiazide-type drugs should find an alternative method of feeding their infants since these diuretics are known to pass into breast milk.

Possible Side Effects

Loss of body potassium, leading to dry mouth, thirst, weakness, drowsiness, restlessness, muscle pains and cramps or tiredness, low blood pressure, decreased frequency of urination, abnormal heart rhythm, and upset stomach. Other side effects are loss of appetite, nausea, vomiting, stomach bloating or cramps, diarrhea, constipation, yellowing of the skin o whites of the eyes, pancreas inflammation, liver inflammation (hepatitis), frequent urination (especially at night), headache, dizziness, fatigue, loss of energy, a feeling of ill health numbness in the hands or feet, nervousness, tension, anxiety, irritability, and agitation.

Possible Adverse Drug Effects

Kidney inflammation, male impotence, reduced sex drive light-headedness, drowsiness, fainting, difficulty sleeping, depression, tingling in the hands or feet, blurred vision, reduced levels of white blood cells and platelets, dizziness when rising quickly from a sitting or lying position, heart palpitations, chest pain, gout attacks, chills, stuffy nose, facial flushing, and weight loss.

Drug Interactions

Metolazone increases the effects of other blood-pressure-lowering drugs. This interaction is beneficial and often used to help treat people with high blood pressure.

The chances of losing body potassium are increased if you take Metolazone with Digoxin or with a corticosteroid anti-inflammatory drug. If you are taking medicine to treat diabetes and begin taking Metolazone, the dose of your diabetes medicine may have to be adjusted.

Metolazone will enhance the effects of Lithium and increase the chances of developing Lithium toxicity by preventing it from passing out of your body.

People taking Metolazone for high blood pressure or heart failure should take care to avoid nonprescription medicines that might aggravate your condition, such as decongestants cold or allergy treatments, and diet pills, all of which may contain stimulants. If you are unsure about which medicine to choose, ask your pharmacist.

Dizziness when rising from a sitting or lying position may

be worsened by taking Metolazone with alcoholic beverages, barbiturate-type sleeping pills, and narcotic pain relievers.

The effects of Metolazone may be counteracted by Indomethacin because of its effect on the kidneys. Taking Colestipol or Cholestyramine (cholesterol-lowering drugs) at the same time as Metolazone will reduce the drug's effect by preventing it from being absorbed into the bloodstream.

Taking more than one diuretic drug at a time can result in an excessive and prolonged diuretic effect. This is especially true when a thiazide-type diuretic is combined with a "loop" diuretic such as Bumetanide, Ethacrynic Acid, or Furosemide.

Taking Metolazone and other thiazide-type diuretics with calcium or Vitamin D could result in excessive levels of calcium in the blood.

Sulfa drugs may increase the effects of Metolazone by increasing the amount of diuretic drug in the bloodstream.

Metolazone may increase the effect of Quinidine, for abnormal heart rhythms, by interfering with its release from the body via the kidneys.

Food Interactions

Metolazone may cause loss of body potassium (hypokalemia), a complication that can be avoided by adding foods rich in potassium to your diet. Some potassium-rich foods are tomatoes, citrus fruits, melons, and bananas. Hypokalemia can also be prevented by taking a potassium supplement in pill, powder, or liquid form. Metolazone may be taken with food or meals if it upsets your stomach.

Usual Dose

2.5 to 5 milligrams per day.

Overdosage

The primary symptom of overdose is potassium deficiency by dehydration: confusion, dizziness, muscle weakness, upset stomach, excessive thirst, loss of appetite, lethargy (rare), drowsiness, restlessness (rare), tingling in the hands or feet, rapid hearbeat, nausea and vomiting. Patients taking an overdose of this drug must be made to vomit with Syrup of Ipecac (available at any pharmacy) to remove any remaining drug from the stomach, if the overdose was taken within the past hour. Call your doctor or a Poison Control Center before doing this. If more than an hour has passed, go to a hospital emergency room. ALWAYS bring the medicine bottle.

Special Information

Always take your daily dose of Metolazone by 10 A.M. Taking it later in the day will increase the chances of being kept awake at night by the need to urinate frequently.

Call your doctor if muscle weakness, cramps, nausea, dizziness, or other severe side effects develop.

Generic Name

Metoprolol

Brand Name

Lopressor

Type of Drug

Beta-adrenergic blocking agent.

Prescribed for

High blood pressure, treatment after a heart attack.

General Information

This drug is very much like Propranolol but it has a more specific effect on the heart and a less specific effect on receptors in the blood vessels and respiratory tract. This means that the drug causes fewer problems in asthmatics and has a more specific effect on heart functions.

Cautions and Warnings

Metoprolol should be used with care if you have a history of asthma, upper respiratory disease, or seasonal allergy, which may be made worse by the effects of this drug.

Drugs similar to Metoprolol have been shown to cause problems during pregnancy in animal studies when used in very high amounts. Pregnant and lactating women should use this drug only if it is essential.

Possible Side Effects

Metoprolol may decrease the heart rate; may aggravate a condition of congestive heart failure; and may produce lowered blood pressure, tingling in the extremities, light-headedness, mental depression including inability to sleep, weakness, and tiredness. It may also produce a mental depression which is reversible when the drug is withdrawn, visual disturbances, hallucinations, disorientation, and short-term memory loss. Patients taking Metoprolol may experience nausea, vomiting, stomach upset, abdominal cramps and diarrhea, or constipation. If you are allergic to this drug, you may show typical reactions associated wth drug allergies, including sore throat, fever, difficulty in breathing, and various effects on the blood system. Metoprolol may induce bronchospasms (spasms of muscles in the bronchi), which will make any existing asthmatic condition or any severe upper respiratory disease worse.

Possible Adverse Drug Effects

Occasionally, patients taking Metoprolol may experience emotional instability, or a feeling of detachment or personality change, or the drug may produce unusual effects on the blood system.

Drug Interactions

This drug will interact with any psychotropic drug, including the MAO inhibitors, which stimulates one of the adrenergic segments of the nervous system. Since this information is not generally known, you should discuss the potential problem of using Metoprolol with your doctor if you are taking any psychotropic or psychiatric drug.

Metoprolol may cause increased effectiveness of Insulin or oral antidiabetic drugs. If you are diabetic, discuss the situation with your doctor; a reduction in dose of antidiabetic medication will probably be made.

Metoprolol may reduce the effectiveness of Digitalis on your heart. Any dose of Digitalis medication will have to be altered. If you are taking Digitalis for a purpose other than congestive heart failure, the effectiveness of the Digitalis may be increased by Metoprolol, and the dose of Digitalis may have to be reduced.

Metoprolol may interact with certain other drugs to produce lowering of blood pressure. This interaction often has positive results in the treatment of patients with high blood pressure.

Do not self-medicate with over-the-counter cold, cough, or allergy remedies which may contain stimulant drugs that will aggravate certain types of heart disease and high blood pressure, or other ingredients that may antagonize the effects of Metoprolol. Double-check with your doctor or pharmacist before taking any over-the-counter medication.

Usual Dose

100 to 450 milligrams per day. The dosage of this drug must be tailored to patient's need.

Overdosage

Symptoms are slowed heart rate, heart failure, lowered blood pressure, and spasms of the bronchial muscles which make it difficult to breathe. The patient should be taken to a hospital emergency room where proper therapy can be given. ALWAYS bring the medicine bottle with you.

Special Information

This drug may make you tired, so take care when driving or when operating machinery. Call your doctor if you become dizzy or develop diarrhea. Do not stop taking this medicine abruptly unless you are told to do so by your doctor, or serious heart pain (angina) may develop.

Generic Name

Metronidazole

Brand Names

Flagyl
Metryl
Protostat
Satric

(Also available in generic form)

Type of Drug

Amoebicide.

Prescribed for

Acute amoebic dysentery; vaginal infections (trichomonas); diseases caused by some parasites; any specific types of bacterial infections.

General Information

Metronidazole may be prescribed for asymptomatic disease when the doctor feels that the use of this drug is indicated; specifically, asymptomatic females may be treated with this drug when vaginal examination shows evidence of trichomonas. Because trichomonas infection of the vaginal area is a veneral disease, asymptomatic sexual partners of treated patients should be treated simultaneously if the organism has been found to be present in the woman's genital tract, in order to prevent reinfection of the partner. The decision to treat an asymptomatic male partner who does not have the organism present is an individual one and must be made by the doctor.

Cautions and Warnings

If you have a history of blood disease or if you know that you are sensitive or allergic to Metronidazole you should not use this drug.

Metronidazole has been shown to be carcinogenic (cancer-inducing) in mice and possibly in rats. This drug should not be used unnecessarily and should only be used in specific conditions for which it is normally prescribed.

This drug may cause birth defects or interfere with your baby's development. Check with your doctor before taking it if you are, or might be, pregnant.

Breast-feeding while taking Metronidazole may cause unwanted side effects in your infant. If you must take Metronidazole, you should temporarily stop nursing and discard pumped breast milk. Nursing can resume 1 or 2 days after stopping Metronidazole.

Possible Side Effects

Most common: symptoms in the gastrointestinal tract, including nausea (sometimes accompanied by headache), loss of appetite, occasional vomiting, diarrhea, stomach upset, abdominal cramping, and constipation. A sharp, unpleasant metallic taste is also associated with the use of this drug. Dizziness and, rarely, incoordination have been reported. Numbness or tingling in the extremities and occasional joint pains have been associated with Metronidazole therapy as have confusion, irritability, depression, inability to sleep, and weakness. Itching and a sense of pelvic pressure have been reported.

Possible Adverse Drug Effects

Rarely: fever, increased urination, incontinence, decrease of libido.

Drug Interactions

Avoid alcoholic beverages: interaction with Metronidazole may cause abdominal cramps, nausea, vomiting, headaches, and flushing. Modification of the taste of alcoholic beverages has also been reported.

People taking oral anticoagulant (blood-thinning) drugs such as Warfarin will have to have their dose of Warfarin changed, because Metronidazole increases the effect of anticoagulants.

Usual Dose

Adult: for the treatment of amoebic dysentery, 3 tablets 3 times per day for 5 to 10 days.

Child: Amoebic dysentery, 16 to 23 milligrams per pound of body weight daily divided in 3 equal doses, for 10 days.

For trichomonal infections, 1 tablet 3 times per day for 7 days.

Special Information

Follow your doctor's dosage instructions faithfully and don't stop until the full course of therapy has been taken.

The occasional darkening of urine of patients taking Metronidazole is of uncertain clinical significance and is probably not important.

Generic Name

Miconazole Nitrate

Brand Names

Micatin
Monistat-7
Monistat-Derm

(Also available in generic form)

Type of Drug

Antifungal.

Prescribed for

Treatment of fungus infections in the vagina, on the skin, and in the blood.

General Information

Miconazole Nitrate is used as a vaginal cream or topical cream, or by intravenous injection. When given as an injection to hospitalized patients, it is effective against serious fungal infections. When used for vaginal infections, it is effective against several nonfungus types of organisms, as well as fungus-type infections of the vaginal tract. On the skin, it is used for common fungus infections such as athlete's foot or jock itch.

Cautions and Warnings

Do not use Miconazole Nitrate if you know you are allergic to it. Pregnant women should avoid using the vaginal cream during the first 3 months of pregnancy. They should use it during the next 6 months only if it is absolutely necessary.

Miconazole Nitrate has not been shown to cause problems in breast-fed infants.

Possible Side Effects

After intravenous injection: vein irritation, itching, rash, nausea, vomiting, fever, drowsiness, diarrhea, loss of appetite, flushing. After vaginal administration: itching, burning or

irritation, pelvic cramps, hives, rash, headache. After appli
cation to the skin: irritation, burning.

Usual Dose

Intravenous: 200 to 3600 milligrams per day.

Vaginal: One applicatorful into the vagina at bedtime for 7
days.

Topical: Apply to affected areas of skin twice a day for up
to 1 month.

Special Information

When using the vaginal cream, insert the whole applicatorful
of cream high into the vagina and be sure to complete the
full course of treatment prescribed for you. Call your doctor
if you develop burning or itching.

Generic Name

Minocycline

Brand Name

Minocin

Type of Drug

Broad-spectrum tetracycline-type antibiotic effective against
gram-positive and gram-negative organisms.

Prescribed for

Bacterial infections such as gonorrhea, infections of the mouth
gums, teeth, Rocky Mountain spotted fever and other fevers
caused by ticks and lice from a variety of carriers, urinary
tract infections, and respiratory system infections such as
pneumonia and bronchitis.

These diseases are produced by gram-positive and gram-
negative organisms such as diplococci, staphylococci, strep
tococci, gonococci, E. coli, and Shigella.

Minocycline has also been successfully used to treat some
skin infections, but it is not considered the first-choice anti
biotic for the treatment of general skin infections or wounds

General Information

Minocycline works by interfering with the normal growth cycle of the invading bacteria, preventing them from reproducing and thus allowing the body's normal defenses to fight off the infection. This process is referred to as bacteriostatic action. Minocycline has also been used along with other medicines to treat amoebic infections of the intestinal tract, known as amoebic dysentery. It is also prescribed for diseases caused by ticks, fleas, and lice.

Minocycline has been successfully used for the treatment of adolescent acne, in small doses over a long period of time. Adverse effects or toxicity in this type of therapy are almost unheard of.

Since the action of this antibiotic depends on its concentration within the invading bacteria, it is imperative that you completely follow your doctor's directions.

Cautions and Warnings

You should not use Minocycline if you are pregnant, especially during the last half of pregnancy or during breastfeeding when bones and teeth are being formed. Minocycline when used in children has been shown to interfere with the development of the long bones and may retard growth.

Exceptions would be when Minocycline is the only effective antibiotic available and all risk factors have been made known to the patient.

Minocycline should not be given to people with known liver disease or kidney or urine excretion problems. You should avoid taking high doses of Minocycline or undergoing extended Minocycline therapy if you will be exposed to sunlight for a long period because this antibiotic can interfere with your body's normal sun-screening mechanism, possibly causing a severe sunburn. If you have a known history of allergy to Minocycline you should avoid taking this drug or other drugs within this category such as Aureomycin, Terramycin, Rondomycin, Vibramycin, Demeclocycline, and Tetracycline.

Possible Side Effects

As with other antibiotics, the common side effects of Minocycline are stomach upset, nausea, vomiting, diarrhea, and skin rash. Less common side effects include hairy tongue and itching and irritation of the anal and/or vaginal region. If these symptoms appear, consult your physician immediately. Periodic physical examinations and laboratory tests should be given to patients who are on long-term Minocycline.

Possible Adverse Drug Effect

Loss of appetite, peeling of the skin, sensitivity to the sun, fever, chills, anemia, possible brown spotting of the skin, decrease in kidney function, damage to the liver.

Drug Interactions

Minocycline (a bacteriostatic drug) may interfere with the action of bactericidal agents such as Penicillin. It is not advisable to take both during the same course of therapy.

Don't take multivitamin products containing minerals at the same time as Minocycline, or you may reduce the antibiotic's effectiveness. You may take these two medicines at least 2 hours apart.

People receiving anticoagulation therapy (blood-thinning agents) should consult their doctor, since Minocycline will interfere with this form of therapy. An adjustment in the anticoagulant dosage may be required.

Food Interactions

The antibacterial effect of Minocycline is neutralized when taken with food, some dairy products (such as milk and cheese), and antacids.

Usual Dose

Adult: first dose, 200 milligrams, followed by 100 milligrams every 12 hours. Or 100 to 200 milligrams may be given to start, followed by 50 milligrams 4 times per day.

Child (age 9 and over): approximately 2 milligrams per pound of body weight initially, followed by 1 milligram per pound every 12 hours.

Child (up to age 8): not recommended, as the drug has been shown to produce serious discoloration of the permanent teeth.

Storage

Minocycline can be stored at room temperature.

Special Information

Do *not* take after the expiration date on the label. The decomposition of Minocycline produces a highly toxic substance which can cause serious kidney damage.

Generic Name

Minoxidil

Brand Name

Loniten

Type of Drug

Antihypertensive.

Prescribed for

Severe high blood pressure not controllable with other drugs. Early male-pattern baldness.

General Information

This drug can cause severe adverse effects on the heart. It is usually given together with a beta-blocking antihypertensive drug (Propranolol, Metoprolol, Nadolol, etc.) to prevent rapid heartbeat and a diuretic to prevent fluid accumulation. Some patients may have to be hospitalized when treatment with this drug is started, to avoid too rapid a drop in blood pressure.

Minoxidil works by dilating peripheral blood vessels and allowing more blood to flow through arms and legs. This increased blood flow reduces the resistance levels in central vessels (heart, lungs, kidneys, etc.) and therefore reduces blood pressure. Its effect on blood pressure can be seen ½ hour after a dose is taken and lasts up to 3 days. Patients usually take the medicine once or twice a day. Maximum drug effect occurs as early as 3 days after the drug is started, if the dose is large enough (40 milligrams per day).

Researchers have formulated a 1% solution of Minoxidil for application to the scalp to treat male-pattern baldness taking advantge of the side effect of causing hair growth. Applying this solution does not work for all people who try it and it is necessary to continue Minoxidil applications to maintain any new hair growth stimulated by the drug. This form of Minoxidil is currently being researched and may not become an approved form of therapy until 1986 or 1987.

Cautions and Warnings

This drug should not be used by people with pheochromo cytoma, a rare tumor in which extra body stimulants (cate cholamines) are made. Minoxidil may cause the accumulation of water and sodium in the body, leading to heart failure. It also increases heart rate. To protect you from these side effects, Minoxidil must be given with other drugs, a diuretic and a beta-adrenergic blocker.

Do not use Minoxidil if you are planning to become preg nant. This drug should be avoided by pregnant women or nursing mothers unless taking it is absolutely necessary. The effect of this drug on the unborn baby is not known.

It has not been carefully studied in patients who have suffered a heart attack within the past month.

Possible Side Effects

Water and sodium retention can develop, leading to heart failure. Also, some patients taking this drug may develop fluid in the sacs surrounding the heart. This is treated with diuretic drugs.

Eighty percent of people taking this drug experience thickening, elongation, and darkening of body hair within 3 to 6 weeks after starting Minoxidil. This is usually first noticed on the temples, between the eyebrows, between the eyebrows and hairline, or on the upper cheek. Later on it will extend to the back, arms, legs, and scalp. This effect stops when the drug is stopped and symptoms will disappear in 1 to 6 months. Electrocardiogram changes occur in 60 percent of patients but are usually not associated with any symptoms. Some other laboratory tests (blood, liver, kidney) may be affected by Minoxidil.

Possible Adverse Drug Effects

Minoxidil may interact with Guanethidine to produce dizziness when rising from a sitting or lying position.

Drug Interactions

Do not take over-the-counter drugs containing stimulants. If you are unsure which drugs to avoid, ask your pharmacist.

Food Interactions

This drug may be taken at any time. It is not affected by food or liquid intake.

Usual Dose

Adult and child (age 12 and over): 5 milligrams to start; may be increased to 40 milligrams per day. Do not take more than 100 milligrams per day. The daily dose of Minoxidil must be tailored to each patient's needs.

Child (under age 12): 0.1 milligram per pound per day to start; may be increased to 0.5 milligram per pound per day. Do not use more than 50 milligrams per day. The daily dose of Minoxidil must be tailored to each patient's needs.

Minoxidil is usually given together with a diuretic (Hydrochlorothiazide, 100 milligrams per day; Chlorthalidone, 50 to 100 milligrams per day; or Furosemide, 80 milligrams per day) and a beta-adrenergic blocker (Propranolol, 80 to 160 milligrams per day; or the equivalent dose of another drug). People who cannot take a beta-adrenergic blocker may take Methyldopa, 500 to 1500 milligrams per day, instead. 0.2 to 0.4 milligram per day of Clonidine may also be used.

Overdosage

Symptoms may be those associated with too low blood pressure. Contact your doctor or Poison Control Center if an overdose of Minoxidil occurs.

Special Information

Since Minoxidil is usually given with two other medications, a beta-adrenergic blocker and a diuretic, do not discontinue any of these drugs unless told to do so by your doctor. Take all medication exactly as prescribed.

The effect of this drug on body hair (see "Possible Side Effects") is a nuisance but not dangerous. Do not stop taking Minoxidil because of it.

Call your doctor if you experience an increase in your pulse of 20 or more beats per minute, weight gain of more than 5 pounds, unusual swelling of your arms and/or legs, face, or stomach, chest pain, difficulty in breathing, dizziness, or fainting spells.

Brand Name

Moduretic

Ingredients

Amiloride
Hydrochlorothiazide

Type of Drug

Diuretic.

Prescribed for

High blood pressure or any condition where it is desirable to eliminate excess fluid from the body.

General Information

Moduretic is a combination of two diuretics and is a convenient, effective approach for the treatment of diseases where the elimination of excess fluids is required. One of the ingredients in Moduretic, Amiloride, holds potassium in the body while producing a diuretic effect. This balances the Hydrochlorothiazide, which often causes a loss of potassium.

Combination drugs such as Moduretic should only be used when you need the exact amount of ingredients contained in the product and when your doctor feels you would benefit from taking one dose per day.

Cautions and Warnings

This drug should not be used by people with diabetes or kidney disease or those who are allergic to either of these ingredients or to sulfa drugs. This drug may cause abnormally high blood potassium levels. Since too much potassium in your blood can be fatal, your doctor should test blood potassium levels periodically.

This drug should only be used by pregnant women or nursing mothers if absolutely necessary.

This drug may cause birth defects or interfere with your baby's development. Check with your doctor before taking it if you are, or might be, pregnant.

Possible Side Effects

Headache, weakness, tiredness, dizziness, difficulty in breathing, abnormal heart rhythms, nausea, loss of appetite, diarrhea, stomach and abdominal pains, decrease in blood potassium, rash, itching, leg pains.

Possible Adverse Drug Effects

Feeling sick, chest and back pain, heart palpitations, dizziness when rising from a sitting or lying position, angina pain, constipation, stomach bleeding, stomach upset, appetite changes, feeling of being bloated, hiccups, thirst, vomiting, stomach gas, gout, dehydration, flushing, muscle cramps or spasms, joint pain, tingling in the arms or legs, feeling of numbness, stupor, sleeplessness, nervousness, depression, sleepiness, confusion, visual disturbances, bad taste in the mouth, stuffy nose, sexual impotence, urinary difficulties, dry mouth, adverse effects on the blood system, fever, shock, allergic reactions, jaundice, liver damage, sugar in the blood or urine, unusual sensitivity to the sun, restlessness.

Drug Interactions

Moduretic will add to (potentiate) the action of other blood-pressure-lowering drugs. Since this is beneficial, it is frequently used to help lower blood pressure in patients with hypertension.

The possibility of developing imbalances in body fluids (electrolytes) is increased if you take other medications such as Digitalis and adrenal corticosteroids while you are taking Moduretic.

If you are taking an oral antidiabetic drug and begin taking Moduretic, the antidiabetic dose may have to be altered.

Lithium Carbonate should not be taken with Moduretic because the combination may increase the risk of Lithium toxicity.

Avoid over-the-counter cough, cold, or allergy remedies containing stimulant drugs which can aggravate your condition.

Moduretic may interfere with the oral blood-thinning drugs such as Warfarin by making the blood more concentrated (thicker).

Usual Dose

1 to 2 tablets per day.

Overdosage

Signs are tingling in the arms or legs, weakness, fatigue, slow heartbeat, a sickly feeling, dryness of the mouth, lethargy, restlessness, muscle pains or cramps, low blood pressure, rapid heartbeat, urinary difficulty, nausea, or vomiting. A patient who has taken a Moduretic overdose should be taken to a hospital emergency room. ALWAYS bring the medicine bottle.

Special Information

This drug can affect your concentration. Do not drive or operate machinery while taking it.

Brand Name

Mycolog Cream/Ointment

Ingredients

Gramicidin	Nystatin
Neomycin	Triamcinolone Acetonide

Other Brand Names

Mycogen	Mytrex
Myco-Triacet	Tri-Statin
Mykacet	

(Also available in generic form)

Type of Drug

Topical adrenal corticosteroid combination.

Prescribed for

Relief of infected rash or inflammation.

General Information

Mycolog Cream/Ointment is used to relieve the symptoms of itching, rash, or inflammation of the skin. It does not treat the underlying cause of the skin problem, but only the symptoms. It exerts this effect by interfering with natural body mechanisms that produced the rash, itching, etc., in the first place. If you use this drug without finding the cause of the problem, you may find that the problem returns after you stop using it. Mycolog Cream/Ointment should not be used without your doctor's consent because it could cover an important reaction, one that may be of value to him in treating you.

Cautions and Warnings

Do not use Mycolog Cream/Ointment if you are allergic to any of its ingredients. This drug should not be used in the eyes, or the external ear if the eardrum is perforated, unless you are specifically directed to do so by your doctor. Severe local infections require antibiotic therapy. If you have some Mycolog Cream/Ointment left over from an old prescription, do not use it without first contacting your doctor. If this medication fails to help you or a new infection develops on your skin while you are using it, contact your doctor so that appropriate treatment can be given.

This drug has been found to be safe for use during pregnancy. Remember, you should check with your doctor before taking any drug if you are pregnant.

Possible Side Effects

Most frequent: burning sensation, itching, irritation of the skin, dryness, secondary infection after prolonged use of this medication.

Usual Dose

Apply to affected areas several times daily.

Special Information

Clean the skin before applying Mycolog Cream/Ointment, to prevent secondary infection. Apply in a very thin film (effectiveness is based on contact area and not on thickness of the layer applied).

Brand Name

Mysteclin-F

Other Brand Name

Tetrastatin

Ingredients

Amphotericin-B
Tetracycline

(Also available in generic form)

Type of Drug

Broad-spectrum antibiotic antifungal combination.

Prescribed for

Bacterial infections such as gonorrhea, infections of the mouth,
gums and teeth, Rocky Mountain spotted fever and other
fevers caused by ticks and lice from a variety of carriers,
urinary tract infections, and respiratory system infections
such as pneumonia and bronchitis.

  These diseases may be produced by gram-positive or gram-
negative organisms such as diplococci, staphylococci, streptococci, gonococci, *E. coli*, and *Shigella*.

  Mysteclin-F has also been successfully used to treat some
skin infections, but is not considered the first-choice antibiotic for the treatment of general skin infections or wounds.

General Information

Mysteclin-F works by interfering with the normal growth
cycle of the invading bacteria, preventing them from reproducing and thus allowing the body's normal growth defenses to fight off the infection. This process is referred to as
bacteriostatic action. Mysteclin-F has also been used along
with other medicines to treat amoebic infections of the intestinal tract, known as amoebic dysentery. It is also prescribed
for diseases caused by ticks, fleas, and lice. This combination should be used only by people who are susceptible to
developing candida (fungus) when taking Tetracycline.

  Since the action of this antibiotic depends on its concenration within the invading bacteria, it is imperative that you, the patient, completely follow the doctor's directions.

Cautions and Warnings

You should not use Mysteclin-F if you are pregnant or nursing. Mysteclin-F, when used in children, has been shown to interfere with the development of the long bones and may retard growth.

Exceptions would be when Mysteclin-F is the only effective antibiotic available and all risk factors have been made known to the patient.

Mysteclin-F should not be given to people with known liver disease or to people with kidney or urine excretion problems. You should avoid taking high doses of Mysteclin-F or undergoing extended Mysteclin-F therapy if you will be exposed to sunlight for a long period because this antibiotic can interfere with your body's normal sun-screening mechanism, possibly causing severe sunburn. If you have a known history of allergy to Mysteclin-F you should avoid taking this drug or other drugs within this category such as Aureomycin, Terramycin, Rondomycin, Vibramycin, Tetracycline, Demeclocycline, and Minocycline.

Possible Side Effects

Amphotericin-B, when given by mouth, is not absorbed into the blood system. For this reason there are few side effects associated with Amphotericin-B in this combination.

As with other antibiotics, the common side effects of Mysteclin-F are stomach upset, nausea, vomiting, diarrhea, and rash. Less common side effects include hairy tongue and itching and irritation of the anal and/or vaginal region. If these symptoms appear, consult your physician immediately. Periodic physical examinations and laboratory tests should be given to patients who are on long-term Mysteclin-F.

Possible Adverse Drug Effects

Loss of appetite, peeling of the skin, sensitivity to the sun, fever, chills, anemia, possible brown spotting of the skin, decrease in kidney function, damage to the liver.

Drug Interactions

Mysteclin-F (a bacteriostatic drug) may interfere with the

action of bactericidal agents such as Penicillin. It is not advisable to take both.

Don't take multivitamin products containing minerals at the same time as Mysteclin-F, or you will reduce the antibiotic's effectiveness. Space the taking of these two medicines at least 2 hours apart.

People receiving anticoagulation therapy (blood-thinning agents) should consult their doctor, since Mysteclin-F will interfere with this form of therapy. An adjustment in the anticoagulant dosage may be required.

Food Interactions

The antibacterial effect of Mysteclin-F is neutralized when taken with food, some dairy products including milk and cheese, and antacids.

Usual Dose

Adult: 250 to 500 milligrams 4 times per day.

Child (age 9 and over): 10 to 20 milligrams per pound of body weight per day in divided doses taken 1 hour before or 2 hours after meals.

Child (up to age 8): should avoid Mysteclin-F, as it has been shown to produce serious discoloration of the permanent teeth.

Special Information

Do not take outdated Mysteclin-F under any circumstances. Its decomposition produces a highly toxic substance which can cause serious kidney damage.

The only difference between Mysteclin-F and Tetracycline is that Mysteclin-F contains a small amount of Amphotericin-B to prevent the growth of fungal organisms in the intestine. Since the Amphotericin-B in Mysteclin-F is often ineffective in reducing the incidence of fungal infections, you may be better off taking plain Tetracycline. Discuss it with your doctor.

Generic Name

Nadolol

Brand Name

Corgard

Type of Drug

Beta-adrenergic blocking agent.

Prescribed for

High blood pressure; angina pectoris (a specific type of chest pain).

General Information

This drug is quite similar to Propranolol, another beta-blocking agent. It has not been studied in as many kinds of problems as Propranolol, but it is very useful because it can be taken once a day. When used for high blood pressure, it is usually given with a diuretic such as Hydrochlorothiazide.

Cautions and Warnings

Nadolol should be used with care if you have a history of asthma or other upper respiratory disease or of heart failure. You should stop taking the drug several days before major surgery, if possible. Do not do this without telling your doctor. Nadolol can hide some symptoms of diabetes or thyroid disease.

Pregnant women should use this drug only if it is absolutely necessary. Although no adverse effects on the unborn child have been reported, drugs similar to Nadolol have been shown to cause problems during pregnancy in animal studies when used in very high amounts. Studies in humans are not definitive.

Possible Side Effects

Nadolol may decrease the heart rate; may aggravate a condition of congestive heart failure; and may produce lowered blood pressure, tingling in the extremities, light-headedness, mental depression including inability to sleep, weakness, and tiredness. It may also produce a mental depression which is reversible when the drug is withdrawn, visual disturbances, hallucinations, disorientation, and short-term memory loss. Patients taking Nadolol may experience nausea, vomiting, stomach upset, abdominal cramps and diarrhea, or constipation. If you are allergic to this drug, you may show typical reactions associated with drug allergies, including sore throat, fever, difficulty in breathing, and various effects on the blood system. Nadolol may induce bronchospasms (spasms of muscles in the bronchi), which will make any existing asthmatic condition or any severe upper respiratory disease worse.

Possible Adverse Drug Effects

Occasionally, patients taking Nadolol may experience emotional instability, or a feeling of detachment or personality change, or the drug may produce unusual effects on the blood system.

Drug Interactions

This drug will interact with any psychotropic drug, including the MAO inhibitors, which stimulates one of the adrenergic segments of the nervous system. Since this information is not generally known, you should discuss the potential problem of using Nadolol with your doctor if you are taking any psychotropic or psychiatric drug.

Nadolol may cause increased effectiveness of Insulin or oral antidiabetic drugs. If you are diabetic, discuss the situation with your doctor; a reduction in dose of antidiabetic medication will probably be made.

Nadolol may reduce the effectiveness of Digitalis on your heart. Any dose of Digitalis medication will have to be altered. If you are taking Digitalis for a purpose other than congestive heart failure, the effectiveness of the Digitalis may be increased by Nadolol, and the dose of Digitalis may have to be reduced.

Nadolol may interact with certain other drugs to lower blood pressure. This interaction often has positive results in the treatment of patients with high blood pressure.

Do not self-medicate with over-the-counter cold, cough, or allergy remedies which may contain stimulant drugs that will aggravate certain types of heart disease and high blood pressure, or other ingredients that may antagonize the effects of Nadolol. Double-check with your doctor or pharmacist before taking any over-the-counter medication.

Usual Dose

40 to 640 milligrams per day. Patients with bad kidneys may take their medication dosage as infrequently as once every 60 hours.

Overdosage

Symptoms are slowed heart rate, heart failure, lowered blood pressure, and spasms of the bronchial muscles which make it difficult to breathe. The patient should be taken to a hospital emergency room where proper therapy can be given. ALWAYS bring the medicine bottle with you.

Special Information

Nadolol may be taken at any time, without regard to meals. Since this drug is taken only once a day, be sure to take it at the same time every day. Do not stop taking the drug abruptly unless your doctor tells you to, or serious heart pain and other effects can occur. Call your doctor if you have trouble breathing when you exert yourself or are lying down, have a nighttime cough, or develop swollen ankles, arms, or legs.

Brand Name

Naldecon Tablets

Ingredients

Chlorpheniramine Maleate
Phenylephrine Hydrochloride
Phenylpropanolamine Hydrochloride
Phenytoloxamine Citrate

Other Brand Names

Amaril "D"	Sinocon
Decongestabs	Tri-phen-chlor
Nalgest	Tudecon
Quarda-Hist	Vasomimic T.D.

(Also available in generic form)

Type of Drug

Long-acting combination antihistamine-decongestant.

Prescribed for

Relief of sneezing, runny nose, and nasal congestion associated with the common cold, allergy, or other upper respiratory condition.

General Information

Naldecon Tablets are one of many products marketed to relieve the symptoms of the common cold. Most of these products contain ingredients to relieve nasal congestion or to dry up runny noses or relieve a scratchy throat; and several of them may contain ingredients to suppress cough, or to help eliminate unwanted mucus. All these products are good only for the relief of symptoms and do not treat the underlying problem such as a cold virus or other infections.

Cautions and Warnings

This drug may cause birth defects or interfere with your baby's development. Check with your doctor before taking it if you are, or might be, pregnant.

Possible Side Effects

Mild drowsiness.

Possible Adverse Drug Effects

Infrequent: restlessness, tension, nervousness, tremor, weakness, inability to sleep, headache, palpitations, elevation of blood pressure, sweating, sleeplessness, loss of appetite, nausea, vomiting, dizziness, constipation.

Drug Interactions

Interaction with sedatives, tranquilizers, antihistamines, sleeping pills, thyroid medicine, and antihypertensive drugs such as Reserpine or Guanethidine may produce excessive drowsiness and/or sleepiness, or inability to concentrate.

Do not self-medicate with over-the-counter drugs for the relief of cold symptoms; taking Naldecon Tablets with such drugs may aggravate high blood pressure, heart disease, diabetes, or thyroid disease.

Do not take Naldecon Tablets if you are taking or suspect you may be taking a monoamine oxidase (MAO) inhibitor: severe elevation in blood pressure may result.

Drug Interactions

Naldecon and other similar cold products interact with alcoholic beverages and can cause excessive drowsiness.

Food Interactions

If this drug upsets your stomach it should be taken with food.

Usual Dose

Adult and child (age 12 and over): 1 tablet 3 times per day.
Child (under age 12): not recommended.

Special Information

Since drowsiness may occur during use of Naldecon Tablets, be cautious while performing mechanical tasks requiring alertness.

Generic Name

Naproxen

Brand Name

Anaprox
Naprosyn

(Also available in generic form)

Type of Drug

Nonsteroid anti-inflammatory.

Prescribed for

Relief of pain and inflammation of joints and muscles; arthritis, mild to moderate pain of menstrual cramps, dental surgery and extractions, rheumatoid and osteoarthritis, ankylosing spondylitis, tendonitis, bursitis, and acute gout.

General Information

Naproxen is one of several nonsteroid anti-inflammatory drugs used to reduce inflammation, relieve pain, or reduce fever. All non steroid anti-inflammatory drugs share the same side effects and may be used by patients who cannot tolerate Aspirin. Choice of one of these drugs over another depends on disease response, side effects seen in a particular patient, convenience of times to be taken, and cost. Different drugs or different doses of the same drug may be tried until the greatest effectiveness is seen with the fewest side effects.

Cautions and Warnings

Do not take Naproxen if you are allergic or sensitive to this drug, Aspirin, or other nonsteroid anti-inflammatory drugs. Naproxen may cause stomach ulcers. This drug should not be used by patients with severe kidney or liver disease.

This drug is not recommended for pregnant women. Naproxen may have unwanted effects on the heart and blood of the unborn child. The length of pregnancy may be increased if Naproxen is taken late in pregnancy.

Naproxen has not been shown to cause problems during breast-feeding.

Possible Side Effects

Stomach upset, blurred vision, darkening of stool, changes in color vision, rash, itching, weight gain, retention of fluids.

Possible Adverse Drug Effects

Most frequent: stomach upset, dizziness, headache, drowsiness, ringing in the ears. Others: heartburn, nausea, vomiting, bloating, gas in the stomach, stomach pain, diarrhea, constipation, dark stool, nervousness, insomnia, depression, confusion, tremor, loss of appetite, fatigue, itching, rash, double vision, abnormal heart rhythm, anemia or other changes in the composition of the blood, changes in liver function, loss of hair, tingling in the hands and feet, fever, breast enlargement, lowered blood sugar, effects on the kidneys. If symptoms appear, stop taking the medicine and see your doctor immediately.

Drug Interactions

Naproxen increases the action of Phenytoin, sulfa drugs, drugs used to control diabetes, and drugs used to thin the blood. If you are taking any of these medicines, be sure to discuss it with your doctor, who will probably change the dose of the other drug.

An adjustment in the dose of Naproxen may be needed if you take Phenobarbital.

Do not take Aspirin while you are taking Naproxen. This combination offers no advantage and may be detrimental.

Usual Dose

Adult: 250 milligrams to 375 milligrams morning and night, to start. Dose may be adjusted up to 1250 milligrams per day, if needed. Mild to moderate pain: 250 milligrams every 6 to 8 hours.

Child: not recommended.

Brand Name
Natalins

Ingredients

Calcium	Vitamin B$_3$ (Niacin)
Folic Acid (Vitamin B$_9$)	Vitamin B$_6$ (Pyridoxine)
Iodine	Vitamin B$_{12}$ (Cyanocobalmin)
Magnesium	Vitamin C
Vitamin A	Vitamin D
Vitamin B$_1$ (Thiamine)	Vitamin E
Vitamin B$_2$ (Riboflavin)	

Type of Drug

Vitamin (with minerals).

Prescribed for

Prenatal vitamin supplement.

General Information

Natalins is one of many prenatal vitamin formulas which can be bought without a prescription. It does not contain Vitamin B_5, Biotin, Copper, or Zinc. The rationale for using prenatal vitamins is to see that the expectant mother receives sufficient vitamins and minerals to keep her healthy and support the growth of the baby she is carrying. Some people state that what vitamin pills provide can be obtained by eating the right foods. However, practical experience has told us that pregnant women can't eat everything they need to satisfy nutritional requirements. Therefore, most obstetricians prescribe a prenatal vitamin supplement for pregnant patients. There are many different combinations of these same vitamins with actions similar to Natalins, including Natabec RX, Materna, Stuart Pre-Natal and Mission Pre-Natal.

Cautions and Warnings

Do not take Natalins if you are allergic or sensitive to any of its ingredients.

This drug has been found to be safe for use during pregnancy. Remember, you should check with your doctor before taking any drug if you are pregnant.

Possible Side Effects

Indigestion, gastrointestinal intolerance.

Possible Adverse Drug Effects

Serious adverse effects are rare.

Usual Dose

1 tablet per day.

Brand Name

Neosporin Ophthalmic Solution

Ingredients

Gramicidin
Neomycin Sulfate
Polymyxin-B Sulfate

(Also available in generic form)

Type of Drug

Topical antibiotic for use in the eye.

Prescribed for

Superficial infections of the eye.

General Information

Neosporin Ophthalmic Solution is a combination of antibiotics which are effective against the most common eye infections. It is most useful when the infecting organism is one known to be sensitive to one of the three antibiotics contained in Neosporin Ophthalmic Solution. It is also useful when the infecting organism is not known, because of the drug's broad range of coverage.

Prolonged use of any antibiotic product in the eye should be avoided because of the possibility of developing sensitivity to the antibiotic. Frequent or prolonged use of antibiotics in the eye may result in the growth of other organisms such as fungi. If the infection does not clear up within a few days, contact your doctor.

Cautions and Warnings

Neosporin Ophthalmic Solution should not be used if you know you are sensitive to or have an allergy to this product or to any of the ingredients in it.

This drug has been found to be safe for use during pregnancy. Remember, you should check with your doctor before taking any drug if you are pregnant.

Possible Side Effects

Occasional local irritation after application to the eye.

Usual Dose

1 to 2 drops in the affected eye or eyes 2 to 4 times per day; more frequently if the infection is severe.

Generic Name

Nicotine

Brand Name

Nicorette Chewing Gum

Type of Drug

Smoking deterrent.

Prescribed for

People addicted to cigarettes who need another source of their drug (Nicotine) to help break the smoking habit.

General Information

Nicotine is known to affect many brain functions, including improving memory, increasing one's ability to perform a number of different tasks, reducing hunger, and increasing tolerance to pain. This chewing gum, a source of noninhaled Nicotine, makes cigarette withdrawal much easier for many people. Although this product is designed to fulfill a specific need in those trying to quit smoking, there are a great many other social and psychological needs filled by smoking. These must be dealt with through counseling or other psychological support in order for a program to be successful.

You may be addicted to Nicotine if you smoke more than 15 cigarettes per day; prefer unfiltered cigarettes or those with a high nicotine content; usually inhale the smoke; have your first cigarette within 30 minutes of getting up in the morning; find the first morning cigarette the hardest to give up; smoke most frequently in the morning hours; find it hard to obey "no smoking" signs or rules; smoke even when you are sick in bed.

Cautions and Warnings

Nicotine Chewing Gum should not be used by nonsmokers or others who are not addicted to the effects of this drug. It should not be used during the period immediately following a heart attack or if severe abnormal heart rhythms, angina pains, or severe temperomandibular joint (TMJ) disease are present. People with other heart conditions must be evaluated by a cardiologist (heart doctor) before starting treatment with Nicotine Chewing Gum.

This product should be used with caution by diabetics being treated with Insulin or people with an overactive thyroid, pheochromocytoma, high blood pressure, stomach ulcers, and chronic dental problems that might be worsened by Nicotine Chewing Gum.

It is possible for Nicotine addiction to be transferred from cigarettes to the gum or for the addiction actually to worsen while using the product.

This product should not be used by women who are pregnant or who might become pregnant because Nicotine is known to harm the developing baby when taken during the last 3 months of pregnancy. Nicotine, whether from cigarettes or chewing gum, interferes with the newborn baby's ability to breath properly. Additionally, one miscarriage has occurred in a woman using Nicotine Chewing Gum. Mothers should not breast-feed while using this product since Nicotine passes into breast milk and can be harmful to a growing infant.

Possible Side Effects

Injury to gums, jaw, or teeth; stomach growling due to swallowing air. Other common systemic side effects are nausea, vomiting, hiccups, and upset stomach.

Possible Adverse Drug Effects

Excessive salivation, dizziness, light-headedness, irritability, headache, increased bowel movement, diarrhea, constipation, gas pains, dry mouth, hoarseness, facial flushing, sneezing, coughing, feeling "high" and sleeplessness.

Drug Interactions

Heavy smokers who suddenly stop smoking may experience

an increase in the effects of a variety of drugs whose break-downs are known to be stimulated by cigarettes. If you are taking any of the following medications, your dosage may have to be reduced to account for this effect: Theophylline, Imipramine, Pentazocine, Furosemide, Propranolol, Propoxyphene Hydrochloride.

Smoking increases the rate at which your body breaks down caffeine. Stopping Nicotine may make you more sensitive to the effects of the caffeine in coffee or tea.

Usual Dose

1 piece of gum whenever you feel the urge for a cigarette, not more than 30 per day. Each piece contains 2 milligrams of Nicotine.

Overdosage

Nicotine overdosage can be deadly. Symptoms include salivation, nausea, vomiting, diarrhea, abdominal pains, headache, cold sweats, dizziness, hearing and visual disturbances, weakness, and confusion. In untreated, these symptoms will be followed by fainting, very low blood pressure, a pulse that is weak, rapid, and irregular, convulsions, and death by paralysis of the muscles that control breathing. The lethal dose of Nicotine is about 50 milligrams.

Nicotine stimulates the brain's vomiting center, making this reaction common, but not automatic. Spontaneous vomiting may be sufficient to remove the poison from the victim's system. If this has not occurred, call your doctor or Poison Control Center for instructions on how to make the victim vomit by giving Syrup of Ipecac. If the victim must be treated in a hospital emergency room, ALWAYS bring the chewing gum package with you.

Special Information

Follow the instructions on the Patient Information Sheet included in each package of the gum.

Chew each piece of the gum slowly and intermittently for about 30 minutes to promote slow and even absorption of the Nicotine through the tissues in your mouth. Too-rapid chewing releases the Nicotine too quickly and can lead to side effects of nausea, hiccups, or throat irritation.

You will learn to control your daily dose of Nicotine chewing gum so that your smoking habit is broken and side effects are minimized. Do not chew more than 30 pieces of gum per day. The amount of gum chewed each day should be gradually reduced after 3 months of successful treatment.

Nicotine Chewing Gum is not recommended for more than 6 months at a time.

Generic Name

Nicotinic Acid (Niacin)

Brand Names

Niac	Nico-Span
Nicobid	Nicotinex
Nico 400	Span-Niacin
Nicolar	Tega-Span

(Also available in generic form)

Type of Drug

Vitamin.

Prescribed for

Treatment of Nicotinic Acid deficiency (pellagra). Also, prescribed to help lower high blood levels of lipids or fats, and to help dilate or enlarge certain blood vessels.

General Information

Nicotinic Acid or Niacin, also known as Vitamin B_3, is essential to normal body function through the part it plays in enzyme activity. It is effective in lowering blood levels of fats and can help enlarge or dilate certain blood vessels, but we do not know exactly how it does these things. Normally, individual requirements of Nicotinic Acid are easily supplied in a well-rounded diet.

Cautions and Warnings

Do not take this drug if you are sensitive or allergic to it or to any related drugs or if you have liver disease, stomach ulcer, severely low blood pressure, or hemorrhage (bleeding).

When used in normal doses Nicotinic Acid can be taken by pregnant women, but if it is used in high doses (to help lower blood levels of fats) there may be some problems. Although Niacin has not been shown to cause birth defects or problems in breast-fed infants, if you are pregnant or nursing consult with your doctor.

Possible Side Effects

Most common: flushing (redness and a warm sensation in the face and hands).

Possible Adverse Drug Effects

Decreased sugar tolerance in diabetics, activation of stomach ulcers, jaundice (yellowing of the whites of the eyes and skin), stomach upset, oily skin, dry skin, possible aggravation of skin conditions such as acne, itching, high blood levels of uric acid, low blood pressure, temporary headache, tingling feeling, skin rash, abnormal heartbeats, dizziness.

Drug Interactions

Nicotinic Acid, which can enlarge blood vessels, can intensify the effect of antihypertensive (blood-pressure-lowering) drugs, causing postural hypotension (getting dizzy when you rise quickly from a sitting or lying position).

If you are diabetic, large doses of Nicotinic Acid can throw your blood sugar slightly out of control and your doctor may have to adjust either your diet or your drug therapy.

Usual Dose

Supplementary vitamin product: 25 milligrams per day.

Treatment of high blood levels of lipids or fats: initial dose, 500 milligrams to 3 grams per day with or after meals. (Take with cold water to assist in swallowing.) If 3 grams does not prove effective the dose may be increased slowly to a maximum of 6 grams per day.

The dose should be built up slowly so you can watch carefully for common side effects: flushing or redness of the face and extremities, itching, and stomach upset.

Generic Name

Nifedipine

Brand Name

Procardia

Type of Drug

Calcium channel blocker.

Prescribed for

Angina pectoris and Prinzmetal's angina.

It has also been prescribed to treat high blood pressure, asthma and Raynaud's Disease.

General Information

Nifedipine was the first member of a new drug group to be marketed in the United States. It works by blocking the passage of calcium into heart and smoothe muscle. Since calcium is an essential factor in muscle contraction, any drug that affects calcium in this way will interfere with the contraction of these muscles. When this happens the amount of oxygen used by the muscles is also reduced. Therefore, Nifedipine is used in the treatment of angina, a type of heart pain related to poor oxygen supply to the heart muscles. Also, Nifedipine dilates the vessels that supply blood to the heart muscles and prevents spasm of these arteries. Nifedipine only affects the movement of calcium into muscle cells. It does not have any affect on calcium in the blood.

Cautions and Warnings

Nifedipine may cause lowered blood pressure in some patients. Patients taking a beta-blocking drug who begin taking Nifedipine may develop heart failure or increased angina pain. Do not take this drug if you have had an allergic reaction to it. This drug may cause birth defects or interfere with your baby's development. Check with your doctor before taking it if you are, or might be, pregnant.

Possible Side Effects

Dizziness, light-headedness, flushing, a feeling of warmth,

headache, weakness, nausea, heartburn, muscle cramps, tremors, swelling of the arms or legs, nervousness, mood changes, heart palpitations, difficulty breathing, coughs, wheezing, stuffy nose, sore throat.

Possible Adverse Drug Effects

Less frequently: shortness of breath, diarrhea, cramps, stomach gas, muscle cramps, stiffness and inflammation of the joints, shakiness, jitteriness, blurred vision, difficulty sleeping, difficulty maintaining balance, itching, rash, fever, sweating, chills, sexual difficulties. In addition, some patients taking Nifedipine have experienced heart attack, heart failure, fluid in the lungs, and abnormal heart rhythms. The occurrence of these serious effects have not been directly related to taking Nifedipine. Future research may tell us whether Nifedipine actually causes these problems or if the occurrence is merely coincidental. Nifedipine can cause increases in certain blood enzyme tests.

Drug Interactions

Nifedipine may interact with the beta-blocking drugs to cause heart failure, very low blood pressure, or an increased incidence of angina pain. However, in many cases these drugs have been taken together with no problem. Nifedipine may cause a lowering of blood pressure in patients already taking medicine to control their high blood pressure through interaction with the other antihypertensive drugs.

Food Interactions

Take this drug 1 hour before or 2 hours after meals.

Usual Dose

30 to 120 milligrams per day. No patient should take more than 180 milligrams per day. If you have been taking Nifedipine, do not stop taking the drug abruptly. The dosage should be gradually reduced over a period of time.

Overdosage

Overdose of Nifedipine can cause low blood pressure. If you think you have taken an overdose of Nifedipine, call your doctor or go to a hospital emergency room. ALWAYS bring the medicine bottle.

Special Information

Call your doctor if you develop swelling in the arms or legs, difficulty breathing, increased heart pains, dizziness or light-headedness, or lowered blood pressure.

Generic Name

Nitrofurantoin

Brand Names

Furadantin	Furatoin
Furalan	Macrodantin
Furan	Nitrofan
Furanite	

(Also available in generic form)

Type of Drug

Urinary anti-infective.

Prescribed for

Urinary tract infections by organisms susceptible to Nitrofurantoin. These organisms cause pyelonephritis, pyelitis, and cystitis.

General Information

Nitrofurantoin, like several other drugs (including Naladixic Acid [NegGram]), is of value in treating urinary tract infections because it appears in large amounts in the urine. It should not be used to treat infections in other parts of the body.

Cautions and Warnings

Do not take Nitrofurantoin if you have kidney disease, or if you are allergic to this agent. This drug may cause birth defects or interfere with your baby's development. Check with your doctor before taking it if you are, or might be, pregnant. It may cause problems during breast-feeding.

Possible Side Effects

Loss of appetite, nausea, vomiting, stomach pain, and diarrhea. Some people develop hepatitis symptoms.

Side effects are less prominent when Macrodantin (large crystal form of Nitrofurantoin) is used rather than Furadantin (regular crystal size).

Possible Adverse Drug Effects

Fever, chills, cough, chest pain, difficulty in breathing, development of fluid in the lungs; if these occur in the first week of therapy they can generally be resolved by stopping the medication. If they develop after a longer time they can be more serious because they develop more slowly and are more difficult to associate with the drug. If you develop chest pains or difficulty in breathing while taking Nitrofurantoin, report the effects to your physician immediately. Other adverse effects: rashes, itching, asthmatic attacks in patients with history of asthma, drug fever, symptoms similar to arthritis, jaundice (yellowing of the whites of the eyes and/or skin), effects on components of the blood, headache, dizziness, drowsiness, temporary loss of hair. The oral liquid form of Nitrofurantoin can stain your teeth if you don't swallow the medicine rapidly.

This drug is known to cause changes in the blood. Therefore, it should be used only under strict supervision by your doctor.

Food Interactions

Nitrofurantoin may be given with food or milk to help decrease stomach upset, loss of appetite, nausea, or other gastrointestinal symptoms.

Usual Dose

Adult: 50 to 100 milligrams 4 times per day.

Child (over age 3 months): 2 to 3 milligrams per pound of body weight in 4 divided doses.

Child (under age 3 months): not recommended.

Nitrofurantoin may be used in lower doses over a long period by people with chronic urinary infections.

Continue to take this medicine at least 3 days after you stop experiencing symptoms of urinary tract infection.

Special Information

Nitrofurantoin may give your urine a brownish color: this is not dangerous.

Generic Name

Nitroglycerin

Brand Names

Klavikordal	Nitrolin
N-G-C	Nitro-Long
Niong	Nitronet
Nitro-Bid	Nitrong
Nitro-Bid Plateau Caps	Nitrospan
Nitrocap	Nitrostat
Nitrodisc Patches	Nitrostat SR
Nitro-Dur Patches	Transderm Nitro Patches
Nitroglyn	Trates Granucaps
Nitrol	

(Also available in generic form)

Type of Drug

Antianginal agent.

Prescribed for

Prevention and treatment of chest pains associated with angina pectoris.

General Information

Nitroglycerin is available in several dosage forms, including sublingual tablets (which are taken under the tongue and are allowed to dissolve), capsules (which are swallowed), transmucosal tablets (which are placed between lip or cheek and gum and are allowed to dissolve), patches (which deliver Nitroglycerin through the skin over a 24-hour period), and ointment (which is usually spread over the chest wall, although it can be spread on any area of the body). Frequently patients may take one or more dosage forms of Nitroglycerin to prevent and/or treat the attack of chest pain associated with angina.

Cautions and Warnings

You should not take Nitroglycerin if you are known to be allergic to it. Also, because Nitroglycerin will increase the pressure of fluid inside your head, it should be taken with great caution if head trauma or bleeding in the head is present.

This drug has been found to be safe for use during pregnancy. Remember, you should check with your doctor before taking any drug if you are pregnant.

Possible Side Effects

The most frequent side effect of Nitroglycerin is flushing of the skin. Headache is common and may be severe or persistent. Once in a while, episodes of dizziness and weakness have been associated with the use of Nitroglycerin. There is a possibility that you will experience blurred vision. If this occurs, stop taking the drug and call your physician.

Possible Adverse Drug Effects

Occasionally an individual exhibits a marked sensitivity to the blood-pressure-lowering effect of Nitroglycerin, causing severe responses of nausea, vomiting, weakness, restlessness, loss of facial color or pallor, perspiration, and collapse even with the usual therapeutic dose. Drug rash occasionally occurs.

Drug Interactions

If you are taking Nitroglycerin continuously, avoid excessive alcohol intake, which may cause lowering of blood pressure and resulting faintness and dizziness.

Avoid over-the-counter drugs containing stimulants, which may aggravate your heart disease. Such drugs are used to treat coughs, colds, and allergies, and as appetite suppressants.

Usual Dose

Only as much as is necessary to control chest pains. Since

the sublingual dosage form (tablet taken under the tongue) acts within 10 to 15 seconds of being taken, the drug is only taken when necessary.

Long-acting (sustained-release) capsules or tablets are generally used to prevent chest pains associated with angina, with the dose being 1 capsule or tablet every 8 to 12 hours.

1 to 2 inches of Nitroglycerin ointment are squeezed from the tube onto a prepared piece of paper with markings on it. (Some patients may require as much as 4 to 5 inches.) The ointment is spread on the skin every 3 to 4 hours as needed for control of chest pains. The drug is absorbed through the skin. Application sites should be rotated to prevent skin inflammation and rash.

Patches are placed on the chest once a day and left on for 24 hours.

Special Information

The sublingual form (tablets which are dissolved under the tongue) should be acquired from your pharmacist only in the original, unopened bottle, and the tablets must not be transferred to a secondary bottle or container; otherwise the tablets may lose potency. Close the bottle tightly after each use or the drug may evaporate from the tablets.

The sublingual form should produce a burning sensation under the tongue, which indicates that the drug is potent and will produce the desired effect. If there is no such sensation you must have the tablets replaced immediately.

When applying Nitroglycerin ointment, do not rub or massage into the skin. Any excess ointment should be washed from hands after application.

Orthostatic hypotension, where more blood stays in the extremities and less becomes available to the brain, resulting in light-headedness or faintness if you rise suddenly from the prone position, can be a problem if you take Nitroglycerin over a long period of time. Avoid prolonged standing and be careful to stand up slowly.

Generic Name

Nomifensine

Brand Name

Merital

Type of Drug

Antidepressant.

Prescribed for

Depression.

General Information

Nomifensine has a potent effect on two important neuro-hormones in the brain, norepinephrine and dopamine. Low doses of Nomifensine may produce a mild sedation, but higher doses cause a stimulant effect. It is absorbed into the blood very quickly and, because of this, may start working sooner than other antidepressants. However, you should expect to take Nomifensine for up to 6 weeks before deciding whether or not it is working for you.

Nomifensine may be effective in people who cannot take other antidepressants because of prostate disease or a heart condition. People with seizure disorders may be able to tolerate Nomifensine when other antidepressants aggravate their condition.

Cautions and Warnings

Nomifensine should not be used if you have had a previous allergic reaction to it. Very high fevers have occurred during Nomifensine treatment. About 7 out of every 100 people taking Nomifensine will develop fevers of 104° or more, but the drug can also cause lower level fevers. Fevers usually occur during the first month or two of treatment and correct themselves within 2 days of stopping the medicine. The fever may be accompanied by headache, muscle aches, and other flulike symptoms. Call your doctor at once if an unexplained fever develops.

Nomifensine may cause a particular type of anemia. Because of this, your doctor should have blood counts performed before you start the drug and while you are continuing on it.

Animal studies with doses 10 times larger than those prescribed in humans have failed to produce an adverse effect on the developing fetus. Nevertheless this drug, like all others, should be avoided by pregnant women or women who may become pregnant while using it. In those situations where it is deemed essential, the potential risk of the drug must be carefully weighed against any benefit it might produce. Nomifensine passes into mother's milk. Nursing mothers must observe for any possible drug effect on their infants while taking Nomifensine, or use another feeding method.

Possible Side Effects

Most common: difficulty sleeping, restlessness, headache, drowsiness, dry mouth, bad taste in mouth, nausea, vomiting, skin reactions.

Possible Adverse Drug Effects

Drug allergy, flulike symptoms, rapid heart rate, heart palpitations, delusions, blurred vision, tremors, numbness or tingling in the hands or feet, emotional instability, constipation, upset stomach, diarrhea, generalized aches and pains, loss of appetite, weight loss, sweating. Nomifensine may cause elevations in levels of body enzymes used to measure liver function. Nomifensine's inherent stimulant effect may activate a latent psychosis or manic reaction in susceptible people.

Drug Interactions

Nomifensine may make you more sensitive to drugs that work by stimulating the nervous system, such as nonprescription cold medicines, decongestants and diet pills.

Nomifensine may interfere with medicines used to lower blood pressure. If you are taking medicine for high blood pressure and begin to take Nomifensine, you may find that a minor dosage modification of your blood pressure medicine may be required. This interaction must be evaluated by your doctor. Do not change any blood pressure medicines on your own.

Nomifensine may interact with the monamine oxidase (MAO) inhibitor drugs, and they should be used together with caution. In most cases, one drug should be discontinued for 2 weeks before the other is begun to avoid excessive stimulation and toxic reaction.

Food Interactions

Nomifensine is best taken on an empty stomach, 1 hour before or 2 hours after eating.

Usual Dose

100 milligrams per day to start. This dose may be increased as required to a maximum of 400 milligrams per day, although most people respond to 100 to 200 milligrams per day. Nomifensine is eliminated from your body almost entirely through the kidneys. Therefore, lower doses should be prescribed for people with kidney disease, expecially senior citizens.

Overdosage

Symptoms are drowsiness, tremors, rapid heart beat, high blood pressure, and coma. You may induce vomiting by giving Syrup of Ipecac, but the victim must be taken to a hospital for treatment as quickly as possible. ALWAYS bring the medicine bottle.

Special Information

Take care while driving or doing anything else requiring concentration or alertness. Avoid alcohol or any other depressant while taking Nomifensine.

Senior citizens may be effectively treated with lower doses of this medication and should avoid doses in the high range because of the increased chance of drug side effects.

Call your doctor if any side effects develop, especially high fever, weight loss, loss of appetite, nausea, vomiting, headache, or drowsiness.

Brand Name

Norgesic Forte

Ingredients

Aspirin
Caffeine
Orphenadrine Citrate

Type of Drug

Muscle relaxant combination.

Prescribed for

Muscle spasms.

General Information

The primary ingredient in Norgesic Forte is Orphenadrine Citrate, a derivative of the antihistamine Diphenhydramine Hydrochloride (Benadryl). It is a moderately effective muscle relaxant which works by exerting a general sedative effect. The Aspirin in Norgesic Forte is there only for pain relief.

Norgesic Forte cannot solve the problems of pain due to muscle spasm: it can only temporarily relieve the pain. You must follow any additional advice given regarding exercise, diet, or immobilization to help solve the underlying problem.

Cautions and Warnings

Norgesic Forte should not be used if you have a history of glaucoma, stomach ulcer, intestinal obstruction, difficulty in passing urine, or known sensitivity or allergy to this drug or any of its ingredients. It should not be used by children or pregnant women. This drug may cause birth defects or interfere with your baby's development. Check with your doctor before taking it if you are, or might be, pregnant.

Possible Side Effects

Dryness of the mouth is usually the first side effect to appear. As the daily dose increases, other possible side effects include rapid heartbeat, palpitations, difficulty in urination, blurred vision, enlarged pupils, weakness, nausea, vomiting, headache, dizziness, constipation, drowsiness, rash, itching, running or stuffy nose, hallucinations, agitation, tremor, and stomach upset. Elderly patients taking this drug may occasionally experience some degree of mental confusion. Large doses or prolonged therapy may result in Aspirin intoxication with symptoms of ringing in the ears, headache, dizziness, fever, confusion, sweating, thirst, drowsiness, dimness of vision, rapid breathing, increased pulse rate, or diarrhea.

Drug Interactions

One of the ingredients in Norgesic Forte is Aspirin, which may significantly affect the effectiveness of oral anticoagulant (blood-thinning) drugs, may increase the effect of Probenecid, and may increase the blood-sugar-lowering effects of oral antidiabetic drugs such as Chlorpropamide and Tolbutamide.

Interaction with Propoxyphene (Darvon) may cause confusion, anxiety, tremors, or shaking.

Long-term users should avoid excessive alcohol intake, which may aggravate stomach upset and bleeding.

Food Interactions

Take with food or at least 1/2 glass of water to prevent stomach upset.

Usual Dose

1 to 2 tablets 3 to 4 times per day.

Generic Name

Nortriptyline

Brand Names

Aventyl
Pamelor

Type of Drug

Antidepressant.

Prescribed for

Depression with or without symptoms of anxiety.

General Information

Nortriptyline and other members of this group are effective in treating symptoms of depression. They can elevate your mood, increase physical activity and mental alertness, improve appetite and sleep patterns. These drugs are mild sedatives and therefore useful in treating mild forms of depression associated with anxiety. You should not expect instant results with this medicine: benefits are usually seen after 1 to 4 weeks. If symptoms are not affected after 6 to 8 weeks, contact your doctor. Occasionally this drug and other members of the group of drugs have been used in treating nighttime bed-wetting in the young child, but they do not produce long-lasting relief and therapy with one of them for nighttime bed-wetting is of questionable value.

Cautions and Warnings

Do not take Nortriptyline if you are allergic or sensitive to this or other members of this class of drug: Doxepin, Protriptyline, Imipramine, Desipramine, and Amitriptyline. The drugs should not be used if you are recovering from a heart attack. Nortriptyline may be taken with caution if you have a history of epilepsy or other convulsive disorders, difficulty in urination, glaucoma, heart disease, or thyroid disease. Nortriptyline can interfere with your ability to perform tasks which require concentration, such as driving or operating machinery.

Nortriptyline will pass from mother to unborn child: consult your doctor before taking this medicine if you are pregnant. This drug can pass into breast milk. Nursing mothers should consider alternate feeding methods.

Possible Side Effects

Changes in blood pressure (both high and low), abnormal heart rates, heart attack, confusion (especially in elderly patients), hallucinations, disorientation, delusions, anxiety, restlessness, excitement, numbness and tingling in the extremities, lack of coordination, muscle spasms or tremors, seizures and/or convulsions, dry mouth, blurred vision, constipation, inability to urinate, rash, itching, sensitivity to bright light or sunlight, retention of fluids, fever, allergy, changes in composition of blood, nausea, vomiting, loss of appetite, stomach upset, diarrhea, enlargement of the breasts in males and females, increased or decreased sex drive, increased or decreased blood sugar.

Possible Adverse Drug Effects

Infrequent: agitation, inability to sleep, nightmares, feeling of panic, development of a peculiar taste in the mouth, stomach cramps, black coloration of the tongue, yellowing eyes and/or skin, changes in liver function, increased or decreased weight, perspiration, flushing, frequent urination, drowsiness, dizziness, weakness, headache, loss of hair, nausea, not feeling well.

Generic Name

Noscapine

Brand Name

Tusscapine

Type of Drug

Nonnarcotic cough suppressant.

Prescribed for

Coughs due to colds or other respiratory infections.

Cautions and Warnings

Do not use this drug if you are allergic to Noscapine (which is rare). Do not use this drug for a serious cough or a cough with severe mucus congestion.

This drug may cause birth defects or interfere with your baby's development. Check with your doctor before taking it if you are, or might be, pregnant.

General Information

This drug is chemically related to Papaverine but has cough

suppressant potency similar to that of Codeine, a narcotic drug. Noscapine does not have all the side effects associated with Codeine because it is not a narcotic.

Possible Side Effects

Nausea, drowsiness.

Drug Interactions

This drug can cause drowsiness when taken in high doses. Do not drink alcoholic beverages or take other drugs which can also cause drowsiness.

Usual Dose

Syrup doses are as follows.
   Adult: 1 to 2 teaspoons 3 to 4 times per day.
   Child (age 2 to 6): ½ to 1 teaspoon 3 to 4 times per day.
Chewable tablet doses are as follows.
   Adult: 1 to 2 every 4 to 6 hours. Do not take more than 8 per day.
   Child (age 6 to 12): 1 tablet 3 to 4 times per day. Do not take more than 4 per day.

Overdosage

Primary sign of overdosage is drowsiness. In case of overdose, call your doctor or local Poison Control Center.

Special Information

Take care while driving or operating equipment if you are taking Noscapine.

Brand Name

Novahistine Elixir

Ingredients

Chlorpheniramine
Phenylephrine Hydrochloride

Other Brand Names

Bayhistine
Dihistine
Histor-D
Phenhist
Ru-Tuss Plain

(Also available in generic form)

Type of Drug

Decongestant combination.

Prescribed for

Relief of cough, nasal congestion, runny nose, and other symptoms associated with the common cold, viruses, or other upper respiratory diseases. The drug may also be used to treat allergies, asthma, ear infections, or sinus infections.

General Information

Novahistine Elixir is one of more than 100 products marketed to relieve the symptoms of the common cold and other upper respiratory infections. These products may contain medicine to relieve congestion, act as an antihistamine, relieve or suppress cough, and help you to cough up mucus. They may contain medicine for a single purpose, or may contain a combination of medicines. Some combinations leave out the antihistamine, the decongestant, or the expectorant. You must realize while taking Novahistine Elixir or similar products that these drugs are only for the relief of symptoms and will not treat the underlying problem, such as a cold virus or other infections.

Cautions and Warnings

Can cause excessive tiredness or drowsiness.

This product should not be used for newborn infants or taken by pregnant or nursing mothers. People with glaucoma or difficulty in urinating should avoid this drug and other drugs containing antihistamines.

Possible Side Effects

Dry mouth, blurred vision, difficulty passing urine, headache, palpitations, (possibly) constipation, nervousness, dizziness, restlessness or even inability to sleep.

Drug Interactions

Taking Novahistine Elixir with MAO inhibitors can produce severe interaction. Consult your doctor first.

Novahistine Elixir contains Chlorpheniramine. Drinking alcoholic beverages while taking this drug may produce excessive drowsiness and/or sleepiness, or inability to concentrate.

Usual Dose

1 to 2 teaspoons every 4 to 6 hours.

Special Information

Take with a full glass of water to reduce stomach upset and help remove excessive mucus from the throat.

Brand Name

Novahistine LP

Ingredients

Chlorpheniramine
Phenylephrine Hydrochloride

Other Brand Names

*Demazin Repetabs
Dristan 12 Hour
**Histaspan Plus

(Also available in generic form)
*Contains the same ingredients in different concentration.

Type of Drug

Long-acting combination antihistamine-decongestant.

Prescribed for

Relief of sneezing, runny nose, and nasal congestion associated with the common cold, allergy, or other upper respiratory condition.

General Information

Novahistine LP is one of many products marketed to relieve the symptoms of the common cold. Most of these products contain ingredients to relieve nasal congestion or dry up runny noses or relieve a scratchy throat; several of them may contain ingredients to suppress cough or to help eliminate unwanted mucus. All these products are good only for the relief of symptoms and do not treat the underlying problem such as the cold virus or other infections.

Cautions and Warnings

This drug may cause birth defects or interfere with your baby's development. Check with your doctor before taking it if you are, or might be, pregnant.

Possible Side Effects

Mild drowsiness.

Possible Adverse Drug Effects

Infrequent: restlessness, tension, nervousness, tremor, weakness, insomnia, headache, palpitations, elevation of blood pressure, sweating, loss of appetite, nausea, vomiting, dizziness, constipation.

Drug Interactions

Interaction with alcoholic beverages may cause excessive drowsiness and/or sleepiness, or inability to concentrate. Do not take this drug with alcohol, sedatives, tranquilizers, antihistamines, sleeping pills, thyroid medicine, or antihypertensive drugs such as Reserpine or Guanethidine. Do not self-medicate with over-the-counter drugs for the relief of cold symptoms: taking Novahistine LP with such drugs may aggravate high blood pressure, heart disease, diabetes, or thyroid disease.

Do not take Novahistine LP if you are taking or suspect you may be taking a monoamine oxidase (MAO) inhibitor; severe elevation in blood pressure may result.

Food Interactions

If this drug upsets your stomach it should be taken with food.

Usual Dose

Adult and child (age 12 and over): 1 tablet every 8 to 12 hours.

Child (under age 12): not recommended.

Special Information

Since drowsiness may occur during use of Novahistine LP, be cautious while performing mechanical tasks requiring alertness.

Generic Name

Nystatin Vaginal Tablets

Brand Names

Korostatin
Mycostatin
Nilstat
O-V Statin

(Also available in generic form)

Type of Drug

Vaginal anti-infective.

Prescribed for

Fungal infection of the vagina.

General Information

Generally you will have relief of symptoms in 1 to 3 days. Nystatin Vaginal Tablets effectively control troublesome and unpleasant symptoms such as itching, inflammation, and discharge. In most cases, 2 weeks of therapy is sufficient for treatment, but prolonged treatment may be necessary. It is important that you continue using this medicine during menstruation. This drug has been used to prevent thrush or candida infection in the newborn infant by treating the mother for 3 to 6 weeks before her due date. At times the vaginal tablet has been used to treat candida infections of the mouth:

the vaginal tablet is used as a lozenge and is allowed to be dissolved in the mouth and then swallowed.

Cautions and Warnings

Do not take this drug if you know you may be sensitive or allergic to Nystatin Vaginal Tablets.

This drug may cause birth defects or interfere with your baby's development. Check with your doctor before taking it if you are, or might be, pregnant.

Possible Side Effects

Nystatin Vaginal Tablets are virtually nontoxic, and are generally well tolerated. The only side effect reported has been intravaginal irritation: if this occurs, discontinue the drug and contact your doctor.

Usual Dose

1 to 2 tablets inserted high in the vagina daily.

Special Information

Do not stop taking the medication just because you begin to feel better. All the medication prescribed must be taken for at least 2 days after the relief of symptoms.

Generic Name

Oral Contraceptives (Combination)

Brand Names

Low Dose Single-Phase Combinations (by estrogen content)

Brevicon	Modicon
Demulen 1/35	Nordette
Loestrin	Norinyl 1 + 35
Loestrin 1/20	Ortho-Novum 1/35
Lo/Ovral	Ovcon-35

Regular Dose Single-Phase Combinations (by estrogen content)

Demulen	Ovcon-50
Norlestrin 1/50 and 2.5/50	Ovral

High Dose Single-Phase Combinations (by estrogen content)

Demulen 1/35	Norinyl 2
Enovid-E	Ortho-Novum 2
Enovid 5 mg.	Ovulen

Low Dose Two-Phase Combinations (by estrogen content)

Ortho-Novum 10/11

Triple-Phase Combinations

Ortho-Novum 7/7/7
Tri-Norinyl
TriPhasil

Progestin-only Products (mini-pill)

Low Dose:
  Ovrette
High Dose:
  Micronor
  Nor-Q.D.

Type of Drug

Oral contraceptive.

Prescribed for

Prevention of pregnancy.

General Information

Oral contraceptives (the Pill) are synthetic hormones, either Progestin alone or Progestin combined with Estrogen. These hormones are similar to natural female hormones that control the menstrual cycle and prepare a woman's body to accept a fertilized egg. The natural hormones cannot be used as contraceptives because very large doses would be needed. Once a fertilized egg is accepted (implanted in the womb) no more eggs may be released from the ovaries until the pregnancy is over. Oral contraceptives interfere with these natural processes; they may not allow sperm to reach the unfertilized egg; not allow the acceptance of a fertilized egg and/or not allow ovulation (the release of an unfertilized egg).

Oral contraceptives provide a very high rated protection from pregnancy. They are from 97 to 99 percent effective, depending upon which product is used and your compliance with taking the Pill regularly. No contraceptive at all is only about 40 percent effective.

The many different combination products available contain different amounts of Estrogen and Progestin. Products containing the least amount of Estrogen may be less effective in some women than others. In general, the product that contains the lowest amount of hormones but is effective and keeps side effects to a minimum is preferred.

The mini-pill, Progestin-only products, may cause irregular menstrual cycles and may be less effective than combination products. Mini-pills may be used in older women or women who should avoid Estrogens. (See Cautions and Warnings)

Single-phase products provide a fixed amount of Estrogen and Progestin throughout the entire pill cycle.

In the two-phase combination, the amount of Progestin first increases and then decreases. This is supposed to allow normal changes to take place in the uterus. The amount of Estrogen remains at a steady low level throughout the cycle. The newest combination products are triple-phase in design. Throughout the cycle, the Estrogen portion remains the same, but the Progestin changes to create a wave pattern in three parts. The three-phase products are supposed to act like normal hormones and reduce breakthrough bleeding. Breakthrough bleeding may be seen with the older combination products beginning with the eighth through sixteenth days. The amount of Estrogen in these new products is considered to be in the low category.

Every woman taking or thinking of taking the Pill should be fully aware of the problems associated with this type of contraception. The highest risk is in women over 40 who smoke and have high blood pressure.

Cautions and Warnings

You should not use oral contraceptives if you have or have had blood clots of the veins or arteries, have a disease affecting blood coagulation, have known or suspected cancer of the breast or sex organs, irregular or scanty menstrual periods, or suspect you are pregnant.

Women who should avoid Estrogen-containing products are those with a history of headaches, high blood pressure, and varicose veins. Older women and women who have experienced side effects from Estrogen also should not take Estrogen products.

This drug is known to cause birth defects or interfere with your baby's development. It is not considered safe for use during pregnancy.

Possible Side Effects

Nausea, abdominal cramps, bloating, vaginal bleeding, change in menstrual flow, possible infertility after coming off the Pill, breast tenderness, weight change, headaches, rash, vaginal itching and burning, general vaginal infection, nervousness, dizziness, formation of eye cataract, changes in sex drive, changes in appetite, loss of hair.

Possible Adverse Drug Effects

Women who take oral contraceptives are more likely to develop several serious conditions including the formation of blood clots in the deep veins, stroke, heart attack, liver cancer, gallbladder disease, and high blood pressure. Women who smoke cigarettes are much more likely to develop some of these adverse effects.

Drug Interactions

Interaction with Rifampin decreases the effectiveness of oral contraceptives. The same may be true of barbiturates, Phenylbutazone, Phenytoin, Ampicillin, Neomycin, Penicillin V, Tetracycline, Chloramphenicol, sulfa drugs, Nitrofurantoin, tranquilizers, and antimigraine medication.

Another interaction reduces the effect of anticoagulant (blood-thinning) drugs. Discuss this with your doctor.

The Pill can also increase blood cholesterol (fat), and can interfere with blood tests for thyroid function and blood sugar.

Usual Dose

The first day of bleeding is the first day of the menstrual cycle. At the start, 1 tablet, beginning on the fifth day of the menstrual cycle, is taken every day for 20 to 21 days according to the number of contraceptive tablets supplied by the manufacturer. If 7 days after taking the last tablet menstrual flow has not begun, begin the next month's cycle of pills. Progestin-only mini pills are taken every day, 365 days a year.

Overdosage

Overdosage may cause nausea and withdrawal bleeding in adult females. Accidental overdosage in children who take their mother's pills has not shown serious adverse effects.

Special Information

Some manufacturers have included 7 blank or 7 iron pills in their packages, to be taken on days when the Pill is not taken. These pills have the number 28 as part of the brand name and a pill should be taken every day.

If you forget to take the Pill for 1 day, take 2 pills the following day. If you miss 2 consecutive days, take 2 pills for the next 2 days. Then continue to take 1 pill daily. If you miss 3 consecutive days, don't take any more pills for the next 7 days; then start a new cycle.

Forgetting to take the Pill reduces your protection: if you keep forgetting to take it, you should consider other means of birth control.

All oral contraceptive prescriptions must come with a "patient package insert" for you to read. It gives detailed information about the drug and is required by federal law.

Brand Name

Ornade

Ingredients

Chlorpheniramine Maleate
Phenylpropanolamine Hydrochloride

Other Brand Names

Condrin   Oraminic Spancaps
Deconade   Resaid
Dehist   Rhinolar-Ex 12 Capsules
Drize   Ru-Tuss II
Neotep   Triaminic-12
Oragest   Tuss-Genade Modified
Orahist Capsules

(Also available in generic form)

Type of Drug

Long-acting combination antihistamine-decongestant.

Prescribed for

Relief of sneezing, runny nose, and nasal congestion associated with the common cold, allergy, or other upper respiratory condition.

General Information

Ornade is one of many products marketed to relieve the symptoms of the common cold. Most of these products contain ingredients to relieve nasal congestion or to dry up runny noses or relieve a scratchy throat; and several of them may contain ingredients to suppress cough, or to help eliminate unwanted mucus. All these products are only for the relief of symptoms and do not treat the underlying problem, such as a cold virus or other infections.

Cautions and Warnings

This drug may cause birth defects or interfere with your baby's development. Check with your doctor before taking it if you are, or might be, pregnant.

Possible Side Effects

Mild drowsiness has been seen in patients taking Ornade.

Possible Adverse Drug Effects

Infrequent: restlessness, tension, nervousness, tremor, weakness, inability to sleep, headache, palpitations, elevation of blood pressure, sweating, sleeplessness, loss of appetite, nausea, vomiting, dizziness, constipation.

Drug Interactions

One of the ingredients in Ornade may cause drowsiness and/or sleepiness and other signs of central nervous system depression. Do not take this drug with alcohol, sedatives, tranquilizers, antihistamines, sleeping pills, thyroid medicine, or antihypertensive drugs such as Reserpine or Guanethidine.

Do not self-medicate with over-the-counter drugs for the relief of cold symptoms along with Ornade, as this may aggravate high blood pressure.

Food Interactions

If this drug upsets your stomach when taken alone, it should be taken with food.

Usual Dose

Adult and child (age 12 and over): 1 tablet or capsule every 12 hours.

Child (under age 12): not recommended.

Special Information

Since drowsiness may occur while using Ornade, be cautious while performing mechanical tasks requiring alertness.

Brand Name

Os-Cal

Ingredients

Calcium Carbonate
Vitamin D

Other Brand Names

Caltro
De-Cal

(Also available in generic form)

Type of Drug

Calcium supplement.

Prescribed for

Calcium deficiency, osteoporosis prevention

General Information

This drug is used as an aid in the treatment of any disorder associated with calcium deficiency. The Vitamin D helps promote more efficient absorption of the calcium.

This drug has been found to be safe for use during pregnancy. Remember, you should check with your doctor before taking any drug if you are pregnant.

Usual Dose

1 or 2 tablets 3 times per day.

Drug Interactions

Do not take together with tetracycline-type antibiotic; it may interfere with that drug's absorption into the body.

Food Interactions

Take with meals.

Generic Name

Oxacillin Sodium

Brand Names

Bactocill
Prostaphlin

(Also available in generic form)

Type of Drug

Broad-spectrum antibiotic.

Prescribed for

Gram-positive bacterial infections. Gram-positive bacteria

(pneumococci, streptococci, and staphylococci) are organisms which usually cause diseases such as pneumonia, infections of the tonsils and throat, venereal disease, meningitis (infection of the spinal column), and septicemia (infection of the bloodstream). This drug is best used to treat infections resistant to Penicillin, although it may be used as initial treatment for some patients.

General Information

Oxacillin Sodium is manufactured in the laboratory by fermentation and by general chemical reaction, and is classified as a semisynthetic antibiotic. Because the effectiveness of the antibiotic is determined by the drug's ability to affect the cell wall of the invading bacteria, it is very important that the patient completely follow the doctor's prescribing directions. These directions include spacing of doses as well as the number of days the patient should continue taking the medicine. If they are not followed, the effect of the antibiotic is severely reduced.

Cautions and Warnings

If you have a known history of allergy to Penicillin you should avoid taking Oxacillin Sodium, since the drugs are chemically similar. The most common allergic reaction to Oxacillin Sodium, as well as to the other penicillins, is a hivelike rash over the body with itching and redness. It is important to tell your doctor if you have ever taken Oxacillin Sodium or penicillins before and if you have experienced any adverse reaction to the drug such as rash, itching, or difficulty in breathing.

    Pregnant women should use Oxacillin Sodium only if clearly needed. The drug passes into breast milk and should be used with caution by nursing mothers.

Possible Side Effects

Common: stomach upset, nausea, vomiting, diarrhea, possible rash. Less common: hairy tongue, itching or irritation around the anus and/or vagina. If these symptoms occur, contact your doctor immediately.

Drug Interactions

The effect of Oxacillin Sodium can be significantly reduced

when it is taken with other antibiotics. Consult your doctor if you are taking both during the same course of therapy. Otherwise, Oxacillin Sodium is generally free of interactions with other medications.

Usual Dose

Adult and child (88 pounds or more): 500 to 1000 milligrams every 4 to 6 hours.

Child (less than 88 pounds): 20 to 40 milligrams per pound of body weight per day in divided doses.

This drug is frequently used in higher doses when given intravenously. It must be given intravenously for serious infections because of the unusually high doses required.

Food Interactions

To ensure the maximum effect, you should take the medication on an empty stomach, either 1 hour before or 2 hours after meals.

Storage

Oxacillin Sodium can be stored at room temperature.

Special Information

Do not take Oxacillin Sodium after the expiration date on the label.

Generic Name

Oxazepam

Brand Name

Serax

Type of Drug

Tranquilizer.

Prescribed for

Relief of symptoms of anxiety, tension, fatigue, or agitation.

General Information

Oxazepam is a member of the chemical group of drugs known as benzodiazepines. These drugs are used as either antianxiety agents, anticonvulsants, or sedatives (sleeping pills). They exert their effects by relaxing the large skeletal muscles and by a direct effect on the brain. In doing so, they can relax you and make you either more tranquil or sleepier, depending on the drug and how much you use. Many doctors prefer Oxazepam and the other members of this class to other drugs that can be used for the same effect. Their reason is that the benzodiazepines tend to be safer, have fewer side effects, and are usually as, if not more, effective.

These drugs are generally used in any situation where they can be a useful adjunct.

Benzodiazepine tranquilizing drugs can be abused if taken for long periods of time and it is possible to develop withdrawal symptoms if you discontinue the therapy abruptly. Withdrawal symptoms include convulsions, tremor, muscle cramps, stomach cramps, vomiting, and sweating.

Cautions and Warnings

Do not take Oxazepam if you know you are sensitive or allergic to this drug or other benzodiazepines such as Chlordiazepoxide, Prazepam, Clorazepate, Diazepam, Lorazepam, Flurazepam, and Clonazepam.

Oxazepam and other members of this drug group may aggravate narrow angle glaucoma, but if you have open angle glaucoma you may take the drugs. In any case, check this information with your doctor. Oxazepam can cause tiredness, drowsiness, inability to concentrate, or similar symptoms. Be careful if you are driving, operating machinery, or performing other activities which require concentration.

Do not take Oxazepam if you are planning to become pregnant and avoid taking it if you are pregnant or nursing. An increased chance of birth defects has not been seen, however there is a risk factor to be considered. Other drugs similar to Oxazepam have been shown to cause birth defects.

The baby may become dependent on Oxazepam if it is used continually during pregnancy. If used during the last weeks of pregnancy or during breast-feeding, the baby may be overly tired, be short of breath, or have a low heartbeat.

Use during labor may cause weakness in the newborn.

Possible Side Effects

Most common: mild drowsiness during the first few days of therapy, especially in the elderly or debilitated. If drowsiness persists, contact your doctor.

Possible Adverse Drug Effects

Major adverse reactions: confusion, depression, lethargy, disorientation, headache, lack of activity, slurred speech, stupor, dizziness, tremor, constipation, dry mouth, nausea, inability to control urination, changes in sex drive, irregular menstrual cycle, changes in heart rhythm, lowered blood pressure, retention of fluids, blurred or double vision, itching, rash, hiccups, nervousness, inability to fall asleep, (occasional) liver dysfunction. If you experience any of these reactions stop taking the medicine and contact your doctor immediately.

Drug Interactions

Oxazepam is a central nervous system depressant. Avoid alcohol, tranquilizers, narcotics, sleeping pills, barbiturates, MAO inhibitors, antihistamines, and other medicines used to relieve depression.

Usual Dose

Adult: 10 to 120 milligrams per day as individualized for maximum benefit, depending on symptoms and response to treatment, which may require a dose outside the range given.

Elderly: usually require less of the drug to control anxiety and tension.

Overdosage

Symptoms are confusion, sleep or sleepiness, lack of response to pain such as a pin stick, shallow breathing, lowered blood pressure, and coma. The patient should be taken to a hospital emergency room immediately. ALWAYS bring the medicine bottle.

Generic Name

Oxtriphylline

Brand Names

Choledyl
Choledyl SA

(Also available in generic form)

Type of Drug

Xanthine bronchodilator.

Prescribed for

Relief of bronchial asthma and spasms of bronchial muscles associated with emphysema, bronchitis, and other diseases.

General Information

Oxtriphylline is one of several drugs known as xanthine derivatives which are the mainstay of therapy for bronchial asthma and similar diseases. Other members of this group are Aminophylline, Dyphylline, and Theophylline. Although the dosage for each of these drugs is different, they all work by relaxing bronchial muscles and helping reverse spasms in these muscles.

Cautions and Warnings

Do not use this drug if you are allergic or sensitive to it or to any related drug, such as Aminophylline. If you have a stomach ulcer or heart disease, you should use this drug with caution. If you are pregnant or think that you may be pregnant or are lactating, you should carefully discuss the use of this drug with your doctor, since Oxtriphylline may cause a rapid heartbeat, irritability, vomiting or breathing problems in the unborn and/or nursing child if too much is used.

Possible Side Effects

Possible side effects from Oxtriphylline or other xanthine derivatives are nausea, vomiting, stomach pain, diarrhea, irritability, restlessness, difficulty sleeping, excitability, muscle twitching or spasms, heart palpitations, other unusual heart rates, low blood pressure, rapid breathing, and local irritation (particularly if a suppository is used).

Possible Adverse Drug Effects

Infrequent: vomiting blood, fever, headache, dehydration.

Drug Interactions

Taking Oxtriphylline at the same time as another xanthine derivative may increase side effects. Don't do it except under the direct care of a doctor.

Oxtriphylline is often given in combination with a stimulant drug such as Ephedrine. Such combinations can cause excessive stimulation and should be used only as specifically directed by your doctor.

Some reports have indicated that combining Erythromycin and Oxtriphylline will give you higher blood levels of Oxtriphylline. Remember that higher blood levels mean the possibility of more side effects. Other drugs that may increase blood levels are: Cimetidine flu vaccine and Allopurinol. Cigarette smoking may decrease this drug's effectiveness.

Food-Drug Interactions

Take on an empty stomach, at least 1 hour before or 2 hours after meals; but occasional mild stomach upset can be minimized by taking the dose with some food (note if you do this, a reduced amount of drug will be absorbed into your bloodstream).

The way Oxtriphylline acts in your body may be influenced by your diet. Charcoal-broiled beef, for example, may cause a greater amount of Oxtriphylline to be eliminated in the urine. Therefore you may experience a decreased effect of the drug. This effect also occurs in people whose diet is low in carbohydrates and high in protein or in people who smoke. Caffeine (also a xanthine derivative) may add to the side effects of Oxtriphylline. It is recommended that you avoid large amounts of caffeine-containing foods such as coffee, tea, cocoa, cola, or chocolate.

Usual Dose

Adult: 200 milligrams 4 times per day. SA (Sustained Action): 400 to 600 milligrams every 12 hours.

Child (age 2 to 12): 100 milligrams for every 60 pounds of body weight taken four times a day.

Note: Each 100 milligrams of Oxtriphylline is equal to 64 milligrams of Theophylline in potency.

Overdosage

The first symptoms are loss of appetite, nausea, vomiting, difficulty sleeping, and restlessness, followed by unusual behavior patterns, frequent vomiting, and extreme thirst, with delirium, convulsions, very high temperature, and collapse. These serious toxic symptoms are rarely experienced after overdose by mouth, which produces loss of appetite, nausea, vomiting, and stimulation. The overdosed patient should be taken to a hospital emergency room where proper treatment can be given. ALWAYS bring the medicine bottle.

Generic Name

Oxymetazoline Hydrochloride

Brand Names

Afrin (nose drops and spray)

Dristan Long Lasting (nose drops and spray)

Duramist Plus (nose spray)

Duration (nose drops and spray)

Neo-Synephrine 12 Hour (nose spray)

Nostrilla (4 way Long Acting)

NTZ Long Acting

Sinex Long-Acting (nose spray)

(Also available in generic form)

Type of Drug

Nasal decongestant.

Prescribed for

Relief of stuffy nose secondary to allergy, the common cold, or any other cause.

Cautions and Warnings

Do not use Oxymetazoline Hydrochloride if you are taking an MAO inhibitor or antidepressant, if you are allergic to Oxymetazoline or any similar preparations, or if you have glaucoma, high blood pressure, heart disease, chest pains, thyroid disease, or diabetes.

This drug may cause birth defects or interfere with your

baby's development. Check with your doctor before taking it if you are, or might be, pregnant.

Possible Side Effects

Common side effects are burning, stinging, dryness of the mucosa inside the nose, and sneezing.

Possible Adverse Drug Effects

Oxymetazoline Hydrochloride may produce abnormal heart rhythms, increase in blood pressure, headache, feeling of light-headedness, nervousness, difficulty in sleeping, blurred vision, and some drowsiness or lethargy.

Adverse effects are more likely to occur in the elderly.

Drug Interactions

Oxymetazoline Hydrochloride is a stimulant drug which will increase the effect of any other stimulant. It may block some of the effect of depressant drugs such as tranquilizers or sleeping medications, but this is unusual if recommended doses are observed.

Interaction with MAO inhibitor drugs may cause severe stimulation.

Usual Dose

Adult and child (age 6 and over): 2 to 3 drops or sprays of the (generally 0.05 percent) solution in each nostril no more than twice a day.

Child (age 2 to 5): 2 to 3 drops of half-strength (0.025 percent) solution in each nostril no more than twice a day.

Overdosage

Symptoms are sedation, desire to go to sleep, possible coma—or with extreme overdosage, high blood pressure, low heart rate, other effects on the heart, with even collapse of the cardiovascular system, and depressed breathing. The patient should be taken to a hospital emergency room immediately, where proper care can be provided. ALWAYS bring the medicine bottle.

Special Information

Use this drug exactly as directed—not more frequently. If

Oxymetazoline Hydrochloride is used more than twice a day or in excessive quantities, "rebound congestion" will occur. The nose will produce excessive amounts of mucus in reaction to the medication, which may lead to overdosage and possible toxicity.

Generic Name

Oxyphenbutazone

Brand Names

Oxalid

(Also available in generic form)

Type of Drug

Anti-inflammatory agent.

Prescribed for

Local inflammation related to gout, rheumatoid arthritis, osteoarthritis, painful shoulder such as bursitis or arthritis of a joint, or other inflammatory diseases which cause pain that cannot be controlled by Aspirin, and when severe disability, because of the inflammation, is not relieved by usual treatment.

General Information

This drug should never be taken without strict medical supervision. Oxyphenbutazone should be used only for the short-term relief of pain due to inflammation of muscles, tendons, and joint area.

Oxyphenbutazone and its sister drug Phenylbutazone are toxic and dangerous and should only be used when absolutely necessary. The list of potential side effects is long. Therefore, any change in habits or unusual effect which may be even remotely connected with the use of these drugs should be reported immediately to your doctor.

Cautions and Warnings

You should not take Oxyphenbutazone if you have a history

of symptoms associated with gastrointestinal inflammation or ulcer, including severe, recurrent, or persistent upset stomach. This drug is not a simple pain reliever and should never be taken casually. It should not be prescribed before a careful and detailed history, plus physical and laboratory tests, have been completed by the doctor. If your problem can be treated by a less toxic drug such as Aspirin, use that first and try to stay away from Oxyphenbutazone. Never take more than the recommended dosage: this would lead to toxic effects. If you have blurred vision, fever, rash, sore throat, sores in the mouth, upset stomach or pain in the stomach, feeling of weakness, bloody, black, or tarry stool, water retention, or a significant or sudden weight gain, report this to the doctor immediately. In addition, stop taking the drug. If the drug is not effective after 1 week, stop taking it. Use Oxyphenbutazone with caution and in consultation with a doctor if you are a pregnant or lactating woman.

Possible Side Effects

Most common: stomach upset, drowsiness, water retention.

Possible Adverse Drug Effects

Infrequent: acute gastric or duodenal ulcer, ulceration or perforation of the large bowel, bleeding from the stomach, anemia, stomach pain, vomiting, vomiting of blood, nausea, diarrhea, changes in the components of the blood, water retention, disruption of normal chemical balance of the body. This drug can cause fatal or nonfatal hepatitis, black-and-blue marks on the skin, serum sickness, drug allergy serious enough to cause shock, itching, serious rashes, fever, and signs of arthritis. It has been known to cause kidney effects including bleeding and kidney stones. Oxyphenbutazone may be a cause of heart disease, high blood pressure, blurred vision, bleeding in the back of the eye, detachment of a retina, hearing loss, high blood sugar, thyroid disease, agitation, confusion, or lethargy.

Drug Interactions

Oxyphenbutazone increases the effects of blood-thinning drugs, Phenytoin, Insulin, and oral antidiabetic agents. If you are taking any of these drugs, discuss this matter with your doctor immediately.

Food Interactions

Oxyphenbutazone causes stomach upset in many patients; take your dose with food or antacids, and if stomach pain continues, notify your doctor.

Usual Dose

Adult and child (age 14 years or over): depending upon the condition being treated, 300 to 600 milligrams per day in 3 to 4 equal doses for 7 days. If dose is effective it can then be reduced to 100 to 400 milligrams per day, depending on the condition being treated.

Elderly: drug to be given only for 7 days because of high risk of severe reactions. Not to be given to senile patients.

Child (under age 14): not recommended.

Overdosage

Symptoms are convulsions, euphoria, depression, headache, hallucinations, giddiness, dizziness, coma, rapid breathing rate, and insomnia or sleeplessness. Contact your doctor immediately. If you must go to a hospital emergency room, ALWAYS bring the medicine bottle.

Special Information

Oxyphenbutazone is a central nervous system depressant that can cause drowsiness and tiredness: be careful when driving or operating other equipment, and avoid large quantities of alcoholic beverages, which will aggravate the situation.

Generic Name

Papaverine Hydrochloride

Brand Names

Cerespan	Pava-Par
Delapav	Pava-Rx
Dilart	Pavased
Myobid	Pavasule
P-200	Pavatine
Papacon	Pavatym
Pavabid HP	Pavarine-Spancaps
Pavabid Plateau Caps	Paverolan Lanacaps
Pavacap Unicelles	PT-300
Pavacen Cenules	Vasal Granucaps
Pavadur	Vasocap
Pavadyl	Vasospan
Pavagen	

(Also available in generic form)

Type of Drug

Vasodilator.

Prescribed for

Relief of spasms of arteries in the heart, brain, arms, and legs.

General Information

Papaverine Hydrochloride relaxes various smooth muscles: it slows their normal degree of responsiveness but does not paralyze them. Papaverine Hydrochloride may directly widen blood vessels in the brain and other areas, increasing the flow of blood and oxygen to those areas.

Cautions and Warnings

Papaverine Hydrochloride may aggravate glaucoma. If you develop stomach upset, yellowing of the skin, and/or the whites of the eyes, call your doctor immediately.

This drug may cause birth defects or interfere with your baby's development. Check with your doctor before taking it if you are, or might be, pregnant.

Possible Side Effects

Most frequent: nausea, stomach upset, loss of appetite, sweating, flushing of the face, not feeling well, dizziness, drowsiness, headache, skin rash, constipation, diarrhea. In general, few side effects are experienced by people taking Papaverine Hydrochloride.

Alcohol may increase all of these possible side effects.

Usual Dose

Plain tablet, 100 to 300 milligrams 3 to 5 times per day. Time-release tablets or capsules, 150 milligrams every 12 hours; if patients do not respond to this, medication may be increased to 150 milligrams every 8 hours, or 300 milligrams every 12 hours.

Brand Name

Parafon Forte

Ingredients

Acetaminophen
Chlorzoxazone

Other Brand Names

Chlorofon-F   Polyflex
Chlorzone Forte   Zoxaphen
Paracet Forte

(Also available in generic form)

Type of Drug

Skeletal muscle relaxant.

Prescribed for

Relief of pain and spasm of muscular conditions, including lower back pain, strains, sprains, or muscle bruises.

General Information

Parafon Forte is one of several drugs used to treat the aches and pains associated with muscle aches, strains, or a bad back. It gives only temporary relief and is not a substitute for other types of therapy such as rest, surgery, or physical therapy.

Cautions and Warnings

Do not take Parafon Forte if you are allergic to either of its ingredients. Do not take more than the exact amount of medication prescribed.

This drug may cause birth defects or interfere with your baby's development. Check with your doctor before taking it if you are, or might be, pregnant. Parafon Forte passes into breast milk. Nursing mothers should use an alternate feeding method.

Possible Side Effects

The major side effects are stomach upset and other gastrointestinal problems. If this occurs you may take the drug with food. Parafon Forte has been associated with bleeding from the stomach, drowsiness, dizziness, light-headedness, not feeling well, and overstimulation.

Possible Adverse Drug Effects

Both ingredients in Parafon Forte have been associated with liver disease: this is especially true when the medicine is taken in large doses for a long time. If you have been taking it for several weeks, your doctor should perform routine tests to be sure that your liver is functioning properly; but if you take Parafon Forte for a short time (several days or less), the problem should not bother you.

Notify your physician if itching or skin rash develops.

Usual Dose

2 tablets 4 times per day.

Overdosage

Symptoms of massive overdosage are sleepiness, weakness tiredness, turning blue of lips, fingertips, or other areas, and signs of liver damage such as nausea, vomiting, diarrhea and severe abdominal pain. Contact your doctor immediately or go to a hospital emergency room where appropriate therapy can be provided. ALWAYS bring the medicine bottle

Special Information

Parafon Forte can make you sleepy, dull your senses, or disturb your concentration, so be extremely careful while driving or operating equipment or machinery. Drinking alcoholic beverages further complicates this problem and enhances the sedative effects of Parafon Forte.

A breakdown product of the Chlorzoxazone ingredient in Parafon Forte can turn your urine orange to purple-red: this is not dangerous.

Generic Name

Paregoric

Other Brand Names

Camphorated Tincture of Opium

(Also available in generic form)

Type of Drug

Antidiarrheal.

Prescribed for

Symptomatic treatment of diarrhea.

General Information

Paregoric and other antidiarrheal agents should only be used for short periods: they will relieve the diarrhea, but not its underlying causes. Sometimes these drugs should not be used even though there is diarrhea present: people with some kinds of bowel, stomach, or other disease may be harmed by taking antidiarrheal drugs. Obviously, the decision to use Paregoric must be made by your doctor. Do not use Paregoric without his advice.

Cautions and Warnings

Paregoric is a derivative of Morphine; the cautions and warnings that go with the use of narcotics also go with the use of Paregoric. When taken in the prescribed dose, however, there should be no serious problems.

This drug may cause birth defects or interfere with your baby's development. Check with your doctor before taking it if you are, or might be, pregnant.

Possible Side Effects

Most people do not experience side effects from Paregoric, but some may experience nausea, upset stomach, and other forms of gastrointestinal disturbance.

Possible Adverse Drug Effects

Most adverse drug effects associated with narcotic drugs are not experienced with Paregoric because of the limited amount of narcotic contained in the medication and the unappealing taste of the drug. Prolonged use of Paregoric may produce some of the narcotic effects such as difficulty in breathing, light-headedness, dizziness, sedation, nausea, and vomiting.

Drug Interactions

Paregoric, a depressant on the central nervous system, may cause tiredness or inability to concentrate, and may thus increase the effect of sleeping pills, tranquilizers, and alcohol. Avoid large amounts of alcoholic beverages.

Food Interactions

To help mask the taste, Paregoric can be mixed with a small amount of water or juice immediately before it is taken. The milky color of the mixture is of no consequence.

Usual Dose

Adult: for diarrhea, 1 to 2 teaspoons 4 times per day.
Infant: for diarrhea, 2 to 10 drops up to 4 times per day.
Paregoric is only a symptomatic treatment: it should be

accompanied by fluids and other therapy prescribed by your doctor.

Overdosage

A patient with Paregoric overdose should be taken to a hospital emergency room immediately. ALWAYS bring the medicine bottle.

Special Information

Take care while driving, or operating any appliance or machine.

Brand Name

Pediazole

Ingredients

Erythromycin Ethylsuccinate
Sulfisoxazole

Type of Drug

Antibiotic anti-infective.

Prescribed for

Middle-ear infections in children.

General Information

This combination of an antibiotic and a sulfa drug has been specifically formulated for its effect against Hemophilus Influenza, an organism responsible for many cases of difficult-to-treat middle-ear infection in children. At present, Pediazole is approved by the Food and Drug Administration only for this specific use, although common sense would indicate that the combination might also be useful for other infections against which both drugs are effective.

The two drugs work by completely different mechanisms and complement each other by working against organisms that the other is unable to affect. Pediazole is especially valuable in cases of Hemophilus Influenza middle-ear infection that do not respond to Ampicillin, a widely used and generally effective antibiotic.

Cautions and Warnings

This combination should not be given to infants under 2 months of age because their systems are not yet sufficiently developed to break down sulfa drugs. Children who are allergic to any sulfa drug or to any form of Erythromycin should not be given this product.

Possible Side Effects

It is possible for children given this combination to develop any side effect known to be caused by either Erythromycin or Sulfisoxazole. However, the most common side effects are upset stomach, cramps, drug allergy, and rashes.

Possible Adverse Drug Effects

Nausea, vomiting, and diarrhea. Sulfa drugs may make your child more sensitive to sunlight, an effect that can last for many months after the medicine has been discontinued.

Drug Interactions

Pediazole may increase the effects of Digoxin (a heart medicine), Tolbutamide and Chlorpropamide (antidiabetes drugs), Methotrexate (an immune suppressant), Theophylline (for asthma), Warfarin (an anticoagulant), Phenylbutazone (a potent anti-inflammatory agent), Aspirin or other Salicylates, Carbamazepine and Phenytoin (for control of seizures), and Probenecid (for gout). The potential results of such an interaction are an increase in drug side effects and a possible need for dosage adjustment of the interacting drug.

Food Interactions

This combination is best taken on an empty stomach, at least 1 hour before or 2 hours after meals. However, if it causes upset stomach, take each dose with food or meals, and be sure to drink lots of water while using Pediazole.

Usual Dose

The dosage of Pediazole depends on your child's body weight and varies from ½ teaspoonful to 2 teaspoonsful every 6 hours. Each teaspoonful of the medicine contains 200 milligrams of Erythromycin and 600 milligrams of Sulfisoxazole.

Overdosage

The strawberry-banana flavoring of this product makes it a good candidate for accidental overdosage, so be sure it is stored in an area of your refrigerator that is least accessible to your child. Overdosage with Pediazole is most likely to result in blood in the urine, nausea, vomiting, stomach upset and cramps, dizziness, headache, and drowsiness. Sulfisoxazole overdosage is more dangerous than Erythromycin overdosage. Patients taking an overdose of this drug must be made to vomit with Syrup of Ipecac (available at any pharmacy) to remove any remaining drug from the stomach. Call your doctor or a Poison Control Center before doing this. If you must go to a hospital emergency room, ALWAYS bring the medicine bottle.

Special Information

This product must be stored under refrigeration and discarded after 2 weeks.

Sulfa drugs may make your child more sensitive to the burning effects of the sun's rays. Avoid excessive exposure to the sun while giving your child Pediazole.

Each dose of Pediazole should be followed by a full glass of water. Do not stop giving your child this medicine when the symptoms disappear. It must be taken for the complete course of treatment prescribed by your doctor.

Call your doctor if nausea, vomiting, diarrhea, stomach cramps, discomfort, or other symptoms persist, especially after giving the dosage with meals or food. Your child may be unable to tolerate the antibiotic and will have to receive different therapy.

Severe or unusual side effects should be reported to your doctor at once. Especially important are yellow discoloration of the eyes or skin, darkening of the urine, pale stools, or unusual tiredness, which can be signs of liver irritation.

Generic Name

Pemoline

Brand Name

Cylert

Type of Drug

Psychotherapeutic.

Prescribed for

Children with attention deficit syndrome who are also in a program that includes social, psychological, and educational counseling.

General Information

This drug stimulates the central nervous system, although its mechanism of action is not known in children with attention deficit disorder (formerly called hyperactivity). It should always be used as part of a total therapeutic program and only when prescribed by a qualified pediatrician.

Cautions and Warnings

Do not use if the patient is allergic or sensitive to Pemoline. Children under age 6 should not receive this medication. Psychotic children may experience worsening of symptoms while taking Pemoline. Patients taking this drug should have periodic blood tests for the liver. Pregnant women and nursing mothers should not use this drug.

Possible Side Effects

Sleeplessness, appetite loss, stomachache, rash, irritability, depression, nausea, dizziness, headache, drowsiness, hallucination. Drug hypersensitivity may occur.

Possible Adverse Drug Effects

Uncontrolled movements of lips, face, tongue, and the extremities; wandering eye may also occur.

Usual Dose

37.5 to 75 milligrams per day. Do not take more than 112.5 milligrams per day.

Overdosage

Symptoms are rapid heartbeat, hallucinations, agitation, uncontrolled muscle movements, and restlessness. Patients suspected of taking an overdose of Pemoline must be taken to a hospital. ALWAYS bring the medicine bottle with you.

Special Information

Take the daily dose at the same time each morning. Call your doctor if sleeplessness develops.

Generic Name

Penicillin G

Brand Names

M-Cillin B-400   Pfizerpen G
Penicillin GK   SK-Penicillin G
Pentids

(Also available in generic form)

Type of Drug

Antibiotic.

Prescribed for

Bacterial infections susceptible to this drug.

General Information

Because the effectiveness of the antibiotic is determined by the drug's ability to destroy the cell wall of the invading bacteria, it is very important that the patient completely follow the doctor's prescribing directions. These directions include spacing of doses as well as the number of days the patient should continue taking the medicine. If they are not followed, the effect of the antibiotic is severely reduced.

Cautions and Warnings

Serious and occasionally fatal hypersensitivity reaction has been reported to Penicillin G. Although this is more common following injection of the drug, it has occurred with oral use. It is more likely to occur in individuals with a history of sensitivity to this drug or sensitivity in general as indicated by multiple allergies.

This drug has been found to be safe for use during pregnancy. Remember, you should check with your doctor before taking any drug if you are pregnant.

Penicillin G is generally safe during breast-feeding, however it is possible for the baby to receive enough of this drug to cause upset stomach and diarrhea.

Possible Side Effects

The most important side effect seen with Penicillin G is sensitivity or allergic reaction.

Possible Adverse Drug Effects

Occasional: stomach upset, nausea, vomiting, diarrhea, coating of the tongue, rash, itching, various types of anemia, other effects on the blood system, oral or rectal infestation with fungal diseases.

Drug Interactions

Penicillin G should not be given at the same time as one of the bacteriostatic antibiotics such as Erythromycin, Tetracycline, or Neomycin, which may diminish the effectiveness of Penicillin G.

Aspirin or Phenylbutazone will increase the level of free Penicillin G in the blood by making more of it available from blood proteins.

Food Interactions

Do not take Penicillin G with fruit juice or carbonated beverages, because the acid in these beverages can destroy the Penicillin.

Penicillin G is best absorbed on an empty stomach. It can be taken 1 hour before or 2 hours after meals, or first thing in the morning and last thing at night with the other doses spaced evenly through the day.

Usual Dose

200,000 to 600,000 units every 6 to 8 hours for 10 days.

Storage

Oral Penicillin G may have to be stored in a refrigerator. The bottle should be labeled to that effect and the information should be available on the prescription label.

Special Information

It takes 7 to 10 days for Penicillin G to be effective against most susceptible organisms; be sure to take all the medicine prescribed for the full period prescribed.

Generic Name

Penicillin V (Phenoxymethyl Penicillin)

Brand Names

Beepen-VK	Pfizerpen VK
Betapen-VK	Repen-VK
Deltapen-VK	Robicillin VK
Ledercillin VK	SK-Penicillin VK
Penapar VK	Uticillin VK
Penicillin VK	V-Cillin K
Pen-Vee K	Veetids

(Also available in generic form)

Type of Drug

Antibiotic.

Prescribed for

Bacterial infections susceptible to this drug.

General Information

General use of Penicillin V is identical to that of Penicillin G, the difference being that Penicillin V is not destroyed by the acids of the stomach, and thus is more effective when taken by mouth than Penicillin G.

Cautions and Warnings

Serious and occasionally fatal hypersensitivity reaction has been reported to Penicillin V. Although it is more common following injection of the drug, it has occurred with oral use. It is more likely to occur in individuals with a history of sensitivity to this drug or sensitivity in general as indicated by multiple allergies.

This drug has been found to be safe for use during pregnancy. Remember, you should check with your doctor before taking any drug if you are pregnant.

Possible Side Effects

The most important side effect seen with Penicillin V is sensitivity or allergic reaction.

Possible Adverse Drug Effects

Occasional: stomach upset, nausea, vomiting, diarrhea, coating of the tongue, rash, itching, various types of anemia, other effects on the blood system, oral or rectal infestation with fungal diseases.

Drug Interactions

Penicillin V should not be given at the same time as one of the bacteriostatic antibiotics such as Erythromycin, Tetracycline, or Neomycin, which may diminish the effectiveness of Penicillin V.

Aspirin or Phenylbutazone will increase the level of free Penicillin V in the blood by making more of it available from blood proteins.

Food Interactions

Penicillin V is best absorbed on an empty stomach. It can be taken 1 hour before or 2 hours after meals, or first thing in the morning and last thing at night with the other doses spaced evenly through the day.

Usual Dose

125 to 500 milligrams every 6 to 8 hours for 10 days.

Storage

Oral Penicillin V may have to be stored in a refrigerator. The bottle should be labeled to that effect and the information should be available on the prescription label.

Special Information

It takes 7 to 10 days for Penicillin V to be effective against most susceptible organisms; be sure to take all the medicine prescribed for the full period prescribed.

Generic Name

Pentazocine

Brand Names

Talacen (Pentazocine with Acetaminophen)
Talwin
Talwin Compound (Pentazocine with aspirin)
Talwin NX (Pentazocine with Naloxone)

Type of Drug

Nonnarcotic analgesic.

Prescribed for

Relief of moderate to severe pain.

General Information

Pentazocine is used for mild to moderate pain. Fifty to 100 milligrams of Pentazocine is approximately equal in pain-relieving effect to 2 Aspirin tablets (650 milligrams). Pentazocine may be less active than Aspirin for types of pain associated with inflammation, since Aspirin reduces inflammation but Pentazocine does not. Talwin NX was formulated to prevent drug abuse.

Cautions and Warnings

Do not use Pentazocine if you believe that you are allergic to it. It is possible to develop addiction to or dependence on Pentazocine but addiction is much more likely to occur with people who have a history of abusing narcotics or other drugs. Abrupt stoppage of Pentazocine after extended periods of therapy has produced withdrawal symptoms such as stomach cramps, fever, stuffy or runny nose, restlessness, anxiety, and tearing of the eyes. The drug may cause visual hallucinations or make you disoriented and confused; if this happens, stop taking the drug immediately and contact your physician. Never give this drug or any other potent painkillers to a patient with a head injury.

This drug may cause birth defects or interfere with your baby's development. Check with your doctor before taking it if you are, or might be, pregnant.

Possible Side Effects

Nausea, vomiting, constipation, cramps, stomach upset, loss of appetite, diarrhea, dry mouth, alteration of taste, dizziness, light-headedness, sedation, euphoria, headache, difficulty sleeping, disturbed dreams, hallucinations, muscle spasms, irritability, excitement, nervousness, apprehension and depression, feeling of being disoriented and detached from your body.

Possible Adverse Drug Effects

Blurred vision, difficulty in focusing the eyes, double vision, sweating, flushing chills, rash, itching, swelling of the face, flushing and reddening of the skin, changes in blood pressure, abnormal heart rate, difficulty in breathing, effects on components of the blood, difficult urination, tingling in the arms and legs.

Drug Interactions

Avoid interaction with drugs that have a sedative or depressive effect, such as alcohol, barbiturates, sleeping pills, and some pain-relieving medications. The combination will produce extreme sedation, sleepiness, and difficulty concentrating.

Pentazocine has the unusual effect of being a mild narcotic antagonist. If you must take narcotics for pain relief, do not take Pentazocine at the same time, because it will reverse the effect of the narcotic drug. This can be a special problem for patients in Methadone treatment programs. If one of these patients takes Pentazocine, he will experience narcotic withdrawal effects.

Usual Dose

50 milligrams every 3 to 4 hours. Maximum dose, 600 milligrams per day to control pain.

This drug is not recommended for children.

Overdosage

Symptoms resemble those of narcotic overdose: decreased breathing, sleepiness, lassitude, low blood pressure, and even coma. The patient should be taken to a hospital emergency room immediately. ALWAYS bring the medicine bottle.

Generic Name

Pentobarbital

Brand Names

Nembutal

(Also available in generic form)

Type of Drug

Hypnotic; sedative.

Prescribed for

Daytime sedation; sleeping medication.

General Information

Pentobarbital, like the other barbiturates, appears to act by interfering with nerve impulses to the brain.

Cautions and Warnings

Pentobarbital may slow down your physical and mental reflexes, so you must be extremely careful when operating machinery, driving an automobile, or performing other potentially dangerous tasks. Pentobarbital is classified as a barbiturate; long-term or unsupervised use may cause addiction. Elderly people taking Pentobarbital may exhibit nervousness and confusion at times. Barbiturates are neutralized in the liver and eliminated from the body through the kidneys;

consequently, people who have liver or kidney disorders—namely, difficulty in forming or excreting urine—should be carefully monitored by their doctor when taking Pentobarbital.

If you have known sensitivities or allergies to barbiturates, or if you have previously been addicted to sedatives or hypnotics, or if you have a disease affecting the respiratory system, you should not take Pentobarbital.

This drug may cause birth defects or interfere with your baby's development. Check with your doctor before taking it if you are, or might be, pregnant.

Breast-feeding while using Pentobarbital may cause increased tiredness, shortness of breath, or a slow heartbeat in the baby.

Possible Side Effects

Difficulty in breathing, rash, and general allergic reaction such as running nose, watering eyes, and scratchy throat.

Possible Adverse Drug Effects

Drowsiness, lethargy, dizziness, hangover, nausea, vomiting, diarrhea. More severe adverse reactions may include anemia and yellowing of the skin and eyes.

Drug Interactions

Interaction with alcohol, tranquilizers, or other sedatives increases the effect of Pentobarbital.

Interaction with anticoagulants (blood-thinning agents) can reduce their effect. This is also true of muscle relaxants and painkillers.

Usual Dose

Daytime sedative: 30 milligrams 3 to 4 times per day.

Hypnotic for sleep: 100 milligrams at bedtime; this may be repeated once if necessary (occasionally) to induce sleep.

Overdosage

Symptoms are difficulty in breathing, decrease in size of the pupils of the eyes, lowered body temperature progressing to fever as time passes, fluid in the lungs, and eventually coma.

Anyone suspected of having taken an overdose must be taken to the hospital for immediate care. ALWAYS bring the medicine bottle to the emergency room physician so he or she can quickly and correctly identify the medicine and start treatment. Severe overdosage of this medication can kill; the drug has been used many times in suicide attempts.

Generic Name

Pentoxifylline

Brand Name

Trental

Type of Drug

Blood viscosity reducer.

Prescribed for

Relief of intermittent claudication, or blood vessel spasms and painful leg cramps, caused by poor blood supply associated with arteriosclerotic disease. It has also been used to treat cases of inadequate blood flow to the brain.

General Information

This medicine, available in Europe since 1972, is the first true "blood thinner." It reduces the blood's viscosity, or thickness, and improves the ability of red blood cells to modify their shape. In doing so, this medication may help people who experience severe leg pains when they walk by improving blood flow to their leg muscles. Leg cramps occur when muscles are deprived of oxygen. When blood flow is improved, the cramps are less severe or do not occur at all. Studies of Pentoxifylline's effectiveness have yielded mixed results, but it may be helpful for people who do not respond to other treatments.

It should be noted that physical training is probably a more effective treatment for intermittent claudication than is Pentoxifylline. However, the medicine may be helpful for people who cannot follow a training program and who are not candidates for surgery, which is another treatment for this condition.

Cautions and Warnings

Pentoxifylline has damaged animal fetuses. Although there is no evidence of a direct effect on humans, this medicine should only be taken by pregnant women when it is absolutely necessary and the possible risk to the unborn child has been taken into account. It is not known if Pentoxifylline passes into breast milk and nursing mothers should decide whether to discontinue breast-feeding or discontinue the drug.

People who cannot tolerate Caffeine, Theophylline, or Theobromine should not use this medicine, since Pentoxifylline is chemically related to those products.

Possible Side Effects

Most common: mild nausea, upset stomach, dizziness, and headache.

Possible Adverse Drug Effects

Less frequently encountered reactions to Pentoxifylline include chest pains, difficulty breathing, swelling of the arms or legs, low blood pressure, stomach gas, loss of appetite, constipation, dry mouth, excessive thirst, tremors, anxiety, confusion, stuffy nose, nose bleeds, flu symptoms, sore throat, laryngitis, swollen glands, itching, rash, brittle fingernails, blurred vision, conjunctivitis (red-eye), earache, a bad taste in the mouth, a general feeling of ill health, and changes in body weight.

The rarest side effects of Pentoxifylline are rapid or abnormal heart rhythms, hepatitis, yellow discoloration of the skin, reduction in white-blood-cell count, and small hemorrhages under the skin.

Food Interactions

It is preferable to take each dose of Pentoxifylline on an empty stomach. However, if it causes stomach upset or gas, the medicine may be taken with food.

Usual Dose

400 milligrams 3 times per day.

Overdosage

The severity of symptoms is directly related to the amount

of drug taken. Symptoms of overdosage usually appear 4 to 5 hours after the medicine was taken and can last for about 12 hours. Some of the reported effects of Pentoxifylline overdose are flushing, low blood pressure, fainting, depression of the nervous system, and convulsions. Patients taking an overdose of this drug must be made to vomit with Syrup of Ipecac (available at any pharmacy) to remove any remaining drug from the stomach. Call your doctor or a Poison Control Center before doing this. If you must go to a hospital emergency room, ALWAYS bring the medicine bottle.

Special Information

Call your doctor if any side effects develop. Some people may have to stop using this medicine if side effects become intolerable. You may feel better within 2 weeks after starting to take Pentoxifylline, but the treatments should be continued for at least 2 months to gain maximum benefit.

Brand Name

Percocet

Ingredients

Acetaminophen
Oxycodone Hydrochloride

(Also available in generic form)

Other Brand Names

SK-Oxycodone with Acetaminophen
Tylox

Type of Drug

Narcotic analgesic combination.

Prescribed for

Relief of mild to moderate pain.

General Information

Percocet is generally prescribed for the patient who is in pain but is allergic to Aspirin. Percocet is probably not effective for arthritis or other pain associated with inflammation because the Acetaminophen ingredient does not produce an anti-inflammatory effect.

Cautions and Warnings

Do not take Percocet if you know you are allergic or sensitive to any of its components. Use this drug with extreme caution if you suffer from asthma or other breathing problems. Long-term use of this drug may cause drug dependence or addiction. The Oxycodone Hydrochloride component of Percocet is a respiratory depressant, and affects the central nervous system, producing sleepiness, tiredness, and/or inability to concentrate. Be careful if you are driving, operating machinery, or performing other functions requiring concentration.

This drug may cause birth defects or interfere with your baby's development. Check with your doctor before taking it if you are, or might be, pregnant.

Possible Side Effects

Most frequent: light-headedness, dizziness, sleepiness, nausea, vomiting, loss of appetite, sweating. If these effects occur, consider calling your doctor and asking him about lowering your dose of Percocet. Usually the side effects disappear if you simply lie down.

More serious side effects of Percocet are shallow breathing or difficulty in breathing.

Possible Adverse Drug Effects

Adverse effects of Percocet include euphoria (feeling high), weakness, sleepiness, headache, agitation, uncoordinated muscle movement, minor hallucinations, disorientation and visual disturbances, dry mouth, loss of appetite, constipation, flushing of the face, rapid heartbeat, palpitations, faintness, urinary difficulties or hesitancy, reduced sex drive and/or potency, itching, rashes, anemia, lowered blood sugar, and a yellowing of the skin and/or whites of the eyes. Narcotic analgesics may aggravate convulsions in those who have had convulsions in the past.

Drug Interactions

Because of its depressant effect and potential effect on breathing, Percocet should be taken with extreme care in combination with alcohol, sleeping medicine, tranquilizers, or other depressant drugs.

Usual Dose

Adult: 1 to 2 tablets every 4 hours.
Child: not recommended for children.

Overdosage

Symptoms are depression of respiration (breathing), extreme tiredness progressing to stupor and then coma, pinpointed pupils of the eyes, no response to stimulation such as a pin stick, cold and clammy skin, slowing down of the heart rate, lowering of blood pressure, yellowing of the skin and/or whites of the eyes, bluish color in skin of hands and feet, fever, excitement, delirium, convulsions, cardiac arrest, and liver toxicity (shown by nausea, vomiting, pain in the abdomen, and diarrhea). The patient should be taken to a hospital emergency room immediately. ALWAYS bring the medicine bottle.

Food Interactions

Percocet is best taken with food or at least ½ glass of water to prevent stomach upset.

Brand Name

Percodan

Ingredients

Aspirin
Oxycodone Hydrochloride
Oxycodone Terephthalate

Other Brand Names

Codoxy
Oxycodone with Aspirin
Percodan-Demi

(Also available in generic form)

Type of Drug

Narcotic analgesic combination.

Prescribed for

Relief of mild to moderate pain.

General Information

Percodan is one of many combination products containing narcotics and analgesics. These products often also contain barbiturates or tranquilizers, and Acetaminophen which may be substituted for Aspirin.

Cautions and Warnings

Do not take Percodan if you know you are allergic or sensitive to any of its components. Use this drug with extreme caution if you suffer from asthma or other breathing problems. Long-term use of this drug may cause drug dependence or addiction. The Oxycodone component of Percodan is a respiratory depressant and affects the central nervous system, producing sleepiness, tiredness, and/or inability to concentrate.

This drug may cause birth defects or interfere with your baby's development. Check with your doctor before taking it if you are, or might be, pregnant.

Possible Side Effects

Most frequent: light-headedness, dizziness, sleepiness, nausea, vomiting, loss of appetite, sweating. If these effects occur, consider calling your doctor and asking him about lowering the dose of Percodan you are taking. Usually the side effects disappear if you simply lie down.

More serious side effects of Percodan are shallow breathing or difficulty in breathing.

Possible Adverse Drug Effects

Euphoria (feeling high), weakness, sleepiness, headache, agitation, uncoordinated muscle movement, minor hallucinations, disorientation and visual disturbances, dry mouth, loss of appetite, constipation, flushing of the face, rapid heartbeat, palpitations, faintness, urinary difficulties or hesitancy, reduced sex drive and/or potency, itching, skin rashes, anemia, lowered blood sugar, yellowing of the skin and/or whites of the eyes. Narcotic analgesics may aggravate convulsions in those who have had convulsions in the past.

Drug Interactions

Interaction with alcohol, tranquilizers, barbiturates, or sleeping pills produces tiredness, sleepiness, or inability to concentrate, and seriously increases the depressive effect of Percodan.

The Aspirin component of Percodan can affect anticoagulant (blood-thinning) therapy. Be sure to discuss this with your doctor so that the proper dosage adjustment can be made.

Interaction with adrenal cortical steroids, Phenylbutazone, or alcohol can cause severe stomach irritation with possible bleeding.

Food Interactions

Take with food or ½ glass of water to prevent stomach upset.

Usual Dose

1 tablet every 6 hours as needed for relief of pain.

Overdosage

Symptoms are depression of respiration (breathing), extreme tiredness progressing to stupor and then coma, pinpointed pupils of the eyes, no response to stimulation such as a pin stick, cold and clammy skin, slowing down of the heartbeat, lowering of blood pressure, convulsions, and cardiac arrest. The patient should be taken to a hospital emergency room immediately. ALWAYS bring the medicine bottle.

Special Information

Drowsiness may occur: be careful when driving or operating hazardous machinery.

Brand Name

Peri-Colace

Ingredients

Casanthranol
Docusate Sodium

Other Brand Names

Afko-Lube Lax	Disanthrol
Bu-Lax Plus	Di-Sosul Forte
Dialose Plus	DSMC Plus
Dioctalose	D-S-S plus
Diocto-K Plus Opolax	Molatoc-CST
Diolax	Pro-Sof Plus
Diothron	Regulance

(Also available in generic form)

Type of Drug

Laxative and stool-softener combination.

Prescribed for

Treatment or prevention of constipation. Also used to clear intestines before X-ray procedures.

General Information

This is one of many laxative combinations available without a prescription. Composed of a stool-softener and a stimulant which makes the stool easier to pass by acting directly on the intestine to move the stool through it, such laxatives should be used for short periods only when necessary. Long-term use of a stimulant laxative can produce laxative dependency, where normal bowel function is lost and the stimulant is required to pass any stool.

Cautions and Warnings

Patients with abdominal pain, nausea, vomiting, or symptoms of appendicitis should not take a laxative.

This drug has been found to be safe for use during pregnancy. Remember, you should check with your doctor before taking any drug if you are pregnant.

Possible Side Effects

Severely constipated patients may experience stomach cramps. Nausea, vomiting, and diarrhea may occur after excessive amounts have been taken.

Usual Dose

1 to 2 capsules at bedtime with an 8-ounce glass of water.

Special Information

If this laxative is not effective after 7 days, stop taking it and call your doctor.

Generic Name

Phenazopyridine Hydrochloride

Brand Names

Azodine	Phenazodine
Azo-Standard	Pyridiate
Baridium	Pyridium
Di-Azo	

(Also available in generic form)

Type of Drug

Urinary analgesic.

Prescribed for

Relief of pain and discomfort associated with urinary tract infections.

General Information

Phenazopyridine Hydrochloride is used only to relieve the pain associated with urinary infections. It has little antibacterial action and cannot be used, therefore, to cure a urinary infection. It is usually used in combination with an antibacterial sulfa drug.

Cautions and Warnings

This drug should not be used if you have kidney disease or are experiencing decrease in urination.

This drug has been found to be safe for use during pregnancy. Remember, you should check with your doctor before taking any drug if you are pregnant.

Possible Side Effects

Occasional stomach upset.

Usual Dose

200 milligrams 3 times per day after meals.

Special Information

Phenazopyridine Hydrochloride may produce an orange-red color in the urine. This is normal, but the color change may interfere with urine tests to monitor diabetes.

Generic Name

Phendimetrazine Tartrate

Brand Names

Adipost	Obeval
Adphen	Phenzine
Anorex	Plegine
Bacarate	Prelu-2
Bontril PDM	Slyn-LL
Bontril Slow Release	Sprx
Di-Ap-Trol	Statobex
Dyrexan-OD	Trimcaps
Hyrex	Trimstat
Melfiat	Trimtabs
Metra	weh-less
Obalan	Weightrol

(Also available in generic form)

Type of Drug

Nonamphetamine appetite suppressant.

Prescribed for

Suppression of appetite and treatment of obesity.

General Information

Although Phendimetrazine Tartrate is not an amphetamine, it can produce the same adverse effects as the amphetamine appetite suppressants. There are several other nonamphetamine appetite suppressants. One, Phenmetrazine Tartrate

(Preludin), is closely related to Phendimetrazine Tartrate and has similar actions and effects.

Cautions and Warnings

Do not use Phendimetrazine Tartrate if you have heart disease, high blood pressure, thyroid disease, or glaucoma, or if you are sensitive or allergic to this or similar drugs. Prolonged use of this drug may be habit-forming.

This drug may cause birth defects or interfere with your baby's development. Check with your doctor before taking it if you are, or might be, pregnant.

Possible Side Effects

Palpitations, high blood pressure, overstimulation, nervousness, restlessness, drowsiness, sedation, weakness, dizziness, inability to sleep, tremor, headache, dry mouth, nausea, vomiting, diarrhea and other intestinal disturbances, rash, itching, changes in sex drive, hair loss, muscle pain, difficulty in passing urine, sweating, chills, blurred vision, fever.

Drug Interactions

Do not take Phendimetrazine Tartrate if you take other stimulants or antidepressants.

This drug may reduce the effectiveness of antihypertensive drugs.

Usual Dose

Tablets: 35 milligram tablet 1 hour before meals 2 to 3 times per day.

Sustained-release capsules: 105 miligrams once per day in the morning.

Overdosage

Symptoms are restlessness, tremor, shallow breathing, confusion, hallucinations, and fever, followed by fatigue and depression, with additional symptoms such as high or possibly low blood pressure, cold and clammy skin, nausea, vomiting, diarrhea, and stomach cramps. The patient should be taken to a hospital emergency room immediately. ALWAYS bring the medicine bottle.

Special Information

Use only for a few weeks as an adjunct to diet, under strict supervision of your doctor.

Medicine alone will not take off weight. You must limit and modify your food intake, preferably under medical supervision.

Brand Name

Phenergan with Dextromethorphan Syrup

Ingredients

Alcohol
Dextromethorphan Hydrobromide
Promethazine Hydrochloride

Other Brand Names

Promethazine with Dextromethorphan Syrup

Type of Drug

Cough suppressant combination.

Prescribed for

Relief of coughs and symptoms associated with the common cold.

General Information

Phenergan with Dextromethorphan Syrup is one of many products marketed for the relief of coughs. The major active ingredient is an antihistamine Promethazine. Therefore the drug is most effective in relieving the symptoms of excess histamine production. It cannot help you recover more quickly, only more comfortably.

Cautions and Warnings

Drowsiness or sleepiness may occur. Do not use this product with similar products such as sedatives, tranquilizers, sleeping pills, antihistamines, or other drugs which can cause sleepiness or drowsiness.

Phenergan with Dextromethorphan Syrup used by pregnant women has caused side effects in newborns such as jaundice (yellowing of skin and eyes) and twitching. These medications should be stopped 1 to 2 weeks before expected delivery to avoid this. Phenergan has not been shown to cause problems during breast-feeding.

Possible Side Effects

Dryness of the mouth, blurred vision, occasional dizziness.

Drug Interactions

Avoid alcohol, which increases central nervous system depression and will increase drowsiness, sleepiness, or similar problems.

Usual Dose

1 teaspoon every 4 to 6 hours.

Special Information

Take with a full glass of water to help reduce any stomach upset caused by the drug.

Brand Name

Phenergan Syrup with Codeine

Ingredients

Alcohol
Ccdeine Phosphate
Prothazine Hydrochloride
Prometh with Codeine Syrup

Other Brand Names

Promethazine with Codeine Syrup
Promethazine-DC Liquid

Type of Drug

Cough suppressant combination.

Prescribed for

Coughs, symptoms of the common cold.

General Information

Phenergan Syrup with Codeine is one of almost 100 products marketed to treat symptoms of the common cold or other upper respiratory problems. It is useful in helping to relieve symptoms but does not treat the basic problem.

Cautions and Warnings

Do not take this medicine if you are allergic to any of its ingredients.

Phenergan Syrup with Codeine when used by pregnant women has caused side effects in newborns such as jaundice (yellowing of skin and eyes) and twitching. These medications should be stopped 1 to 2 weeks before expected delivery to avoid this. This drug has not been shown to cause problems during breast-feeding.

Possible Side Effects

Drowsiness, dry mouth, blurred vision, difficulty in urination, constipation.

Possible Adverse Drug Effects

Palpitations—pounding of the heart.

Drug Interactions

Avoid alcohol, sedatives, tranquilizers, antihistamines, or other medication which can cause tiredness and/or drowsiness.

Taking Phenergan Syrup with Codeine with Isocarboxazid (Marplan), Tranylcypromine Sulfate (Parnate), Phenelzine Sulfate (Nardil), or other MAO inhibitor drugs can produce a severe interaction. Consult your doctor first.

Usual Dose

Adult: 1 to 2 teaspoons 4 times per day.
Child (over age 1): ½ to 1 teaspoon 3 to 4 times per day.

Special Information

Be aware of the potential depressive effects of Phenergan

Syrup with Codeine; be careful when driving, or operating heavy or dangerous machinery.

Take with a full glass of water to reduce stomach upset.

Brand Name

Phenergan VC Syrup

Ingredients

Alcohol
Phenylephrine Hydrochloride
Promethazine Hydrochloride

(Also available in generic form)

Type of Drug

Cough suppressant and decongestant combination.

Prescribed for

Coughs.

General Information

Phenergan VC Syrup is one of many products marketed to relieve the symptoms of the common cold or other upper respiratory infections, relieve runny nose, and unclog nasal and sinus passages.

Cautions and Warnings

Drowsiness, dry mouth, blurred vision, difficulty in urination, and/or constipation can occur.

Phenergan VC Syrup when used by pregnant women has caused side effects in newborns such as jaundice (yellowing of skin and eyes) and twitching. These medications should be stopped 1 to 2 weeks before expected delivery to avoid this. This drug has not been shown to cause problems during breast-feeding.

Possible Side Effects

The drug may cause mild stimulation and you may experience nervousness, restlessness, or even inability to sleep.

Drug Interactions

Avoid alcohol, sedatives, tranquilizers, antihistamines, or other medication which can cause tiredness and/or drowsiness. Taking Phenergan VC Syrup with MAO inhibitor drugs can produce severe interaction. Consult your doctor first.

Usual Dose

1 teaspoon every 4 to 6 hours as needed for the relief of cough.

Special Information

Be aware of the potential depressive effects of this drug; take care when driving, or operating heavy or dangerous machinery.

Brand Name

Phenergan VC Syrup with Codeine

Ingredients

Alcohol   Phenylephrine
Codeine Phosphate   Promethazine Hydrochloride

Other Brand Names

Mallergan VC with Codeine Syrup
Promethazine VC with Codeine Syrup

Type of Drug

Cough suppressant and decongestant combination.

Prescribed for

Relief of cough, nasal congestion, runny nose, and other symptoms associated with the common cold, viruses, or other upper respiratory diseases. The drug may also be used to treat allergies, asthma, ear infections, or sinus infections.

General Information

Phenergan VC Syrup with Codeine is one of almost 100 products marketed to relieve the symptoms of the common cold and other respiratory infections. These products contain medicine to relieve congestion, act as an antihistamine, and relieve or suppress cough. They may contain medicine for each purpose, or may contain a combination of medicines. Some combinations leave out the antihistamine, the decongestant, or add an expectorant. You must realize while taking Phenergan VC Syrup with Codeine or similar products that these drugs only relieve symptoms and will not treat the underlying problem, such as a cold virus or other infections.

Cautions and Warnings

Phenergan VC Syrup with Codeine when taken by pregnant women has caused side effects in newborns such as jaundice (yellowing of skin and eyes) and twitching. These medications should be stopped 1 to 2 weeks before expected delivery to avoid this. This drug has not been shown to cause problems during breast-feeding.

Possible Side Effects

Dry mouth, blurred vision, difficulty passing urine, (possibly) constipation, nervousness, restlessness, or even inability to sleep. Can cause excessive tiredness or drowsiness.

Drug Interactions

Taking Phenergan VC Syrup with Codeine with MAO inhibitor drugs can produce severe interaction. Consult with your doctor first.

Drinking alcoholic beverages while taking Codeine may produce excessive drowsiness and/or sleepiness, or inability to concentrate.

Usual Dose

1 to 2 teaspoons 4 times per day.

Special Information

Take with a full glass of water to reduce stomach upset.

Generic Name

Phenobarbital

Brand Names

Barbita
Luminal
PBR/12

Sedadrops
SK-Phenobarbital
Solfoton

(Also available in generic form)

Type of Drug

Hypnotic; sedative; anticonvulsive.

Prescribed for

Epileptic seizures, convulsions, as an anticonvulsive or a daytime sedative; as a mild hypnotic (sleeping medication); for eclampsia (toxemia in pregnancy).

General Information

Phenobarbital, like the other barbiturates, appears to act by interfering with nerve impulses to the brain. When used as an anticonvulsive, Phenobarbital is not very effective by itself, but when used with anticonvulsive agents such as Phenytoin, the combined action of Phenobarbital and Phenytoin is dramatic. This combination has been used very successfully to control epileptic seizures.

Cautions and Warnings

Phenobarbital may slow down your physical and mental reflexes, so you must be extremely careful when operating machinery, driving an automobile, or performing other potentially dangerous tasks. Phenobarbital is classified as a barbiturate; long-term or unsupervised use may cause addiction. Elderly patients on Phenobarbital exhibit nervousness and confusion at times. Barbiturates are neutralized in the liver and eliminated from the body through the kidneys: consequently, people who have liver or kidney disorders—namely, difficulty in forming or excreting urine—should be carefully monitored by their doctor when taking Phenobarbital.

If you have known sensitivities or allergies to barbiturates, or have previously been addicted to sedatives or hypnotics, or if you have a disease affecting the respiratory system, you should not take Phenobarbital.

There is an increased chance of birth defects when women use Phenobarbital during pregnancy. Phenobarbital may be required to be used if a serious situation arises which threatens the mother's life.

Regularly using Phenobarbital during the last 3 months of pregnancy may cause drug dependency of the newborn. Labor may be prolonged and delivery may be delayed. There may be breathing problems in the newborn if Phenobarbital is used.

Breast-feeding while using Phenobarbital may cause increased tiredness, shortness of breath, or a slow heartbeat in the baby.

Possible Side Effects

Difficulty in breathing, skin rash, and general allergic reaction such as running nose, watering eyes, and scratchy throat.

Possible Adverse Drug Effects

Drowsiness, lethargy, dizziness, hangover, nausea, vomiting, diarrhea. More severe adverse reactions may include anemia and yellowing of the skin and eyes.

Drug Interactions

Interaction with alcohol, tranquilizers, the antibiotic Chloramphenicol, or other sedatives increases the sedative effect of Phenobarbital.

Interaction with anticoagulants (blood-thinning agents) can reduce their effect. This is also true of muscle relaxants and painkillers. Phenobarbital has been shown to reduce the potency of the antibiotic Doxycycline.

Usual Dose

Anticonvulsant: 15 to 100 milligrams 3 times per day. Hypnotic (for sleep): 30 to 320 milligrams at bedtime. Sedative: 15 to 120 milligrams 3 times per day.

Specific dose is determined by patient's size, weight, and physical condition.

Overdosage

Symptoms are difficulty in breathing, decrease in size of the pupils of the eyes, lowered body temperature progressing to fever as time passes, fluid in the lungs, and eventually coma.

Anyone suspected of having taken an overdose must be taken to the hospital for immediate care. ALWAYS bring the medicine bottle to the emergency room physician so he can quickly and correctly identify the medicine and start treatment. Severe overdosage of this medication can kill; the drug has been used many times in suicide attempts.

Generic Name

Phensuximide

Brand Name

Milontin

Type of Drug

Anticonvulsant.

Prescribed for

Control of petit mal seizures.

General Information

Phensuximide and the other succinimide-type anticonvulsants control petit mal seizures by slowing the transmission of impulses through certain areas of the brain. Generally, Ethosuximide is prescribed first for this type of seizure. Phensuximide may be prescribed if Ethosuximide does not work. If the succinimides are ineffective, the condition may then be treated with Clonazepam.

Cautions and Warnings

Phensuximide may be associated with severe reductions in white-blood-cell and platelet counts. Your doctor should perform periodic blood counts while you are taking this medicine.

In patients with grand mal and petit mal, succinimide-type anticonvulsants, when used alone, may increase the number of grand mal seizures and necessitate more medicine to control those seizures.

Abrupt withdrawal of any anticonvulsant may lead to severe seizures. It is important that your dosage be reduced gradually by your doctor.

This drug should be avoided by women who may become pregnant while using it and by pregnant and nursing mothers, since it will cross into the developing baby, and possible adverse effects on the infant are not known. In those situations where it is deemed essential, the potential risk of the drug must be carefully weighed against any benefit it might produce.

Recent reports suggest a strong association between the use of anticonvulsant drugs and birth defects. Although most of the information pertains to Phenytoin and Phenobarbital, not Phensuximide, other reports indicate a general association between all anticonvulsant drug treatments and birth defects. It is possible that the epileptic condition itself or genetic factors common to people with seizure disorders may also figure in the higher incidence of birth defects. Mothers taking Phensuximide should not breast-feed because of the possibility that the drug will pass into their breast milk and affect the baby. Use an alternative feeding method.

Possible Side Effects

Nausea, vomiting, upset stomach, stomach cramps and pain, loss of appetite, diarrhea, constipation, weight loss, drowsiness, dizziness, and poor muscle control.

Possible Adverse Drug Effects

Reductions in white-blood-cell and platelet counts, nervousness, hyperactivity, sleeplessness, irritability, headache, blurred vision, unusual sensitivity to bright lights, hiccups, a euphoric feeling, a dreamlike state, lack of energy, fatigue, confusion, mental instability, mental slowness, depression, sleep disturbances, nightmares, loss of the ability to concentrate, aggressiveness, constant concern with well-being and health, paranoid psychosis, suicidal tendencies, increased sex drive, rash, itching, frequent urination, kidney damage, blood in the urine, swelling around the eyes, hair loss, hairiness, muscle weakness, nearsightedness, vaginal bleeding, and swelling of the tongue and/or gums.

Drug Interactions

The depressant effects of Phensuximide are increased by tranquilizers, sleeping pills, narcotic pain relievers, antihistamines, alcohol, MAO inhibitors, antidepressants, and other anticonvulsants.

Phensuximide may increase the action of Phenytoin by increasing the blood levels of that drug. Your doctor should be sure that your dosages of the two drugs are appropriate to your condition.

Carbamazepine, another medicine prescribed to treat seizure disorders, may interfere with Phensuximide action by increasing the rate at which it is removed from the body.

The action of Phensuximide may be increased by Isoniazid, prescribed for tuberculosis prevention, and by Valproic Acid, another anticonvulsant drug, possibly leading to an increase in drug side effects when both drugs are taken together.

Avoid alcoholic beverages, which increase the depressant effects of this medicine.

Food Interactions

Phensuximide is best taken on an empty stomach but may be taken with food if it upsets your stomach.

Usual Dose

500 to 1000 milligrams 2 or 3 times per day, with weekly adjustments to meet your individual needs.

Dosage adjustments may be required for people with reduced kidney or liver function.

Overdosage

Phensuximide overdose will cause exaggerated side effects. If the overdose is discovered immediately, it may be helpful to make the victim vomit. But all victims of Phensuximide overdose must be taken to a hospital emergency room for treatment. ALWAYS bring the prescription bottle with you.

Special Information

Phensuximide will color your urine pink or red-brown. This is harmless and should be ignored.

Call your doctor if side effects become intolerable. Especially important are sore throat, joint pains, unexplained fever, rashes, unusual bleeding or bruising, drowsiness, dizziness, and blurred vision. Be sure to tell your doctor if you become pregnant while taking this medicine.

Phensuximide may interfere with your ability to drive a car or perform other complex tasks because it can cause drowsiness and difficulty concentrating.

Your doctor should perform periodic blood counts while you are taking this drug to check for possible adverse drug effects.

Do not suddenly stop taking this medicine, since to do so can result in severe seizures. The dosage must be discontinued gradually by your doctor.

Carry identification or wear a bracelet indicating that you suffer from a seizure disorder for which you take Phensuximide.

Generic Name

Phentermine Hydrochloride

Brand Names

Adipex	Obestin-30
Dapex 37.5	Parmine
Fastin	Phentamine
Ionamin	Phentrol
Obe-Nix	Tora
Obephen	Unifast Unicelles
Obermine	Wilpowr

(Also available in generic form)

Type of Drug

Nonamphetamine appetite suppressant.

Prescribed for

Suppression of appetite and treatment of obesity.

General Information

Although Phentermine Hydrochloride is not an amphetamine, it can produce the same adverse effects as the amphetamine appetite suppressants.

Cautions and Warnings

Do not use Phentermine Hydrochloride if you have heart disease, high blood pressure, thyroid disease, or glaucoma, or if you are sensitive or allergic to this or similar drugs. Prolonged use of this drug may be habit-forming.

This drug may cause birth defects or interfere with your baby's development. Check with your doctor before taking it if you are, or might be, pregnant.

Possible Side Effects

Palpitations, high blood pressure, overstimulation, nervousness, restlessness, drowsiness, sedation, weakness, dizziness, inability to sleep, tremor, headache, dry mouth, nausea, vomiting, diarrhea and other intestinal disturbances, rash, itching, changes in sex drive, hair loss, muscle pain, difficulty in passing urine, sweating, chills, blurred vision, and fever.

Drug Interactions

Do not take Phentermine Hydrochloride if you take other stimulants or antidepressants.

Phentermine Hydrochloride may reduce the effectiveness of antihypertensive drugs.

Usual Dose

Adult: 8 milligrams ½ hour before meals, or 15 to 37.5 milligrams once a day before breakfast.
Child: not recommended.

Overdosage

Symptoms are restlessness, tremor, shallow breathing, confusion, hallucinations, and fever followed by fatigue and depression, with additional symptoms such as high or possibly low blood pressure, cold and clammy skin, nausea, vomiting, diarrhea, and stomach cramps. The patient should be taken to a hospital emergency room immediately. ALWAYS bring the medicine bottle.

Special Information

Use only for a few weeks as an adjunct to diet, under strict supervision of your doctor.

Medicine alone will not take off weight. You must limit and modify your food intake, preferably under medical supervision.

Generic Name

Phenylbutazone

Brand Names

Azolid
Butazolidin

(Also available in generic form)

Type of Drug

Anti-inflammatory agent.

Prescribed for

Local inflammation of bone joints such as gout, rheumatoid arthritis, osteoarthritis, painful shoulder such as bursitis or arthritis of a joint, or other inflammatory diseases that cause pain which cannot be controlled by Aspirin, and when severe disability, because of the inflammation, is not relieved by usual treatment.

General Information

This drug should never be taken without strict medical supervision. Phenylbutazone should be used only for the short-term relief of pain due to inflammation of muscles, tendons, and joint area. It has anti-inflammatory, analgesic, and fever-reducing properties. This drug is quite useful but is limited by its side effects and adverse drug reactions.

Phenylbutazone and its sister drug Oxyphenbutazone are toxic and dangerous and should only be used when absolutely necessary. The list of potential side effects is long. Therefore, any change in habits or unusual effect which may be even remotely connected with the use of these drugs should be reported immediately to your doctor.

Cautions and Warnings

You should not take Phenylbutazone if you have a history of symptoms associated with gastrointestinal inflammation or ulcer, including severe, recurrent, or persistent upset stomach. This drug is not a simple pain reliever and should never be taken casually. It should not be prescribed before a careful and detailed history, plus physical and laboratory tests, have been completed by the doctor. Always discuss your state of health and medical history with your doctor completely before taking this medicine. If your problem can be treated by a less toxic drug such as Aspirin, use that first and try to avoid taking Phenylbutazone. Never take more than the recommended dosage: this would lead to toxic effects. If you have blurred vision, fever, rash, sore throat, sores in the mouth, upset stomach or pain in the stomach, feeling of weakness, bloody, black, or tarry stool, water retention, or a significant or sudden weight gain, report this to the doctor immediately. In addition, stop taking the drug. If the drug is not effective after 1 week, stop taking it.

This drug is known to cause birth defects or interfere with your baby's development. It is not considered safe for use by pregnant or lactating women.

Possible Side Effects

Most common: stomach upset, drowsiness, water retention.

Possible Adverse Drug Effects

Gastric or duodenal ulcer, ulceration or perforation of the large bowel, bleeding from the stomach, anemia, stomach pain, vomiting, vomiting of blood, nausea, diarrhea, changes in the components of the blood, water retention, disruption of normal chemical balance of the body. This drug can cause fatal or nonfatal hepatitis, black-and-blue marks on the skin, serum sickness, drug allergy serious enough to cause shock, itching, serious rashes, fever, and signs of arthritis. It has been known to cause kidney effects including bleeding and kidney stones. Phenylbutazone may be a cause of heart disease, high blood pressure, blurred vision, bleeding in the

back of the eye, detachment of a retina, hearing loss, high
blood sugar, thyroid disease, agitation, confusion, or lethargy.

Drug Interactions

Phenylbutazone increases the effects of blood-thinning drugs,
Phenytoin, Insulin, and oral antidiabetic agents. If you are
taking any of these drugs, discuss this matter with your
doctor immediately.

Food Interactions

Avoid alcoholic beverages. Phenylbutazone causes stomach
upset in many patients; take your dose with food or antacids,
and if stomach pain continues, notify your doctor.

Usual Dose

Adult and child (age 14 or over): 300 to 600 milligrams per
day in 3 to 4 equal doses for 7 days. If dose is effective it can
then be reduced to 100 to 400 milligrams per day, depending
on the condition being treated.

Elderly: drug to be given only for 7 days because of high
risk of severe reactions. Not to be given to senile patients.

Child (under age 14): not recommended.

Overdosage

If symptoms of convulsions, euphoria, depression, headache, hallucinations, giddiness, dizziness, coma, rapid breathing rate, continued stomach pain, and insomnia or sleeplessness appear, contact your doctor immediately.

Special Information

This drug can make you drowsy and/or tired: be careful
when driving or operating equipment.

This drug should be avoided by pregnant women.

Generic Name

Phenytoin

Brand Names

Dilantin (extended action)
Diphenylan Sodium (prompt acting)
Ditan (prompt acting)

(Also available in generic form)

Type of Drug

Anticonvulsant.

Prescribed for

Control of epileptic seizures.

General Information

Phenytoin is one of several drugs of the same chemical group used to control convulsions. All these drugs act by the same mechanism, although some patients may respond to some and not another.

Cautions and Warnings

If you have been taking Phenytoin for a long time and no longer need it, the dosage should be reduced gradually over a period of about a week. Stopping abruptly may bring on severe epileptic seizures. Pregnant women who use anticonvulsive medicine are said to tend to give birth to children with birth defects, but the data available are somewhat questionable. If you become pregnant and you are taking this medicine, consult your doctor immediately.

Mothers who breast-feed their babies may see some unwanted effects, such as yellowing of the eyes or skin, upset stomach, and constipation.

Possible Side Effects

Most common: slurred speech, mental confusion, nystagmus (a rhythmic, uncontrolled movement of the eyeballs), dizziness, insomnia, nervousness, uncontrollable twitching, double vision, tiredness, irritability, depression, tremors, headaches. These side effects will generally disappear as therapy continues and the dosage is reduced.

Possible Adverse Drug Effects

Nausea, vomiting, diarrhea, constipation, fever, rashes, balding, weight gain, numbness of the hands and feet, chest pains, retention of water, sensitivity to bright lights, especially sunlight, conjunctivitis, changes of the blood system including anemia, swollen glands. Phenytoin can cause an abnormal growth of the gums surrounding the teeth, so good oral hygiene including gum massage, frequent brushing, and appropriate dental care is very important. Occasionally Phenytoin produces unusual hair growth over the body, and liver damage, including hepatitis.

Drug Interactions

A barbiturate taken with Phenytoin may increase the rate at which Phenytoin is excreted from the body; then if the barbiturate is discontinued the patient may show an increased response to Phenytoin, and the dose may have to be reduced slightly.

Warfarin, Isoniazid, Chloramphenicol, Disulfiram, Phenylbutazone, and Oxyphenbutazone can cause Phenytoin to remain in the body for a longer time, increasing the incidence of Phenytoin side effects. Folic acid or high doses of tricyclic antidepressant drugs may increase seizures. The dose of Phenytoin may have to be adjusted by your doctor.

Food Interactions

The amount of Phenytoin that is absorbed from the small intestine can be decreased if you eat foods high in calcium or take calcium supplements. This may result in less Phenytoin available for action in the body.

If you get upset stomach after taking Phenytoin, take the medicine with meals.

Usual Dose

Adult: initial dose, 300 milligrams per day. If this does not result in satisfactory control, gradually increase to 600 milligrams per day. (The most frequent maintenance dose is 300 to 400 milligrams per day.) Only Dilantin may be taken once daily. The other brands of Phenytoin must be taken throughout the day, as convenient.

Child: initial dose, 2.5 milligrams per pound of body weight per day in 2 to 3 equally divided doses; then adjust according to needs and response of child (normal maintenance dose, 2 to 4 milligrams per pound of body weight per day). Children over age 6 may require the same dose as an adult, but no child should be given more than 300 milligrams per day.

Overdosage

Symptoms are listed in "Possible Side Effects" and "Possible Adverse Drug Effects" above. The patient should be taken to a hospital emergency room immediately. ALWAYS bring the medicine bottle.

Special Information

If you develop a rash, sore throat, fever, unusual bleeding, or bruising, contact your doctor immediately. Phenytoin sometimes produces a pink-brown color in the urine; don't worry about it. Do not change brands of Phenytoin without notifying your doctor.

Generic Name

Pilocarpine Ophthalmic Solution

Brand Names

Adsorbocarpine
Akarpine
Almocarpine
Isopto Carpine
Ocusert Pilo
Pilocar
Pilocel
Pilomiotin

P.V. Carpine Liquifilm
Combination Products:
E-Pilo (with epinephrine)
Isopto P-ES (with physostigmine)
Miocel (with physostigmine)
P E (with epinephrine)

(Also available in generic form)

Type of Drug

Miotic agent.

Prescribed for

Management of glaucoma (increased pressure in the eye).

General Information

Pilocarpine Ophthalmic Solution is the drug of choice in the treatment of open angle glaucoma. It works on muscles in the eye to open passages so that fluid can normally flow out of the eye chamber, reducing fluid pressure inside the eye. Pilocarpine Ophthalmic Solution may also help reduce the amount of fluid produced within the eye.

Although used as eyedrops, the drug can affect other parts of the body, especially after long use. When this drug is prescribed, it is usually given for long periods of time, as long as eye pressure does not increase or eyesight does not worsen. The concentration of Pilocarpine Ophthalmic Solution is determined by the physician, and is based on the severity of the disease. This drug is also marketed in a special form called Pilo-Ocusert—a thin football-shaped wafer designed to continuously release the drug for 1 week. This eliminates the need for putting drops in your eyes 3 to 4 times a day. The wafer is placed under the eyelid similarly to the way contact lenses are placed.

If you use the conventional eyedrops, be very careful not to touch the eyelids or surrounding area with the dropper tip; otherwise you will contaminate the dropper and cause the medicine to become unsterile. Be sure you recap the bottle tightly in order to preserve the sterility of the medicine.

Cautions and Warnings

Pilocarpine Ophthalmic Solution should only be used when prescribed by an eye specialist (ophthalmologist). This drug should not be used if you are allergic to it.

This drug has been found to be safe for use during pregnancy. Remember, you should check with your doctor before taking any drug if you are pregnant.

Possible Side Effects

This drug may produce spasms of the eye muscles resulting

in an aching feeling over the brow. You may also find it hard to focus your eyes. These effects are seen in younger people and will disappear with continued use. Some people may complain of decreased vision in low light.

Possible Adverse Drug Effects

Allergy or itching and tearing of the eye may develop after prolonged use.

Usual Dose

Initial dose, 1 to 2 drops in the affected eye up to 6 times per day, then according to severity of disease.

Ocusert Pilo: insert into eye sac and replace weekly.

At first Pilocarpine Ophthalmic Solution is also placed in the healthy eye to keep it from becoming diseased.

The usual concentration of the drug is 0.5 to 4 percent. Concentrations above 4 percent are used less often. The most frequently used concentrations are 1 and 2 percent.

Overdosage

After long-term use, small amounts of Pilocarpine Ophthalmic Solution may be absorbed by the drainage systems of the eye. If symptoms of stomach upset, nausea, vomiting, diarrhea, and cramps appear, contact your doctor immediately.

Special Information

After placing drops in your eye you may feel a stinging sensation; this is normal in the Pilocarpine solutions. You should not close your eyes tightly or blink more than normal, which removes the drops from the eye.

Generic Name

Pindolol

Brand Name

Visken

Type of Drug

Beta-adrenergic blocking agent.

Prescribed for

High blood pressure.

General Information

Pindolol is a unique beta-adrenergic blocker. It is similar to Propranolol, Nadolol, and Timolol Maleate in that it works on both beta receptors in the heart and those in blood vessels. But it differs from those medications in its ability to increase the heart's activity. As a result, this drug causes less of a reduction in heart rate than the other beta blockers, making it useful for people with heart failure, who cannot take other beta blockers. Pindolol can be taken with a diuretic drug or by itself to treat high blood pressure.

Unlike other beta blockers, which can be used to treat a variety of heart conditions, migraine headaches, schizophrenia, tremors, panic, and other symptoms, Pindolol should not be taken for any purpose other than treating high blood pressure.

Cautions and Warnings

Heart failure, although far less likely with Pindolol than with the other beta blockers, is the most important caution for people taking this drug. Pindolol should not be discontinued abruptly because of the possibility of developing tremors, sweating, heart pain, palpitations, headache, and a feeling of ill health. The drug should be discontinued gradually over a period of several weeks.

Pindolol must be used with extreme caution by asthmatics and others with respiratory disease, since this and other beta blockers can worsen bronchial spasms. This effect is less prominent with Pindolol than some other drugs, but is still possible.

This drug should be stopped several days or weeks before major surgery to prevent the risk of its affecting the ability of your heart to respond during the surgical procedure.

There have been no adequate studies undertaken on the effects of Pindolol on the human fetus. This drug should be avoided by pregnant women or women who may become pregnant while using it. In those situations where it is deemed essential, the potential risk of the drug must be carefully weighed against any benefit it might produce. Nursing mothers who must take Pindolol should use an alternative method of feeding their infants since the drug definitely passes into breast milk.

All beta blockers can mask the signs or symptoms of diabetes and low blood sugar and an overactive thyroid. Be sure the doctor prescribing Pindolol knows your complete medical history.

This drug must be used with caution by people with severe liver disease.

Possible Side Effects

Most side effects are mild and will pass on their own. The most common are anxiety, bizarre dreams, hallucinations, dizziness, fatigue or tiredness, lethargy, difficulty sleeping, nervousness, weakness, visual disturbances, tingling in the hands or feet, breathing difficulty, retention of fluid, heart failure, heart palpitations, weight gain (when the drug is taken alone), chest and joint pains, muscle cramps and pain, nausea, abdominal discomfort and pain, itching, and rash.

Possible Adverse Drug Effects

Sore throat, fever, slowing of the heart, coldness of the arms or legs, leg pains, stroke, fainting, low blood pressure, rapid heartbeat, abnormal heart rhythms, depression, loss of the ability to concentrate, sedation, odd behavior (especially in the elderly), memory loss, disorientation (especially in the elderly), emotional upset, slurred speech, ringing or buzzing in the ears, light-headedness, changes in blood-sugar level (up or down), stomach gas and pain, constipation, diarrhea, dry mouth, vomiting, loss of appetite, bloating, loss of sexual potency and/or drive, difficulty urinating, skin discoloration, sweating, hair loss, dry skin, eye irritation or discomfort, and dry or burning eyes.

Drug Interactions

Chlorpromazine, Cimetidine, Furosemide, Hydralazine Hydrochloride, oral contraceptive pills, and Reserpine increase Pindolol's effect on the body.

Indomethacin and Aspirin or Aspirin-containing drugs may counteract the blood-pressure-reducing effect of Pindolol.

Beta blockers can antagonize the effects of Theophylline.

They can increase the effects of Insulin and can worsen the body's reaction to the sudden discontinuation of Clonidine (taken for high blood pressure) and the usual "first dose" reaction to Prazosin Hydrochloride.

Usual Dose

10 to 15 milligrams per day.

Overdosage

The symptoms of Pindolol overdose can include a drastic reduction in heart rate, heart failure, very low blood pressure, breathing difficulty because of bronchial muscle spasm, seizures, delerium, coma, and possible loss of consciousness. Very large Pindolol overdoses can cause your heart to beat faster and blood pressure to increase. Patients taking an overdose of this drug must be made to vomit with Syrup of Ipecac (available at any pharmacy) to remove any remaining drug from the stomach. Call your doctor or a Poison Control Center before doing this. If you must go to a hospital emergency room, ALWAYS bring the medicine bottle.

Special Information

Don't stop taking this medicine without your doctor's specific knowledge and approval. Sudden discontinuation could result in heart pains or other symptoms.

Call your doctor if it becomes gradually more difficult to breathe while you are taking Pindolol, especially when you are lying down, when you cough at night, or when you retain fluid in your legs. These may be signs of heart failure. Other symptoms to tell your doctor about are slow pulse, dizziness, light-headedness, depression, confusion, rash, fever, sore throat, and unusual bleeding or bruising.

Since Pindolol can cause loss of concentration and visual disturbances, be careful while driving or operating machinery.

Generic Name

Piroxicam

Brand Name

Feldene

Type of Drug

Nonsteroid anti-inflammatory.

Prescribed for

Arthritis and other forms of bone and joint inflammation.

General Information

This new nonsteroid anti-inflammatory agent represents an entirely different chemical class than any of its predecessors. It is long-acting and given only once a day, characteristics that have made Piroxicam the most widely prescribed nonsteroid anti-inflammatory drug in America. Like other nonsteroid anti-inflammatories, it is thought to work by preventing the body from manufacturing hormones called prostaglandins, thus reducing pain, inflammation and fever.

Cautions and Warnings

Piroxicam should not be used by infants or children.

Do not take this drug if you are allergic to it, to Aspirin or to other nonsteroid anti-inflammatory drugs. It may cause stomach ulcers.

This drug may cause birth defects or interfere with your baby's development. Check with your doctor before taking it if you are, or might be, pregnant.

Piroxicam has not been shown to cause problems during breast-feeding.

All patients taking this drug should have regular eye examinations since it may cause blurred vision or other problems.

Possible Side Effects

Most common: upset stomach, nausea, iron deficiency, and blood loss through the gastrointestinal tract.

Piroxicam may also cause loss of appetite, abdominal discomfort, constipation, diarrhea, stomach gas or pains, indigestion, adverse effects on the blood system, reduced kidney function, dizziness, sleepiness, ringing or buzzing in the ears, headache, a sickly feeling, fluid in the arms or legs, itching, and rash. The elderly are more likely to experience side effects.

Possible Adverse Drug Effects

Piroxicam may cause reduced liver function, vomiting with or without blood, blood in the urine or stool, bleeding from the stomach, dry mouth, sweating, unusual bruising, loss of patches of skin, swollen eyes, blurred vision, eye irritations, high blood pressure, lowered blood sugar, body weight changes (either up or down), depression, nervousness, sleeplessness, heart palpitations, difficulty breathing and difficulty in urination.

Drug Interactions

Avoid alcohol, since this may increase upset stomach associated with Piroxicam or aggravate any problems with drowsiness or lack of alertness.

Piroxicam may interact with anticoagulant (blood-thinning) drugs. Although you will probably not experience a serious interaction, your doctor should monitor your anticoagulant therapy during the first few weeks of Piroxicam therapy in case any adjustment is needed.

Aspirin, in doses of 12 tablets per day or more, will reduce the effect of Piroxicam by reducing its level in the blood. These drugs should not be taken together since there is no special benefit from the combination and it may cause unwanted side effects.

Since Piroxicam may cause lowered blood-sugar levels, diabetics taking Piroxicam may need to have the dose of their antidiabetic drug reduced.

Usual Dose

10 to 20 milligrams per day.

Special Information

You will not feel the maximum effects of Piroxicam until you have taken the drug for 2 to 3 months, although you may begin to experience some relief as early as 2 weeks after beginning treatment.

If you get an upset stomach after taking Piroxicam, take the medicine with meals. If you develop swollen hands or feet, itching, rash, black tarry stools, vomiting, blurred vision or other visual disturbances, or unusual bruises, contact your doctor immediately.

Brand Name

Poly-Vi-Flor Chewable Tablets

Ingredients

Folic Acid (Vitamin B9)	Vitamin B6 (Pyridoxine)
Sodium Fluoride	Vitamin B12 (Cyanocobalmin)
Vitamin A	Vitamin C
Vitamin B1 (Thiamine)	Vitamin D
Vitamin B2 (Riboflavin)	Vitamin E
Vitamin B3 (Niacin)	

Other Brand Names

Florvite
Poly-Tabs-F
Vi-Daylin/F

(Also available in generic form)

Type of Drug

Multivitamin supplement with a fluoride.

Prescribed for

Vitamin deficiencies and prevention of dental cavities in infants and children.

General Information

Fluorides taken in small daily doses have been effective in preventing cavities in children by strengthening their teeth and making them resistant to cavity formation. Too much fluoride can damage the teeth. Because of this, vitamins with a fluoride should only be used in areas where the water supply is not fluoridated.

Cautions and Warnings

Poly-Vi-Flor Chewable Tablets should not be used in areas where the fluoride content exceeds 0.7 ppm (part per million). Your pediatrician or local water company can tell you the fluoride content of the water you drink.

This drug has been found to be safe for use during pregnancy. Remember, you should check with your doctor before taking any drug if you are pregnant.

Possible Side Effects

Occasional skin rash, itching, stomach upset, headache, weakness.

Usual Dose

1 tablet chewed per day.

Generic Name

Potassium Chloride

Brand Names

Liquids	Powders (to be dissolved)
Cena-K	KATO
EM-K	Kay Ciel
Kaochlor	K-Lor
Kaon-Cl	KLOR-CON
Kay Ciel	Klorvess Granules
Klor	K-Lyte/Cl
Klor-con	Kolyum
Potachlor	Potage
Potasalan	*Effervescent tablets*
Potassine	Kaochlor-Eff
Rum-K	Klorvess Oral tablets
S.K. Potassium Chloride	K-Lyte

Swallow Tablets
  Kaon-Cl (wax matrix)
  Klotrix (wax matrix)
  K-Tab (wax matrix)

Micro-K Extencaps;
Potassium C (coated)
Slow-K (wax matrix)

(Also available in generic form)

Type of Drug

Potassium supplement.

Prescribed for

Replacement of potassium in the body.

General Information

Potassium Chloride is a very important component of the body and has a major effect on maintaining the proper tone of all body cells. Potassium Chloride is also important for the maintenance of normal kidney function; it is required for the passage of electrical impulses in the nervous system, and has a major effect on the heart and all other muscles of the body.

Cautions and Warnings

Potassium replacement should always be monitored and controlled by your physician. Potassium Chloride tablets have produced ulceration in some patients with compression of the esophagus. Potassium Chloride supplements for these patients should be given in liquid form. Potassium Chloride tablets have been reported to cause ulcers of the small bowel, leading to hemorrhage, obstruction, and/or perforation.

Do not take Potassium Chloride supplements if you are dehydrated or experiencing muscle cramps due to excessive sun exposure. The drug should be used with caution in patients who have kidney and/or heart disease.

This drug has been found to be safe for use during pregnancy. Remember, you should check with your doctor before taking any drug if you are pregnant. However, breast-feeding while taking Potassium Chloride may cause unwanted side effects in your infant. If you must take Potassium Chloride, you should temporarily stop nursing and discard pumped breast milk. Nursing can resume 1 to 2 days after stopping Potassium Chloride.

Possible Side Effects

Potassium Chloride toxicity, or overdose, is extremely rare. Toxicity can occur when high doses of Potassium Chloride supplements are taken in combination with foods high in Potassium Chloride. Common side effects are nausea, vomiting, diarrhea, and abdominal discomfort. Less common side effects are tingling of hands and feet, listlessness, mental confusion, weakness and heaviness of legs, decreased blood pressure, and/or heart rhythm changes.

Drug Interactions

Potassium Chloride supplements should not be taken with Spironolactone, Triamterene, or combinations of these drugs, as Potassium Chloride toxicity may occur.

Food Interactions

Salt substitutes may contain large amounts of Potassium. You should discuss their use with your doctor.

Usual Dose

As regulated by physician; generally 20 to 60 milliequivalents per day.

Special Information

Directions for taking Potassium Chloride supplements should be followed closely. Liquid Potassium Chloride supplement should be diluted properly. Effervescent tablets and Potassium Chloride supplement powders should be dissolved completely.

Directions for taking and using Potassium supplements should be followed closely. Effervescent tablets, powders, and liquids should be properly and completely dissolved or diluted in cold water or juice and drunk slowly. Oral tablets or capsules should not be chewed or crushed and are intended to be swallowed whole.

Generic Name

Prazepam

Brand Name

Centrax

Type of Drug

Tranquilizer.

Prescribed for

Relief of symptoms of anxiety, tension, fatigue, or agitation.

General Information

Prazepam is a member of the chemical group of drugs known as benzodiazepines. These drugs are used as either antianxiety agents, anticonvulsants, or sedatives (sleeping pills). They exert their effects by relaxing the large skeletal muscles and by a direct effect on the brain. In doing so, they can relax you and make you either more tranquil or sleepier, depending on the drug and how much you use. Many doctors prefer Prazepam and the other members of this class to other drugs that can be used for the same effect. Their reason is that the benzodiazepines tend to be safer, have fewer side effects, and are usually as, if not more, effective.

These drugs are generally used in any situation where they can be a useful adjunct.

Benzodiazepine tranquilizing drugs can be abused if taken for long periods of time and it is possible to develop withdrawal symptoms if you discontinue the therapy abruptly. Withdrawal symptoms include convulsions, tremor, muscle cramps, stomach cramps, vomiting, and sweating.

Cautions and Warnings

Do not take Prazepam if you know you are sensitive or allergic to this drug or other benzodiazepines such as Chlordiazepoxide, Oxazepam, Clorazepate, Diazepam, Lorazepam, Flurazepam, and Clonazepam.

Prazepam and other members of this drug group may aggravate narrow angle glaucoma, but if you have open angle glaucoma you may take the drugs. In any case, check this information with your doctor. Prazepam can cause tiredness, drowsiness, inability to concentrate, or similar symptoms. Be careful if you are driving, operating machinery, or performing other activities which require concentration.

This drug may cause birth defects or interfere with your baby's development. Check with your doctor before taking it if you are, or might be, pregnant.

Possible Side Effects

Most common: mild drowsiness during the first few days of therapy, especially in the elderly or debilitated. If drowsiness persists, contact your doctor.

Possible Adverse Drug Effects

Major adverse reactions: confusion, depression, lethargy, disorientation, headache, lack of activity, slurred speech, stupor, dizziness, tremor, constipation, dry mouth, nausea, inability to control urination, changes in sex drive, irregular menstrual cycle, changes in heart rhythm, lowered blood pressure, retention of fluids, blurred or double vision, itching, rash, hiccups, nervousness, inability to fall asleep, (occasional) liver dysfunction. If you experience any of these reactions stop taking the medicine and contact your doctor immediately.

Drug Interactions

Prazepam is a central nervous system depressant. Avoid alcohol, tranquilizers, narcotics, sleeping pills, barbiturates, MAO inhibitors, antihistamines, and other medicines used to relieve depression.

Usual Dose

Adult: 20 to 60 milligrams per day as individualized for maximum benefit, depending on symptoms and response to treatment, which may require a dose outside the range given. 20 milligrams may be taken at bedtime for sleep.

Elderly: usually require less of the drug to control anxiety and tension.

Overdosage

Symptoms are confusion, sleep or sleepiness, lack of response to pain such as a pin stick, shallow breathing, lowered blood pressure, and coma. The patient should be taken to a hospital emergency room immediately. ALWAYS bring the medicine bottle.

Generic Name

Prazosin Hydrochloride

Brand Name

Minipress

Type of Drug

Antihypertensive.

Prescribed for

High blood pressure.

General Information

Prazosin Hydrochloride works by dilating and reducing pressure in blood vessels. It is quite effective when used in combination with a thiazide diuretic and/or beta-adrenergic blocker. It is much safer than other drugs which work in the same way because it does not directly affect the heart.

Cautions and Warnings

This drug can cause dizziness and fainting, most often due to an effect called "postural hypotension" where blood supply to the brain is reduced when rising suddenly from a sitting or lying-down position. This often occurs after taking first dose of 2 milligrams or more of Prazosin Hydrochloride.

This drug may cause birth defects or interfere with your baby's development. Check with your doctor before taking it if you are, or might be, pregnant.

Possible Side Effects

The most common side effects of Prazosin Hydrochloride are dizziness, headache, drowsiness, lack of energy, weakness, heart palpitations, and nausea. Usually these side effects subside and people become more tolerant to the drug.

Possible Adverse Drug Effects

Vomiting, diarrhea, constipation, stomach upset or pain, unusual swelling in the arms or legs, shortness of breath, passing out, rapid heart rate, increased chest pain (angina), nervousness, depression, tingling in the hands or feet, rash, itching, frequent urination, poor urinary control, sexual impotence, blurred vision, redness of the eyes, ringing or buzzing in the ears, dry mouth, stuffy nose, sweating.

Usual Dose

1 milligram 2 to 3 times per day to start; the dose may be increased to 20 milligrams a day, and 40 milligrams has been used in some cases. The daily dose of Prazosin Hydrochloride must be tailored to patient's needs.

Overdosage

Overdosage may lead to very low blood pressure. Call your doctor or Poison Control Center for advice. If you go to a hospital emergency room, remember, ALWAYS bring the medicine bottle.

Special Information

Take this drug exactly as prescribed. Do not stop taking Prazosin Hydrochloride unless directed to do so by your doctor. Do not take over-the-counter medicines containing stimulants. If you are unsure which ones to avoid, ask your pharmacist.

Prazosin Hydrochloride can cause dizziness, drowsiness, or headache, especially when you begin taking the drug. Avoid driving or operating any equipment 4 hours after the first dose and take care for the first few days. You may want to take the first dose before you go to bed. If you experience severe dizziness, lie down and wait for the episode to pass.

Generic Name

Prednisone

Brand Names

Cortan	Orasone
Deltasone	Prednicen-M
Liquid Pred	SK-Prednisone
Meticorten	Sterapred

(Also available in generic form)

Type of Drug

Adrenal cortical steroid.

Prescribed for

The variety of disorders for which Prednisone is prescribed is almost endless, from skin rash to cancer. The drug may be used as a treatment for adrenal gland disease, since one of the hormones produced by the adrenal gland is very similar to Prednisone. If patients are not producing sufficient adrenal hormones, Prednisone may be used as replacement therapy. It may also be prescribed for the treatment of bursitis, arthritis, severe skin reactions such as psoriasis or other rashes, severe allergic conditions, asthma, drug or serum sickness, severe, acute, or chronic allergic inflammation of the eye and surrounding areas such as conjunctivitis, respiratory diseases including pneumonitis, blood disorders, gastrointestinal diseases including ulcerative colitis, and inflammation of the nerves, heart, or other organs.

General Information

Prednisone is one of many adrenal cortical steroids used in medical practice today. The major differences between Prednisone and other adrenal cortical steroids are potency of medication and variation in some secondary effects. Choice of an adrenal cortical steroid to be used for a specific disease is usually a matter of doctor preference and past experience. Other adrenal cortical steroids include Cortisone, Hydrocortisone, Prednisolone, Triamcinolone, Methylprednisolone, Meprednisone, Paramethasone, Fluprednisolone, Dexamethasone, Betamethasone, and Fludrocortisone.

Cautions and Warnings

Because of the effect of Prednisone on your adrenal gland, it is essential that the dose be tapered from a large dose down to a small dose over a period of time. Do not stop taking this medication suddenly or without the advice of your doctor. If you do, you may cause a failure of the adrenal gland with extremely serious consequences.

Prednisone has a strong anti-inflammatory effect, and may mask some signs of infections. If new infections appear during the use of Prednisone therapy, they may be difficult to discover and may grow more rapidly due to your decreased resistance. If you think you are getting an infection during the time that you are taking Prednisone, you should contact your doctor, who will prescribe appropriate therapy.

If you are taking Prednisone, you should not be vaccinated against any infectious diseases, because of inability of the body to produce the normal reaction to vaccination. Discuss this with your doctor before he administers any vaccination.

If you suspect that you are pregnant and are taking Prednisone, report it immediately to your doctor. If you are taking Prednisone and have just given birth, do not nurse; use prepared formulas instead.

Large amounts of Prednisone taken by the mother during pregnancy or breast-feeding may slow the growth of new-born babies.

Possible Side Effects

Stomach upset is one of the more common side effects of Prednisone, which may in some cases cause gastric or duodenal ulcers. Other side effects: retention of water, heart failure, potassium loss, muscle weakness, loss of muscle mass, loss of calcium which may result in bone fractures and a condition known as aseptic necrosis of the femoral and humoral heads (this means the ends of the large bones in the hip may degenerate from loss of calcium), slowing down of wound healing, black-and-blue marks on the skin, increased sweating, allergic skin rash, itching, convulsions, dizziness, headache.

Possible Adverse Drug Effects

May cause irregular menstrual cycles, slowing down of growth in children, particularly after the medication has been taken for long periods of time, depression of the adrenal and/or pituitary glands, development of diabetes, increased pressure of the fluid inside the eye, hypersensitivity or allergic reactions, blood clots, insomnia, weight gain, increased appetite, nausea, and feeling of ill health. Psychic derangements may appear which range from euphoria to mood swings, personality changes, and severe depression. Prednisone may also aggravate existing emotional instability.

Drug Interactions

Prednisone and other adrenal corticosteroids may interact with Insulin and oral antidiabetic drugs, causing an increased requirement of the antidiabetic drugs.

Interaction with Phenobarbital, Ephedrine, and Phenytoin may reduce the effect of Prednisone by increasing its removal from the body.

If a doctor prescribes Prednisone you should discuss any oral anti-coagulant (blood-thinning) drugs you are taking: the dose of them may have to be changed.

Interaction with diuretics such as Hydrochlorothiazide may cause you to lose blood potassium. Be aware of signs of lowered potassium level such as weakness, muscle cramps, and tiredness, and report them to your physician. Eat high potassium foods such as bananas, citrus fruits, melons, and tomatoes.

Prednisone and other steroids can intefere with laboratory tests. You should notify your physician that you are taking these drugs so that the tests can be properly analyzed.

Food Interactions

If you notice a slight stomach upset when you take your dose of Prednisone, take this medication with food or a small amount of antacid. If stomach upset continues or bothers you, notify your doctor.

Usual Dose

Initial dose, 5 to 60 or even more milligrams; maintenance dose, 5 to 60 milligrams depending on patient's response. Dose also varies according to disease being treated. The lowest effective dose is desirable. Stressful situations may cause a need for a temporary increase in your Prednisone dose.

This drug must be tapered off slowly, not stopped abruptly. Prednisone may be given in alternate day therapy; twice the usual daily dose is given every other day.

Overdosage

There is no specific treatment for overdosage of adrenal cortical steroids. Symptoms are anxiety, depression and/or stimulation, stomach bleeding, increased blood sugar, high blood pressure, and retention of fluid. The patient should be taken to a hospital emergency room immediately, where stomach pumping, oxygen, intravenous fluids, and other supportive treatments are available. ALWAYS bring the medicine bottle.

Generic Name

Primidone

Brand Names

Mysoline
Primoline

(Also available in generic form)

Type of Drug

Anticonvulsant.

Prescribed for

Control of epileptic and other seizures.

General Information

Although this drug is not a barbiturate, it is a close chemical cousin to the barbiturates and possesses many of their characteristics. It acts on a portion of the brain that inhibits the unusual nerve transmissions that are present in seizure disorders.

Cautions and Warnings

If you have been taking Primidone for a long time and no longer need it do not stop abruptly, but reduce the dosage gradually over a period of about a week. Stopping abruptly may bring on severe epileptic seizures.

This drug may cause birth defects or interfere with your baby's development. Check with your doctor before taking it if you are, or might be, pregnant. Most mothers have delivered normal children, but there is an increased chance for birth defects. Primidone may also cause bleeding problems and increased tiredness in the newborn and breast-fed baby.

Possible Side Effects

Dizziness and some loss of muscle coordination. Side effects tend to disappear with time.

Possible Adverse Drug Effects

Fatigue, loss of appetite, nystagmus (a rhythmic, uncontrolled movement of the eyeballs), irritability, emotional upset, sexual impotence, double vision, rash. If side effects are persistent or severe, your doctor may have to discontinue treatment or use a different medication.

Drug Interactions

This drug, because of its relation to barbiturates, may affect oral anticoagulants, Doxycycline, corticosteroids, or Griseofulvin. Special care should be taken if you need any sedative, sleeping pill, antidepressant, or strong analgesic, because of the possibility of drug interaction. Consult your physician or pharmacist for more information. Avoid alcoholic beverages, which may enhance the side effects of fatigue and dizziness normally experienced with Primidone.

Food Interactions

If you get an upset stomach after taking Primidone, take the medicine with meals.

Usual Dose

Adult (and child age 8 and over): 250 milligrams per day to start. Dose may be increased in steps of 250 milligrams per day up to 1500 milligrams per day, according to patient's need.

Child (under age 8): 125 milligrams per day to start. Dose may be increased in steps of 125 milligrams per day up to 750 milligrams per day, according to patient's need. Doses may be divided 3 to 6 times per day.

Overdosage

Symptoms are listed in "Possible Side Effects" and "Possible Adverse Drug Effects" above. The patient should be taken to a hospital emergency room immediately. ALWAYS bring the medicine bottle.

Special Information

If you develop a rash, sore throat, fever, or unusual bleeding or bruising, contact your doctor immediately. Primidone sometimes produces a pink-brown color in the urine; this is normal, and not a cause for worry.

Brand Name

Pro-Banthine with Phenobarbital

Ingredients

Phenobarbital
Propantheline

Type of Drug

Gastrointestinal anticholinergic agent.

Prescribed for

Symptomatic relief of stomach upset, spasms, and peptic ulcers.

General Information

Pro-Banthine with Phenobarbital works by reducing spasms in muscles of the stomach and other parts of the gastrointestinal tract. In doing so, it helps relieve some of the uncomfortable symptoms associated with peptic ulcer, irritable bowel and/or colon, spastic colon, and other gastrointestinal disorders. It only relieves symptoms. It does not cure the underlying disease. There are many other combinations of anticholinergics and tranquilizers used to treat stomach ulcers and similar disorders. One such combination product is Pathibamate.

Cautions and Warnings

Pro-Banthine with Phenobarbital should not be used if you know you are sensitive or allergic to Propantheline or Phenobarbital. Do not use this medicine if you have glaucoma, asthma, obstructive disease of the gastrointestinal tract, or other serious gastrointestinal disease. This drug reduces your ability to sweat; its use in hot climates may cause heat exhaustion.

This drug may cause birth defects or interfere with your baby's development. Check with your doctor before taking it if you are, or might be, pregnant.

Possible Side Effects

Occasional: difficulty in urination, blurred vision, rapid heartbeat, palpitations, sensitivity to light, headache, flushing of the skin, nervousness, dizziness, weakness, drowsiness, nausea, vomiting, fever, nasal congestion, heartburn, constipation, loss of taste, feeling of being bloated; also a drug allergy or a drug idiosyncratic reaction, which may include itching or other skin manifestations.

Possible Adverse Drug Effects

Elderly patients taking this drug may develop mental confusion or excitement.

Drug Interactions

Interaction with antihistamines, phenothiazines, long-term use of corticosteroids, tranquilizers, antidepressants, and some narcotic painkillers may cause blurred vision, dry mouth, or drowsiness. Antacids should not be taken together with Pro-Banthine with Phenobarbital, or they will reduce the absorption of the Pro-Banthine with Phenobarbital. Space doses of antacids and Pro-Banthine with Phenobarbital by 2 hours.

Do not use with MAO inhibitor drugs, which will tend to

prevent excretion of Pro-Banthine with Phenobarbital from the body and thus potentiate it (increase its effect).

Usual Dose

1 to 2 tablets 3 to 4 times per day.

Special Information

Dry mouth from Pro-Banthine with Phenobarbital can be relieved by chewing gum or sucking hard candy; constipation can be treated by using a stool-softening laxative (rather than a harsh cathartic).

Generic Name

Probucol

Brand Name

Lorelco

Type of Drug

Antihyperlipidemic (blood-fat reducer).

Prescribed for

People with excessively high levels of blood cholesterol.

General information

Probucol consistently reduces blood cholesterol levels, but is prescribed only for people who have not responded to diet changes or other therapies. Probucol has little effect on blood triglycerides.

Probucol increases the body's breakdown of cholesterol, reduces the amount of cholesterol manufactured by the liver, and reduces the amount of cholesterol absorbed from foods.

Cautions and Warnings

Probucol should not be taken by people who have had allergic reactions to the drug. Probucol users may have an increased chance of developing abnormal heart rhythms and should realize that this drug, like other blood-fat reducers, including Clofibrate and Gemfibrozil, have not been proven to reduce the chances of fatal heart attacks.

Animal studies of this drug have revealed no harmful effects on the developing fetus. However, because there have been no controlled studies of pregnant women, Probucol should be avoided by pregnant women or women who may become pregnant while using it. Women who are trying to become pregnant should discontinue the drug and use birth control for at least 6 months before they want to conceive, because the drug remains in the body for extended periods. It is not known if Probucol passes into human breast milk, but this has been observed in animal studies. Nursing mothers should not breast-feed while taking this drug.

Possible Side Effects

Most side effects are mild and last for only short periods of time. The most common are diarrhea or loose stools, headaches, dizziness, and reduction in some white-blood-cell counts.

Possible Adverse Drug Effects

Abnormal heart rhythms, heart palpitations, chest pains, stomach and abdominal pains or gas, nausea, vomiting, anemia, itching, rash, male impotence, sleeplessness, conjunctivitis (red-eye), tearing, blurred vision, ringing or buzzing in the ears, loss of appetite, reduced senses of taste and/or smell, heartburn, indigestion, stomach or intestinal bleeding, easy bruising, goiter, nighttime waking to urinate, and excessive and possibly malodorous sweat.

Food Interactions

Take each dose with food or a meal to ensure better drug absorption.

Usual Dose

500 milligrams twice per day with breakfast and evening meal.

Overdosage

There are no reports of Probucol overdosage, but victims might be expected to develop exaggerated versions of the drug's side effects. Less than 10 percent of each dose of Probucol is absorbed from the stomach and intestines. Because of this, the chances are that few symptoms other than those affecting the stomach and intestines will develop. Patients taking an overdose of this drug must be made to vomit with Syrup of Ipecac (available at any pharmacy) to remove any remaining drug from the stomach. Call your doctor or a Poison Control Center before doing this. If you must go to a hospital emergency room, ALWAYS bring the medicine bottle.

Special Information

Follow your doctor's dietary guidelines.

Probucol occasionally causes dizziness and blurred vision. Use caution while driving or doing anything else that requires concentration and alertness.

Call your doctor if any drug side effects become severe or intolerable, especially diarrhea, nausea, vomiting, or stomach pains and/or gas. These may be resolved with a reduction in drug dose.

Generic Name

Procainamide Hydrochloride

Brand Names

Procan SR
Promine
Pronestyl
Pronestyl SR

(Also available in generic form)

Type of Drug

Antiarrhythmic.

Prescribed for

Abnormal heart rhythms.

General Information

Procainamide Hydrochloride is frequently used as the primary treatment for arrythmias (abnormal heart rhythms), which it controls by affecting the response of heart muscle to nervous system stimulation. It also slows the rate at which nervous system impulses are carried through the heart. It may be given to patients who do not respond to or cannot tolerate other antiarrhythmic drugs.

Cautions and Warnings

Tell your doctor if you have the disease myasthenia gravis. If you do, you should be taking a drug other than Procainamide Hydrochloride. Tell your doctor if you are allergic to Procainamide Hydrochloride or to the local anesthetic Procaine. Patients taking this drug should be under strict medical supervision.

This drug is eliminated from the body through the kidney and liver. Therefore, if you have either kidney or liver disease your dose of Procainamide Hydrochloride may have to be adjusted.

This drug may cause birth defects or interfere with your baby's development. Check with your doctor before taking it if you are, or might be, pregnant.

Possible Side Effects

Large oral doses of Procainamide Hydrochloride may produce loss of appetite, nausea, or itching. A group of symptoms resembling the disease lupus erythematosus has been reported in patients taking the drug: fever and chills, nausea, vomiting, and abdominal pains. Your doctor may detect enlargement of your liver and changes in blood tests indicating a change in the liver. Soreness of the mouth or throat, unusual bleeding, rash, or fever may also occur. If any of these symptoms occur while you are taking Procainamide Hydrochloride, tell your doctor immediately.

Possible Adverse Drug Effects

Bitter taste in the mouth, diarrhea, weakness, mental depression, giddiness, hallucinations, drug allergy (such as rash and drug fever).

Drug Interactions

Avoid over-the-counter cough, cold, or allergy remedies containing drugs which have a direct stimulating effect on your heart. Ask your pharmacist to tell you about the ingredients in over-the-counter remedies.

Usual Dose

Adult: Initial dose, 1000 milligrams; maintenance dose, 25 milligrams per pound per day in divided doses every 3 hours, around the clock, adjusted according to individual needs.

Generic Name

Prochlorperazine

Brand Names

Compazine
Compa-Z

(Also available in generic form)

Type of Drug

Phenothiazine antipsychotic, antinauseant.

Prescribed for

Severe nausea, vomiting, psychotic disorders, excessive anxiety, tension, and agitation.

General Information

Prochlorperazine and other members of the phenothiazine group act on a portion of the brain called the hypothalamus. They affect parts of the hypothalamus that control metabolism, body temperature, alertness, muscle tone, hormone balance, and vomiting, and may be used to treat problems related to any of these functions.

Cautions and Warnings

Sudden death has occurred in patients who have taken this drug, because of its effect on the cough reflex. In some cases the patients choked to death because of failure of the cough reflex to protect them. Prochlorperazine, because of its effect in reducing vomiting, can obscure signs of toxicity due to overdose of other drugs or symptoms of disease.

Prochlorperazine should not be taken if you are allergic to one of the drugs in the broad classification known as phenothiazine drugs. Do not take Prochlorperazine if you have any blood, liver, kidney, or heart disease, very low blood pressure, or Parkinson's disease. This medication is a tranquilizer and can have a depressive effect, especially during the first few days of therapy. Care should be taken when performing activities requiring a high degree of concentration, such as driving.

If you are taking this medication and become pregnant contact your doctor immediately. Prochlorperazine when taken by pregnant women has caused side effects in newborns such as jaundice (yellowing of skin and eyes) and twitching. These medications should be stopped 1 to 2 weeks before expected delivery to avoid this. Prochlorperazine has not been shown to cause problems during breast-feeding.

This drug should be used with caution and under strict supervision of your doctor if you have glaucoma, epilepsy, ulcers, or difficulty passing urine.

Avoid exposure to extreme heat, since this drug can affect your body's normal temperature mechanism.

Possible Side Effects

Most common: drowsiness, especially during the first or second week of therapy. If the drowsiness becomes troublesome, contact your doctor.

Possible Adverse Drug Effects

Prochlorperazine can cause jaundice (yellowing of the whites of the eyes or skin), usually in 2 to 4 weeks. The jaundice usually goes away when the drug is discontinued, but there have been cases when it did not. If you notice this effect or if you develop symptoms such as fever and generally not feeling well, contact your doctor immediately. Less frequent: changes in components of the blood including anemias, raised or lowered blood pressure, abnormal heart rates, heart attack, feeling faint or dizzy.

Phenothiazines can produce "extrapyramidal effects," such as spasm of the neck muscles, rolling back of the eyes, convulsions, difficulty in swallowing, and symptoms associated with Parkinson's disease. These effects look very serious but disappear after the drug has been withdrawn; however, symptoms of the face, tongue, and jaw may persist for as long as several years, especially in the elderly with a history of brain damage. If you experience extrapyramidal effects contact your doctor immediately.

Prochlorperazine may cause an unusual increase in psychotic symptoms or may cause paranoid reactions, tiredness, lethargy, restlessness, hyperactivity, confusion at night, bizarre dreams, inability to sleep, depression, and euphoria. Other reactions are itching, swelling, unusual sensitivity to bright lights, red skin, and rash. There have been cases of breast enlargement, false positive pregnancy tests, changes in menstrual flow, impotence and changes in sex drive in males, as well as stuffy nose, headache, nausea, vomiting, loss of appetite, change in body temperature, pallor, excessive salivation, excessive perspiration, constipation, diarrhea, changes in urine and stool habits, worsening of glaucoma, blurred vision, weakening of eyelid muscles, and spasms in bronchial and other muscles, increased appetite, fatigue, excessive thirst, and changes in the coloration of skin, particularly in exposed areas.

Drug Interactions

Prochlorperazine should be taken with caution in combination with barbiturates, sleeping pills, narcotics, other tranquilizers, or any other medication which may produce a depressive effect.

Alcoholic beverages should be avoided. They can increase the depressant effects of Prochlorperazine.

Food Interactions

Antipsychotic effectiveness of Prochlorperazine or other members of the phenothizaine drug group may be counteracted by alcohol- or caffeine-containing food, such as coffee, tea, cola drinks, or chocolate.

Usual Dose

Adult: 15 to 150 milligrams per day, depending on disease

and patient's response. For nausea and vomiting, 15 to 40 milligrams per day by mouth, 25 milligrams twice per day in rectal suppositories.

Child (40 to 85 pounds): 10 to 15 milligrams per day; (30 to 40 pounds), 2.5 milligrams 2 to 3 times per day; (20 to 30 pounds), 2.5 milligrams 1 to 2 times per day; not recommended for children under age 2 or weight 20 pounds, except to save life. Usually only 1 to 2 days of therapy is needed for nausea and vomiting. For psychosis, doses of 25 milligrams or more per day may be required.

Overdosage

Symptoms are depression, extreme weakness, tiredness, desire to go to sleep, coma, lowered blood pressure, uncontrolled muscle spasms, agitation, restlessness, convulsions, fever, dry mouth, and abnormal heart rhythms. The patient should be taken to a hospital emergency room immediately. ALWAYS bring the medicine bottle.

Special Information

This drug may turn the color of your urine pink or reddish brown; this is normal and not a cause for worry.

Generic Name

Propantheline Bromide

Brand Names

Norpanth
Pro-Banthine
SK-Propantheline Bromide

(Also available in generic form)

Type of Drug

Gastrointestinal anticholinergic agent.

Prescribed for

Relief of stomach upset, spasms, and peptic ulcers. This

medication is sometimes prescribed to treat morning sickness during the early months of pregnancy.

General Information

Propantheline Bromide works by reducing spasms in muscles of the stomach and other parts of the gastrointestinal tract. In doing so, it helps relieve some of the uncomfortable symptoms associated with peptic ulcer, irritable bowel and/or colon, spastic colon, and other gastrointestinal disorders. It only relieves symptoms, but does not cure the underlying disease.

Cautions and Warnings

Propantheline Bromide should not be used if you know you are sensitive or allergic to it. Do not use this medicine if you have glaucoma, asthma, obstructive disease of the gastrointestinal tract, or other serious gastrointestinal disease. Because this drug reduces your ability to sweat, its use in hot climates may cause heat exhaustion.

This drug may cause birth defects or interfere with your baby's development. Check with your doctor before taking it if you are, or might be, pregnant.

Possible Side Effects

Difficulty in urination, blurred vision, rapid heartbeat, skin rash, sensitivity to light, headache, flushing of the skin, nervousness, dizziness, weakness, drowsiness, nausea, vomiting, fever, nasal congestion, heartburn, constipation, loss of taste.

Possible Adverse Drug Effects

Elderly patients taking this drug may develop mental confusion or excitement.

Drug Interactions

Interaction with antihistamines, phenothiazines, long-term use of corticosteroids, tranquilizers, antidepressants, and some narcotic painkillers may cause blurred vision, dry mouth, or drowsiness. Antacids should not be taken together with Propantheline Bromide, or they will reduce the absorption of the Propantheline Bromide; doses of Antacids and Propantheline Bromide should be taken 2 hours apart.

Do not use with Tranylcypromine Sulfate (Parnate), Isocarboxazid (Marplan), Phenelzine Sulfate (Nardil), or other MAO inhibitor drugs, which will tend to prevent excretion of Propantheline Bromide from the body and thus potentiate it (increase its effect).

Usual Dose

30 milligrams at bedtime or 7.5 to 15 milligrams 3 to 4 times per day.

Special Information

Dry mouth from Propantheline Bromide can be relieved by chewing gum or sucking hard candy; constipation can be treated by using a stool-softening laxative.

Generic Name

Propoxyphene Hydrochloride

Brand Names

Darvon	Profene
Dolene	SK-65
Doxaphene	

Combination Products with Aspirin and Caffeine:

Darvon Compound	Doxaphene Compound
Bexophene	SK-65 Compound
Dolene Compound	

Combination Products with Acetaminophen:

Dolene AP-65	Wygesic
SK-65 APAP	

(Also available in generic form)

Type of Drug

Analgesic.

Prescribed for

Relief of pain.

General Information

Propoxyphene Hydrochloride is a chemical derivative of Methadone, a narcotic used for pain relief. It is estimated that Propoxyphene Hydrochloride is about half to two-thirds as strong a pain reliever as Codeine and about as effective as Aspirin. Propoxyphene Hydrochloride is widely used for mild pain; it can produce drug dependence when used for extended periods of time.

Cautions and Warnings

Propoxyphene Hydrochloride may interfere with your ability to concentrate. Therefore, be very careful when driving an automobile or operating complicated or dangerous machinery. Do not drink alcohol when taking this medicine. As there is a possibility that Propoxyphene Hydrochloride may affect the development of unborn children, do not take this medicine, except under your doctor's advice, if you are pregnant or suspect that you may be pregnant. Never take more medicine than is prescribed by your doctor.

Do not take Propoxyphene Hydrochloride if you are allergic to this or similar drugs. This drug can produce psychological or physical drug dependence (addiction). The major sign of dependence is anxiety when the drug is suddenly stopped. Propoxyphene Hydrochloride can be abused to the same degree as Codeine.

Possible Side Effects

Dizziness, sedation, nausea, vomiting. These effects usually disappear if you lie down and relax for a few moments.

Possible Adverse Drug Effects

Infrequent: constipation, stomach pain, skin rashes, lightheadedness, headache, weakness, euphoria, minor visual disturbances. Taking Propoxyphene Hydrochloride over long periods of time and in very high doses has caused psychotic reactions and convulsions.

Drug Interactions

Propoxyphene Hydrochloride may cause drowsiness. Therefore, avoid other drugs which also cause drowsiness, such as tranquilizers, sedatives, hypnotics, narcotics, alcohol, and possibly antihistamines.

There may be an interaction between Propoxyphene Hydrochloride and Orphenadrine. However, this reaction is only a probability and only for patients who have a tendency toward low blood sugar.

Food Interactions

Take with a full glass of water or with food to reduce the possibility of stomach upset.

Usual Dose

65 milligrams every 4 hours as needed.

Overdosage

Symptoms resemble those of a narcotic overdose: decrease in rate of breathing (in some people breathing rate is so low that the heart stops), changes in breathing pattern, extreme sleepiness leading to stupor or coma, pinpointed pupils, convulsions, abnormal heart rhythms, and development of fluid in the lungs. The patient should be taken to a hospital emergency room immediately. ALWAYS bring the medicine bottle.

Special Information

A "patient package insert" which provides detailed information about the drug is available for you to read from your pharmacist.

Generic Name

Propranolol Hydrochloride

Brand Name

Inderal
Inderal LA (long acting)

(Also available in generic form)

Type of Drug

Beta-adrenergic blocking agent.

Prescribed for

High blood pressure, angina pectoris (a specified type of chest pain), abnormal heart rhythm, thyroid disease, and pheochromocytoma, a tumor associated with hypertension. In addition, Propranolol Hydrochloride has been studied for its ability to reduce the possibility of a second heart attack, its effect on migraine headaches, diarrhea, stagefright, and schizophrenia.

General Information

Propranolol Hydrochloride was the first beta-adrenergic blocking agent available in the United States. The drug acts to block a major chemical reaction of the nervous system in our bodies. For this reason, it can exert a broad range of effects, as is evident from the wide variety of diseases in which it can be used effectively. Because of this spectrum of effects, it is impossible to say specifically what you will be taking this drug for. Therefore, this information must be discussed with your doctor. This drug has been used, for example, in low (5-10 milligrams) doses by musicians and others to treat nervousness and "butterflies" experienced before going on stage.

Cautions and Warnings

Propranolol Hydrochloride should be used with care if you have a history of asthma, upper respiratory disease, or seasonal allergy, which may be made worse by the effects of this drug.

This drug may cause birth defects or interfere with your baby's development. Check with your doctor before taking it if you are, or might be, pregnant. This drug is excreted in breast milk. A nursing mother should consult her physician.

Possible Side Effects

Propranolol Hydrochloride may decrease the heart rate; may aggravate a condition of congestive heart failure; and may produce lowered blood pressure, tingling in the extremities, light-headedness, mental depression including inability to sleep, weakness, and tiredness. It may also produce a mental depression which is reversible when the drug is withdrawn, visual disturbances, hallucinations, disorientation, and short-term memory loss. Patients taking Propranolol Hydrochloride may experience nausea, vomiting, stomach upset, abdominal cramps and diarrhea, or constipation. If you are allergic to this drug, you may show typical reactions associated with drug allergies, including sore throat, fever, difficulty in breathing, and various effects on the blood system. Propranolol Hydrochloride may induce bronchospasms (spasms of muscles in the bronchi), which will aggravate any existing asthmatic condition or any severe upper respiratory disease.

Possible Adverse Drug Effects

Occasionally, patients taking Propranolol Hydrochloride may experience emotional instability, may appear to be somewhat detached or show other unusual personality changes, or the drug may produce unusual effects on the blood system.

Drug Interactions

This drug will interact with any psychotropic drug, including the MAO inhibitors, which stimulates one of the adrenergic segments of the nervous system. Since this information is not generally known, you should discuss the potential problem of using Propranolol Hydrochloride with your doctor if you are taking any psychotropic or psychiatric drug.

Propranolol Hydrochloride may cause increased effectiveness of Insulin or oral antidiabetic drugs. If you are diabetic, discuss the situation with your doctor, who will probably reduce the dose of antidiabetic medication.

Propranolol Hydrochloride may reduce the effectiveness of Digitalis on your heart. Any dose of Digitalis medication will have to be altered. If you are taking Digitalis for a purpose other than congestive heart failure, the effectiveness of the Digitalis may be increased by Propranolol Hydrochloride, and the dose of Digitalis may have to be reduced.

Propranolol Hydrochloride may interact with certain other drugs to produce lowering of blood pressure. This interaction often has positive results in the treatment of patients with high blood pressure.

Do not self-medicate with over-the-counter cold, cough, or allergy remedies which may contain stimulant drugs that will aggravate certain types of heart disease and high blood pressure, or other ingredients that may antagonize the effects of Propranolol Hydrochloride. Double-check with your doctor or pharmacist before taking any over-the-counter medication.

Food Interactions

Take Propranolol Hydrochloride before meals for maximum effectiveness.

Usual Dose

30 to 700 milligrams per day, depending on disease treated and patient's response. The drug is given in the smallest effective dose, that is, the smallest dose which will produce the desired therapeutic effect.

Overdosage

Symptoms are slowed heart rate, heart failure, lowered blood pressure, and spasms of the bronchial muscles which make it difficult to breathe. The patient should be taken to a hospital emergency room where proper therapy can be given. ALWAYS bring the medicine bottle with you.

Special Information

There have been reports of serious effects on the heart when this drug is stopped abruptly. Instead, the dose should be lowered gradually from what you are taking to nothing over a period of 2 weeks.

Generic Name

Protriptyline Hydrochloride

Brand Name

Vivactil

Type of Drug

Antidepressant.

Prescribed for

Depression with or without symptoms of anxiety.

General Information

Protriptyline Hydrochloride and other members of this group are effective in treating symptoms of depression. They can elevate your mood, increase physical activity and mental alertness, improve appetite and sleep patterns. These drugs are mild sedatives and therefore useful in treating mild forms of depression associated with anxiety. You should not expect instant results with this medicine: benefits are usually seen after 1 to 4 weeks. If symptoms are not affected after 6 to 8 weeks, contact your doctor. Occasionally this drug and other members of the group of drugs have been used in treating nighttime bed-wetting in the young child, but they do not produce long-lasting relief and therapy with one of them for nighttime bed-wetting is of questionable value.

Cautions and Warnings

Do not take Protriptyline Hydrochloride if you are allergic or sensitive to this or other members of this class of drug: Doxepin, Nortriptyline, Imipramine, Desipramine, and Amitriptyline. The drugs should not be used if you are recovering from a heart attack. Protriptyline Hydrochloride may be taken with caution if you have a history of epilepsy or other convulsive disorders, difficulty in urination, glaucoma, heart disease, or thyroid disease. Protriptyline Hydrochloride can interfere with your ability to perform tasks which require concentration, such as driving or operating machinery.

This drug may cause birth defects or interfere with your baby's development. Check with your doctor before taking it if you are, or might be, pregnant. Protriptyline may pass into breast milk. Nursing mothers should use an alternate feeding method.

Possible Side Effects

Changes in blood pressure (both high and low), abnormal heart rates, heart attack, confusion, especially in elderly patients, hallucinations, disorientation, delusions, anxiety, restlessness, excitement, numbness and tingling in the extremities, lack of coordination, muscle spasms or tremors, seizures and/or convulsions, dry mouth, blurred vision, constipation, inability to urinate, rash, itching, sensitivity to bright light or sunlight, retention of fluids, fever, allergy, changes in composition of blood, nausea, vomiting, loss of appetite, stomach upset, diarrhea, enlargement of the breasts in males and females, increased or decreased sex drive, increased or decreased blood sugar.

Possible Adverse Drug Effects

Infrequent: agitation, inability to sleep, nightmares, feeling of panic, a peculiar taste in the mouth, stomach cramps, black coloration of the tongue, yellowing eyes and/or skin, changes in liver function, increased or decreased weight, perspiration, flushing, frequent urination, drowsiness, dizziness, weakness, headache, loss of hair, nausea, not feeling well.

Drug Interactions

Interaction with monoamine oxidase (MAO) inhibitors can cause high fevers, convulsions, and occasionally death. Don't take MAO inhibitors until at least 2 weeks after Protriptyline Hydrochloride has been discontinued.

Protriptyline Hydrochloride interacts with Guanethidine, a drug used to treat high blood pressure: if your doctor prescribes Protriptyline Hydrochloride and you are taking medicine for high blood pressure, be sure to discuss this with him.

Protriptyline Hydrochloride increases the effects of barbiturates, tranquilizers, other depressive drugs, and alcohol. Don't drink alcoholic beverages if you take this medicine.

Taking Protriptyline Hydrochloride and thyroid medicine will enhance the effects of the thyroid medicine. The combination can cause abnormal heart rhythms.

Large doses of Vitamin C (Ascorbic Acid) can reduce the effect of Protriptyline Hydrochloride. Drugs such as Bicarbonate of Soda or Acetazolamide will increase the effect of Protriptyline Hydrochloride.

Usual Dose

Adult: 15 to 60 milligrams per day in 3 or 4 divided doses. *Adolescent and elderly:* lower doses are recommended, usually up to 20 milligrams per day. An elderly patient taking more than 20 milligrams per day should have regular heart examinations.

The dose of this drug must be tailored to the patient's need.

Overdosage

Symptoms are confusion, inability to concentrate, hallucinations, drowsiness, lowered body temperature, abnormal heart rate, heart failure, large pupils of the eyes, convulsions, severely lowered blood pressure, stupor, and coma (as well as agitation, stiffening of body muscles, vomiting, and high fever). The patient should be taken to a hospital emergency room immediately. ALWAYS bring the medicine bottle.

Generic Name

Pseudoephedrine

Brand Names

Afrinol	Neo-Synephrinol Day Relief
Cenafed	Novafed
Decofed	Sudafed
Deedee Dose	Sudafed S.A.
Dorcol Pediatric Formula	Sudagest Decongestant
Halofed	Sudrin
NeoFed	

(Also available in generic form)

Type of Drug

Bronchodilator-decongestant.

Prescribed for

Symptomatic relief of stuffy nose, upper respiratory congestion, or bronchospasm associated with asthma, asthmatic bronchitis, or a similar disorder.

General Information

There are almost 200 products available that contain Pseudoephedrine. These combinations range from pain relievers to antihistamines to cough suppressants; some can be obtained only with a prescription while others are available over the counter. These products provide symptomatic relief of respiratory conditions, but do not treat the underlying disease. If you are taking an over-the-counter (available without a prescription) Pseudoephedrine medication, you should always inform your doctor.

Pseudoephedrine produces central nervous system stimulation, and it should not be taken by people with heart disease or high blood pressure. Elderly people are more likely to experience adverse effects from this and other stimulant drugs; overdosage of stimulants in this age group may cause hallucinations, convulsions, depression, and even death.

Cautions and Warnings

Do not take Pseudoephedrine if you are allergic or sensitive to this or similar drugs or if you have severe high blood pressure, coronary artery disease (angina pectoris), abnormal heart rhythms, or closed angle glaucoma.

This drug should be used with caution and only under medical supervision if you have chest pain, stroke, high blood pressure, diabetes, overactive thyroid, glaucoma, or history of convulsions.

This drug may cause birth defects or interfere with your baby's development. Check with your doctor before taking it if you are, or might be, pregnant. Pseudoephedrine may cause unwanted side effects in nursing infants and should by avoided by nursing mothers.

Possible Side Effects

Excessive tiredness or drowsiness, restlessness, nervousness with an inability to sleep. Less frequent: tremor, headache, palpitations, elevation of blood pressure, sweating, sleeplessness, loss of appetite, nausea, vomiting, dizziness, constipation.

Drug Interactions

Pseudoephedrine may increase the effect of antidepressant drugs and antihistamines, and reduce the effect of some high blood pressure medicine like Reserpine or Guanethidine.

Do not self-medicate with additional over-the-counter drugs for the relief of cold symptoms: taking Pseudoephedrine with such drugs may result in aggravation of high blood pressure, heart disease, diabetes, or thyroid disease.

Do not take Pseudoephedrine if you are taking or suspect you may be taking a monoamine oxidase (MAO) inhibitor: severe elevation in blood pressure may result.

Interaction with alcoholic beverages may produce excessive drowsiness and/or sleepiness, and/or inability to concentrate.

Usual Dose

Adult: 60 milligrams every 4 hours.
Child (age 6 to 12): 30 milligrams every 4 hours.
Child (age 2 to 6): 15 milligrams every 4 hours.

Liquid form contains 30 milligrams per teaspoon; tablets contain 30 or 60 milligrams depending on strength prescribed; time-release dosage contains 60 to 120 milligrams (taken twice per day).

Combination products provide a fixed amount of drug per dose and should be taken according to recommendations.

Brand Name

Quibron

Ingredients

Guaifenesin
Theophylline

Other Brand Names

Bronchial Capsules	Quiagen
Glyceryl T	Slo-Phyllin GG
Lanophyllin GG	Theocolate liquid

Other Brand Names

(same ingredients but different amounts)

Asbron G   Synophylate-GG
Elixophyllin-GG   Theolair-Plus
Quibron-300

(Also available in generic form)

Type of Drug

Antiasthmatic combination product.

Prescribed for

Relief of asthma symptoms or other upper respiratory disorders.

General Information

Quibron, a xanthine combination, is one of several antiasthmatic combination products prescribed for the relief of asthmatic symptoms and other breathing problems. These products contain drugs which help relax the bronchial muscles, drugs which increase the diameter of the breathing passages, and a mild tranquilizer to help relax the patient. Other products in this class may contain similar ingredients along with other medicine to help eliminate mucus from the breathing passages.

Cautions and Warnings

Do not use this drug if you are allergic or sensitive to it or to any related drug, such as Aminophylline. If you have stomach ulcer or heart disease, you should use this drug with caution.

If you are pregnant or think that you may be pregnant you should carefully discuss the use of this drug with your doctor, since Quibron may induce an adverse effect in the unborn child.

Quibron may be required by a woman during pregnancy. However, there is an increased chance of birth defects while using Quibron during pregnancy. Regularly using Quibron during the last 3 months of pregnancy may cause drug dependency of the newborn. Labor may be prolonged and delivery may be delayed, and there may be breathing problems in the newborn if Quibron is used.

Breast-feeding while using Quibron may cause increased tiredness, shortness of breath, or a slow heartbeat in the baby.

Theophylline, an ingredient in Tedral, may cause a fast heartbeat, irritability, vomiting or breathing problems in the unborn or nursing child if too much is used by the mother.

This drug should not be taken if you have severe kidney or liver disease.

Possible Side Effects

Large doses of Quibron can produce excitation, shakiness, sleeplessness, nervousness, rapid heartbeat, chest pains, or irregular heartbeat, Occasionally people have been known to develop hesitation or difficulty in urination.

Possible Adverse Drug Effects

Excessive urination, heart stimulation, drowsiness, muscle weakness, muscle twitching, unsteady walk. These effects can usually be controlled by having your doctor adjust the dose.

Drug Interactions

Quibron may cause sleeplessness and/or drowsiness.

Taking Quibron or similar medicines with an MAO inhibitor can produce severe interaction. Consult your doctor first.

Quibron or similar products taken together with Lithium Carbonate will increase the excretion of Lithium; they have neutralized the effect of Propranalol. Erythromycin and similar antibiotics cause the body to hold Theophylline, leading to possible side effects.

Do not take this drug with alcoholic beverages.

Food Interactions

The way Quibron acts in your body may be influenced by your diet. Charcoal-broiled beef, for example, may cause the amount of Quibron that is being eliminated in the urine to increase. Therefore you may experience a decreased effect of the drug. This is also true for people whose diet is low in carbohydrates and high in protein or for people who smoke.

Caffeine (also a xanthine derivative) may add to the side effects of Quibron. It is recommended that you avoid large amounts of caffeine-containing foods, such as coffee, tea, cocoa, colas, or chocolate.

Take this drug with food to avoid upset stomach.

Usual Dose

Capsules: 1 to 2 every 6 to 8 hours.
Elixir: 1 to 2 tablespoons every 6 to 8 hours.

Generic Name

Quinidine Sulfate

Brand Names

Cin-Quin
Quinidex Extentabs
Quinora
SK-Quinidine Sulfate

(Also available in generic form)

Type of Drug

Antiarrhythmic.

Prescribed for

Abnormal heart rhythms.

General Information

Derived from the bark of the cinchona tree (which gives us Quinine), the drug works by affecting the flow of potassium into and out of cells of the heart muscle (myocardium). Its basic action is to slow down the pulse. Its action allows normal control mechanisms in the heart to take over and keep the heart beating at a normal rate and rhythm.

Cautions and Warnings

Do not take Quinidine Sulfate if you are allergic to it or a related drug.

This drug may cause birth defects or interfere with your baby's development. Check with your doctor before taking it if you are, or might be, pregnant. Quinidine Sulfate does not cause problems while breast-feeding and may be used by nursing mothers.

Possible Side Effects

High doses of Quinidine Sulfate can give you rash, changes in hearing, dizziness, ringing in the ears, headache, nausea, or disturbed vision: this group of symptoms, called cinchonism, is due to ingestion of large amounts of Quinidine Sulfate and is not necessarily a toxic reaction. However, report signs of cinchonism to your doctor immediately. Do not stop taking this drug unless instructed to do so by your doctor.

Possible Adverse Drug Effects

Quinidine Sulfate may cause unusual heart rhythms, but such effects are generally found by your doctor during routine examination or electrocardiogram. It can cause nausea, vomiting, stomach pain, and diarrhea. It may affect components of the blood system and can cause headache, fever, dizziness, feeling of apprehension or excitement, confusion, delirium, disturbed hearing, blurred vision, changes in color perception, sensitivity to bright lights, double vision, difficulty seeing at night, flushing of the skin, itching, cramps, unusual urge to defecate or urinate, and cold sweat.

Drug Interactions

If you are taking an oral anticoagulant (blood-thinning medicine) and have been given a new prescription for Quinidine Sulfate, be sure your doctor knows about the blood-thinning medication, because Quinidine Sulfate may affect the ability of the anticoagulant to do its job. The anticoagulant dose may have to be adjusted for the effect of Quinidine Sulfate.

Either Phenobarbital or Phenytoin may reduce the time that Quinidine Sulfate is effective in your body, and may increase your need for it. Quinidine Sulfate in combination with Digoxin can increase the effects of the Digoxin causing possible Digoxin toxicity. This combination should be monitored closely by your doctor.

Avoid over-the-counter cough, cold, allergy, or diet preparations. These medications may contain drugs which will stimulate your heart; this can be dangerous while you are taking Quinidine Sulfate. Ask your pharmacist, if you have any questions about the contents of a particular cough, cold, or allergy remedy.

Food Interactions

If Quinidine Sulfate gives you stomach upset, take it with food. Quinidine is also available in forms that are supposed to be less irritating to the stomach; contact your doctor if upset stomach persists.

Usual Dose

Extremely variable, depending on disease and patient's response. Most doses are 800 to 1200 milligrams per day.

Overdosage

Produces abnormal effects on the heart and symptoms of cinchonism. Patient should be taken to a hospital emergency room where proper therapy can be given. ALWAYS bring the medicine bottle.

Generic Name

Ranitidine

Brand Name

Zantac

Type of Drug

Antiulcer, histamine H_2 antagonist.

Prescribed for

Short-term treatment of duodenal (intestinal) and gastric (stomach) ulcers. Also prescribed for other conditions characterized by the secretions of large amounts of gastric fluids. A surgeon may prescribe Ranitidine for a patient under anesthesia when it is desirable for the production of stomach acid to be stopped completely.

General Information

Ranitidine is only the second histamine H_2 antagonist to be released in the United States. It is more potent that Cimetidine, the original histamine H_2 antagonist, and has less potential for causing drug interactions than Cimetidine. The elderly respond to Ranitidine about as well as younger adults, although smaller doses may be required.

Cautions and Warnings

Although studies with laboratory animals have revealed no damage to a developing fetus, it is recommended that Ranitidine be avoided by pregnant women or women who might become pregnant while using it. When its use is considered essential, Ranitidine's potential risk must be carefully weighed against any benefit it might produce. Nursing mothers should avoid taking Ranitidine because it is known to pass into breast milk.

Possible Side Effects

Most common: headache, dizziness, constipation, abdominal discomfort, rash, and a feeling of ill health.

Possible Adverse Drug Effects

Ranitidine may rarely cause a reduction in the levels of either white blood cells or blood platelets. Hepatitis is another rare consequence of Ranitidine treatment.

Drug Interactions

The effects of Ranitidine may be reduced if it is taken together with antacids. This minor interaction may be avoided by separating doses of Ranitidine and antacid by about 3 hours.

Ranitidine may interfere with the absorption of Diazepam tablets into the blood. This interaction is considered of only minor importance and is unlikely to affect many people.

Ranitidine may decrease the effect of Theophylline, prescribed for asthma and other respiratory conditions, while the two drugs are being taken together and for several days after the Ranitidine has been discontinued. This interaction is far less severe than the Cimetidine-Theophylline interaction, which may require temporary dosage adjustments.

Food Interactions

You may take each dose with food or meals if Ranitidine upsets your stomach.

Usual Dose

Adult: 150 milligrams twice per day. However, several studies have shown that smaller doses may be as effective, especially in the elderly or people with impaired kidney function. People with severe ulcers or other conditions may require more than the average dose.

Overdosage

There is little information on Ranitidine overdosage. Overdose victims might be expected to show exaggerated side-effect symptoms, but little else is known. Patients taking an overdose of this drug must be made to vomit with Syrup of Ipecac (available at any pharmacy) to remove any remaining drug from the stomach. Call your doctor or a Poison Control Center before doing this. If you must go to a hospital emergency room, ALWAYS bring the medicine bottle.

Special Information

You must take this medicine exactly as directed and follow doctor's instructions for diet and other treatments in order to get the maximum benefit from it.

Brand Name

Regroton

Ingredients

Chlorthalidone
Reserpine

Other Brand Name

Demi-Regroton

Type of Drug

Antihypertensive combination.

Prescribed for

High blood pressure.

General Information

Regroton is a good example of a drug taking advantage of a drug interaction. Each of the drug ingredients works by different mechanisms to lower your blood pressure. The Chlorthalidone relaxes the muscles in your veins and arteries and also helps reduce the volume of blood flowing through those blood vessels. Reserpine works on the nervous system to reduce the efficiency of nerve transmissions which are contributing to the increased pressure. These drugs complement each other so that their combined effect is better than the effect of either one alone.

It is essential that you take your medicine exactly as prescribed, for maximum benefit.

An ingredient in this drug may cause excessive loss of potassium, which may lead to a condition called hypokalemia. Warning signs are dryness of mouth, excessive thirst, weakness, drowsiness, restlessness, muscle pains or cramps, muscular fatigue, lack of urination, abnormal heart rhythms, and upset stomach. If warning signs occur, call your doctor. You may need potassium from some outside source. This may be done by taking a potassium supplement or by eating foods such as bananas, citrus fruits, melons, and tomatoes, which have high concentrations of potassium.

This drug should be stopped at the first sign of despondency, early morning insomnia, loss of appetite, or sexual impotence. Drug-induced depression may persist for several months after the drug has been discontinued; it has been known to be severe enough to result in suicide attempts. This drug should be used with care by women of childbearing age.

Cautions and Warnings

Do not take this drug if you are sensitive or allergic to either of its ingredients or if you have a history of mental depression, active peptic ulcer, or ulcerative colitis.

Pregnant and nursing women should avoid this drug. The Reserpine in Regroton may cause unwanted effects (breathing problems, appetite loss, low temperature) in the baby if too much is taken during pregnancy or breast-feeding.

Possible Side Effects

Loss of appetite, stomach irritation, nausea, vomiting, cramps, diarrhea, constipation, dizziness, headache, tingling in the arms and legs, restlessness, chest pains, abnormal heart rhythms, drowsiness, depression, nervousness, anxiety, nightmares, glaucoma, blood disorders, itching, fever, difficulty in breathing, muscle spasms, weakness, high blood sugar, sugar in the urine, blurred vision, stuffy nose, dryness of the mouth, rash. Occasional: impotence or decreased sex drive.

Drug Interactions

Interaction with Digitalis or Quinidine may cause abnormal heart rhythms.

Caution must be taken if this drug is given with other antihypertensive agents such as Guanethidine, Veratrum, Methyldopa, Chlorthalidone or Hydralazine: the dose of these drugs must be monitored carefully by your physician. It is strongly advised not to take MAO antidepressant drugs while taking Regroton.

Interaction with drugs containing Lithium may lead to toxic effects of Lithium.

Avoid over-the-counter cough, cold, or allergy remedies containing stimulant drugs which may raise your blood pressure.

Food Interactions

Take Regroton with food if it upsets your stomach.

Usual Dose

Must be individualized to patient's response.

Generic Name

Rifampin

Brand Names

Rifadin
Rimactane

Type of Drug

Antitubercular.

Prescribed for

Tuberculosis. Also used to treat people who are carriers of certain infections rather than infected patients.

General Information

This is an important drug for the treatment of tuberculosis. It is always used together with Isoniazid or another antitubercular drug because it is not effective by itself. It also eradicates an organism which causes meningitis in people who are carriers: although they are not infected, they carry the organism and spread it to others.

Cautions and Warnings

Do not take this drug if you are allergic to it. It may cause liver damage and should not be used by people with liver disease or those taking other drugs which may cause liver damage.

This drug should only be used by pregnant women or nursing mothers if absolutely necessary. Animal studies indicate that Rifampin may cause backbone problems (spina bifida) in the fetus. Rifampin has not been shown to cause problems to the infant while the mother is breast-feeding.

Possible Side Effects

Flulike symptoms, heartburn, upset stomach, loss of appetite, nausea, vomiting, stomach gas cramps, diarrhea, headache, drowsiness, tiredness, menstrual disturbances, dizziness, fever, pains in the arms and legs, confusion, visual disturbances, numbness, hypersensitivity to the drug.

Possible Adverse Drug Effects

Adverse effects on the blood, kidneys, or liver.

Drug Interactions

When this is taken with other drugs that cause liver toxicity, severe liver damage may develop.

Rifampin will increase patient requirements for oral anticoagulant drugs and may affect Methadone, oral antidiabetic drugs, digitalis drugs, or adrenal corticosteroids. Women taking oral contraceptives and Rifampin should supplement with other contraceptive methods while taking the two drugs together.

Food Interactions

Take this medicine 1 hour before or 2 hours after a meal, at the same time every day.

Usual Dose

Adult: 600 milligrams once daily.

Child: 1 to 2 milligrams per pound, or up to 600 milligrams per day.

Overdosage

Signs are nausea, vomiting, and tiredness. Unconsciousness may develop, with severe liver damage. A brown-red or orange discoloration of the skin may develop. Patients suspected of taking a Rifampin overdose must be taken to the hospital at once. ALWAYS take the medicine bottle with you.

Special Information

This drug may cause a red-brown or orange coloration of the urine, stool, saliva, sweat, and tears.

Soft contact lenses may become permanently stained.

Call your doctor if you develop the flu, fever, chills, muscle pains, headache, tiredness or weakness, loss of appetite, nausea, vomiting, sore throat, unusual bleeding or bruising, or yellow discoloration of the skin or eyes, rash, or itching.

If you take daily doses of Rifampin and you miss a dose, consult your doctor. Reactions may occur if you start again.

Generic Name

Ritodrine Hydrochloride

Brand Name

Yutopar

Type of Drug

Uterine relaxant.

Prescribed for

Controlling preterm labor to prevent premature delivery.

General Information

This drug stimulates the beta nerve receptors in muscles in the uterus and prevents them from contracting. This drug must be used only under the direction of your doctor and only after the fifth month of pregnancy. It should be started with intravenous dosage and then continued as oral tablets.

Cautions and Warnings

This drug should not be used until after the twentieth week of pregnancy or if the mother has any complicating factors.

Possible Side Effects

Increased heart rate and blood pressure in both mother and child, palpitations, tremor, nausea, vomiting, headache, swelling of the extremities.

Possible Adverse Drug Effects

Nervousness, jitteriness, restlessness, emotional anxiety, upset, feeling of ill health, chest pains, abnormal heart rates, rash, heart murmur, upset stomach, bloating, constipation, diarrhea, sweating, chills, drowsiness, weakness, difficulty breathing, sugar in the urine.

Drug Interactions

Adrenal corticosteroids may lead to fluid in the lungs when given together with Ritodrine Hydrochloride.

All beta-adrenergic blocking drugs will directly inhibit the effect of Ritodrine Hydrochloride.

Usual Dose

After intravenous therapy, tablets are taken in a dose of 10 milligrams every 2 hours on the first day, then 10 to 20 milligrams every 4 to 6 hours. The drug may be used as long as it is desirable to prolong the pregnancy.

Overdosage

Signs are rapid heart rate, palpitation, abnormal heartbeats, low blood pressure, nervousness, tremor, nausea, and vomiting. Take the patient to a hospital emergency room. ALWAYS bring the medicine bottle.

Special Information

Take only as directed by your doctor. Report any unusual effect immediately.

Brand Name

Salutensin

Ingredients

Hydroflumethiazide
Reserpine

Other Brand Names

Hydropine
Salazide
Salutensin-Demi

(Also available in generic form)

Type of Drug

Antihypertensive combination.

Prescribed for

High blood pressure.

General Information

Salutensin is a good example of a drug taking advantage of a drug interaction. Each of the drug ingredients works by different mechanisms to lower your blood pressure. The Hydroflumethiazide relaxes the muscles in your veins and arteries and also helps reduce the volume of blood flowing through those blood vessels. Reserpine works on the nervous system to reduce the efficiency of nerve transmissions which are contributing to the increased pressure. These drugs complement each other so that their combined effect is better than the effect of either one alone.

It is essential that you take your medicine exactly as prescribed, for maximum benefit.

An ingredient in this drug may cause excessive loss of potassium, which may lead to a condition called hypokalemia. Warning signs are dryness of mouth, excessive thirst, weakness, drowsiness, restlessness, muscle pains or cramps, muscular fatigue, lack of urination, abnormal heart rhythms, and upset stomach. If warning signs occur, call your doctor.

This drug should be stopped at the first sign of despondency, early morning insomnia, loss of appetite, or sexual impotence. Drug-induced depression may persist for several months after the drug has been discontinued; it has been known to be severe enough to result in suicide attempts. This drug should be used with care by women of childbearing age.

Cautions and Warnings

Do not take this drug if you are sensitive or allergic to either of its ingredients or if you have a history of mental depression, active peptic ulcer, or ulcerative colitis.

Do not take this drug if you are pregnant or nursing. The Reserpine in Salutensin may cause unwanted effects in the baby if too much is taken during pregnancy or breast-feeding (breathing problems, appetite loss, low temperature).

Salutensin, if used during pregnancy, may cause side effects in the newborn infant such as jaundice, (blood problems) and low potassium. Birth defects have not been seen in animal studies.

Possible Side Effects

Loss of appetite, stomach irritation, nausea, vomiting, cramps, diarrhea, constipation, dizziness, headache, tingling in the arms and legs, restlessness, chest pains, abnormal heart rhythms, drowsiness, depression, nervousness, anxiety, nightmares, glaucoma, blood disorders, itching, fever, difficulty in breathing, muscle spasms, weakness, high blood sugar, sugar in the urine, blurred vision, stuffy nose, dryness of the mouth, rash. Occasional: impotence or decreased sex drive.

Drug Interactions

Interaction with Digitalis or Quinidine may cause abnormal heart rhythms.

Caution must be taken if this drug is given with other antihypertensive agents such as Guanethidine, Veratrum, Methyldopa, Chlorthalidone, or Hydralazine: the dose of these drugs must be monitored carefully by your physician. It is strongly advised not to take MAO antidepressant drugs while taking Salutensin.

Interaction with drugs containing Lithium may lead to toxic effects of Lithium.

Avoid over-the-counter cough, cold, or allergy remedies containing stimulant drugs which may raise your blood pressure.

Food Interactions

If Salutensin upsets your stomach, take it with food.

Usual Dose

Must be individualized to patient's response.

Special Information

You may need potassium from some outside source. This may be done by taking a potassium supplement or by eating foods such as bananas, citrus fruits, melons, and tomatoes, which have high concentrations of potassium.

Generic Name

Secobarbital

Brand Name

Seconal

(Also available in generic form)

Type of Drug

Hypnotic; sedative.

Prescribed for

Daytime sedation, sleeplessness, sedation before surgery.

General Information

Secobarbital, like the other barbiturates, works by interfering with the passage of certain nerve impulses to the brain. It is useful in any situation where a fast-acting sedative or hypnotic (sleep-producing) effect is needed. This drug can be addicting if taken for a period of time in large enough doses, especially if more than 400 milligrams a day is taken for 3 months. Larger doses will produce barbiturate addiction in a shorter time.

Cautions and Warnings

Secobarbital may slow down your physical and mental reflexes; be extremely careful when operating machinery, driving an automobile, or performing other potentially dangerous tasks. Secobarbital is classified as a barbiturate; long-term or unsupervised use may cause addiction. Elderly people on Secobarbital may exhibit nervousness and confusion at times. Barbiturates are neutralized in the liver and eliminated from the body through the kidneys; consequently, people who have liver or kidney disorders—namely, difficulty in forming or excreting urine—should be carefully monitored by their doctor when taking Secobarbital.

If you have known sensitivities or allergies to barbiturates, or if you have previously been addicted to sedatives or hypnotics, or if you have a disease affecting the respiratory system, you should not take Secobarbital.

This drug is known to cause birth defects or interfere with your baby's development. It is not considered safe for use during pregnancy. Breast-feeding while using Secobarbital may cause increased tiredness, shortness of breath, or a slow heartbeat in the baby.

Possible Side Effects

Difficulty in breathing, rash, and general allergic reaction such as running nose, watery eyes, and scratchy throat.

Possible Adverse Drug Effects

Drowsiness, lethargy, dizziness, hangover, nausea, vomiting, diarrhea. More severe adverse reactions may include anemia and yellowing of the skin and eyes.

Drug Interactions

Interaction with alcohol, tranquilizers, or other sedatives increases the effect of Secobarbital.

Interaction with anticoagulants (blood-thinning agents) can reduce their effect. This is also true of muscle relaxants and painkillers.

Usual Dose

Daytime sedative: 30 to 50 milligrams.

Hypnotic for sleep: 100 to 200 milligrams.

Sedation before surgery: 200 to 500 milligrams 1 to 2 hours before surgery.

Child: sedative, 2.7 milligrams per pound per day; sedation before surgery, 50 to 100 milligrams.

Overdosage

Symptoms are difficulty in breathing, decrease in size of the pupils of the eyes, lowered body temperature progressing to fever as time passes, fluid in the lungs, and eventually coma.

Anyone suspected of having taken an overdose must be taken to the hospital for immediate care. ALWAYS bring the medicine bottle to the emergency room physician so he can quickly and correctly identify the medicine and start treatment. Severe overdosage of this medication can kill; the drug has been used many times in suicide attempts.

Brand Name

Septra

Ingredients

Sulfamethoxazole
Trimethoprim

Other Brand Names

Bactrim	SMZ-TMP
Bethaprim SS	Sulfatrim
Cotrim	

(Also available in generic form)

Type of Drug

Anti-infective.

Prescribed for

Urinary tract infections. Septra can also be used to treat bronchitis or ear infections in children caused by susceptible organisms.

General Information

Septra is one of many combination products used to treat infections. This is a unique combination because it attacks the infecting organism in two ways; it is effective in many situations where other drugs are not.

Cautions and Warnings

Do not take this medication if you have a folic acid deficiency, are allergic or sensitive to either ingredient or to any sulfa drug, or are pregnant or nursing. Septra has been shown to cause birth defects in animals but not humans. However, rare liver problems may occur. Unwanted effects while breast-feeding may occur if your baby has the disease known as G6PD (glucose-6-phosphate dehydrogenose deficiency). Infants under age 2 months should not be given this combination product. Symptoms such as unusual bleeding or bruising, extreme tiredness, rash, sore throat, fever, pallor, or yellowing of the skin or whites of the eyes may be early indications of serious blood disorders. If any of these effects occur, contact your doctor immediately and stop taking the drug.

Possible Side Effects

Effects on components of the blood system, allergic reactions including itching, rash, drug fever, swelling around the eyes, arthritislike pains. Septra can also cause nausea, stomach upset, vomiting, abdominal pain, diarrhea, coating on the tongue, headache, tingling in the arms and/or legs, depression, convulsions, hallucinations, ringing in the ears, dizziness, difficulty sleeping, feeling of apathy, tiredness, weakness, and nervousness. Septra may affect your kidneys and cause you to produce less urine.

Drug Interactions

This drug may prolong the effects of blood-thinning agents (such as Warfarin) and antidiabetic oral drugs.

Usual Dose

1 to 2 tablets every 12 hours for 10 to 14 days. Oral suspension, 2 to 4 teaspoons every 12 hours for 10 to 14 days.

Special Information

Take Septra in the exact dosage and for the exact period of time prescribed. Do not stop taking it just because you are beginning to feel better.

You may develop unusual sensitivity to sun or bright light. If you have a history of light sensitivity or if you have sensitive skin, avoid prolonged exposure to sunlight while using Septra.

Take each dose with a full glass of water and continue to drink fluids throughout the day. This is to decrease the chances of a stone forming in your kidneys.

Brand Name

Ser-Ap-Es Tablets

Ingredients

Hydralazine
Hydrochlorothiazide
Reserpine

Other Brand Names

Cam-ap-es	Hyserp
Cherapas	Rezide
H-H-R	Ser-A-Gen

Seralazide   Tri-Hydroserpine
Serpazide   Unipres

(Also available in generic form)

Type of Drug

Antihypertensive combination.

Prescribed for

High blood pressure.

General Information

Ser-Ap-Es Tablets take advantage of three drugs working together to give enhanced action.

Be sure to take this medicine exactly as prescribed: if you don't, the medicine will not be able to work best for you.

One of the ingredients in Ser-Ap-Es Tablets may cause mental depression. If you have a history of depressive problems, make sure your doctor knows, so that the appropriate changes can be made. Stop taking this drug at the first sign of despondency, early morning insomnia, loss of appetite, or sexual impotence. Drug-induced depression may persist for several months after the drug has been stopped; it has been known to be severe enough to result in suicide attempts.

Cautions and Warnings

Do not take Ser-Ap-Es Tablets if you are sensitive or allergic to any of its ingredients or if you have a history of mental depression, active peptic ulcer, or ulcerative colitis. Long-term administration in large doses may produce symptoms similar to arthritis in a few patients. This usually resolves itself when you stop taking the drug. The recurrence of fever, chest pains, not feeling well, or other unexplained problems should be investigated further by your doctor.

An ingredient in this drug may cause you to lose an excessive amount of potassium, which may lead to a condition known as hypokalemia. Warning signs of hypokalemia are dryness of the mouth, excessive thirst, weakness, drowsiness, restlessness, muscle pain or cramps, muscular fatigue, lack of urination, abnormal heart rhythms, and upset stomach. If you notice these warning signs, call your doctor.

This drug may cause birth defects or interfere with your baby's development. Check with your doctor before taking it if you are, or might be, pregnant. Problems have not been seen in breast-fed infants, even though Hydrochlorthiazide passes into breast milk.

Possible Side Effects

Common: headache, loss of appetite, vomiting, nausea, diarrhea, abnormal heart rate, chest pains, stomach upset, cramps, tingling in the arms and legs, restlessness, drowsiness, depression, nervousness, anxiety, nightmares, glaucoma, blood disorders, rash, itching, fever, difficulty in breathing, muscle spasms, weakness, high blood sugar, sugar in the urine, blurred vision, stuffy nose, dry mouth, rash. Impotence and decreased sex drive have also been reported.

Possible Adverse Drug Effects

Flushing of the skin, tearing of the eyes, conjunctivitis, disorientation, and anxiety are infrequent. Rarely, long-term users have developed symptoms of hepatitis.

Drug Interactions

Ser-Ap-Es Tablets may interact with MAO inhibitor drugs, Digitalis, or Quinidine.

Ser-Ap-Es Tablets will interact with drugs containing Lithium, producing a higher incidence of adverse effects from the Lithium products.

Avoid over-the-counter cough, cold, or allergy remedies which contain stimulant drugs, as these can counteract the antihypertensive medication.

You may need to take extra potassium to replace the loss caused by the drug. You may do this either by taking a potassium supplement (liquid, powder, or tablet), or by increasing the amounts of foods in your diet which are high in potassium. Some of these foods are bananas, citrus fruits, melons, and tomatoes.

Food Interactions

Slight stomach upset from Ser-Ap-Es Tablets can be overcome by taking each dose with some food. If stomach pain continues or becomes severe, call your doctor.

Usual Dose

Must be individualized to patient's response.

Overdosage

Symptoms are extreme lowering of blood pressure, rapid heartbeat, headache, generalized skin flushing, chest pains, and poor heart rhythms. The patient should be treated in a hospital where proper facilities and procedures are available. ALWAYS bring the medicine bottle to the emergency room.

Special Information

It is important to eat a well-balanced diet or follow the special diet given to you by your doctor. You must take your medicine exactly as prescribed.

Brand Name
Sinemet

Ingredients

Carbidopa
Levodopa

Type of Drug

Anti-Parkinsonian.

Prescribed for

Parkinson's disease.

General Information

The two ingredients in Sinemet interact for a beneficial drug interaction. Levodopa is the active ingredient that aids treatment of Parkinson's disease. Vitamin B_6 (Pyridoxine) destroys Levodopa, but Carbidopa prevents this. This allows more Levodopa to get into the brain, where it works.

This combination is so effective that the amount of Levodopa can be reduced by about 75 percent, which results in fewer side effects and, generally, safer drug treatment.

Cautions and Warnings

Do not take this drug if you are allergic to either of the ingredients. Patients being switched from Levodopa to Sinemet should stop taking Levodopa 8 hours before their first dose of Sinemet. It can be increased gradually, as needed. Side effects with Sinemet can occur at much lower dosages than with Levodopa, because of the effect of Carbidopa.

These drugs are known to cause birth defects in laboratory animals. The effect in humans is not known. However, women who are pregnant or breast-feeding should use this drug only if it is absolutely necessary.

Possible Side Effects

Uncontrolled muscle movements, loss of appetite, nausea, vomiting, stomach pain, dry mouth, difficulty swallowing, dribbling saliva from the side of the mouth, shaking of the hands, headache, dizziness, numbness, weakness, feeling faint, grinding of the teeth, confusion, sleeplessness, nightmares, hallucinations, anxiety, agitation, tiredness, feeling of ill health, feeling of euphoria (high).

Possible Adverse Drug Effects

Adverse effects on the heart including palpitations, dizziness when rising quickly from a sitting or lying position, and sudden extreme slowness of movement (on-off phenomenon); mental changes including paranoia, psychosis and depression, and slowdown of mental functioning; also difficult urination, muscle twitching, spasms of the eyelids, lockjaw, burning sensation on the tongue, bitter taste, diarrhea, constipation, stomach gas, flushing of the skin, rash, sweating, unusual breathing, double or blurred vision, dilation of the pupils of the eyes, hot flashes, changes in body weight, darkening of the urine or sweat.

Occasionally Sinemet may cause bleeding of the stomach or development of an ulcer, high blood pressure, adverse effects on components of the blood, irritation of blood vessels, convulsions, inability to control movements of the eye muscles, hiccups, feeling of being stimulated, retention of body fluid, hair loss, hoarseness of the voice, or persistent penile erection. The drug may affect blood tests for kidney and liver function.

Drug Interactions

The effectiveness of Sinemet may be increased by taking drugs with an anticholinergic effect, such as Trihexyphenidyl. Methyldopa, an antihypertensive drug, has the same effect on Levodopa as Carbidopa. It can increase the amount of Levodopa available in the central nervous system, and it may have a slight effect on Sinemet as well.

Patients taking Guanethidine or a diuretic to treat high blood pressure may find they need less medication to control their pressure.

Reserpine, benzodiazepine tranquilizers, major tranquilizers, Phenytoin, and Papaverine may interfere with the effects of Sinemet. Vitamin BF will interfere with Levodopa but not with Sinemet.

Diabetics who start taking Sinemet may need adjustments in their antidiabetic drugs.

Patients taking Sinemet together with an MAO inhibitor drug may experience a rapid increase in blood pressure. MAO inhibitors should be stopped 2 weeks before Sinemet.

Sinemet may increase the effects of Ephedrine, amphetamines, Epinephrine, and Isoproterenol. This interaction can result in adverse effects on the heart. This reaction may also occur with some of the antidepressants.

Food Interactions

This drug may be taken with food to reduce upset stomach.

Usual Dose

Dose must be tailored to individual need. For patients who have been taking Levodopa, the starting dose of Sinemet should contain 20 to 25 percent of the amount of Levodopa that was taken previously.

For patients who have not been taking Levodopa 3 times per day, the dose is 9 10/100 tablets a day. Dosage may be adjusted slowly thereafter.

Overdosage

Patients taking an overdose of Sinemet should be taken to a hospital emergency room. ALWAYS bring the medicine bottle. The most worrisome effect of an overdosage with Sinemet is the development of abnormal heart rhythms.

Special Information

Take care while driving or operating machinery; Sinemet can cause tiredness or lack of concentration. Call your doctor if you experience dizziness, light-headedness or fainting spells, uncontrollable movements of the face, eyelids, mouth, tongue, neck, arms, hands, or legs, mood changes, mental changes, abnormal heartbeats or heart palpitations, difficult urination, or persistent nausea or vomiting or other stomach complaints.

This drug may cause darkening of the urine or sweat. This effect is not harmful, but may interfere with urine tests for diabetes.

Call your doctor before making any adjustments in your treatment.

Brand Name
Singlet Tablets

Ingredients

Acetaminophen
Chlorpheniramine Maleate
Phenylephrine Hydrochloride

Other Brand Names

(same combination with different concentrations)
Cerose Compound   Histagesic Modified
Colrex   Papzans Modified
Dristan Advanced Formula

Type of Drug

Decongestant antihistamine combination.

Prescribed for

Relief of congestion, runny nose, and other general symptoms associated with the common cold, influenza, or other upper respiratory diseases.

General Information

Singlet Tablets is one of many products marketed to alleviate the symptoms of the common cold. These products contain medicine to relieve nasal congestion or to dry up runny noses or soothe scratchy throats; and several of them may contain ingredients to suppress cough, or to help eliminate unwanted mucus. All these products are only for the relief of symptoms and will not treat the underlying problem, such as a cold virus or other infections.

Cautions and Warnings

Can cause excessive tiredness or drowsiness. This product should not be used for newborn infants or taken by pregnant or nursing women.

People with glaucoma or difficulty in urinating should avoid this drug and other drugs containing antihistamines.

Possible Side Effects

Excessive tiredness or drowsiness, restlessness, tension, nervousness, tremor, weakness, inability to sleep, headache, palpitations, elevation of blood pressure, sweating, sleeplessness, loss of appetite, nausea, vomiting, dizziness, constipation.

Drug Interactions

Interaction with alcoholic beverages may produce excessive drowsiness and/or sleepiness, or inability to concentrate. Also avoid sedatives, tranquilizers, antihistamines, and sleeping pills.

Do not self-medicate with additional over-the-counter drugs for the relief of cold symptoms; taking Singlet Tablets with such drugs may result in aggravation of high blood pressure, heart disease, diabetes, or thyroid disease.

Do not take Singlet Tablets if you are taking or suspect you may be taking a monoamine oxidase (MAO) inhibitor: severe elevation in blood pressure may result.

Usual Dose

1 tablet 3 times per day.

Special Information

Since drowsiness may occur during use of Singlet Tablets, be cautious while performing mechanical tasks requiring alertness.

Brand Name

Sinubid

Ingredients

Acetaminophen
Phenyltoloxamine Citrate
Phenylpropanolamine Hydrochloride

Other Brand Names

(same combinations with different concentrations)
Phenapap
Sinus Relief
Sinutrex
Sinutrol

Type of Drug

Decongestant antihistamine combination.

Prescribed for

Relief of congestion, runny nose, and other general symptoms associated with the common cold, influenza, or other upper respiratory diseases.

General Information

Sinubid is one of many products marketed to relieve the symptoms of the common cold. These products contain medicine to relieve nasal congestion or dry up runny noses or relieve scratchy throats, and several of them may contain ingredients to suppress cough, or to help eliminate unwanted mucus. All these products are good only for the relief of symptoms and will not treat the underlying problem, such as cold virus, or other infections.

Cautions and Warnings

This drug can cause excessive tiredness or drowsiness. Sinubid should not be used for newborn infants or taken by pregnant or nursing mothers. People with glaucoma or difficulty in urinating should avoid this drug and other drugs containing antihistamines.

Possible Side Effects

Excessive tiredness or drowsiness, restlessness, tension, nervousness, tremor, weakness, inability to sleep, headache, palpitations, elevation of blood pressure, sweating, loss of appetite, nausea, vomiting, dizziness, constipation.

Drug Interactions

Interaction with alcoholic beverages may produce excessive drowsiness and/or sleepiness, or inability to concentrate. Also avoid sedatives, tranquilizers, other antihistamines, and sleeping pills.

Do not self-medicate with over-the-counter drugs for the relief of cold symptoms; taking Sinubid with such drugs may result in aggravation of high blood pressure, heart disease, diabetes, or thyroid disease.

Do not take Sinubid if you are taking or suspect you may be taking a monoamine oxidase (MAO) inhibitor: severe elevation in blood pressure may result.

Usual Dose

1 tablet morning and night.

Special Information

Since drowsiness may occur during use of Sinubid, be cautious while performing mechanical tasks requiring alertness.

Generic Name

Spironolactone

Brand Names

Alatone
Aldactone

(Also available in generic form)

Type of Drug

Diuretic.

Prescribed for

High blood pressure; excess fluid in the body due to other diseases.

General Information

Spironolactone is a specific physiologic antagonist of aldosterone. Therefore, it is extremely useful for the treatment of excess fluid in the body related to the presence of high levels of aldosterone (hyperaldosteronism) when used alone or in combination with other diuretics.

Cautions and Warnings

Do not use this drug if you know you have kidney failure or high blood levels of potassium. This drug has been shown to cause tumors when given in very high doses to experimental rats. This drug may cause birth defects or interfere with your baby's development. Check with your doctor before taking it if you are, or might be, pregnant.

Possible Side Effects

Drowsiness, lethargy, headache, gastrointestinal upset, cramps and diarrhea, rash, mental confusion, fever, feeling of ill health, enlargement of the breasts, inability to achieve or maintain erection in males, irregular menstrual cycles or deepening of the voice in females. These side effects are generally reversible.

Drug Interactions

Spironolactone will potentiate (increase the action of) other antihypertensive drugs; frequently it is used for this effect. The dosage of other antihypertensive drugs may be reduced as much as 50 percent when Spironolactone is added to the regimen.

Patients taking Spironolactone for the treatment of high blood pressure should not self-medicate with over-the-counter cough, cold, or allergy remedies containing stimulant drugs which may counteract its effectiveness and have an adverse effect on their hearts.

Food Interactions

Patients taking Spironolactone should not eat potassium or food rich in potassium.

Usual Dose

Adult: for high blood pressure, initial dose is 50 to 100 milligrams per day in divided doses; for excess fluids related to other diseases, 100 milligrams per day in divided doses.

Child: 1 to 1.5 milligrams per pound of body weight, if deemed necessary.

Special Information

Take the drug exactly as it has been prescribed for maximum therapeutic effect. High blood levels of potassium associated with use of Spironolactone may cause weakness, lethargy, drowsiness, muscle pains or cramps, and muscular fatigue. Patients should be careful when driving or performing jobs that require alertness. Spironolactone does not cause the loss of potassium as do other diuretics. Therefore, potassium supplements are unnecessary.

Generic Name

Sucralfate

Brand Name

Carafate

Type of Drug

Local anti-ulcer therapy.

Prescribed for

Duodenal ulcer.

General Information

Sucralfate is minimally absorbed into the body from the gastrointestinal (GI) tract, but instead works within the GI tract by exerting a soothing local effect. After the drug binds to proteins in the damaged mucous tissue within the ulcer, it forms a barrier to acids and enzymes normally found in the gastrointestinal tract, protecting the ulcerated tissue from further damage and allowing it to begin to heal naturally.

Although its mechanism of action is completely different from Cimetidine, Sucralfate is equally effective in treating duodenal ulcer disease.

Cautions and Warnings

This drug should not be used by pregnant women or nursing mothers unless absolutely necessary. The use of Sucralfate in children is not recommended because the drug has only been studied in adults.

Possible Side Effects

Most frequent: constipation. Others are: diarrhea, nausea, upset stomach, indigestion, dry mouth, rash, itching, back pain, dizziness, sleepiness. The incidence of reported side effects to Sucralfate is only about 5 percent.

Drug Interactions

Sucralfate may decrease the action of Tetracycline, Phenytoin, or Cimetidine. To avoid this, separate doses by 2 hours.

Usual Dose

One tablet 4 times per day on an empty stomach.

Overdosage

There have been no reports of human overdoses of Sucralfate. Animals given the equivalent of 5.5 grams per pound of body weight did not experience any unusual effects, and therefore the risk associated with Sucralfate overdose is thought to be minimal.

Special Information

Each dose may be taken 1 hour before meals or 2 hours after meals and before bedtime. Be sure to take the medicine for a full 6 to 8 week course of treatment. Notify your doctor if you develop constipation, diarrhea, or other gastrointestinal side effects. If you are taking antacids as part of your ulcer therapy, separate antacid doses from Sucralfate by at least 2 hours.

eneric Name

ulfamethizole

and Names

oklar

iosulfil

pe of Drug

inary anti-infective.

escribed for

inary tract infections.

eneral Information

lfamethizole is one of the sulfa drugs, some of which are
ed for the treatment of urinary tract infections. Others may
used for high blood pressure, diabetes mellitus, or as
uretic (urine-producing) drugs. When taking Sulfamethizole
urinary tract infections, it is essential that you take your
edicine for the full course prescribed by your doctor. If you
n't, your infection will not be cured and may actually
come more difficult to treat. Sulfa drugs are usually the
st choice for urinary infections.

utions and Warnings

not take Sulfamethizole if you know you are allergic to
lfa drugs, Salicylates, or similar agents. Do not take this
ug if you are pregnant or nursing, since the drug can pass
m the mother to child. Sulfamethizole should not be
nsidered if you have advanced kidney disease, or intes-
al or urinary obstruction.

ssible Side Effects

adache, itching, rash, sensitivity to strong sunlight, nau-
a, vomiting, abdominal pains, feeling of tiredness or lassi-
de, hallucinations, dizziness, ringing in the ears, chills,
eling of ill health.

Possible Adverse Drug Effects

Blood diseases or alterations of normal blood components, itching of the eyes, arthritic pain, diarrhea, loss of appetite, stomach cramps or pains, hearing loss, drowsiness, fever, chills, loss of hair, yellowing of the skin and/or eyes, reduction in sperm count.

Drug Interactions

When Sulfamethizole is taken with an anticoagulant (blood thinning) drug, any drug used to treat diabetes, or Methotrexate, it will cause unusually large amounts of these drugs to be released into the bloodstream, producing symptoms of overdosage. If you are going to take Sulfamethizole for an extended period, your physician should reduce the dosage of these interactive drugs. Also avoid large doses of Vitamin C.

Usual Dose

Adult: .5 to 1 gram 3 to 4 times per day.

Child and infant (age over 2 months): 3 to 5 milligrams per pound 4 times per day.

Overdosage

Induce vomiting and give a rectal enema; then take the patient to a hospital emergency room. ALWAYS bring the medicine bottle.

Special Information

Avoid prolonged exposure to strong sunlight while you are taking Sulfamethizole, which can cause photosensitivity—severe reaction to strong sunlight.

Sore throat, fever, unusual bleeding or bruising, rash, and feeling tired are early signs of serious blood disorders and should be reported to your doctor immediately.

Take each dose with a full glass of water.

Therapy should continue 1 to 2 days after symptoms have subsided. Take the medicine for the time prescribed by your doctor; do not stop just because you have begun to feel better.

Sulfa drugs may interfere with tests for urine glucose.

Generic Name

Sulfamethoxazole

Brand Names

Gamazole
Gantanol
Gantanol DS
Urobak

(Also available in generic form)

Type of Drug

Anti-infective.

Prescribed for

Urinary tract infections; ear infections in children.

General Information

Sulfamethoxazole is a member of the group called sulfa drugs. Some sulfa drugs are used for the treatment of infections, while others may be used for high blood pressure or diabetes mellitus, or as diuretic (water-losing) drugs. When taking Sulfamethoxazole for urinary tract infections it is essential that you take your medicine for the full course prescribed by your doctor. If you don't, your infection will not be cured and may become more difficult to treat. Sulfa drugs are usually the best choice for urinary infections, and may also be used to treat other infections.

Cautions and Warnings

Do not take Sulfamethoxazole if you know you are allergic to sulfa drugs, salicylates, or similar agents. Do not take this drug if you are pregnant or nursing a young child, since the drug can pass from the mother into the child. Sulfamethoxazole has not been shown to cause birth defects. However, rare liver problems may occur. Unwanted effects while breast-feeding may occur if your baby has the disease known as G6PD (glucose-6-phosphate dehydrogenose deficiency). Sulfamethoxazole should not be considered if you have advanced kidney disease or intestinal or urinary obstruction.

Possible Side Effects

Headache, itching, rash, sensitivity to strong sunlight, nausea, vomiting, abdominal pains, feeling of tiredness or lassitude, hallucinations, dizziness, ringing in the ears, chills, feeling of ill health.

Possible Adverse Drug Effects

Blood diseases or alterations of normal blood components, itching of the eyes, arthritic pain, diarrhea, loss of appetite, stomach cramps or pains, hearing loss, drowsiness, fever, chills, loss of hair, yellowing of the skin and/or eyes, reduction in sperm count.

Drug Interactions

When Sulfamethoxazole is taken with an anticoagulant (blood-thinning) drug, any drug used to treat diabetes, or Methotrexate, it will cause unusually large amounts of these drugs to be released into the bloodstream, producing symptoms of overdosage. If you have to take Sulfamethoxazole for an extended period, your physician should reduce the dosage of these interactive drugs. Also avoid large doses of Vitamin C.

Usual Dose

Adult: first dose, 4 tablets; then 2 tablets 2 to 3 times per day.

Child (suspension): first dose, 25 to 30 milligrams per pound of body weight; then 12.5 to 15 milligrams per pound morning and evening. No more than 34 milligrams per pound per day.

Therapy should continue 1 to 2 days after symptoms have subsided. Take the medicine for the time prescribed by your doctor; do not stop just because you have begun to feel better.

Overdosage

Induce vomiting and give a rectal enema; then take the patient to a hospital emergency room. ALWAYS bring the medicine bottle.

Special Information

Sulfamethoxazole can cause photosensitivity—a severe reaction to strong sunlight. Avoid prolonged exposure to strong sunlight while you are taking it.

Sore throat, fever, unusual bleeding or bruising, rash, and feeling tired are early signs of serious blood disorders and should be reported to your doctor immediately.

Sulfa drugs may interfere with tests for urine glucose.

Take each dose with a full glass of water.

Generic Name

Sulfasalazine

Brand Names

Azaline
Azulfidine
Azulfidine EN-tabs
S.A.S.-500

(Also available in generic form)

Type of Drug

Sulfonamide.

Prescribed for

Treatment of ulcerative colitis.

General Information

Sulfasalazine is a member of the group called sulfa drugs. Some sulfa drugs are used for their effects as anti-infectives, others are diuretics or can be used to treat diabetes mellitus. Sulfasalazine has a unique effect in that it reduces the intestinal inflammation of ulcerative colitis.

Cautions and Warnings

Do not take Sulfasalazine if you know you are allergic to sulfa drugs, salicylates, or similar agents. Do not take this drug if you are pregnant or nursing a young child, since the drug can pass from the mother into the child. Sulfasalazine has not been shown to cause birth defects. However, rare liver problems may occur. Unwanted effects while breast-feeding may occur if your baby has the disease known as

G6PD (glucose-6-phosphate dehydrogenose deficiency). Sulfasalazine should not be considered if you have advanced kidney disease.

Possible Side Effects

Headache, itching, skin rash, sensitivity to strong sunlight, nausea, vomiting, abdominal pains, feeling of tiredness or lassitude, hallucinations, dizziness, ringing in the ears, chills, feeling of ill health.

Possible Adverse Drug Effects

Blood diseases or changes in normal blood components, itching of the eyes, arthritis-type pain, diarrhea, loss of appetite, stomach cramps or pains, hearing loss, drowsiness, fever, chills, loss of hair, yellowing of the skin and/or eyes, reduction in sperm count.

Drug Interactions

When Sulfasalazine is taken with an anticoagulant (blood-thinning) drug, any drug used to treat diabetes, or Methotrexate, it will cause unusually large amounts of these drugs to be released into the bloodstream, producing symptoms of overdosage. If you are going to take Sulfasalazine for an extended period, your physician should reduce the dosage of these interactive drugs. Also avoid large doses of Vitamin C.

Usual Dose

Adult: 6 to 8 tablets per day to start. Adjust dose as needed. Usual maintenance dose is 4 tablets per day.

Child: 1 to 19 milligrams per pound of body weight per day to start. Adjust dose as needed. Usual maintenance dose is 15 milligrams per pound per day.

Overdosage

Induce vomiting and give a rectal enema; then take the patient to a hospital emergency room. ALWAYS bring the medicine bottle.

Special Information

Sulfasalazine can cause photosensitivity—a severe reaction

to strong sunlight. Avoid prolonged exposure to strong sunlight while you are taking it.

Sore throat, fever, unusual bleeding or bruising, rash, and feeling tired are early signs of serious blood disorders and should be reported to your doctor immediately.

Sulfa drugs may interfere with tests for urine glucose.

Generic Name

Sulfisoxazole

Brand Names

Gantrisin
Gulfasin
Lipo Gantrisin
SK-Soxazole

(Also available in generic form)

Type of Drug

Urinary anti-infective.

Prescribed for

Urinary tract infections.

General Information

Sulfisoxazole is a member of the group called sulfa drugs. Some sulfa drugs are used for the treatment of urinary tract infections. Others may be used for high blood pressure or diabetes mellitus, or as diuretic (water-losing) drugs. When taking Sulfisoxazole for urinary tract infections it is essential that you take your medicine for the full course prescribed by your doctor. If you don't, your infection will not be cured and may become more difficult to treat. Sulfa drugs are usually the best choice for urinary infections, and may also be used to treat other infections.

Cautions and Warnings

Do not take Sulfisoxazole if you know you are allergic to sulfa drugs, salicylates, or similar agents. Do not take this drug if you are pregnant or nursing a young child, since the drug can pass from the mother into the child. Sulfisoxazole has not been shown to cause birth defects. However, rare liver problems may occur. Unwanted effects while breast-feeding may occur if your baby has the disease known as G6PD (glucose-6-phosphate dehydrogenose deficiency). Sulfisoxazole should not be considered if you have advanced kidney disease.

Possible Side Effects

Headache, itching, rash, sensitivity to strong sunlight, nausea, vomiting, abdominal pains, feeling of tiredness or lassitude, hallucinations, dizziness, ringing in the ears, chills, feeling of ill health.

Possible Adverse Drug Effects

Blood diseases or alterations of normal blood components, itching of the eyes, arthritis-type pain, diarrhea, loss of appetite, stomach cramps or pains, hearing loss, drowsiness, fever, chills, loss of hair, yellowing of the skin and/or eyes, reduction in sperm count.

Drug Interactions

When Sulfisoxazole is taken with an anticoagulant (blood-thinning) drug, any drug used to treat diabetes, or Methotrexate, it will cause unusually large amounts of these drugs to be released into the bloodstream, producing symptoms of overdosage. If you are going to take Sulfisoxazole for an extended period, your physician should reduce the dosage of these interactive drugs. Also avoid large doses of Vitamin C.

Usual Dose

Adult: first dose, 4 to 8 tablets; then 2 to 3 tablets 4 times per day (not to exceed 12 tablets daily).

Child (over 50 pounds): liquid suspension (Lipo Gantrisin), 1 teaspoon 4 times per day; liquid syrup (Gantrisin Syrup), 2 teaspoons 4 times per day.

Overdosage

Induce vomiting and give a rectal enema; then take the

patient to a hospital emergency room. ALWAYS bring the medicine bottle.

Special Information

Sulfisoxazole can cause photosensitivity—a severe reaction to strong sunlight. Avoid prolonged exposure to strong sunlight while you are taking it.

Sore throat, fever, unusual bleeding or bruising, rash, and feeling tired are early signs of serious blood disorders and should be reported to your doctor immediately.

Sulfa drugs may interfere with tests for urine glucose.

Generic Name

Sulindac

Brand Name

Clinoril

Type of Drug

Nonsteroid anti-inflammatory.

Prescribed for

Arthritis, bursitis and other forms of inflammatory diseases.

General Information

Sulindac is one of ten drugs available in the United States for arthritis and joint pain. As with the other members of this group, patient response to Sulindac is individual. For some, this drug will work wonders; for others, it will do nothing. We do not know how Sulindac works.

Sulindac is one of several nonsteroid anti-inflammatory drugs used to reduce inflammation, relieve pain, or reduce fever. Nonsteroid anti-inflammatory drugs share the same side effects and may be used by patients who cannot tolerate Aspirin. Choice of one of these drugs over another depends on disease response, side effects seen in a particular patient, convenience of times to be taken, and cost. Different drugs or different doses of the same drug may be tried until the greatest effectiveness is achieved with the fewest side effects.

Cautions and Warnings

Use Sulindac with extra caution if you have a history of ulcers, bleeding diseases, or allergic reaction to Aspirin. Sulindac should be avoided by pregnant women, nursing mothers, children under age 14, and those who have nasal polyps. Sulindac when used by a pregnant woman may have unwanted effects on the heart and blood of the unborn child. If this drug is taken late in the pregnancy, the length of the pregnancy may be increased. It is not a simple pain reliever; it should be used only under the strict supervision of your doctor.

Possible Side Effects

Upset stomach, nausea, vomiting, constipation, loss of appetite, gas, stomach cramps and pain, itching and rash, dizziness, headache, nervousness, buzzing or ringing in the ears, swelling of the feet, legs, hands, or arms.

Possible Adverse Drug Effects

Stomach bleeding, irritation, and ulcer, as well as abnormal liver function, jaundice, and hepatitis have been reported. Heart failure in patients with already weak hearts, palpitations, blurred vision, and allergic reactions have occurred.

Drug Interactions

May increase the effect of anticoagulant (blood-thinning) drugs. Probenecid (Benemid) may increase the amount of Sulindac in your blood by reducing its elimination from the body.

Usual Dose

Adult: up to 200 milligrams twice per day, with food.

Overdosage

Patients taking an overdose of Sulindac must be made to vomit to remove any remaining drug from the stomach. Call your doctor or Poison Control Center before doing this. If you must go to a hospital emergency room, ALWAYS bring the medicine bottle.

Special Information

If you are allergic to Aspirin, you may be allergic to Sulindac. Since this drug can irritate the stomach, take each dose with food. While taking Sulindac, avoid taking Aspirin or alcoholic beverages. Sulindac may cause blurred vision or dizziness. Take care while driving or performing any task requiring alertness.

Call your doctor if you develop rash, itching, hives, yellowing of the skin or whites of the eyes, black or tarry stools, swelling of hands or feet, sore throat, mouth sores, unusual bleeding or bruising, or shortness of breath.

Brand Name

Synalgos-DC

Ingredients

Aspirin
Caffeine
Dihydrocodeine Bitartrate

Other Brand Names

Compal Capsules

(Also available in generic form)

Type of Drug

Narcotic analgesic combination.

Prescribed for

Relief of mild to moderate pain.

General Information

Synalgos-DC is one of many combination products containing narcotics and analgesics. These products often also contain barbiturates or tranquilizers, and Acetaminophen may be substituted for Aspirin, or Caffeine may be omitted.

Cautions and Warnings

Do not take Synalgos-DC if you know you are allergic or sensitive to it. Use this drug with extreme caution if you suffer from asthma or other breathing problems. Long-term use of Synalgos-DC may cause drug dependence or addiction. Synalgos-DC is a respiratory depressant and affects the central nervous system, producing sleepiness, tiredness, and/or inability to concentrate. If you are pregnant or suspect that you are pregnant do not take this drug.

Synalgos-DC may cause birth defects or interfere with your baby's development. Check with your doctor before taking it if you are, or might be, pregnant.

Aspirin used regularly may affect the heart of the newborn and if taken within the last 2 weeks of pregnancy may cause bleeding in the child. Problems may also be seen in the mother herself, such as bleeding, increasing the length of pregnancy or labor.

Caffeine can cause birth defects in animals but has not been shown to cause problems in humans.

Codeine can cause addiction in the unborn child if used regularly during pregnancy.

Dihydrocodeine may cause the unborn infant to become dependent on it and cause unwanted side effects. Dihydrocodeine, taken at the time of delivery, may cause breathing problems in the newborn.

Possible Side Effects

Most frequent: light-headedness, dizziness, sleepiness, nausea, vomiting, loss of appetite, sweating. If these effects occur, consider asking your doctor about lowering your dose. Usually the side effects disappear if you simply lie down.

More serious side effects of Synalgos-DC are shallow breathing or difficulty in breathing.

Possible Adverse Drug Effects

Euphoria (feeling high), weakness, sleepiness, headache, agi-

ation, uncoordinated muscle movement, minor hallucinations, disorientation and visual disturbances, dry mouth, loss
of appetite, constipation, flushing of the face, rapid heartbeat, palpitations, faintness, urinary difficulties or hesitancy,
reduced sex drive and/or potency, itching, rashes, anemia,
lowered blood sugar, yellowing of the skin and/or whites of
the eyes. Narcotic analgesics may aggravate convulsions in
those who have had convulsions in the past.

Drug Interactions

Interaction with alcohol, tranquilizers, barbiturates, or sleeping pills produces tiredness, sleepiness, or inability to concentrate and seriously increases the depressive effect of
Synalgos-DC.

The Aspirin component of Synalgos-DC can affect anticoagulant (blood-thinning) therapy. Be sure to discuss this
with your doctor so that the proper dosage adjustment can
be made.

Interaction with adrenal cortical steroids, Phenylbutazone,
or alcohol can cause severe stomach irritation with possible
bleeding.

Food Interactions

Take with food or ½ glass of water to prevent stomach
upset.

Usual Dose

2 capsules every 4 hours.

Overdosage

Symptoms are depression of respiration (breathing), extreme
tiredness progressing to stupor and then coma, pinpointed
pupils of the eyes, no response to stimulation such as a pin
stick, cold and clammy skin, slowing down of heartbeat,
lowering of blood pressure, convulsions, and cardiac arrest.
The patient should be taken to a hospital emergency room
immediately. ALWAYS bring the medicine bottle.

Special Information

Drowsiness may occur: be careful when driving or operating
hazardous machinery.

Brand Name

Tedral

Ingredients

Ephedrine Hydrochloride
Phenobarbital
Theophylline

Other Brand Names

Azma Aid	Thalfed
Phedral C.T.	Theodrine
Primatene "P" Formula	Theofedral
Tedral S.A.	Theophenyllin
T.E.P. Tablets	Theoral
Tedrigen	

(Also available in generic form)

Type of Drug

Antiasthmatic combination product.

Prescribed for

Relief of asthma symptoms or other upper respiratory disorders.

General Information

Tedral is one of several antiasthmatic combination products prescribed for the relief of asthmatic symptoms and other breathing problems. These products contain drugs which help relax the bronchial muscles, drugs which increase the diameter of the breathing passages, and a mild tranquilizer to help relax the patient. Other products in this class may contain similar ingredients along with other medicine to help eliminate mucus from the breathing passages.

Cautions and Warnings

Take the drug with food to help prevent stomach upset.

This drug should not be taken if you have severe kidney or liver disease.

Tedral may be required for a woman during pregnancy or

nursing. However, there is an increased chance of birth defects while using Tedral during pregnancy. Regularly using Tedral during the last 3 months of pregnancy may cause drug dependency of the newborn. Labor may be prolonged and delivery may be delayed as well as breathing problems in the newborn if Tedral is used. Breast-feeding while using Tedral may cause increased tiredness, shortness of breath, or a slow heartbeat in the baby.

Possible Side Effects

Large doses of Tedral can produce excitation, shakiness, sleeplessness, nervousness, rapid heartbeat, chest pains, irregular heartbeat, dizziness, dryness of the nose and throat, headache, and sweating. Occasionally people have been known to develop hesitation or difficulty in urination.

Possible Adverse Drug Effects

Excessive urination, heart stimulation, drowsiness, muscle weakness, muscle twitching, unsteady walk. These effects can usually be controlled by having your doctor adjust the dose.

Drug Interactions

Tedral may cause sleeplessness and/or drowsiness. Do not take this drug with alcoholic beverages.

Taking Tedral or similar medicines with an MAO inhibitor can produce severe interaction. Consult your doctor first.

Tedral or similar products taken together with Lithium Carbonate will increase the excretion of Lithium; they have neutralized the effect of Propranolol. Erythromycin and similar antibiotics cause the body to hold Theophylline, leading to possible side effects.

Usual Dose

1 to 2 tablets every 4 hours.

Sustained-action tablet: 1 tablet every 12 hours.

Elixir or suspension: 1 teaspoon per 60 pounds of body weight every 4 hours.

Generic Name

Temazepam

Brand Name

Restoril

Type of Drug

Sedative; hypnotic.

Prescribed for

Insomnia or sleeplessness, frequent nighttime awakening, or waking up too early in the morning.

General Information

Temazepam is a member of the chemical group of drugs known as benzodiazepines. These drugs are used as antianxiety agents, anticonvulsants, or sedatives (sleeping pills). They exert their effects by relaxing the large skeletal muscles and by a direct effect on the brain. In doing so, they can relax you and make you either more tranquil or sleepier, depending on the drug and how much you use. Many doctors prefer Temazepam and the other members of this class to other drugs that can be used for the same effect. Their reason is that the benzodiazepines tend to be safer, have fewer side effects, and are usually as, if not more, effective.

These drugs are generally used in any situation where they can be a useful adjunct.

Benzodiazepine tranquilizing drugs can be abused if taken for long periods of time and it is possible to develop withdrawal symptoms if you discontinue the therapy abruptly. Withdrawal symptoms include convulsions, tremor, muscle cramps, stomach cramps, insomnia, agitation, diarrhea, vomiting, sweating, and convulsions.

Cautions and Warnings

Do not take Temazepam if you know you are sensitive or allergic to this drug or other benzodiazepines such as Chlordiazepoxide, Oxazepam, Chlorazepate, Diazepam, Lorazepam, Prazepam, and Clonazepam.

Temazepam and other members of this drug group may aggravate narrow angle glaucoma, but if you have open angle glaucoma you may take the drugs. In any case, check this information with your doctor. Temazepam can cause tiredness, drowsiness, inability to concentrate, and similar symptoms. Be careful if you are driving, operating machinery, or performing other activities which require concentration.

This drug may cause birth defects or interfere with your baby's development. Check with your doctor before taking it if you are, or might be, pregnant. Your baby may become dependent on Temazepam if it is used continually during pregnancy. If used during the last weeks of pregnancy or during breat-feeding, the baby may be overly tired, be short of breath, or have a low heartbeat. Use during labor may cause weakness in the newborn.

Possible Side Effects

Most common: mild drowsiness during the first few days of therapy, especially in the elderly or debilitated. If drowsiness persists, contact your doctor.

Possible Adverse Drug Effects

Major adverse reactions: confusion, depression, lethargy, disorientation, headache, tiredness, slurred speech, stupor, dizziness, tremor, constipation, dry mouth, nausea, inability to control urination, changes in sex drive, irregular menstrual cycle, changes in heart rhythm, lowered blood pressure, retention of fluids, blurred or double vision, itching, rash, hiccups, nervousness, inability to fall asleep, (occasional) liver dysfunction. If you experience any of these reactions, stop taking the medicine and contact your doctor immediately.

Drug Interactions

Temazepam is a central nervous system depressant. Avoid alcohol, tranquilizers, narcotics, sleeping pills, barbiturates, MAO inhibitors, antihistamines, and other medicines used to relieve depression.

Usual Dose

15 to 30 milligrams at bedtime. Must be individualized for maximum benefit.

Overdosage

Symptoms are confusion, sleep or sleepiness, lack of response to pain such as a pin stick, shallow breathing, lowered blood pressure, and coma. The patient should be taken to a hospital emergency room immediately. ALWAYS bring the medicine bottle.

Generic Name

Terbutaline Sulfate

Brand Names

Brethine
Bricanyl

Type of Drug

Bronchodilator.

Prescribed for

Asthma and spasm of the bronchial muscles. This drug has been used experimentally to prevent or slow down premature labor in pregnant women.

General Information

This is one of the newer bronchodilator drugs in use in the United States. It has a more specific effect than some of the older drugs and so can cause a somewhat lower incidence of side effects on the heart. Often Terbutaline Sulfate is used with other drugs to enhance beneficial effects. The tablet takes effect 30 minutes after it has been taken and continues working for 4 to 8 hours. Therefore it is not used for an acute asthma attack, but rather to prevent one.

Cautions and Warnings

This drug should be used with caution by patients who have angina, heart disease, high blood pressure, a history of stroke or seizures, diabetes, thyroid disease, prostate disease, or glaucoma.

This drug should be used by women who are pregnant or breast-feeding only when absolutely necessary. The potential hazard to the unborn child or nursing infant is not known at this time.

Older patients, over age 60, are more likely to experience the adverse effects of this drug.

Possible Side Effects

Restlessness, anxiety, fear, tension, sleeplessness, tremors, convulsions, weakness, dizziness, headache, flushing, pallor, sweating, nausea and vomiting, loss of appetite, muscle cramps, urinary difficulties.

Possible Adverse Drug Effects

Terbutaline Sulfate can cause some side effects on the heart and cardiovascular system, including high blood pressure, abnormal heart rhythms, and angina. It is less likely to cause these effects than some of the older drugs.

Drug Interactions

The effect of this drug may be increased by antidepressant drugs, some antihistamines, and Levothyroxine. It may antagonize the effects of Reserpine or Guanethidine.

Food Interactions

If the drug causes upset stomach, take each dose with food.

Usual Dose

Adult: 5 milligrams 3 time per day, every 6 hours. No more than 15 milligrams per day.

Child (age 12 to 15): 2.5 milligrams 3 times per day every 6 hours. No more than 7.5 milligrams per day.

Child (under age 12): not recommended.

Overdosage

Symptoms include palpitation, abnormal heart rhythms, rapid heartbeat, slow heartbeat, chest pain, high blood pressure, fever, chills, cold sweat, blanching of the skin, nausea, vomiting, sleeplessness, delirium, tremor, pinpoint pupils, convulsions, coma, and collapse. If you or someone you know has taken an overdose of this drug call your doctor or bring the patient to a hospital emergency room. ALWAYS remember to bring the prescription bottle with you.

Special Information

Do not take more than the amount prescribed for you.
Terbutaline Sulfate is also available in an oral spray.

Generic Name

Terfenadine

Brand Name

Seldane

Type of Drug

Antihistamine.

Prescribed for

Seasonal allergy, stuffy and runny nose, itching of the eyes, scratchy throat caused by allergies, and other allergic symptoms such as rash, itching or hives.

General Information

Terfenadine is the first truly nonsedating antihistamine approved for use in the United States. Available in Europe and Canada for several years, this drug has been widely used and accepted by people who find other antihistamines unacceptable because of the drowsiness and tiredness they cause. Terfenadine appears to work in exactly the same way as Chlorpheniramine and other widely used antihistamines.

Cautions and Warnings

Do not take Terfenadine if you have had an allergic reaction to it in the past. People with asthma or other deep-breathing problems, glaucoma (pressure in the eye), stomach ulcer or other stomach problems should avoid Terfenadine because its side effects may aggravate these problems.

Terfenadine has been studied in lab animals and found to cause no damage to a developing fetus. Nevertheless, this drug should only be used by pregnant women if it is absolutely necessary. Nursing mothers should avoid using this drug. Temporarily suspend breast-feeding if you must use Terfenadine.

Possible Side Effects

Occasional: headache, nervousness, weakness, upset stomach, nausea, vomiting, dry mouth, nose or throat, sore throat, nosebleeds, cough, stuffy nose, nervousness, weakness, change in bowel habits. In scientific studies, Terfenadine was found to cause the same amount of drowsiness as a placebo (inactive pill) and about half that caused by other antihistamines. It is considered safe for use by people who cannot tolerate the sedating effects of other anithistamine drugs.

Possible Adverse Drug Effects

Hair loss, allergic reactions, depression, sleeplessness, menstrual irregularities, muscle aches, sweating, tingling in the hands or feet, frequent urination, visual disturbances. A few people taking this drug have developed liver damage.

Drug Interactions

No interactions have been found between Terfenadine and other drugs. Unlike other antihistamines, Terfenadine does not interact with alcohol or other nervous system depressants to produce drowsiness or loss of coordination.

Food Interactions

Terfenadine should be taken on an empty stomach, 1 hour before or 2 hours after food or meals.

Usual Dose

Adult and child (age 12 and over): 60 milligrams twice a day. Not recommended for children under age 12.

Overdosage

Terfenadine overdose is likely to cause exaggerated side effects. Victims of Terfenadine overdose should be given Syrup of Ipecac to make them vomit and be taken to a hospital emergency room for treatment. ALWAYS bring the prescription bottle with you.

Special Information

Report any unusual side effects to your doctor. Since this is a new drug in the United States, he or she will want to know anything that happens to learn more about the drug and its effects. Terfenadine's only disadvantage is its cost. Equally effective antihistamines are sold over-the-counter without a prescription and can be purchased for relatively little money.

Generic Name

Terpin Hydrate with Codeine

Brand Name

SK-Terpin Hydrate & Codeine

(Also available in generic form)

Type of Drug

Cough suppressant and expectorant combination.

Prescribed for

Relief of coughs due to colds or other respiratory infections.

General Information

Terpin Hydrate decreases the production of mucus and other bronchial secretions which can cause coughs. The cough suppressant effect of Terpin Hydrate with Codeine is primarily due to the Codeine.

Cautions and Warnings

Do not take Codeine if you know you are allergic or sensitive to this drug. Use this drug with extreme caution if you suffer from asthma or other breathing problems. Long-term use of Codeine may cause drug dependence or addiction. Codeine is a respiratory depressant and affects the central nervous system, producing sleepiness, tiredness, and/or inability to concentrate. Be careful if you are driving, operating machinery, or performing other functions requiring concentration. If you are pregnant or suspect that you are pregnant do not take this drug.

Terpin Hydrate with Codeine is 80 proof (40 percent alcohol). Too much alcohol taken by the mother during pregnancy and lactation may cause birth defects and unwanted problems during breast-feeding.

Terpin Hydrate has not been shown to cause birth defects. Too much (large amounts taken for a long time) narcotics used during pregnancy and breast-feeding may cause the baby to become dependent on the narcotic. Narcotics may also cause breathing problems in the infant during delivery.

Possible Side Effects

Most frequent: light-headedness, dizziness, sedation or sleepiness, nausea, vomiting, sweating. Terpin Hydrate with Codeine elixir contains 40 percent alcohol (80 proof), and it is an easily abused drug product.

Possible Adverse Drug Effects

Euphoria (feeling high), weakness, sleepiness, headache, agitation, uncoordinated muscle movement, minor hallucinations, disorientation and visual disturbances, dry mouth, loss of appetite, constipation, flushing of the face, rapid heartbeat, palpitations, faintness, urinary difficulties or hesitancy, reduced sex drive and/or potency, itching, rashes, anemia, lowered blood sugar, yellowing of the skin and/or whites of the eyes. Narcotic analgesics may aggravate convulsions in those who have had convulsions in the past.

Drug Interactions

Codeine has a depressant effect and potential effect on breathing, and it should be taken with extreme care in combination with alcohol, sedatives, tranquilizers, antihistamines, or other depressant drugs.

Usual Dose

1 to 2 teaspoons every 3 or 4 hours as needed for relief of cough.

Special Information

To help reduce the cough, try to cough up as much mucus as possible while taking this medication.

Brand Name

Terrastatin

Ingredients

Nystatin
Oxytetracycline

Type of Drug

Broad-spectrum antibiotic antifungal combination.

Prescribed for

Bacterial infections such as gonorrhea, infections of the mouth, gums, and teeth, Rocky Mountain spotted fever and other fevers caused by ticks and lice from a variety of carriers, urinary tract infections, and respiratory system infections such as pneumonia and bronchitis.

These diseases may be produced by gram-positive or gram-negative organisms such as diplococci, staphylococci, streptococci, gonococci, *E. coli*, and *Shigella*.

Terrastatin has also been successfully used to treat some skin infections, but is not considered the first-choice antibiotic for the treatment of general skin infections or wounds.

Terrastatin has been used along with other medicines to treat amoebic infections of the intestinal tract, known as amoebic dysentery. It is also prescribed for diseases caused by ticks, fleas, and lice.

Terrastatin has been successfully used in the treatment of adolescent acne, using small doses over a long period of time. Adverse effects or toxicity in this type of therapy are almost unheard of.

General Information

Terrastatin works by interfering with the normal growth cycle of the invading bacteria, preventing them from reproducing and thus allowing the body's normal defenses to fight off the infection. This process is called bacteriostatic action.

Since the action of this antibiotic depends on its concentration within the invading bacteria, it is imperative that the patient completely follow the doctor's directions.

The Nystatin component of Terrastatin is to prevent fungal infections while taking Oxytetracylcine.

Cautions and Warnings

Do not use Terrastatin if you are pregnant. Terrastatin, when used in children, has been shown to interfere with the development of the long bones and may retard growth. Exceptions would be when Terrastatin is the only effective antibiotic available and all risk factors have been made known to the patient.

Terrastatin should not be given to people with known liver disease or to people with kidney or urine excretion problems. You should avoid taking high doses of Terrastatin or undergoing extended Terrastatin therapy if you will be exposed to sunlight for a long period, because this antibiotic can interfere with your body's normal sun-screening mechanism, possibly resulting in a severe sunburn. If you have a known history of allergy to Terrastatin, you should avoid taking this drug or other drugs within this category such as Aureomycin, Terramycin, Rondomycin, Doxycyline, Demeclocycline, and Minocycline.

Possible Side Effects

Nystatin, when given by mouth, is not absorbed into the blood system. For this reason, there are few side effects associated with Nystatin in this combination.

As with other antibiotics, the common side effects of Terrastatin are stomach upset, nausea, vomiting, diarrhea, and rash. Less common side effects include hairy tongue and itching and irritation of the anal and/or vaginal region. If these symptoms appear, consult your physician immediately. Periodic physical examinations and laboratory tests should be given to patients who are receiving long-term Terrastatin treatment.

Possible Adverse Drug Effects

Loss of appetite, peeling of the skin, sensitivity to the sun, fever, chills, anemia, possible brown spotting of the skin, decrease in kidney function, damage to the liver.

Drug Interactions

Terrastatin (a bacteriostatic drug) may interfere with the action of bactericidal agents such as Penicillin. It is not advisable to take both together.

Don't take multivitamin products containing minerals at the same time as Terrastatin, or you will reduce the antibiotic's effectiveness. Space the taking of the two medicines at least 2 hours apart.

If you are receiving anticoagulants (blood-thinning agents), consult your doctor, since Terrastatin will interfere with this form of therapy. An adjustment in the anticoagulant dosage may be required.

Food Interactions

The antibacterial effect of Terrastatin may be neutralized if taken with food, some dairy products (such as milk or cheese), or antacids.

Usual Dose

Adult: 1 to 2 capsules 4 times per day.

Child (age 9 and over): 10 to 20 milligrams per pound of body weight per day in divided doses taken 1 hour before or 2 hours after meals.

Child (up to age 8): not recommended, since Terrastatin has been shown to produce serious discoloration of the permanent teeth.

Special Information

Like other Tetracyclines, this drug is always dated. Do not take outdated Terrastatin under any circumstances. Its decomposition produces a highly toxic substance which can cause serious kidney damage.

Generic Name

Tetracycline Hydrochloride

Brand Names

Achromycin V	SK-Tetracycline
Cycline-250	Sumycin
Cyclopar	Tetra-C
Deltamycin	Tetracap
Nor-Tet	Tetracyn
Panmycin	Tetralan
Retet	Tetram
Robitet	

(Also available in generic form)

Type of Drug

Broad-spectrum antibiotic effective against gram-positive and gram-negative organisms.

Prescribed for

Bacterial infections such as gonorrhea, infections of the mouth, gums, teeth, Rocky Mountain spotted fever and other fevers caused by ticks and lice from a variety of carriers, urinary tract infections, and respiratory system infections such as pneumonia and bronchitis.

These diseases are produced by gram-positive and gram-negative organisms such as diplococci, staphylococci, streptococci, gonococci, *E. coli,* and *Shigella.*

Tetracycline has also been successfully used to treat some skin infections, but it is not considered the first-choice antibiotic for the treatment of general skin infections or wounds.

General Information

Tetracycline Hydrochloride works by interfering with the normal growth cycle of the invading bacteria, preventing them from reproducing and thus allowing the body's normal defenses to fight off the infection. This process is referred to as bacteriostatic action. Tetracycline Hydrochloride has also been used along with other medicines to treat amoebic infections of the intestinal tract, known as amoebic dysentery. It is also prescribed for diseases caused by ticks, fleas, and lice.

Tetracycline Hydrochloride has been successfully used for the treatment of adolescent acne, in small doses over a long period of time. Adverse effects or toxicity in this type of therapy are almost unheard of.

Since the action of this antibiotic depends on its concentration within the invading bacteria, it is imperative that you completely follow the doctor's directions. Another form of Tetracycline Hydrochloride is Oxytetracycline (Terramycin) which is given in the same dose and has the same effects as Tetracycline Hydrochloride.

Cautions and Warnings

You should not use Tetracycline Hydrochloride if you are pregnant, especially during the last half of pregnancy or when breast-feeding, when the child's bones and teeth are being formed. Tetracycline Hydrochloride when used in children has been shown to interfere with the development of the long bones and may retard growth. Exceptions would be when Tetracycline Hydrochloride is the only effective antibiotic available and all risk factors have been made known to the patient.

Tetracycline Hydrochloride should not be given to people with known liver disease or kidney or urine excretion problems. You should avoid taking high doses of Tetracycline Hydrochloride or undergoing extended Tetracycline Hydrochloride therapy if you will be exposed to sunlight for a long period because this antibiotic can interfere with your body's normal sun-screening mechanism, possibly causing a severe sunburn. If you have a known history of allergy to Tetracycline Hydrochloride you should avoid taking this drug or other drugs within this category such as Aureomycin, Terramycin, Rondomycin, Doxycycline, Demeclocycline, and Minocycline.

Possible Side Effects

As with other antibiotics, the common side effects of Tetracycline Hydrochloride are stomach upset, nausea, vomiting, diarrhea, and rash. Less common side effects include hairy tongue and itching and irritation of the anal and/or vaginal region. If these symptoms appear, consult your physician immediately. Periodic physical examinations and laboratory

ests should be given to patients who are on long-term
Tetracycline Hydrochloride.

Possible Adverse Drug Effects

Loss of appetite, peeling of the skin, sensitivity to the sun,
fever, chills, anemia, possible brown spotting of the skin,
decrease in kidney function, damage to the liver.

Drug Interactions

Tetracycline Hydrochloride (a bacteriostatic drug) may interfere with the action of bactericidal agents such as Penicillin.
It is not advisable to take both during the same course of
therapy.

Don't take multivitamin products containing minerals at
the same time as Tetracycline Hydrochloride, or you may
reduce the antibiotic's effectiveness. Space the taking of
these two medicines at least 2 hours apart.

People receiving anticoagulation therapy (blood-thinning
agents) should consult their doctor, since Tetracycline Hydrochloride will interfere with this form of therapy. An adjustment in the anticoagulant dosage may be required.

Food Interactions

Take on an empty stomach 1 hour before or 2 hours after
meals and with 8 ounces of water. The antibacterial effect of
Tetracycline Hydrochloride may be neutralized when taken
with food, some dairy products (such as milk or cheese), or
antacids.

Usual Dose

Adult: 250-500 milligrams 4 times per day.
Child (age 9 and over): 50 to 100 milligrams 4 times per
day.
Child (up to age 8): should avoid Tetracycline Hydrochloride, as it has been shown to produce serious discoloration
of the permanent teeth.

Special Information

Do not take after the expiration date on the label. The decomposition of Tetracycline Hydrochloride produces a highly toxic
substance which can cause serious kidney damage.

Generic Name

Theophylline

Brand Names

Accurbron	Lixolin
Aerolate	Quibron-T
Aquaphyllin	Slo-Phyllin
Asmalix	Somophyllin-T
Bronkodyl	Theoclear
Elixicon	Theolair
Elixomin	Theolix
Elixophyllin	Theolixir
Lanophyllin	Theophyl
Liquophylline	Theostat
Timed-Release Products:	
Aerolate Capsules	Theobid Duracaps
Broncodyl S-R	Theobid Jr. Duracaps
Constant-T	Theobron SR
Duraphyl	Theoclear L.A. Cenules
Elixophyllin SR	Theo-Dur
LāBID	Theo-Dur Sprinkle
Lodrane	Theolain-SR
Quibron-T/SR Dividose	Theophyl-SR
Respbid	Theospan-SR
Slo-Bid Gyrocaps	Theo-Time
Slo-Phyllin Gyrocaps	Theo-24
Somophyllin-CRT	Theovent
Sustaire	Uniphyl

(Also available in generic form)

Type of Drug

Xanthine bronchodilator.

Prescribed for

Relief of bronchial asthma and spasms of bronchial muscle associated with emphysema, bronchitis, and other diseases

General Information

Theophylline is one of several drugs known as xanthine

derivatives which are the mainstay of therapy for bronchial asthma and similar diseases. Other members of this group are Aminophylline, Dyphylline, and Oxtriphylline. Although the dosage for each of these drugs is different, they all work by relaxing bronchial muscles and helping reverse spasms in these muscles.

Timed-release products allow Theophylline to act continually throughout the day. This usually allows you to decrease the total number of different doses to be taken during a 24-hour period.

Theophylline, or another xanthine, can be found combined in almost 100 prescription or nonprescription drugs.

Cautions and Warnings

Do not use this drug if you are allergic or sensitive to it or to any related drug, such as Aminophylline. If you have a stomach ulcer or heart disease, you should use this drug with caution.

If you are pregnant or think that you may be pregnant you should carefully discuss the use of this drug with your doctor, since Theophylline may induce an adverse effect in the unborn child. Theophylline may cause a rapid heartbeat, irritability, vomiting, or breathing problems in the unborn and nursing child if too much is used by the mother.

Possible Side Effects

Possible side effects from Theophylline or other xanthine derivatives are nausea, vomiting, stomach pain, diarrhea, irritability, restlessness, difficulty sleeping, excitability, muscle twitching or spasms, heart palpitations, other unusual heart rates, low blood pressure, rapid breathing, and local irritation (particularly if a suppository is used).

Possible Adverse Drug Effects

Infrequent: vomiting blood, fever, headache, dehydration.

Drug Interactions

Taking Theophylline at the same time as another xanthine derivative may increase side effects. Don't do it except under the direct care of a doctor.

Theophylline is often given in combination with a stimulant drug such as Ephedrine. Such combinations can cause excessive stimulation and should be used only as specifically directed by your doctor.

Reports have indicated that combining Erythromycin, Flu vaccine, Allopurinol, Cimetidine, and Theophylline will give you higher blood levels of Theophylline. Remember that higher blood levels mean the possibility of more side effects. Smoking cigarettes or marijuana makes Theophylline less effective.

Food Interactions

Take on an empty stomach, at least 1 hour before or 2 hours after meals; but occasional mild stomach upset can be minimized by taking the dose with some food (note that if you do this, a reduced amount of drug will be absorbed into your bloodstream).

The way Theophylline acts in your body may be influenced by your diet. Charcoal-broiled beef, for example, may cause the amount of Theophylline that is being eliminated in the urine to increase. Therefore you may experience a decreased effect of the drug. This is also true for people with a diet low in carbohydrates and high in protein or for people who smoke.

Caffeine (also a xanthine derivative) may add to the side effects of Theophylline. It is recommended that you avoid large amounts of caffeine-containing foods such as coffee, tea, cocoa, cola, or chocolate.

Usual Dose

Adult: 100 to 200 milligrams every 6 hours.

Child: 50 to 100 milligrams every 6 hours. On the basis of body weight, 1 to 2.5 milligrams per pound every 6 hours.

Timed-release products are usually taken 1 to 3 times per day depending on your response.

The best dose of Theophylline is tailored to your needs and the severity of your disease: it is the lowest dose that will produce maximum control of your symptoms.

Overdosage

The first symptoms are loss of appetite, nausea, vomiting, difficulty sleeping, and restlessness, followed by unusual behavior patterns, frequent vomiting, and extreme thirst, with delirium, convulsions, very high temperature, and collapse. These serious toxic symptoms are rarely experienced after overdose by mouth, which produces loss of appetite, nausea, vomiting, and stimulation. The overdosed patient should be taken to a hospital emergency room where proper treatment can be given. ALWAYS bring the medicine bottle.

Generic Name

Thioguanine

Type of Drug

Antimetabolite, antineoplastic.

Prescribed for

Treatment of leukemias.

General Information

Thioguanine is a member of the antimetabolite group of drugs used to treat neoplastic diseases. These drugs work by interfering with the metabolism of the cancerous cells. In doing so, they disrupt the cell reproduction cycle of the disease and slow its progress.

Cautions and Warnings

Blood counts should be taken once a week while on Thioguanine to avoid excessive lowering of white-cell counts. It should be used with extreme care by pregnant women (and then only after the first 3 months of pregnancy) and patients with kidney or liver disease. Nursing mothers should use an alternate feeding method.

Possible Side Effects

Nausea, vomiting, loss of appetite, stomach irritation or pains.

Usual Dose

1 to 1.5 milligrams per pound of body weight per day given in a single dose; adjusted to patient's response.

Overdosage

Overdosage with Thioguanine leads to an excessive drop in white-blood-cell counts. In case of overdosage, bring the patient to a hospital emergency room immediately. ALWAYS bring the medicine bottle.

Special Information

Due to the nature of the disease treated with this drug, it is absolutely essential that you remain in close contact with the doctor providing your treatment, to obtain maximum benefit with minimum side effect.

Contact your doctor if you experience swelling of the feet, joint or stomach pain, sore throat, fever, chills, unusual bleeding, bruising, or yellow discoloration of skin.

Generic Name

Thioridazine Hydrochloride

Brand Names

Mellaril
Mellaril-S
Mellazine
Sk-Thioridazine

(Also available in generic form)

Type of Drug

Phenothiazine antipsychotic.

Prescribed for

Psychotic disorders, moderate to severe depression with anxiety, control of agitation or aggressiveness of disturbed children, alcohol withdrawal symptoms, intractable pain, and senility.

General Information

Thioridazine Hydrochloride and other members of the phenothiazine group act on a portion of the brain called the
hypothalamus. They affect parts of the hypothalamus that
control metabolism, body temperature, alertness, muscle tone,
hormone balance, and vomiting, and may be used to treat
problems related to any of these functions.

Cautions and Warnings

Thioridazine Hydrochloride should not be taken if you are
allergic to one of the drugs in the broad classification known
as phenothiazine drugs. Do not take Thioridazine Hydrochloride if you have any blood, liver, kidney, or heart disease,
very low blood pressure, or Parkinson's disease. This medication is a tranquilizer and can have a depressive effect,
especially during the first few days of therapy. Care should
be taken when performing activities requiring a high degree
of concentration, such as driving.

If you are taking this medication and become pregnant
contact your doctor immediately. Thioridazine Hydrochloride
when used by pregnant women has caused side effects in
newborns such as jaundice (yellowing of skin and eyes) and
twitching. These medications should be stopped 1 to 2 weeks
before expected delivery to avoid this. Thioridazine Hydrochloride has not been shown to cause problems during
breast-feeding.

This drug should be used with caution and under strict
supervision of your doctor if you have glaucoma, epilepsy,
ulcers, or difficulty passing urine.

Avoid insecticides and extreme exposure to heat, as this
drug can affect your body's temperature control center.

Possible Side Effects

Most common: drowsiness, especially during the first or second week of therapy. If the drowsiness becomes troublesome, contact your doctor.

Possible Adverse Drug Effects

Thioridazine Hydrochloride can cause jaundice (yellowing of
the whites of the eyes or skin), usually in 2 to 4 weeks. The
jaundice usually goes away when the drug is discontinued,
but there have been cases when it did not. If you notice this

effect or if you develop symptoms such as fever and generally not feeling well, contact your doctor immediately. Less frequent: changes in components of the blood including anemias, raised or lowered blood pressure, abnormal heart rates, heart attack, feeling faint or dizzy.

Phenothiazines can produce "extrapyramidal effects," such as spasm of the neck muscles, rolling back of the eyes, convulsions, difficulty in swallowing, and symptoms associated with Parkinson's disease. These effects look very serious but disappear after the drug has been withdrawn; however, symptoms of the face, tongue, and jaw may persist for as long as several years, especially in the elderly with a history of brain damage. If you experience extrapyramidal effects contact your doctor immediately.

Thioridazine Hydrochloride may cause an unusual increase in psychotic symptoms or may cause paranoid reactions, tiredness, lethargy, restlessness, hyperactivity, confusion at night, bizarre dreams, inability to sleep, depression, and euphoria. Other reactions are itching, swelling, unusual sensitivity to bright lights, red skin, and rash. There have been cases of breast enlargement, false positive pregnancy tests, changes in menstrual flow in females, and impotence and changes in sex drive in males, as well as stuffy nose, headache, nausea, vomiting, loss of appetite, change in body temperature, loss of facial color, excessive salivation, excessive perspiration, constipation, diarrhea, changes in urine and stool habits, worsening of glaucoma, blurred vision, weakening of eyelid muscles, spasms in bronchial and other muscles, increased appetite, fatigue, excessive thirst, and changes in the coloration of skin, particularly in exposed areas.

Drug Interactions

Thioridazine Hydrochloride should be taken with caution in combination with barbiturates, sleeping pills, narcotics, other tranquilizers, or any other medication which may produce a depressive effect. Avoid alcohol.

Food Interactions

Caffeine-containing foods, such as coffee, tea, cola drinks, or chocolate may counteract the effects of Thioridazine Hydrochloride.

Usual Dose

Adult: for treatment of psychosis, 50 to 100 milligrams per day at first, then 50 to 800 milligrams per day as required to control symptoms effectively without overly sedating the patient.

Child: 20 to 75 milligrams per day.

Overdosage

Symptoms are depression, extreme weakness, tiredness, desire to go to sleep, coma, lowered blood pressure, uncontrolled muscle spasms, agitation, restlessness, convulsions, fever, dry mouth, and abnormal heart rhythms. The patient should be taken to a hospital emergency room immediately. ALWAYS bring the medicine bottle.

Special Information

This drug may turn the color of your urine pink or reddish brown; this is normal and not a cause for worry.

Liquid concentrate may be diluted in water or fruit juices.

Generic Name

Thiothixene

Brand Name

Navane

Type of Drug

Thioxanthene antipsychotic.

Prescribed for

Psychotic disorders.

General Information

Thiothixene is one of many nonphenothiazine agents used in the treatment of psychosis. The drugs in this group are usually about equally effective when given in therapeutically equivalent doses. The major differences are in type and severity of side effects. Some patients may respond well to one and not at all to another: this variability is not easily explained and is thought to relate to inborn biochemical differences.

Cautions and Warnings

Thiothixene should not be used by patients who are allergic to it. Patients with blood, liver, kidney or heart disease, very low blood pressure, or Parkinson's disease should avoid this drug.

This drug may cause birth defects or interfere with your baby's development. It may decrease your chances to have a successful pregnancy. Check with your doctor before taking it if you are, or might be, pregnant. No breast-feeding problems have been seen.

Possible Side Effects

Most common: drowsiness, especially during the first or second week of therapy. If the drowsiness becomes troublesome, contact your doctor.

Possible Adverse Drug Effects

Thiothixene can cause jaundice (yellowing of the whites of the eyes or skin), usually in 2 to 4 weeks. The jaundice usually goes away when the drug is discontinued, but there have been cases when it did not. If you notice this effect or if you develop symptoms such as fever and generally do not feel well, contact your doctor immediately. Less frequent: changes in components of the blood including anemias, raised or lowered blood pressure, abnormal heartbeat, heart attack, feeling faint or dizzy.

Thioxanthene drugs can produce "extrapyramidal effects," such as spasms of the neck muscles, severe stiffness of the back muscles, rolling back of the eyes, convulsions, difficulty in swallowing, and symptoms associated with Parkinson's disease. These effects look very serious but disappear after the drug has been withdrawn; however, symptoms of the face, tongue, and jaw may persist for several years, especially in the elderly with a long history of brain damage. If you experience extrapyramidal effects contact your doctor immediately.

Thiothixene may cause an unusual increase in psychotic

symptoms or may cause paranoid reactions, tiredness, lethargy, restlessness, hyperactivity, confusion at night, bizarre dreams, inability to sleep, depression, or euphoria. Other reactions are itching, swelling, unusual sensitivity to bright lights, red skin, and rash. There have been cases of breast enlargement, false positive pregnancy tests, changes in menstrual flow in females, and impotence and changes in sex drive in males.

Thiothixene may also cause dry mouth, stuffy nose, headache, nausea, vomiting, loss of appetite, change in body temperature, loss of facial color, excessive salivation, excessive perspiration, constipation, diarrhea, changes in urine and stool habits, worsening of glaucoma, blurred vision, weakening of eyelid muscles, and spasms in bronchial and other muscles, as well as increased appetite, fatigue, excessive thirst, and changes in the coloration of skin, particularly in exposed areas.

Drug Interactions

Thiothixene should be taken with caution in combination with barbiturates, sleeping pills, narcotics, other tranquilizers, or any other medication which produces a depressive effect. Avoid alcohol.

Usual Dose

Adult and child (age 12 and over): 2 milligrams 3 times per day, to start. Dose is increased according to patient's need and may go to 60 milligrams per day.

Child (under age 12): not recommended.

Overdosage

Symptoms are depression, extreme weakness, tiredness, desire to go to sleep, coma, lowered blood pressure, uncontrolled muscle spasms, agitation, restlessness, convulsions, fever, dry mouth, and abnormal heart rhythms. The patient should be taken to a hospital emergency room immediately. ALWAYS bring the medicine bottle.

Generic Name

Thyroglobulin

Brand Name

Proloid

Type of Drug

Thyroid replacement.

Prescribed for

Replacement of thyroid hormone or low output of hormone from the thyroid gland.

General Information

Thyroglobulin is used to replace the normal output of the thyroid gland when it is unusually low. The drug is obtained from purified extract of frozen hog thyroid and is chemically standardized according to its iodine content. Thyroglobulin, or other forms of thyroid therapy, may be used for short periods in some people or for long periods in others. Some people take a thyroid replacement drug for their entire lives. It is important for your doctor to check periodically that you are receiving the correct dose. Occasionally a person's need for thyroid replacement changes, in which case, the dose should also be changed: your doctor can do this only by checking certain blood tests.

Thyroglobulin is one of several thyroid replacement products available. The major difference between these products is in effectiveness in treating certain phases of thyroid disease.

Cautions and Warnings

If you have hyperthyroid disease or high output of thyroid hormone you should not use Thyroglobulin. Symptoms of hyperthyroid disease include headache, nervousness, sweating, rapid heartbeat, chest pains, and other signs of central nervous system stimulation. If you have heart disease or high blood pressure, thyroid replacement therapy should not be used unless it is clearly indicated and supervised by your doctor. If you develop chest pains or other signs of heart disease while you are taking thyroid medication, contact your doctor immediately.

This drug has been found to be safe for use during pregnancy. Remember, you should check with your doctor before taking any drug if you are pregnant.

Possible Side Effects

Most common: palpitations of the heart, rapid heartbeat, abnormal heart rhythms, weight loss, chest pains, menstrual irregularity, shaking hands, headache, diarrhea, nervousness, inability to sleep, heat discomfort, and sweating. These symptoms may be controlled by adjusting the dose of the medication. If you are suffering from one or more side effects, you must contact your physician immediately so that the proper dose adjustment can be made.

Drug Interactions

Interaction of Thyroglobulin with Cholestyramine (Questran) can be avoided by spacing the two doses at least 4 hours apart.

Avoid over-the-counter products containing stimulant drugs, such as many drugs used to treat coughs, colds, or allergies, which will affect your heart and may cause symptoms of overdosage.

Thyroid replacement therapy may increase the effect of anticoagulant (blood-thinning) drugs such as Warfarin or Bishydroxycoumarin. Be sure you report this to your physician as it will be necessary to reduce the dose of your anticoagulant drug by approximately one-third at the beginning of thyroid therapy (to avoid hemorrhage). Further adjustments may be made later, after your doctor reviews your blood tests.

Diabetics may have to increase their dose of Insulin or oral antidiabetic drugs. Changes in dose must be made by a physician.

Usual Dose

Initial dose, 16 milligrams (¼ grain) per day, then increase at intervals of 1 to 2 weeks until response is satisfactory. Maintenance dose, 32 to 190 milligrams per day or even higher.

Overdosage

Symptoms are headache, irritability, nervousness, sweating, rapid heartbeat with unusual stomach rumbling and with or without cramps, chest pains, heart failure, and shock. The patient should be taken to a hospital emergency room immediately. ALWAYS bring the medicine bottle.

Generic Name

Thyroid Hormone

Brand Names

Armour Thyroid
S-P-T
Thyrar
Thyroid strong

(Also available in generic form)

Type of Drug

Thyroid replacement.

Prescribed for

Replacement of thyroid hormone or low output of hormone from the thyroid gland.

General Information

Thyroid Hormone is one of several thyroid replacement products available. The major difference between them is in effectiveness in treating certain phases of thyroid disease.

Other drugs, such as Methimazole (Tapazole) and Propylthiouracil (PTU) are given to people whose thyroid gland is overactive. Their effect on the thyroid gland is exactly the opposite of Thyroid Hormones. Check with your doctor if you are uncertain about why you have been given drugs which affect the thyroid gland.

Cautions and Warnings

If you have hyperthyroid disease or high output of thyroid hormone you should not use Thyroid Hormone. Symptoms of hyperthyroid disease include headache, nervousness, sweating, rapid heartbeat, chest pains, and other signs of central nervous system stimulation. If you have heart disease or high blood pressure, thyroid therapy should not be used unless it is clearly indicated and supervised by your physician. If you develop chest pains or other signs of heart disease while you are taking thyroid medication, contact your doctor immediately.

This drug has been found to be safe for use during pregnancy. Remember, you should check with your doctor before taking any drug if you are pregnant. Some of the hormone passes into breast milk. Consult your physician if you are lactating and must use this drug.

Possible Side Effects

Most common: palpitations of the heart, rapid heartbeat, abnormal heart rhythms, weight loss, chest pains, shaking hands, headache, diarrhea, nervousness, menstrual irregularity, inability to sleep, sweating, inability to stand heat. These symptoms may be controlled by adjusting the dose of the medication. If you are suffering from one or more side effects, you must contact your doctor immediately so that the proper dose adjustment can be made.

Drug Interactions

Interaction of Thyroid Hormone with Cholestyramine (Questran) can be avoided by spacing the two doses at least 4 hours apart.

Avoid over-the-counter products containing stimulant drugs, such as many drugs used to treat coughs, colds, or allergies, which will affect your heart and may cause symptoms of overdosage.

Thyroid replacement therapy may increase the affect of anticoagulant (blood-thinning) drugs such as Warfarin or Bishydroxycoumarin. Be sure you report this to your physician as it will be necessary to reduce the dose of your anticoagulant drug by approximately one-third at the beginning of thyroid therapy (to avoid hemorrhage). Further adjustments may be made later, after your doctor reviews your blood tests.

Diabetics may have to increase their dose of Insulin or oral antidiabetic drugs. Changes in dose must be made by a doctor.

Usual Dose

The dose is tailored to the individual.

Adult: Initial dose, 15 to 30 milligrams per day, depending on severity of disease; may be increased gradually to 195 milligrams per day.

Child: Initial dose, same as adult; but children may require greater maintenance doses because they are growing.

Take in 1 dose before breakfast.

Overdosage

Symptoms are headache, irritability, nervousness, sweating, rapid heartbeat with unusual stomach rumbling with or without cramps, chest pains, heart failure, and shock. The patient should be taken to a hospital emergency room immediately. ALWAYS bring the medicine bottle.

Generic Name

Timolol Maleate

Brand Name

Timoptic Eye Drops
Blocadren Tablets

Type of Drug

Beta-adrenergic blocking agent.

Prescribed for

High blood pressure; reducing the possibility of a second heart attack. Open angle glaucoma (increased fluid pressure inside the eye).

General Information

When applied directly to the eye, Timolol Maleate reduces fluid pressure inside the eye by reducing the production of eye fluids and increasing slightly the rate at which eye fluids leave the eye. Studies have shown Timolol Maleate to produce a greater reduction in eye fluid pressure than either Pilocarpine or Epinephrine.

Women who are pregnant or breast-feeding should not use this drug unless it is absolutely necessary. Timolol Maleate Eye Drops should not be used by people who cannot take oral beta-blocking drugs, such as Propranolol.

Recent studies have shown Timolol Maleate to be very effective for treating heart pain called angina. It has also been used to treat high blood pressure.

The most famous Timolol Maleate study was published in April 1981 in the prestigious *New England Journal of Medicine.* This study showed that people who had a heart attack and took 20 milligrams of Timolol Maleate per day by mouth had fewer additional heart attacks and fewer additional heart problems, and survived longer. The death rate in non-Timolol Maleate patients was 1.6 times that in the Timolol Maleate group. Other beta-adrenergic blockers currently available, Propranolol, Metoprolol, Atenolol, and Pindolol, may also have this effect on heart attack patients.

Cautions and Warnings

Timolol Maleate should be used with care if you have a history of asthma or upper respiratory disease, seasonal allergy, which may become worsened by the effects of this drug. Do not use Timolol Maleate if you are allergic to it.

This drug may cause birth defects or interfere with your baby's development. Check with your doctor before taking it if you are, or might be, pregnant. To date, Timolol Maleate has not been shown to cause birth defects or problems in breast-feeding infants.

Possible Side Effects

Timolol Maleate may decrease the heart rate, aggravate or worsen a condition of congestive heart failure, and may produce lowered blood pressure, tingling in the extremities, light-headedness, mental depression, inability to sleep, weakness, and tiredness. It can also produce visual disturbances, hallucinations, disorientation, and loss of short-term memory. People taking Timolol Maleate may experience nausea, vomiting, upset stomach, abdominal cramps and diarrhea, or constipation. If you are allergic to Timolol Maleate, you may show typical reactions associated with drug allergies including sore throat, fever, difficulty breathing, and various effects on the blood system. Timolol Maleate may induce spasm of muscles in the bronchi, which will aggravate any existing asthma or respiratory disease.

Possible Adverse Drug Effects

Occasionally, people taking Timolol Maleate may experience emotional instability, become detached, or show unusual personality change. Timolol Maleate may cause adverse effects on the blood system.

Drug Interactions

Timolol Maleate will interact with any psychotropic drug, including the MAO inhibitors, which stimulates one of the segments of the central nervous system. Since this information is not often available to doctors, you should discuss this potential problem with your doctor if you are taking any psychotropic or psychiatric drug.

Timolol Maleate may cause increased effectiveness of Insulin or oral antidiabetic drugs. If you are diabetic, discuss the situation with your doctor. A reduction in dosage of your antidiabetic drug may be required.

Timolol Maleate may reduce the effectiveness of Digitalis on your heart. Any dose of Digitalis will have to be altered if you are taking Timolol Maleate. If you are taking Digitalis for a purpose other than heart failure, the effectiveness of the Digitalis may be increased by Timolol Maleate, and the dose of Digitalis reduced.

Timolol Maleate may interact with other drugs to cause lowering of blood pressure. This interaction often has positive effects in the treatment of patients with high blood pressure.

Do not self-medicate with over-the-counter drugs for colds, coughs, or allergy which may contain stimulants that will aggravate certain types of heart disease and high blood pressure, or other ingredients that may antagonize the effects of Timolol Maleate. Check with your doctor or pharmacist before taking any over-the-counter medication.

Food Interactions

Take Timolol Maleate tablets before meals for maximum effect. The eye drops may be used at any time.

Usual Dose

Eyedrops: One drop twice a day.
Tablets: 20 to 60 milligrams per day divided into 2 doses.

Overdosage

Symptoms are slowed heart rate, heart failure, lowered blood pressure, and spasms of the bronchial muscles which make it difficult to breathe. The patient should be taken to a hospital emergency room where proper therapy can be given. ALWAYS bring the medicine bottle with you.

Special Information

There have been reports of serious effects when Timolol Maleate is stopped abruptly. The dose should be lowered gradually over a period of two weeks.

If you are using Timolol Maleate Eye Drops, press your finger lightly just below the eye for one minute following the instillation of the eyedrops.

Generic Name

Tocainide Hydrochloride

Brand Name

Tonocard

Type of Drug

Antiarrhythmic.

Prescribed for

Abnormal heart rhythms.

General Information

First available in late 1984, Tocainide Hydrochloride is the first chemical derivative of Lidocaine, one of the most widely used injectable antiarrhythmic drugs, that can be taken orally. It affects the speed with which nerve impulses are carried through the heart's ventricle. Tocainide Hydrochloride affects different areas of your heart than other widely used oral antiarrrhythmic drugs like Quinidine Sulfate, Procainamide Hydrochloride, and Disopyramide. Unlike those drugs, it does not interact negatively with Digoxin. Tocainide Hydrochloride is usually prescribed for people who have been given Lidocaine in the hospital and who require some form of oral follow-up treatment.

Cautions and Warnings

This drug should not be used by people who are allergic to Tocainide Hydrochloride, Lidocaine, or to local anesthetics. Some people using Tocainide Hydrochloride may develop respiratory difficulties, including fluid buildup in the lungs, pneumonia, and irritation of the lungs. Report any cough or difficulty breathing to your doctor immediately. Tocainide Hydrochloride should not be used by people with heart failure, since the drug can actually worsen that condition.

Animal studies employing doses 1 to 4 times larger than the human equivalent reveal no adverse effect on the developing fetus, but they did result in an unusually high rate of stillbirth and spontaneous abortion. This drug should be avoided by pregnant women or women who may become pregnant while using it. In those situations where its use is essential, the potential risks must be carefully weighed against any benefits. Nursing mothers must be aware of any possible drug effect on their infants while taking this medicine, since it is not known if the active ingredients in it pass into breast milk. Consider an alternative infant feeding method if you must take Tocainide Hydrochloride to control an abnormal heart rhythm.

Possible Side Effects

Nausea, vomiting, tingling in the hands or feet, light-headedness, dizziness, fainting, giddiness, tremors, confusion, disorientation, hallucinations, restlessness, blurred or double vision, visual disturbances, poor muscle coordination, anxiety, low blood pressure, slowing of the heart rate, heart palpitations, chest pains, cold sweats, headache, drowsiness, and lethargy.

Possible Adverse Drug Effects

Ringing or buzzing in the ears, rolling the eyes, loss of

appetite, diarrhea, rash, unusual feelings of hot or cold, joint inflammation and pain, and muscle aches. Other adverse reactions may include seizures, depression, psychosis, mental changes, alterations of taste (including a metallic taste) and/or smell, agitation, difficulty concentrating, memory loss, slurred speech, difficulty sleeping, nightmares, unusual thirst, weakness, upset stomach or abdominal pains and discomfort, difficulty swallowing, breathing difficulty (see Cautions and Warnings), changes in white-blood-cell counts, anemia, urinary difficulty, hair loss, cold hands or feet, leg pains after minor exercise, dry mouth, earache, fever, hiccups, aching, a feeling of ill health, muscle twitches or spasms, neck or shoulder pains, facial flushing or pallor, and yawning.

Drug Interactions

The combination of Tocainide Hydrochloride and Metoprolol, prescribed for high blood pressure, can cause too rapid a drop in blood pressure and slowing of the heart.

Unlike other oral antiarrhythmic drugs, Tocainide Hydrochloride does not interact with Digoxin. However, it is likely that the wide usage this drug will receive over the next several years will disclose other, previously unknown, interactions.

Food Interactions

You may take Tocainide Hydrochloride with food or meals if it causes upset stomach, nausea, or vomiting when taken alone.

Usual Dose

Adult: 1200 to 1800 milligrams per day, in divided doses.
Elderly and people with kidney or liver disease: less than 1200 milligrams per day.

Overdosage

There are no reports of overdosage. However, the symptoms can be expected to be exaggerated versions of Tocainide Hydrochloride side effects or adverse drug effects. Patients taking an overdose of this drug must be made to vomit with Syrup of Ipecac (available at any pharmacy) to remove any remaining drug from the stomach. Call your doctor or a

Poison Control Center before doing this. If you must go to a hospital emergency room, ALWAYS bring the medicine bottle.

Special Information

Be sure to report any side effects to your doctor. Most of them are minor or will respond to minor dosage adjustments. Especially important symptoms are difficulty breathing, coughing, unusual or easy bruising, and frequent infections.

Do not take more or less of this drug than prescribed.

Generic Name

Tolazamide

Brand Name

Tolinase

(Also available in generic form)

Type of Drug

Oral antidiabetic.

Prescribed for

Diabetes mellitus (sugar in the urine).

General Information

Tolazamide is one of several oral antidiabetic drugs that work by stimulating the production and release of Insulin from the pancreas. The primary difference between the oral antidiabetic drugs lies in their duration of action. Because these drugs do not lower blood sugar directly, they require some function of pancreas cells.

Cautions and Warnings

Mild stress such as infection, minor surgery, or emotional upset reduces the effectiveness of Tolazamide. Remember that while you are taking this drug you should be under your doctor's continuous care.

Tolazamide is an aide to, not a substitute for, a diet. Diet remains of primary importance in the treatment of your diabetes. Follow the diet plan your doctor has prescribed for you.

Tolazamide and similar drugs are not oral Insulin, nor are they a substitute for Insulin. They do not lower blood sugar by themselves.

The treatment of diabetes is your responsibility. You should follow all instructions about diet, body weight, exercise, personal hygiene, and all measures to avoid infection. If you are not feeling well, or if you have symptoms such as itching, rash, yellowing of the skin or eyes, abnormally light-colored stools, a low-grade fever, sore throat, or diarrhea—contact your doctor immediately.

This drug should not be used if you have serious liver, kidney, or endocrine disease.

This drug may cause birth defects or interfere with your baby's development. Check with your doctor before taking it if you are, or might be, pregnant. Nursing mothers should use an alternative feeding method.

Possible Side Effects

Common: loss of appetite, nausea, vomiting, stomach upset. At times you may experience weakness or tingling in the hands and feet. These effects can be eliminated by reducing the daily dose of Tolazamide or, if necessary, by switching to a different oral antidiabetic drug. This decision must be made by your doctor.

Possible Adverse Drug Effects

Tolazamide may produce abnormally low levels of blood sugar when too much is taken for your immediate requirements. (Other factors which may cause lowering of blood sugar are liver or kidney disease, malnutrition, age, drinking alcohol, and diseases of the glands.)

Tolazamide may cause a yellowing of the whites of the eyes or skin, itching, rash, or changes in the results of laboratory tests made by your doctor. Usually these reactions will disappear in time. If they persist, you should contact your doctor.

Drug Interactions

Thiazide diuretics may call for a higher dose of Tolazamide, while Insulin, sulfa drugs, Oxyphenbutazone, Phenylbutazone, Aspirin and other salicylates, Probenecid, Dicoumarol, Bishydroxycoumarin, Warfarin, Phenyramidol, and MAO inhibitor drugs prolong and enhance the action of Tolazamide, possibly requiring dose reduction.

Interaction with alcoholic beverages will cause flushing of the face and body, throbbing pain in the head and neck, difficult breathing, nausea, vomiting, sweating, thirst, chest pains, palpitations, lowered blood pressure, weakness, dizziness, blurred vision, and confusion. If you experience these reactions, contact your doctor immediately.

Because of the stimulant ingredients in many over-the-counter drug products for the relief of coughs, colds, and allergies, avoid them unless your doctor advises otherwise.

Usual Dose

Moderate diabetes, 100 to 250 milligrams daily. Severe diabetes, 500 to 1000 milligrams daily.

Overdosage

A mild overdose of Tolazamide lowers the blood sugar, which can be treated by consuming sugar in such forms as candy, orange juice, or glucose tablets. A patient with a more serious overdose should be taken to a hospital emergency room immediately. ALWAYS bring the medicine bottle.

Generic Name

Tolbutamide

Brand Name

Orinase

(Also available in generic form)

Type of Drug

Oral antidiabetic.

Prescribed for

Diabetes mellitus (sugar in the urine).

General Information

Tolbutamide is one of several oral antidiabetic drugs that work by stimulating the production and release of Insulin from the pancreas. The primary difference between the oral antidiabetic drugs lies in their duration of action. Because they do not lower blood sugar directly, they require some function of pancreas cells.

Cautions and Warnings

Mild stress such as infection, minor surgery, or emotional upset reduces the effectiveness of Tolbutamide. Remember that while taking this drug you should be under your doctor's continuous care.

Tolbutamide is an aide to, not a substitute for, a diet. Diet remains of primary importance in the treatment of your diabetes. Follow the diet plan your doctor has prescribed for you.

Tolbutamide and similar drugs are not oral Insulin, nor are they a substitute for Insulin. They do not lower blood sugar by themselves.

The treatment of diabetes is your responsibility. You should follow all instructions about diet, body weight, exercise, personal hygiene, and all measures to avoid infection. If you are not feeling well, or if you have symptoms such as itching, rash, yellowing of the skin or eyes, abnormally light-colored stools, a low-grade fever, sore throat, or diarrhea—contact your doctor immediately.

This drug should be used with caution and under strict supervision of your doctor if you have glaucoma, epilepsy, ulcers, or difficulty passing urine. Avoid insecticides and extreme exposure to heat.

This drug may cause birth defects or interfere with your baby's development. Check with your doctor before taking it if you are, or might be, pregnant. Nursing mothers should use an alternative feeding method.

Possible Side Effects

Common: loss of appetite, nausea, vomiting, stomach upset. At times you may experience weakness or tingling in the hands and feet. These effects can be eliminated by reducing the daily dose of Tolbutamide or, if necessary, by switching to a different oral antidiabetic drug. This decision must be made by your doctor.

Possible Adverse Drug Effects

Tolbutamide may produce abnormally low levels of blood sugar when too much is taken for your immediate requirements. (Other factors which may cause lowering of blood sugar are liver or kidney disease, malnutrition, age, drinking alcohol, and diseases of the glands.)

Tolbutamide may cause a yellowing of the whites of the eyes or skin, itching, rash, or changes in the results of laboratory tests made by your doctor. Usually these reactions will disappear in time. If they persist you should contact your doctor.

Drug Interactions

Thiazide diuretics may call for a higher dose of Tolbutamide, while Insulin, sulfa drugs, Oxyphenbutazone, Phenylbutazone, Aspirin and other salicylates, Probenecid, Dicoumarol, Bishydroxycoumarin, Warfarin, Phenyramidol, and MAO inhibitor drugs prolong and enhance the action of Tolbutamide, possibly requiring dose reduction.

Interaction with alcoholic beverages will cause flushing of the face and body, throbbing pain in the head and neck, difficult breathing, nausea, vomiting, sweating, thirst, chest pains, palpitations, lowered blood pressure, weakness, dizziness, blurred vision, and confusion. If you experience these reactions contact your doctor immediately.

Because of the stimulant ingredients in many over-the-counter drug products for the relief of coughs, colds, and allergies, avoid them unless your doctor advises otherwise.

Usual Dose

Begin with 1 to 2 grams per day; then increase or decrease according to patient's response. Maintenance dose, 250 milligrams to 2 (or, rarely, 3) grams per day.

Overdosage

A mild overdose of Tolbutamide lowers the blood sugar, which can be treated by consuming sugar in such forms as candy, orange juice, or glucose tablets. A patient with a more serious overdose should be taken to a hospital emergency room immediately. ALWAYS bring the medicine bottle.

Generic Name

Tolmetin Sodium

Brand Name

Tolectin
Tolectin DS

Type of Drug

Nonsteroid anti-inflammatory.

Prescribed for

Relief of pain and inflammation of joints and muscles; arthritis.

General Information

Tolmetin Sodium is one of several new drugs used to treat various types of arthritis. These drugs reduce inflammation and share side effects, the most common of which is possible formation of ulcers and upset stomach. The drugs are roughly comparable to Aspirin in controlling the symptoms of arthritis, and are used by some people who cannot tolerate Aspirin.

Cautions and Warnings

Do not take Tolmetin Sodium if you are allergic or sensitive to this drug, Aspirin, or other nonsteroid anti-inflammatory drugs. Tolmetin Sodium may cause stomach ulcers.

This drug may cause birth defects or interfere with your baby's development. Check with your doctor before taking it if you are, or might be, pregnant.

Possible Side Effects

Stomach upset, blurred vision, darkening of stool, changes in color vision, rash, weight gain, retention of fluids.

Possible Adverse Drug Effects

Most frequent: stomach upset, dizziness, headache, drowsiness, ringing in the ears. Others: heartburn, nausea, vomiting, bloating, gas in the stomach, stomach pain, diarrhea, constipation, dark stool, nervousness, insomnia, depression, confusion, tremor, lack of appetite, fatigue, itching, rash, double vision, abnormal heart rhythm, anemia or other changes in the composition of the blood, changes in liver function, loss of hair, tingling in the hands and feet, fever, breast enlargement, lowered blood sugar, occasional effects on the kidneys. If symptoms appear, stop taking the medicine and see your doctor immediately.

Drug Interactions

Tolmetin Sodium increases the action of Phenytoin, sulfa drugs, drugs used to control diabetes, and drugs used to thin the blood. If you are taking one of these drugs, be sure you discuss it with your doctor, who will probably change the dose of the drug whose action is increased.

Avoid taking Aspirin while taking Tolmetin Sodium.

Food Interactions

If upset stomach occurs, take with food or milk.

Usual Dose

Adult: 400 milligrams 3 times per day, to start. Dosage must then be adjusted to individual need. Do not take more than 2000 milligrams per day.

Child (age 2 and over): 9 milligrams per pound of body weight given in divided doses 3 to 4 times per day, to start. Adjust dose to individual need. Do not give more than 13.5 milligrams per pound of body weight to a child.

Child (under age 2): not recommended.

Generic Name

Trazodone

Brand Name

Desyrel

Type of Drug

Antidepressant.

Prescribed for

Depression with or without anxiety.

General Information

Trazodone is as effective in treating the symptoms of depression as are other antidepressant tablets. However, it is chemically different from the other antidepressants and may be less likely to cause side effects.

Cautions and Warnings

Do not use Trazodone if you are allergic to it. It is not recommended during the initial stages of recovery from a heart attack. People with a previous history of heart disease should not use Trazodone because it may cause abnormal heart rhythms.

This drug should not be taken by women who may become pregnant while using it or by pregnant or nursing mothers, since this drug may pass into breast milk. In situations where it is deemed essential, the potential risk of the drug must be carefully weighed against any benefit it might produce.

Possible Side Effects

Most common: upset stomach, constipation, abdominal pains, a bad taste in your mouth, nausea, vomiting, diarrhea, palpitations, rapid heartbeat, rashes, swelling of the extremities, elevated or depressed blood pressure, difficulty breathing, dizziness, anger, hostility, nightmares and/or vivid dreams, confusion, disorientation, loss of memory or concentration, drowsiness, fatigue, light-headedness, difficulty sleeping, nervousness, excitement, headache, loss of coordination, tingling in the hands or feet, tremor of the hands or arms, ringing or buzzing in the ears, blurred vision, red, tired, and itchy eyes, stuffy nose or sinuses, loss of sex drive, muscle aches and pains, loss of appetite, changes in body weight (up or down), sweating, clamminess, a feeling of ill health.

Possible Adverse Drug Effects

Less frequent reactions to Trazodone include drug allergy, chest pain, heart attack, delusions, hallucinations, agitation, difficulty speaking, restlessness, numbness, weakness, seizures, increased sex drive, a sustained and painful male erection, reverse ejaculation, impotence, missed or early menstrual periods, stomach gas, increased salivation, anemia, reduced levels of some white blood cells, muscle twitches, blood in the urine, reduced urine flow, increased urinary frequency, incresed appetite. Trazodone may cause elevations in levels of body enzymes used to measure liver function.

Drug Interactions

Trazodone, when taken together with Digoxin or Phenytoin, may increase the amount of those drugs in your blood, leading to a greater possibility of drug side effects.

Trazodone may make you more sensitive to drugs that work by depressing the nervous system, including sedatives, tranquilizers, and alcohol.

This medicine may cause a slight reduction in blood pressure. If you are taking medicine for high blood pressure and begin to take Trazodone, you may find that a minor reduction in the dosage of your blood-pressure medicine is required. On the other hand, the action of Clonidine, a high-blood-pressure medicine, can be inhibited by Trazodone. These interactions must be evaluated by your doctor. Do not change any blood-pressure medicines on your own.

Little is known about the potential interaction between Trazodone and the MAO inhibitor drugs. With most antidepressants, it is suggested that one drug be discontinued for 2 weeks before the other is begun. If these drugs are used together, they should be used cautiously.

Food Interactions

Take each dose of Trazodone with a meal or snack to increase the amount of drug absorbed into your bloodstream and to minimize the possibility of upset stomach, dizziness, or light-headedness. For many people, symptoms will be relieved as soon as 2 weeks after starting the medicine, but 4 weeks or more may be required to achieve maximum benefit.

Usual Dose

Adult: 150 milligrams per day with food, to start. This dose may be increased by 50 milligrams per day every 3 to 4 days, to a maximum of 400 milligrams per day. Severely depressed people may be given as much as 600 milligrams per day.

Overdosage

Drowsiness and vomiting are the most frequent signs of Trazodone overdose. The other signs are simply more severe side-effects symptoms, especially those affecting the heart and mood. Fever may develop at first, but body temperature will drop below normal as time passes. ALL victims of antidepressant overdosage, especially children, must be taken to a hospital for treatment as quickly as possible. ALWAYS bring the medicine bottle with you.

Special Information

Use care while driving or doing anything else requiring concentration or alertness, and avoid alcohol or any other depressant while taking Trazodone.

Call your doctor if any side effects develop, especially blood in the urine, dizziness, or light-headedness. Trazodone may cause dry mouth, irregular heartbeat, nausea, vomiting, or difficulty breathing. Call your doctor if these symptoms become severe.

Generic Name

Tretinoin Cream/Gel/Liquid

Other Names

Retinoic Acid
Vitamin A Acid

Brand Name

Retin-A

Type of Drug

Antiacne.

Prescribed for

The early stages of acne. This drug is usually not effective in treating severe acne.

General Information

This drug works by acting as an irritant to the skin, causing the skin to peel, which is helpful in acne treatment. Because it is an irritant, any other skin irritant, such as extreme weather or wind, cosmetics, and some soaps, can cause severe irritation. Excessive application of Tretinoin will cause more peeling and irritation but will not give better results.

Cautions and Warnings

Do not use this drug if you are allergic to it or any of its components. This drug may increase the skin-cancer-causing effects of ultraviolet light. Therefore, people using this drug must avoid exposure to the sun. If you can't avoid exposure to the sun, use sunscreen products and protective covering. Do not apply to areas around the eyes, corner of the mouth, or sides of the nose.

This drug has been found to be safe for use during pregnancy. Remember, you should check with your doctor before taking any drug if you are pregnant.

Possible Side Effects

Redness, swelling, blistering, or formation of crusts on the

skin near the areas to which the drug has been applied.
Overcoloration of the skin, greater sensitivity to the sun.

All side effects disappear after the drug has been stopped.

Drug Interactions

Other skin irritants will cause excessive sensitivity, irritation,
and side effects. Among the substances that cause this interaction are medication and abrasive soaps or skin cleansers,
cosmetics or other creams, ointments, etc., with a severe
drying effect, products with a high alcohol, astringent, spice,
or lime content.

Usual Dose

Apply a small amount to the affected area when you go to
bed, and after thoroughly cleansing the area.

Special Information

You may experience an increase in acne lesions during the
first couple of weeks of treatment, because the drug is acting
on deeper lesions which you had not seen before. This is
beneficial and is not a reason to stop using the drug.

Results should be seen in 2 to 6 weeks.

Keep this drug away from your eyes, nose, mouth, and
mucous membranes.

Avoid exposure to sunlight or sunlamp.

You may feel warmth and slight stinging when you apply
Tretinoin. If you develop an excessive skin reaction or are
uncomfortable, stop using this product for a short time.

Generic Name

Triamcinolone Acetonide Ointment/Cream/Lotion/Aerosol

Brand Names

Aristocort	Kenalog-H
Aristocort A	Triacet
Flutex	Triderm
Kenac	Trymex
Kenalog	

(Also available in generic form)

Type of Drug

Topical corticosteroid.

Prescribed for

Relief of inflammation in a local area, itching, or other dermatological (skin) problems.

General Information

Triamcinolone Acetonide is used to relieve the symptom of any itching, rash, or inflammation of the skin. It does not treat the underlying cause of the skin problem, only the symptoms. It exerts this effect by interfering with natural body mechanisms that produced the rash, itching, etc., in the first place. If you use this drug without finding the cause of the problem, the condition may return after you stop using the drug. Triamcinolone Acetonide should not be used without your doctor's consent because it could cover an important reaction, one that may be valuable to him in treating you.

Cautions and Warnings

Triamcinolone Acetonide should not be used if you have viral diseases of the skin (herpes), fungal infections of the skin (athlete's foot), or tuberculosis of the skin, nor should it be used in the ear if the eardrum has been perforated. People with a history of allergies to any of the components

the ointment, cream, lotion, or aerosol should not use this
drug.

This drug has been found to be safe for use during pregnancy. Remember, you should check with your doctor before taking any drug if you are pregnant.

Possible Side Effects

After topically applying this drug, some people may experience burning sensations, itching, irritation, dryness, and secondary infection.

Special Information

Clean the skin before applying Triamcinolone Acetonide, to
prevent secondary infection. Apply in a very thin film (effectiveness is based on contact area and not on the thickness of
the layer applied).

Brand Name

Triavil

Ingredients

Amitriptyline Hydrochloride
Perphenazine

Other Brand Names

Etrafon

(Also available in generic form)

Type of Drug

Antidepressant tranquilizer combination.

Prescribed for

Relief of symptoms of anxiety and/or depression associated
with chronic physical or psychiatric disease.

General Information

Triavil and other psychotherapeutic agents are effective in

treating various symptoms of psychological or psychiatr
disorders, which may result from organic disease or may
signs of psychiatric illness. Triavil must be used only und
the supervision of a doctor. It will take a minimum of
weeks to 1 month for this medication to show benefic
effect, so don't expect instant results. If you feel there h
been no change in symptoms after 6 to 8 weeks, conta
your doctor and discuss it with him. He may tell you
continue taking the medicine and give it more time, or
may give you another drug which he feels will be mo
effective.

Cautions and Warnings

Do not take Triavil if you are allergic to it or to any relate
compound. For more information on drugs related to th
ingredients found in Triavil, consult the entries for Amitript
line and Chlorpromazine. Do not take Triavil if you hav
glaucoma or difficulty pasing urine, unless you are speci
cally directed to by your physician. This drug is usually n
recommended for patients who are recovering from hea
attacks. Triavil may make you sleepy or tired and it may als
cause difficulty in concentration. Be extremely careful whe
driving a car or operating machinery while taking this dru
especially during the first couple of weeks of therapy.

This drug may cause birth defects or interfere with yo
baby's development. Check with your doctor before taking
if you are, or might be, pregnant. Triavil may pass into brea
milk. Nursing mothers should use an alternative feedir
method.

Possible Side Effects

Most frequent: dry mouth, difficulty in urination, constip
tion, blurred vision, rapid heartbeat, numbness and tinglir
sensation in the arms and legs, yellowing of the skin and/
whites of the eyes, unusually low blood pressure, drows
ness, sleepiness.

Possible Adverse Drug Effects

Infrequent: dizziness, nausea, excitement, fainting, slig
twitching of the muscles, jittery feeling, weakness, hea
ache, heartburn, loss of appetite, stomach cramps, increase
perspiration, loss of coordination, skin rash with unusu

ensitivity to bright lights, itching, redness, peeling away of
arge sections of skin. You may experience an allergic reaction: difficulty in breathing, retention of fluids in arms and
legs, drug fever, swelling of the face and tongue.

Also infrequent: effects on the hormone and blood system, convulsions, development of unusual skin colorations
and spots, effect on sex drive and sexual performance.

Drug Interactions

Quinidine or Procainamide, drugs which are used to control
heart rhythm, will strongly increase the effects of this drug.
Avoid depressive drugs such as other tranquilizers, sleeping
pills, antihistamines, barbiturates, or alcohol. Interaction will
cause excessive drowsiness, inability to concentrate, and/or
sleepiness. Some patients may experience changes in heart
rhythm when taking this drug along with thyroid medication.

One of the ingredients in Triavil may increase your response to common stimulant drugs found in over-the-counter
cough and cold preparations, causing stimulation, nervousness, and difficulty in sleeping.

Avoid large amounts of Vitamin C, which may cause you to
release larger than normal amounts of Triavil from your body.

Both of the ingredients in Triavil may neutralize drugs
used to treat high blood pressure. If you have high blood
pressure and are taking Triavil, discuss this potential difficulty with your doctor or pharmacist to be sure that you are
taking adequate doses of blood pressure medicine.

If you are taking a drug which is an MAO inhibitor, discuss
this matter with your doctor, because there have been severe interactions.

Usual Dose

1 or 2 tablets 3 to 4 times per day.

Overdosage

Symptoms are central nervous system depression to the
point of possible coma, low blood pressure, agitation, restlessness, convulsions, fever, dry mouth, abnormal heart
rhythms, confusion, hallucinations, drowsiness, unusually low
body temperature, dilated eye pupils, and abnormally rigid
muscles. The patient should be taken to a hospital emergency room immediately. ALWAYS bring the medicine bottle.

Generic Name

Triazolam

Brand Name

Halcion

Type of Drug

Sedative.

Prescribed for

Short-term treatment of insomnia or sleeplessness, frequent nighttime awakening, waking too early in the morning.

General Information

Triazolam, used only as a sleep inducer, is a member of the group of drugs known as benzodiazepines. Characterized by Diazepam (Valium), other benzodiazepine drugs are used as antianxiety agents, anticonvulsants, and sedatives (sleeping pills). They exert their effects by relaxing large skeletal muscles and through a direct effect on the brain. In doing so they can relax you and make you either more tranquil or sleepier, depending on the specific drug taken and how much of it has been prescribed. Many doctors prefer Triazolam and the other members of this class to other drugs that can be used for the same effect, because the benzodiazepines tend to be safer, have fewer side effects, and are usually as if not more, effective.

Triazolam is distinguished from other benzodiazepines by the fact that it has a very short duration of action and produces less hangover than other sleeping pills. However, some people who use it on a regular basis find that, because of the drug's short duration of effect, they still get up early in the morning or become anxious during the day.

Benzodiazepines can be abused if taken for long periods of time and it's possible to develop drug-withdrawal symptoms if therapy is suddenly discontinued. Withdrawal symptoms include convulsions, tremors, muscle cramps, insomnia, agitation, diarrhea, vomiting, sweating, and convulsions.

Cautions and Warnings

Older patients are more susceptible to drug side effects than are younger adults and should take the lowest possible dosage of Triazolam. It is not intended for children under age 18.

Triazolam may interfere with daily tasks by producing some daytime drowsiness, although this is less of a problem than with other sedatives. Clinical depression may be increased by Triazolam or any other drug that has an ability to depress the nervous system. Intentional overdosage is more common among depressed people who take sleeping pills.

This drug should not be used by pregnant women or women who may become pregnant while using it. Animal studies have shown that it passes easily into the blood system of a developing baby.

Triazolam and the products of its metabolism pass into mother's milk and the drug is not recommended for nursing mothers.

Possible Side Effects

Drowsiness, headache, dizziness, nervousness, poor muscle coordination, light-headedness, nausea, and vomiting.

Possible Adverse Drug Effects

A "high" feeling, rapid heartbeat, tiredness, confusion, temporary memory loss, cramps and pain, depressing, blurred or double vision. The least often experienced adverse effects of Triazolam are constipation, changes in taste perception, stuffy nose, diarrhea, dry mouth, allergic reactions, rash, nightmares or strange dreams, difficulty sleeping, tingling in the hands or feet, temporary loss of normal sensation, and ringing or buzzing in the ears.

Drug Interactions

As for all other benzodiazepines, the effects of Triazolam may be enhanced if it is taken together with alcoholic beverages, antihistamines, tranquilizers, barbiturates, anticonvulsant medicines, antidepressants, and MAO inhibitor drugs (most often prescribed for severe depression).

Oral contraceptives, Cimetidine (for ulcers), and Disulfiram (for alcoholism) may increase the effect of Triazolam by interfering with the drug's breakdown in the liver.

Cigarette smoking may reduce the effect of Triazolam on your body, as it does the other benzodiazepines.

The effectiveness of Levodopa (for Parkinson's disease) may be increased by benzodiazepine drugs, including Triazolam.

Food Interactions

Triazolam may be taken with food if it upsets your stomach.

Usual Dose

Adult: 0.25 to 0.5 milligrams about 30 minutes before you want to go to sleep.

Elderly: 0.125 milligrams to start, then increase in 0.125-milligram increments until the desired effect is achieved.

Overdosage

The most common symptoms of Triazolam overdose are confusion, sleepiness, depression, loss of muscle coordination, and slurred speech. Coma may develop if the overdose was particularly large. Overdose symptoms can develop if a single dose of 2 milligrams (4 times the maximum daily dose) is taken. Patients taking an overdose of this drug must be made to vomit with Syrup of Ipecac (available at any pharmacy) to remove any remaining drug from the stomach. Call your doctor or a Poison Control Center before doing this. If 30 minutes has passed since the overdose was taken or symptoms have begun to develop, the victim must be immediately transported to a hospital emergency room for treatment. ALWAYS bring the medicine bottle.

Special Information

Never take more of this medication than your doctor has prescribed. If you have been taking Triazolam for several months and decide to stop using it, your daily dosage should be gradually reduced, rather than stopping it all at once, to avoid drug-withdrawal symptoms.

Generic Name

Trifluoperazine

Brand Names

Stelazine
Suprazine

(Also available in generic form)

Type of Drug

Phenothiazine antipsychotic.

Prescribed for

Psychotic disorders, moderate to severe depression with anxiety, control of agitation or aggressiveness of disturbed children, alcohol withdrawal symptoms, intractable pain, and senility.

General Information

Trifluoperazine and other members of the phenothiazine group act on a portion of the brain called the hypothalamus. They affect parts of the hypothalamus that control metabolism, body temperature, alertness, muscle tone, hormone balance, and vomiting, and may be used to treat problems related to any of these functions.

Cautions and Warnings

Trifluoperazine should not be taken if you are allergic to one of the drugs in the broad classification known as phenothiazine drugs. Do not take Trifluoperazine if you have any blood, liver, kidney, or heart disease, very low blood pressure, or Parkinson's disease. This medication is a tranquilizer and can have a depressive effect, especially during the first few days of therapy. Care should be taken when performing activities requiring a high degree of concentration, such as driving.

This drug should be used with caution and under strict supervision of your doctor if you have glaucoma, epilepsy, ulcers, or difficulty passing urine.

Avoid insecticides and extreme exposure to heat.

If you are taking this medication and become pregnant contact your doctor immediately. Trifluoperazine when used by pregnant women has caused side effects in newborns: jaundice (yellowing of skin and eyes) and twitching. This drug should be stopped 1 to 2 weeks before expected delivery to avoid this. Nursing mothers should use an alternative feeding method.

Possible Side Effects

Most common: drowsiness, especially during the first or second week of therapy. If the drowsiness becomes troublesome, contact your doctor.

Possible Adverse Drug Effects

Trifluoperazine can cause jaundice (yellowing of the whites of the eyes or skin), usually in 2 to 4 weeks. The jaundice usually goes away when the drug is discontinued, but there have been cases when it did not. If you notice this effect or if you develop symptoms such as fever and generally not feeling well, contact your doctor immediately. Less frequent: changes in components of the blood including anemias, raised or lowered blood pressure, abnormal heart rates, heart attack, feeling faint or dizzy.

Phenothiazines can produce "extrapyramidal effects," such as spasm of the neck muscles, rolling back of the eyes, convulsions, difficulty in swallowing, and symptoms associated with Parkinson's disease. These effects look very serious but disappear after the drug has been withdrawn; however, symptoms of the face, tongue, and jaw may persist for as long as several years, especially in the elderly with a history of brain damage. If you experience extrapyramidal effects contact your doctor immediately.

Trifluoperazine may cause an unusual increase in psychotic symptoms or may cause paranoid reactions, tiredness, lethargy, restlessness, hyperactivity, confusion at night, bizarre dreams, inability to sleep, depression, and euphoria. Other reactions are itching, swelling, unusual sensitivity to bright lights, red skin, and rash. There have been cases of breast enlargement, false positive pregnancy tests, changes in menstrual flow in females, and impotence and changes in sex drive in males, as well as stuffy nose, headache, nausea, vomiting, loss of appetite, change in body temperature, loss of facial color, excessive salivation, excessive perspiration, constipation, diarrhea, changes in urine and stool habits, worsening of glaucoma, blurred vision, weakening of eyelid muscles, spasms in bronchial and other muscles, increased appetite, fatigue, excessive thirst, and changes in the coloration of skin, particularly in exposed areas.

Drug Interactions

Trifluoperazine should be taken with caution in combination with barbiturates, sleeping pills, narcotics, other tranquilizers, or any other medication which may produce a depressive effect. Avoid alcohol.

Usual Dose

Adult: 2 to 40 milligrams per day (the lowest effective dose should be used). This long-acting drug will then be taken once or twice per day.

Elderly: lower dose, because of greater sensitivity to phenothiazines.

Child (age 6 to 12): 1 to 15 milligrams per day, slowly increased until satisfactory control is achieved.

Overdosage

Symptoms are depression, extreme weakness, tiredness, desire to go to sleep, coma, lowered blood pressure, uncontrolled muscle spasms, agitation, restlessness, convulsions, fever, dry mouth, and abnormal heart rhythms. The patient should be taken to a hospital emergency room immediately. ALWAYS bring the medicine bottle.

Special Information

This drug may turn the color of your urine to pink or reddish brown; this is normal and not a cause for worry.

Generic Name

Trihexyphenidyl Hydrochloride

Brand Names

Aphen	Trihexane
Artane	Trihexidyl
Artane Sequels (Long Acting)	Trihexy
Tremin	

(Also available in generic form)

Type of Drug

Anticholinergic.

Prescribed for

Treatment of Parkinson's disease or prevention or control of muscle spasms caused by other drugs, particularly the phenothiazine drugs.

General Information

The drug has an action on the body similar to that of Atropine Sulfate. As an anticholinergic it has the ability to reduce muscle spasm, which makes the drug useful in treating Parkinson's disease and other diseases associated with spasm of skeletal muscles.

Cautions and Warnings

Trihexyphenidyl Hydrochloride should be used with caution if you have narrow angle glaucoma, stomach ulcers, obstructions in the gastrointestinal tract, prostatitis, or myasthenia gravis.

    This drug may cause birth defects or interfere with your baby's development. Check with your doctor before taking it if you are, or might be, pregnant.

Possible Side Effects

The same as with any other anticholinergic drug: dry mouth, difficulty in urination, constipation, blurred vision, rapid or pounding heartbeat, possible mental confusion, and increased sensitivity to strong light. The effects may increase if Trihexyphenidyl Hydrochloride is taken with antihistamines, phenothiazines, antidepressants, or other anticholinergic drugs.

Side effects are less frequent and severe than those seen with Atropine Sulfate, to which this drug is therapeutically similar.

Drug Interactions

Interaction with other anticholinergic drugs, including tricyclic antidepressants, may cause severe stomach upset or unusual abdominal pain. If this happens, contact your doctor.

Avoid over-the-counter remedies which contain Atropine Sulfate or similar drugs. Your pharmacist can tell you the ingredients of over-the-counter drugs.

This drug should not be taken with alcohol.

Usual Dose

1 to 15 milligrams per day, depending on disease and patient's response. Can be taken with food if stomach upset occurs.

Special Information

Side effects of dry mouth, constipation, and increased sensitivity to strong light may be relieved by, respectively, chewing gum or sucking on hard candy, taking a stool softener, and wearing sunglasses. Such side effects are easily tolerated in the absence of undesirable drug interaction.

Generic Name

Trimethobenzamide Hydrochloride

Brand Names

Tigan
Tegamide

(Also available in generic form)

Type of Drug

Antiemetic.

Prescribed for

Control of nausea and vomiting.

General Information

Trimethobenzamide Hydrochloride works on the "chemo-receptor trigger zone" of the brain through which impulses are carried to the vomiting center. It can help control nausea and vomiting.

Cautions and Warnings

Do not use this drug if you are allergic or sensitive to it. Trimethobenzamide Hydrochloride rectal suppositories contain a local anesthetic and should not be used for newborn infants or patients who are allergic to local anesthetics. Some drugs, when taken by children with a viral illness that causes vomiting, may contribute to the development of Reye's syndrome, a potentially fatal, acute childhood disease. Although this relationship has not been confirmed, caution must be exercised. Reye's syndrome is characterized by a rapid onset of persistent severe vomiting, tiredness, and irrational behavior. It can progress to coma, convulsions, and death—usually following a nonspecific illness associated with a high fever. It has been suspected that Trimethobenzamide Hydrochloride and other drugs which can be toxic to the liver may unfavorably alter the course of Reye's syndrome; such drugs should be avoided in children exhibiting signs and symptoms associated with Reye's syndrome.

Trimethobenzamide Hydrochloride can obscure the signs of overdosage by other drugs or signs of disease because of its effect of controlling nausea and vomiting.

Do not use this drug if you are pregnant because Trimethobenzamide Hydrochloride may decrease your chances to have a successful pregnancy. No breast-feeding problems have been seen.

Possible Side Effects

Muscle cramps and tremors, low blood pressure (especially

after an injection of this medication), effects on components of the blood, blurred vision, drowsiness, headache, jaundice (yellowing of skin or whites of the eyes). If you experience one of these side effects report it to your doctor. If you develop a rash or other allergic effects from Trimethobenzamide Hydrochloride, stop taking the drug and tell your doctor. Usually these symptoms will disappear by themselves, but additional treatment may be necessary.

Drug Interactions

Trimethobenzamide Hydrochloride may make you sleepy or cause you to lose concentration, therefore, avoid alcoholic beverages, antihistamines, sleeping pills, tranquilizers, and other depressant drugs which may aggravate these effects.

Usual Dose

Adult: 250-milligram capsule 3 to 4 times per day. Rectal suppository form, 200 milligrams 3 to 4 times per day.

Child (30 to 90 pounds): 100 to 200 milligrams 3 to 4 times per day, rectal suppository or oral capsule.

Child (under 30 pounds): Rectal suppository form, 100 milligrams 3 to 4 times per day.

Dose must be adjusted according to disease severity and patient's response.

Special Information

Severe vomiting should not be treated with an antiemetic drug alone: the cause of vomiting should be established and treated. Overuse of antiemetic drugs may delay diagnosis of the underlying condition or problem and obscure the signs of toxic effects from other drugs. Primary emphasis in the treatment of vomiting is on reestablishment of body fluid and electrolyte balance, relief of fever if present, and treatment of the causative disease process.

If you have taken Trimethobenzamide Hydrochloride, use special care when driving.

Generic Name

Trimethoprim

Brand Names

Cotrim
Proloprim
Trimpex

(Also available in generic form)

Type of Drug

Anti-infective.

Prescribed for

Urinary tract infections.

General Information

This drug works by blocking the effects of folic acid in micro
organisms which may infect the urinary tract. It is often used
in combination with a sulfa drug and was first made avail
able in the United States only as a combination. However, i
is effective by itself.

Cautions and Warnings

Do not take Trimethoprim if you are allgeric to it. This drug
should not be used by pregnant or nursing women.

This drug may cause birth defects or interfere with you
baby's development. Check with your doctor before taking i
if you are, or might be, pregnant.

Patients with a possible folic acid deficiency should no
take this drug.

Possible Side Effects

Itching, rash, peeling of the skin.

Possible Adverse Drug Effects

Stomach upset, nausea, vomiting, fever, adverse effects or
the blood, elevation of blood enzymes.

Drug Interactions

The anticonvulsant Phenytoin may have increased effects i
you take Trimethoprim.

Usual Dose

200 milligrams every day for 10 days. Patients with kidney disease will take less medication.

Overdosage

Signs may appear after taking 10 or more tablets. They are nausea, vomiting, dizziness, headache, depression, confusion, and adverse effects on the blood system. People taking high doses of this drug or those taking it for long periods of time may develop adverse effects on the blood system.

Special Information

Take exactly as directed. Call your doctor if you develop sore throat, fever, blood clots, black-and-blue marks, or a very pale sickly skin coloration.

Generic Name

Trimipramine Maleate

Brand Name

Surmontil

Type of Drug

Antidepressant.

Prescribed for

Depression with or without symptoms of anxiety.

General Information

Trimipramine Maleate and other members of this group are effective in treating symptoms of depression. They can elevate your mood, increase physical activity and mental alertness, improve appetite and sleep patterns. These drugs are mild sedatives and therefore useful in treating mild forms of depression associated with anxiety. You should not expect instant results with this medicine: benefits are usually seen after 1 to 4 weeks. If symptoms are not affected after 6 to 8 weeks, contact your doctor. Occasionally other members of this group of drugs have been used in treating nighttime bed-wetting in the young child, but they do not produce long-lasting relief and therapy with one of them for night time bed-wetting is of questionable value.

Cautions and Warnings

Do not take Trimipramine Maleate if you are allergic or sensitive to this or other members of this class of drug: Doxepin, Nortriptyline, Imipramine, Desipramine, Protriptyline, and Amitriptyline. The drugs should not be used if you are recovering from a heart attack. Trimipramine Maleate may be taken with caution if you have a history of epilepsy or other convulsive disorders, difficulty in urination, glaucoma, heart disease, or thyroid disease. Trimipramine Maleate can interfere with your ability to perform tasks which require concentration, such as driving or operating machinery.

Trimipramine Maleate will pass from mother to unborn child: consult your doctor before taking this medicine if you are pregnant. Trimipramine Maleate may pass into breast milk. Nursing mothers should use an alternative feeding method.

Possible Side Effects

Changes in blood pressure (both high and low), abnormal heart rates, heart attack, confusion, especially in elderly patients, hallucinations, disorientation, delusions, anxiety, restlessness, excitement, numbness and tingling in the extremities, lack of coordination, muscle spasms or tremors, seizures and/or convulsions, dry mouth, blurred vision, constipation, inability to urinate, rash, itching, sensitivity to bright light or sunlight, retention of fluids, fever, allergy, changes in composition of blood, nausea, vomiting, loss of appetite, stomach upset, diarrhea, enlargement of the breasts in males and females, increased or decreased sex drive, increased or decreased blood sugar.

Possible Adverse Drug Effects

Infrequent: agitation, inability to sleep, nightmares, feeling of panic, peculiar taste in the mouth, stomach cramps, black coloration of the tongue, yellowing eyes and/or skin, changes in liver function, increased or decreased weight, perspira-

on, flushing, frequent urination, drowsiness, dizziness, weak-
ess, headache, loss of hair, nausea, not feeling well.

rug Interactions

teraction with monoamine oxidase (MAO) inhibitors can
ause high fevers, convulsions, and occasionally death. Don't
ke MAO inhibitors until at least 2 weeks after Trimipramine
aleate has been discontinued.

Trimipramine Maleate interacts with Guanethidine, a drug
sed to treat high blood pressure: if your doctor prescribes
rimipramine Maleate and you are taking medicine for high
lood pressure, be sure to discuss this with him.

Trimipramine Maleate increases the effects of barbiturates,
anquilizers, other depressive drugs, and alcohol. Don't drink
lcoholic beverages if you take this medicine.

Taking Trimipramine Maleate and thyroid medicine will
nhance the effects of the thyroid medicine. The combina-
on can cause abnormal heart rhythms.

Large doses of Vitamin C (Ascorbic Acid) can reduce the
ffect of Trimipramine Maleate. Drugs such as Bicarbonate
f Soda or Acetazolamide will increase the effect of Trimi-
ramine Maleate.

sual Dose

Adult: 150 to 200 milligrams per day in divided doses or
s a single bedtime dose. Hospitalized patients may need up
300 milligrams per day. The dose of this drug must be
ailored to patient's need.

Adolescent or elderly: lower doses are recommended; for
eople over 60 years of age, usually 50 to 100 milligrams per
ay.

verdosage

ymptoms are confusion, inability to concentrate, hallucina-
ons, drowsiness, lowered body temperature, abnormal heart
ate, heart failure, large pupils of the eyes, convulsions,
everely lowered blood pressure, stupor, and coma (as well
s agitation, stiffening of body muscles, vomiting, and high
ever). The patient should be taken to a hospital emergency
oom immediately. ALWAYS bring the medicine bottle.

Brand Name

Trinalin

Ingredients

Azatidine Maleate
Pseudoephedrine Sulfate

Type of Drug

Antihistamine-decongestant.

Prescribed for

Relief of runny nose, sneezing, and nasal congestion assoc
ated with the common cold, allergy, or other respirator
ailments.

General Information

Trinalin is one of many products sold to relieve symptoms (
the common cold. Its formula is similar to most other:
except the antihistamine, Azatidine Maleate, has a long du
ration of action. When Azatidine Maleate is combined with
large dose of Pseudoephedrine Sulfate, the final product is
long-lasting antihistamine-decongestant that can be conve
niently used only twice a day. The major difference betwee
this and other cough and cold products is that the antihista
mine is more sedating than many others. Like other suc
combinations, Trinalin can relieve the symptoms of a cold
but can't cure it.

Cautions and Warnings

This product can cause excessive drowsiness. It also ca
cause you to become overly anxious and nervous and ma
interfere with sleep. Older patients are more likely to suffe
from dizziness, sedation, low blood pressure, and confusio
than are younger adults using it. This drug should not b
taken by women who may become pregnant while using
or by pregnant or nursing mothers, since both ingredient
may pass into breast milk.

Possible Side Effects

Restlessness, sleeplessness, excitation, nervousness, drows

ness, sedation, dizziness, poor coordination, upset stomach,
and worsening or bronchial congestion (if present before the
pill is taken).

Possible Adverse Drug Effects

Low blood pressure, heart palpitations, chest pain, rapid
heartbeat and abnormal heart rhythm, anemia, fatigue, confusion, tremors, headache, irritability, feeling "high", tingling or heaviness in the hands, tingling in the feet or legs,
blurred or double vision, convulsions, hysterical reactions,
ringing or buzzing in the ears, fainting, changes in appetite,
nausea, vomiting, diarrhea and constipation, frequent urination, difficulty urinating, early menstrual periods, loss of sex
drive, difficulty breathing, wheezing with chest tightness,
stuffy nose, dry mouth, nose, and throat, itching, rashes,
unusual sensitivity to the sun, chills, and excessive sweating.

Drug Interactions

Interaction with alcoholic beverages, tranquilizers, antianxiety drugs, and narcotic-type pain relievers can lead to excessive drowsiness or inability to concentrate.

Avoid Trinalin if you are taking an MAO inhibitor for depression or high blood pressure, because the MAO inhibitor
may cause a very rapid rise in blood pressure or increase
some side effects (dry mouth and nose, blurred vision, abnormal heart rhythms).

The decongestant portion of this product may interfere
with the normal effects of blood-pressure-lowering medicines and can aggravate diabetes, heart disease, hyperthy-
oid disease, high blood pressure, a prostate condition,
stomach ulcers, and urinary blockage.

Food Interactions

Take your pill with food if it causes an upset stomach.

Usual Dose

1 tablet every 12 hours.

Overdosage

The main symptoms of Trinalin overdose are drowsiness,
chills, dry mouth, fever, nausea, nervousness, irritability, rapid

or irregular heartbeat, heart pains, and urinary difficulty. Most cases of overdose are not severe. Patients taking an overdose of this drug must be made to vomit with Syrup of Ipecac (available at any pharmacy) to remove any remaining drug from the stomach. Call your doctor or a Poison Control Center before doing this. If you must go to a hospital emergency room, ALWAYS bring the medicine bottle.

Special Information

Since the antihistamine component of this medicine can slow down your central nervous system, use extra caution when doing anything that requires concentration like driving a car or operating other machinery.

Call your doctor if side effects become severe or gradually become intolerable. There are so many different cold and allergy products available to choose from that one is sure to be the right combination for you.

Generic Name

Tripelennamine Hydrochloride

Brand Names

PBZ
PBZ-SR (Long Acting)
Pelamine
Pyribenzemine

(Also available in generic form)

Type of Drug

Antihistamine.

Prescribed for

Seasonal allergy, stuffy and runny nose, itching of the eyes, scratching of the throat caused by allergy, and other allergic symptoms such as itching, rash, or hives.

General Information

Antihistamines generally, and Tripelennamine Hydrochloride

specifically, act by blocking the release of the chemical substance histamine from the cell. Antihistamines work by drying up the secretions of the nose, throat, and eyes.

Cautions and Warnings

Tripelennamine Hydrochloride should not be used if you are allergic to this drug. It should be avoided or used with extreme care if you have narrow angle glaucoma (pressure in the eye), stomach ulcer or other stomach problems, enlarged prostate, or problems passing urine. It should not be used by people who have deep-breathing problems such as asthma.

Tripelennamine Hydrochloride can cause dizziness, drowsiness, and lowering of blood pressure, particularly in the elderly patient. Young children can show signs of nervousness, increased tension, and anxiety.

This drug may cause birth defects or interfere with your baby's development. Check with your doctor before taking it if you are, or might be, pregnant. The ingredients in Tripelennamine Hydrochloride cross over to breast-fed infants and may cause excitement or irritability. Tripelennamine Hydrochloride is not recommended for nursing mothers.

Possible Side Effects

Occasional: itching, rash, sensitivity to light, perspiration, chills, dryness of the mouth, nose and throat, lowered blood pressure, headache, rapid heartbeat, sleeplessness, dizziness, disturbed coordination, confusion, restlessness, nervousness, irritability, euphoria (feeling high), tingling of the hands and feet, blurred vision, double vision, ringing in the ears, stomach upset, loss of appetite, nausea, vomiting, constipation, diarrhea, difficulty in urination, tightness of the chest, wheezing, nasal stuffiness.

Possible Adverse Drug Effects

Use with care if you have a history of asthma, glaucoma, thyroid disease, heart disease, high blood pressure, or diabetes.

Drug Interactions

Tripelennamine Hydrochloride should not be taken with MAO inhibitors.

Interaction with tranquilizers, sedatives, and sleeping medication will increase the effects of these drugs; it is extremely important that you discuss this with your doctor so that doses of these drugs can be properly adjusted.

Be extremely cautious when drinking while taking Tripelennamine Hydrochloride, which will enhance the intoxicating effect of alcohol. Alcohol also has a sedative effect.

Usual Dose

Adult: 25 to 50 milligrams every 4 to 6 hours. Up to 600 milligrams per day may be used. Adult patient may take up to 3 of the 100-milligram long-acting (PBZ-SR) tablets per day, although this much is not usually needed.

Infant and child: 2 milligrams per pound of body weight per day in divided doses. No more than 300 milligrams should be given per day. Older children may take up to 3 of the extended-release (long-acting) tablets per day, if needed.

Overdosage

Symptoms are depression or stimulation (especially in children), fixed or dilated pupils, flushing of the skin, and stomach upset. Patients taking an overdose of this drug must be made to vomit with Syrup of Ipecac (available at any pharmacy) to remove any remaining drug from the stomach. Call your doctor or a Poison Control Center before doing this. If you must go to a hospital emergency room, ALWAYS bring the medicine bottle.

Special Information

Antihistamines produce a depressing effect: be extremely cautious when driving or operating heavy equipment.

Brand Name

Tri-Vi-Flor Drops

Ingredients

Sodium Fluoride
Vitamin A
Vitamin C
Vitamin D

Other Brand Names

Adeflor
Tri-Bay-Flor
Tri-Vitamin w/Fluoride
Vi-Daylin/F ADC

(Also available in generic form)

Type of Drug

Multivitamin supplement with a fluoride.

Prescribed for

Vitamin deficiencies and prevention of dental cavities in infants and children.

General Information

Tri-Vi-Flor Drops is a vitamin supplement containing a fluoride. Fluorides taken in small daily doses have been effective in preventing cavities in children by strengthening their teeth and making them resistant to cavity formation. Too much of a fluoride can cause damage to the teeth. Because of this, vitamins with a fluoride should only be used in areas where the water supply is not fluoridated.

Tri-Vi-Flor is also available with iron for those patients who need it.

Cautions and Warnings

Tri-Vi-Flor Drops should not be used in areas where the water fluoride content exceeds 0.7 ppm (part per million). Your pediatrician or local water company can tell you the fluoride content of the water you drink.

Possible Side Effects

Occasional skin rash, itching, stomach upset, headache, weakness.

Usual Dose

1 milliliter per day (measured with provided calibrated dropper).

Brand Name

Tuinal

Ingredients

Amobarbital
Secobarbital

(Also available in generic form)

Type of Drug

Hypnotic combination.

Prescribed for

Daytime sedation, or sleeping medication.

General Information

This drug is a combination of a short- and intermediate-acting barbiturate. The combination takes advantage of the fast-acting nature of Secobarbital and the longer duration of action of Amobarbital (about 8 hours). Although the combination works well, it can be addicting if taken daily for 3 months in sufficient doses (about 100 milligrams). Larger doses will result in addiction in a shorter period of time.

Cautions and Warnings

Tuinal may slow down your physical and mental reflexes, so you must be extremely careful when operating machinery, driving an automobile, or performing other potentially dangerous tasks. Tuinal is classified as a barbiturate; long-term or unsupervised use may cause addiction. Elderly people taking Tuinal may exhibit nervousness and confusion at times.

Barbiturates are neutralized in the liver and eliminated from the body through the kidneys; consequently, people who have liver or kidney disorders—namely, difficulty in forming or excreting urine—should be carefully monitored by their doctor when taking Tuinal.

If you have known sensitivities or allergies to barbiturates, or if you have previously been addicted to sedatives or hypnotics, or if you have a disease affecting the respiratory system, you should not take Tuinal.

This drug is known to cause birth defects or interfere with your baby's development. It is not considered safe for use during pregnancy.

Breast-feeding while using Tuinal may cause increased tiredness, shortness of breath, or a slow heartbeat in the baby. It should be avoided by nursing mothers.

Possible Side Effects

Difficulty in breathing, skin rash, and general allergic reaction such as running nose, watery eyes, and scratchy throat.

Possible Adverse Drug Effects

Drowsiness, lethargy, dizziness, hangover, nausea, vomiting, diarrhea. More severe adverse reactions may include anemia and yellowing of the skin and eyes.

Drug Interactions

Interaction with alcohol, tranquilizers, or other sedatives increases the effect of Tuinal.

Interaction with anticoagulants (blood-thinning agents) can reduce their effect. This is also true of muscle relaxants and painkillers.

Usual Dose

Up to 200 milligrams.

Overdosage

Symptoms are difficulty in breathing, decrease in size of the pupils of the eyes, lowered body temperature progressing to fever as time passes, fluid in the lungs, and eventually coma.

Anyone suspected of having taken an overdose must be taken to the hospital for immediate care. ALWAYS bring the medicine bottle to the emergency room physician so he can quickly and correctly identify the medicine and start treatment. Severe overdosage of this medication can kill; the drug has been used many times in suicide attempts.

Brand Name

Tussionex

Ingredients

Hydrocodone
Phenyltoloxamine

Type of Drug

Cough suppressant antihistamine combination.

Prescribed for

Relief of cough and other symptoms of a cold or other respiratory condition.

General Information

This drug may be prescribed to treat a cough or congestion that has not responded to other medication. The suppressant ingredient (Hydrocodone) in this combination is more potent than Codeine.

Cautions and Warnings

Do not use Tussionex if you are allergic to any of the ingredients. Patients allergic to Codeine may also be allergic to Tussionex. Long-term use of this or any other narcotic-containing drug can lead to drug dependence or addiction. Both ingredients in Tussionex can cause drowsiness, tiredness, or loss of concentration. Use with caution if you have a history of convulsions, glaucoma, stomach ulcer, high blood pressure, thyroid disease, heart disease, or diabetes.

This drug may cause birth defects or interfere with your baby's development. Check with your doctor before taking it if you are, or might be, pregnant. The newborn infant may be dependent on Hydrocodone after birth if large amounts are used during pregnancy.

Possible Side Effects

Light-headedness, dizziness, sleepiness, nausea, vomiting, sweating, itching, rash, sensitivity to light, excessive perspiration, chills, dryness of the mouth, nose, and throat.

Possible Adverse Drug Effects

Euphoria (feeling high), weakness, agitation, uncoordinated muscle movement, minor hallucinations, disorientation and visual disturbances, loss of appetite, constipation, flushing of the face, rapid heartbeat, palpitations, faintness, difficult urination, reduced sexual potency, low blood sugar, anemia, yellowing of the skin or whites of the eyes, blurred or double vision, ringing or buzzing in the ears, wheezing, nasal stuffiness.

Drug Interactions

Do not use alcohol or other depressant drugs because they will increase the depressant effect of the Tussionex. This drug should not be taken in combination with MAO inhibitor drugs.

Usual Dose

Tablet or capsule: 1 every 8 to 12 hours.
Suspension: 1 teaspoon every 8 to 12 hours.

Overdosage

Signs of overdose are depression, slowed breathing, flushing of the skin, upset stomach. In case of overdose, bring the patient to a hospital emergency room. ALWAYS bring the medicine bottle.

Special Information

Be careful while driving or operating any equipment.
The liquid form of Tussionex does not contain any sugar.

Brand Name

Tuss-Ornade Spansules/Liquid

Ingredients

Caramiphen Edisylate
Phenylpropanolamine Hydrochloride

Other Brand Names

Detuss
Rescaps-D.S.R.
Tuss-Ade
Tuss Allergine Modified T.D.
Tussogest

(Also available in generic form)

Type of Drug

Decongestant; expectorant.

Prescribed for

Relief of cough, nasal congestion, runny nose, and other symptoms associated with the common cold, viruses, or other upper respiratory diseases. The drug may also be used to treat allergies, asthma, ear infections, or sinus infections.

General Information

Tuss-Ornade is one of almost 100 products marketed to relieve the symptoms of the common cold and other respiratory infections. These products contain ingredients to relieve congestion, act as an antihistamine, relieve or suppress cough, and help you to cough up mucus. They may contain medicine for each purpose, or may contain a combination of medicines. Some combinations leave out the antihistamine, the decongestant, or the expectorant. You must realize while taking Tuss-Ornade or similar products that these drugs are good only for the relief of symptoms and do not treat the underlying problem such as a cold virus or other infections.

Cautions and Warnings

Can cause excessive tiredness or drowsiness.

This drug may cause birth defects or interfere with your baby's development. Check with your doctor before taking it if you are, or might be, pregnant.

Possible Side Effects

Dry mouth, blurred vision, difficulty passing urine, (possibly) constipation, nervousness, restlessness or even inability to sleep.

Drug Interactions

Taking Tuss-Ornade with an MAO inhibitor can produce severe interaction, so consult your doctor before combining them.

Do not take this drug with sedatives, tranquilizers, antihistamines, sleeping pills, thyroid medicine, or antihypertensive drugs such as Reserpine or Guanethidine.

Since Tuss-Ornade contains ingredients which may cause sleepiness or difficulty in concentration, do not drink alcoholic beverages while taking this drug. The combination can cause excessive drowsiness or sleepiness, and result in inability to concentrate and carry out activities requiring extra concentration and coordination.

Usual Dose

Spansules: 1 every 12 hours.

Liquid: 1 to 2 teaspoons every 4 hours as needed for relief of cough, nasal congestion, runny nose, or other symptoms associated with the common cold or other upper respiratory diseases.

Special Information

Take with a full glass of water to remove excessive mucus from the throat and reduce stomach upset.

Brand Name

Tylox

Ingredients

Acetaminophen
Oxycodone Hydrochloride
Oxycodone Terephthalate

Type of Drug

Narcotic analgesic combination.

Prescribed for

Relief of mild to moderate pain.

General Information

Tylox is generally prescribed for the patient who is in pain
but is allergic to Aspirin. Tylox is probably not effective for
arthritis or other pain associated with inflammation because
the ingredient Acetaminophen does not produce an anti-
inflammatory effect.

Cautions and Warnings

Do not take Tylox if you know you are allergic or sensitive to
it. Use this drug with extreme caution if you suffer from
asthma or other breathing problems. Long-term use of Tylox
may cause drug dependence or addiction. Oxycodone is a
respiratory depressant and affects the central nervous system, producing sleepiness, tiredness, and/or inability to
concentrate. Be careful if you are driving, operating machinery
or performing other functions requiring concentration.

   If you are pregnant or suspect that you are pregnant do
not take this drug. Too much narcotic taken during pregnancy and breast-feeding may cause the baby to become
dependent on the narcotic. These drugs may also cause
breathing problems in the infant during delivery.

Possible Side Effects

Most frequent: light-headedness, dizziness, sleepiness, nausea, vomiting, loss of appetite, sweating. If these effects

occur, consider calling your doctor and asking him about lowering the dose of Tylox you are taking. Usually the side effects disappear if you simply lie down.

More serious side effects of Tylox are shallow breathing or difficulty in breathing.

Possible Adverse Drug Effects

Euphoria (feeling "high"), weakness, sleepiness, headache, agitation, uncoordinated muscle movement, minor hallucinations, disorientation and visual disturbances, dry mouth, loss of appetite, constipation, flushing of the face, rapid heartbeat, palpitations, faintness, urinary difficulties or hesitancy, reduced sex drive and/or potency, itching, rashes, anemia, lowered blood sugar, yellowing of the skin and/or whites of the eyes. Narcotic analgesics may aggravate convulsions in those who have had convulsions in the past.

Drug Interactions

Because of its depressant effect and potential effect on breathing, Tylox should be taken with extreme care in combination with alcohol, sleeping medicine, tranquilizers, or other depressant drugs.

Food Interactions

Tylox is best taken with food or at least ½ glass of water to prevent stomach upset.

Usual Dose

Adult: 1 to 2 capsules every 4 hours.
Child: not recommended for children.

Overdosage

Symptoms are depression of respiration (breathing), extreme tiredness progressing to stupor and then coma, pinpointed pupils of the eyes, no response to stimulation such as a pin stick, cold and clammy skin, slowing down of the heart rate, lowering of blood pressure, yellowing of the skin and/or whites of the eyes, bluish color in skin of hands and feet, fever, excitement, delirium, convulsions, cardiac arrest, and liver toxicity (shown by nausea, vomiting, pain in the abdomen, and diarrhea). The patient should be taken to a hospital emergency room immediately. ALWAYS bring the medicine bottle.

Generic Name

Valproic Acid

Brand Names

Depakene
Depakote

Type of Drug

Anticonvulsant.

Prescribed for

Various kinds of seizures.

General Information

Valproic Acid is used to treat the special kind of seizures called petit-mal. It can also be used to treat absence seizures, where the patient loses memory of the seizure but does not lose consciousness.

Cautions and Warnings

Do not take Valproic Acid if you are allergic to it. Take this drug with caution if you have a history of liver problems. Some cases of liver failure have occurred in people taking Valproic Acid.

Pregnant women should avoid this drug. Although no cases of adverse effect on the human fetus have been reported, studies in animals strongly suggest that Valproic Acid has such effects.

Possible Side Effects

Nausea, vomiting and indigestion, sedation or sleepiness, weakness, skin rash, emotional upset, depression, psycho-

is, aggression, hyperactive behavor. Valproic Acid can cause
adverse effects on the blood system. The frequency of side
effects increases as your dose of Valproic Acid increases.

Possible Adverse Drug Effects

Diarrhea, stomach cramps, constipation, appetite changes
(either increase or decrease), headache, loss of control of
eye muscles, drooping eyelids, double vision, spots before
the eyes, loss of muscle control and coordination, tremors.

Drug Interactions

Valproic Acid may increase the depressive effects of alcohol,
sleeping pills, tranquilizers, or other depressant drugs.

If you begin taking Valproic Acid while taking Phenytoin,
your Phenytoin dosage may have to be adjusted. Use of
Valproic Acid together with Clonazepam may produce a certain kind of seizure. This combination should be used with
extreme caution.

Valproic Acid may affect oral anticoagulant (blood-thinning)
drugs. If you begin taking Valproic Acid and have been
taking an anticoagulant, your anticoagulant dose may have
to be changed.

Aspirin may increase the chances of toxicity due to Valproic
Acid.

Valproic Acid may cause a false positive interpretation of
the test for ketones in the urine (used by diabetics).

Food Interactions

Valproic Acid may be taken with food to reduce upset stomach.

Usual Dose

to 27 milligrams per pound per day; up to 250 milligrams
per day.

Overdosage

Call your doctor or take the patient to a hospital emergency
room immediately. ALWAYS bring the medicine bottle.

Special Information

This medicine may cause drowsiness; be careful while driving or operating machinery. Do not chew or crush Valproic
Acid capsules or tablets.

Valproic Acid can cause mouth and throat irritation. A
seizure patients should carry special identification indicatin
their disease and the medicine being taken for it.

Generic Name

Verapamil

Brand Names

Calan
Isoptin

Type of Drug

Calcium channel blocker.

Prescribed for

Angina pectoris and Prinzmetals's angina, as well as hig
blood pressure, asthma, or Raynaud's disease.

General Information

Verapamil is a member of a new drug class to be markete
in the United States. It works by blocking the passage c
calcium into heart and smooth muscle. Since calcium is a
essential ingredient in muscle contraction, blocking calciun
reduces both muscle contraction and oxygen use by th
muscle. This is why Verapamil is used in the treatment o
angina, a kind of heart pain related to poor oxygen supply t
the heart muscles. Verapamil also dilates the vessels tha
supply blood to the heart muscles and prevents spasm o
these arteries. Verapamil only affects the movement of cal
cium into muscle cells. It does not have any effect on cal
cium in the blood.

Cautions and Warnings

Verapamil may cause lowered blood pressure in some pa
tients. Patients taking a beta-blocking drug who begin takin
Verapamil may develop heart failure or increased angin

pain. Do not take this drug if you have had an allergic reaction to it.

Pregnant women or nursing mothers should only use this drug if absolutely necessary. This drug may cause birth defects or interfere with your baby's development. Check with your doctor before taking it if you are, or might be, pregnant.

Possible Side Effects

Low blood pressure, swelling of the arms or legs, heart failure, slowed heartbeat, dizziness, light-headedness, weakness, fatigue, headache, constipation, nausea, liver damage, especially in patients with previous liver damage.

Possible Adverse Drug Effects

Confusion, tingling in the arms or legs, difficulty sleeping, blurred vision, muscle cramps, shakiness, leg pains, difficulty maintaining balance, hair loss, spotty menstruation. In addition, some patients taking Verapamil have experienced heart attack and abnormal heart rhythms, but the occurrence of these effects has not been directly linked to Verapamil.

Drug Interactions

Long-term Verapamil use will cause the blood levels of digitalis drugs to increase by 50 to 70 percent. The dose of digitalis drugs will have to be drastically lowered. Disopyramide should not be given within 48 hours of taking Verapamil because of possible interaction. Patients taking Verapamil together with Quinidine may experience very low blood pressure.

Verapamil's effectiveness may be decreased by taking calcium.

Food Interactions

Take this drug 1 hour before or 2 hours after meals.

Usual Dose

240 to 480 milligrams per day. The dose must be individualized to patient's need.

Overdosage

Overdosage of Verapamil can cause low blood pressure Symptoms are dizziness, weakness, and (possibly) slowed heartbeat. If you have taken an overdose of Verapamil, call your doctor or go to a hospital emergency room. ALWAYS bring the medicine bottle.

Special Information

Call your doctor if you develop swelling in the arms or legs difficulty breathing, increased heart pains, dizziness, light headedness, or low blood pressure.

Brand Name

Vicodin

Ingredients

Acetaminophen
Hydrocodone Bitartrate

Other Brand Names

Amacodone	Hycodaphen
Bancap HC	Hydrogesic
Cogesic	Lortab 5
Damacet-P	Lortab 7
Dolacet	Norcet
Dolo-Pap	T-Gesic Forte
Duradyne DHC	

Type of Drug

Narcotic analgesic combination.

Prescribed for

Relief of mild to moderate pain.

General Information

Vicodin may be prescribed for anyone who is allergic to Aspirin or who requires a narcotic pain reliever more potent than Codeine. This combination will relieve virtually any kind of pain, but is probably not effective for pain caused by arthritis or other inflammation because the Acetominophen ingredient does not produce an anti-inflammatory effect. A better choice would be a drug that contains Aspirin instead of Acetaminophen.

Cautions and Warnings

Do not take Vicodin if you are allergic to Acetaminophen or to Codeine or any other narcotic pain reliever. People with asthma or other breathing problems should use this combination with caution. The long-term use of Vicodin can lead to drug dependence or addiction. Hydrocodone Bitartrate is a respiratory depressant and affects the central nervous system, producing sleepiness, tiredness, and an inability to concentrate.

This drug should not be taken by women who may become pregnant while using it or by pregnant or nursing mothers.

Possible Side Effects

Light-headedness, dizziness, sleepiness, nausea, vomiting, loss of appetite, and sweating. These side effects usually can be controlled by taking a preparation with a lower narcotic dose.

Possible Adverse Drug Effects

Feeling "high", weakness, headache, agitation, loss of coordinated muscle movements, minor hallucinations, disorientation, blurred vision, dry mouth, constipation, facial flushing, rapid heartbeat, faintness, urinary difficulty or hesitancy, reduced sex drive and/or potency, itching, rash, anemia, low blood sugar, and yellowing of the skin or whites of the eyes. Narcotic drugs may aggravate convulsions in those who have had them in the past.

Drug Interactions

Alcohol, tranquilizers, sleeping pills, antihistamines, and other medicines that can depress the central nervous system should be avoided if you are taking Vicodin, because of the possibility of severe difficulty breathing. This interaction can be severe enough to make you stop breathing or can result in death.

Food Interactions

This combination may be taken with food or meals if it upsets your stomach.

Usual Dose

1 tablet every 6 hours.

Overdosage

The major signs of Vicodin overdose are extreme tiredness progressing to stupor and coma, difficulty breathing, pin-point pupils of the eyes, loss of response to simple stimulation such as the prick of a pin, cold clammy skin, and reduced heart rate. Massive Acetaminophen overdose or chronic use of the maximum daily dose of Acetaminophen can result in liver failure, indicated by yellowing of the skin or whites of the eyes, nausea, vomiting, abdominal pain, and diarrhea.

Victims of Vicodin overdose, if discovered within 1 hour of the incident, should be given Syrup of Ipecac to induce vomiting to remove any remaining drug from the stomach. Call your doctor or Poison Control Center before doing this. DO NOT try to induce vomiting if the victim is unconscious or having convulsions. If Vicodin overdose is discovered later than 1 hour after the medicine is taken, the victim will have to be taken to the hospital for treatment of narcotic overdose. Acetaminophen poisoning takes 24 to 36 hours to develop and requires continuous monitoring by a doctor. ALWAYS bring the medicine bottle with you.

Special Information

Use care while driving or doing anything else that requires concentration or alertness. Avoid alcohol and other nervous system depressants while taking Vicodin.

Call your doctor if you have trouble breathing normally or if this product causes nausea, vomiting, constipation, or any other side effect that becomes unusually severe.

Brand Name

Vioform-Hydrocortisone Cream/Lotion/Ointment/Jelly

Ingredients

Hydrocortisone
Iodochlorhydroxyquin (or Iodoquinol)

Other Brand Names

AP Creme	Hysone
Caquin	Iodosone
Corque	Lanvisone
Cortin	Mity-Quin
Epiform-HC	Pedi-Cort
HC-Form	Racet
Hydrocortisone with	Viodo
Iodochlorhydroxyquin	Vytone

(Also available in generic form)

Type of Drug

Topical corticosteroid anti-infective combination.

Prescribed for

Inflamed conditions of the skin such as eczema, athlete's foot, and other fungal infections.

General Information

Hydrocortisone is used to relieve the symptom of any itching, rash, or inflammation of the skin. It does not treat the underlying cause of the skin problem, only the symptom. It exerts this effect by interfering with natural body mechanisms that produced the rash, itching, etc., in the first place. If you use this drug without finding the cause of the problem, the condition may return after you stop using the drug. Hydrocortisone should not be used without your doctor's consent because it could cover an important reaction, one that may be valuable to him in treating you. Iodochlorhydroxyquin is used because of its antifungal, antibacterial, and antieczema effects.

Cautions and Warnings

Keep this medication away from the eyes. Because there is some question about the safety of topical Hydrocortisone in pregnant females, these products should not be used extensively or in large amounts for a long time if you are pregnant. Generally, this drug is safe for use during pregnancy. However, large amounts of Vioform-Hydrocortisone used during pregnancy or breast-feeding may slow the growth of newborn babies. If local irritation worsens, or develops where there was none, stop using the drug and contact your physician immediately.

Possible Side Effects

Burning sensation, itching, irritation, dryness, secondary infection, pimples similar to acne.

Usual Dose

Apply to affected area only, 2 to 3 times per day.

Special Information

Iodochlorhydroxyquin will stain fabric, skin, and hair and may not wash out of clothing.

Generic Name

Warfarin Sodium or Potassium

Brand Names

Athrombin-K
Panwarfin

(Also available in generic form)

Type of Drug

Oral anticoagulant.

Prescribed for

Anticoagulation (thinning of the blood). This is generally a secondary form of treatment for other diseases—such as blood clots in the arms and legs, pulmonary embolism, heart attack, or abnormal heart rhythms—in which the formation of blood clots may cause serious problems.

Under investigation is the use of Warfarin to reduce the risk of recurring heart attack. It may also be of benefit in the treatment of lung cancer.

General Information

Anticoagulants act by depressing the body's normal production of various factors which are known to take part in the coagulation mechanism. If you are taking Warfarin it is absolutely essential that you take the exact dose in the exact way prescribed by your doctor. Notify your doctor at the earliest sign of unusual bleeding or bruising (that is, the formation of black-and-blue marks), if you pass blood in your urine or stool, and/or if you pass a black tarry stool. The interactions of this class of drugs are extremely important and are discussed in detail below.

Warfarin can be extremely dangerous if not used properly. Periodic blood tests of the time it takes your blood or various factors in your blood to begin to coagulate are required for proper control of oral anticoagulant therapy.

If you are pregnant or think that you may be pregnant, you must discuss this with your doctor immediately: Warfarin can cause problems with the mother and will also pass into the fetus. It can cause and has caused bleeding and death of the fetus. A nursing mother should be careful, since the Warfarin will appear in the mother's milk. There are situations where the potential benefits to be gained from the use of Warfarin or one of the other anticoagulants may outweigh possible negative effects of these drugs in the pregnant patient: the decision to use one of these drugs is an important one which should be made cooperatively by you and your doctor.

Cautions and Warnings

Warfarin must be taken with care if you have a preexisting blood disease associated with coagulation or lack of coagulation. Other conditions in which the use of Warfarin should be discussed with your doctor are threatened abortion, Vitamin C deficiency, stomach ulcers or bleeding from the genital or urinary areas, severe high blood pressure, disease of the large bowel such as diverticulitis or ulcerative colitis, and subacute bacterial endocarditis.

People taking Warfarin should be extremely cautious about being exposed to cuts, bruises, or other types of injury which might cause bleeding.

Warfarin is not recommended to be taken during pregnancy or breast-feeding. Warfarin can cause birth defects and bleeding problems in the unborn child, mother, and newborn baby.

Possible Side Effects

The principal side effect experienced by patients taking Warfarin or other oral anticoagulant drugs is bleeding, which may occur within therapeutic dosage ranges and even when blood tests normally used to monitor anticoagulant therapy are within normal limits. If you bleed abnormally while you are taking anticoagulants and have eliminated the possibility of drug interactions, you should discuss this matter immediately with your doctor: it may indicate the presence of an underlying problem.

Possible Adverse Drug Effects

People taking oral anticoagulant drugs have reported bleeding from peptic ulcers, nausea, vomiting, diarrhea, blood in the urine, anemia, adverse effects on components of the blood, hepatitis, jaundice or yellowing of the skin and whites of the eyes, itching, rash, loss of hair, sore throat and mouth, and fever.

Drug Interactions

Warfarin and other oral anticoagulant (blood-thinning) drugs are probably involved in more drug interactions than any other kind of drug. Contact your pharmacist or doctor to discuss any other medications which you may be taking in order to avoid serious adverse interactions, which may increase the effectiveness of Warfarin to the point of causing severe bleeding or hemorrhage, or decrease its effectiveness to the point of causing formation of blood clots. Your doctor and your pharmacist should have records of all medications which you are taking.

Drugs that may increase the effect of Warfarin include broad-spectrum antibiotics such as Neomycin or others which will act on the normal bacterial contents of the stomach and intestines to eliminate Vitamin K, the body's natural antidote to Warfarin; mineral oil; Cholestyramine; Phenylbutazone; Oxyphenbutazone; Clofibrate; Indomethacin; sulfa drugs; Chloral Hydrate; Ethacrynic Acid; Mefenamic Acid; Nalidixic Acid; Aspirin; oral antidiabetic drugs (Tolbutamide, Chlorpropamide, Tolazamide); Chloramphenicol; Allopurinol; Nortriptyline; Methylphenidate; alcohol; Cimetidine, Disulfiram; Chlortetracycline; Quinidine; Haloperidol; Ascorbic Acid in large quantities; MAO inhibitors; Meperidine; and Thyroid Hormone and antithyroid drugs such as Propylthiouracil and Methylthiouracil will also increase the effects of oral anticoagulants.

There are fewer drugs that will decrease the effect of Warfarin, but the potential interaction can be just as dangerous with barbiturates, Glutethimide, Ethchlorvynol, Meprobamate, Griseofulvin, estrogens, oral contraceptive drugs, Chlorthalidone, corticosteroids, Phenytoin (see p. 528 for interaction resulting in Phenytoin toxicity), Carbamazepine, Vitamin K, and Rifampin.

No matter what the interaction, it is essential that you discuss all medications you are taking with your doctor or pharmacist, including not only prescription drugs but over-the-counter drugs containing Aspirin or other ingredients which may interact with Warfarin. Consult your physician or pharmacist before buying any over-the-counter drugs.

Food Interactions

Vitamin K is the antidote for Warfarin. Therefore, you should refrain from eating large quantities of foods rich in Vitamin K, like green leafy vegetables.

It should also be noted that any change in dietary habits or alcohol intake can effect Warfarin's action in your body.

Usual Dose

2 to 10 or more milligrams daily; but dose is extremely variable and must be individualized for maximum effect.

Overdosage

The primary symptom is bleeding. A laboratory test will show longer blood-clotting time, and bleeding can make itself known by appearance of blood in the urine or stool, an unusual number of black-and-blue marks, oozing of blood from small cuts made while shaving or from other trivial nicks or cuts, or bleeding from the gums after brushing the teeth. If bleeding does not stop within 10 to 15 minutes, your doctor should be called. He may tell you to skip a dose of anticoagulant and continue normal activities, or to go to a local hospital or doctor's office where blood evaluations can be made; or he may give you a prescription for Vitamin K, which antagonizes the effect of Warfarin. The latter has dangers because it can complicate subsequent anticoagulant therapy, but this is a decision that your doctor must make.

THE TOP 200 PRESCRIPTION DRUGS

**DISPENSED IN U.S. COMMUNITY PHARMACIES
BRAND NAME AS DISPENSED
NEW AND REFILL PRESCRIPTIONS—ALL STRENGTHS**

Rank 1984	Rank 1983	Drug Product	Manufacturer
1	1	Inderal	Ayerst
2	2	Dyazide	SKF
3	3	Lanoxin	Burroughs
4	4	Valium	Roche
5	6	Tylenol w/Codeine	McNeil
6	8	Ortho-Novum	Ortho
7	7	Tagamet	SKF
8	5	Lasix	Hoechst
9	11	Amoxil	Beecham
10	9	Motrin	Upjohn
11	10	Aldomet	MSD
12	12	Darvocet-N	Lilly
13	13	Keflex	Dista
14	15	Diabinese	Pfizer
15	14	Slow-K	CIBA
16	17	Lo/Ovral	Wyeth
17	18	Premarin	Ayerst
18	19	Lopressor	Geigy
19	16	Dilantin	Parke Davis
20	28	Tenormin	Stuart
21	20	Synthroid	Flint
22	24	Theo-Dur	Key
23	26	Ativan	Wyeth
24	21	E.E.S.	Abbott
25	27	Naprosyn	Syntex
26	23	Dimetapp	Robins
27	25	Indocin	MSD
28	29	Feldene	Pfizer

*Not in top 200 in 1983

Rank 1984	Rank 1983	Drug Product	Manufacturer
29	22	Dalmane	Roche
30	32	Timoptic	MSD
31	34	Procardia	Pfizer
32	62	Xanax	Upjohn
33	35	Minipress	Pfizer
34	30	Benadryl	Parke Davis
35	37	Monistat-7	Ortho
36	31	Tranxene	Abbott
37	49	Norinyl	Syntex
38	48	Ceclor	Lilly
39	40	Ovral	Wyeth
40	33	Isordil	Ives
41	39	E-Mycin	Upjohn
42	*	Zantac	Glaxo
43	47	Corgard	Squibb
44	38	Persantine	Boehringer
45	79	Rufen	Boots
46	41	Clinoril	MSD
47	98	Ledercillin VK	Lederle
48	*	Polymox	Bristol
49	42	Aldoril	MSD
50	57	Restoril	Sandoz
51	55	Catapres	Boehringer
52	52	Fiorinal	Sandoz
53	36	Hygroton	USV
54	44	Hydrodiuril	MSD
55	43	Omnipen	Wyeth
56	102	Micro-K	Robins
57	50	Zyloprim	Burroughs
58	56	Hydrochlorothiazide	Lederle
59	59	Tolinase	Upjohn
60	46	Empirin w/Codeine	Burroughs
61	45	Mellaril	Sandoz
62	53	Pen Vee K	Wyeth
63	63	Nitrostat	Parke Davis
64	51	Donnatal	Robins
65	58	Naldecon	Bristol
66	54	Thyroid	USV
67	75	Alupent	Boehringer
68	60	Bactrim DS	Roche

Rank 1984	Rank 1983	Drug Product	Manufacturer
69	77	Tetracycline	Parke Davis
70	*	Hydrochlorothiazide	Rugby
71	*	Hydrochlorothiazide	Barr
72	145	Nordette	Wyeth
73	196	Halcion	Upjohn
74	116	Demulen	Searle
75	111	EryC	Parke Davis
76	80	Wymox	Wyeth
77	83	Ventolin	Glaxo
78	64	Percodan	Du Pont
79	93	Moduretic	MSD
80	190	Cardizem	Marion
81	105	Haldol	McNeil
82	69	Coumadin	Du Pont
83	67	Septra DS	Burroughs
84	92	Proventil	Schering
85	61	Elavil	MSD
86	65	Triavil	MSD
87	*	Beepen VK	Beecham
88	71	Sinequan	Roerig
89	74	Cortisporin	Burroughs
90	84	K-Tab	Abbott
91	87	Flexeril	MSD
92	141	Transderm-Nitro	CIBA
93	66	Atarax	Roerig
94	68	Antivert	Roerig
95	70	Lotrimin	Schering
96	73	Phenobarbital	Lilly
97	76	Valisone	Schering
98	140	Nitro-Dur	Key
99	137	Capoten	Squibb
100	78	Achromycin V	Lederle
101	72	V-Cillin K	Lilly
102	95	Macrodantin	Norwich
103	100	Nalfon	Dista
104	109	Fiorinal w/Codeine	Sandoz
105	146	Reglan	Robins
106	121	Provera	Upjohn
107	85	Brethine	Geigy
108	108	Erythromycin	Abbott

Rank 1984	Rank 1983	Drug Product	Manufacturer
109	82	Lomotil	Searle
110	*	Acetaminophen w/Codeine	Zenith
111	110	Erythrocin Stearate	Abbott
112	103	Bactrim	Roche
113	128	Dolobid	MSD
114	89	Librax	Roche
115	126	Parafon Forte	McNeil
116	101	Septra	Burroughs
117	129	Anaprox	Syntex
118	150	Percocet	Du Pont
119	*	Nicorette	Merrell Dow
120	86	Amcill	Parke Davis
121	133	Tegretol	Geigy
122	166	Entex LA	Norwich
123	122	Bentyl	Merrell Dow
124	96	Apresoline	CIBA
125	99	Ornade	SKF
126	114	Tolectin	McNeil
127	88	Librium	Roche
128	97	Aldactazide	Searle
129	91	Mycolog	Squibb
130	144	Klotrix	Mead Johnson
131	117	Cogentin	MSD
132	119	Sinemet	MSD
133	94	Synalgos-DC	Ives
134	155	Desyrel	Mead Johnson
135	90	Amoxicillin	Parke Davis
136	*	Procan	Parke Davis
137	120	K-Lyte	Mead Johnson
138	134	Norpace	Searle
139	107	Nitro-Bid	Marion
140	138	Minocin	Lederle
141	112	Enduron	Abbott
142	135	Kenalog	Squibb
143	127	Serax	Wyeth
144	142	Centrax	Parke Davis
145	136	Lidex	Syntex
146	*	Phenergan Exp w/Codeine	Wyeth
147	123	Orinase	Upjohn
148	158	Meclomen	Parke Davis

Rank 1984	Rank 1983	Drug Product	Manufacturer
149	118	Slo-Phyllin	Rorer
150	197	Tylox	McNeil
151	152	Adapin	Pennwalt
152	143	Compazine	SKF
153	132	Inderide	Ayerst
154	*	Neosporin	Burroughs
155	81	Penicillin VK	Parke Davis
156	*	Polycillin	Bristol
157	*	Trinalin	Schering
158	106	Ser-Ap-Es	CIBA
159	162	Medrol	Upjohn
160	124	Phenaphen w/Codeine	Robins
161	113	Vibramycin	Pfizer
162	195	Vicodin	Knoll
163	200	Lopurin	Boots
164	131	Sumycin	Squibb
165	*	Tri-Vi-Flor	Mead Johnson
166	*	Ampicillin	Purepac
167	125	Deltasone	Upjohn
168	165	Pediazole	Ross
169	191	Duricef	Mead Johnson
170	130	Esidrix	CIBA
171	153	Stuartnatal 1+1	Stuart
172	*	Calan	Searle
173	169	Pyridium	Parke Davis
174	159	Vanceril	Schering
175	115	Ilosone	Dista
176	170	Quinaglute	Berlex
177	149	Kwell	Reed & Carnrick
178	151	Nitroglycerin	Lilly
179	164	Limbitrol	Roche
180	179	Anusol HC	Parke Davis
181	*	Talwin NX	Winthrop-Breon
182	175	Phenergan VC w/Cod.	Wyeth
183	147	Darvon Compound-65	Lilly
184	163	Zaroxolyn	Pennwalt
185	*	Furosemide	Lederle
186	*	Gyne-Lotrimin	Schering
187	*	Dipyridamole	Rugby
188	154	Hydergine	Dorsey

Rank 1984	Rank 1983	Drug Product	Manufacturer
189	148	Sorbitrate	Stuart
190	181	Materna 1.60	Lederle
191	193	Tussi-Organidin	Wallace
192	176	Phenobarbital	Parke Davis
193	180	Hytone	Dermik
194	156	Diuril	MSD
195	177	Ludiomil	CIBA
196	184	Navane	Roerig
197	*	Rondec DM	Ross
198	194	Topicort	Hoechst
199	168	Thorazine	SKF
200	187	Isopto Carpine	Alcon

Data supplied by Pharmaceutical Data Services, Scottsdale, AZ a wholly-owned subsidiary of McKesson Corporation.

How Different Drug Types Work in the Body

During the last 50 years there have been many dramatic medical advances, particularly in the development of new drugs which have improved our health and extended our life expectancy. Many products of recent drug research, including the antibiotics, oral contraceptives, psychotropic drugs, and newer heart medicines, have changed our life-styles. Today both brand-name and generic versions of these drugs are available; they dry up runny noses, curb pain, and, very often, arrest serious disease.

Although most newer drugs are "synthetic" products, concocted in the laboratory, others, and many older drugs, are derived from plants, herbs, roots, and other naturally occurring minerals and substances which have been known and used for centuries. Digoxin, for example, was derived from digitalis which has been used for over 200 years to treat heart disease and other ailments such as "fits" and comes from the foxglove family; Quinine is derived from tree bark; Insulin and other hormones are produced from animal glands; and, of course, Penicillin originally came from simple bread mold. In some ways, today's giant pharmaceutical industry is a direct descendant of the medicine men of earlier times who mixed their exotic "potions."

An important difference between the drugs we use today and potions of past eras is standardization. Except for compounded prescriptions prepared by your local pharmacist and mixutres of intravenous medicines made by hospital pharmacists, all of today's pills are made in modern manufacturing facilities strictly supervised and required to meet exacting government standards. Because of these stringent laws and regulations, which have come into force in the United States only since the early part of this century, all drugs are carefully made. Each new drug must pass through

715

many testing levels before it can be marketed. A drug cannot reach your mouth until the federal agency that supervises this activity, the Food and Drug Administration (FDA), is satisfied that it has been proved both safe and effective. The FDA requires that drugs be tested on lab animals and a relatively small number of people before they can be marketed. For some drugs, studies are continued after their introduction to see if they can be used to treat other diseases; or if they will produce previously unreported side effects.

Some examples of this follow-up or postmarketing surveillance are studies conducted on oral contraceptives (the Pill), the antiarthritis drug Piroxicam (Feldene), and the beta blocker Propranolol (Inderal). Serious potential side effects of the Pill were not revealed until after millions of women had used the drug for 10 to 20 years. Scientists had been unable to fully evaluate oral contraceptives until these long-term effects on the body were uncovered. On the other hand, Propranolol had already been shown to be very effective in the treatment of abnormal heart rhythms, angina, high blood pressure, and other diseases. Recent tests demonstrated its effectiveness in preventing second heart attacks and were so successful that a long-range study was stopped at midpoint to allow those in the control group (who were getting placebos) to benefit from the drug's newly uncovered properties. Piroxicam has been associated with several deaths over the years and postmarketing studies have been undertaken to determine if the drug contributed to those deaths or was simply an innocent bystander in the process.

The drug introduction process can take 3 to 10 years and costs millions of dollars. Until recently, even drugs available outside the United States were required to undergo extensive retesting to meet FDA standards. Critics have suggested that United States drug laws are too tough, producing a "drug lag" in which medicines often are not introduced into the United States until after they have been used in other countries for many years. Recently, the FDA revised its regulations to permit the submission of a limited amount of foreign drug data in the approval process. The drug still must be proved safe and effective in the United States, but the foreign data does save drug manufacturers time and money by not forcing them to reproduce the results of already accepted medical studies. The FDA closely examines all the data and submits both foreign and domestic studies to rigorous tests. As a result, the United States has yet to suffer a drug tragedy on the scale of the Thalidomide scandal of the 1960s in Europe. At that time, many women were given the sedative during the first months of pregnancy. The drug caused many horrible birth defects and led directly to stronger FDA regulations in the 1960s.

ORPHAN DRUGS

Each year hundreds of drugs are tested, but only a small percentage ever reach general distribution. Some of these drugs can be used to treat rare medical conditions. But others are never released because they do not have a commercial potential large enough to justify the financial investment required to move a drug product through the approval process. These drugs are called "orphan drugs" but can be obtained through the FDA under a "compassionate IND," a special application procedure which can be undertaken by your doctor; it's wise to check with your doctor before taking any medication not regularly prescribed in the United States.

A major step toward making more orphan drugs available for their limited application occurred when, in 1983, federal legislation was passed easing the process of approval for these special medicines. Since that time, several new medications have been made available, but the impact has not been as great as expected by the sponsors of the legislation.

GENERIC VS. BRAND NAME DRUGS

When a new drug is approved by FDA, it is known by two different names. The generic name, also known as the official name, is used by FDA and others who write about or refer to the drug because it does not denote a particular manufacturer. The generic name is usually complex and may be related to the drug's chemical name or formula. The other name is the drug's brand name, assigned by the pharmaceutical company. Brand names are usually catchy and designed to be remembered with ease or to indicate a particular characteristic of the drug. For example, one drug used to lower high blood pressure is known by the generic name Metoprolol and the brand name Lopressor.

atent law allows pharmaceutical companies the right to sell a new drug for as long as 25 years. In most cases, it takes between 7 and 10 years for a pharmaceutical manufacturer to obtain new drug approval, leaving 15 to 18 years of exclusive right to sell the drug product. During this period, a drug is known as a sole source (available from only one manufacturer or distributor) or brand name product.

After the originator's period of exclusive right to sell the drug product expires, other manufacturers or distributors may enter the market and sell the same drug. These products are called generic drugs, even though they are often given brand names of their own by the companies which make or distribute them.

Some generic drug products require special manufacturing procedures to insure the drug's potency and effectiveness. In these cases, FDA requires drug manufacturers to submit biological studies to prove that the generic drug product is equivalent to the original in the effect it can be expected to produce in your body. The approval process is much less complicated for most drugs because they do not require special studies.

Companies that market generic drugs usually sell them for less money than the brand name product because they are competing with the original drug manufacturer for drug sales. Because of this, generic drug products offer you the opportunity of saving a great deal of money on prescription drugs. Unfortunately, few of the most often prescribed drugs are available from more than one manufacturer. You can determine if your medicine is available under more than one brand name by simply looking under the section, "Other Brand Names," in each drug profile.

HOW DO PILLS WORK?

Drugs work by altering a normal function in the body or by correcting an abnormal function. Generally they are taken by mouth in either solid (capsule or tablet) or liquid form, depending on their chemical makeup. Some drugs are injected directly into the bloodstream for quicker action or are not made in oral form.

When a pill is taken, it is first broken down in the stomach by the gastric juices. The drug passes through the walls of the stomach or intestines into the bloodstream. (Food already in the stomach may slow this absorption process, so it's important to ask your doctor or pharmacist if your drug should be taken with or before meals.) Once in the bloodstream, drugs, along with foods and other substances, are sent to and metabolized by the liver. When the liver has done its work it may have turned the drug into its most useful form, or it may have deactivated the drug. In either case, the drug is then sent back out into the bloodstream and then to its site of action.

Once the drug has exerted its effect it returns to the bloodstream and is excreted. We have to take medicines in repeated doses because they work on the body for only a limited period of time. Taking more of the medicine replenishes your internal supply and allows the drug effect to continue. Therefore, you must take all drugs exactly as prescribed to avoid overloading or overdosing your body.

The following information will give you a brief idea of how various drug types work in the body.

ANTIBIOTICS

Antibiotics are used to treat infections which can by caused by any of hundreds of microorganisms. You must take an antibiotic specific for the organism causing your problem; otherwise, your infection can not be cured.

How do we identify the trouble-making organism? By running specific tests called "cultures." Your doctor, or nurse, or a trained technician takes a small sample of infected fluid or tissue and places it in a medium containing specific nutrients. Here, the organism can multiply and grow. The culture then is placed in an incubator to stimulate bacterial growth. Within 2 days the organisms multiply to form a colony; samples of the colony can be examined under a microscope and identified.

The organisms can be tested against various antibiotics to see which is the best choice for treatment. This process is called testing for sensitivity.

Your doctor may have a good idea of what the infecting organisms are most likely to be after evaluating the location and appearance of the infection and correlating this information with your symptoms. However, this hypothesis should be confirmed by taking a culture.

Starting to take an antibiotic BEFORE your infection is cultured can lead to a falsely negative infection report. This happens because even the smallest amounts of antibiotic can prevent the infecting organism from growing in the culture environment. Small amounts of antibiotic in your body can grossly interfere with this test.

Many infections, including the common cold, flu, and some other upper respiratory (lung) infections, are caused by viruses. Viruses are simpler organisms than bacteria; they are not affected by antibiotics, so taking an antibiotic will not cure your virus infection. You must depend upon your doctor to distinguish between bacterial and virus infections, which can present similar symptoms. Often the only way to tell them apart is through a culture. Viruses don't grow in a bacterial culture.

Can taking an antibiotic when you don't need one hurt you? Yes. Taking any drug unnecessarily exposes you to potential side effects and adverse reactions. Also, unwarranted use of an antibiotic can sensitize you to it, so that the next time you use it, perhaps in a situation where you badly need it, you may develop an allergic reaction. Self-medication with antibiotics is unwise for other reasons: you may take too much or too little, or you may have an infection caused by an organism not affected by the antibiotic. Do not take any antibiotic unless specifically directed to do so by your doctor.

In general, antibiotics are considered either bactericidal or bacteriostatic. Batericidal antibiotics kill the microorganisms they affect by interfering with natural processes such as development of the cell wall or normal chemical reactions. Bactericidal antibiotics include Penicillin, Ampicillin, Amoxcillin, Cefadroxil (Duricef), Cephalexin, Carbenicillin (Geocillin), Polymyxin, Bacitracin, Amphotericin, and Nystatin.

Bacteriostatic antibiotics interfere with microorganisms by disturbing chemical processes (usually, stages of protein production) necessary to their reproduction. Bacteriostatic antibiotics include Tetracycline, Doxycycline, Minocycline, Erythromycin, Griseofulvin, and Chloramphenicol (Chloramphenicol may be bactericidal in some situations.)

ANTIHYPERTENSIVE DRUGS

High blood pressure is a major problem in the United States, since many people have it and there are problems associated with treating it. Twelve percent of Americans have high blood pressure but don't know it. Of those who know they have high blood pressure, only half have achieved constant pressure readings in the acceptable range.

High blood pressure can cause heart attack, heart failure, stroke, aneurysm (ballooning out of a major blood vessel—death can result if the blood vessel wall bursts like a balloon), and kidney failure.

How do you know if you have high blood pressure?

For diagnosis a series of blood pressure readings, on at least three visits, are taken to be sure that the high pressure is persistent. The way your high blood pressure is treated depends upon how high the pressure is and also on an evaluation of how much damage has already been done.

Drugs usually play a major role in the treatment of high blood pressure. Four types of drugs are used to help reduce muscle tension in veins and arteries: diuretics, vasodilators, drugs that interfere with nervous system activity, and one drug that interferes with body hormone function.

Diuretics help lower blood pressure by lowering the amount of water in the body. They decrease the amount of fluid that must be handled by the circulatory system and lower the blood pressure by reducing fluid volume inside blood vessels. They also increase the amount of sodium lost through your kidneys and affect levels of sodium and calcium in the muscles of your small arteries. Diuretics alone can control mild or moderate hypertension in as many as half of all people with high blood pressure. Some diuretics used to treat hypertension are Hydrochlorothiazide, Chlorothiazide, Chlorthalidone, Ethacrynic Acid (Edecrin), Furosemide, Indapamide, Metalazone, and Polythiazide, (Renese), Qunethazone (Hydomox) and Bendroflumethazide (Naturetin).

Vasodilators work directly on the muscles in the walls of arteries to relax them, keeping your blood in the arteries of your arms and legs and reducing blood pressure. One vasodilator is Hydralazine, which can be taken by itself in tablet form and as an ingredient in the drug Ser-Ap-Es; it is always used in combination with another antihypertensive drug. Another vasodilator is Prazosin, which is most effective when taken with a beta blocker or diuretic drug.

The third group of drugs act on the nervous system to help control muscle tone in blood vessels. Some of these drugs work in the brain or spinal cord (central nervous system); some at intermediate centers for nervous system control called autonomic ganglia; some at nerve endings where control of muscle tone actually takes place; and some at points in muscle tissue (receptor sites) where chemical messages from the nervous system are received. Some of the more important drugs in this group are Reserpine, which works by depleting natural stimulants from blood vessel nerve endings, Rauwiloid Methyldopa, Guanethidine, and the beta blockers. Guanadrel works by blocking nerve impulses traveling to muscles in blood vessel walls. Guanabenz, a newer antihypertensive drug, and Clonidine work on special receptors in the brain to reduce the amount of natural stimulant produced, lowering blood pressure. Beta blockers deserve special mention here because they are used more widely than any other antihypertensive drug group except the diuretics. Beta blockers lower blood pressure by reducing the amount of blood pumped by your heart with each stroke, by reducing the amount of blood circulating in your veins and arteries, and by reducing the nerve impulses in the muscles of your veins and arteries that keep your pressure high. Beta blockers also inhibit the enzyme renin produced by your kidney. Renin is converted to another substance, angiotensin, a potent elevator of blood pressure and an important ingredient in maintaining normal blood pressure. The beta blockers include Acebutelol, Atenolol, Labetolol, Metoprolol, Nadolol, Pindolol, Propranolol, and Timolol. Metoprolol and Labetolol are used exclusively for high blood pressure. The others are used for a variety of other conditions as well as high blood pressure.

The fourth group is represented by Captopril, which prevents the conversion of a potent hormone called angiotensin inhibitors and can drastically lower blood pressure.

Usually, more than one drug is prescribed for treatment of hypertension. Mixing medications allows your doctor to use drugs that complement each other, resulting in more efficient lowering of blood pressure.

One of the problems in the treatment of high blood pressure is that people often don't do what is best for them. They don't take their medicines as directed, they don't follow special diets given to them, and they don't follow other instructions relating to exercise and weight control. In high blood pressure, as in many other diseases, effective treatment can only be accomplished by you. The medication prescribed for your hypertension can help only if taken exactly as directed.

HEART DRUGS

This section deals with drugs that have a direct effect on the heart rather than drugs that have only a secondary effect, such as those which affect your heart by reducing high blood pressure. We will discuss digitalis drugs, drugs used to correct abnormal heart rhythm, and drugs used to treat angina pectoris.

Digitalis Group

The members of the digitalis group are chemically similar. Originally derived from the garden plant Digitalis Purpurea (foxglove), they are chemically synthesized today. Most commonly used are Digoxin and Digitoxin. Digitalis drugs may differ in how long it takes the drug to start working, how long the drug effect lasts, how the drug is eliminated from the body, and how well the drug is tolerated by patients.

What are the effects of digitalis on your heart? First, it makes your heart beat more forcefully, which helps people with congestive heart failure by helping the heart to work more efficiently and increase the amount of blood pumped with each contraction, or beat. The heart is essentially a pump; the more efficiently it works, the better off we are.

Second, digitalis slows the rate at which the heart beats. This is also important in helping the heart to be more efficient. When a person suffers from heart failure, the heart muscle contracts with less force and pumps less blood with each beat. The normal response of the heart is to try to work faster and keep a sufficient supply of blood flowing. But a faster heartbeat creates another problem: like any pump, the heart can only work when there is sufficient fluid (blood) inside the pump chamber. When the heart beats too rapidly, the pump chambers of the heart (ventricles) do not fill enough between beats, reducing the potential output of the heart.

Correcting Abnormal Heart Rhythms

When abnormalities in the conduction of nervous impulses through the heart muscle are present, they cause the heart

to beat in uneven cycles or in an uncoordinated manner. Arrhythmias (abnormal heart rhythms) have many causes, including:
• Imbalances in body levels of potassium or sodium.
• Thyroid or other disease
• Adverse drug effects
• Cardiac disease directly affecting nerve pathways in the heart.

Arrhythmias, which come in many sizes, shapes, and styles are classified according to heart area affected, cause (if one can be found), and severity. This classification helps your doctor to choose the most appropriate drug therapy. In general, all antiarrhythmic drugs slow the conduction of nerve impulses through cardiac tissue. But, since each agent affects your heart's nervous system differently, the determination of which drug is most appropriate for your condition can be made only by your doctor after complete analysis of electrocardiogram, symptoms, medical history, and other conditions.

When drugs do not satisfactorily control abnormal heart rhythms, an electrical device called a pacemaker may be surgically inserted. The pacemaker controls heart rate by sending out an electrical impulse of its own that overrides or counterbalances abnormal imulses being transmitted within the heart. It may be permanently implanted if short-term use does not convert your heart to a normal rhythm of its own.

Treatment of Angina

Angina Pectoris is characterized by a squeezing, choking, or heavy pain or discomfort in the chest. These symptoms can also be found in or extend to the arm, shoulder, back, neck, or lower jaw. Angina usually sets in or gets worse while or immediately after the victim has undergone strenuous physical activity. It is thought to be caused by a decrease in oxygen supply to the heart, or oxygen deficit. Oxygen deficit develops when blood flow to the heart is partially blocked by cholesterol or other deposits in blood vessels. This kind of blockage is called atherosclerosis and the disease (such as angina) resulting from it is called atherosclerotic heart disease. Oxygen defect can also occur if the muscles in cardiac blood vessel walls go into spasm and temporarily choke off blood supply. Until recently, it has been widely accepted that anyone experiencing angina will develop the painful symptoms described above. However, it is now recognized that several hundred thousand fatal heart attacks each year occur in people with angina who do not experience these painful symptoms. Since the pain serves as a warning to see a doctor for treatment, people with angina who do not feel pain are unable to seek treatment and progress rapidly to an untreatable condition. People with this condition may be identified by stress testing techniques. However, often they don't get to a doctor until it is too late.

Drugs used to treat angina work by dilating (opening) blood vessels that serve the heart. Nitroglycerin, the prime example of this group of drugs, is taken in tablets which dissolve under the tongue and can provide almost immediate relief as the medicine is absorbed directly into the bloodstream. From there is quickly goes to the heart and can relax the muscles in blood vessel walls, increasing blood supply to heart tissue. Nitroglycerin can also be taken to prevent angina as a long-acting pill or as a medication-saturated patch that you place on your skin. Nitroglycerin is released from the patch in controlled doses, providing a steady and consistent supply of the drug to your bloodstream. Other drugs in this group are: Isosorbide Dinitrate and Pentaerythrityl Tetranitrate.

Other drugs that can be used to treat angina are the beta blockers Nadolol or Propranolol and the calcium or slow-channel blockers.

Beta Blockers

The beta blockers work by blocking the effects of naturally occurring stimulants such as norepinephrine or the "beta" receptors of your heart and blood vessels. Since beta receptors can be found in many parts of your body, these drugs have been found to have profound effects on other conditions than heart disease.

Two beta blockers are routinely used as part of the long-term treatment of angina. They reduce the heart's workload, thus reducing its need for oxygen. When the need for oxygen is reduced, angina is less likely to occur.

Beta blockers are used for a variety of other purposes as well, including high blood pressure, abnormal heart rhythms, prevention of second heart attacks after a first one has been experienced, migraine headaches, stomach bleeding, schizophrenia, tremors resulting from unknown causes, panic, and stage fright. Some studies indicate that Propranolol may be an effective contraceptive when inserted into the vaginal tract.

Calcium or Slow-Channel Blockers

These drugs are quite effective in the long-term treatment of angina and have become routine therapy for many people whose condition cannot be controlled with Nitroglycerine alone. A calcium channel blocker such as Diltiazem, Nifedipine, or Verapamil may be used together with Nitroglycerine or other nitrate and with a beta blocker. Calcium or slow-channel blockers prevent calcium from moving into muscle cells. This results in a reduction in the rate at which muscle cells contract or flex. Since less muscle flexion translates into less work for the heart, the need for oxygen is also reduced, thereby contributing to the treatment of angina. Calcium blockers are also used to treat arrhythmias (abnormal heart rhythms) and high blood pressure. They are being studied for their positive effects on blood clotting, asthma, migraine headaches, and gastrointestinal spasms.

ANTICOAGULANTS

Popularly known as "blood thinners," these drugs work by interfering with the clotting mechanism. They have been in use for some 400 years and are prescribed to people who have any disease that increases the chance of forming a blood clot or who have had some damage from a blood clot in the brain (stroke), heart, lung, or other critical area. Those who have had a myocardial infarction (heart attack) may be given an anticoagulant to keep heart damage from causing the formation of a blood clot.

The clotting process is a complex set of chemical reactions; anything that upsets one or more of these reactions will prevent clot formation.

If you are taking an anticoagulant, its effectiveness should be carefully monitored by blood tests, which can easily and conveniently be performed in your doctor's office and are used to help decide if you need more or less medication. Anticoagulants should not be used if you have a history of severe bleeding episodes, have an active bleeding ulcer, have had a recent stroke with continued bleeding in the head, or are pregnant (especially if your doctor feels you may spontaneously lose your baby).

Most people taking anticoagulant drugs have no major problems so long as they take care of themselves, follow instructions, and avoid unnecessary medications, including over-the-counter drugs containing Aspirin. (Guidance on specific over-the-counter drugs can be obtained from your doctor or pharmacist.) Aspirin and over-the-counter drugs containing Aspirin as an ingredient interact with oral anticoagulants to increase the action of the anticoagulant, causing bleeding, most commonly at first from the nose or gums. If you are taking an anticoagulant and begin oozing blood from the nose or gums, contact your doctor *immediately*.

Other drug interactions may decrease the effect of the anticoagulant, which increases the risk of a blood clot—exactly what you were trying to prevent in the first place. The best policy is to avoid drugs (if possible) which can interfere with anticoagulant activity, including barbiturates, Glutethimide, oral contraceptive drugs, and Phenytoin.

Interactions with anticoagluant drugs can be compensated for by adjusting the dosage of anticoagulant. For example, if you must take Phenytoin on a long-term basis, the doctor can give you more anticoagulant drug than you would ordinarily take.

ANTINEOPLASTICS (Anticancer Drugs)

Drugs used to treat cancer are designed to slow or completely stop the abnormal growth of cancerous cells. Basically, cancerous cells grow uncontrollably at a much faster rate than others in surrounding tissues. The abnormal growth rate causes functional problems and interferes with normal life processes. A great deal of time, effort, and money has gone into research aimed at discovering more about the growth process of human cells so that drugs could be designed which would interfere with specific phases in the growth of the cancerous cells. Drugs which do this are called "cell cycle specific" drugs. Other anticancer drugs work on cells that are growing or resting; they are called "cell cycle nonspecific." In other words, these drugs do not work on a specific phase of cell growth. In reviewing the antineoplastic drugs, we will only provide a brief description of the various classes of drugs used. Also, many drugs given to cancer patients are not given to treat the basic disease. Rather, they are used to relieve other symptoms which may have developed as a result of cancer (pain, constipation, nutritional deficiency, etc.) or to relieve the stress caused by the disease (tranquilizers, antianxiety drugs, etc.).

Alkylating Agents

These drugs interfere with DNA and render it powerless to carry out its normal function in cell duplication. Members of this group include Mechlorethamine, Chlorambucil (Leukeran), Melphalan, Cyclophosphamide (Cytoxan), Lomustine, Carmustine, Uracil Mustard, Thiotepa, Busulfan, and Pipobroman. These drugs all have severe side effects and can be as dangerous as the disease against which they are used if not taken under the strict supervision of a doctor who has been trained to use these medications. The alkylating agents are cell cycle nonspecific.

Antimetabolites

These drugs can also interfere with normal cells and cause their eventual destruction. They can accomplish this by either substituting for a normal component of the cell, thereby rendering that part of the cell nonfunctional, or by blocking a key enzyme directly within the cell. Members of this group include Methotrexate, Fluorouracil, Floxuridine, Cytarabine, Mercaptopurine, and Thioguanine. The antimetabolites are cell cycle specific agents and only work on the so-called "s phase" of cell growth.

Hormones

Hormone therapy has been successfully used as part of the treatment of various cancers although the exact mechanism of action is not known. Adrenocortical steroids (Prednisone, Hydrocortisone, Dexamethasone, etc.) are used most

dely. Male (androgens) and female (estrogens) hormones
e used to counterbalance the overproduction of sex hor-
ones produced by some tumors, thereby restricting their
owth. For example, androgens such as Dromostanolone,
alusterone, or Testolactone are used in the treatment of
east cancer in women. Estrogens such as Diethylstilbestrol
ay be given to men with prostate cancer to counterbalance
e overproduction of male hormone resulting from that
mor. Other hormones used in cancer treatment are the
ogestins (Megestrol Acetate and Medroxyprogesterone Ac-
ate). One drug has been developed which counters the
fect of estrogen. This "anti-estrogen" is Tamoxifen and
n be used to neutralize excessive estrogen.

One interesting application of the relationship between
ody hormones and cancer is the analysis of cancerous
east tissue for male and female hormone receptors. Women
ith so called "estrogen sensitive" disease are more likely
respond to certain treatment programs than women whose
ncers are estrogen negative or progesterone sensitive. To-
ay, hormone sensitivity is widely used as part of the process
determining the most appropriate breast cancer treatment.

ntibiotics

Several antineoplastic drugs are derived from natural
urces and have antimicrobial activity. These drugs work
disrupting cellular functions in normal tissues as well as
invading microorganisms. When used in cancer treat-
ent, the drug is taken up by the cancerous tissue because
ose cells are dividing at a much more rapid pace than
rmal cells. These drugs are cell cycle nonspecific. They
hibit DNA-dependent cell functions and delay or inhibit the
ocess by which cells divide. The members of this group
e Bleomycin, Doxorubicin, Daunorubicin, Mitomycin, Dac-
omycin, and Mithramycin.

itotic Inhibitors

There are only two drugs in this group: Vincristine and
nblastine. They work by interfering with a specific phase of
ll duplication, that point at which the two strands of DNA
parate to form the nuclei of the two new cells. These
ugs are cell cycle specific and are used frequently because

of their relatively low incidence of serious toxic effects ∘
the bone marrow.

Radioactive Drugs

Radiation is used to kill cancerous cells. Drugs tagged wi
a radioactive component are used when the drug is a
sorbed by a specific organ that is cancerous and in need
treatment. Examples of this type of drug are Iodine 1.
(thyroid cancer) and Phosphorous 32 (leukemias, polycyth
mia vera, lung cancer).

Immunosuppressants

Azathioprine (Imuran) is a unique medicine used to suppre
the body's immune response mechanism, which normal
allows us to respond to infection, outside agents that cau
allergies, or other foreign objects. When it is artificially su
pressed with this medication, as in the case of a transplant∘
kidney, it permits the new kidney to continue functioning
the body of the transplant patient. Without Azathioprine t∎
body would react to a new kidney as a foreign object a∎
soon destroy it. People taking this drug are unusually su
ceptible to infection and must be constantly alert to a∎
changes. Normal responses (fever, etc.) may not be prese
or may be delayed by Azathioprine treatment.

Other

Other drugs have been developed which do not fall in
any of the other previously discussed groups, although son
of them act similarly to members of specific drug group
Hydroxyurea inhibits DNA synthesis. It is cell cycle specif
Procarbazine inhibits protein DNA and RNA synthesis. It
cell cycle specific and used only for Hodgkins diseas
Dacarbazine inhibits DNA and acts very similarly to the alk∘
ating agents. It is cell cycle nonspecific. Cisplatin also wor
similarly to the alkylating agents. It is used in the treatme
of tumors of the ovary and testicle and is cell cycle nonsp
cific. Mitotane is used in cancer of the adrenal cortex (t∎
part of the body that produces adrenal corticosteroids). ∎
action is very specific and, therefore, it does not have ma∎
severe side effects. Asparaginase is used in the treatment

kemia. It is a highly toxic drug that must be used only
der strict supervision in a hospital.

Newer agents are continuously being investigated for their
ect against cancer. Several have shown promise but many
ve received more notoriety and publicity than they de-
rve. Two examples are Laetrile and Interferon. Laetrile was
ently found to be worthless in cancer treatment. Inter-
on is still undergoing preliminary studies in several differ-
t types of cancer. The premise in using Interferon is that
any cancers are caused by viruslike particles. Interferon,
eoretically, interrupts virus activity and thus can treat
ncer.

DRUGS FOR THE COMMON COLD

ve you ever felt unwell and had a runny or stuffy nose,
stnasal drip, muscle aches, cough, headache, or fever? If
, you probably have been told, "It's just a cold." The com-
on cold is a catchall name given to a set of symptoms that
n be caused by over 150 different viruses. Although we
ow what causes a cold we cannot prevent or cure it: we
n only let it run its course and take medicine to make us
ore comfortable and help relieve the symptoms. Antibiotic
ugs are not effective against cold viruses. How, then, can
u make yourself more comfortable during a cold? You can
ke nasal decongestants, antihistamines, cough suppressants,
pectorants, analgesics (pain relievers), or antipyretics (fe-
r reducers). Usually, if you get a prescription for a cold
medy it will contain drugs in two or three of these catego-
es. Let us consider each type of drug and how it helps
lieve our suffering.

sal Decongestants

When your nose is stuffy or runny, tissue in the lining of
e nose and blood vessels are dilated and produce more
cretions (mucus) than normal. There has to be some place
r the extra material to go, so it either goes out the front
ay (runny nose) or the back way (postnasal drip). Dilated
sues give one of the feeling of nasal congestion or stuffi-
ss. Decongestant drugs are stimulants which, when they
ach the congested area, act on the swollen vessels and
sues to cause them to return to normal size by vasocon-

striction, allowing nasal passages to clear. This can improv
sinus drainage and help relieve sinus headache.

Decongestants can be applied topically as nose drops (
sprays, or can be swallowed in tablet or liquid form. Peop
often use the drug in both forms—the tablet or liquid 1
produce a deeper, longer-lasting constriction, and the spra
to produce almost immediate response by constriction
surface vessels and tissues. In tablet or liquid form, deco
gestants are frequently combined with antihistamines.

People with high blood pressure, diabetes, heart diseas
or thyroid disease should avoid decongestants because the
could worsen their their disease. People taking antidepressa
drugs or MAO inhibitors should not take decongestants b
cause of possible drug interaction.

Antihistamines

Antihistamines block the effect of histamine, a natural
occurring chemical in the body which is released into th
bloodstream as part of its response to outside challeng
This response is sometimes called the allergic response, ar
when we experience it we say we have an allergy, wheth
the challenge is from an insect bite or from pollen or som
other allergenic (allergy-provoking) substance. There is litt
histamine released by the common cold viruses, therefo
antihistamines exert only a minor effect on cold symptom
Antihistimines can only block histamine after it is in th
bloodstream; they cannot prevent histamine from bein
released.

Individual response to any drug is variable and antihist
mines are no exception. There are 17 different antihist
mines currently available in the United States, which can l
divided into five major chemical groups.

Cough Suppressants

Coughing can be good for you. It is a natural reflex d
signed to protect you by helping to clear the respiratory tra
of any unwanted material, be it foreign matter or unusual
heavy natural secretions. When you take a cough medicine
suppresses this natural reflex. The medicine cannot cure th
cause of your cough.

Cough medicine is helpful when it allows you to get

restful night's sleep when you might otherwise have been kept up by a cough. It is also beneficial in reducing the amount of coughing because frequent, deep coughing tends to cause irritation of the respiratory tract. Cough suppressants act either on the cough control center (there actually is such a place) in the part of the brain called the medulla, or on the source of irritation in your throat causing the cough center to be activated. Most commercial cough suppressants (both prescription and over-the-counter) tend to combine a centrally acting drug (such as Codeine or Dextromethorphan) with an ingredient that will help reduce local irritation (such as glycerine, honey, or some other soothing syrupy medicine). Expectorants such as Terpin Hydrate, Guiafenesin, and Potassium Iodide are often used in cough formulas on the theory that by making mucus secretions in the throat thinner and perhaps easier to bring up, they will help reduce cough.

Expectorants

Expectorants are supposed to stimulate the production of mucus and other respiratory secretions, helping loosen thick, tenacious secretions by diluting them with more secretory material. Once diluted, they can be removed by natural action. Expectorants may work in respiratory diseases that cause very thick secretions. However, their effectiveness with coughs due to colds is questionable because thickness of secretions is not a major problem for most people with a cold. If you take a cough medicine, especially one sold over the counter, be sure that if there is an expectorant in it, there is also a cough suppressant. If you are not sure, consult your pharmacist.

Analgesics and Antipyretics

The two antipyretic analgesics (reducing fever, reducing pain) commonly used in cold medicines are Aspirin and Acetaminophen (Tylenol, Datril, etc.). Aspirin also reduces inflammation. Aspirin or Acetaminophen should be used only if you have fever, pain, or inflammation (Aspirin only, not Acetaminophen). Taking these drugs unnecessarily may expose you to drug-induced side effects without gaining any counterbalancing benefit. If you have been given a prescription drug to relieve pain, fever, or inflammation, don't take the medicine later on for another illness unless you consult your doctor first.

PSYCHOTROPIC DRUGS

Psychotropic drugs are used to alleviate symptoms in psychiatric disorders, from minor anxiety or major psychoses. They are extremely useful in today's stressful society and often enable people to function normally on a day-to-day basis.

Psychotropic drugs affect brain chemicals or chemical systems called neurotransmitters, which mediate such basic functions as sleep, wakefullness, and memory, by increasing or blocking their effects. There are three major classes of psychotropic drugs: antianxiety drugs, antipsychotic drugs, and antidepressants.

Antianxiety Drugs

These drugs, including Diazepam (Valium), Chlordiazepoxide (Librium), Oxazepam (Serax), and related benzodiazepines, and Meprobamate, are used to treat anxiety neurosis. People with an anxiety neurosis experience waves of anxiety characterized by apprehension, tension, sudden fatigue, and a panic reaction; these feelings may be accompanied by sweating, rapid heartbeat (palpitation), weakness, dizziness, and irritability, which are defenses set up by the brain to avoid the actual source of the anxiety. Formerly known as minor tranquilizers, antianxiety drugs generally direct their activity at the brain centers involved with emotion.

The benzodiazapine tranquilizers can also be used as anticonvulsant drugs. In fact, one of that class, Clonazepam (Clonopin) is used solely for that purpose. Its other effects are similar to Diazepam and other members of that group.

Special care should be used by patients with a family and/or personal history of alcohol or substance abuse when taking benzodiazapine or other antianxiety drugs. Recent research studies indicate that these people are at greater risk to become dependent on these drugs.

Antipsychotic Drugs

The antipsychotic (neuroleptic) drugs alter the activity of dopamine, norepinephrine, and serotonin in the brain, with a profound effect on psychotic disorder, whether paranoid or schizophrenic. People with psychotic disorders show severe personality disintegration and distortion of the world around them, have difficulty separating reality from fantasy, and often suffer from hallucinations and delusions.

The major groups of antipsychotic drugs, formerly known as major tranquilizers, are the phenothiazines, such as Chlorpromazine (Thorazine), Trifluoperazine (Stelazine), and Thioridazine (Mellaril); the butyrophenones, such as Haloperidol (Haldol); and the thioxanthenes, such as Thiothixene (Navane). All antipsychotic drugs tend to exhibit more side effects than antianxiety drugs and are reserved for more severe situations. Other groups of antipsychotic drugs are the dibenzoxazepines: (Loxitane) Loxapine; and the dihydroindolones: Molindone (Moban, Lidone).

Antidepressants

Depressed people tend to be self-critical, self-depreciating, brooding; they have a feeling of extreme helplessness. Loss of self-esteem, withdrawal from personal relationships, and inhibition of normal aggressive activity may result. Those suffering from depression also frequently suffer from anxiety. Here the depression is thought to be a defense against the underlying anxiety and is accompanied by physical complaints of headache, tiredness, loss of appetite, and constipation.

The three classes of antidepressant drugs are the tricyclic antidepressants, such as Amitriptyline (Elavil and Endep) and Imipramine (Tofranil), the tetracyclic antidepressant Trazodone (Desyrel) and the MAO inhibitors, such as Isocarboxazid (Marplan), Tranylcypromine Sulfate (Parnate), and Phenelzine Sulfate (Nardil). Each class is effective in relieving depressive symptoms, but they do not cure depression; they only help the patient to deal more effectively with his or her problems.

MAO INHIBITORS

MAO inhibitor drugs block a naturally occurring enzyme system called monoamine oxidase, from which the name MAO comes. One of its more important functions is to break down other naturally occurring chemicals called amines. Amines are responsible for much of the stimulating effects of the central nervous system. By giving an MAO inhibitor we increase the amount of amines available. Too much MAO inhibitor can produce excess amine effects such as over-stimulation, very high blood pressure, agitation, changes in heart rate and rhythm, muscle spasms and tremors, and sleeplessness; but taken under the supervision of a physician, MAO inhibitors can be valuable, relatively safe therapeutic agents.

Because of their high potential for drug interaction and side effects, MAO inhibitor drugs are prescribed only for patients who are severely depressed and do not respond to tricyclic therapy (Tranylcypromine [Parmante] and Isocarboxazid [Marplan]), or for people with severe high blood pressure (Pargyline [Eutony]), Hodgkin's disease (Procarbazine [Matulane]), and infections (Furazolidone [Furoxone]); here the beneficial effects may not be related directly to MAO inhibition, but many of the adverse effects and all the drug interactions are so related. These drugs are not included in *The Pill Book* because of their relatively limited use.

When an MAO inhibitor is given along with a drug which is broken down, at least in part, by the MAO enzyme system, the result is *higher concentration* of the second drug. For example, when antidepressant drugs are given with an MAO inhibitor, unusually high antidepressant levels resulting from this combination can cause fever and convulsions. Similarly, when a diabetic patient is given an MAO inhibitor drug, his blood sugar will be lowered if he is taking either an oral antidiabetic drug or Insulin.

MAO inhibitors have also been implicated in serious interactions with certain foods—those containing large amounts of naturally occurring amines (tyramine or dopa). The MAO inhibitor makes you lose the ability to rapidly destroy these chemicals, with possible results of headache, rapid rise in blood pressure, hemorrhaging due to bursting of small blood vessels, and general stimulation. Several deaths have been caused by this interaction.

Some foods to be avoided if you are taking an MAO inhibitor are broad beans, Chianti wine, chicken or beef liver, pickled herring, and cheddar cheese, as well as Camembert, Stilton, Brie, Emmentaler, and Gruyère cheese. Avoid large amounts of chocolate, sour cream, canned figs, raisins, soy sauce, pineapple, and bananas.

CORTICOSTEROIDS

orticosteroid drugs are chemically related to hydrocorti-
one, corticosterone, aldosterone, and deoxycorticosterone
naturally produced hormones that are essential to normal
ody functions). The first two hormones control the storage
f carbohydrates (sugars) in the body, affect the breakdown
f body proteins, and reduce inflammation. The last two
ormones primarily affect the regulation of sodium and po-
assium in the body, although they possess some activity
imilar to that of hydrocortisone and corticosterone.

Some of the corticosteroid drugs most commonly used in
atient treatment are related to the hormones hydrocorti-
one and corticosterone: Betamethasone, Cortisone, Dexamethasone, Fluprednisolone, Hydrocortisone, Meprednisone,
Methylprednisolone, Paramethasone, Prednisolone, Predni-
one, and Triamcinolone.

Others are related to the hormone deoxycorticosterone:
Deoxycorticosterone and Fludrocortisone.

Corticosteroids are used to treat a wide variety of condi-
ions. They can replace naturally produced hormones in pa-
ients who cannot make enough of their own. They can also
e used to treat diseases in which it is desirable to adminis-
er a potent anti-inflammatory drug. Some of the host of
iseases in which corticosteroids are used for this effect are
hose which affect collagen (connective) tissue such as lupus
rythematosus and pemphigus vulgaris; allergic disorders
ncluding asthma, hay fever, and allergic rhinitis (nasal in-
ammation due to allergy); and reactions to drugs, serum,
nd blood transfusions. Skin rashes of various types, causes,
nd severities are also treated with corticosteroids. The drugs
an be especially helpful in treating itchy, inflamed rashes
nd in psoriasis, neurodermatitis, and similar conditions.
Corticosteroids are also given to treat inflammation of areas
f the body including tendons, muscles, eye, brain, and liver.
They are of great value in shock and are often used as part
f the treatment of certain cancers.

Because of the wide variety of diseases for which cortico-
teroids are used, your doctor must individualize treatment
or you, depending upon the drug being used and the dis-
ase being treated.

Corticosteroids can have many serious side effects. The

possibility of experiencing side effects increases with th
amount of drug being taken and the length of time it i
taken. Some of the possible side effects of corticosteroid
are irritation of the stomach (possibly leading to peptic u
cer), loss of body potassium, infection (due to temporar
disabling of body defense mechanisms), behavioral and pe
sonality changes, loss of calcium from bone leading to sub
sequent bone weakness and increased possibility of fractur
in elderly patients, increased pressure inside the eye, exces
sive breakdown of body proteins, change in the quality an
appearance of skin to which corticosteroids are topicall
applied, muscle weakness, aggravation of diabetes, and un
usual or excessive retention of water in the body, leading t
fluid accumulation under the skin.

Corticosteroids are remarkable drugs which can be lifesav
ing. They should only be used under the direct supervisio
of your doctor because of the many serious side effect
which can develop. The carefully supervised use of cortico
steroids is quite safe, in most cases. If you must take one o
these drugs, be sure to follow your doctor's directions ex
plicitly: only then will you get the maximum benefit.

ANALGESICS

Analgesics are drugs used to relieve pain. They act on cer
ters in the nervous system to affect your response to painfu
stimuli. They don't take the pain away, they simply reduc
the response produced by the pain.

Analgesics are classified by the severity of pain they re
lieve. Those that relieve severe pain are called strong ana
gesics; those that relieve mild to moderate pain are calle
mild analgesics.

Strong analgesics have an additional quality of alterin
the psychological response to pain and alleviating the anx
ety and apprehension which often accompany the painfu
situation. Some drugs considered to be strong analgesic
are narcotics, such as Morphine, Meperidine (Demerol
Opium, Oxymorphone (Numorphan), Oxycodone (found i
Percodan), Pentazocine (Talwin), and Methotrimeprazin
(Levoprome). They all exert basically the same effect on th
central nervous system. Their usefulness is related to th
length of their effective pain relief, how fast they start work

ing, and the type and degree of side effects and adverse reactions. The differences among them are not great and a doctor will usually choose one based on his training and experience. Patients may express a strong feeling for one of these drugs according to past experience.

Strong analgesics should not be used for mild to moderate pain because of their relative potency and the definite potential for addiction after prolonged use. Other side effects associated with these drugs are difficulty in breathing, nausea, vomiting, constipation, lowered blood pressure, slowed heart rate, and drug reaction or allergy.

Mild analgesics are divided into two categories: those which are chemical derivatives of one of the strong analgesics such as Codeine Sulfate, Mefenamic Acid (Ponstel), Propoxyphene (Darvon, Dolene, SK-65), Ethoheptazine (Zactane), and those considered to be antipyretic (fever-reducing) such as Aspirin, Sodium Salicylate, Salicylamide, Salsalate (Disalcid), Acetaminophen, Phenacetin, Ibuprofen Dipyrone, and Mefenamic Acid (Ponstel).

Of the mild analgesics which are derivatives of one of the strong analgesics, Codeine Sulfate is the most effective, although it can become addicting after long periods of use. It is generally considered more effective than Aspirin, and is therefore held in reserve by most doctors for patients who either cannot be effectively treated by the milder drugs or who cannot take them for some reason.

The analgesic-antipyretic drugs are among the most widely used in the world, primarily because most members of this group are available without a prescription. They are used to treat any mild or moderate pain of headache or muscle ache, or from arthritis (inflammation of bone joints), sprains, strains, and so on. They may also be prescribed as part of the treatment of pain due to surgical procedures, cancer, and periodic cramps, and for the reduction of fever. The two most widely used drugs are Aspirin and Acetaminophen, but one of the NSAID drugs, which can be used for all the same purposes as Aspirin, Ibuprofen, was approved for sale without a prescription during 1984.

See page 114 for information on Acetaminophen, and page 65 for Aspirin. Information on Ibuprofen, which is available both with and without a prescription in a milder form, can be found on page 317.

Some analgesics are used for relief or prevention of severe vascular (migraine) headaches. One of these drugs, Methysergide (Sansert) blocks the effect of serotonin, a naturally occurring chemical thought to be involved in producing these headaches.

Other analgesics are reserved for a special purpose. One of these is Carbamazepine (Tegretol), a potent pain reliever used to treat trigeminal neuralgia (tic doloreaux). It has also been used to treat certain forms of epilepsy. This is a potent drug with some very severe side effects and must be taken with caution and only while under a doctor's direction. Another is Hydroxychloroguine (Plaquenil), used for severe rheumatoid arthritis.

Drugs and . . .

The increased interest of many Americans in diet and nutrition has focused attention on how diet affects drug therapy and the effect of drugs on diet and nutrition.

How Does Diet Affect Drug Therapy?

Foods can interfere with the ability of drugs to be absorbed into the blood through the gastrointestinal system. For this reason, most medications are best taken at least 1 hour before or 2 hours after meals, unless specific characteristics of the drug dictate that it is better taken with or immediately following meals. Check each drug profile for information as to the best time to take your medicine and check with your doctor or pharmacist if you are unsure about how to best take your medicine.

Some drugs which are taken with meals because the food reduces the amount of drug-related stomach irritation are Indomethacin, Phenylbutazone, and Oxyphenbutazone. Other drugs such as Amoxicillin, may not be affected at all by food.

Some food effects interfere with a drug by reducing the amount of medication available to be absorbed. Juice or milk taken to help you swallow drugs can interfere with them. Many fruit juices, because of their acid content, breakdown Penicillin-G, Erythromycin, and other antibiotics. Milk or milk products (like ice cream) can interfere with the absorption of Tetracycline antibiotics through the gastrointestinal tract.

Investigators have questioned the seriousness of such effects and, it is generally difficult to prove that people who experience these food-drug interactions don't get well as

741

fast as others who did not. There probably is some effect, but its extent is not known.

Some medications react with specific diets. People taking anticoagulant (blood-thinning) drugs should avoid fat-rich foods because they may reduce anticoagulant effectiveness. People taking Levodopa (L-dopa) should avoid high-protein diets rich in Vitamin B_6 (Pyridoxine), which can reduce the effectiveness of Levodopa.

Raw vegetables (cabbage, okra, and some others) contain Vitamin K, which interferes with oral anticoagulant drugs. This interaction can contribute to the development of potentially fatal blood clots.

An ingredient in licorice can cause you to retain sodium and lose potassium. This can be dangerous if you have high blood pressure (increased sodium = increased water = higher blood pressure) or if you are taking a digitalis drug for your heart (less potassium = more digitalis drug side effects).

Many foods interact with MAO inhibitors (see p. 735).

Foods containing potassium can be useful to people taking diuretics who need to add potassium to their diet:

Apricots (dried)	Peaches (dried)
Bananas	Prune juice
Cantaloupe	Raisins
Dates	Steak
Figs (dried)	Turkey
Milk	Watermelon
Orange juice	

How Do Drugs Affect Diet and Nutrition?

Drugs can affect your appetite. Some medicines that can stimulate your appetite include tricyclic antidepressants and phenothiazine tranquilizers.

Drugs that can cause you to lose your appetite include antibiotics (especially Penicillin) and any medication with a possible side effect of nausea and vomiting.

Many drugs can interfere with the normal absorption of one or more body nutrients:

ntacids	Colchicine
nticholinergics	Glutethimide
(Atropine, etc.)	Isoniazid
nticonvulsants	Methotrexate
arbiturates	Neomycin Sulfate
athartics (laxatives)	Oral contraceptives
hloramphenicol	Sulfa drugs
lofibrate	

DRUGS AND ALCOHOL

rug interactions with alcohol, itself a potent drug, are a ignificant problem and can be experienced by anyone, even nose who avoid drinking near the time that they take pre- cription pills. Many over-the-counter medicines are alcohol- ased and have the potential to interact with prescription rugs: there are more than 500 pharmaceutical items that ontain alcohol, some in concentrations up to 68 percent. lcohol is used to dissolve drugs, as in vitamin tonics and ntitussive-decongestant liquids, and also to enhance seda- ve effects. Alcohol is found in almost all decongestant cold- uppressing mixtures.

Alcohol's action in the body is simply that of a central ervous system depressant. It may either enhance or reduce he effect of a drug. In some drug interactions, the amount f alcohol consumed may not be as important as the chemi- al reaction it causes in your body. Small concentrations can ause excess stomach secretions, while larger amounts can nhibit stomach secretions, eroding the stomach's lining. Use f over-the-counter alcohol-based products by the elderly is specially dangerous, since their systems may be more sen- itive to alcohol. People with stomach disorders such as eptic or gastric ulcer should be fully aware of the alcohol evels in products they use.

The effects of alcohol on certain classes of drugs are de- cribed below.

One drug, Disulfiram (Antabuse) is used to treat alcohol- sm. Alcoholics using this medication will experience ab- lominal cramps, nausea, vomiting, headaches, and flushing f they drink any alcohol, including beer, wine, whiskey, or nedication with alcohol base such as cough medications. hese effects help alcoholics abstain from drinking. Some

other drugs also produce this effect, but they are not used i
primary treatment programs. They include the oral antidia
betics and Metrondiazole.

Analgesics

Certain pain relievers such as Aspirin (Salicylates) hav
been linked with intestinal bleeding. Use of alcohol wit
these products can aggravate an already existing condition
Strong narcotic pain relievers have a sedative effect on th
central nervous system. Adding alcohol can lead to seriou
central nervous system depression, respiratory arrest, an
death.

Alcohol should never be used with narcotic drugs.

Anticoagulants

Alcohol may interact with blood-thinning drugs, extendin
coagulation time. This is especially true for heavy drinkers
Those taking anticoagulant drugs should avoid alcohol an
alcohol-based products.

Antihistamines

Alcohol enhances the sedative effects of antihistamines
even in small doses. Be especially careful, when taking anti
histamines, to avoid driving a car or operating machinery.

Antihypertensive Drugs

Some antihypertensive drugs will interact with alcohol to
cause orthostatic hypotension (dizziness, fainting). Be sure
that the effectiveness of antihypertensive combinations i
not being counteracted by alcohol-based over-the-counte
products and remember, take all antihypertensive medica
tion exactly as prescribed by your doctor.

Antianxiety Drugs and Antidepressants

Phenothiazines and other antipsychotic medicines like
Thorazine work by depressing the central nervous system
Alcohol will increase this effect, leading to severely impaired
ability to drive or operate machinery. Judgment, alertness
and coordination will be diminished. When taken in excess

mounts, phenothiazines and alcohol can depress the respiratory control center, leading to death. Since phenothiazines are metabolized in the liver, they may impair livers already damaged by alcohol abuse.

Tricyclic antidepressants (Elavil, for example) have similar interactions when combined with alcohol; the drugs' central nervous system depressant effect is enhanced. Psychomotor skills—driving, etc.—are affected by alcohol combined with antidepressants; such combinations have led to serious accidents or death. Antidepressant drugs are also metabolized in the liver; they can reach toxic levels if a damaged liver cannot fully metabolize them.

MAO Inhibitors

Chianti wines, vermouth, and unpasteurized beer can cause serious drug interactions with MAO inhibitors. These drugs, which block a naturally occurring enzyme system called monoamine oxidase, are sometimes used to treat severe depression or high blood pressure. Using alcohol-based products with MAO inhibitors can result in increased blood pressure, headache, and fever; such use should be avoided.

Sedatives/Hypnotics

This frequently prescribed group of drugs is one of the most dangerous to mix with alcohol. Drugs like Chloral Hydrate, Carbromal, Methyprylon, Glutethimide, Ethclorvynol, Ethinamate, and Flurazepam, when taken with alcohol, can cause excessive sedation and potentiate central nervous system effects. Barbiturates, Diazepam (Valium), and other sedative drugs can cause impairment of motor abilities when taken in combination with alcohol. Some studies have shown that Diazepam and alcohol abuse can lead to addiction, even at prescribed doses.

Before you use alcohol and sedative/hypnotic drugs together, check with your doctor.

Stimulants/Amphetamines

Alcohol in combination with Amphetamine or stimulant drugs can lead to a sudden, dangerous rise in blood pressure. The combination should be avoided.

Antidiabetics

Use of alcohol with antidiabetic drugs such as Insulin or oral antidiabetic pills such as Diabenese or Tolbutamide can be dangerous. The combination can cause excessive hypoglycemia, a dangerous lowering of the glucose (sugar) level in the blood, which can lead to coma.

DRUGS AND SEXUAL ACTIVITY

Sexual activity is usually not limited by drugs; however, some drugs can have an effect on libido and their side effects can lead to impotence. This is especially true in men taking some high blood pressure drugs which affect the central nervous or circulatory system. It's important to discuss such effects with your doctor: a simple reduction in dosage or the change to another drug in the same class may solve the problem.

Many antihypertensives can impair potency and cause retrograde ejaculation in the male. Antidepressants, amphetamines, and sedatives have similar effects on libido and can reduce potency. Oral contraceptives have been linked to reduced libido in some women. Anticancer drugs don't affect sex drive but will reduce sperm count in many men.

Some drugs, such as Levodopa, have been reported to increase libido; note that this is age- and dose-related.

DRUGS AND PREGNANCY

Today we are acutely aware of the potential damage to a fetus from drugs of all kinds. In order for a drug to affect the fetus, it must cross the placental barrier from the mother's bloodstream to that of the fetus. Once in the baby's bloodstream, the drug may affect any of the normal growth and development processes. Because a fetus grows much more rapidly than a fully developed human, the effects of a drug on this process are exaggerated. Adverse results can range from physcial disfigurement to severe mental and/or physical damage to death.

An illustration of the damage caused by drug use during pregnancy is the discovery of the latent effect of DES (Diethylstilbestrol). This hormone, given to many women during the 1940s and '50s to prevent miscarriage, has been linked to aginal cancer in the daughters of the women who used it. The Thalidomide scandal of the 1960s was caused by a drug which was intended to help pregnant women but which resulted in birth defects and deformities in children. This led to a complete reevaluation of the use of drugs during pregnancy.

Many obstetricians now recommend that pregnant women avoid all unnecessary medication during pregnancy and after birth while lactating. This includes analgesics such as Aspirin. Unfortunately, potential damage to a fetus is greatest during the first three months of pregnancy, when a woman may not be aware that she is pregnant. If you are considering becoming pregnant, it is wise to curtail any drug use immediately and discuss it fully with your ob/gyn specialist.

Today, most doctors suggest that pregnant women use only vitamins or iron supplements and limit their alcohol, tobacco, and caffeine intake.

The Food and Drug Administration has classified all prescription drugs according to their safety for use during pregnancy. Many profiles in *The Pill Book* contain specific information on drug safety for use by both pregnant and breast-feeding women.

DRUGS AND CHILDREN

Medications for children should only be given on direct orders from a pediatrician or other doctor. Of course, children suffer from colds and runny noses and there are many over-the-counter medicines which parents use frequently. Parents should be aware of the ingredients of such products—for example, the alcohol content—and of possible side effects.

Children are at greater risk for drug side effects and interactions because their body systems are not fully developed. This is espcially true of infants and young children. Some drugs like tetracyclines have been linked to serious side effects in children and should be avoided. It's wise to ask your doctor whether side effects such as fever or rash are to be expected when he prescribes a drug for a child.

Some drugs have opposite effects on adults and children. Ritalin, which is given to children to calm hyperactivity, acts as a stimulant in adults.

Drug doses for children are usually lower and are often

determined by body weight. Be sure you know all there is to know about a drug before you give it to your child. If you can, check with your doctor about over-the-counter products unless you've used them before and are sure they can't interact with other drugs the child is taking.

DRUGS AND THE ELDERLY

Changes in the body caused either by age or disease make older adults three times as likely to have adverse drug reactions—nausea, dizziness, blurred vision, and others—as younger people. Drug interactions are another potential source of great danger for the elderly. Since many elderly are on multiple drug regimens for more than one chronic condition, the potential for drug interaction is much greater.

Older adults often suffer from "asymptomatic drug reaction," silent undetected reactions caused by slowly building amounts of drugs that are not being properly metabolized by the older, less efficient systems.

Most people over the age of 65 take prescription drugs regularly; in fact, 25 percent of all prescriptions are filled for elderly customers, who make up only 11 percent of the population. Many spend up to $100 a year to get an average of 13 prescriptions filled. The 1.5 million elderly in nursing homes are also at great risk for drug interactions: 54 percent of them take 6 or more pills per day, and some receive as many as 23.

Studies have shown that 70 to 90 percent of the elderly take pills and over-the-counter medicines with little knowledge of their dangerous effects. Often elderly people who have speech or hearing problems, are absentminded, or are experiencing other symptoms we attribute to aging, are really suffering from drug reactions. This condition is called reversible dementia.

The elderly are often victims of overdose, and not necessarily because of mistaken dosages. Often body weight fluctuations and normal changes in body composition lead to overdose unless the dosage of a drug is altered accordingly.

Antihistamines, phenothiazines, and tricyclic antidepressants are known to cause frequent adverse reactions in the elderly. Older people are sometimes unknowing victims of a drug reaction that causes another disease state. For examle, gout can be precipitated by certain diuretics, and kidney disease can be caused by long overuse of anti-inflammatories ke Aspirin.

It's important to make sure that elderly people understand heir drugs completely. Follow the tips for safe drug use on ages 760 to 761 to assist an older person in managing drug ntake properly. Install a drug control system which lists the ills prescribed, the sequence in which they should be taken, he time of day, how they should be taken, and a place to ndicate what was taken.

Some more specific suggestions, classified by type of drug:

Analgesics

Pain relievers can be especially dangerous to older adults who tend to increase the dosages in order to manage pain. This can lead to overdose, since the drugs are excreted more slowly by aging kidneys. The adverse effects vary with the pain reliever used.

Antiarthritics

Antiarthritics are widely used by the elderly and are generally effective to control pain caused by swollen or inflamed joints. Side effects are gastric upset, blurred vision, and nausea.

Mild anti-inflammatories used by the elderly to combat arthritis include Motrin, Nalfon, Indocin, Naprosyn, and Clinoril. Stronger anti-inflammatories include Oxalid, Tandearil, Azolid, and Butazolidin.

The mild analgesics most commonly used to combat the effects of arthritis are the salicylates, mainly Aspirin. There are hundreds of brand-name products which have been shown to be effective in reducing the pain of mild arthritic conditions. Main drawbacks are stomach irritation, Aspirin's link to blood thinning which may increase the effect of anticoagulants, and Aspirin's excretion through the kidneys.

Strong analgesics such as Codeine Sulfate, Talwin, and narcotics such as Demerol, are especially dangerous to the elderly and should be carefully monitored by a doctor. They can provoke serious drug interactions with glaucoma drugs, tranquilizers, antidepressants, and antihypertensives, and should only be used under a doctor's close supervision.

Oral Antidiabetics

Although most diabetic conditions in the elderly can be controlled by dietary supervision, oral antidiabetics like Diabenese, DiaBeta, Glucotrol, Micronase, Tolinase, Orinase, and Dymelor are also used. These drugs differ in their length of effect; oftena doctor will tailor the dosage to the individual. Side effects include loss of appetite, nausea, and general gastric distress. Minor infections and emotional problems can affect the actions of these drugs. They should be used carefully when taken with thiazide diuretics, sulfa drugs, Aspirin, anticoagulants, or MAO inhibitors.

Antihypertensive Drugs

Hypertension (high blood pressure) is experienced by 40 to 50 percent of those over 65. This condition, often linked to heart problems, is treated by control of diet and proper, consistent use of medication. The drugs used to treat high blood pressure are discussed on page 720, "Antihypertensive Drugs."

Some side effects can be serious, including depression, light-headedness, and dizziness or feeling faint. Contact your doctor immediately if any of these occur.

Antihypertensives must be taken exactly as prescribed.

Heart Drugs

Heart disease is the leading cause of death in the United States. For many of the elderly, treatment programs for heart disease are the focus of their lives. They must use their drugs exactly as prescribed, often in combination with strict dietary restrictions and technical equipment like pacemakers.

Digitalis drugs are commonly prescribed for congestive heart failure in the elderly. Digitalis intoxication occurs when digitalis drugs are excreted too slowly from the body and is more likely in the elderly because of reduced kidney function. Early symptoms include loss of appetite, vomiting, and nausea. They are serious and a doctor should be contacted immediately.

Diuretics eliminate excess fluid from the body and are often called water pills. The elderly should take the lowest dose possible when using these drugs, and a doctor should carefully monitor their use. They often are used in combination with other drugs; check with a doctor about potential side effects. Diuretics can cause potassium depletion which often results in dry mouth, thirst, weakness, lethargy, drowsiness, restlessness, and muscle pains or cramps.

Other Drugs

Some drugs are more often prescribed for elderly people because certain conditions are found more frequently in this group. One example is Hydergine, often used to treat the symptoms of Alzheimer-like diseases. (see pg. 250—Ergot Alkaloids). Another example of this would be Methandrostenolone (Dianabol), an anabolic steroid, which has been shown to be somewhat effective as secondary therapy in treating senile and post-menopausal osteoporosis (bone disease). Conditions like osteoporosis are treated primarily with diet, calcium balance, and physiotherapy.

Twenty Questions to Ask Your Doctor and Pharmacist About Your Prescription

1. What is the name of this medicine?

2. What results can be expected from taking it?

3. How long should I wait before reporting if this medicine does not help me?

4. How does the medicine work?

5. What is the exact dose of the medicine?

6. What time of day should I take it?

7. Can I drink alcoholic beverages while taking this medicine?

8. Do I have to take special precautions with this medicine in combination with other prescription drugs I am taking?

9. Do I have to take special precautions with this medicine in combination with nonprescription (over-the-counter) drugs?

10. Can I take this medicine without regard to food or mealtimes?

11. Are there any special instructions I should have about how to use this medicine?

12. How long should I continue to take this medicine?

13. Is my prescription renewable?

14. For how long a period can my prescription be renewed?

15. Which side effects should I report and which can I disregard?

16. Can I save any unused portion of this medicine for future use?

17. How should I store this medicine?

18. How long can I keep this medicine without its losing strength?

19. What should I do if I forget to take a dose of this medicine?

20. Is this medicine available in a less expensive, generic form? If so, is the less expensive form of equal quality?

Drug Interactions and Side Effects

A drug side effect is an effect of the drug other than that for which you are taking the drug. In *The Pill Book,* the most common drug reactions are listed under the heading of side effects. One example of a side effect is antihistamine sleepiness. If you are taking the antihistamine to relieve the symptoms of an allergy, the sleepiness is a side effect. But if you are taking the antihistamine to help you go to sleep, the sleepiness becomes the primary drug effect, not its side effect. Another example of a drug side effect is the upset stomach associated with Aspirin or another of the anti-inflammatory drugs.

Most side effects are considered undesirable. Occasionally though, we learn of some unexpected benefits from taking medicines. For example, women taking oral contraceptives (the Pill) have less chance of getting cancer of the ovaries than non-users; what's more, the protective effect seems to increase with the length of time the Pill is taken. Women taking the Pill for at least 12 consecutive months during their lives have half the risk of developing cancer of the uterus as women not taking the Pill.

How common are drug side effects? If they are listed in *The Pill Book,* they occur in more than 1 percent (1 out of 100) of people taking the drug. It is difficult, however, to make a general statement about your chances of experiencing a drug side effect. On average, a drug side effect can be expected in 5 to 10 percent of people taking a medication. Your chances of experiencing a side effect increase with the number of drugs taken, the type and variety of medical conditions present, and your age.

For example, drowsiness occurs in about ⅓ of all people taking an antihistamine. But the severity of the reaction varies with the drug and can be different from one person to the next. Many common gastrointestinal (stomach or intestinal) reactions occur in anywhere from 1 to 25 to 50 percent of people taking medicines. Older people are more likely to experience drug side effects. Some studies have shown that elderly people can experience 7 times as many drug side effects as younger adults given the same medication. Although the statistics vary, the trend is always the same: the older we get, the more likely we are to suffer from the medicines that are supposed to cure our ills.

ADVERSE DRUG EFFECTS

Since the majority of drug reactions are undesirable, or cause adverse effects on the body, medical professionals generally use the terms adverse reaction, side effect and adverse effect interchangeably. In *The Pill Book,* the term "Adverse Drug Effects" is used to indicate those reactions which occur least often. In all cases, the listings under this section include drug effects that occur in *less than 1 percent* of people taking a particular medication. Your chances of actually experiencing an Adverse Drug Effect are far less than your chances of experiencing a side effect. Fewer than ½ percent (5 out of every 1000) of people who take a drug will actually experience an Adverse Drug Effect.

What Can You Do About Drug Side Effects and Adverse Drug Effects?

Be aware of any changes in your body and report them at once to your doctor. You may be more susceptible to certain side effects or adverse drug effects, like drug allergy or sensitivity. Common sense dictates that you avoid any medicine to which you have had a previous reaction. Reading over the profile for each of your medicines in *The Pill Book* will help alert you as to what to look for and determine whether or not a particular effect may be caused by a drug. But only your doctor can make the final decision about this and then decide if the problem should be treated by changing medicines, reducing the dosage, or prescribing a second drug to treat the problem created by the first.

DRUG INTERACTIONS

Drug interaction is that effect which occurs when two or

more medications are taken together. The interaction of drugs with foods, diseases (other than the one being treated) and the environment are also considered to be a part of the overall problem, but the major focus of drug interaction is on the potential problems that exist between two or more medications. Several different things can happen when drugs are taken together.

Drug Interactions That Decrease a Drug's Effect

One drug can completely or partially antagonize the effects of another. This drug interaction is fairly common and easy to understand. It can happen when one drug interferes with the absorption of another into the body, as when antacids swallowed together with a tetracycline antibiotic interfere with the absorption of the antibiotics into the blood. It can be caused by the effect of one drug stimulating the body to eliminate a second one from the body more rapidly than normal. This interaction can occur with drugs that are broken down in the liver or eliminated from your body by the kidneys. One drug can also antagonize another simply through a normal pharmacologic effect. For example, people with high blood pressure should never use anything that will counteract the effects of their high blood pressure medicines, such as some of the common antidepressant drugs.

Drug Interactions That Increase a Drug's Effect

The second possible result of a drug interaction is potentiation. This means that one drug can increase the effect of another.

Some drugs are bound to albumin, a protein, circulating in the blood. Anything, including another drug, that can pry the first drug loose from its binding site on the albumin molecule will increase the drug's effect. This happens when Warfarin (an anticoagulant) and Clofibrate (a blood cholesterol lowering agent) are taken together. If you were taking Warfarin and then begin taking Clofibrate, your daily dose of Warfarin would have to be cut by about 50 percent. The Clofibrate causes so much Warfarin to be released from blood albumin that only one-half of the usual dose is required.

Another kind of drug interaction that produces drug potentiation is associated with drugs eliminated by the kidney. One excellent example is an interaction that takes place between the antigout drug Probenecid and Penicillin antibiotics. Probenecid interferes with the elimination process for

Penicillin, resulting in a vast increase in the amount of Penicillin in the blood. This interaction has been employed in developing pharmaceutical products designed to produce a prolonged antibiotic blood level.

Additive effects are a third kind of potentiation interaction. This is probably the simplest of all drug interactions and is the easiest to understand. If you take two tranquilizers instead of one, you will experience a definite increase in the depressive effects of the drugs. If you take two drugs that contain Aspirin, you run a greater risk of developing ringing in the ears, upset stomach or other side effect associated with Aspirin. If you take two drugs with a stimulant effect, you can expect to experience jitteriness, nervousness or other side effects commonly associated with central nervous system stimulants.

There are other ways that drugs can interact to lead to a potentiation of one of the drugs involved. One drug can interfere with the breakdown of another in the liver. Interference with the metabolic process leads to higher blood levels of the drug and an increase in the drug's effect. Some drugs that are eliminated through the kidneys are sensitive to changes in the acid content of the urine. Drugs that can change the acid content of the urine, like Ascorbic Acid—Vitamin C—(which makes the urine more acid) and Sodium Bicarbonate or Acetazolamide (which make the urine less acid), will affect the kidneys' ability to eliminate medicines that are sensitive to those changes.

Synergistic Drug Interactions

Synergism is a very rare drug interaction and happens when the effect produced by the interaction is greater than the effect to be expected from both drugs taken separately.

Drug Interactions with the Environment

The interaction of drugs with our environment is an extremely interesting area, and one into which there has been relatively little research. Environmental effects tend to stimulate the liver to produce more enzymes, with the result that the liver breaks down drugs more rapidly. This effect has been proven in people exposed to insecticides or air pollution and in cigarette smokers. Clinically, the people who were studied needed more medication to achieve a desired effect than those who had not been exposed to these effects.

Drug Interactions with Food

In general, food will either interfere with or prolong the time it takes for a drug to be absorbed into the bloodstream. This happens because food prevents the drug molecules from getting to the wall of the intestine, or stomach, where drug absorption takes place. In most cases, the absorption of drugs is only delayed, not prevented or decreased. You should try to take your medication on an empty stomach to avoid any interference caused by food. However, drugs that are irritating to the stomach and intestines should be taken with food, as this will reduce the irritating effect.

Some foods can directly interfere with the absorption of drugs from the gastrointestinal tract. The drugs most often involved are antibiotics. In the case of the tetracyclines, any food product that contains large amounts of calcium interferes with the drug's action, because a complex is formed between the antibiotic and the calcium. This interaction can be avoided by simply separating your dose of antibiotic from the time that you eat ice cream, milk or other dairy products by about 2 hours. This will allow sufficient time for the drug to be absorbed. Other foods do not contain enough calcium to effectively interfere with the drug's action.

Another important drug-food interaction involves foods that contribute to the body's manufacture of chemicals that control central nervous system activity. Some drugs affect the enzyme system most responsible for breaking down these chemicals and removing them from the nerve endings. This enzyme is called MonAmine Oxidase (capitals added), and abbreviated MAO.

Warfarin, an anticoagulant or blood-thinning drug, works by interfering with chemical reactions in the blood coagulation mechanism that depend upon the presence of Vitamin K. The effect of Warfarin, and other oral anticoagulant drugs, can be completely reversed by taking Vitamin K. In fact, Vitamin K is given by injection as an antidote to an overdose of these anticoagulants. We get most of our Vitamin K from micro-organisms in the gut that manufacture it. However, we can also get Vitamin K from some raw vegetables such as cabbage and okra. If you eat too much of these vegetables, the Vitamin K content can interfere with the anticoagulant effect of Warfarin.

Specific information on drug/food interaction, where relevant, is contained in each pill profile.

What You Can Do About Drug Interactions

Drug interactions must be dealt with on an individual basis, since not everyone will respond in the same way to the same set of circumstances or medications. Your doctor and pharmacist should play a primary role by screening your medications every time a new one is added to see if there are any potential problems. Most interactions can be avoided or minimized by either changing the dose of one or more medications, or by changing the time at which medicines are taken. Some situations may require changing a medication to one that will not interact. Information on potential interactions of the medicines you take is included in each drug profile.

As with side effects and adverse drug effects, it is important that you observe any unexpected reactions while you are on medication and report them to your doctor.

Other Points to Remember for Safe Drug Use

- Store your medicines in a sealed, light resistant container to maintain maximum potency and be sure to follow any special storage instructions listed on your medicine bottle such as refrigerate, do not freeze, protect from light, or keep in a cool place. Protect all medicines from excessive humidity.

- Make sure you tell the doctor everything that is wrong. The more information he has, the more effectively he can treat you.

- Make sure each doctor you see knows all the medicines you use regularly, including prescription and nonprescription drugs.

- Keep a record of any bad reaction you have had to a medicine.

- Fill each prescription you are given. If you don't fill a prescription, make sure the doctor knows it.

- Don't take extra medicine without consulting your doctor or pharmacist.

- Follow the label instructions *exactly*. If you have any questions, call your doctor or pharmacist.

- Report any unusual symptoms that develop after taking medicine.

- Don't save unused medicine for future use unless you have consulted your doctor. Dispose of unused medicine by flushing it down the toilet.

- Never keep medicine where children can see or reach it.

- Always read the label before taking your medicine. Don't trust your memory.

Consult your pharmacist for guidance on the use of over-the-counter (nonprescription) drugs.

Don't share your medicine with anyone. Your prescription was written for you and only you.

Be sure the label stays on the container until the medicine is used or destroyed.

Keep the label facing up when pouring liquid medicine from the bottle.

Don't use a prescription medicine unless it has been specifically prescribed for you.

When you travel, take your prescription with you in its original container.

If you move to another city, ask your pharmacist to forward your prescription records to your new pharmacy.

Carry important medical facts about you in your wallet. Such things as drug allergies, chronic diseases (diabetes, etc.), and special requirements can be very useful.

Don't hesitate to discuss the cost of medical care with your doctor or pharmacist.

Exercise your right to make decisions about buying medicines:

1. If you suffer from a chronic condition, you can probably save by buying in larger quantities.

2. Choose your pharmacist as carefully as you choose your doctor.

3. Remember, the cost of your prescription includes the professional services offered by your pharmacy. If you want more service you will have to pay for it.

Glossary of Drug-Related Words

Addiction—Habituation to the use of a drug or other substance. Withdrawal of the addicting agent gives rise to physical symptoms and an overwhelming desire for the agent.

Adrenal corticosteroid—Drug related to hydrocortisone, corticosterone, or deoxycorticosterone used primarily for its ability t reduce inflammation. Also used to replace natural corticosteroids in deficient patients.

Allergy—Unusual response produced in some people when exposed to a drug, food, or other substance. The response ca vary widely from a simple rash to life-threatening symptoms.

Amoebicide—Drug used to treat infections caused by amoebas, tiny microorganisms commonly found in nature.

Analgesic—Pain-relieving.

Androgen—Drug or hormone that stimulates activity in male se organs or prevents changes in male sex characteristics already present.

Anemia—Condition in which the number or size of red blood cell or the amount of oxygen-carrying hemoglobin contained in re blood cells is deficient. Anemia is usually further defined according to the causative agent or disease.

Anesthetic—Drug that produces loss of sensation or of response t stimulation.

Angina pectoris—Severe chest pain, often extending down the lef shoulder and arm, relieved by Nitroglycerin.

Antacid—Drug used to neutralize excess acid in the stomach.

Antianxiety drug—Drug used to treat symptoms of anxiety (feeling of apprehension or danger accompanied by restlessness).

Antiarrhythmic drug—Drug used to help regulate unusual or ab normal heart rhythms.

Antiasthmatic drug—Drug used to treat symptoms of asthma, including difficulty in breathing, with wheezing.

Antibacterial drug—Drug that is destructive to or prevents the growth of bacteria.

Antibiotic—Substance derived from a mold or bacteria which slow or stops the growth of other bacteria.

Anticholinergic drug—Drug that antagonizes or counteracts the effects of acetylcholine, a natural hormone responsible for certain nervous system activities.

Anticoagulant drug—Drug used to extend the time it normally takes for blood to clot.

Anticonvulsant drug—Drug used to prevent or treat any disease associated with violent involuntary muscle contractions.

Antidepressant—Drug used to treat the symptoms of depression (dejection, sinking of one's spirits).

Antidiabetic drug—Drug used to treat diabetes mellitus.

Antidiarrheal drug—Drug used to treat diarrhea.

Antidote—Drug used to counteract the adverse effects of a drug or chemical.

Antiemetic drug—Drug to control vomiting.

Antiflatulent drug—Drug used to relieve discomfort due to excessive gas in the stomach or intestines.

Antihelminthic drug—Drug used to treat infections caused by helminths (worms).

Antihistamine—Drug used for its ability to neutralize or antagonize the effects of histamine, a naturally occurring substance; used to relieve the symptoms of allergy.

Antihyperlipidemic drug—Drug used to help control high levels of fats (cholesterol; triglycerides) in the blood.

Anti-infective—Relating to any agent used to treat an infection.

Antineoplastic drug—Drug used to treat neoplasms (unusual growths of tissue). Cancers are neoplastic diseases. Benign (noncancerous) growths are also neoplastic.

Antipruritic drug—Drug used to relieve itching.

Antipyretic drug—Drug used to reduce fever.

Antirheumatic drug—Drug used to treat or prevent rheumatism.

Antitoxin—Drug that neutralizes the effects of toxins (poisons, usually produced by bacteria invading the body).

Antitussive drug—Drug used to relieve cough.

Arrhythmia—Unusual or irregular heartbeat.

Ataxia—Loss of ability to coordinate muscular movements.

Bacteria—Living organisms, visible only under a microscope, which may infect humans and cause disease. Bacteria are classified according to shape, chemical reactivity, and nutrients they require.

Bactericidal drug—Drug that kills bacteria.

Bacteriostatic drug—Drug that inhibits the reproduction of bacteria.

Blood count—Number of red and white blood cells found in a standard sample of blood.

Blood dyscrasia—General term for any blood disease.

Blood sugar—Sugar normally found in the blood and burned for energy. Normal level of blood sugar is approximately 100 mg of glucose in approximately 3 oz of blood.

Bradycardia—Slowing of the heartbeat, usually to less than 60 beats per minute.

Bronchodilator—Drug used to help relax the bronchial muscles and to widen the bronchial passages.

Calorie—Unit of measure used to determine the energy (heat) value of foods to the body.

Cancer—General term used to describe malignant neoplasms which tend to spread rapidly and will result in illness and death if left untreated.

Capillary—Microscopic blood vessel connecting veins with arteries.

Carcinoma—Cancer.

Cardiac—Having to do with the heart.

Cardiac arrest—Stoppage of heart activity.

Cardiac glycoside—Type of drug that has the ability to increase the strength of and help regulate the rate of the heartbeat.

Cataract—Condition in which the lens of the eye loses its transparency, so that light cannot pass through it normally.

Cerebrum—Portion of the brain that is the seat of conscious mental processes.

Cerumen—Earwax.

Chilblain—Frostbite.

Climacteric—Menopause.

Coagulant drug—Drug which causes clotting of the blood.

Coma—State of unconsciousness from which one cannot be awakened. Causes include diabetes, liver disease, and thyroid disease.

Conception—Act of becoming pregnant.

Congestion—Presence of abnormal amounts of fluids due to increased flow into the area or decreased drainage.

Corticosteroid—See **Adrenal corticosteroid**.

Decongestant—Drug that reduces congestion.

Decubitus—Bedsore.

Delirium—Condition of extreme mental excitement marked by a stream of confused, unconnected ideas.

Dementia—General mental deterioration.

Demulcent—Agent applied to the skin or mucous membranes to relieve an irritation.

Dermatologic drug—Agent applied directly to the skin.

Dextrose—See **Glucose**.

Diabetes—Disease of body metabolism in which there is an insufficient supply of natural Insulin. This reduces the body's ability to store or burn glucose.

Diagnostic drug—Agent used by a physician to assist in the diagnosis of a disease.

Dilate—To enlarge a cavity, canal, blood vessel, or opening.

Disinfectant—Agent that inhibits or destroys bacteria which cause disease.

Diuretic—Drug that stimulates the production and passing of urine.

Dose—Quantity of a drug or medicine to be taken or applied all at once or over a designated period.

Drug dependence—Term used to describe drug habituation or addiction.

Drug interaction—What occurs when one drug affects (increases or decreases) the ability of a second drug to exert a therapeutic effect.

Drug sensitivity—Reaction or allergy to a drug.

Edema—Accumulation of clear watery fluid.

EEG—Electroencephalogram.

EKG—Electrocardiogram.

Electrolytes—Chemicals such as sodium, potassium, calcium, and bicarbonate found in body tissues and fluids.

Embolism—Obstruction of a blood vessel, caused by a blood clot or a large mass of bacterial or foreign material.

Emollient—Agent that softens or smooths irritated skin or mucous membranes.

Endocarditis—Inflammation of the membrane lining the heart.

Endocrine glands—Glands that produce hormones and release them directly into the bloodstream.

Enzyme—Protein, produced by body cells, which stimulates a chemical reaction in the body and remains unchanged during the reaction.

Epilepsy—Chronic disease characterized by periods of unconsciousness, convulsions, or both.

Eruption—Redness, spotting, or breaking out in a rash on the skin.

Estrogen—Drug or hormone that stimulates activity in female sex organs or prevents changes in female sex characteristics already present.

Euphoria—Feeling of exaggerated well-being.

Exfoliation—Profuse scaling of large areas of skin.

Expectorant—Drug that stimulates the production of secretions from mucous membranes.

Extrapyramidal effects—Spasm of neck muscles, rolling of the eyeballs, convulsions, difficulty swallowing, and other symptoms associated with Parkinson's disease, but also seen as an adverse drug effect.

Fever—Body temperature above 98.6°F (37°C).

Ganglia—Aggregations or groups of nerve cells.

Gastritis—Inflammation of the stomach.

Generic name—Standard name accepted for a drug. Manufacturers often use their own trade names that correspond to the generic name.

Glucose—Principal sugar used by the body for energy; also called dextrose.

Gonad—Sexual gland.

Hallucination—Perception of something which does not exist.

Hemorrhoids—Piles.

Hepatitis—Inflammation of the liver.

Histamine—Substance produced by the body as part of an allergic reaction; it causes dilation of blood vessels, lowered blood pressure, and stimulation of secretions from the stomach and other organs.

Hyperacidity—Abnormally large amounts of acid in the stomach.

Hyperglycemia—Presence of high level of sugar (glucose) in the blood.

Hyperkalemia—Presence of high potassium level in the blood.

Hyperlipidemia—High blood level of cholesterol and/or triglycerides.

Hypertension—High blood pressure.

Hypoacidity—Unusually low level of stomach acid.

Hypoglycemia—Low blood sugar (glucose) level.

Hypokalemia—Low blood potassium level.

Hypotension—Low blood pressure.

Immunity—Resistance to the effects of a specified disease or of some other abnormal condition.

Ketonuria—The passage of ketone bodies (acetone) in the urine. This condition may be present in diabetes or as a result of an unbalanced high-protein diet.

Laudanum—Tincture of opium.

Laxative—Drug that can loosen the bowels (act as a cathartic). Types of laxatives are bulk, saline, and stimulant.

Lesion—Wound or injury.

Lethargy—Drowsiness.

Malaise—Feeling of general discomfort or of being out of sorts.

Metastasis—Shifting of a disease, or its local effect, from one part of the body to another.

Migraine headache—Pain on one side of the head; complex of effects consisting of head pain, dizziness, nausea and vomiting, and extreme sensitivity to bright light.

Myopia—Nearsightedness.

Nebulizer—Atomizer or vaporizer.

Neoplasm—New or abnormal growth of tissue usually associated with a tumor.

Normotension—Blood pressure in the normal range.

Nystagmus—Rapid uncontrolled eye movement.

Obesity—Body weight at least 10 to 20 percent greater than the expected value.

Over-the-counter drug—Medication sold without a prescription. May be purchased in pharmacies and other outlets.

Palpitation—Rapid heart beat in which the patient feels throbbing in his chest.

Paralysis—Loss of power in one or more muscles because of injury or disease.

Pill—Small mass of material containing a medication and taken by swallowing.

Plasma—Fluid portion of circulating blood.

Platelet—Component of the blood whose primary role is in the clotting mechanism.

Pneumonia—Inflammation of the lungs, from any cause.

Polydipsia—Excessive thirst.

Polyuria—Excessive urination.

Prescription—Written formula for the preparation and administration of any remedy or medicine, by a qualified, licensed medical practitioner.

Progestins—Female hormones that cause changes in the uterus to prepare it for the fertilized egg. Progestins may also affect other female sex characteristics.

Pruritis—Itching.

Psychotherapeutic drug—Drug used as treatment or part of the treatment of emotional disorders.

Rash—Local or generalized eruption.

Respiration—Breathing.

Rhinorrhea—Running nose.

Somnifacient drug—Drug that produces sleep.

Sulfa drug—Drug belonging to the chemical group of sulfonamides. Members of this group can have anti-infective, diuretic, and antidiabetic properties.

Sulfonamide—See **Sulfa drug**.

Sympathomimetic drug—Drug with stimulating action, also causing relief of congestion, increase in blood pressure, and other effects.

Symptom—Any change in function, appearance, or sensation related to a disease.

Syndrome—Group of symptoms which, when taken together, indicate the presence of a specific disease.

Tablet—Solid dosage form containing medicine. Tablets from different manufacturers may vary in size, color, shape, and content.

Testosterone—Male sex hormone.

Tinnitus—Ringing or noise in the ears, often as a drug side effect.

Toxic—Poisonous or harmful.

Toxin—Substance produced by a cell or group of cells, or by bacteria during their growth, that produces a poisonous effect.

Toxoid—Toxin that has been treated with chemicals to destroy its harmful properties. After this treatment it can be injected into the human body and will provide immunity to the original toxin.

Tremor—Involuntary trembling or quivering.

Tumor—Swelling or neoplasm that grows at an unusual rate.

Ulcer—Lesion on the surface of the skin or mucous membrane.

Urticaria—Hives or itching rash.

Vaccine—Solution of modified virus or bacteria that, when injected, provides immunity to the original virus or bacteria.

Vasodilator—Drug that causes opening or widening of the blood vessels.

Vitamin—Chemical present in foods that is essential to normal body functions and to normal chemical reactions in the body.

Sources

Abramowicz, Mark, ed., *The Medical Letter on Drugs and Therapeutics,* Medical Letter, New Rochelle, N.Y., 1980, 1981.

Adams, George, *Essentials of Geriatric Medicine,* 4th ed., Oxford Medical Publications, London, 1981.

American Medical Association, Department of Drugs, *AMA Drug Evaluations,* 3d ed., Publishing Sciences Group, Acton, Mass., 1977.

American Medical Association, Department of Mental Health, *Drug Abuse, A Guide for the Primary Care Physician,* 1st ed., Chicago, 1981.

American Pharmaceutical Association, *Evaluations of Drug Interactions,* 2d ed., American Pharmaceutical Association, Washington, D.C., 1976.

American Pharmaceutical Association, *Handbook of Nonprescription Drugs,* 6th ed., American Pharmaceutical Association, Washington, D.C., 1979.

American Society of Hospital Pharmacists, *American Hospital Formulary Service,* American Society of Hospital Pharmacists, Washington, D.C., 1981.

Consumer Guide, Gossel, T. A., and Stansloski, D. W., *Prescription Drugs,* Beekman House, New York, 1979.

Conn, H. F., ed., *Current Therapy 1977,* W. B. Saunders, Philadelphia.

Deichman, W. B., and Gerarde, H. W., *Toxicology of Drugs and Chemicals,* Academic Press, New York, 1969.

Dorlands Illustrated Medical Dictionary, 24th ed., W. B. Saunders Co., Philadelphia, 1965.

Dukes, G. E., Kuhn, J. G. and Evens, R. P. "Alcohol in Pharmaceutical Products," *Family Practice,* September, 1977.

Gleason, M. N., Gosselin, R. E., Hodge, H. C., and Smith, R. P., *Clinical Toxicology of Commercial Products,* 3d ed., Williams & Wilkins, Baltimore, 1969.

Goldstein, A., Aronow, L., and Kalman, S., *Principles of Drug Action: The Basis of Pharmacology,* 2d ed., John Wiley & Sons, New York, 1974.

Goodman, L. S., and Gilman, A., *The Fnarmacological Basis of Therapeutics,* 6th ed., Macmillan, New York, 1980.

Graedon, J., *The People's Pharmacy, A Guide to Prescription Drugs, Home Remedies and Over-the-Counter Medications,* St. Martin's Press, New York, 1976.

Graedon, J., with Graedon, T., *The People's Pharmacy-2,* Avon Books, New York, 1980.

Greenblatt, D. J., and Shader, R. I., *Benzodiazepines in Clinical Practice,* Raven Press, New York, 1974.

Hansten, P. D., *Drug Interactions,* 3d ed., Lea & Febiger, Philadelphia, 1975.

Hodkinson, H. M., *Common Symptoms of Disease in the Elderly,* 2d ed., Blackwell Scientific Publications, London, 1979.

Jones, Judith K., *Family Guide to Medications,* Hearst Books, New York, 1980.

Kastrup, E. K., and Schwach, G., eds., *Facts and Comparisons,* Facts and Comparisons, St. Louis, 1981.

Kastrup, E. K. and Olin, B. R., eds. *Facts and Comparisons,* J.B. Lippincott Company, St. Louis, Missouri, 1985.

Lamy, P. P., *Prescribing for the Elderly,* PSG Publishing Company, Littleton, Mass., 1980.

Langley, L., Cheraskin, F., and Sleeper, R., *Dynamic Anatomy and Physiology,* 2d ed., McGraw-Hill, New York, 1963.

Long, J. S., *The Essential Guide to Prescription Drugs,* 3d. ed. Harper & Row, New York, 1982.

Medical Economics, *Physicians' Desk Reference,* 39th ed., Medical Economics, Oradell, N.J., 1985.

Mortality Statistics Branch, Division of Vital Statistics, *Vital Statistics of the United States,* Vol. 2, Mortality, National Center for Health Services, Hyattsville, Maryland, 1982.

National Clearing House for Poison Control Centers, *Bulletin,* Vol. 25, No. 6, U.S. Department of Health and Human Services, Food and Drug Administration, August, 1981.

National Institute on Drug Abuse, *Sex and Race Differentials in Acute Drug Abuse,* (NIDA Statistical Series H #1) 1982.

Parish, P., *The Doctors and Patients Handbook of Medicines and Drugs,* Alfred A. Knopf, New York, 1977.

Silverman, H. M., "Anticoagulant Therapy," *New Environment of Pharmacy* 3:5 (Nov./Dec.) 1976.

Silverman, H. M., "Antineoplastic Therapy," *Physician Assistant* 1:23 (May/June) 1976.

Silverman, H. M., "Classification of Antibiotics," *Hospital Formulary Management* 7:26 (Feb.) 1972.

Silverman, H. M., "Fetal and Newborn Adverse Drug Reactions," *Drug Intelligence and Clinical Pharmacy* 8:690 (Dec.) 1974.

Silverman, H. M., "MAO Inhibitors," *Hospital Formulary Management* 8:14 (March) 1973.

Silverman, H. M., "The Proper Time for Taking Drugs," *Hospital Formulary Management* 9:18 (Feb.) 1974.

Strauss, S., *Your Prescription and You*, 3d ed., Medical Business Services, Ambler, Pa., 1978.

Thomas, C. L., ed., *Tabers Cyclopedic Medical Dictionary*, 12th ed., F. A. Davis, Philadelphia, 1973.

United States Department of Health, Education and Welfare, "Health Status of the Elderly."

United States Pharmacopeial Convention, Inc., *About Your Medicines*, United States Pharmacopeial Convention, Inc., Rockville, Maryland, 1981.

Wesson, Donald R., M.D., and Smith, David E., M.D., "Low Dose Benzodiazapine Withdrawal Syndrome: Receptor Site Mediated," NEWS, California Society for the Treatment of Alcoholism and Other Drug Dependencies, Vol. 9, No. 1, (Feb.) 1982.

Index of Generic and Brand Name Drugs

Index of Drug Types

ABOUT THE MEDICAL WRITERS

GILBERT I. SIMON, Sc.D., is Director of the Department of Pharmacy at Beth Israel Medical Center, New York City. From 1961 to 1982 he was Director of the Department of Pharmacy, Lenox Hill Hospital, New York City. Dr. Simon received his B.S. from Fordham University, his M.S. from Long Island University, Doctorate, Honoris Causa, from the College of Pharmacy Sciences, City of New York (Columbia University) and an MPA in Health from Pace University. He was an associate professor of pharmaceutical sciences at Columbia University from 1964 to 1976. Dr. Simon has served as president to both the New York State and the New York City societies. In 1973 he was honored with the Award of Merit from the New York City Society of Hospital Pharmacists for his contribution to the practice of institutional pharmacy. He has been a member of the Pharmacy Advisory Committee of the Greater New York Hospital Association, a member of The Govenor's (NYS) Medical Advisory Committee and served on committees of the Hospital Association of the State of New York. Dr. Simon has served as a consultant to the pharmaceutical industry, publishers, advertising agencies and government. He has been a principal speaker on contemporary hospital pharmacy practice throughout the United States and in Europe. In 1975, Drs. Simon and Silverman coauthored *Med-File*, a book on common nonprescription drugs and their interactions. Dr. Simon lives in Bronxville, New York with his wife Sheila.

HAROLD M. SILVERMAN, PHARM.D., is a hospital pharmacist, author, educator, and consultant to the pharmaceutical industry. As an author, his guiding principle is that health reference books should help people to understand why medicines are prescribed and how they can best be used to guarantee their safety and effectiveness. In addition to THE PILL BOOK, Dr. Silverman is co-author of THE VITAMIN BOOK: A No-Nonsense Consumer Guide. He is author of THE CONSUMER'S GUIDE TO POISON PROTECTION, THE WOMAN'S DRUG STORE, and TRAVEL HEALTHY. Dr. Silverman's contributions to professional pharmaceutical literature include many articles, research papers, and textbook chapters. He has been involved with many professional organizations, including the New York State Council of Hospital Pharmacists, of which he is past-President. Dr. Silverman holds two degrees from Columbia University and has taught at several colleges and universities and has won numerous awards for his work. He and his family reside in a suburb of New York City.

BANTAM'S
PILL BOOK LIBRARY

NEED MORE INFORMATION ON YOUR HEALTH AND NUTRITION?

Read the books that will lead you to
a happier and healthier life.